OXFORD READINGS IN FEMINISM

FEMINISM AND PORNOGRAPHY

PUBLISHED IN THIS SERIES:

Feminism and Science
edited by Evelyn Fox Keller and Helen E. Longino

Feminism, the Public and the Private
edited by Joan Landes

Feminism and Politics
edited by Anne Phillips

Feminism and History
edited by Joan Wallach Scott

Feminism and Cultural Studies
edited by Morag Shiach

Feminism and Renaissance Studies
edited by Lorna Hutson

OXFORD READINGS IN FEMINISM

Feminism and Pornography

Edited by

Drucilla Cornell

OXFORD
UNIVERSITY PRESS

Great Clarendon Street, Oxford OX2 6DP

Oxford University Press is a department of the University of Oxford.
It furthers the University's objective of excellence in research, scholarship,
and education by publishing worldwide in

Oxford New York

Athens Auckland Bangkok Bogotá Buenos Aires Calcutta
Cape Town Chennai Dar es Salaam Delhi Florence Hong Kong Istanbul
Karachi Kuala Lumpur Madrid Melbourne Mexico City Mumbai
Nairobi Paris São Paulo Singapore Taipei Tokyo Toronto Warsaw

with associated companies in Berlin Ibadan

Oxford is a trade mark of Oxford University Press
in the UK and in certain other countries

Published in the United States
by Oxford University Press Inc., New York

British Library Cataloguing in Publication Data
Data available

British Library Cataloging in Publication Data
(Data applied for)
ISBN 0–19–878250–0

1 3 5 7 9 10 8 6 4 2

Typeset in Minion
by RefineCatch Limited, Bungay, Suffolk
Printed in Great Britain by
TJ International Ltd, Padstow, Cornwall

Preface

Given how divisive the issue of pornography in the second wave of feminism has been, it is not surprising that it took the committed effort of a great number of people to bring this book to fruition. I want to thank all of them. Judith Butler's wisdom was crucial to me in thinking through how to be fair to the different points of view on pornography. Wendy Brown's generosity and intellectual integrity was essential in helping me see through what compromises could be made to make this volume as inclusive as it is. Ann Scales gave of her time to do research on the aftermath of the *Butler* decision in Canada, thus making sure that I accurately represented current Canadian Obscenity Law. Norma Ramos was helpful in explaining why a Latina could embrace anti-pornography legislation. Catharine MacKinnon threw herself into the project and taught me a lot about what anti-pornography feminism stands for. Donna Hughes played an important role through her effort in collecting international materials. Andrea Dworkin's cooperation from the beginning of the project was unyielding. It is this kind of sisterly cooperation that makes a project like this possible. I would like to thank my editor, Tim Barton, for his patience and understanding of the importance of putting together the collection which we ultimately achieved.

Teresa Brennan was by my side through all of the twists and turns that this book took. Her devoted support and belief that a feminist volume containing diverse views on pornography was possible, helped me see the light of day. She went way beyond her responsibilities as a series editor. From the beginning of its conception, she embraced the spirit of the collection, which would include not only diverse perspectives on pornography, but also voices which are not usually heard on the topic, particularly perspectives from former colonial nations. Teresa also graciously provided the translation for pieces which were written in Spanish and had to be translated into English. Throughout this process, she represented the best kind of support and sustenance.

Isabelle Barker, my assistant, in a very real sense took the journey with me as we struggled together, not only to figure out what should be included in the book, but also to discuss the differences between her generation and mine about pornography. Isabelle spent months on the internet so we could reach organizations, such as the El Salvador Sex Workers Union. Isabelle also helped me conceive of the overarching structure of the collection and poured over book after book on pornography to help me select the materials. It is no exaggeration to say that without her assistance, this book could not have gone forward. Her own response to 'Editing Pornography' is included as an essay in this volume because of the lessons she brought to this project and taught me.

Evelyn Alsultany took over from Isabelle and saw the book through its completion. Her dedication to the project was shown in her diligence in taking care of all the nitty gritty details that a manuscript like this demands. Our discussions about the complex relationship between ethnic and national identity to questions of sexuality were indispensable.

Dorchen Leidholdt was extraordinarily helpful in my search for international materials. More importantly, she embraced the spirit I was trying to achieve in the book which was that of respect for the different views of the feminists on pornography in all their complexity. Dorchen Leidholdt and my long-time friend, Mary Elizabeth Bartholomew, are both anti-pornography feminists. Dorchen was one of the founders of anti-pornography feminism and helped to conceptualize it as a movement. Although we have often disagreed about what role law should play in feminist struggles, including over exploitation of women in the sex industry, we have been able to strengthen a bond of alliance and cooperation that is so necessary if feminism is able to embrace disagreement amongst women without taking such a disagreement as a sign that the other side is no longer part of the feminist community. It is the spirit of solidarity in the discussions between Dorchen, Mary Elizabeth, and myself that sustains feminism. Mary Elizabeth and Dorchen also represent the unflagging commitment to the liberation of women without which a feminist movement could not get off the ground. They are untiring fighters for the rights of battered women. It is this day to day work in the trenches which often goes unsung which I would like to recognize here by dedicating this book to them.

D.C.

New York City
November 1999

Contents

Part IV. Breaking Open the Ground of Sex and Gender

Part V. Erotic Hope, Feminine Sexuality, and the Beginnings of Sexual Freedom

Notes on Contributors

M. JACQUI ALEXANDER is Chair of the Department of Gender and Women's Studies at Connecticut College and holds the Fuller-Maathai Chair there. She teaches courses grounded in feminist critiques of imperialism, colonization, and hetrosexuality. She has been actively involved in feminist movements inthe Caribbean as well as in feminist and lesbian and gay movements in the United States of North America. Professor Alexander is a recent recipient of a Guggenheim fellowship for a study on Kongo memory and spiritual practices in the Caribbean.

MALEK ALLOULA was born in Oran, Algeria, in 1937. He received a Master Of Arts degree in Letters after having studies in Algeria and at the Sorbonne. He has been living in Paris since 1967 and works in publishing. He has published articles of literary criticism in numerous publications and journals, both in France and Algeria. He has published three collections of poems (*Villes et Autres leux; Rêveurs Sépultures; mesures du vent*) and the essay (*Le harem colonial. Images d'un sous-esotisme*).

ISABELLE V. BARKER is a doctoral candidate in political science at Rutgers University, where she studies women and politics, political theory, and comparative politics. She is also a freelance writer and activist involved in feminist and anti-racist violence prevention and education work in New York City.

WENDY BROWN is Professor of Political Science and Women's Studies at the University of California, Berkeley. Her most recent books include *States of Injury: Power and freedom in Late Modernity* (Princeton, 1995) and *Liberalism Out of History: Political Possibilities After Progress* (Princeton, forthcoming).

JUDITH BUTLER is Maxine Elliot Professor in the Departments of Rhetoric and Comparative Literature at the University of California, Berkeley. She is the author of *Subjects of Desire* (Columbia University Press, 1987), *Gender Trouble* (Routledge, 1990), *Bodies That Matter* (Routledge, 1993), *The Psychic Lift of Power* (Stanford University Press, 1997), *Excitable Speech* (Routledge, 1997), as well as numerous articles and contributions on philosophy, feminist and queer theory. She is currently finishing a manuscript on Antigone and the politics of kinship.

DEBORAH CAMERON has taught linguistics and women's studies in England, Scotland, Sweden, and the US and is now professor of languages at the Institute of Education, London University. Her publications include *Feminism and Linguistic Theory* (Macmillan 1985), *Verbal Hygiene* (Routledge 1995), and, with Elizabeth Frazer, *The Lust To Kill: A Feminist Investigation of Sexual Murder* (Polity 1987).

Rey Chow is Andrew W. Mellon Professor of the Humanities at Brown University. She is the author of many essays and several books, the most recent of which is *Ethics after Idealism: Theory, Culture, Ethnicity, Reading* (1998). In 2000 the journal *Differences* will publish a special issue guest-edited by her entitled 'Writing in the Realm of the Senses'.

Drucilla Cornell is a professor of law, women's studies, and political science at Rutgers University. Prior to beginning her academic life, Professor Cornell was a union organizer for a number of years, working for the UAW, the UE, and the IUE in California, New Jersey, and New York. She played a key role in organizing the conferences on Deconstruction and Justice with Jacques Derrida, held at Cardozo in 1989, 1990, and 1993. In addition, she has worked to coordinate the Law and Humanism Speakers Series with the Jacob Burns Institute for Advanced Legal Studies and the Committee on Liberal Studies at the New School for Social Research. Professor Cornell was professor at the Benjamin N. Cardozo School of Law from 1989 to 1994 and spent the 1991–2 academic year at the Institute for Advanced Study at Princeton. She has authored numerous articles on critical theory, feminism and 'Postmodern' theories of ethics. She is the co-editor, with Seyla Benhabib, of *Feminism as Critique: On the Politics of Gender*; with Michel Rosenfeld and David Gray Carlson, of *Deconstruction and the Possibility of Justice*; and has published five books: *At the Heart of Freedom: Feminism, Sex, and Equality; The Imaginary Domain: Abortion, Pornography and Sexual Harassment; Beyond Accommodation: Ethical Feminism, Deconstruction and the Law; The Philosophy of the Limit;* and *Transformations: Recollective Imagination and Sexual Difference.* She is part of a published philosophical exchange with Seyla Benhabib, Judith Butler, and Nancy Fraser entitled *Feminist Contentions.* She is also a produced playwright—productions of her plays *The Dream Cure* and *Background Interference* have been performed in New York and Los Angeles.

Kimberle Crenshaw has lectured and written extensively on civil rights, Black feminist legal theory, and race and the law. A founding member of the Critical Race Theory workshop; co-editor of *Critical Race Theory: A Reader.* Her work has appeared in *Harvard Law Review, National Black Law Journal, Stanford Law Review*, and *Southern California Law Review.* She serves on the governing board of the Law and Society Association and the Society of American Law Teachers, is a specialist on legal issues confronting Black women (assisting the legal team that represented Anita Hill). A frequent commentator on political and cultural issues and an international lecturer, Ms. Crenshaw is twice honored as Professor of the Year at UCLA Law School and has lectured throughout the national and international community with recent visits to South Africa, Brazil, Spain, France, Germany, and Holland.

ANDREA DWORKIN has spoken at colleges, universities, and rallies around the world. With Catharine A. McKinnon, she authored civil rights legislation recognizing pornography as legally actionable sex discrimination. She has written ten books, including such seminal works as *Intercourse* and *Pornography*. Her next book, *Scapegoat*, will be published by the Free Press in Spring 2000. She lives in New York City.

RONALD DWORKIN is Sommer Professor of Law and Philosophy, NYC; and Quain Professor of Jurisprudence at University College, London.

EL SALVADOR SEX WORKER'S UNION is an organization affiliated with the FMLN in El Salvador. The Union is part of a broader coalition of worker's organizations that have fought for national liberation as well as struggling to obtain rights and economic benefits for workers within their own industry and in the country more broadly.

PETER ESTERHAZY is one of the most popular and prolific writers in Hungary today. His *Book of Harabal* was named by *The New York Times* as one of the most notable books of 1994.

ELIZABETH FRAZER is now Fellow and Tutor in Politics, New College, and university lecturer in Politics at the University of Oxford.

MARY JOE FRUG practised poverty law in Washington, D.C. and New York City before she began her 20-year career teaching women and the law, contracts, professional responsibility, and family law at Villanova Law School and the New England School of Law. She is the author of many law review articles and two posthumously published books, *Postmodern Feminism* (Routledge 1992) and *Women in the Law* (Foundation Press 1992). She was murdered in 1991.

AMBER HOLLIBAUGH has 30 years's experience as a national organizer, educator, filmmaker, and writer. She has worked as a theoretician and activist on issues such as prisoners' rights, homophobia, women's rights, incest, domestic violence, rape, race and class oppression, and sexuality. For the last ten years she has worked as a health educator: as a pre- and post-test supervisor of New York City's AIDS hotline, in the New York City Commission on Human Rights AIDS Discrimination Unit, and finally, as Director of the lesbian AIDS project at Gay men's Health Crisis in New York. Her documentary, *The Heart of the Matter*, focuses attention on Women's sexuality through the prism of premiered nationwide on PBS's POV series in 1994.

BELL HOOKS, cultural critic, feminist theorist and poet, has written widely on feminism and popular culture, the civil rights movement, and capitalism. Her more recent texts, *Remembered Rapture: The Writer at Work* (1999), and *Wounds of Passion: A Writing Life* (1997) embody both memoire and social critique: they examine not only the field of publishing, but also the creative writing process and the powerful relationship between the author and the word. Her latest book is *All About Love: New Visions.*

LYNN HUNT is Eugen Weber Professor of Modern European History at the University of California, Los Angeles. She is author of *The Family Romance of the French Revolution* and *Telling the Truth about History* (with Joyce Appleby and Margaret Jacob), and editor of *Histories: French Constructions of the Past* (with Jaques Revel). She is now working on the origins of human rights.

DORCHEN LEIDHOLDT is founder of The Sanctuary for Families, one of the major shelters for battered women in New York City. Dorchen is also a leading member in the Coalition Against Trafficking in Women. She's written numerous feminist essays and has been an activist in feminist politics for over 20 years.

LLIANE LOOTS is a lecturer in the Drama and Performance Studies Programme at the University of Natal (Durban) campus in South Africa. She also teaches, in an interdisciplinary capacity, in the Gender Studies Centre where she lectures on modules on gender, power and the workings of the 'new' South African Constitution. She has a Master's Degree in Women's Studies which focused specifically on feminism and the South African media.

AUDRE LORDE 1934–1992. A self-described 'Black lesbian, mother, warrior, poet,' Lorde's celebrated works continue to inspire. Her works include books, essays, and poetry volumes such as *Zami: A New Spelling of My Name* (1982), *The Uses of the Erotic: The Erotic As Power* (1978), and *Our Dead Behind Us* (1986). Lorde was a co-founder of 'Kitchen Table: Women of Color Press'.

CATHARINE A. MACKINNON, J.D., Ph.D., is a lawyer, teacher, writer, activist, and expert on sex equality. She and Andrea Dworkin concieved and wrote civil rights ordinances making the harms of pornography civilly actionable as sex discrimination. She is Elizabeth A. Long Professor of Law at the University of Michigan and long-term Visiting Professor of Law at the University of Chicago.

KOBENA MERCER is a writer and lecturer on the visual arts of the black diaspora. He is author of *Welcome to the Jungle* (1994) and is currently Fellow at the Society for the Humanities, Cornell University.

CHERRIE MORAGA is a poet, playwright and essayist, and the co-editor of *This Bridge Called My Back: Writings by Radical Women of Color*. She is the author of numerous plays including 'Shadow of a Man' and 'Watsonville: Some Place Not Here,' (both won the Fund for New American Plays Award in 1991 and 1995, respectively) and 'Heroes and Saints', which earned the Pen West Award for Drama in 1992. Her two most recent books include a collection of poems and essays entitled *The Last Generation* and a memoir, *Waiting in the Wings: Portrait of a Queer Motherhood*, released in October 1997. Ms. Moraga is also a recipient of the National Endowment for the Arts' Theatre Playwrights' Fellowship and is the Artist-in-Residence in the Departments of Drama and Spanish & Portuguese at Stanford University.

VICTORIA ORTIZ is a feminist legal scholar and historian focusing on: women of colour; queer history and theory; gender, sexual orientation, race and the family; and slave women's resistance. She is Dean of Students at Boalt Hall School of Law, University of California at Berkeley.

CATHERINE PORTUGES is Professor of Comparative Literature and Director of the Interdepartmental Program in Film Studies at the University of Massachusetts, Amherst. She is co-editor of *Gendered Subjects: the Dynamics of Feminist Pedagogy* (Routledge, 1985) and of *Post-Communist East-Central European Cinema in Transition* (Flicks Books/London, 2000), and author of *Screen Memories: the Hungarian Cinema of Márta Mészáros* (Indiana, 1993), as well as articles in *Cinema Colonialism Postcolonialism* (Texas, 1996), *Lacan/Politics/Aesthetics* (SUNY, 1995) and *Re-Writing New Identities* (Minnesota, 1997).

NORMA RAMOS is an environmental attorney who practices in New York City. She is a self-described eco-feminist who is active in the movement to end violence against women and is a founding activist in the environmental justice movement.

ZORAIDA ESPERANZA RAMÍREZ RODRÍGUEZ, economist, born in Caracas, Venezuela in 1949. She is author of *Prostitution and Underdevelopment: A Feminist Approach* (1994). Ms. Ramírez has been the Latin American and Caribbean representative for The Coalition Against Trafficking in Women, and since July 1997 is a Vice President of the same institution, a Non-Governmental Organization with consultative status to the United Nations Economic and Social Council. She has worked as a representative for Latin America and the Caribbean for the Third World Movement Against the Exploitation of Women (TW-MAE-W), and as the Venezuelan National Consultant to UNIFEM in the United Nations Programs for Development (PNUD). Ms. Ramírez is active in groups such as The Liberation Movement of Women and is a founding member of others, among them, "Conjura" and "La Mala Vida". Some of her greatest contributions to the movement are the only two feminist magazines in Venezuela, *Boletín Una Mujer Cualquiera* and *Revista La Mala Vida*.

DIANA H. RUSSELL, Ph.D., is an Emerita Professor of Sociology at Mills College, Oakland, California, where she taught for 22 years. She is the author/co-author/editor/so-editor of fifteen books, most of them on sexual violence. Her book, *The Secret Trauma: Incest in the Lives of Girls and Women* (1986), was winner of the 1986 C. Wright Mills Award for outstanding social science research. Russell has also written/edited three books on pornography: *Making*

Violence Sexy: Feminist Views on Pornography (1993), *Against Pornography: The Evidence of Harm* (1994), and *Dangerous Relationships: Pornography, Misogyny, and Rape* (1998).

ANN SCALES is an activist and lawyer. For twenty years, she taught law on various faculties, including the University of New Mexico, the University of British Columbia, Boston College, and the University of Iowa. She testified as an expert witness on pornography in the landmark Canadian case, *Little Sisters Book and Art Emporium v. Canada.*

ALICE WALKER is a Pulitzer Prize winning novelist, essayist, and poet. Her 1997 collection, *Anything We Love Can be Saved: A Writer's Activism* includes pieces on religion and the spirit, writing and language, families and identity, politics and social change.

Introduction

Drucilla Cornell

The politics of sexuality generates violent tensions because a deeply intimate part of ourselves is engaged in debates about such issues as pornography. This collection of essays seeks to provide an alternative to the divisive 'which side are you on?' mentality that has held sway over much of the feminist discussion and analysis of pornography in the United States and, to a lesser extent, in England, Canada, and Europe. The parameters of the debate must be expanded so that we may at last begin to confront the complex challenges presented by sexually explicit material. As many of these essays point out, pornography is not one clearly designatable pedagogical object. In order to understand what pornography is, we need to look at what it means to those who consume it, to those who fight against it, to those who are used in it, and to those engaged in changing its meaning. Crucial to an expansion of the debate beyond the Northern 'First World' is a grasp of the way emerging post-colonial nations have dealt with pornography, as well as sex work in general, in their effort to constitute new nation-states and in some instances to build socialist societies. We in the Northern hemisphere have much to learn from grass-roots feminist organizations in the nations in the Southern hemisphere that have tackled these issues. In the essays compiled here, pornography is shown to be a dynamic construct continually shaped and reshaped, in part by the feminist debate over what should be done about it legally and politically.

There are at least four central questions that the contributions in this book seek to address. First, what is pornography? How is the meaning of pornography shaped by changing historical and political realities? These are crucial questions in a world so obviously wrought by political change as ours. I have sought, for example, to include essays that explore the personal, political, and legal significance of the availability of 'Western' pornography in the post-socialist states of Europe, as well as in the post-colonial states in the South. Further, what happens to the way societies produce and view pornography when the censorship of all sorts of literature—including that considered pornographic and thus part of bourgeois decadence—is at last lifted? How is the pornographic other to be differentiated from culturally valued literature, film, and music and how is such differentiation culturally specific? How is this process different, for example, in Hungary and China, countries that were bound together as the 'socialist other' to Northern capitalism, but are obviously different in almost all other aspects of culture?

Secondly, what role should law play, if any, in providing a 'solution' to pornography (if a 'solution' needs to be found)? It is no surprise that feminist struggles against pornography, in whatever form they take, have become a favoured example to bolster the charge that feminism has a deeply totalitarian impulse. The liberal legal concern often voiced by feminists themselves, particularly those in law, is that nothing is more personal than a person's intimate sexual fantasies and that, if legal privacy is to mean anything, the state must stay out of a person's sexual imagination and the expression he or she gives to it. Feminists who have marked pornography as a crucial political issue have militantly disagreed with the presentation of pornography as private or as speech or as representation.[1] Instead, pornography has been condemned as part of a larger public institution of sexual slavery, which involves worldwide trafficking in women and children.[2] If pornography is a form of sexual slavery, then the question of what should be legally done about it seems to answer itself—it should be outlawed with all other forms of slavery.

But is pornography sexual slavery? If not, is the harm involved in its production and distribution nonetheless too great for any society to tolerate legally? Should the ultimate decision about pornography be put in the hands of women who are used by it? Is there, after all, a causal relationship between pornography and the horrifying reality of brutal violence against women throughout the world? Do men who consume pornography have an increased propensity to rape? The answers to such questions have been as divergent as the definitions of pornography that feminists have offered. That is why the first two central questions addressed in this volume are necessarily tied together. Legal regulation demands a definition of what is to be regulated. Civil rights, in turn, demands a definition of civil violation.

Further, we need to ask: is pornography all sexually explicit material, whether written or visual, no matter how produced, and no matter for what stated purpose? For example, is sex education pornography?

Some conservative groups in the United States have unabashedly advocated so sweeping a definition of pornography that sex education materials would be curbed legally or outright censored. Alternatively, should the legal definition of pornography be limited to the big business which produces millions of dollars worth of videos a year in the United States, Canada, Europe, and some countries in the South? Could the concern here be mainly about the regulation of the conditions of work in the production of those videos, rather than in the censorship of the videos themselves? Should Andrea Dworkin and Catharine MacKinnon's definition be embraced instead?

Dworkin and MacKinnon battled legally and politically to have ordinances enacted in several cities in the United States, ordinances which have since been declared unconstitutional, although not in a legally final way, in part because their definition of pornography was considered overbroad. These ordinances would have provided women in the industry with a course of action if they had been abused in any way on a production set. But the ordinances were not only for them. A woman who was physically harmed by a consumer of pornography and could show that this act was the result of his reading or viewing pornography could have sued under the ordinance. So too could a woman whose treatment as an equal citizen was undermined by undesired exposure to pornographic images that presented her exclusively as a sexually viable commodity and thus silenced other forms of her self-presentation. Here is how MacKinnon and Dworkin defined pornography: 'On the basis of its reality, Andrea Dworkin and I have proposed a law against pornography that defines it as graphic sexually explicit materials that subordinate women through pictures or words.'[3] MacKinnon and Dworkin define in the ordinance what kinds of material constitute subordination of women and sexually explicit materials. What follows are the ordinance's attempts to list what could be inclusive of the words 'subordination of women graphically depicted':

> (i) women are presented dehumanized as sexual objects, things, or commodities; or (ii) women are presented as sexual objects who enjoy pain or humiliation; or (iii) women are presented as sexual objects who experience sexual pleasure in being raped; or (iv) women are presented as sexual objects tied up or cut up or mutilated or bruised or physically hurt; or (v) women are presented in postures or positions of sexual submission, servility, or display; or (vi) women's body parts — including but not limited to, vaginas, breasts, or buttocks — are exhibited such that women are reduced to those parts; or (vii)

women are presented as whores by nature; or (viii) women are presented as being penetrated by objects or animals; or (ix) women are presented in scenarios of degradation, injury, torture, shown as filthy or inferior, bleeding, bruised, or hurt in a context that makes these conditions sexual.[4]

MacKinnon and Dworkin sought to change the legal definition of pornography from an obscenity standard, which appealed to the public morality, to that of the subordination of women. The ordinance's success in Minneapolis and Indianapolis created an extraordinary sense of empowerment for the women who mobilized for its passage.[5] But those very mobilizations left many feminists wary because they believed conservative allies had been necessary for the ordinance's initial political success. The fierceness of the divide among feminists within law was evidenced by the group of feminists, lawyers, and professors who submitted an amicus brief in the case that challenged the constitutionality of the ordinance. When both ordinances were struck down as unconstitutional, the feminists behind the amicus brief hailed the result as a victory for feminism. At that time I was a young law professor and refused to sign the brief or support the ordinance. I had a lot of questions about the ordinance, as I am sure many other feminists did. I felt strongly that our political and ethical disagreements over the ordinance should be aired amongst ourselves to a much greater extent than they were before any of us chose legal recourse to the federal courts to resolve them for us. I was moved by that experience to reflect on the dangers of feminist investment in the mythical positivity of law. I have since written extensively about how a feminist should tailor a conception of right of personality that will allow women the freedom they need to claim their own person and to represent themselves in the political realm, including that of feminist politics. I have called that right of personality the imaginary domain.[6] The imaginary domain is the moral and psychic space of free exploration of our sexual identifications and representations that we as sexuate creatures need if we are to find our way to a life that we can claim as our own. It is precisely because we are inevitably formed by our basic identifications, because our freedom is inevitably relational and thus so fragile, that we need to be recognized by the state as the moral source of the narration and representation of our sexual difference and our erotic lives, including the 'materials' from out of which we form and express them.

The question of what should legally count as pornography is not easily answered even by those advocating divergent programmes for its reform or prohibition, particularly when we try to rethink what either of these efforts might mean in the light of the importance of women's sexual freedom. If pornography is defined as sexual slavery, should literature necessarily be excluded simply because no one is being paid for actually having sex in the author's work? What about photographs in which no sex acts take place? What about sex clubs in which sex acts are performed? What about sex clubs where there is stripping, but no 'sex' acts? Must there be filmed, paid for sex acts in order for there to be pornography? The question of sex clubs is explicitly not addressed by Dworkin and MacKinnon's ordinance. But in other countries with less economic resources and where VCRs are not prevalent, struggles over the exploitation of women in the sex industry have focused on sex clubs and live performance.

The Adult Film Makers Association has an easy answer to the question of whether or not you need filmed sex acts for erotic materials to constitute pornography. The answer is 'yes', with one caveat. A film is not pornography unless it includes a 'cum' shot. Some lesbians who have sought to have their films distributed by the association have under this definition been excluded. The leaders of the Adult Film Makers Association have what many film makers would consider a hetero-sexist fantasy; they argued that lesbian 'pornographic' films do not have 'cum' shots because there is no filmed male ejaculation. Whether or not one is excluded in the distribution network of the Association has a clear impact on the economics of production. Obviously then, women, lesbians, and many gay men cannot benefit from the mainstream industry in the United States with its worldwide distribution network, even though they are involved in the production of sexually explicit materials. As a result, some pornographers, such as Candida Royalle are choosing to primarily work outside of the industry. Royalle also declares that she runs her sets differently, without the abuse associated with corporate porn production. Royalle's own analysis of her work is included in this collection.

Some gay and lesbian activists in Canada, the USA and in Europe, who wished to produce independently of the industry, argued that their sexually explicit videos should not be legally regulated because they were outside the heterosexual matrix of subordination described in MacKinnon and Dworkin's definition of the industry. Obviously, there are gay films in which women are not present at all. Some independent lesbian S/M makers of sexually explicit videos argue that the exploitative working conditions so pervasive in the mainstream heterosexual industry are not present on their sets. They insist that lesbian S/M has nothing to do with Dworkin and MacKinnon's definition of subordination. They expressed the fear that their work would be read through a heterosexual lens that would in turn be used to deny them sexual freedom. Some activists felt that their fears were given reality in Canada, after a decision of the Canadian Supreme Court in 1992 that reinterpreted a country's criminal prohibition on 'obscenity' to focus not on morality (as in the United States), but on harm to women. Those activists claimed that the court's decision allowed Canadian police and customs to target gay and lesbian erotic literature, and that the decision constituted a new 'censorship'. The Canadian situation is more complex than that, and is ongoing.[7] What transpired in Canada will be most instructive to the larger question here, whether gays, lesbians, and the transgendered will be targeted in any such attempts at legal regulation of sexually explicit material because their sexuality is so threatening to the heterosexual majority.

Fear of lesbian sexuality, for example, is ironically present in the so-called 'anything goes' mainstream pornography industry. Is it just the literalness of the pornography industry that has led them to exclude lesbians and include some gay filmmakers, because at least they have 'cum' shots? What is the lurking danger of lesbian sexuality when it is publicly expressed which makes it so transgressive that it cannot even be a 'legitimate' part of the pornography industry? However one answers these questions, it is clear that there is a divide amongst gays and lesbians over the ordinance and legal regulation of sexually explicit materials more generally. We all clearly need to confront why this division exists if we are not to make a mockery of the oft-stated feminist claim that feminism begins by heeding rather than ignoring the experience of other women. Who 'counts' as women worthy of being listened to in feminist debates about pornography and sex work is a question that this collection takes up, particularly as addressed in Ortiz's discussion of the efforts of Cuba, El Salvador, and Nicaragua to end sex work without recourse to legal prohibition or other more direct forms of coercion deployed against either prostitutes or Johns or both. Ortiz tellingly titled her essay 'We Are Women, Too: Prostitution after the Cuban Revolution'.

In post-colonial emerging nation-states, the question of legal regulation of pornography remains extremely complicated. The irony is that sexual tourism both promotes explicit sexual imagery and demands a particular kind of inviting sexual environment. As a result, for example, laws in the Bahamas have often sought to regulate what is seen as behaviour that is sexually threatening to tourists. Thus, several countries in the Caribbean have passed laws that seek to 'clean up' sexuality by regulating and so making heterosexual prostitution 'safe' for tourists, and at the same time outlawing gay and lesbian sexuality. Although pornography is rarely the sole target—indeed, I could not find a single example from the Third World[8] where laws were directed *just* at pornography—these laws attempt to sweep the streets of uncontrolled 'perversion', 'perversion' which might create the wrong image for a successful tourist industry. Thus, M. Jacqui Alexander, whose essay is included in edited form in this volume, argues strongly against such laws, laws which deny gays, lesbians, and transgendered people citizenship in their own countries. Alexander also argues strongly for erotic autonomy as a crucial component of the struggle for decolonization.

Although Alexander writes more broadly of the struggle against legal regulation of sexualities designated 'suspect' by the government, including prostitution, and not of pornography per se, I have included an essay by her because it raises two important issues. The first is that, in some contexts, neither the government nor feminists, nor gay or lesbian activists in opposition have targeted pornography as central to the regulation of 'suspect sexualities'. This is at least in part due to the attention given to other forms of sex work in countries in the southern hemisphere.

Much government concern about suspect sexualities in countries promoting sex tourism focuses on regulating prostitution and sex clubs, not on pornography. Of course, the efforts here are often not to outlaw prostitution, but to regulate it so that it will be a source of attraction to tourists.[9] Exactly how pornography and prostitution are connected is the second larger issue that must be addressed. Oppositional theatres have been closed down by governments that purport to be post-colonial on the basis that they presented 'indecent' material. At times, these closures have led to the arrest of the actors and actresses involved as pimps and prostitutes. There is a history behind this kind of state action. Some of the former African colonies designated certain 'native' women as prostitutes, available not only to be preyed on, but to be regulated in their freedom of movement.[10] Suspicion of legal regulation of prostitution has to be viewed differently in the context of the particular practices of colonization and the struggle against them. This suspicion, however should in no way invalidate the important work of human rights feminists in drafting legislation to end the trafficking in female children as the increase in this trafficking is inseparable from a global sweatshop economy. Even feminists most wary of legal regulation of sexuality might well join in the effort to outlaw the trafficking in female children as a grotesque violation of human rights. The question of whom is to be included in the moral community of persons worthy of human rights is obviously crucial to these debates. Female children, and of course adult women, have all too long been thought of as things to be used or destroyed rather than as persons whose inviolability must be respected by the moral community constituted by the international human rights treaties.[11] The political and economic connection that is being brought to our attention by activists throughout the world between the global sweatshop economy and the increase in trafficking of female children is one that can allow feminists to build new alliances in their struggle to end the economic exploitation and sexual abuse of all females.

Again, another issue considered here is the way feminists involved in post-colonial movements have sought to elaborate on the significance of 'pornography' in their feminist struggles for erotic autonomy. Towards this, I have included several essays that would not necessarily come under some current definitions of pornography. I write 'necessarily' because whether or not some of the pieces included in this volume are beyond the scope of pornography turns on how one defines pornography. If, for example, all pornography is prostitution, then pornography and prostitution are easily collapsed into one. Still, since most of the essays challenge this collapse of the two, I have tried to open the discussion up to prostitution and sex clubs, and legal regulation of suspect sexualities more generally, as they are relevant to the central questions of pornography around which the volume is organized.

The third question addressed by many of the authors is whether representational politics can be a force in the struggle against pornography, as developed into the form of a union movement or into efforts to change the conditions of production of videos as well as the scripts of these videos. What about the role of sex clubs? Can the participation in performances in sex clubs be considered art? Can these clubs be places where new forms of performance art can be developed? Can sex clubs serve sexual freedom, *especially* women's sexual freedom more directly by giving us the space to act out?

It is perhaps a sign of the narrowness of the legal debate in the USA and its class bias, that sex worker Ona Zee Wigger's effort to organize the pornography industry, an effort concurrent with the legal debate over the Dworkin/MacKinnon ordinance, never received any general media publicity. Ona Zee's organizing effort took place within the mainstream corporate pornography industry that is undoubtedly tied to organized crime.

That the legal debates failed to note the distinctions between the multibillion-dollar porn industry and alternative pornography industries shows us why many feminists and gay and lesbian activists perceived the debate over law and regulation as irrelevant to their own complex struggle with the significance of sexually explicit material in their own lives. Part of the goal of this volume is to recognize the complexity of the debate—in all of its political manifestations—as to what the role of sexually explicit material, as well as sex clubs, is now and should be in an ideal society. What is sought here, then, is to give the legal debate its proper place, while recognizing that the feminist concern with pornography has always reached far beyond 'law's empire'.[12]

Was it 'false consciousness' for Ona Zee to attempt to organize a union because such an effort necessarily accepts the labour model of sex work when it is inappropriate to do so? Or was it class bias on the part of middle-class feminists to fail to even note the presence of this effort, or address it seriously? Was the failure to note the effort a sign of unconscious fantasies about who prostitutes are? Fantasies about 'good girls' and 'bad girls' have played themselves out over and over again in efforts on the part of well-meaning middle class women to reform prostitution.[13] This collection explores these fantasies and what psychoanalysis has to say in this debate. Ona Zee's union effort failed for many of the same reasons union efforts fail more generally—lack of funding, blacklisting, and other more brutal forms of repression. Would it have failed if feminists had rallied around Ona Zee's effort rather than around the ordinance? The answer to that is lost in history. But it is not only for rhetorical purposes that we need to ask this question. Clearly, history has taught us that the more political support, the more who rally behind the union effort, the more likely the union is to win.[14] But, Ona Zee's efforts ran against the ambivalent status of porn workers. If porn workers are prostitutes, they are also outlaws and so their unions cannot be recognized as legitimate. Whether or not prostitution, and with it porn work, should be decriminalized is a question that has to be addressed if union efforts are to proceed. In El Salvador, a union organization has been formed that demands decriminalization as the first step in the effort to organize prostitutes. The sex workers organization in El

Salvador has been influenced by the success of Cuba's efforts to end prostitution after the revolution. Thus, the efforts in the unions in those countries are significantly different from those undertaken in the USA because they are developed in connection with programmes of far-reaching redistribution of wealth, and the restructuring of private property. These programmes allow prostitutes to choose new ways of life by offering them other jobs and careers as alternatives to prostitution.

Again, in most of the world's countries, union-like organizations do not have a special category or group just for porn workers. In discussions with members of these organizations, I explicitly asked about whether or not there were separate organizations for porn workers. The answer I was often given was that in these countries there was no porn industry per se. El Salvador does not have a pornography video industry. Neither does Paraguay. Brazil does. But the union organizations in Brazil have been built around solidarity among sex workers and have not separated out porn workers from prostitutes or workers in sex clubs. From a Brazilian union perspective, there is nothing to be gained politically by making distinctions between workers, which would limit the reach of the union's organizing efforts. Even if one accepts that sex workers are not sexual slaves, the question remains whether or not such union organizations are transitional, or if their programme will change as occurred in Cuba with the formation of a nation-state with socialist aspirations. If a just society were organized, would prostitution need to be outlawed, or would it wither away with the gross economic inequalities that undoubtedly push many women into it? If so, how would this happen?

How it *should* happen is a question that has been addressed by some of the post-colonial states of the Southern hemisphere. If the reasons for prostitution are not simply economic, if prostitution, and pornography and heterosexual sex clubs are all also implicated in a cultural order which reinforces rigid gender identity and heterosexual hegemony, then what steps could be taken to undermine the sedimented symbolic forms in which certain forms of sex work have become engraved? These questions have been asked and answered by women's organizations associated with national liberation movements. Putting these questions forward allows us to see that, for some purposes, it is useful to distinguish between prostitution and sexually explicit material. At the least, certain kinds of sexually explicit material would be needed for sex education in any society.

This leads us to the second half of the question about political organization and pornography and opens us up to the fourth question: what kinds of representational politics are available for redefining pornography, to shift explicit sexual materials away from the frozen violence and rigid gender identities associated with the mainstream heterosexual industry as it has developed in a number of the world's countries? Many union organizations insist on all-condom sets. Some unions in South America have insisted that sex workers in sex clubs have their work limited to 'performance' on stage and have been willing to lend organizational protection so women can enforce this rule themselves. With this change, some of these clubs have a different kind of setting for 'sexual' performance. Just this simple reform changes representational possibilities, since the message of safe sex has been condemned by some mainstream pornographers as running counter to the kind of masculinity they seek to portray in their films. Sexually explicit material can also be used to challenge the limits of representation that some artists, writers, and activists have claimed lie at the heart of totalitarianism. For Peter Esterházy, for example, pornography is a metaphor for the enclosed social and political environments that shut down the individual's imaginary domain,[15] forcing him to sexually, politically, and morally 'hide out'. To quote Esterházy, from his work *A Little Hungarian Pornography*, excerpted for this collection, '. . . pornography should be understood as meaning lies, the lies of the body, the lies of the soul, our lies'.[16] To refuse to hide out, even if only to escape to the small crevices left open by sexuality, can paradoxically, at least under this definition, be a challenge to pornography, even if it proceeds through what others might consider to be pornographic writing.

Thus, our last question is: how can sexually explicit literature, videos, art, and music serve the purpose of sexual freedom? Can we think of such materials as serving the creation of a feminist symbolic, if such a new symbolic order is sought as desirable? Is the protection of sexual freedom, on the contrary, against the impulse to give it order? Essays in Parts IV and V of the collection address these questions, among others.

By opening space for divergent points of view to be addressed, and questions addressing the complexity of sexual material to be heard, we may also allow new forms of organizing and solidarity to get off the ground—ones that do not pit feminists against each other, white middle-class women against women of colour, or prostitutes against porn workers organizations. I have sought to present fairly the divergent voices in both the feminist and queer communities, as they have explored the relationship between sexually explicit material, sex education, and the challenge to rigid gender identities. I felt that to do so meant taking into account the complex class and racial relationships that have often haunted legal and political discussions of how and when sexually explicit materials are labelled sordid, obscene, and/or pornographic.

But I have also sought to be fair to anti-pornography feminism which has undoubtedly shaped so much of the debate within feminism over the last ten years. If there is a central ethical premiss behind the selection of the essays in this book it is that the complexity of sexuality demands that we accord each other respect for our equal dignity. We particularly need to accord each other respect given how intensely invested we are in our own sexuality. This investment makes it difficult for many of us to struggle towards programmes of legal and political reform of prostitution, pornography and trafficking in women more generally. Whatever political or ethical opinion one has about Dworkin and MacKinnon's ordinances, for example, it should remain just that, an ethical and political opinion about the ordinance. But those of us who have participated in the debate know that it has not always remained within those ethical parameters. Both Dworkin and MacKinnon have been demonized in the press and in some academic work. Their political and legal position has at times been read as an expression of their sexuality or a repressed longing for the very sexual abuse they criticize. The sexualization of women who come into the public eye has a long history.[17] Vulnerability to sexual ridicule appeals to an unconscious shame that is symbolically encoded with established meanings of femininity. To discredit a woman can only too easily be done by an appeal to stereotypes of female sexuality. When an idea or reform programme is unattractive, so incompatible with one's sexual-political disposition that it has to be rejected, the rejection can be done either through argument or through displacement and projection. Both displacement and projection often can occur when no good counter argument comes to mind, either because there isn't one or because those who are offended by the idea are too invested in its disposal from the public realm that they are unable to debate it at all. Displacement and projection take all the anxiety and aggression a challenging idea or reform programme evokes and directs those effects not towards the idea or programme but to the person or people who propose it. People who strongly advocate gay and lesbian freedom and equality often have to endure this kind of attack in our current political climate. Displacement or projection shifts the ideological goalpost from the terrain of debate towards the ad homineum. We all know what this move to the ad homineum means. We do not have to listen to her because she is a 'dyke'. We do not have to take her seriously because she slept her way into prominence. She is only advocating that position because she is too unattractive to 'get laid'. In our heart of hearts all of us know why we are afraid of such attacks. It is a long struggle to separate feminine sexual difference from shame; to dare to be 'out there' as ourselves. This is why public reticence and civility are central feminist demands. We have been the targets too often of breaches of public reticence and civility.[18]

Furthermore, we need to support each other in our struggle to claim our person and the best way that we can do that is to adhere to the respect that equal dignity demands. If this dignity is to mean anything it must start with taking each other's self-representations seriously, whether we are representing who we take ourselves to be sexually, how we view pornography, or how we see ourselves as feminists. It is a commonplace insight of feminists of many different schools of thought that women internalize the wounds of femininity so as to disavow their own worth as persons. The solution to this within feminism can only be that by treating each other with equal dignity we can bring into 'being' the world we dream of, a world in which women are finally freed from imposed personas that mark us out as those who can be excluded from the respect due to all those who are included in the moral community of persons.

If we are to tackle effectively the issue of pornography we must first and foremost recognize that any fixed definition of what pornography is will be inadequate. Lecturing at people has always been a detriment to organizing. Open discussion is no replacement for organizing, but it can be a first step. My hope for this collection is that it can help us to take that step.

Notes

1. Catharine MacKinnon, *Only Words* (Cambridge, Mass.: Harvard University Press, 1993).
2. For an excellent discussion of the relationship between the pornography industry in the United States and Europe and its relationship to the worldwide institutionalized sexual slavery of women and children, see Kathleen Barry, *Female Sexual Slavery* (New York: New York University Press, 1979) ch. 9, 205–52. For Barry, and many feminists have agreed with her, pornography is a form of prostitution and therefore there can be no separation of pornography from the institution of prostitution more generally.

3. MacKinnon, *Only Words*, 22.
4. Andrea Dworkin and Catharine MacKinnon, *Pornography and Civil Rights: A New Day* (Minneapolis: Organizing Against Pornography, 1988).
5. The Indianapolis ordinance was ruled unconstitutional in *American Booksellers* v. *Hudnut*, 771 F.2d 323 (7th Cir. 1985), *aff'd*, 475 U.S 1001 (1986).
6. For a more extensive discussion on what role the imaginary domain is to play in feminist theory and the development of a concept of rights, see Drucilla Cornell, *The Imaginary Domain: Abortion, Pornography, Sexual Harassment* (New York: Routledge, 1995) and *At the Heart of Freedom: Feminism, Sex, and Equality* (Princeton: Princeton University Press, 1998).
7. In *R.* v. *Butler*, 1 S. C. R. 452 (S. C. C. 1992), the Canadian Supreme Court reinterpreted 'obscenity', as prohibited by the criminal code, to focus on the harms it inflicts. Pursuant to a bust shortly thereafter, one piece of short fiction in one issue of *Bad Attitude* (a US lesbian magazine) was held to be criminally obscene. *R.* v. *Scythes*, O. J. No. 537 Ont. Prov. Ct. (16 January 1993). Few North American feminists have endorsed the finding of obscenity there, and the case illustrates the peril of criminalizing pornography, in contrast to the civil rights approach of the MacKinnon/Dworkin ordinance. More far-reaching are two civil challenges brought by gay/lesbian bookstores against arbitrary and discriminatory seizures by Canadian Customs of materials imported for them. Both cases were brought before the *Butler* decision: Customs had long discriminated against gay/lesbian materials, back when 'obscenity' was a moral issue. In the first case, an Ontario court held that nine seized items were obscene, purportedly relying on *Butler*, but deploying expressly morality-based reasoning. *Glad Day Bookshop, Inc.* v. *M. N. R. Canada*, O.J. No. 1466 Ont. H. C. Gen. Div. (14 July 1992). That reasoning was later expressly rejected by a higher court in the same province, in finding gay materials not obscene within the meaning of *Butler. R.* v. *Ronish*, 26 C. R. 4th 75 (Ont. C. A. 1993). More recently, in the case involving Customs' seizure of 370 gay/lesbian titles destined for Little Sisters bookstore in Vancouver, a court had stated that the materials were not obscene, and that Customs' practice in seizing them was inconsistent with *Butler. Little Sisters Art and Book Emporium* v. *A. G. Canada*, 131 D. L. R. 4th (B. C. Sup. Ct. 1996). Thus, though *Butler* can be problematic if misused, its harm-based focus has generally relieved gay/lesbian publications from the moral opprobrium and legal assaults previously imposed by both Canadian police and Customs.
8. I use the expression Third World reluctantly because it brings together countries with very different cultural traditions, strategies for economic and national independence, and linguistic traditions, and defines them in a relationship of hierarchy to the First World. See M. Jacqui Alexander and Chandra Talpade Mohanty, 'Genealogies, Legacies, Movements' in id. (eds.) *Feminist Genealogies, Colonial Legacies, Democratic Futures* (New York: Routledge, 1997) for an analysis of why First World feminists should be careful of designating the now Northern world as the Third World.
9. See Barry, *Female Sexual Slavery*, 163–204.
10. Amina Mama, 'Sheroes and Villains: Conceptualizing Colonial and Contemporary Violence Against Women in Africa', in Alexander and Mohanty (eds.) *Feminist Genealogies, Colonial Legacies, Democratic Futures*, 46–62
11. The difference between adult women and children is not that I do not

consider children persons in the moral community at birth. I do, and they have as a result at least two basic rights: the right not to be sold and the right not to be killed. Their scope of rights increases with age. If anything, children because they are so vulnerable to adults are in desperate need of the protection of their imaginary domain. But given their youth and inexperience, the question of their right to the self representation of their sexuate being is differently answered. As I have argued elsewhere, it undermines the dignity of adult women to deny them their right to the self-representation of their sexuate being as a matter of law. See Cornell, *At the Heart of Freedom*, ch. 2.

12. I am adopting Ronald Dworkin's well-known title of his book on legal interpretation, *Law's Empire* (Cambridge, Mass.: Belknap Press, 1986)
13. See Cornell, *At the Heart of Freedom*, ch. 2., for a discussion of the history of such reform efforts in 19th century England and France.
14. See John Hevener, *Which Side Are You On?* (Urbana: University of Illinois Press, 1978).
15. See Cornell, *The Imaginary Domain.*
16. Peter Esterházy, *A Little Hungarian Pornography*, trans. Judith Sollosy (Evanston, I 11.: Northwestern University Press, 1995).
17. See Joan Wallace Scott's discussion of how women are exposed to ridicule when they seek to enter the public domain in ways considered inappropriate to proper female behaviour. See ch. 1 in *Only Paradoxes to Offer: French Feminists and the Rights of Man* (Cambridge, Mass.: Harvard University Press, 1996).
18. For an excellent discussion of the importance of concealment and reticence in a civil public life, see Thomas Nagel's 'Concealment and Exposure' *Philosophy and Public Affairs*, 27: 1 (1998), 3 30.

Part I. Anti-Pornography Feminism

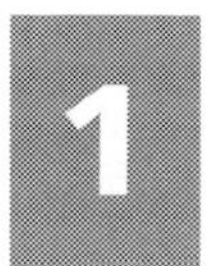

Against the Male Flood

Censorship, Pornography, and Equality

Andrea Dworkin

To say what one thought—that was my little problem—against the prodigious Current; to find a sentence that could hold its own against the male flood.

(Virginia Woolf)

I want to say right here, that those well-meaning friends on the outside who say that we have suffered these horrors of prison, of hunger strikes and forcible feeding, because we desired to martyrise ourselves for the cause, are absolutely and entirely mistaken. We never went to prison in order to be martyrs. We went there in order that we might obtain the rights of citizenship. We were willing to break laws that we might force men to give us the right to make laws.

(Emmeline Pankhurst)

CENSORSHIP

Censorship is a real thing, not an abstract idea or a word that can be used to mean anything at all.

In ancient Rome, a censor was a magistrate who took the census (a count of the male population and an evaluation of property for the purpose of taxation done every fifth year), assessed taxes, and inspected morals and conduct. His power over conduct came from his power to tax. For instance, in 403 B.C. the censors Camillus and

Andrea Dworkin, 'Against the Male Flood: Censorship, Pornography, and Equality', in *Letters for a War Zone* (Martin Secker and Warburg, 1997). Version printed in this collection is from *Pornography: Woman, Violence, and Civil Liberties*, ed. Catherine Itzin (Oxford University Press, 1994), 515–35, reprinted by permission of Elaine Markson Literary Agency Inc.

Postimius heavily fined elderly bachelors for not marrying. The power to tax, then as now, was the power to destroy. The censor, using the police and judicial powers of the state, regulated social behaviour.

At its origins, then, censorship had nothing to do with striking down ideas as such; it had to do with acts. In my view, real state censorship still does. In South Africa, and the Soviet Union, for instance, writing is treated entirely as an act and writers are viewed as persons who engage in an act (writing) that by its very nature is dangerous to the continued existence of the state. The police do not try to suppress ideas. They are more specific, more concrete, more realistic. They go after books and manuscripts (writing) and destroy them. They go after writers as persons who have done something that they will do again and they persecute, punish, or kill them. They do not worry about what people think—not, at least, as we use the word *think*: a mental event, entirely internal, abstract. They worry about what people do: and writing, speaking, even as evidence that thinking is going on, are seen as things people *do*. There is a quality of immediacy and reality in what writing is taken to be. Where police power is used against writers systematically, writers are seen as people who by writing do something socially real and significant, not contemplative or dithering. Therefore, writing is never peripheral or beside the point. It is serious and easily seditious. I am offering no brief for police states when I say that virtually all great writers, cross-culturally and trans-historically, share this view of what writing is. In countries like the USA, controlled by a bourgeoisie to whom the police are accountable, writing is easier to do and valued less. It has less impact. It is more abundant and cheaper. Less is at stake for reader and writer both. The writer may hold writing to be a life-or-death matter, but the police and society do not. Writing is seen to be a personal choice, not a social, political, or aesthetic necessity fraught with danger and meaning. The general view in these pleasant places* is that writers think up ideas or words and then other people read them and all this happens in the head, a vast cavern somewhere north of the eyes. It is all air, except for the paper and ink, which are simply banal. Nothing happens.

Police in police states and most great writers throughout time see

* 'Well, you know, it amazes me . . .', says dissident South African writer Nadine Gordimer in an interview. I come to America, I go to England, I go to France . . . nobody's at risk. They're afraid of getting cancer, losing a lover, losing their jobs, being insecure . . . It's only in my own country that I find people who voluntarily choose to put everything at risk — in their personal life' Nadine Gordimer, *Writers at Work: The Paris Review Interviews* 261 (G. Plimpton ed., 6th ser., 1984).

writing as act, not air—as act, not idea; concrete, specific, real, not insubstantial blather on a dead page. Censorship goes after the act and the actor: the book and the writer. It needs to destroy both. The cost in human lives is staggering, and it is perhaps essential to say that human lives destroyed must count more in the weighing of horror than books burned. This is my personal view, and I love books more than I love people.

Censorship is deeply misunderstood in the United States, because the fairly spoiled, privileged, frivolous people who are the literate citizens of this country think that censorship is some foggy effort to suppress ideas. For them, censorship is not something in itself—an act of police power with discernible consequences to hunted people; instead, it is about something abstract—the suppressing or controlling of ideas. Censorship, like writing itself, is no longer an act. Because it is no longer the blatant exercise of police power against writers or books because of what they do, what they accomplish in the real world, it becomes vague, hard to find, except perhaps as an attitude. It gets used to mean unpleasant, even angry frowns of disapproval or critiques delivered in harsh tones; it means social disapproval or small retaliations by outraged citizens where the book is still available and the writer is entirely unharmed, even if insulted. It hangs in the air, ominous, like the threat of drizzle. It gets to be, in silly countries like this one, whatever people say it is, separate from any material definition, separate from police power, separate from state repression (jail, banning, exile, death), separate from devastating consequences to real people (jail, banning, exile, death). It is something that people who eat fine food and wear fine clothes worry about frenetically, trying to find it, anticipating it with great anxiety, arguing it down as if it were real—an argument would make it go away; not knowing that it has a clear, simple, unavoidable momentum and meaning in a cruel world of police power that their privilege cannot comprehend.

OBSCENITY

In the nineteenth and twentieth centuries, in most of Western Europe, England, and the United States, more often than not (time-out for Franco, for instance), writing has been most consistently viewed as an act warranting prosecution when the writing is construed to be obscene.

The republics, democracies and constitutional monarchies of the

West, now and then do not smother writers in police violence; they prefer to pick off writers who annoy and irritate selectively with fairly token prosecutions. The list of writers so harassed is elegant, white, male (therefore the pronoun he is used throughout this discussion), and remarkably small. Being among them is more than a ceremoinial honour. As Flaubert wrote to his brother in 1857:

> My persecution has brought me widespread sympathy. If my book is bad, that will serve to make it seem better. If, on the other hand, it has lasting qualities, that will build a foundation for it. There you are!
>
> I am hourly awaiting the official document which will name the day when I am to take my seat (for the crime of having written in French) in the dock in the company of thieves and homosexuals.[1]

A few months later that same year, Baudelaire was fined 300 francs for publishing six obscene poems. They also had to be removed from future editions of his book. In harder, earlier days, Jean-Jacques Rousseau spent eight years as a fugitive after his *Émile* was banned and a warrant was issued for his arrest. English censors criminally prosecuted Swinburne's *Poems and Ballads* in 1866. They were particularly piqued at Zola, even in translation, so his English publisher, 70 years old, went to jail for three months. In 1898, a bookseller was arrested for selling Havelock Ellis' work and received a suspended sentence. This list is representative, not exhaustive. While prosecutions of writers under obscenity laws have created great difficulties for writers already plagued with them (as most writers are), criminal prosecutions under obscenity law in Europe and the United States are notable for how narrowly they reach writers, how sanguine writers tend to be about the consequences to themselves, and how little is paid in the writer's life-blood to what D. H. Lawrence (who paid more than most modern Western writers) called the 'censor-moron'.[2] In South Africa, one would hardly be so flip. In our world, the writer gets harassed, as Lawrence did; the writer may be poor or not—the injury is considerably worse if he is; but the writer is not terrorized or tortured, and writers do not live under a reign of terror as writers, because of what they *do*. The potshot application of criminal law for writing is not good, nice, or right; but it is important to recognize the relatively narrow scope and marginal character of criminal prosecution under obscenity law in particular—especially compared with the scope and character of police-state censorship. Resisting obscenity law does not require hyperbolic renderings of what it is and how it has been used. It can be fought or repudiated on its own terms.

The use of obscenity laws against writers, however haphazard or insistent, is censorship and it does hold writing to be an act. This is a unique perception of what writing is, taking place, as it does, in a liberal context in which writing is held to be ideas. It is the obscene quality of the writing, the obscenity itself, that is seen to turn writing from idea into act. Writing of any kind or quality is idea, except for obscene writing, which is act. Writing is censored, even in our own happy little land of Oz, as act, not idea.

What is obscenity, such that it turns writing, when obscene, into something that actually happens—changes it from internal wind somewhere in the elevated mind into a genuinely offensive and utterly real fart, noticed, rude, occasioning pinched fingers on the nose?

There is the legal answer and the artistic answer. Artists have been consistently pushing on the boundaries of obscenity because great writers see writing as an act, and in liberal culture, only obscene writing has that social standing, that quality of dynamism and heroism. Great writers tend to experience writing as an intense and disruptive act; in the West, it is only recognized as such when the writing itself is experienced as obscene. In liberal culture, the writer has needed obscenity to be perceived as socially real.

What is it that obscenity does? The writer uses what the society deems to be obscene because the society then reacts to the writing the way the writer values the writing: as if it does something. But obscenity itself is socially constructed; the writer does not invent it or in any sense originate it. He finds it, knowing that it is what society hides. He looks under rocks and in dark corners.

There are two possible derivations of the word *obscenity*: the discredited one, *what is concealed*; and the accepted one, *filth*. Animals bury their filth, hide it, cover it, leave it behind, separate it from themselves: so do we, going way way back. Filth is excrement; from down there. We bury it or hide it; also, we hide where it comes from. Under male rule, menstrual blood is also filth, so women are twice dirty. Filth is where the sexual organs are and because women are seen primarily as sex, existing to provide sex, women have to be covered: our naked bodies being obscene.

Obscenity law uses both possible root meanings of *obscene* intertwined: it typically condemns nudity, public display, lewd exhibition, exposed genitals or buttocks or pubic areas, sodomy, masturbation, sexual intercourse, excretion. Obscenity law is applied to pictures and words: the artefact itself exposes what should be hidden; it shows dirt.

The human body and all sex and excretory acts are the domain of obscenity law.

But being in the domain of obscenity law is not enough. One must feel alive there. To be obscene, the representations must arouse prurient interest. *Prurient* means *itching* or *itch*; it is related to the Sanskrit for *he burns*. It means sexual arousal. Judges, law-makers, and juries have been, until very recently, entirely male: empirically, *prurient* means *causes erection*. Theologians have called this same quality of obscenity 'venereal pleasure', holding that

> if a work is to be called obscene it must, of its nature, be such as actually to arouse or calculated to arouse in the viewer or reader such venereal pleasure. If the work is *not* of such a kind, it may, indeed, be vulgar, disgusting, crude, unpleasant, what you will—but it will *not* be, in the strict sense which Canon Law obliges us to apply, obscene.[3]

A secular philosopher of pornography isolated the same quality when he wrote: 'Obscenity is our name for the uneasiness which upsets the physical state associated with self-possession.'[4]

Throughout history, the male has been the standard for obscenity law: erection is his venereal pleasure or the uneasiness which upsets the physical state associated with his self-possession. It is not surprising, then, that in the same period when women became jurors, lawyers, and judges—but especially jurors, women having been summarily excluded from most juries until perhaps a decade ago—obscenity law fell into disuse and disregard. In order for obscenity law to have retained social and legal coherence, it would have had to recognize as part of its standard women's sexual arousal, a more subjective standard than erection. It would also have had to use the standard of penile erection in a social environment that was no longer sex-segregated, an environment in which male sexual arousal would be subjected to female scrutiny. In my view, the presence of women in the public sphere of legal decision-making has done more to undermine the efficacy of obscenity law than any self-conscious movement against it.

The act that obscenity recognizes is erection, and whatever writing produces erection is seen to be obscene—act, not idea—because of what it makes happen. The male sexual response is seen to be involuntary, so there is no experientially explicable division between the material that causes erection and the erection itself. That is the logic of obscenity law used against important writers who have pushed against the borders of the socially defined obscene, because they wanted writing to have that very quality of being a socially recognized act. They wanted the inevitability of the response—the social response. The erection makes the writing socially real from the society's point of view, not from the writer's. What the writer needs is to be taken seriously, by any means necessary. In liberal societies, only obscenity law comprehends writing as an act. It defines the nature and quality of the act narrowly—not writing itself, but producing erections. Flaubert apparently did produce them; so did Baudelaire, Zola, Rousseau, Lawrence, Joyce, and Nabokov. It's that simple.

What is at stake in obscenity law is always erection: under what conditions, in what circumstances, how, by whom, by what materials men want it produced in themselves. Men have made this public policy. Why they want to regulate their own erections through law is a question of endless interest and importance to feminists. Nevertheless, that they do persist in this regulation is simple fact. There are civil and social conflicts over how best to regulate erection through law, especially when caused by words or pictures. Arguments among men notwithstanding, high culture is phallocentric. It is also, using the civilized criteria of jurisprudence, not infrequently obscene.

Most important writers have insisted that their own uses of the obscene as socially defined are not pornography. As D. H. Lawrence wrote: 'But even I would censor genuine pornography rigorously. It would not be very difficult . . . [Y]ou can recognize it by the insult it offers, invariably, to sex, and to the human spirit.'[5] It was also, he pointed out, produced by the underworld. Nabokov saw in pornography 'mediocrity, commercialism, and certain strict rules of narration . . . [A]ction has to be limited to the copulation of clichés. Style, structure, imagery should never distract the reader from his tepid lust'.[6] They knew that what they did was different from pornography, but they did not entirely know what the difference was. They missed the heart of an empirical distinction because writing was indeed real to them but women were not.

The insult pornography offers, invariably, to sex is accomplished in the active subordination of women: the creation of a sexual dynamic in which the putting-down of women, the suppression of women, and ultimately the brutalization of women, *is* what sex is taken to be. Obscenity in law, and in what it does socially, is erection. Law recognizes the act in this. Pornography, however, is a broader, more comprehensive act, because it crushes a whole class of people through violence and subjugation: and sex is the vehicle that does the crushing. The penis is not the test, as it is in obscenity. Instead, the status of women is the issue. Erection is implicated in the subordinating, but who it reaches and how are the pressing legal and social questions. Pornography, unlike obscenity, is a discrete, identifiable system of sexual exploitation that hurts women as a class by creating inequality and abuse. This is a new legal idea, but it is the recognition and naming of an old and cruel injury to a dispossessed and coerced underclass. It is the sound of women's words breaking the longest silence.

PORNOGRAPHY

In the United States, it is an $8 billion trade in sexual exploitation.

It is women turned into subhumans, beaver, pussy, body parts, genitals exposed, buttocks, breasts, mouths opened and throats penetrated, covered in semen, pissed on, shitted on, hung from light fixtures, tortured, maimed, bleeding, disembowelled, killed.

It is some creature called female, used.

It is scissors poised at the vagina and objects stuck in it, a smile on the woman's face, her tongue hanging out.

It is a woman being fucked by dogs, horses, snakes.

It is every torture in every prison cell in the world, done to women and sold as sexual entertainment.

It is rape and gang rape and anal rape and throat rape: and it is the woman raped, asking for more.

It is the woman in the picture to whom it is really happening and the women against whom the picture is used, to make them do what the woman in the picture is doing.

It is the power men have over women turned into sexual acts men do to women, because pornography is the power and the act.

It is the conditioning of erection and orgasm in men to the powerlessness of women; our inferiority, humiliation, pain, torment; to us as objects, things, or commodities for use in sex as servants.

It sexualizes inequality and in doing so creates discrimination as a sex-based practice.

It permeates the political condition of women in society by being the substance of our inequality however located—in jobs, in education, in marriage, *in life.*

It is women, kept a sexual underclass, kept available for rape and battery and incest and prostitution.

It is what we are under male domination; it is what we are for under male domination.

It is the heretofore hidden (from us) system of subordination that women have been told is just life.

Under male supremacy, it is the synonym for what being a woman is.

It is access to our bodies as a birthright to men: the grant, the gift, the permission, the licence, the proof, the promise, the method, how-to; it is us accessible, no matter what the law pretends to say, no matter what we pretend to say.

It is physical injury and physical humiliation and physical pain: to the women against whom it is used after it is made; to the women used to make it.

As words alone, or words and pictures, moving or still, it creates systematic harm to women in the form of discrimination and physical hurt. It creates harm inevitably by its nature because of what it is and what it does. The harm will occur as long as it is made and used. The name of the next victim is unknown, but everything else is known.

Because of it—because it is the subordination of women perfectly achieved—the abuse done to us by any human standard is perceived as using us for what we are by nature: women are whores; women want to be raped; she provoked it; women like to be hurt; she says no but means yes because she wants to be taken against her will which is not really her will because what she wants underneath is to have anything done to her that violates or humiliates or hurts her; she wants it, because she is a woman, no matter what it is, because she is a woman; that is how women are, what women are, what women are for. This view is institutionally expressed in law. So much for equal protection.

If it were being done to human beings, it would be reckoned an atrocity. It is being done to women. It is reckoned fun, pleasure, entertainment, sex, somebody's (not something's) civil liberty no less.

What do you want to be when you grow up? *Doggie Girl*? *Gestapo Sex Slave*? *Black Bitch in Bondage*? Pet, bunny, beaver? In dreams begin responsibilities,[7] whether one is the dreamer or the dreamed.

PORNOGRAPHERS

Most of them are small-time pimps or big-time pimps. They sell women: the real flesh-and-blood women in the pictures. They like the excitement of domination; they are greedy for profit; they are sadistic in their exploitation of women; they hate women, and the pornography they make is the distillation of that hate. The photographs are what they have created live, for themselves, for their own enjoyment. The exchanges of women among them are part of the fun, too: so that the fictional creature 'Linda Lovelace', who was the real woman Linda Marciano, was forced to 'deep-throat' every pornographer her owner-pornographer wanted to impress. Of course, it was the woman, not the fiction, who had to be hypnotized so that the men could penetrate to the bottom of her throat, and who had to be beaten and terrorized to get her compliance at all. The finding of new and terrible things to do to women is part of the challenge of the vocation: so the inventor of 'Linda Lovelace' and 'deep-throating' is a genius in the field, a pioneer. Or, as Al Goldstein, a colleague, referred to him in an interview with him in *Screw* several years ago: a pimp's pimp.

Even with written pornography, there has never been the distinction between making pornography and the sexual abuse of live women that is taken as a truism by those who approach pornography as if it were an intellectual phenomenon. The Marquis de Sade, as the world's foremost literary pornographer, is archetypal. His sexual practice was the persistent sexual abuse of women and girls, with occasional excursions into the abuse of boys. As an aristocrat in a feudal society, he preyed with near impunity on prostitutes and servants. The pornography he wrote was an urgent part of the sexual abuse he practised: not only because he did what he wrote, but also because the intense hatred of women that fuelled the one also fuelled the other: not two separate engines, but one engine running on the same tank. The acts of pornography and the acts of rape were waves on the same sea: that sea, becoming for its victims however it reached them, a tidal wave of destruction. Pornographers who use words know that what they are doing is both aggressive and destructive: sometimes they philosophize about how sex inevitably ends in death, the death of a woman being a thing of sexual beauty as well as excitement. Pornography, even when written, is sex because of the dynamism of the sexual hatred in it; and for pornographers, the sexual abuse of women as commonly understood and pornography are both acts of sexual predation, which is how they live.

One reason that stopping pornographers and pornography is not censorship is that pornographers are more like the police in police states than they are like the writers in police states. They are the instruments of terror, not its victims. What police do to the powerless in police states is what pornographers do to women, except that it is entertainment for the masses, not dignified as political. Writers do not do what pornographers do. Secret police do. Torturers do. What pornographers do to women is more like what police do to political prisoners than it is like anything else: except for the fact that it is watched with so much pleasure by so many. Intervening in a system of terror where it is vulnerable to public scrutiny to stop it is not censorship; it is the system of terror that stops speech and creates abuse and despair. The pornographers are the secret police of male supremacy: keeping women subordinate through intimidation and assault.

SUBORDINATION

In the amendment to the Human Rights Ordinance of the City of Minneapolis written by Catharine A. MacKinnon and myself, pornography is defined as the graphic, sexually explicit subordination of women whether in pictures or in words that also includes one or more of the following: women are presented dehumanized as sexual objects, things, or commodities; or women are presented as sexual objects who enjoy pain or humiliation; or women are presented as sexual objects who experience sexual pleasure in being raped, or women are presented as sexual objects tied up or cut up or mutilated or bruised or physically hurt; or women are presented in postures of sexual submission; or women's body parts are exhibited such that women are reduced to those parts; or women are presented being penetrated by objects or animals; or women are presented in scenarios of degradation, injury, abasement, torture, shown as filthy or inferior, bleeding, bruised, or hurt in a context that makes these conditions sexual.

This statutory definition is an objectively accurate definition of what pornography is, based on an analysis of the material produced by the $8 billion-a-year industry, and also on extensive study of the whole range of pornography extant from other eras and other cultures. Given the fact that women's oppression has an ahistorical character—a sameness across time and cultures expressed in rape, battery, incest and prostitution—it is no surprise that pornography, a central phenomenon in that oppression, has precisely that quality of sameness. It does not significantly change in what it is, what it does, what is in it, or how it works, whether it is, for instance, classical or feudal or modern, Western or Asian; whether the method of manufacture is words, photographs or video. What has changed is the public availability of pornography and the numbers of live women used in it because of new technologies: not its nature. Many people note what seems to them a qualitative change in pornography—that it has become more violent, even grotesquely violent, over the last two decades. The change is only in what is publicly visible: not in the range or preponderance of violent pornography (e.g. the place of rape in pornography stays constant and central, no matter where, when, or how the pornography is produced); not in the character, quality, or content of what the pornographers actually produce; not in the harm caused; not in the valuation of women in it, or the metaphysical definition of what women are; not in the sexual abuse promoted, including rape, battery, and incest; not in the centrality of its role in subordinating women. Until recently, pornography operated in private, where most abuse of women takes place.

The oppression of women occurs through sexual subordination. It is the use of sex as the medium of oppression that makes the subordination of women so distinct from racism or prejudice against a group based on religion or national origin. Social inequality is created in many different ways. In my view, the radical responsibility is to isolate the material means of creating the inequality so that material remedies can be found for it.

This is particularly difficult with respect to women's inequality because that inequality is achieved through sex. Sex as desired by the class that dominates women is held by that class to be elemental, urgent, necessary, even if or even though it appears to *require* the repudiation of any claim women might have to full human standing. In the subordination of women, inequality itself is sexualized: made into the experience of sexual pleasure, essential to sexual desire. Pornography is the material means of sexualizing inequality; and that is why pornography is a central practice in the subordination of women.

Subordination itself is a broad, deep, systematic dynamic discernible in any persecution based on race or sex. Social subordination has four main parts. First, there is *hierarchy*, a group on top and a group on the bottom. For women, this hierarchy is experienced both socially and sexually, publicly and privately. Women are physically integrated into the society in which we are held to be inferior, and our low status is both put in place and maintained in the sexual usage of us by men; and so women's experience of hierarchy is incredibly intimate and wounding.

Second, subordination is *objectification*. Objectification occurs when a human being, through social means, is made less than human, turned into a thing or commodity, bought and sold. When objectification occurs, a person is depersonalized, so that no individuality or integrity is available socially or in what is an extremely circumscribed privacy (because those who dominate determine its boundaries). Objectification is an injury right at the heart of discrimination: those who can be used as if they are not fully human are no longer fully human in social terms; their humanity is hurt by being diminished.

Third, subordination is *submission.* A person is at the bottom of a hierarchy because of a condition of birth; a person on the bottom is dehumanized, an object or commodity; inevitably, the situation of that person requires obedience and compliance. That diminished person is expected to be submissive; there is no longer any right to self-determination, because there is no basis in equality for any such right to exist. In a condition of inferiority and objectification, submission is usually essential for survival. Oppressed groups are known for their abilities to anticipate the orders and desires of those who have power over them, to comply with an obsequiousness that is then used by the dominant group to justify its own dominance: the master, not able to imagine a human like himself in such degrading servility, thinks the servility is proof that the hierarchy is natural and that the objectification simply amounts to seeing these lesser creatures for what they are. The submission forced on inferior, objectified groups precisely by hierarchy and objectification is taken to be the proof of inherent inferiority and subhuman capacities.

Fourth, subordination is *violence.* The violence is systematic, endemic enough to be unremarkable and normative, usually taken as an implicit right of the one committing the violence. In my view, hierarchy, objectification, and submission are the preconditions for systematic social violence against any group targeted because of a condition of birth. If violence against a group is both socially pervasive and socially normal, then hierarchy, objectification, and submission are already solidly in place.

The role of violence in subordinating women has one special characteristic congruent with sex as the instrumentality of subordination: the violence is supposed to be sex for the woman too—what women want and like as part of our sexual nature; it is supposed to give women pleasure (as in rape); it is supposed to mean love to a woman from her point of view (as in battery). The violence against women is seen to be done not just in accord with something compliant in women, but in response to something active in and basic to women's nature.

Pornography uses each component of social subordination. Its particular medium is sex. Hierarchy, objectification, submission, and violence all become alive with sexual energy and sexual meaning. A hierarchy, for instance, can have a static quality; but pornography, by sexualizing it, makes it dynamic, almost carnivorous, so that men keep imposing it for the sake of their own sexual pleasure—for the sexual pleasure it gives them to impose it. In pornography, each element of subordination is conveyed through the sexually explicit usage of women: pornography in fact is what women are and what women are for and how women are used in a society premised on the inferiority of women. It is a metaphysics of women's subjugation: our existence delineated in a definition of our nature; our status in society predetermined by the uses to which we are put. The woman's body is what is materially subordinated. Sex is the material means through which the subordination is accomplished. Pornography is the institution of male dominance that sexualizes hierarchy, objectification, submission, and violence. As such, pornography creates inequality, not as artefact but as a system of social reality; it creates the necessity for and the actual behaviours that constitute sex inequality.

SPEECH

Subordination can be so deep that those who are hurt by it are utterly silent. Subordination can create a silence quieter than death. The women flattened out on the page are deathly still, except for *hurt me. Hurt me* is not women's speech. It is the speech imposed on women by pimps to cover the awful, condemning silence. The Three Marias of Portugal went to jail for writing this: 'Let no one tell me that silence gives consent, because whoever is silent dissents.'[8] The women say the pimps' words: the language is another element of the rape; the language is part of the humiliation; the language is part of the forced sex. Real silence might signify dissent, for those reared to understand its sad discourse. The pimps cannot tolerate literal silence—it is too eloquent as testimony—so they force the words out of the woman's mouth. The women say pimps' words: which is worse than silence. The silence of the women not in the picture, outside the pages, hurt but silent, used but silent, is staggering in how deep and wide it goes. It is a silence over centuries: an exile into speechlessness. One is shut up by the inferiority and the abuse. One is shut up by the threat and the injury. In her memoir of the Stalin period, *Hope Against Hope*, Nadezhda Mandelstam wrote that screaming

> is a man's way of leaving a trace, of telling people how he lived and died. By

his screams he asserts his right to live, sends a message to the outside world demanding help and calling for resistance. If nothing else is left, one must scream. Silence is the real crime against humanity.[9]

Screaming is a man's way of leaving a trace. The scream of a man is never misunderstood as a scream of pleasure by passers-by or politicians or historians, nor by the tormentor. A man's scream is a call for resistance. A man's scream asserts his right to live, sends a message; he leaves a trace. A woman's scream is the sound of her female will and her female pleasure in doing what the pornographers say she is for. Her scream is a sound of celebration to those who overhear. Women's way of leaving a trace is the silence, centuries' worth: the entirely inhuman silence that surely one day will be noticed, someone will say that something is wrong, some sound is missing, some voice is lost; the entirely inhuman silence that will be a clue to human hope denied, a shard of evidence that a crime has occurred, the crime that created the silence; the entirely inhuman silence that is a cold, cold condemnation of hurt sustained in speechlessness, a cold, cold condemnation of what those who speak have done to those who do not.

But there is more than the *hurt me* forced out of us, and the silence in which it lies. The pornographers actually use our bodies as their language. Our bodies are the building blocks of their sentences. What they do to us, called speech, is not unlike what Kafka's Harrow machine '"The needles are set in like the teeth of a harrow and the whole thing works something like a harrow, although its action is limited to one place and contrived with much more artistic skill"'[10]—did to the condemned in 'In the Penal Colony':

'Our sentence does not sound severe. Whatever commandment the prisoner has disobeyed is written upon his body by the Harrow. This prisoner, for instance'—the officer indicated the man—'will have written on his body: HONOUR THY SUPERIORS!'[11]

'. . . The Harrow is beginning to write; when it finishes the first draft of the inscription on the man's back, the layer of cotton wool begins to roll and slowly turns the body over, to give the Harrow fresh space for writing . . . So it keeps on writing deeper and deeper.'[12]

Asked if the prisoner knows his sentence, the officer replies 'There would be no point in telling him. He'll learn it on his body.'[13]

This is the so-called speech of the pornographers, protected now by law.

Protecting what they 'say' means protecting what they do to us, how they do it. It means protecting their sadism on our bodies, because that is how they write: not like a writer at all; like a torturer. Protecting what they 'say' means protecting sexual exploitation, because they cannot 'say' anything without diminishing, hurting, or destroying us. Their rights of speech express their rights over us. Their rights of speech require our inferiority: and that we be powerless in relation to them. Their rights of speech mean that *hurt me* is accepted as the real speech of women, not speech forced on us as part of the sex forced on us but originating with us because we are what the pornographers 'say' we are.

If what we want to say is not *hurt me*, we have the real social power only to use silence as eloquent dissent. Silence is what women have instead of speech. Silence is our dissent during rape unless the rapist, like the pornographer, prefers *hurt me*, in which case we have no dissent. Silence is our moving persuasive dissent during battery unless the batterer, like the pornographer, prefers *hurt me*. Silence is a fine dissent during incest and for all the long years after.

Silence is not speech. We have silence, not speech. We fight rape, battery, incest, and prostitution with it. We lose. But someday someone will notice: that people called women were buried in a long silence that meant dissent and that the pornographers—with needles set in like the teeth of a harrow—chattered on.

EQUALITY

> To get that word, male, out of the Constitution cost the women of this country 52 years of pauseless campaign; 56 state referendum campaigns; 480 legislative campaigns to get state suffrage amendments submitted; 47 state constitutional convention campaigns; 277 state party convention campaigns; 30 national party convention campaigns to get suffrage planks in the party platforms; 19 campaigns with 19 successive Congresses to get the federal amendment submitted, and the final ratification campaign.
>
> Millions of dollars were raised, mostly in small sums, and spent with economic care. Hundreds of women gave the accumulated possibilities of an entire lifetime, thousands gave years of their lives, hundreds of thousands gave constant interest and such aid as they could. It was a continuous and seemingly endless chain of activity. Young suffragists who helped forge the last links

> of that chain were not born when it began. Old suffragists who helped forge the first links were dead when it ended.
>
> (Carrie Chapman Catt)

Feminists have wanted equality. Radicals and reformists have different ideas of what equality would be, but it has been the wisdom of feminism to value equality as a political goal with social integrity and complex meaning. The Jacobins also wanted equality, and the French Revolution was fought to accomplish it. Conservatism as a modern political movement actually developed to resist social and political movements for equality, beginning with the egalitarian imperatives of the French Revolution.

Women have had to prove human status, before having any claim to equality. But equality has been impossible to achieve, perhaps because, really, women have not been able to prove human status. The burden of proof is on the victim.

Not one inch of change has been easy or cheap. We have fought so hard and so long for so little. The vote did not change the status of women. The changes in women's lives that we can see on the surface do not change the status of women. By the year 2000, women are expected to be 100 per cent of this nation's poor. We are raped, battered, and prostituted: these acts against us are in the fabric of social life. As children, we are raped, physically abused, and prostituted. The country enjoys the injuries done to us, and spends $8 billion a year on the pleasure of watching us being hurt (exploitation as well as torture constituting substantive harm). The subordination gets deeper: we keep getting pushed down further. Rape is an entertainment. The contempt for us in that fact is immeasurable; yet we live under the weight of it. Discrimination is a euphemism for what happens to us.

It has plagued us to try to understand why the status of women does not change. Those who hate the politics of equality say they know: we are biologically destined for rape; God made us to be submissive unto our husbands. We change, but our status does not change. Laws change, but our status stays fixed. We move into the marketplace, only to face there classic sexual exploitation, now called sexual harassment. Rape, battery, prostitution, and incest stay the same in that they keep happening to us as part of what life is: even though we name the crimes against us as such and try to keep the victims from being destroyed by what we cannot stop from happening to them. And the silence stays in place too, however much we try to dislodge it with our truths. We say what has happened to us, but newspapers, governments, the culture that excludes us as fully human participants, wipe us out, wipe out our speech: by refusing to hear it. We are the tree falling in the desert. Should it matter: they are the desert.

The cost of trying to shatter the silence is astonishing to those who do it: the women, raped, battered, prostituted, who have something to say and say it. They stand there, even as they are erased. Governments turn from them; courts ignore them; this country disavows and dispossesses them. Men ridicule, threaten, or hurt them. Women jeopardized by them—silence being safer than speech—betray them. It is ugly to watch the complacent destroy the brave. It is horrible to watch power win.

Still, equality is what we want, and we are going to get it. What we understand about it now is that it cannot be proclaimed; it must be created. It has to take the place of subordination in human experience: physically replace it. Equality does not co-exist with subordination, as if it were a little pocket located somewhere within it. Equality has to win. Subordination has to lose. The subordination of women has not even been knocked loose, and equality has not materially advanced, at least in part because the pornography has been creating sexualized inequality in hiding, in private, where the abuses occur on a massive scale.

Equality for women requires material remedies for pornography, whether pornography is central to the inequality of women or only one cause of it. Pornography's antagonism to civil equality, integrity, and self-determination for women is absolute; and it is effective in making that antagonism socially real and socially determining.

The law that Catharine A. MacKinnon and I wrote making pornography a violation of women's civil rights recognizes the injury that pornography does: how it hurts women's rights of citizenship through sexual exploitation and sexual torture both.

The civil rights law empowers women by allowing women to civilly sue those who hurt us through pornography by trafficking in it, coercing people into it, forcing it on people, and assaulting people directly because of a specific piece of it.

The civil rights law does not force the pornography back underground. There is no prior restraint or police power to make arrests, which would then result in a revivified black market. This respects the reach of the first amendment, but it also keeps the pornography from getting sexier—hidden, forbidden, dirty, happily back in the land of the obscene, sexy slime oozing on great books. Wanting to cover the pornography up, hide it, is the first response of those who need pornography to the civil rights law. If pornography is hidden, it is still accessible to men as a male right of access to women; its injuries to the status of women are safe and secure in those hidden rooms, behind those opaque covers; the abuses of women are sustained as a private right supported by public policy. The civil rights law puts a flood of light on the pornography, what it is, how it is used, what it does, those who are hurt by it.

The civil rights law changes the power relationship between pornographers and women: it stops the pornographers from producing discrimination with the total impunity they now enjoy, and gives women a legal standing resembling equality from which to repudiate the subordination itself. The secret-police power of the pornographers suddenly has to confront a modest amount of due process.

The civil rights law undermines the subordination of women in society by confronting the pornography, which is the systematic sexualization of that subordination. Pornography is inequality. The civil rights law would allow women to advance equality by removing this concrete discrimination and hurting economically those who make, sell, distribute, or exhibit it. The pornography, being power, has a right to exist that we are not allowed to challenge under this system of law. After it hurts us by being what it is and doing what it does, the civil rights law would allow us to hurt it back. Women, not being power, do not have a right to exist equal to the right the pornography has. If we did, the pornographers would be precluded from exercising their rights at the expense of ours, and since they cannot exercise them any other way, they would be precluded period. We come to the legal system beggars: though in the public dialogue around the passage of this civil rights law we have the satisfaction of being regarded as thieves.

The civil rights law is women's speech. It defines an injury to us from our point of view. It is premised on a repudiation of sexual subordination which is born of our experience of it. It breaks the silence. It is a sentence that can hold its own against the male flood. It is a sentence on which we can build a paragraph, then a page.

It is my view, learned largely from Catharine MacKinnon, that women have a right to be effective. The pornographers, of course, do not think so, nor do other male supremacists; and it is hard for women to think so. We have been told to educate people on the evils of pornography: before the development of this civil rights law, we were told just to keep quiet about pornography altogether; but now that we have a law we want to use, we are encouraged to educate and stop there. Law educates. This law educates. It also allows women to *do* something. In hurting the pornography back, we gain ground in making equality more likely, more possible—some day it will be real. We have a means to fight the pornographers' trade in women. We have a means to get at the torture and the terror. We have a means with which to challenge the pornography's efficacy in making exploitation and inferiority the bedrock of women's social status. The civil rights law introduces into the public consciousness an analysis: of what pornography is, what sexual subordination is, what equality might be. The civil rights law introduces a new legal standard: these things are not done to citizens of this country. The civil rights law introduces a new political standard: these things are not done to human beings. The civil rights law provides a new mode of action for women through which we can pursue equality and because of which *our* speech will have social meaning. The civil rights law gives us back what the pornographers have taken from us: hope rooted in real possibility.

Notes

1. Gustave Flaubert, *Letters*, trans. J. M. Cohen (London: George Weidenfeld & Nicolson, 1950), p.94.
2. D. H. Lawrence, *Sex, Literature and Censorship* (New York: Twayne Publishers, 1953), p.9.
3. Harold Gardiner (SJ), *Catholic Viewpoint on Censorship* (Garden City: Hanover House, 1958), p. 65.
4. Georges Bataille, *Death and Sensuality* (New York: Ballantine Books, Inc., 1969), p.12.
5. Lawrence, op. cit., p. 74.
6. Vladimir Nabokov, 'Afterward', *Lolita* (New York: Berkeley Publishing Corporation, 1977), p. 284.
7. The actual line is 'In dreams begins responsibility', quoted by Yeats as an epigram to his collection, *Responsibilities.*
8. Maria Isabel Barreno, Maria Teresa Horta, and Maria Velho da Costa, *The Three Marias: New Portuguese Letters*, trans. Helen R. Lane (New York: Bantam Books, 1976), p. 291.
9. Nadezhda Mandelstam, *Hope Against Hope*, trans. Max Hayward (New York: Atheneum, 1978), pp. 42–3.
10. Franz Kafka, 'In the Penal Colony', *The Penal Colony*, trans. Willa and Edwin Muir (New York: Schocken Books, 1965), p. 194.
11. Ibid., p. 197.
12. Ibid., p. 203.
13. Ibid., p. 197.

2 Pornography and Grief

Andrea Dworkin

'Pornography and Grief' was written as a speech for a Take Back the Night March that was part of the first feminist conference on pornography in the United States in San Francisco, November 1978. Organized by the now defunct Women Against Violence in Pornography and Media (WAVPM), over 5,000 women from thirty states participated and we shut down San Francisco's pornography district for one night. The ground was taken but not held.

I searched for something to say here today quite different from what I am going to say. I wanted to come here militant and proud and angry as hell. But more and more, I find that anger is a pale shadow next to the grief I feel. If a woman has any sense of her own intrinsic worth, seeing pornography in small bits and pieces can bring her to a useful rage. Studying pornography in quantity and depth, as I have been doing for more months than I care to remember, will turn that same woman into a mourner.

The pornography itself is vile. To characterize it any other way would be to lie. No plague of male intellectualisms and sophistries can change or hide that simple fact. Georges Bataille, a philosopher of pornography (which he calls 'eroticism'), puts it clearly: 'In essence, the domain of eroticism is the domain of violence, of violation.'[1] Mr Bataille, unlike so many of his peers, is good enough to make explicit that the whole idea is to violate the female. Using the language of grand euphemism so popular with male intellectuals who write on the subject of pornography, Bataille informs us that '[t]he passive, female side is essentially the one that is dissolved as a separate entity.'[2] To

Andrea Dworkin, 'Pornography and Grief', in *Letters from a War Zone* (Martin Secker and Warburg, 1987). Reprinted by permission of Elaine Markson Literary Agency Inc.

be 'dissolved'—by any means necessary—is the role of women in pornography. The great male scientists and philosophers of sexuality, including Kinsey, Havelock Ellis, Wilhelm Reich, and Freud, uphold this view of our purpose and destiny. The great male writers use language more or less beautifully to create us in self-serving fragments, half-'dissolved' as it were, and then proceed to 'dissolve' us all the way, by any means necessary. The biographers of the great male artists celebrate the real life atrocities those men have committed against us, as if those atrocities are central to the making of art. And in history, as men have lived it, they have 'dissolved' us—by any means necessary. The slicing of our skins and the rattling of our bones are the energizing sources of male-defined art and science, as they are the essential content of pornography. The visceral experience of a hatred of women that literally knows no bounds has put me beyond anger and beyond tears; I can only speak to you from grief.

We all expected the world to be different than it is, didn't we? No matter what material or emotional deprivation we have experienced as children or as adults, no matter what we understood from history or from the testimonies of living persons about how people suffer and why, we all believed, however privately, in human possibility. Some of us believed in art, or literature, or music, or religion, or revolution, or in children, or in the redeeming potential of eroticism or affection. No matter what we knew of cruelty, we all believed in kindness; and no matter what we knew of hatred, we all believed in friendship or love. Not one of us could have imagined or would have believed the simple facts of life as we have come to know them: the rapacity of male greed for dominance; the malignancy of male supremacy; the virulent contempt for women that is the very foundation of the culture in which we live. The Women's Movement has forced us all to face the facts, but no matter how brave and clear-sighted we are, no matter how far we are willing to go or are forced to go in viewing reality without romance or illusion, we are simply overwhelmed by the male hatred of our kind, its morbidity, its compulsiveness, its obsessiveness, its celebration of itself in every detail of life and culture. We think that we have grasped this hatred once and for all, seen it in its spectacular cruelty, learned its every secret, got used to it or risen above it or organized against it so as to be protected from its worst excesses. We think that we know all there is to know about what men do to women, even if we cannot imagine why they do what they do, when something happens that simply drives us mad, out of our minds, so that we are again imprisoned like caged animals in the numbing reality of male control, male revenge against no one knows what, male hatred of our very being.

One can know everything and still not imagine snuff films. One can know everything and still be shocked and terrified when a man who attempted to make snuff films is released, despite the testimony of the women undercover agents whom he wanted to torture, murder, and, of course, film. One can know everything and still be stunned and paralyzed when one meets a child who is being continuously raped by her father or some close male relative. One can know everything and still be reduced to sputtering like an idiot when a woman is prosecuted for attempting to abort herself with knitting needles, or when a woman is imprisoned for killing a man who has raped or tortured her, or is raping or torturing her. One can know everything and still want to kill and be dead simultaneously when one sees a celebratory picture of a woman being ground up in a meat grinder on the cover of a national magazine, no matter how putrid the magazine. One can know everything and still somewhere inside refuse to believe that the personal, social, culturally sanctioned violence against women is unlimited, unpredictable, pervasive, constant, ruthless, and happily and unselfconsciously sadistic. One can know everything and still be unable to accept the fact that sex and murder are fused in the male consciousness, so that the one without the imminent possibility of the other is unthinkable and impossible. One can know everything and still, at bottom, refuse to accept that the annihilation of women is the source of meaning and identity for men. One can know everything and still want desperately to know nothing because to face what we know is to question whether life is worth anything at all.

The pornographers, modern and ancient, visual and literary, vulgar and aristocratic, put forth one consistent proposition: erotic pleasure for men is derived from and predicated on the savage destruction of women. As the world's most honored pornographer, the Marquis de Sade (called by male scholars 'The Divine Marquis'), wrote in one of his more restrained and civil moments: 'There's not a woman on earth who'd ever have had cause to complain of my services if I'd been sure of being able to kill her afterward.'[3] The eroticization of murder is the essence of pornography, as it is the essence of life. The torturer may be a policeman tearing the fingernails off a victim in a prison cell or a so-called normal man engaged in the project of attempting to fuck a woman to death. The fact is that the process of killing—and both rape and battery are steps in that process—is the prime sexual act for men in reality and/or in imagination. Women as a class must remain in bondage, subject to the sexual will of men, because the knowledge of an imperial right to kill, whether exercised to the fullest extent or just part way, is necessary to fuel sexual appetite and behavior. Without women as potential or actual victims, men are, in the current sanitized jargon, 'sexually dysfunctional'. This same motif also operates among male homosexuals, where force and/or convention designate some males as female or feminized. The plethora of leather and chains among male homosexuals, and the newly fashionable defenses of organized rings of boy prostitution by supposedly radical gay men, are testimony to the fixedness of the male compulsion to dominate and destroy that is the source of sexual pleasure for men.

The most terrible thing about pornography is that it tells male truth. The most insidious thing about pornography is that it tells male truth as if it were universal truth. Those depictions of women in chains being tortured are supposed to represent our deepest erotic aspirations. And some of us believe it, don't we? The most important thing about pornography is that the values in it are the common values of men. This is the crucial fact that both the male Right and the male Left, in their differing but mutually reinforcing ways, want to keep hidden from women. The male Right wants to hide the pornography, and the male Left wants to hide its meaning. Both want access to pornography so that men can be encouraged and energized by it. The Right wants secret access; the Left wants public access. But whether we see the pornography or not, the values expressed in it are the values expressed in the acts of rape and wife-beating, in the legal system, in religion, in art and in literature, in systematic economic discrimination against women, in the moribund academies, and by the good and wise and kind and enlightened in all of these fields and areas. Pornography is not a genre of expression separate and different from the rest of life; it is a genre of expression fully in harmony with any culture in which it flourishes. This is so whether it is legal or illegal. And, in either case, pornography functions to perpetuate male supremacy and crimes of violence against women because it conditions, trains, educates, and inspires men to despise women, to use women, to hurt women. Pornography exists because men despise women, and men despise women in part because pornography exists.

For myself, pornography has defeated me in a way that, at least so far, life has not. Whatever struggles and difficulties I have had in my life, I have always wanted to find a way to go on even if I did not know how, to live through one more day, to learn one more thing, to take one more walk, to read one more book, to write one more paragraph, to see one more friend, to love one more time. When I read or see pornography, I want everything to stop. Why, I ask, why are they so damned cruel and so damned proud of it? Sometimes, a detail drives me mad. There is a series of photographs: a woman slicing her breasts with a knife, smearing her own blood on her own body, sticking a sword up her vagina. *And she is smiling.* And it is the smile that drives me mad. There is a record album plastered all over a huge display window. The picture on the album is a profile view of a woman's thighs. Her crotch is suggested because we know it is there; it is not shown. The title of the album is 'Plug Me to Death.' And it is the use of the first person that drives me mad. 'Plug Me to Death.' The arrogance. The cold-blooded arrogance. And how can it go on like this, senseless, entirely brutal, inane, day after day and year after year, these images and ideas and values pouring out, packaged, bought and sold, promoted, enduring on and on, and no one stops it, and our darling boy intellectuals defend it, and elegant radical lawyers argue for it, and men of every sort cannot and will not live without it. And life, which means everything to me, becomes meaningless, because these celebrations of cruelty destroy my very capacity to feel and to care and to hope. I hate the pornographers most of all for depriving me of hope.

The psychic violence in pornography is unbearable in and of itself. It acts on one like a bludgeon until one's sensibility is pummelled flat and one's heart goes dead. One becomes numb. Everything stops, and one looks at the pages or pictures and knows: this is what men want, and this is what men have had, and this is what men will not give up. As lesbian-feminist Karla Jay pointed out in an article called 'Pot, Porn, and the Politics of Pleasure', men will give up grapes and lettuce and orange juice and Portuguese wine and tuna fish, but men will not give up pornography. And yes, one wants to take it from them, to burn it, to rip it up, bomb it, raze their theaters and publishing houses to the ground. One can be part of a revolutionary movement or one can mourn. Perhaps I have found the real source of my grief: we have not yet become a revolutionary movement.

Tonight we are going to walk together, all of us, to take back the night, as women have in cities all over the world, because in every sense none of us can walk alone. Every woman walking alone is a target. Every woman walking alone is hunted, harassed, time after time harmed by psychic or physical violence. Only by walking together can we walk at all with any sense of safety, dignity, or freedom. Tonight, walking together, we will proclaim to the rapists and pornographers and woman-batterers that their days are numbered and our time has come. And tomorrow, what will we do tomorrow? Because, sisters, the truth is that we have to take back the night every night, or the night will never be ours. And once we have conquered the dark, we have to reach for the light, to take the day and make it ours. This is our choice, and this is our necessity. It is a revolutionary choice, and it is a revolutionary necessity. For us, the two are indivisible, as we must be indivisible in our fight for freedom. Many of us have walked many miles already—brave, hard miles—but we have not gone far enough. Tonight, with every breath and every step, we must commit ourselves to going the distance: to transforming this earth on which we walk from prison and tomb into our rightful and joyous home. This we must do and this we will do, for our own sakes and for the sake of every woman who has ever lived.

Notes

1. Georges Bataille, *Death and Sensuality* (New York: Ballantine Books, Inc., 1969), p. 10.
2. Bataille, *Death and Sensuality*, p. 11.
3. Donatien-Alphonse-François de Sade, *Juliette*, trans. Austryn Wainhouse (New York: Grove Press, Inc., 1976), p. 404.

3 Pornography is a Social Justice Issue

Norma Ramos

For over a decade now, Women Against Pornography has worked to expose the connection between pornography and rape, pornography and the sexual abuse of children, battery, sexual harrassment and a generalized bigotry towards women. In the course of doing this work, we have learned a great deal about the ways in which inequality is rationalized and defended. This goes to the heart of the strategies that have been employed by the pornographers and their lawyers in their efforts to disguise what they do and shield themselves from accountability. We are all painfully aware of the extent to which they have been successful.

It remains a challenge to our movement to peel away the layers of rationalizations and lies, to give voice to the realities of the abuse and exploitation that forms the foundation by which this industry is built. I have often said that the work and politics of our movement are often intentionally distorted and little understood by others, thus making education the most essential component of our strategy. We are faced with not only bringing to the forefront the true nature of sexual exploitation and the thriving industry that profits from this, but we are faced with informing those who have been misinformed.

A chief tool of the pornographers has been to inextricably intertwine unfettered sexual exploitation with freedom of expression, and then skilfully reducing this confusion into simplistic First Amendment rhetoric: you know, we must defend pimping if the Communist Party USA is to have its speech. I for one have never been convinced that strengthening threats to freedom is a form of protecting freedom.

Norma Ramos, 'Pornography is a Social Justice Issue,' originally given as a speech sponsored by the Freedom Forum before a gathering of first amendment scholars at Vanderbilt University on November 4, 1994.

That ACLU doctrine has always been lost on me. In fact it has always felt more like a collaboration with oppressive forces, a sort of suicide pact. It is this confusion that we are challenged with disentangling.

We are also faced with doing this educational work in a culture which for some time now has been saturated with pornography. The expression that came out of the women's movement of the 1970s, 'the personal is political', has even more urgent meaning today. Naomi Wolf, author of *The Beauty Myth*, writes that 'the generation born after the 1960s is the pornographic generation', a generation whose sexuality has been heavily influenced by pornographic imagery.[1]

We are told by human sexuality researchers that human sexuality, specifically what turns a person on, is remarkably almost entirely learned and culturally influenced. In a pornographic culture like ours, domination and subordination are packaged as sex; specifically, the power of men over women (and children) is experienced as sex, as pleasure. And because of pornography's influence on mainstream culture, you do not even have to directly consume the pornography in order for the pornography to impact your sexuality. This is what is unique about gender domination in that the domination of women is linked up with biologic sexuality itself. This is a very dangerous place to have reached. And it means that we are faced with nothing less than reclaiming our sexuality from the pornographers. It has been said to unlearn is more difficult than to learn. It is men, of course, whose sexuality has been specifically targeted by the pornographers. Much work, some of it therapeutic, will have to be done in order to extricate the pornography from our most personal selves.

This leads me to another strategy. At the risk of sounding politically naive, part of what we must do, is to urge, to borrow a phrase from John Stoltenberg, 'men of conscience', to take responsibility in leading their own fight against sexual exploitation in all of its forms. Too often we as feminists think it unfeminist to urge men to do anything. It seems that this is viewed as coming from a position of powerlessness. While I see this as a valid criticism if that is all we do, that is urge men to act. But I argue that this must be part of a larger strategy. We must never lose sight of the fact that the sexploitation industry has been created by men, for men, and it is sustained by men (notwithstanding a small number of female defenders and promoters, i.e. the women of the ACLU, COYOTE, and such) and it is men who will do the most to protect it. Therefore it is men who have a special role in ending the sexploitation industry, just as caucasians have a special role in providing leadership among each other to end white supremacy.

Another strategy must involve working with existing feminist organizations who cannot be allowed to continue to ignore sexual exploitation. We have watched them champion abortion rights to the point of exclusion of all other concerns. We have also watched them begin to embrace sexual harrassment at the work place (nowhere else—yet) as a concern deserving their attention. I have been wondering what National NOW is going to do now that abortion rights have lost their urgency. Just a week ago I received a mailing from National NOW that focused on violence against women that read like a speech that myself or anyone else in this movement would deliver in part, regarding the epidemic of violence against women that we are confronting in this country—I mean it described that state of affairs pretty well— but without once alluding to the causes of this epidemic. It was as if violence against women is a given and we must engage in as Kitty and Andrea described 'the great mop up operation'.

Any politics that takes injustice as a given is destined to failure. The politics of fighting violence against women must be rooted in a deep understanding of the role of violence. Sonia Johnson once remarked that ours has become a species where the male half is destroying the female half. I see the domination of men over women to be the core and central domination. I see it as being the model domination for all other dominations that men have come up with (i.e. race, class, species). Given that domination is achieved and maintained through violence, male domination specifically through battery, rape, incest, sexual harrassment both at work and ON THE STREET, to struggle against the root causes of violence against women is essential.

And of course, a key strategy must include the creation of legal remedies where none exist. And when these remedies do emerge as they did with the Dworkin/MacKinnon Civil Rights Anti-Pornography Ordinance, we must as we have done in the past support these measures, because their success for the most part will depend on the kind of political climate we have created outside of the courtroom. We must build, strengthen, and promote a body of politics that is uncompromising in its definition of justice. We must become the architects of an evolved concept of freedom that eliminates male supremacy, white supremacy, and one that does not leave sexual exploitation intact. A concept that is uncompromising in its value of all human beings. And that will be a freedom worth defending.

Note

1. Naomi Wolf, *The Beauty Myth* (New York: Anchor Books, 1992).

4 Pornography and Rape

A Causal Model

Diana E. H. Russell

I. INTRODUCTION

DEFINING PORNOGRAPHY

Proponents of the anti-pornography-equals-censorship school deliberately obfuscate any distinction between erotica and pornography, using the term *erotica* for all sexually explicit materials (e.g. Pally 1994; Strossen 1995). In contrast, most anti-pornography feminists consider it vitally important to distinguish between pornography and erotica (see Itzin 1992; Lederer 1980; Russell 1993). While condemning pornography, most of us approve of, or even advocate, erotica.

Although women's bodies are the staple of adult pornography, it is important to have a gender-neutral definition that encompasses the various types of pornography, including gay pornography and child pornography. Animals are also targets of pornographic depictions. Hence, I define *pornography as material that combines sex and/or the exposure of genitals with abuse or degradation in a manner that appears to endorse, condone, or encourage such behavior.*[1] However, this book will exclude gay and child pornography, and focus on pornography that abuses or degrades women.

Erotica refers to *sexually suggestive or arousing material that is free of sexism, racism, and homophobia and is respectful of all human beings and animals portrayed.* This definition acknowledges the fact that humans are not the only subject matter of erotica. For example, a

Diana E. H. Russell, 'Pornography and Rape: A Causal Model', revised version of the essay which appeared in Political Psychology 9/1 (1988). Section II. is from *Making Violence Sexy: Feminist Views on Pornography.* New York: Teacher's College Press, 1993.

scene in a documentary on insects titled *Microcosmos*, in which two snails 'make love', was highly sensual and erotic.[2] I remember seeing a short award-winning erotic film depicting the peeling of an orange. The shapes and coloring of flowers or hills can make them appear erotic. Many people find Georgia O'Keeffe's paintings erotic. However, erotica can also include overtly or explicitly sexual images.

Canadian psychologists Charlene Senn and Lorraine Radtke (1986) conducted an experiment using slides that demonstrate the significance and meaningfulness to female subjects of distinguishing between pornography and erotica. First, these researchers categorized the slides into three groups:

- violent pornography
- nonviolent but dehumanizing pornography
- erotica (material that was nonsexist and nonviolent)

Then they administered tests of the mood states of their subjects in response to these three categories of slides. They found that both the violent and the nonviolent dehumanizing slides had a negative effect on the mood states of the women subjects, whereas the erotic images had a positive effect (Senn and Radtke 1986: 15–16; also see Senn 1993). Furthermore, the violent pornographic pictures had a greater negative impact on the women than did the nonviolent dehumanizing pictures.[3] This shows that a conceptual distinction between pornography and erotica is both meaningful and operational. Experiments conducted by psychologist James Check replicate this finding (Check and Guloien 1989).

My definition's requirement that erotica must be nonsexist means that the following types of pictorial materials qualify as pornography:

- Sexually arousing images in which women are consistently shown naked while men are clothed
- Pictures in which women's genitals are displayed but men's are not
- Images in which men are always portrayed in the initiating, dominant role

Racist pornography that focuses on people of color typically combines racism and sexism. Yet racism is also manifested in depictions of white women who embody many white males' narrow concept of beauty (very thin, large-breasted, and blonde), since the obvious inference is that women of color don't qualify as sufficiently attractive or beautiful. This form of sexualized racism pervades pornography.

The term *abusive* sexual behavior in my definition of pornography refers to sexual conduct that ranges from derogatory, demeaning, contemptuous, or damaging to that which is brutal, cruel, exploitative, painful, or violent. *Degrading* sexual behavior refers to sexual conduct that is humiliating, insulting, and/or disrespectful: examples of degrading sexual behavior include urinating or defecating on a woman, ejaculating in her face, treating her as sexually dirty or inferior, depicting her as slavishly following men's orders and eager to engage in whatever sex acts males want, and/or calling her insulting names such as 'bitch', 'cunt', 'nigger', 'whore', while engaging in sex.

Feminist philosopher Helen Longino (1980) describes typically abusive and degrading portrayals of female sexuality in many pornographic books, magazines, and films, as follows:

> Women are represented as passive and as slavishly dependent upon men. The role of female characters is limited to the provision of sexual services to men. To the extent that women's sexual pleasure is represented at all, it is subordinated to that of men and is never an end in itself as is the sexual pleasure of men. What pleases women is the use of their bodies to satisfy male desires. While the sexual objectification of women is common to all pornography, women are the recipients of even worse treatment in violent pornography, in which women characters are killed, tortured, gang-raped, mutilated, bound, and otherwise abused, as a means of providing sexual stimulation or pleasure to the male characters. (p.42)

What is objectionable about pornography, then, is its abusive and degrading portrayal of females and female sexuality, not its sexual content or explicitness.

A particularly important feature of my definition of pornography is the requirement that *it appears to endorse,*[4] *condone, or encourage abusive sexual desires or behaviors.* These attributes differentiate pornography from materials that include such abusive or degrading sexual behavior for educational purposes. Movies such as *The Accused* and *The Rape of Love*, for example, are not pornographic because they present realistic representations of rape with the apparent intention of helping viewers to understand the reprehensible nature of rape, as well as the agony experienced by rape victims.

My definition of pornography differs from the current legal definition, which focuses instead on material that is judged to be obscene. It also differs from the definition that I used in previous publications, which limited pornography to sexually explicit materials (e.g. Russell 1988). I decided to broaden my definition to include materials like slasher films, record covers, and cartoons that meet my definition. In doing so, I am returning to the conception of pornography that we formulated in Women Against Violence in Pornography and Media (WAVPM), the first feminist anti-pornography organization in the United States (see Lederer 1980).

Some other feminists, however, have included sexual explicitness as a defining feature of pornography. Andrea Dworkin and Catharine MacKinnon (1988), for example, define pornography as 'the graphic sexually explicit subordination of women through pictures and/or words' (p. 36). They go on to spell out nine ways in which this overall definition can be met, for example, when '(i) women are presented dehumanized as sexual objects, things, or commodities' (p. 36). Unfortunately, Dworkin and MacKinnon's definition fails to distinguish between materials that depict women as dehumanized sex objects for educational purposes (like the movie *The Accused*—which I consider nonpornographic) and materials that degrade women for males' sexual entertainment and/or sexual gratification.

James Check often uses the term *sexually explicit materials* instead of pornography, presumably in the hope of bypassing the many controversies associated with the term *pornography* (Check and Guloien 1989: 159). However, these scholars have not, to my knowledge, defined what they mean by sexually explicit materials. Because I am unclear about what sex acts qualify as sexually explicit, it is impossible to evaluate the advisability of using this term in my definition.

Some people may object that feminist definitions of pornography that go beyond sexually explicit materials differ so substantially from common usage that they make discussion between feminists and nonfeminists confusing.[5] I would argue, however, that there is no consensus on definitions among either of these groups. Sometimes there is a good reason for feminists to employ the same definition as nonfeminists. For example, in my study of the prevalence of rape, I used a very narrow, legal definition of rape because I wanted to be able to compare the rape rates obtained in my study with those obtained in government studies (see Russell 1984). Had I used a broader definition that included oral and anal penetration, for example, my study could not have been used to show how grossly flawed the methodology of the government's national surveys is in determining meaningful rape rates. If, however, there is no compelling reason to use a definition with which one disagrees, then it makes sense for feminists to define phenomena in ways that best fit feminist principles.

Unlike Andrea Dworkin and Catharine MacKinnon, most feminists have not attempted to create a definition that would meet legal standards. They devised a definition which, if implemented, would enable someone who has been coerced into pornography, assaulted because of it, or subordinated by trafficking in it, to attempt to prove in a court of law that pornography harmed her (1988: 36). More specifically, they defined (and continue to define) pornography as 'the graphic sexually explicit subordination of women through pictures and/or words' that also includes one or more of nine conditions, including the following three examples:

> (i) women are presented dehumanized as sexual objects, things, or commodities; . . . or (vi) women's body parts—including but not limited to vaginas, breasts, or buttocks—are exhibited such that women are reduced to those parts; . . . or (ix) women are presented in scenarios of degradation, injury, torture, shown as filthy or inferior, bleeding, bruised, or hurt in a context that makes these conditions sexual.
> The use of men, children, or transsexuals in the place of women in [the paragraph] above is also pornography.

Unfortunately, the nine conditions formulated by Dworkin and MacKinnon are typically overlooked by those intent on simplifying it.

Returning to my more concise definition, it should be noted that it does not include all the features that commonly characterize such material. For example, even though pornography frequently depicts female desires and sexuality inaccurately,[6] I have not included this feature of pornography in my definition. It has been shown, for example, that pornography consumers are more likely to believe that unusual sexual practices are more common than they really are (Zillmann and Bryant 1989). This is hardly surprising in view of the many distortions about female sexuality that pornography typically contains.[7]

Sexual objectification is another common characteristic of pornography that I have not included in my definition. It refers to *the portrayal of human beings—usually women—as depersonalized sexual things, such as 'tits, cunt, and ass', not as multifaceted human beings deserving equal rights with men.* As Susan Brownmiller (1975) so eloquently noted,

> [In pornography] our bodies are being stripped, exposed and contorted for the purpose of ridicule to bolster that 'masculine esteem' which gets its kick and sense of power from viewing females as anonymous, panting playthings, adult toys, dehumanized objects to be used, abused, broken and discarded. (p. 394)

However, the sexual objectification of females is not confined to pornography. It is also a staple of mainstream movies, ads, record covers, songs, magazines, television programs, art, cartoons, literature, and so on, and influences the way that many males learn to see women and even children. This is why I have not included sexual objectification as a defining feature of pornography.

INCONSISTENCIES IN DEFINITIONS

Many people have commented on the difficulty of defining pornography and erotica, declaring that 'one person's erotica is another person's pornography'. This statement is often used to deride an anti-pornography stance, as if the lack of consensus on a definition of pornography means that its effects cannot be examined.

However, there is no consensus on the definitions of many phenomena that we nonetheless are willing to take a stand on. Rape is one example. Legal definitions of rape vary considerably in different states. The police often have their own definitions, which may differ from legal definitions. If a woman is raped by someone she knows, for example, the police often 'unfound'[8] the case because they are skeptical about many acquaintance and date rapes. Hence, such crimes are rarely investigated. This practice certainly has no basis in the law.

If rape is defined as forced intercourse or attempts at forced intercourse, the problem of figuring out what exactly constitutes force remains. How does one measure it? What is the definition of intercourse? Does it include oral and anal intercourse, intercourse with a foreign object, or digital penetration, or is it defined only as vaginal penetration by the penis? How much penetration is necessary to qualify as intercourse? How does one determine if an attempt at rape has occurred?

How does one deal with the fact that both the rapist and the rape survivor quite often do not believe that a rape has occurred, even when the incident matches the legal definition of rape? Many rapists, for example, do not consider that forcing intercourse on an unwilling woman qualifies as rape because they think the woman's 'no' actually means 'yes'. Many women think they have not been raped when the perpetrator is their husband or lover, even though the law in most states defines such acts as rape.

Fortunately, few people argue that because rape is so difficult to define and because there is no consensus on the best definition of it, it should therefore not be considered a heinous and illegal act.

Similarly, millions of court cases have revolved around arguments as to whether a killing constitutes murder or manslaughter.[9] No one argues that killing should not be subject to legal sanctions just because it takes a court case to decide this question.

The fact that the lack of consensus on how to define pornography is used to discredit any attempt to impose legal restraints on it, or even to express strong opposition to it, whereas no similar argument is made in response to the lack of consensus on definitions of rape and murder, highlights the ideological motivation behind this reasoning. The validity of this point is further substantiated by the fact that nonconsensus on the definition of pornography did not prove to be an obstacle to making pictorial child pornography illegal.

Hence, it is reasonable to conclude that the fixation of pro-pornography advocates on the difficulty of defining pornography is merely a strategy that they employ in their efforts to derail their opponents by making anti-pornography policies appear futile.

ABUSE OF WOMEN IN THE MAKING OF PORNOGRAPHY

Catharine MacKinnon points out the frequently forgotten fact that 'before pornography became the pornographer's speech it was somebody's life' (1987: 179). Many people, including some of the best researchers on pornography in the United States (for example, see Malamuth and Donnerstein 1984), ignore the abuse and/or violence some pornographers use to manufacture these misogynist materials. Testimony by women and men involved in such activity provides numerous examples of this (see Attorney General's Commission on Pornography 1986).

In one case, a man who said he had participated in over a hundred pornographic movies testified at the Commission hearings in Los Angeles as follows: 'I, myself, have been on a couple of sets where the young ladies have been forced to do even anal sex scenes with a guy which [sic] is rather large and I have seen them crying in pain' (1986: 773).

Another witness testified at the Los Angeles hearings as follows:

> Women and young girls were tortured and suffered permanent physical injuries to answer publisher demands for photographs depicting sadomasochistic abuse. When the torturer/photographer inquired of the publisher as to the types of depictions that would sell, the torturer/photographer was instructed

to get similar existing publications and use the depiction therein for instruction. The torturer/photographer followed the publisher's instructions, tortured women and girls accordingly, and then sold the photographs to the publisher. The photographs were included in magazines sold nationally in pornographic outlets (1986: 787–788).

Peter Bogdanovich writes of *Playboy* 'Playmate of the Year' Dorothy Stratten's response to her participation in a pornographic movie: 'A key sequence in *Galaxina* called for Dorothy to be spread-eagled against a cold water tower. The producers insisted she remain bound there for several hours, day and night. In one shot of the completed film, the tears she cries are real' (1984: 59). Although this movie was not made for the so-called adult movie houses, I consider it pornography because of its sexist and degrading combination of sexuality and bondage.

A letter sent to the United States Attorney General's Commission on Pornography provides a final example of abuse in the making of pornography: 'A mother and father in South Oklahoma City forced their four daughters, ages ten to seventeen, to engage in family sex while pornographic pictures were being filmed' (1986: 780).

It should not be assumed that violence occurs only in the making of *violent* pornography. For example, although many people would classify the movie *Deep Throat* as nonviolent pornography because it does not portray rape or other violence, we now know from Linda (Lovelace) Marchiano's two books (*Ordeal*, 1980, and *Out of Bondage*, 1986), as well as from her public testimony (for example, *Public Hearings*, 1983), that this film is in fact a documentary of rape from beginning to end.

Although rape is illegal, the showing and distribution of actual rapes on film is protected as free speech. As Dworkin and MacKinnon (1988: 60) so aptly question: 'If lynchings were done *in order to* make photographs, on a ten-billion-dollar-a-year scale, would that make them protected speech?' And later they ask:

> What would it say about the seriousness with which society regards lynching if actual lynching is illegal but pictures of actual lynching are protected and highly profitable and defended as a form of freedom and a constitutional right? What would it say about the seriousness and effectiveness of laws against lynching if people paid good money to see it and the law looked the other way, so long as they saw it in mass-produced form? What would it say about one's status if the society permits one to be hung from trees and calls it entertainment—calls it what it is to those who enjoy it, rather than what it is to those to whom it is done? (1988: 61).

Although it is disturbing that so many people ignore the harm done to the women who are used in making pornography, this kind of harm should be distinguished from the harm that occurs to the consumers and their victims (Robert Brannon, personal communication 11 March and 28 April 1992). Either kind of harm can occur, with or without the other. The rest of this chapter will focus on the latter kind of harm.

II. PORNOGRAPHY AND RAPE: A CAUSAL MODEL

> 'I don't need studies and statistics to tell me that there is a relationship between pornography and real violence against women. My body remembers.'
>
> Woman's testimony, 1983[10]

The fact that in many instances the actual *making* of pornography involves or even requires violence and sexual assault has already been emphasized. In this section, I will ignore this aspect of the relationship between pornography and rape to present instead my theoretical model on the causal relationship between the consumption of pornography and rape, as well as some of the research that substantiates this theory.

Because it is important to know the proclivities and the state of mind of those who read and view pornography, I will start by discussing some of the data on males' propensity to rape.

MALES' PROPENSITY TO RAPE[11]

> 'Why do I want to rape women? Because I am basically, as a male, a predator and all women look to men like prey. I fantasize about the expression on a woman's face when I 'capture' her and she realizes she cannot escape. It's like I won, I own her.'
>
> (Male respondent, Shere Hite 1981: 718)

Research indicates that 25 to 30% of male college students in the United States and Canada admit that there is some likelihood they would rape a woman if they could get away with it.[12] In the first study of men's self-reported likelihood to rape that was conducted at the University of California at Los Angeles, the word *rape* was not used; instead, an account of rape was read to the male subjects, of whom 53% said there was some likelihood that they would behave in the same fashion as the man described in the story (quoted below), if they could be sure of getting away with it (Malamuth, Haber and Feshbach, 1980). Without this assurance, only 17% said they might emulate the rapist's behavior. It is helpful to know exactly what behavior these students said they might enact.

> Bill soon caught up with Susan and offered to escort her to her car. Susan politely refused him. Bill was enraged by the rejection. 'Who the hell does this bitch think she is, turning me down,' Bill thought to himself as he reached into his pocket and took out a Swiss army knife. With his left hand he placed the knife at her throat. 'If you try to get away, I'll cut you,' said Bill. Susan nodded her head, her eyes wild with terror. (Malamuth et al. 1980: 124)[13]

The story then depicts the rape, describing sexual acts with the victim who is continually portrayed as clearly opposing the assaults.

In another study, 356 male students were asked: 'If you could be assured that no one would know and that you could in no way be punished for engaging in the following acts, how likely, if at all, would you be to commit such acts?' (Briere and Malamuth 1983). Among the sexual acts listed were the two of interest to these researchers: 'forcing a female to do something she really didn't want to do' and 'rape' (Briere and Malamuth 1983). *Sixty per cent of the sample indicated that under the right circumstances, there was some likelihood that they would rape, use force, or do both.*

In a study of high school males, 50% of those interviewed believed it acceptable 'for a guy to hold a girl down and force her to have sexual intercourse in instances such as when "she gets him sexually excited" or "she says she's going to have sex with him and then changes her mind"' (Goodchilds and Zellman 1984).

Some people dismiss the findings from these studies as 'merely attitudinal'. But this conclusion is incorrect. Malamuth has found that male subjects' self-reported likelihood of raping is correlated with physiological measures of sexual arousal by rape depictions. Clearly, erections cannot be considered attitudes. More specifically, the male students who say they might rape a woman if they could get away with it are significantly more likely than other male students to be sexually aroused by portrayals of rape. Indeed, these men were more sexually aroused by depictions of rape than by mutually consenting depictions. And when asked if they would find committing a rape sexually arousing, they said yes (Donnerstein 1983: 7). They were also more likely than the other male subjects to admit to having used actual physical force to impose sex on a woman. These latter data were self-reported, but because they refer to actual behavior they too cannot be dismissed as merely attitudinal.

Looking at sexual arousal data alone (as measured by penile tumescence), not its correlation with self-reported likelihood to rape, Malamuth reports that:

- About 10% of the population of male students are sexually aroused by 'very extreme violence' with 'a great deal of blood and gore' that 'has very little of the sexual element' (1985: 95).
- About 20 to 30% show substantial sexual arousal by depictions of rape in which the woman never shows signs of arousal, only abhorrence (1985: 95).
- About 50 to 60% show some degree of sexual arousal by a rape depiction in which the victim is portrayed as becoming sexually aroused at the end (personal communication, 18 August 1986).

Given these findings, it is hardly surprising that after reviewing a whole series of related experiments, Neil Malamuth concluded that 'the overall pattern of the data is . . . consistent with contentions that many men have a proclivity to rape' (1981*b*: 139).

Shere Hite (1981: 1123) provides information on the self-reported desire of men to rape women in the general population outside the university laboratory. Distinguishing between those men who answered the question anonymously and those who revealed their identities, Hite reports the following answers by the anonymous group to her question 'Have you ever wanted to rape a woman?': 46% answered 'yes' or 'sometimes', 47% answered 'no', and 7% said they had fantasies of rape, but presumably had not acted them out—yet (1981: 1123).

For reasons unknown, the non-anonymous group of men reported slightly more interest in rape: 52% answered 'yes' or 'sometimes', 36% answered 'no', and 11% reported having rape fantasies. Although Hite's survey was not based on a random sample, and therefore, like the experimental work cited above, cannot be generalized to the population at large, her finding that roughly half of the more than 7,000 men she surveyed admitted to having wanted to rape a woman one or more times suggests that men's propensity to rape is probably very widespread indeed. It is interesting that Hite's percentages are quite comparable to my finding that 44% of a probability sample of 930 adult women residing in San Francisco reported having been the victim of one or more rapes or attempted rapes over the course of their lives (Russell 1984).

The studies reviewed here suggest that at this time in the history of our culture, a substantial percentage of the male population has some desire or proclivity to rape females. Indeed, some men in this culture consider themselves deviant for *not* wanting to rape a woman. For example, the answer of one of Hite's male respondents was: 'I have never raped a woman, or wanted to. In this I guess *I am somewhat odd.* Many of my friends talk about rape a lot and fantasize about it. The whole idea leaves me cold' (1981: 719, emphasis added). Another replied: 'I must admit a certain part of me would receive some sort of thrill at ripping the clothes from a woman and ravishing her. But I would probably collapse into tears of pity and weep with my victim, *unlike the traditional man*' (1981: 719, emphasis added).

Feminists are among the optimists who believe that males' proclivity to rape is largely a consequence of social and cultural forces, not biological ones. And, of course, having a *desire* to behave in a certain way is not the same as actually *behaving* in that way, particularly in the case of antisocial behavior. Nevertheless, it is helpful to have this kind of baseline information on the desires and predispositions of males, who are, after all, the chief consumers of pornography.

What, then, is the content of the pornography men consume in this country?

THE CONTENT OF PORNOGRAPHY

> 'I've seen some soft porn movies, which seem to have the common theme that a great many women would really like to be raped, and after being thus "awakened to sex" will become lascivious nymphomaniacs. That . . . provides a sort of rationale for rape: "they want it, and anyway, it's really doing them a favor"'.
>
> (Male respondent, Hite 1981: 787)

Don Smith did a content analysis of 428 'adults only' paperbacks published between 1968 and 1974. His sample was limited to books that were readily accessible to the general public in the United States, excluding paperbacks that are usually available only in so-called adult bookstores (1976). He reported the following findings:

- One-fifth of all the sex episodes involved completed rape. The number of rapes increased with each year's output of newly published books.
- Of the sex episodes, 6% involved incestuous rape. The focus in the rape scenes were almost always on the victim's fear and terror, which became transformed by the rape into sexual passion. Over 97% of the rapes portrayed in these books resulted in orgasm for the victims. In three-quarters of these rapes, multiple orgasm occurred.

A few years later, Neil Malamuth and Barry Spinner undertook a content analysis to determine the amount of sexual violence in cartoons and pictorials in *Penthouse* and *Playboy* magazines from June 1973 to December 1977 (1980). They found that:

- By 1977, about 5% of the pictorials and 10% of the cartoons were rated as sexually violent.
- Sexual violence in pictorials (but not in cartoons) increased significantly over the 5-year period, 'both in absolute numbers and as a percentage of the total number of pictorials'.
- *Penthouse* contained over twice the percentage of sexually violent cartoons as *Playboy* (13 vs. 6%).

In another study of 1,760 covers of heterosexual magazines published between 1971 and 1980, Park Dietz and Barbara Evans reported that bondage and confinement themes were evident in 17% of them (1982).

Finally, in a more recent content analysis of videos in Vancouver, Canada, T. S. Palys found that 19% of all the scenes coded in a sample of 150 sexually oriented home videos involved aggression, and 13% involved sexual aggression (1986: 26–27).[14] Of all the sexually aggressive scenes in the 'adult' videos, 46% involved bondage or confinement; 23%, slapping, hitting, spanking, or pulling hair; 22%, rape; 18%, sexual harassment; 4%, sadomasochism; and 3%, sexual mutilation. In comparison, 38% of all the sexually aggressive scenes in the triple-X videos involved bondage or confinement; 33%, slapping, hitting, spanking, or pulling hair; 31%, rape; 17%, sexual harassment; 14%, sadomasochism; and 3%, sexual mutilation (1986: 31).

While Palys's analysis focuses largely on the unexpected finding that 'adult' videos 'have a significantly greater absolute number of depictions of sexual aggression per movie than [have] triple-X videos', the more relevant point here is that violence against women in both types of pornographic videos is quite common, and that rape is one of the more prevalent forms of sexual violence depicted. Moreover, I would expect a comparable content analysis of videos in the United States to reveal more rape and other sexual violence than was found in this Canadian study, as the Canadian government has played a more active role than the US government in trying to restrict the most abusive categories of pornography.

Palys did not find an increase in the amount of sexual violence portrayed in these videos over time. However, as Palys points out, it was not clear whether this was because some proprietors had become sensitized to issues of sexual violence as a result of protests by Canadian women, or whether they hoped to avoid protests by selecting less violent fare in recent years (1986: 34).

In a comparison of the contents of sexual and nonsexual media violence, Malamuth (1986) points out the following important differences between them:

- The victim is usually female in pornography and male in nonsexual portrayals of violence on television (p. 5).
- 'Victims' of nonsexual aggression are usually shown as outraged by their experience and intent on avoiding victimization. They, and at times the perpetrators of the aggression, suffer from the violence (p. 6). In contrast, 'when sexual violence is portrayed, there is frequently the suggestion that, despite initial resistance, the victim secretly desired the abusive treatment and eventually derived pleasure from it' (p. 6).
- Unlike nonsexual violence, pornography is designed to arouse men sexually. Such arousal 'might result in subliminal conditioning and cognitive changes in the consumer by associating physical pleasure with violence. Therefore, even sexual aggression depicted negatively may have harmful effects because of the sexual arousal induced by the explicitness of the depiction' (pp. 6–7).

In summary: pornography has become increasingly violent over the years—at least in the non-video media—and it presents an extremely distorted view of rape and sexuality.

A THEORY ABOUT THE CAUSATIVE ROLE OF PORNOGRAPHY

Sociologist David Finkelhor (1984) has developed a very useful multi-causal theory to explain the occurrence of child sexual abuse. According to Finkelhor's model, in order for child sexual abuse to occur, four conditions have to be met. First, someone has to *want* to abuse a child sexually. Second, this person's internal inhibitions against acting out this desire have to be undermined. Third, this person's social inhibitions against acting out this desire (e. g. fear of being caught and punished) have to be undermined. Fourth, the would-be perpetrator has to undermine or overcome his or her chosen victim's capacity to avoid or resist the sexual abuse.

According to my theory, these conditions also have to be met in order for rape, battery, and other forms of sexual assault on adult women to occur (Russell 1984). Although my theory can be applied to other forms of sexual abuse and violence against women besides rape, this formulation of it will focus on rape because most of the research relevant to my theory has been on this form of sexual assault.

In *Sexual Exploitation* (1984) I suggest many factors that may predispose a large number of men in the United States to want to rape or assault women sexually. Some examples discussed in this book are (*a*) biological factors, (*b*) childhood experiences of sexual abuse, (*c*) male sex-role socialization, (*d*) exposure to mass media that encourage rape, and (*e*) exposure to pornography. Here I will discuss only the role of pornography.

Although women have been known to rape both men and women, males are by far the predominant perpetrators of sexual assault as well as the biggest consumers of pornography (see e.g. Finkelhor 1984; Russell 1984). Hence, my theory will focus on male perpetrators.

A diagrammatic presentation of this theory appears in Figure 1. As previously noted, in order for rape to occur, a man not only must be predisposed to rape, but his internal and social inhibitions against acting out his rape desires must be undermined. My theory, in a nutshell, is that pornography (*a*) predisposes some men to want to rape women and intensifies the predisposition in other men already so predisposed; (*b*) it undermines some men's internal inhibitions against acting out their desire to rape; and (*c*) it undermines some men's social inhibitions against acting out their desire to rape.

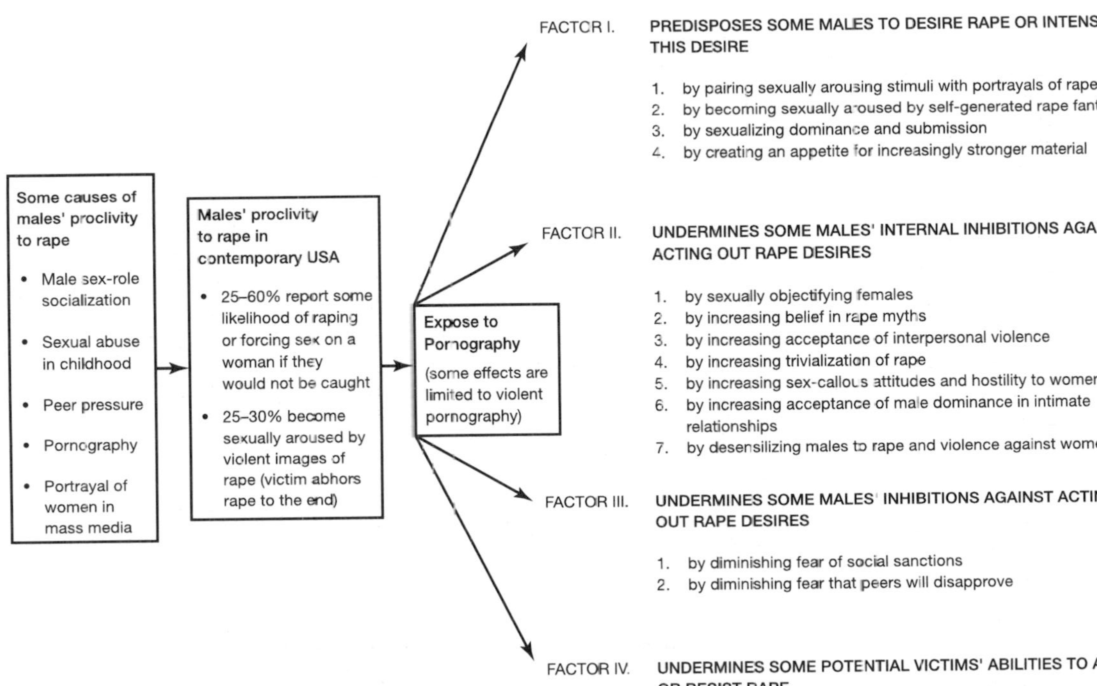

FIGURE 1 Theoretical model of pornography as a cause of rape

The Meaning of 'Cause'

Given the intense debate about whether or not pornography plays a causal role in rape, it is surprising that so few of those engaged in it ever state what they mean by 'cause'. A definition of the concept *simple causation* follows:

> An event (or events) that precedes and results in the occurrence of another event. Whenever the first event (the cause) occurs, the second event (the effect) necessarily or inevitably follows. Moreover, in simple causation the second event does not occur unless the first event has occurred. Thus the cause is both the SUFFICIENT CONDITION and the NECESSARY CONDITION for the occurrence of the effect. (Theodorson and Theodorson 1979)

By this definition, pornography clearly does not cause rape, as it seems safe to assume that some unknown percentage of pornography consumers do not rape women, and that many rapes are unrelated to pornography. However, the concept of *multiple causation* is more relevant to this question than simple causation.

> With the conception of MULTIPLE CAUSATION, various possible causes may be seen for a given event, any one of which may be a sufficient but not necessary condition for the occurrence of the effect, or a necessary but not sufficient condition. In the case of multiple causation, then, the given effect may occur in the absence of all but one of the possible sufficient but not necessary causes; and, conversely, the given effect would not follow the occurrence of some but not all of the various necessary but not sufficient causes (Theodorson and Theodorson 1979).

As I have already presented the research on males' proclivity to rape, I will next discuss some of the evidence that pornography can be a sufficient (though not necessary) condition for men to desire rape (see the list on the far right of Figure 1). I will mention when the research findings I describe apply to violent pornography and when to pornography that appears to the viewer to be nonviolent.

As high as is the percentage of male students who report some likelihood of raping women, the percentage who would admit a *desire* to rape women would likely be significantly higher. There must be at least some men who would like to rape a woman, but who would have moral compunctions about doing so. On the other hand, a desire to rape can be assumed to be present in men who disclose some likelihood of raping women. In addition to this desire they must have succeeded in blunting some of their presumed internal or social inhibitions against rape in order to express some likelihood that they would do it.

The Role of Pornography in Predisposing Some Males to Want to Rape

> 'I went to a porno bookstore, put a quarter in a slot, and saw this porn movie. It was just a guy coming up from behind a girl and attacking her and raping her. That's when I started having rape fantasies. When I seen that movie, it was like somebody lit a fuse from my childhood on up. . . . I just went for it, went out and raped.'
>
> (Rapist interviewed by Beneke 1982: 73–4)

According to Factor I in my theoretical model, pornography can induce a desire to rape women in males who had no such desire previously, and it can increase or intensify the desire to rape in males who have already felt this desire. This section will provide the evidence for the four different ways in which pornography can induce this predisposition that are listed alongside Factor I in Figure 1.

(1) Pairing Sexually Arousing/Gratifying Stimuli with Rape. A simple application of the laws of social learning (e.g. classical conditioning, instrumental conditioning, and social modelling), about which there is now considerable consensus among psychologists, suggests that viewers of pornography can develop arousal responses to depictions of rape, murder, child sexual abuse, or other assaultive behavior. Researcher S. Rachman of the Institute of Psychiatry, Maudsley Hospital, London, has demonstrated that male subjects can learn to become sexually aroused by seeing a picture of a woman's boot after repeatedly seeing women's boots in association with sexually arousing slides of nude females (Rachman and Hodgson 1968). The laws of learning that operated in the acquisition of the boot fetish can also teach men who were not previously aroused by depictions of rape to become so. All it may take is the repeated association of rape with arousing portrayals of female nudity (or clothed females in provocative poses).

Even for men who are not sexually excited during movie portrayals of rape, masturbation subsequent to the movie reinforces the association. This constitutes what R. J. McGuire, J. M. Carlisle, and B. G. Young refer to as 'masturbatory conditioning' (Cline 1914: 210). The pleasurable experience of orgasm—an expected and planned-for activity in many pornography parlors—is an exceptionally potent reinforcer.

(2) Increasing Males' Self-Generated Rape Fantasies. Further evidence that exposure to pornography can create in men a predisposition to rape where none existed before is provided by an experiment conducted by Malamuth. Malamuth classified 29 male students as sexually force-oriented or non-force-oriented on the basis of their responses to a questionnaire (1981*a*). These students were then randomly assigned to view either a rape version or a mutually consenting version of a slide-audio presentation. The account of rape and accompanying pictures were based on a story in a popular pornographic magazine, which Malamuth describes as follows:

> The man in this story finds an attractive woman on a deserted road. When he approaches her, she faints with fear. In the rape version, the man ties her up and forcibly undresses her. The accompanying narrative is as follows: 'You take her into the car. Though this experience is new to you, there is a temptation too powerful to resist. When she awakens, you tell her she had better do exactly as you say or she'll be sorry. With terrified eyes she agrees. She is undressed and she is willing to succumb to whatever you want. You kiss her and she returns the kiss.' Portrayal of the man and woman in sexual acts follows; intercourse is implied rather than explicit. (1981*a*: 38)

In the mutually consenting version of the story the victim was not tied up or threatened. Instead, on her awakening in the car, the man told her that 'she is safe and that no one will do her any harm. She seems to like you and you begin to kiss.' The rest of the story is identical to the rape version (Malamuth 1981*a*: 38).

All subjects were then exposed to the same audio description of a rape read by a female. This rape involved threats with a knife, beatings, and physical restraint. The victim was portrayed as pleading, crying, screaming, and fighting against the rapist (Abel, Barlow, Blanchard, and Guild, 1977: 898). Malamuth reports that measures of penile tumescence as well as self-reported arousal 'indicated that relatively high levels of sexual arousal were generated by all the experimental stimuli' (1981*a*: 33).

After the 29 male students had been exposed to the rape audio tape, they were asked to try to reach as high a level of sexual arousal as possible by fantasizing about whatever they wanted but without any direct stimulation of the penis (1981*a*: 40). Self-reported sexual arousal during the fantasy period indicated that those students who had been exposed to the rape version of the first slide-audio presentation, created more violent sexual fantasies than those exposed to the mutually consenting version *irrespective of whether they had been classified as force-oriented or non-force-oriented* (1981*a*: 33).

As the rape version of the slide-audio presentation is typical of what is seen in pornography, the results of this experiment suggest that similar pornographic depictions are likely to generate rape fantasies even in previously non-force-oriented consumers. And, as Edna Einsiedel points out (1986: 60):

> Current evidence suggests a high correlation between deviant fantasies and deviant behaviors. . . . Some treatment methods are also predicated on the link between fantasies and behavior by attempting to alter fantasy patterns in order to change the deviant behaviors. (1986: 60)

Because so many people resist the idea that a desire to rape may develop as a result of viewing pornography, let us focus for a moment on behavior other than rape. There is abundant testimonial evidence that at least some men decide they would like to perform certain sex acts on women after seeing pornography portraying such acts. For example, one of the men who answered Shere Hite's question on pornography wrote: 'It's great for me. *It gives me new ideas to try and see*, and it's always sexually exciting' (1981: 780; emphasis added). Of course, there's nothing wrong with getting new ideas from pornography or anywhere else, nor with trying them out, as long as they are not actions that subordinate or violate others. Unfortunately, many of the behaviors modelled in pornography *do* subordinate and violate women, sometimes viciously. For example, a respondent in my probability sample survey, said: 'He'd read something in a pornographic book, and then he wanted to live it out. It was too violent for me to do something like that. It was basically getting dressed up and spanking. Him spanking me. I refused to do it.'

When a man engages in a particularly unusual act that he had previously encountered in pornography, it becomes even more likely that the decision to do so was inspired by the pornography. For example, one woman testified to the Attorney General's Commission on Pornography about the pornography related death of her son:

> My son, Troy Daniel Dunaway, was murdered on August 6, 1981, by the greed and avarice of the publishers of *Hustler* magazine. My son read the article 'Orgasm of Death,' set up the sexual experiment depicted therein, followed the explicit instructions of the article, and ended up dead. He would still be

alive today were he not enticed and incited into this action by *Hustler* magazine's 'How to Do' August 1981 article, an article which was found at his feet and which directly caused his death. (1986: 797)

When children do what they see in pornography, it is even more inappropriate than in the case of adults to attribute their behavior entirely to their predispositions.

Psychologist Jennings Bryant testified to the Pornography Commission about a survey he had conducted involving 600 telephone interviews with males and females who were evenly divided into three age groups: students in junior high school, students in high school, and adults aged 19 to 39 years (1985: 133). Respondents were asked if 'exposure to X-rated materials had made them want to try anything they saw' (1985: 140). Two-thirds of the males reported 'wanting to try some of the behavior depicted' (1985: 140). Bryant reports that the desire to imitate what is seen in pornography 'progressively increases as age of respondents *decreases*' (1985: 140; emphasis added). Among the junior high school students, 72% of the males reported that 'they wanted to try some sexual experiment or sexual behavior that they had seen in their initial exposure to X-rated materials' (1985: 140).

In trying to ascertain if imitation had occurred, the respondents were asked: 'Did you actually experiment with or try any of the behaviors depicted' within a few days of seeing the materials (1985: 140)? A quarter of the males answered that they had. A number of adult men answered no but said that some years later they had experimented with the behaviors portrayed. However, only imitations within a few days of seeing the materials were counted (1985: 140). Male high school students were the most likely (31%) to report experimenting with the behaviors portrayed (1985: 141).

Unfortunately, no information is available on the behaviors imitated by these males. Imitating pornography is only cause for concern if the behavior imitated is violent or abusive, or if the behavior is not wanted by the recipient. Despite the unavailability of this information, Bryant's study is valuable in showing how common it is for males to *want* to imitate what they see in pornography, and for revealing that many *do* imitate it within a few days of viewing it. Furthermore, given the degrading and often violent content of pornography, as well as the youthfulness and presumable susceptibility of many of the viewers, how likely it is that these males only imitated or wished to imitate the nonsexist, nondegrading, and nonviolent sexual behavior?

Almost all the research on pornography to date has been conducted on men and women who were at least 18 years old. But as Malamuth points out, there is 'a research basis for expecting that children would be more susceptible to the influences of mass media, including violent pornography if they are exposed to it' than adults (1985: 107). Bryant's telephone interviews show that very large numbers of children now have access to both hard-core and soft-core materials. For example:

- The average age at which male respondents saw their first issue of *Playboy* or a similar magazine was 11 years (1985: 135).
- All of the high school age males surveyed reported having read or looked at *Playboy*, *Playgirl*, or some other soft-core magazine (1985: 134).
- High school males reported having seen an average of 16.1 issues, and junior high school males said they had seen an average of 2.5 issues.
- In spite of being legally under age, junior high students reported having seen an average of 16.3 'unedited sexy R-rated films' (1985: 135). (Although R-rated movies are not usually considered pornographic, many of them meet my definition of pornography.)
- The average age of first exposure to sexually oriented R-rated films for all respondents was 12.5 years (1985: 135).
- Nearly 70% of the junior high students surveyed reported that they had seen their first R-rated film before they were 13 (1985: 135).
- The vast majority of all the respondents reported exposure to hard-core, X-rated, sexually explicit material (1985: 135). Furthermore, 'a larger proportion of high school students had seen X-rated films than any other age group, including adults': 84%, with the average age of first exposure being 16 years, 11 months (1985: 136).

In a more recent anonymous survey of 247 Canadian junior high school students whose average age was 14 years, James Check and Kirstin Maxwell (1992) report that 87% of the boys and 61% of the girls said they had viewed videopornography. The average age at first exposure was just under 12 years.

33% of the boys versus only 2% of the girls reported watching pornography once a month or more often. As well, 29% of the boys versus 1% of the girls reported that pornography was the source that had provided them with the most useful information about sex (i.e., more than parents, school, friends, etc.). Finally, boys who were frequent consumers of pornography and/or reported learning a lot from pornography were also more likely to say that it was 'OK' to hold a girl down and force her to have intercourse.

Clearly, more research is needed on the effects of pornography on young male viewers, particularly in view of the fact that recent studies suggest that 'over 50% of various categories of paraphiliacs [sex offenders] had developed their deviant arousal patterns prior to age 18' (Einsiedel 1986: 53). Einsiedel goes on to say that 'it is clear that the age-of-first-exposure variable and the nature of that exposure needs to be examined more carefully. There is also evidence that the longer the duration of the paraphilia, the more significant the association with use of pornography (Abel, Mittelman, and Becker 1985).'

The first two items listed under Factor I in my theoretical model both relate to the viewing of *violent* pornography. But sexualizing dominance and submission is a way in which nonviolent pornography can also predispose some males to want to rape women.

(3) Sexualizing Dominance and Submission. Canadian psychologists James Check and Ted Guloien (1989) conducted an experiment in which they distinguished between degrading nonviolent pornography and erotica, and compared their effects. Their experiment is rare not only for making this distinction but also for including non-students as subjects; 436 Toronto residents and college students were exposed to one of three types of sexual material over three viewing sessions, or to no material. The sexual materials were constructed from existing commercially available videos and validated by measuring subjects' perceptions of them. The contents of the sexual materials shown to the three groups of respondents were as follows:

1. The *sexual violence* material portrayed scenes of sexual intercourse involving a woman strapped to a table and being penetrated by a large plastic penis.
2. The *sexually explicit dehumanizing but nonviolent* material portrayed scenes of sexual activity that included a man sitting on top of a woman and masturbating into her face.
3. The *sexually explicit non-degrading* material portrayed sexual activities leading up to heterosexual intercourse (Check and Guloien 1989).

Check and Guloien's experiment revealed that the viewing of both the nonviolent dehumanizing materials as well as the violent materials resulted in male subjects reporting a significantly greater likelihood of engaging in rape or other coercive sex acts than the control group.

Although self-reported likelihood of raping is not a proper measure of *desire* to rape, as it also indicates that the internal inhibitions against acting out rape desires have been undermined to some extent, Check and Guloien's experiment does offer tentative support for my theoretical model's claim that pornography sexualizes dominance and submission. In addition, it makes theoretical sense that sexualizing dominance and submission would likely be generalized to include eroticizing rape for some men. Further research is needed on this issue, and more researchers need to follow the lead of the Canadian researchers in going beyond the distinction between violent and nonviolent pornography, and distinguishing also between nonviolent degrading pornography and erotica.

(4) Creating an Appetite for Increasingly Stronger Material. Dolf Zillmann and Jennings Bryant have studied the effects of what they refer to as 'massive exposure' to pornography (1984). (In fact, it was not that massive: 4 hours and 48 minutes per week over a period of 6 weeks.) These researchers, unlike Malamuth and Donnerstein, focus on trying to ascertain the effects of *nonviolent* pornography and, in the study to be described, they use a sample drawn from a non-student adult population.

Subjects in the *massive exposure* condition saw 36 nonviolent pornographic films, 6 per session per week; subjects in the *intermediate* condition saw 18 such movies, 3 per session per week. Subjects in the control group saw 36 nonpornographic movies. Various measures were taken after 1 week, 2 weeks, and 3 weeks of exposure. In the third week the subjects who were told that they were participating in an American Bar Association study, were asked to recommend the prison term they thought most fair in the case of a rape of a female hitchhiker.

Zillmann and Bryant (1984) found that an appetite for stronger material was fostered in their subjects, presumably, Zillmann suggests, 'because familiar material becomes unexciting as a result of habituation' (1984: 127). Hence, 'consumers graduate from common to less common forms of pornography,' that is, to more violent and more degrading materials (1984: 127).

According to this research, then, pornography can transform a male who was not previously interested in the more abusive types of pornography, into one who *is* turned on by such material. In turn,

Malamuth has shown that males who did not previously find rape sexually arousing, generate such fantasies after being exposed to a typical example of violent pornography, as described in (2) above. And men who have rape fantasies are more likely to act them out than men who do not.

I have argued that the laws of social learning apply to pornography, just as they apply to other media. As Donnerstein testified at the hearings in Minneapolis: 'If you assume that your child can learn from Sesame Street how to count one, two, three, four, five, believe me, they can learn how to pick up a gun' (Donnerstein 1983: 11). Presumably, males can learn equally well how to rape, beat, sexually abuse, and degrade females.

The Role of Pornography in Undermining Some Males' Internal Inhibitions Against Acting Out the Desire to Rape

> 'The movie was just like a big picture stand with words on it saying "go out and do it, everybody's doin' it, even the movies."'
>
> (Rapist interviewed by Beneke 1982: 74)

Evidence has been cited showing that many males would like to rape a woman, but for some unknown percentage of these males they have internal inhibitions against doing so. Some males' internal inhibitions are likely to be very weak, others very strong. Presumably, the strength of internal inhibitions also varies in the same individual from time to time. Seven ways in which pornography undermines some males' internal inhibitions against acting out rape desires are listed in Figure 1. Research evidence about these processes will be presented in this section.

(1) Objectifying Women. The first way in which pornography undermines some males' internal inhibitions against acting out their desires to rape is by objectifying women. Feminists have been emphasizing the role of objectification in the occurrence of rape for years (e.g. Medea and Thompson 1974; Russell 1975). Some men in this culture literally do not see women as human beings but as body parts. They are tits, cunts, and asses. This makes it easier to rape them. 'It was difficult for me to admit that I was dealing with a human being when I was talking to a woman,' one rapist reported, 'because, if you read men's magazines, you hear about your stereo, your car, your chick' (Russell 1975: 249–50). After this rapist had hit his victim several times in her face,

she stopped resisting and begged, 'All right, just don't hurt me.' 'When she said that,' he reported, 'all of a sudden it came into my head, "My God, this is a human being!" I came to my senses and saw that I was hurting this person.' Another rapist said of his victim, 'I wanted this beautiful fine *thing* and I got it' (Russell 1975: 245, emphasis added).

Dehumanizing oppressed groups or enemy nations in times of war is an important mechanism for facilitating brutal behavior toward members of those groups. However, the dehumanization of women that occurs in pornography is often not recognized because of its sexual guise and its pervasiveness. And it is important to note that the objectification of women is as common in nonviolent pornography as it is in violent pornography.

Doug McKenzie-Mohr and Mark Zanna conducted an experiment to test whether certain types of males would be more likely to sexually objectify a woman after viewing 15 minutes of nonviolent pornography. They selected 60 male students who they classified into one of two categories: masculine sex-typed or gender schematic—individuals who 'encode all cross-sex interactions in sexual terms and all members of the opposite sex in terms of sexual attractiveness' (Bem 1981: 361); and androgenous or gender aschematic—men who do not encode cross-sex interactions and women in these ways (McKenzie-Mohr and Zanna 1990: 297, 299).

McKenzie-Mohr and Zanna found that after exposure to nonviolent pornography, the masculine sex-typed males 'treated our female experimenter who was interacting with them in a professional setting, in a manner that was both cognitively and behaviorally sexist' (1990: 305). For example, in comparison with the androgynous males, the masculine sex-typed males positioned themselves closer to the female experimenter, and had 'greater recall for information about her physical appearance' and less about the survey she was conducting (1990: 305). The experimenter also rated these men as more sexually motivated based on her answers to questions such as, 'How much did you feel he was looking at your body?' 'How sexually motivated did you find the subject?' (1990: 301).

This experiment confirmed McKenzie-Mohr and Zanna's hypothesis that exposure to nonviolent pornography causes masculine sex-typed men, in contrast to androgynous men, to view and treat a woman as a sex object.

(2) Rape Myths. If males believe that women enjoy rape and find it sexually exciting, this belief is likely to undermine the inhibitions of

some of them who would like to rape women. Sociologists Diana Scully and Martha Burt have reported that rapists are particularly apt to believe rape myths (Burt 1980; Scully 1985). For example, Scully found that 65% of the rapists in her study believed that 'women cause their own rape by the way they act and the clothes they wear'; and 69% agreed that 'most men accused of rape are really innocent'. However, as Scully points out, it is not possible to know if their beliefs preceded their behavior or constitute an attempt to rationalize it. Hence, findings from the experimental data are more telling for our purposes than these interviews with rapists.

As the myth that women enjoy rape is widely held, the argument that consumers of pornography realize that such portrayals are false is totally unconvincing (Brownmiller 1975; Burt 1980; Russell 1975). Indeed, several studies have shown that portrayals of women enjoying rape and other kinds of sexual violence can lead to increased acceptance of rape myths in both men and women. For example, in an experiment conducted by Neil Malamuth and James Check, one group of college students saw a pornographic depiction in which a woman was portrayed as sexually aroused by sexual violence, and a second group was exposed to control materials. Subsequently, all subjects were shown a second rape portrayal. The students who had been exposed to the pornographic depiction of rape were significantly more likely than the students in the control group (*a*) to perceive the second rape victim as suffering less trauma; (*b*) to believe that she actually enjoyed it; and (*c*) to believe that women in general enjoy rape and forced sexual acts (Check and Malamuth 1985: 419).

Other examples of the rape myths that male subjects in these studies are more apt to believe after viewing pornography are as follows: 'A woman who goes to the home or the apartment of a man on their first date implies that she is willing to have sex'; 'Any healthy woman can successfully resist a rapist if she really wants to'; 'Many women have an unconscious wish to be raped, and may then unconsciously set up a situation in which they are likely to be attacked'; 'If a girl engages in necking or petting and she lets things get out of hand it is her own fault if her partner forces sex on her' (Briere, Malamuth, and Check 1985: 400).

In Maxwell and Check's 1992 study of 247 high school students described above, they found very high rates of rape supportive beliefs. The boys who were the most frequent consumers of pornography and/or who reported learning a lot from it, were more accepting of rape myths and violence against women than their peers, who were less frequent consumers and/or who said they had not learned as much from it.

> A full 25% of girls and 57% of boys indicated belief that in one or more situations, it was at least 'maybe okay' for a boy to hold a girl down and force her to have intercourse. Further, only 21% of the boys and 57% of the girls believed that forced intercourse was 'definitely not okay' in any of the situations. The situation in which forced intercourse was most accepted, was that in which the girl had sexually excited her date. In this case 43% of the boys and 16% of the girls stated that it was at least 'maybe okay' for the boy to force intercourse. (1992)

According to Donnerstein, 'After only 10 minutes of exposure to aggressive pornography, particularly material in which women are shown being aggressed against, you find male subjects are much more willing to accept these particular myths' (1983: 6). These men are also more inclined to believe that 25% of the women they know would enjoy being raped (1983: 6).

(3) Acceptance of Interpersonal Violence. Males' internal inhibitions against acting out their desire to rape can also be undermined if they consider male violence against women to be acceptable behavior. Studies have shown that viewing portrayals of sexual violence as having positive consequences increases male subjects' acceptance of violence against women. Examples of some of these items include 'Being roughed up is sexually stimulating to many women'; 'Sometimes the only way a man can get a cold woman turned on is to use force'; 'Many times a woman will pretend she doesn't want to have intercourse because she doesn't want to seem loose, but she's really hoping the man will force her' (Briere, Malamuth, and Check 1985: 401).

Malamuth and Check (1981) conducted an experiment of particular interest because the movies shown were part of the regular campus film program. Students were randomly assigned to view either a feature-length film that portrayed violence against women as being justifiable and having positive consequences (*Swept Away* or *The Getaway*) or a film without sexual violence. The experiment showed that exposure to the sexually violent movies increased the male subjects' acceptance of interpersonal violence against women. (This outcome did not occur with the female subjects.) These effects were measured several days after the films had been seen.

Malamuth suggests several processes by which sexual violence in the media 'might lead to attitudes that are more accepting of violence against women' (1986: 4). Some of these processes also probably facilitate the undermining of pornography consumers' internal inhibitions against acting out rape desires.

1. Labeling sexual violence more as a sexual rather than a violent act.
2. Adding to perceptions that sexual aggression is normative and culturally acceptable.
3. Changing attributions of responsibility to place more blame on the victim.
4. Elevating the positive value of sexual aggression by associating it with sexual pleasure and a sense of conquest.
5. Reducing negative emotional reactions to sexually aggressive acts (1986: 5).

(4) Trivializing Rape; (5) Sex-Callous Attitudes; (6) Acceptance of Male Dominance in Intimate Relationships. According to Donnerstein, in most studies 'subjects have been exposed to only a few minutes of pornographic material' (1985: 341). In contrast, Zillmann and Bryant examined the effects of 'massive exposure' to pornography (this experiment was described on p. 71). As well as creating an appetite for increasingly stronger material, Zillmann and Bryant found that:

- 'Heavy exposure to common nonviolent pornography trivialized rape as a criminal offense' (1984: 117). In addition, sexual aggression and abuse was perceived as causing less suffering for the victims, for example, an adult male having sexual intercourse with a 12-year-old girl (1984: 132).
- 'Males' sexual callousness toward women was significantly enhanced' (1984: 117). For example, there was an increased acceptance of statements such as 'A woman doesn't mean "no" until she slaps you'; 'A man should find them, fool them, fuck them, and forget them'; and 'If they are old enough to bleed, they are old enough to butcher.' Judging by these items, it is difficult to distinguish sexual callousness from a general hostility to women.
- The acceptance of male dominance in intimate relationships was greatly increased (1984: 121), and the notion that women are or ought to be equal in intimate relationships was more likely to be abandoned (1984: 122). Support of the women's liberation movement also sharply declined (1984: 134).

All these effects—both separately and together—are likely to contribute to undermining some males' inhibitions against acting out their desires to rape.

(7) Desensitizing Males to Rape. In an experiment specifically designed to study desensitization, Linz, Donnerstein, and Penrod showed 10 hours of R-rated or X-rated movies over a period of 5 days to male subjects (Donnerstein and Linz 1985: 34A). Some students saw X-rated movies depicting sexual assault; others saw X-rated movies depicting only consenting sex; and a third group saw R-rated sexually violent movies—for example, *I Spit on Your Grave, Toolbox Murders, Texas Chainsaw Massacre.* Donnerstein (1983) describes *Toolbox Murders* as follows: There is an erotic bathtub scene in which a woman massages herself. A beautiful song is played. Then a psychotic killer enters with a nail gun. The music stops. He chases the woman around the room, then shoots her through the stomach with the nail gun. She falls across a chair. The song comes back on as he puts the nail gun to her forehead and blows her brains out. According to Donnerstein, many young males become sexually aroused by this movie (1983: 10).

Donnerstein and Linz point out that, 'It has always been suggested by critics of media violence research that only those who are *already* predisposed toward violence are influenced by exposure to media violence' (1985: 34F). But these experimenters had actually preselected their subjects to ensure that they were not psychotic, hostile, or anxious.

Donnerstein and Linz described the impact of the R-rated movies on their subjects as follows:

> Initially, after the first day of viewing, the men rated themselves as significantly above the norm for depression, anxiety and annoyance on a mood adjective checklist. After each subsequent day of viewing, these scores dropped until, on the fourth day of viewing, the males' levels of anxiety, depression, and annoyance were indistinguishable from baseline norms. (1985: 34F)

By the fifth day, the subjects rated the movies as less graphic and less gory and estimated fewer violent or offensive scenes than after the first day of viewing. They also rated the films as significantly less debasing and degrading to women, more humorous, and more enjoyable, and reported a greater willingness to see this type of film again (1985: 34F). However, their sexual arousal by this material did *not* decrease over this 5-day period (Donnerstein 1983: 10).

On the last day, the subjects went to a law school where they saw a documentary reenactment of a real rape trial. A control group of subjects who had never seen the films also participated in this part of the experiment. Subjects who had seen the R-rated movies: (a) rated the rape victim as significantly more worthless, (b) rated her injury as significantly less severe, and (c) assigned greater blame to her for being raped than did the subjects who had not seen the film. In contrast, these effects were not observed for the X-rated nonviolent films.[15] However, the results were much the same for the violent X-rated films, despite the fact that the R-rated material was 'much more graphically violent' (Donnerstein 1985: 12–13).

In summary: I have presented only a fraction of the research evidence for seven different effects of pornography, all of which are likely to contribute to the undermining of some males' internal inhibitions against acting out rape desires. This list is not intended to be comprehensive. Indeed, I now have several additions to make, but space precludes my including them here.

The Role of Pornography in Undermining Some Males' Social Inhibitions Against Acting Out Their Desire to Rape

> I have often thought about it [rape], fantasized about it. I might like it because of having a feeling of power over a woman. But I never actually wanted to through *fear of being caught and publicly ruined.*
>
> (Hite 1981: 715, emphasis added)

A man may want to rape a woman *and* his internal inhibitions against rape may be undermined by his hostility to women or by his belief in the myths that women really enjoy being raped and/or that they deserve it, but he may still not act out his desire to rape because of his *social* inhibitions. Fear of being caught and convicted for the crime is the most obvious example of a social inhibition. In addition to Hite's respondent quoted above, a second man's answer to her question on whether he had ever wanted to rape a woman illustrates this form of inhibition:

> I have never raped a woman, but have at times felt a desire to—for the struggle and final victory. I'm a person, though, who always thinks before he acts, and *the consequences wouldn't be worth it. Besides, I don't want to be known as a pervert.* (1981: 715, emphasis added)

(1) Diminishing Fear of Social Sanctions. In one of his early experi-

ments, Malamuth, along with his colleagues Haber and Feshbach (1980), reported that after reading the account of a violent stranger rape, 17% of their male student subjects admitted that there was some likelihood that they might behave in a similar fashion in the same circumstances. However, 53% of the same male students said there was some likelihood that they might act as the rapist did *if they could be sure of getting away with it.* This higher percentage reveals the significant role that can be played by social inhibitions against acting out rape desires. My hypothesis is that pornography also plays a role in undermining some males' social inhibitions against acting out their desire to rape.

In his content analysis of 150 pornographic home videos, Palys investigated 'whether aggressive perpetrators ever received any negative consequences for their aggressive activity—if charges were laid, or the person felt personal trauma, or had some form of "just deserts"' (1986: 32). The answer was no in 73% of the cases in which a clear-cut answer was ascertainable. Similarly, Don Smith (1976) found that fewer than 3% of the rapists portrayed in the 428 pornographic books he analyzed were depicted as experiencing any negative consequences as a result of their behavior. Indeed, many of them were rewarded. The common portrayal in pornography of rape as easy to get away with is likely to contribute to the undermining of some males' social inhibitions against the acting out of their rape desires.

(2) Diminishing Fear of Disapproval by Peers. Fear of disapproval by one's peers is another social inhibition that may be undermined by pornography. For example, Zillmann found that 'massive' exposure to nonviolent pornography produced overestimates by the subjects of uncommon sexual practices, such as anal intercourse, group sexual activities, sadomasochism, and bestiality (1985: 118; Zillmann and Bryant 1984: 132). Rape is portrayed as a very common male practice in much violent pornography, and the actors themselves may serve as a kind of pseudo-peer group and/or role models for consumers. Further research is needed to evaluate these hypotheses.

In general, I hypothesize the following disinhibiting effects of viewing violent pornography—particularly in 'massive' amounts: (*a*) viewers' estimates of the percentage of men who have raped women would be likely to increase; (*b*) viewers would be likely to consider rape a much easier crime to commit than they had previously believed; (*c*) viewers would be less likely to believe that rape victims would report their rapes to the police; (*d*) viewers would be more likely to expect that rapists would avoid arrest, prosecution, and conviction in those cases that are reported; (*e*) viewers would become less disapproving of rapists, and less likely to expect disapproval from others if they decide to rape.

The Role of Pornography in Undermining Potential Victims' Abilities to Avoid or Resist Rape

> 'He . . . told me it was not wrong because they were doing it in the magazines and that made it O.K.'
>
> (Attorney General's Commission 1986: 786).

Obviously this fourth factor (the role of pornography in undermining potential victims' abilities to avoid or resist rape) is not necessary for rape to occur. Nevertheless, once the first three factors in my causal model have been met—a male not only wants to rape a woman but is willing to do so because his inhibitions, both internal and social, have been undermined—a would-be rapist may use pornography to try to undermine a woman's resistance. Pornography is more likely to be used for this purpose when men attack their intimates (as opposed to strangers).

(1) Encouraging Females to Get into High Rape-Risk Situations. Most adult rape victims are not shown pornography in the course of being raped, although the testimony reveals that this is quite a common experience for many prostitutes who are raped. Pornography is more often used to try to persuade a woman or child to engage in certain acts, to legitimize the acts, and to undermine their resistance, refusal, or disclosure of these acts. For example, Donald Mosher reported in his 1971 study that 16% of the 'sex calloused' male students had attempted to obtain intercourse by showing pornography to a woman, or by taking her to a 'sexy' movie. To the extent that this strategy succeeds in manipulating some women into sexual engagements that do not include intercourse, it can result in women being very vulnerable to date rape.

In a more recent study conducted in Canada, Charlene Senn found that 'the more pornography women were exposed to, the more likely they were to have been forced or coerced into sexual activity they did not want' (1992). In addition, a male was present in most of the cases in which women were exposed to pornography. This means that most women who consume pornography are doing it because a man wants them to (1992). This is a particularly important finding because the media have made much of the alleged fact that increasing numbers of women are renting pornographic videos.

The positive correlation between the quantity of pornography to which women are exposed and their experiences of forced or coerced sex suggests that women who cooperate with men's requests for them to see it are more likely to be sexually assaulted. This in turn implies that viewing pornography somehow undermines their ability to avoid being sexually assaulted.

Following are two examples of men who used pornography to undermine their victims' resistance. Although these examples do not include rape, the first two cases make it easy to see how being shown pornography can increase a child's vulnerability to rape.

I was sexually abused by my foster father from the time I was seven until I was thirteen. He had stacks and stacks of *Playboys*. He would take me to his bedroom or his workshop, show me the pictures, and say, 'This is what big girls do. If you want to be a big girl, you have to do this, but you can never tell anybody.' Then I would have to pose like the woman in the pictures. I also remember being shown a *Playboy* cartoon of a man having sex with a child. (Attorney General's Commission, 1986: 783)

He encouraged me by showing me pornographic magazines which they kept in the bathroom and told me it was not wrong because they were doing it in the magazines and that made it O.K. He told me all fathers do it to their daughters and said even pastors do it to their daughters. The magazines were to help me learn more about sex. (Attorney General's Commission 1986: 786)

When women are shown such materials, they probably feel more obliged to engage in unwanted sex acts that they mistakenly believe are normative. Evidence for this hypothesis is provided by Zillmann and Bryant's previously quoted finding that massive exposure to pornography distorts the viewers' perceptions of sexuality by producing the lasting impression that relatively uncommon sexual practices are more common than they actually are, for example, 'intercourse with more than one partner at a time, sadomasochistic actions, and animal contacts' (1984: 132–3).

Following is a statement by a woman about how her husband used pornography for this purpose.

Once we saw an X-rated film that showed anal intercourse. After that he insisted that I try anal intercourse. I agreed to do so, trying to be the available, willing creature that I thought I was supposed to be. I found the experience very painful, and I told him so. But he kept insisting that we try it again and again. (Attorney General's Commission 1986: 778)

Women in this situation who try to stop unwanted sex acts are at risk of being raped.

More systematic research is needed to establish how frequently males use pornography to try to undermine the ability of potential victims to avoid or resist rape and other sexual abuse, and how effective this strategy is. Even if pornography could not predispose men to want to rape women, and it could not intensify the desires of men who are already so predisposed, and it could not undermine men's internal and external inhibitions against acting out their desires to rape, the use of pornography to undermine potential victims' abilities to avoid rape would be cause enough to be deeply concerned about its harmfulness.

(2) A Pornography Industry that Requires Female Participation. Because the portrayal of rape is one of the favorite themes of pornography, a large and ever changing supply of girls and women have to be found to provide it. Clearly, some women are voluntary participants in simulated acts of rape. But many of the rapes that are photographed are real.

In summary: A significant amount of research supports my theory that pornography can, and does, cause rape. Nevertheless, much of the research undertaken to date does not adequately examine the four key variables in my theory. For example, Malamuth's self-reported likelihood-of-raping construct merges the desire to rape with the undermining of internal inhibitions against acting out this desire. I hope that more research will be guided in the future by the theoretical distinctions required by my model.

FURTHER EMPIRICAL FINDINGS ON THE CAUSATIVE ROLE OF PORNOGRAPHY IN RAPE

As Donnerstein points out, 'One cannot, for obvious reasons, experimentally examine the relationship between pornography and *actual* sexual aggression' (1984: 53). However, he has conducted experiments that have shown that the level of aggression of male subjects toward females increased after they had been exposed to violent pornography in which a female rape victim was portrayed as becoming aroused by the end of the movie (aggression was measured by the intensity of electric shock subjects were willing to administer; Donnerstein 1984). Violent films that were nonpornographic (depicting, for example, a man hitting a woman) also increased male subjects' levels of aggression toward women, but not to the same extent as violent pornographic films. When Donnerstein used violent pornography in which the victim was portrayed as being distressed by the sexual assault throughout the movie, the levels of aggression of male subjects toward females became increased only when they had first been angered by a confederate of the experimenter before seeing the movie.

To explain these findings, Malamuth suggested that: 'positive victim reactions . . . may act to justify aggression and to reduce general inhibitions against aggression' (1984: 36). This interpretation is consistent with my causal model's emphasis on the important role pornographic depictions play in undermining males' inhibitions against acting out hostile behavior toward women.

Malamuth also undertook an experiment to test whether men's attitudes and sexual arousal to depictions of rape could predict aggression in the laboratory. A week after measuring male subjects' attitudes and sexual arousal to rape, they were angered by a female confederate of the experimenter. When the subjects were given an opportunity to behave aggressively toward her by administering an unpleasant noise as punishment for errors she made in an alleged extrasensory perception experiment, men who had higher levels of sexual arousal to rape and who had attitudes that condoned aggression, 'were more aggressive against the woman and wanted to hurt her to a greater extent' (Malamuth 1986: 16).

On the basis of this experiment, as well as two others, Malamuth concluded that 'attitudes condoning aggression against women related to objectively observable behavior—laboratory aggression against women' (1986: 16).

Both Donnerstein and Malamuth emphasize that their findings on the relationship between pornography and aggression toward women relate to aggressive or violent, not to nonviolent, pornography. For example, Donnerstein maintains that 'nonaggressive materials only affect aggression when inhibitions to aggress are quite low, or with long-term and massive exposure. With a single exposure and normal aggressing conditions, there is little evidence that nonviolent pornography has any negative effects' (1984: 78–9). In the real world, however, inhibitions to aggress are often very low, and long-term and massive exposure to nonviolent material is also quite common.

Furthermore, there is a lot of evidence of harm from nonaggressive pornography, aside from its impact on aggressive behavior (for example, see my earlier discussion of some of Zillmann's findings).

Finally, given how saturated US culture is with pornographic images and how much exposure many of the male subjects being tested have already had, the task of trying to design experiments that can show effects on the basis of one more exposure is challenging indeed. Because of this methodological problem, when no measurable effects result, it would be wrong to interpret the experiment as proving that there are no effects in general. We should therefore focus on the effects that *do* show up, rather than being overly impressed by the effects that do not.

Some people are critical of the fact that most of the experimental research on pornography has been conducted on college students who are not representative of men in the general population. Hence, the research of Richard Frost and John Stauffer (1987) comparing the responses to filmed violence of college students and residents of an inner-city housing project is of particular interest.

In 5 of the 10 violent films shown to these two groups the violence was directed at females. Frost and Stauffer evaluated these men's sexual arousal to these films by applying both self-report and physiological measures. They found that 'there was no single form of violence for which the responses of the college sample exceeded those of the inner city sample on either measure' (1987: 36). Four of the five most physiologically arousing categories of violence were the same for both groups: a female killing another female; a male killing a female; rape/murder; and a female killing a male (1987: 37). Interestingly, depictions of male–female assault were the least exciting of all ten types of violence measured to all subjects (1987: 39). Have men become bored by such a mundane form of violence in movies?

The greatest disparity between the two groups in both physiological and self-reported sexual arousal was to depictions of rape, which 'caused the highest response by inner-city subjects but only the fifth highest by the college sample' (1987: 38). Although it is not acceptable to infer action from arousal, nevertheless men who are aroused by depictions of violence toward women are more likely to act violently toward them than men who are not aroused by such depictions.

Hence, Frost and Stauffer's study suggests that college students are less prone to sexual violence than some other groups of men. While this is hardly surprising for many people, as inner-city environments are more violent than colleges or than the places in which most college students grew up, it does invalidate attempts to discount the pornography researchers' high figures for self-reported likelihood to rape reported by college males.

The 25 to 30% of male students who admit that there is some likelihood that they would rape a woman if they could be assured of getting away with it, increases to 57% after exposure to sexually violent images, particularly sexually violent images depicting women enjoying rape (Donnerstein 1983: 7). This means that *as a result of one brief exposure to pornography, the number of men who are willing to consider rape as a plausible act for them to commit actually doubles.*

One such brief exposure to pornography also increases male subjects' acceptance of rape myths and interpersonal violence against women. Given the hypothesis that such increased acceptance would serve to lower viewers' inhibitions against acting out violent desires, one would expect pornography consumption to be related to rape rates. This is what one ingenious study found.

Larry Baron and Murray Straus (1984) undertook a 50-state correlational analysis of reported rape rates and the circulation rates of eight pornographic magazines: *Chic*, *Club*, *Forum*, *Gallery*, *Genesis*, *Hustler*, *Oui*, and *Playboy*. A highly significant correlation (+0.64) was found between reported rape rates and circulation rates. Baron and Straus attempted to ascertain what other factors might possibly explain this correlation. Their statistical analysis revealed that the proliferation of pornographic magazines and the level of urbanization explained more of the variance in rape rates than the other variables investigated (for example, social disorganization, economic inequality, unemployment, sexual inequality).

In another important study, Mary Koss conducted a large national survey of over 6,000 college students selected by a probability sample of institutions of higher education (Koss, Gidycz, and Wisniewski 1987). She found that college men who reported behavior that meets common legal definitions of rape were significantly more likely than college men who denied such behavior to be frequent readers of at least one of the following magazines: *Playboy*, *Penthouse*, *Chic*, *Club*, *Forum*, *Gallery*, *Genesis*, *Oui*, or *Hustler* (Koss and Dinero 1989).

Several other studies have assessed the correlation between the degree of men's exposure to pornography and attitudes supportive of violence against women. Malamuth reports that in three out of four of these studies 'higher levels of reported exposure to sexually explicit media correlated with higher levels of attitudes supportive of violence against women' (1986: 8).

- 'In a sample of college men, Malamuth and Check (1985) found that higher readership of sexually explicit magazines was correlated with more beliefs that women enjoy forced sex.'
- 'Similarly, Check (1985) found that the more exposure to pornography a diverse sample of Canadian men had, the higher their acceptance of rape myths, violence against women, and general sexual callousness.'
- 'Briere, Corne, Runtz, and Malamuth (1984) reported similar correlations in a sample of college males.'

In her study of male sexuality, Shere Hite found that 67% of the men who admitted that they had wanted to rape a woman reported reading men's magazines, compared to only 19% of those who said that they had never wanted to rape a woman (1981: 1123). With regard to the frequency of exposure to pornography, of the 7,000 men she surveyed, Hite reports that only 11% said that they did not look at pornography, and never had. Thirty-six per cent said they viewed it regularly, 21%, sometimes, 26%, infrequently and 6% simply acknowledged that they used to look at it (1981: 1123). While correlation does not prove causation, and it therefore cannot be concluded from these studies that it was the consumption of the pornography that was responsible for the men's higher acceptance of violence against women, their findings are consistent with a theory that a causal connection exists.

If the rape rate was very low in the United States, or if it had declined over the past few decades, such findings would likely be cited to support the view that pornography does not play a causative role in rape. While drawing such a conclusion would not be warranted, it is nevertheless of interest to note that my probability sample survey in San Francisco shows that a dramatic increase in the rape rate has occurred in the United States over the last several decades during which there has also been a great proliferation of pornography (Russell 1984). Unlike the rapes studied by Straus and Baron, 90% of the rapes and attempted rapes described in my survey were never reported to the police.

Finally, it is significant that many sex offenders claim that viewing pornography affects their criminal behavior. Ted Bundy is perhaps the most notorious of these men. For example, in one study of 89 non-incarcerated sex offenders conducted by William Marshall, 'slightly more than one-third of the child molesters and rapists reported at least occasionally being incited to commit an offense by exposure to forced or consenting pornography' (Einsiedel 1986: 62). Exactly one-third of the rapists who reported being incited by pornography to commit an offense said that they deliberately used pornography in their preparation for committing the rape. The comparable figure for child molesters was much higher—53 versus 33% (Einsiedel 1986: 62).

However, as these sex offenders appear to have used the pornography to arouse themselves after they had already decided to commit an offense, it could be argued that it was not the pornography that incited them. To what extent they actually required the pornography in order to commit their offenses, like some perpetrators require alcohol, we do not know. But even if these perpetrators were eliminated from the data analysis, that still leaves 66% of the rapists and 47% of the child molesters who claimed that they were at least sometimes incited by pornography to commit an offense.

Gene Abel, Mary Mittelman, and Judith Becker (1985) evaluated the use of pornography by 256 perpetrators of sexual offenses, all of whom were undergoing assessment and treatment. Like Marshall's sample, these men were outpatients, not incarcerated offenders. This is important because there is evidence that the data provided by incarcerated and non-incarcerated offenders differ (Einsiedel 1986: 47). It is also likely that incarcerated offenders might be substantially less willing to be entirely frank about their antisocial histories than non-incarcerated offenders, for fear that such information might be used against them.

Abel and his colleagues reported that 56% of the rapists and 42% of the child molesters implicated pornography in the commission of their offenses. Edna Einsiedel, in her review of the social science research for the 1985 Attorney General's Commission on Pornography, concluded that these studies 'are suggestive of the implication of pornography in the commission of sex crimes among *some* rapists and child molesters' (1986: 63).

In another study, Michael Goldstein and Harold Kant found that incarcerated rapists had been exposed to hard-core pornography at an earlier age than men presumed to be non-rapists. Specifically, 30% of the rapists in their sexual offender sample said that they had encountered hard-core pornographic photos in their preadolescence (i.e. before the age of 11; 1973: 55). This 30% figure compares with only 2% of the control group subjects exposed to hard-core pornography as preadolescents. (The control group was obtained by a random household sample that was matched with the offender group for age, race, religion, and education level; 1973: 50.) Could it be that this early exposure of the offenders to hard-core pornography played a role in their becoming rapists? Hopefully, future research will address this question.

CONCLUSION

This chapter describes my theory about how pornography—both violent and nonviolent—can cause rape. I have drawn on the findings of recent research to support my theory. I believe that my theory can be adapted to apply to other forms of sexual assault and abuse, as well as woman battering and femicide (the misogyny-motivated killing of women). I have done the preliminary work on such an adaptation to the causal relationship between pornography and child sexual abuse and plan to publish this work in the future.

Just as smoking is not the only cause of lung cancer, neither is pornography the only cause of rape. I believe there are many factors that play a causal role in this crime (see Russell 1984, for a multicausal theory of rape). I have not attempted here to evaluate the relative importance of these different causal factors, but merely to show the overwhelming evidence that pornography is a major one of them.

Notes

This chapter is a revised version of an article with the same title originally published in *Political Psychology*, 9 (1), 1988.

1. I have incorporated several of Robert Brannon's suggestions into my definition of pornography, as well as the definitions of the concepts within it. Personal communication, 11 March 1992.
2. Claude Nuridsany and Marie Pérennou are the filmmakers of *Microcosmos*, 1996.
3. These differences were significant at $p > 0.05$ (Senn and Radtke 1986: 16).
4. I have used the phrase '*it appears to*' instead of '*it is intended to*' in order to avoid the difficult, if not impossible, task of establishing the intentions of the porn producers.
5. For example, members of the now-defunct organization WAVPM (Women Against Violence in Pornography and Media)—the first feminist anti-pornography organization in the United States—used to refer to record covers, jokes, ads, and billboards as pornography when they were sexually degrading to women, even when nudity or displays of women's genitals were not portrayed (Lederer, 1980)
6. To bring attention to this attribute of pornography, WAVPM designed a sticker to deface pornography which read: 'Pornography Tells Lies about Women.'

7. These distortions often have serious consequences. For example, some viewers act on the assumption that the depictions are accurate and presume that there is something wrong with females who do not behave like those portrayed in pornography. This can result in verbal abuse and/or sexual assault, including rape, by males who consider that they are entitled to the sex acts that they desire or that they believe other men enjoy.
8. This is an FBI euphemism for the frequent police practice of discounting rape cases reported to them.
9. That a sizable proportion of the killing is womanslaughter is essentially obliterated by this term.
10. This woman was a victim of incest through pornography who testified at the Minneapolis Hearings. Catharine MacKinnon, personal communication, 1986.
11. I use the term *males* rather than *men* because many rapists are juveniles.
12. In 1984 Malamuth reported that in several studies an average of about 35% of male students indicated some likelihood of raping a woman (1984: 22). This figure has decreased to 25 to 30% since then, for reasons Malamuth cannot explain (personal communication, July 1986).
13. Unfortunately, this is the only part of the story that Malamuth has described in print.
14. A 'scene' was defined as 'a thematically uninterrupted sequence of activity in a given physical context' (1986: 25). Only scenes involving sex, aggression, or sexual aggression were coded.
15. It is a mystery why Donnerstein finds no effects for non-violent pornographic movies while Zillmann reports many significant effects.

References

Abel, G. G., Barlow, D. H., Blanchard, E. B., and Guild, D. (1977). 'The Components of Rapists' Sexual Arousal'. *Arch. Gen. Psychiatry*, 34: 895–903.

Abel, G., Mittelman, M., and Becker, J. (1985). 'Sexual Offenders: Results of Assessment and Recommendations for Treatment'. In M. H. Ben-Aron, S. J. Hucker, and C. D. Webster (eds.), *Clinical Criminology*. Toronto: Clarke Institute of Psychiatry.

Attorney General's Commission on Pornography (1986). *Final Report*. Vols. I and II. Washington, DC: US Department of Justice.

Baron, L., and Straus, M. A. (1984). 'Sexual Stratification, Pornography, and Rape in the United States'. In N. M. Malamuth and E. Donnerstein (eds.), *Pornography and Sexual Aggression*. New York: Academic Press.

Bem, Sandra (1981). 'Gender Schema Theory: A Cognitive Account of Sex Typing'. *Psychological Review*, 88: 354–64.

Beneke, T. (1982). *Men on Rape*. New York: St Martin's Press.

Bogdanovich, P. (1984). *The Killing of the Unicorn: Dorothy Stratten 1960–1980*. New York: William Morrow.

Brannon, Robert (1992, 11 March and 28 April). Personal communication.

Briere, J., and Malamuth, N. (1983). 'Self-Reported Likelihood of Sexually

Aggressive Behavior: Attitudinal versus Sexual Explanations'. *Journal of Research in Personality*, 17: 315–23.

Briere, J., Malamuth, N. and Check, J. (1985). 'Sexuality and Rape-Supportive Beliefs'. *Int. J. Women's Studies*, 8: 398–403.

Brownmiller, Susan (1975). *Against Our Will: Men, Women and Rape.* New York: Simon and Schuster.

Bryant, J. (1985). Unpublished transcript, pp. 128–57. Testimony to the Attorney General's Commission on Pornography Hearings, Houston, Texas.

Burt, M. R. (1980) 'Cultural Myths and Supports for Rape'. *J. Pers. Soc. Psychology*, 38: 217–30.

Check, J. (1984). 'The Effects of Violent and Nonviolent Pornography'. Canadian Department of Justice, Ottawa, Canada.

—— and Guloien, Ted (1989). 'Reported Proclivity for Coercive Sex Following Repeated Exposure to Sexually Violent Pornography, Non-Violent Dehumanizing Pornography, and Erotica'. In Dolf Zillmann and Jennings Bryant (eds.), *Pornography: Recent Research, Interpretations and Policy Considerations*, 159–84. Hillside, NJ: Lawrence Erlbaum.

—— and Malamuth, N. (1985). 'An Empirical Assessment of Some Feminist Hypotheses about Rape'. *Int. J. Women's Studies*, 8: 414–23.

—— and Maxwell, K. (1992). 'Children's Consumption of Pornography and their Attitudes Regarding Sexual Violence'. Paper to be presented at the Canadian Psychological Association Meetings, Quebec, Canada, 11–13 June.

Cline, V. (1974) (ed.) *Where Do You Draw the Line?* Provo, Utah: Brigham Young University Press.

Dietz, P., and Evans, B. (1982). 'Pornographic Imagery and Prevalence of Paraphilia'. *Am. J. Psychiatry*, 139: 1493–5.

Donnerstein, E. (1983). 'Public Hearings on Ordinances to Add Pornography as Discrimination against Women', Committee on Government Operations, City Council, Minneapolis, Minnesota.

—— (1984). 'Pornography: Its Effects on Violence against Women'. In Neil Malamuth and Edward Donnerstein (eds.), *Pornography and Sexual Aggression*, 53–84. New York: Academic Press.

—— (1985). Unpublished transcript, pp. 5–33. Testimony to the Attorney General's Commission on Pornography Hearings, Houston, Texas.

—— and Linz, D. (1985). Unpublished paper prepared for the Attorney General's Commission on Pornography Hearings, Houston, Texas.

Dworkin, Andrea, and MacKinnon, Catharine (1988). *Pornography and Civil Rights.* Minneapolis: Organizing Against Pornography.

Einsiedel, E. F. (1986). 'Social Science Report'. Prepared for the Attorney General's Commission on Pornography, US Department of Justice, Washington, DC.

Finkelhor, D. (1984). *Child Sexual Abuse: New Theory and Practice.* New York: Free Press.

Frost, R., and Stauffer, J. (1987). 'The Effects of Social Class, Gender, and Personality on Physiological Responses to Filmed Violence'. *Journal of Communication* (Spring).

Goldstein, Michael, and Kant, Harold (1973). *Pornography and Sexual Deviance.* Berkeley: University of California Press.

Goodchilds, J., and Zellman, G. (1984). 'Sexual Signaling and Sexual Aggression in Adolescent Relationships'. In N. Malamuth and E. Donnerstein (eds.), *Pornography and Sexual Aggression.* New York: Academic Press.

Hite, S. (1981). *The Hite Report on Male Sexuality.* New York: Knopf.

Itzin, Catherine (1992) (ed.). *Pornography: Women, Violence and Civil Liberties.* New York: Oxford University Press.

Koss, Mary, and Dinero, Thomas E. (1989). 'Predictors of Sexual Aggression among a Sample of Male College Students'. In V. Quinsey and Robert Prentky (eds.), *Human Sexual Aggression: Current Perspectives,* Annals of the New York Academy of Sciences, 528: 133–47.

—— Gidycz, Christine, and Wisniewski, Nadine, (1987). 'The Scope of Rape: Incidence and Prevalence of Sexual Aggression and Victimization in a National Sample of Higher Education Students'. *Journal of Consulting and Clinical Psychology,* 55: 162–70.

Lederer, Laura (1980) (ed.). *Take Back the Night: Women on Pornography.* New York: William Morrow.

Longino, Helen (1980). 'What is pornography?' In Laura Lederer (ed.), *Take Back the Night,* 40–54. New York: William Morrow.

Lovelace, Linda (1981). *Ordeal.* New York: Berkeley Books.

—— (1986). *Out Of Bondage.* Secaucus, NJ: Lyle Stuart.

McKenzie-Mohr, D., and Zanna, M. (1990). 'Treating Women as Sexual Objects: Look to the (Gender Schematic) Male Who Has Viewed Pornography'. *Personality and Social Psychology Bulletin,* 16 (2): 296–308.

MacKinnon, Catharine A. (1987). *Feminism Unmodified: Discourses on Life and Law.* Cambridge, Mass.: Harvard University Press.

Malamuth, N. (1981*a*). 'Rape Fantasies as a Function of Exposure to Violent Sexual Stimuli'. *Arch. Sex. Behav.,* 10.

—— (1981*b*). 'Rape Proclivity among Males'. *J. Soc. Issues,* 37: 138–57.

—— (1984). 'Aggression against Women: Cultural and Individual Causes'. In N. M. Malamuth and E. Donnerstein (eds.), *Pornography and Sexual Aggression.* New York: Academic Press.

—— (1985). Unpublished transcript, pp. 68–110. Testimony to the Attorney General's Commission on Pornography Hearings, Houston, Texas.

—— (1986). 'Do Sexually Violent Media Indirectly Contribute to Anti-Social Behavior?'. Unpublished paper prepared for the Surgeon General's Workshop on Pornography and Public Health, Arlington, Virginia.

—— and Check, J. (1981). 'The Effects of Mass Media Exposure on Acceptance of Violence against Women: A Field Experiment'. *J. Res. Pers.,* 15.

—— —— (1985). 'The Effects of Aggressive Pornography on Beliefs in Rape

Myths: Individual Differences'. *Journal of Research in Personality*, 19: 299–320.

Malamuth, N. and Donnerstein, Edward (1984) (eds.). *Pornography and Sexual Aggression*. New York: Academic Press.

—— and Spinner, B. (1980). 'A Longitudinal Content Analysis of Sexual Violence in the Best-Selling Erotic Magazines'. *J. Sex Res.*, 16: 226–37.

—— Haber, S., and Feshbach, S. (1980). 'Testing Hypotheses Regarding Rape: Exposure to Sexual Violence, Sex Differences, and the "Normality" of Rapists'. *J. Res. Pers.*, 14: 121–37.

Maxwell, K., and Check, J. (1992). 'Adolescents' Rape Myth Attitudes and Acceptance of Forced Sexual Intercourse'. Paper to be presented at the Canadian Psychological Association Meetings, Quebec, Canada, 11–13 June.

Medea, A., and Thompson, K. (1974). *Against Rape*. New York: Farrar, Straus and Giroux.

Mosher, D. (1971). 'Sex Callousness toward Women'. *Technical Reports of the Commission on Obscenity and Pornography*, Vol. 8. Washington, DC: Government Printing Office.

Pally, Marcia (1994). *Sex and Sensibility*. Hopwell, NJ: The Ecco Press.

Palys, T. S. (1986). 'Testing the Common Wisdom: The Social Content of Video Pornography'. *Can. Psychology*, 27: 22–35.

Rachman, S., and Hodgson, R. J. (1968). 'Experimentally-Induced "Sexual Fetishism": Replication and Development'. *Psychological Record*, 18: 25–7.

Russell, D. E. H. (1975). *The Politics of Rape: The Victim's Perspective*. Chelsea, Mich.: Scarborough House.

—— (1984). *Sexual Exploitation: Rape, Child Sexual Abuse, and Workplace Harassment*. Beverly Hills, Calif.: Sage.

—— (1988). 'Pornography: Towards a Non-Sexist Policy for the New South Africa'. *Agenda: A Journal about Women and Gender*.

—— (1993) (ed.) *Making Violence Sexy: Feminist Views on Pornography*. New York: Teachers College Press.

Scully, D. (1985). 'The Role of Violent Pornography in Justifying Rape'. Unpublished paper prepared for the Attorney General's Commission on Pornography Hearings, Houston, Texas.

Senn, C. (1992). 'Women's Contact with Male Consumers: One Link between Pornography and Women's Experiences of Male Violence'. Paper presented at the Canadian Psychological Association Meetings, Quebec, Canada, 11–13 June.

—— (1993). 'Women's Responses to Pornography'. In Diana Russell (ed.), *Making Violence Sexy: Feminist Views on Pornography*. New York: Teachers College Press.

—— and Radtke, Lorraine (1986). 'A Comparison of Women's Reactions to Violent Pornography, Non-Violent Pornography, and Erotica'. Paper presented at the Canadian Psychological Association, Toronto, June.

Smith, D. (1976). 'Sexual Aggression in American Pornography: The Stereotype of Rape'. Unpublished paper presented at the American Sociological Association Meetings.

Strossen, Nadine (1995). *Defending Pornography: Free Speech, Sex, and the Fight for Human Rights.* New York: Scribner.

Theodorson, G., and Theodorson, A. (1979). *A Modern Dictionary of Sociology.* New York: Barnes & Noble.

Zillmann, Dolf (1985). Unpublished transcript of testimony to the Attorney General's Commission on Pornography, Houston, Tex., pp. 110–57.

—— and Bryant, Jennings (1984). 'Effects of Massive Exposure to Pornography'. In Neil Malamuth and Edward Donnerstein (eds.), *Pornography and Sexual Aggression*, 115–38. New York: Academic Press.

5 Only Words

Catharine A. MacKinnon

Imagine that for hundreds of years your most formative traumas, your daily suffering and pain, the abuse you live through, the terror you live with, are unspeakable—not the basis of literature. You grow up with your father holding you down and covering your mouth so another man can make a horrible searing pain between your legs. When you are older, your husband ties you to the bed and drips hot wax on your nipples and brings in other men to watch and makes you smile through it. Your doctor will not give you drugs he has addicted you to unless you suck his penis.[1]

You cannot tell anyone. When you try to speak of these things, you are told it did not happen, you imagined it, you wanted it, you enjoyed it. Books say this. No books say what happened to you. Law says this. No law imagines what happened to you, the way it happened. You live your whole life surrounded by this cultural echo of nothing where your screams and your words should be.

In this thousand years of silence, the camera is invented and pictures are made of you while these things are being done. You hear the camera clicking or whirring as you are being hurt, keeping time to the rhythm of your pain. You always know that the pictures are out there somewhere, sold or traded or shown around or just kept in a drawer. In them, what was done to you is immortal. He has them; someone, anyone, has seen you there, that way. This is unbearable. What he felt as he watched you as he used you is always being done again and lived again and felt again through the pictures—your violation his arousal, your torture his pleasure. Watching you was how he got off doing it; with the pictures he can watch you and get off any time.[2]

Slowly, then suddenly, it dawns on you: maybe now I will be believed. You find a guarded way of bringing it up. Maybe the pictures are even evidence of rape.[3] You find that the pictures, far from making what happened undeniable, are sex, proof of your desire and your consent.[4] Those who use you through the pictures feel their own pleasure. They do not feel your pain as pain any more than those who watched as they hurt you to make the pictures felt it. The pictures, surrounded by a special halo of false secrecy and false taboo—false because they really are public and are not really against the rules—have become the authority on what happened to you, the literature of your experience, a sign for sex, sex itself. In a very real way, they have made sex *be* what it is to the people who use you and the pictures of you interchangeably. In this, the pictures are not so different from the words and drawings that came before, but your use for the camera gives the pictures a special credibility, a deep verisimilitude, an even stronger claim to truth, to being incontrovertibly about you, because they happened and there you are. And because you are needed for the pictures, the provider has yet another reason to use you over and over and over again.

Finally, somehow, you find other women. Their fathers, husbands, and doctors saw the pictures, liked them, and did the same things to them, things they had never done or said they wanted before. As these other women were held down, or tied up, or examined on the table, pictures like the pictures of you were talked about or pointed to: do what she did, enjoy it the way she enjoyed it. The same acts that were forced on you are forced on them; the same smile you were forced to smile, they must smile. There is, you find, a whole industry in buying and selling captive smiling women to make such pictures, acting as if they like it.

When any one of them tries to tell what happened, she is told it did not happen, she imagined it, she wanted it. Her no meant yes. The pictures prove it. See, she smiles. Besides, why fixate on the pictures, the little artifact, at most a symptom? Even if something wrong was *done* to you, how metaphysically obtuse can you be? The pictures *themselves* do nothing. They are an expression of ideas, a discussion, a debate, a discourse. How repressed and repressive can you be? They are constitutionally protected speech.

Putting to one side what this progression from life to law does to ones sense of reality, personal security, and place in the community, not to mention faith in the legal system, consider what it does to one's relation to expression: to language, speech, the world of thought and communication. You learn that language does not belong to you, that you cannot use it to say what you know, that knowledge is not what you learn from your life, that information is not made out of your experience. You learn that thinking about what happened to you does not count as 'thinking', but doing it apparently does. You learn that your reality subsists somewhere beneath the socially real—totally exposed but invisible, screaming yet inaudible, thought about incessantly yet unthinkable, 'expression' yet inexpressible, beyond words. You learn that speech is not what you say but what your abusers do to you.

Your relation to speech is like shouting at a movie. Somebody stop that man, you scream. The audience acts as though nothing has been said, keeps watching fixedly or turns slightly, embarrassed for you. The action on-screen continues as if nothing has been said. As the echo of your voice dies in your ears, you begin to doubt that you said anything. Soon your own experience is not real to you anymore, like a movie you watch but cannot stop. This is women's version of life imitating art: your life as the pornographer's text. To survive, you learn shame and how to cover it with sexual bravado, inefficacy and how to make it seductive, secrecy and the habit of not telling what you know until you forget it. You learn how to leave your body and create someone else who takes over when you cannot stand it any more. You develop a self who is ingratiating and obsequious and imitative and aggressively passive and silent—you learn, in a word, femininity.

I am asking you to imagine that women's reality is real—something of a leap of faith in a society saturated with pornography, not to mention an academy saturated with deconstruction.[5] In the early 1980s women spoke of this reality, in Virginia Woolf's words of many years before, 'against the male flood':[6] they spoke of being sexually abused. Thirty-eight per cent of women are sexually molested as girls; 24 per cent of us are raped in our marriages. Nearly half are victims of rape or attempted rape at least once in our lives, many more than once, especially women of color, many involving multiple attackers, mostly men we know. Eighty-five per cent of women who work outside the home are sexually harassed at some point by employers.[7] We do not yet know how many women are sexually harassed by their doctors or how many are bought and sold as sex—the one thing men will seemingly always pay for, even in a depressed economy.

A long time before the women's movement made this information available, in the absence of the words of sexually abused women, in the vacuum of this knowledge, in the silence of this speech, the question of pornography was framed and debated—its trenches dug, its moves choreographed, its voices rehearsed. Before the invention of the camera, which requires the direct use of real women; before the rise of a mammoth profitmaking industry of pictures and words acting as pimp; before women spoke out about sexual abuse and were heard, the question of the legal regulation of pornography was framed as a question of the freedom of expression of the pornographers and their consumers. The government's interest in censoring the expression of ideas about sex was opposed to publishers' right to express them and readers' right to read and think about them.

Frozen in the classic form of prior debates over censorship of political and artistic speech, the pornography debate thus became one of governmental authority threatening to suppress genius and dissent. There was some basis in reality for this division of sides. Under the law of obscenity, governments did try to suppress art and literature because it was sexual in content. This was before the camera required live fodder and usually resulted in the books' becoming bestsellers.

Once abused women are heard and—this is the real hitch—become real, women's silence can no longer be the context in which pornography and speech are analyzed. Into the symbiotic dance between left and right, between the men who love to hate each other, enters the captive woman, the terms of access to whom they have been fighting over.[8] Instead of the forces of darkness seeking to suppress what the forces of light are struggling to free, her captivity itself is made central and put in issue for the first time. This changes everything, or should. Before, each woman who said she was abused looked incredible or exceptional; now, the abuse appears deadeningly commonplace. Before, what was done to her was sex; now, it is sexual abuse. Before, she was sex; now, she is a human being gendered female—if anyone can figure out what that is.

In this new context, the expressive issues raised by pornography also change—or should. Protecting pornography means protecting sexual abuse *as* speech, at the same time that both pornography and its protection have deprived women *of* speech, especially speech against sexual abuse. There is a connection between the silence enforced on women, in which we are seen to love and choose our chains because they have been sexualized, and the noise of pornography that surrounds us, passing for discourse (ours, even) and parading under constitutional protection. The operative definition of censorship accordingly shifts from government silencing what powerless people say, to powerful people violating powerless people into silence and hiding behind state power to do it.

In the United States, pornography is protected by the state.[9] Conceptually, this protection relies centrally on putting it back into the context of the silence of violated women: from real abuse back to an 'idea' or 'viewpoint' on women and sex. In this de-realization of the subordination of women, this erasure of sexual abuse through which a technologically sophisticated traffic in women becomes a consumer choice of expressive content, abused women become a pornographer's 'thought' or 'emotion'. This posture unites pornography's apologists from libertarian economist and judge Frank Easterbrook[10] to liberal philosopher-king Ronald Dworkin,[11] from conservative scholar and judge Richard Posner[12] to pornographers' lawyer Edward DeGrazia.[13]

In their approach, taken together, pornography falls presumptively into the legal category 'speech' at the outset through being rendered in terms of 'content', 'message', 'emotion', what it 'says', its 'viewpoint', its 'ideas'. Once the women abused in it and through it are elided this way, its artifact status as pictures and words gets it legal protection through a seemingly indelible categorical formalism that then must be negated for anything to be done.

In this approach, the approach of current law, pornography is essentially treated as defamation rather than as discrimination.[14] That is, it is conceived in terms of what it says, which is imagined more or less effective or harmful as someone then acts on it, rather than in terms of what it does. Fundamentally, in this view, a form of communication cannot, as such, *do* anything bad except offend. Offense is all in the head. Because the purveyor is protected in sending, and the consumer in receiving, the thought or feeling, the fact that an unintended bystander might have offended thoughts or unpleasant feelings is a mere externality, a cost we must pay for freedom. That the First Amendment protects this process of interchange—thought to thought, feeling to feeling—there is no doubt.

Within the confines of this approach, to say that pornography is an act against women is seen as metaphorical or magical, rhetorical or unreal, a literary hyperbole or propaganda device. On the assumption that words have only a referential relation to reality, pornography is defended as only words—even when it is pictures women had to be directly used to make, even when the means of writing are women's bodies, even when a woman is destroyed in order to say it or show it or because it was said or shown.

A theory of protected speech begins here: words express, hence are *presumed* 'speech' in the protected sense. Pictures partake of the same level of expressive protection. But social life is full of words that are legally treated as the acts they constitute without so much as a whimper from the First Amendment. What becomes interesting is when the First Amendment frame is invoked and when it is not. *Saying* 'kill' to a trained attack dog is only words. Yet it is not seen as expressing the viewpoint 'I want you dead'—which it usually does, in fact, express. It is seen as performing an act tantamount to someone's destruction, like saying 'ready, aim, fire' to a firing squad. Under bribery statutes, saying the word 'aye' in a legislative vote triggers a crime that can consist entirely of what people say. So does price-fixing under the antitrust laws. 'Raise your goddamn fares twenty per cent, I'll raise mine the next morning' is not protected speech; it is attempted joint monopolization, a 'highly verbal crime'. In this case, conviction nicely disproved the defendant's view, expressed in the same conversation, that 'we can talk about any goddamn thing we want to talk about'.[15]

Along with other mere words like 'not guilty' and 'I do', such words are uniformly treated as the institutions and practices they constitute, rather than as expressions of the ideas they embody or further. They are not seen as saying anything (although they do) but as doing something. No one confuses discussing them with doing them, for instance discussing a verdict of 'guilty' with a jury's passing a verdict of 'guilty'. Nobody takes an appeal of a guilty verdict as censorship of the jury. Such words are not considered 'speech' at all.

Social inequality is substantially created and enforced—that is, *done*—through words and images. Social hierarchy cannot and does not exist without being embodied in meanings and expressed in communications. A sign *saying* 'White Only'[16] is only words, but is not legally seen as expressing the viewpoint 'we do not want Black people in this store', or as dissenting from the policy view that both Blacks and whites must be served, or even as hate speech, the restriction of which would need to be debated in First Amendment terms. It is seen as the act of segregation that it is, like 'Juden nicht erwünscht!'[17] Segregation cannot happen without someone *saying* 'get out' or 'you don't belong here' at some point. Elevation and denigration are all accomplished through meaningful symbols and communicative acts in which saying it is doing it.

Words unproblematically treated as acts in the inequality context include 'you're fired', 'help wanted—male', 'sleep with me and I'll give you an A', 'fuck me or you're fired', 'walk more femininely, talk more femininely, dress more femininely, wear makeup, have your hair styled, and wear jewelry', and 'it was essential that the understudy to my Administrative Assistant be a man'.[18] These statements are discriminatory acts and are legally seen as such. Statements like them can also evidence discrimination or show that patterns of inequality are motivated by discriminatory animus. They can constitute actionable discriminatory acts in themselves or legally transform otherwise non-suspect acts into bias-motivated ones. Whatever damage is done through such words is done not only through their context but through their content, in the sense that if they did not contain what they contain, and convey the meanings and feelings and thoughts they convey, they would not evidence or actualize the discrimination that they do.

Pornography, by contrast, has been legally framed as a vehicle for the expression of ideas. The Supreme Court of Minnesota recently observed of some pornography before it that 'even the most liberal construction would be strained to find an "idea" in it', limited as it was to 'who wants what, where, when, how, how much, and how often'.[19] Even this criticism dignifies the pornography. The *idea* of who wants what, where, and when sexually can be expressed without violating anyone and without getting anyone raped. There are many ways to say what pornography says, in the sense of its content. But nothing else does what pornography does. The question becomes, do the pornographers—saying they are only saying what it says—have a speech right to do what only it does?

What pornography does, it does in the real world, not only in the mind. As an initial matter, it should be observed that it is the pornography industry, not the ideas in the materials, that forces, threatens, blackmails, pressures, tricks, and cajoles women into sex for pictures. In pornography, women are gang raped so they can be filmed. They are not gang raped by the idea of a gang rape. It is for pornography, and not by the ideas in it, that women are hurt and penetrated, tied and gagged, undressed and genitally spread and sprayed with lacquer and water so sex pictures can be made. Only for pornography are women killed to make a sex movie, and it is not the idea of a sex killing that kills them. It is unnecessary to do any of these things to express, as ideas, the ideas pornography expresses. It *is* essential to do them to make pornography. Similarly, on the consumption end, it is not the ideas in pornography that assault women: men do, men who are made, changed, and impelled by it. Pornography does not leap off the shelf and assault women. Women could, in theory, walk safely past whole warehouses full of it, quietly resting in its jackets. It is what it takes to make it and what happens through its use that are the problem.

Empirically, of all two-dimensional forms of sex, it is only pornography, not its ideas as such, that gives men erections that support aggression against women in particular. Put another way, an erection is neither a thought nor a feeling, but a behavior. It is only pornography that rapists use to select whom they rape and to get up for their rapes. This is not because they are persuaded by its ideas or even inflamed by its emotions, or because it is so conceptually or emotionally compelling, but because they are sexually habituated to its kick, a process that is largely unconscious and works as primitive conditioning, with pictures and words as sexual stimuli. Pornography consumers are not consuming an idea any more than eating a loaf of bread is consuming the ideas on its wrapper or the ideas in its recipe.

This is not to object to primitiveness or sensuality or subtlety or habituation in communication. Speech conveys more than its literal meaning, and its undertones and nuances must be protected. It is to question the extent to which the First Amendment protects unconscious mental intrusion and physical manipulation, even by pictures and words, particularly when the results are further acted out through aggression and other discrimination.[20] It is also to observe that pornography does not engage the conscious mind in the chosen way the model of 'content', in terms of which it is largely defended, envisions and requires. In the words of Judge Easterbrook, describing this dynamic, pornography 'does not persuade people so much as change them'.[21]

Pornography is masturbation material.[22] It is used as sex. It therefore is sex. Men know this. In the centuries before pornography was made into an 'idea' worthy of First Amendment protection, men amused themselves and excused their sexual practices by observing that the penis is not an organ of thought. Aristotle said, 'it is impossible to think about anything while absorbed [in the pleasures of sex.]'[23] The Yiddish equivalent translates roughly as 'a stiff prick turns the mind to shit'.[24] The common point is that having sex is antithetical to thinking. It would not have occurred to them that having sex *is* thinking.

With pornography, men masturbate to women being exposed, humiliated, violated, degraded, mutilated, dismembered, bound, gagged, tortured, and killed. In the visual materials, they experience this *being done* by watching it *being done*. What is real here is not that the materials are pictures, but that they are part of a sex act. The women are in two dimensions, but the men have sex with them in their own three-dimensional bodies, not in their minds alone. Men come doing this. This, too, is a behavior, not a thought or an argument. It is not ideas they are ejaculating over. Try arguing with an orgasm sometime. You will find you are no match for the sexual access and power the materials provide.

The fact that this experience is sexual does not erupt *sui generis* from pornography all by itself, any more than the experience of access and power in rape or child abuse or sexual harassment or sexual murder is sexual in isolation. There is no such thing as pornography, or any social occurrence, all by itself. But, of these, it is only pornography of which it is said that the experience is not one of access and power but one of thought; only of pornography that it is said that unless you can show what it and it alone does, you cannot do anything about it; and only pornography that is protected as a constitutional right. The fact that pornography, like rape, has deep and broad social roots and cultural groundings makes it more rather than less active, galvanizing and damaging.

One consumer of rape pornography and snuff films recently made this point as only an honest perpetrator can: 'I can remember when I get horny from looking at girly books and watching girly shows that I would want to go rape somebody. Every time I would jack off before I come I would be thinking of rape and the women I had raped and remembering how exciting it was. The pain on their faces. The thrill, the excitement.'[25] This, presumably, is what the court that recently protected pornography as speech meant when it said that its effects depend upon 'mental intermediation'.[26] See, he was watching, wanting, thinking, remembering, feeling. He was also receiving the death penalty for murdering a young woman named Laura after raping her, having vaginal and anal intercourse with her corpse, and chewing on several parts of her body.

Sooner or later, in one way or another, the consumers want to live out the pornography further in three dimensions. Sooner or later, in one way or an other, they do. *It* makes them want to; when they believe they can, when they feel they can get away with it *they* do. Depending upon their chosen sphere of operation, they may use whatever power they have to keep the world a pornographic place so they can continue to get hard from everyday life. As pornography consumers, teachers may become epistemically incapable of seeing their women students as their potential equals and unconsciously teach about rape from the viewpoint of the accused. Doctors may molest anesthetized women, enjoy watching and inflicting pain during childbirth, and use pornography to teach sex education in medical school. Some consumers write on bathroom walls. Some undoubtedly write judicial opinions.[27]

Some pornography consumers presumably serve on juries, sit on the Senate Judiciary Committee, answer police calls reporting domestic violence, edit media accounts of child sexual abuse, and produce mainstream films. Some make wives and daughters and clients and students and prostitutes look at it and do what is in it. Some sexually harass their employees and clients, molest their daughters, batter their wives, and use prostitutes—with pornography present and integral to the acts. Some gang rape women in fraternities and at rest stops on highways, holding up the pornography and reading it aloud and mimicking it. Some become serial rapists and sex murderers—using and making pornography is inextricable to these acts—either freelancing or in sex packs known variously as sex rings, organized crime, religious cults, or white supremacist organizations. Some make pornography for their own use and as a sex act in itself, or in order to make money and support the group's habit.[28]

This does not presume that all pornography is made through abuse or rely on the fact that some pornography is made through coercion as a legal basis for restricting all of it.[29] Empirically, all pornography is made under conditions of inequality based on sex, overwhelmingly by poor, desperate, homeless, pimped women who were sexually abused as children. The industry's profits exploit, and are an incentive to maintain, these conditions. These conditions constrain choice rather than offering freedom. They are *what it takes* to make women do what is in even the pornography that shows no overt violence.

I have come to think that there is a connection between these conditions of production and the force that is so often needed to make other women perform the sex that consumers come to want as a result of viewing it. In other words, if it took these forms of force to make a woman do what was needed to make the materials, might it not take the same or other forms of force to get other women to do what is in it? Isn't there, then, an obvious link between the apparent need to coerce some women to perform for pornography and the coercion of other women as a result of its consumption? If a woman had to be coerced to make *Deep Throat*, doesn't that suggest that *Deep Throat* is dangerous to all women anywhere near a man who wants to do what he saw in it?[30]

Pornography contains ideas, like any other social practice. But the way it works is not as a thought or through its ideas as such, at least not in the way thoughts and ideas are protected as speech. Its place in abuse requires understanding it more in active than in passive terms, as constructing and performative[31] rather than as merely referential or connotative.

The message of these materials, and there is one, as there is to all conscious activity, is 'get her', pointing at all women, to the perpetrators' benefit of ten billion dollars a year and counting. This message is addressed directly to the penis, delivered through an erection, and taken out on women in the real world. The content of this message is not unique to pornography. It is the function of pornography in effectuating it that is unique. Put another way, if there is anything that only pornography can say, that is exactly the measure of the harm that only pornography can do. Suppose the consumer could not get in any other way the feeling he gets from watching a woman actually be murdered. What is more protected, his sensation or her life? Should it matter if the murder is artistically presented? Shall we now balance away women's lesser entitlements—not to be raped, dehumanized, molested, invaded, and sold? Do the consequences for many women of doing this to some women, for mass marketing, weigh in this calculus? How many women's bodies have to stack up here even to register against male profit and pleasure presented as First Amendment principle?

On the basis of its reality, Andrea Dworkin and I have proposed a law against pornography that defines it as graphic sexually explicit materials that subordinate women through pictures or words.[32] This definition describes what is there, that is, what must be there for the materials to work as sex and to promote sexual abuse across a broad spectrum of consumers. This definition includes the harm of what pornography says—its function as defamation or hate speech—but defines it and it alone in terms of what it does—its role as subordination, as sex discrimination, including what it does through what it says. This definition is coterminous with the industry, from *Playboy*, in which women are objectified and presented dehumanized as sexual objects or things for use; through the torture of women and the sexualization of racism and the fetishization of women's body parts; to snuff films, in which actual murder is the ultimate sexual act, the reduction to the thing form of a human being and the silence of women literal and complete. Such material combines the graphic sexually explicit—graphically showing explicit sex—with activities like hurting, degrading, violating, and humiliating, that is, actively subordinating, treating unequally, as less than human, on the basis of sex. Pornography is not restricted here because of what it says. It is restricted through what it does. Neither is it protected because it says something, given what it does.

Now, in First Amendment terms, what is 'content'—the 'what it says' element—here?[33] We are told by the Supreme Court that we cannot restrict speech *because* of what it says, but all restricted expression says something. Most recently, we have been told that obscenity and child pornography are content that can be regulated although what distinguishes child pornography is not its 'particular literary theme'.[34] In other words, it has a message, but it does not do its harm through that message. So what, exactly, are the children who are hurt through the use of the materials hurt by?[35]

Suppose that the sexually explicit has a content element: it contains a penis ramming into a vagina. Does that mean that a picture of this conveys the idea of a penis ramming into a vagina, or does the viewer see and experience a penis ramming into a vagina? If a man watches a penis ram into a vagina live, in the flesh, do we say he is watching the idea of a penis ramming into a vagina? How is the visual pornography different? When he then goes and rams his penis into a woman's vagina, is that because he has an idea, or because he has an erection? I am not saying his head is not attached to his body; I am saying his body is attached to his head.

The ideas pornography conveys, construed as 'ideas' in the First Amendment sense, are the same as those in mainstream misogyny: male authority in a naturalized gender hierarchy, male possession of an objectified other. In this form, they do not make men hard. The erections and ejaculations come from providing a physical reality for sexual use, which is what pornography does. Pornography is often more sexually compelling than the realities it presents, more sexually real than reality. When the pimp does his job right, he has the woman exactly where the consumers want her. In the ultimate male bond, that between pimp and john, the trick is given the sense of absolute control, total access, power to take combined with the illusion that it is a fantasy, when the one who actually has that power is the pimp. For the consumer, the mediation provides the element of remove requisite for deniability. Pornography thus offers both types of generic sex: for those who want to wallow in filth without getting their hands dirty and for those who want to violate the pure and get only their hands wet.

None of this starts or stops as a thought or feeling. Pornography does not simply express or interpret experience; it substitutes for it. Beyond bringing a message from reality, it stands in for reality; it is existentially being there. This does not mean that there is no spin on the experience—far from it. To make visual pornography, and to live up to its imperatives, the world, namely women, must do what the pornographers want to 'say'. Pornography brings its conditions of production to the consumer: sexual dominance. As Creel Froman puts it, subordination is 'doing someone else's language'.[36] Pornography makes the world a pornographic place through its making and use, establishing what women are said to exist as, are seen as, are treated as, constructing the social reality of what a woman is and can be in terms of what can be done to her, and what a man is in terms of doing it.

As society becomes saturated with pornography, what makes for sexual arousal, and the nature of sex itself in terms of the place of speech in it, change. What was words and pictures becomes, through masturbation, sex itself. As the industry expands, this becomes more and more the generic experience of sex, the woman in pornography becoming more and more the lived archetype for women's sexuality in men's, hence women's, experience. In other words, as the human becomes thing and the mutual becomes one-sided and the given becomes stolen and sold, objectification comes to define femininity, and one-sidedness comes to define mutuality, and force comes to define consent as pictures and words become the forms of possession and use through which women are actually possessed and used. In pornography, pictures and words are sex. At the same time, in the world pornography creates, sex is pictures and words. As sex becomes speech, speech becomes sex.

The denial that pornography is a real force comes in the guise of many mediating constructions. At most, it is said, pornography reflects or depicts or describes or represents subordination that happens elsewhere. The most common denial is that pornography is 'fantasy'. Meaning it is unreal, or only an internal reality. For whom? The women in it may dissociate to survive, but it *is* happening to their bodies. The pornographer regularly uses the women personally and does not stop his business at fantasizing. The consumer masturbates to it, replays it in his head and onto the bodies of women he encounters or has sex with, lives it out on the women and children around him. Are the victims of snuff films fantasized to death?

Another common evasion is that pornography is 'simulated'. What can this mean? It always reminds me of calling rape with a bottle 'artificial rape'.[37] In pornography, the penis is shown ramming up into the woman over and over; this is because it actually was rammed up into the woman over and over. In mainstream media, violence is done through special effects; in pornography, women shown being beaten and tortured report being beaten and tortured. Sometimes 'simulated' seems to mean that the rapes are not really rapes but are part of the story, so the woman's refusal and resistance are acting. If it is acting, why does it matter what the actress is really feeling? We are told unendingly that the women in pornography are *really* enjoying themselves (but it's simulated?). Is the man's erection on screen 'simulated' too? Is he 'acting' too?

No pornography is 'real' sex in the sense of shared intimacy; this may make it a lie, but it does not make it 'simulated'. Nor is it real in the sense that it happened as it appears. To look real to an observing camera, the sex acts have to be twisted open, stopped and restarted, positioned and repositioned, the come shot often executed by another actor entirely. The women regularly take drugs to get through it. This is not to say that none of this happens in sex that is not for pornography; rather that, as a defense of pornography, this sounds more like an indictment of sex.

One wonders why it is not said that the pleasure is simulated and the rape is real, rather than the other way around. The answer is that the consumer's pleasure requires that the scenario conform to the male rape fantasy, which requires him to abuse her and her to like it. Paying the woman to appear to resist and then surrender does not make the sex consensual; it makes pornography an arm of prostitution. The sex is not chosen for the sex. Money is the medium of force and provides the cover of consent.

The most elite denial of the harm is the one that holds that pornography is 'representation', when a representation is a nonreality. Actual rape arranges reality; ritual torture frames and presents it. Does that make them 'representations', and so not rape and torture? Is a rape a representation of a rape if someone is watching it? When is the rapist *not* watching it? Taking photographs is part of the ritual of some abusive sex, an act of taking, the possession involved. So is watching while doing it and watching the pictures later. The photos are trophies; looking at the photos is fetishism. Is nude dancing a 'representation' of eroticism or is it eroticism, meaning a sex act? How is a live sex show different? In terms of what the men are doing sexually, an audience watching a gang rape in a movie is no different from an audience watching a gang rape that is reenacting a gang rape from a movie, or an audience watching any gang rape.

To say that pornography is categorically or functionally representation rather than sex simply creates a distanced world we can say is not the real world, a world that mixes reality with unreality, art and literature with everything else, as if life does not do the same thing. The effect is to license whatever is done there, creating a special aura of privilege and demarcating a sphere of protected freedom, no matter who is hurt. In this approach, there is no way to prohibit rape if pornography is protected. If, by contrast, representation *is* reality, as other theorists argue, then pornography is no less an act than the rape and torture it represents.[38]

At stake in constructing pornography as 'speech' is gaining constitutional protection for doing what pornography *does*: subordinating women through sex. This is not content as such, nor is it wholly other than content. Segregation is not the content of 'help wanted—male' employment advertisements, nor is the harm of the segregation done without regard to the content of the ad. It is its function. Law's proper concern here is not with what speech says, but with what it does.[39] The meaning *of* pornography in the sense of interpretation may be an interesting problem, but it is not this one. This problem is its meaning *for* women: what it does in and to our lives.

I am not saying that pornography is conduct and therefore not speech, or that it does things and therefore says nothing and is without meaning, or that all its harms are noncontent harms. In society, nothing is without meaning. Nothing has no content. Society is made of words, whose meanings the powerful control, or try to. At a certain point, when those who are hurt by them become real, some words are recognized as the acts that they are. Converging with this point from the action side, nothing that happens in society lacks ideas or says nothing, including rape and torture and sexual murder. This presumably does not make rape and murder protected expression, but, other than by simplistic categorization, speech theory never says why not. Similarly, every act of discrimination is done because of group membership, such as on the basis of sex or race or both, meaning done either with that conscious thought, perception, knowledge, or consequence. Indeed, discriminatory intent, a mental state, is required to prove discrimination under the Fourteenth Amendment.[40] Does this 'thought' make all that discrimination 'speech'?

It is not new to observe that while the doctrinal distinction between speech and action is on one level obvious, on another level it makes little sense. In social inequality, it makes almost none. Discrimination does not divide into acts on one side and speech on the other. Speech acts. It makes no sense from the action side either. Acts speak. In the context of social inequality, so-called speech can be an exercise of power which constructs the social reality in which people live, from objectification to genocide. The words and images are either direct incidents of such acts, such as making pornography or requiring Jews to wear yellow stars, or are connected to them, whether immediately, linearly, and directly, or in more complicated and extended ways.

Together with all its material supports, authoritatively *saying* someone is inferior is largely how structures of status and differential treatment are demarcated and actualized. Words and images are how people are placed in hierarchies, how social stratification is made to seem inevitable and right, how feelings of inferiority and superiority are engendered, and how indifference to violence against those on the bottom is rationalized and normalized.[41] Social supremacy is made, inside and between people, through making meanings. To unmake it, these meanings and their technologies have to be unmade.

A recent Supreme Court decision on nude dancing provides an example of the inextricability of expression with action in an unrecognized sex inequality setting. Chief Justice Rehnquist wrote, for the Court, that nude dancing can be regulated without violating the First Amendment because one can *say* the same thing by dancing in pasties and a G-string.[42] No issues of women's inequality to men were raised in all the pondering of the First Amendment, although the dancers who were the parties to the case could not have been clearer that *they* were not expressing anything.[43] In previous cases like this, no one has ever said what shoving dollar bills up women's vaginas expresses.[44] As a result, the fact that the accessibility and exploitation of women through their use as sex is at once being said *and done* through presenting women dancing nude is not confronted. That women's inequality is simultaneously being expressed and exploited is never mentioned. Given the role of access to women's genitals in gender inequality, dancing in a G string raises similar 'themes' and does similar harms, but neither says nor does exactly the same thing.

Justice Souter, in a separate concurrence, got closer to reality when he said that nude dancing could be regulated because it is accompanied by rape and prostitution.[45] These harms are exactly what is made worse by the difference between dancing in a G-string and pasties, and dancing in the nude. Yet he did not see that these harms are inextricable from, and occur exactly through, what nude dancing *expresses.* Unlike the majority, Justice Souter said that dancing in a G-string does not express the same 'erotic message'[46] as nude dancing. In other words, men are measurably more turned on by seeing women expose their sexual parts entirely to public view than almost entirely.

Nobody said that expressing eroticism is speech-think for engaging in public sex. Justice Souter did say that the feeling nude dancing expresses 'is eroticism'.[47] To express eroticism is to engage in eroticism, meaning to perform a sex act. To say it is to do it, and to do it is to say it. It is also to do the harm of it and to exacerbate harms surrounding it. In this context, unrecognized by law, it is to practice sex inequality as well as to express it.

The legal treatment of crossburning in another recent Supreme Court opinion provides yet another example of the incoherence of distinguishing speech from conduct in the inequality context. Crossburning is nothing but an act, yet it is pure expression, doing the harm it does solely through the message it conveys. Nobody weeps for the charred wood. By symbolically invoking the entire violent history of the Ku Klux Klan, it *says*, 'Blacks get out', thus engaging in terrorism and effectuating segregation. It carries the message of historic white indifference both to this message and to the imminent death for which it stands. Segregating transportation expressed (at a minimum) the view that African-Americans should ride separately from whites; it was not seen to raise thorny issues of symbolic expression. Ads for segregated housing are only words, yet they are widely prohibited outright as acts of segregation.[48]

Like pornography, crossburning is seen by the Supreme Court to raise crucial expressive issues. Its function as an enforcer of segregation, instigator of lynch mobs, instiller of terror, and emblem of official impunity is transmuted into a discussion of specific 'disfavored subjects'.[49] The burning cross is the discussion. The 'subject' is race—discriminating on the basis of it, that is. The bland indifference to reality is underlined by the lack of a single mention of the Ku Klux Klan. Recognizing the content communicated, Justice Stevens nonetheless characterized the crossburning as 'nothing more than a crude form of physical intimidation'.[50]

In this country, nothing has at once expressed racial hatred and effectuated racial subordination more effectively than the murder and hanging of a mutilated body, usually of a Black man. I guess this makes Black male bodies the subject of the discussion. Lynching expresses a clear point of view.[51] Photographs were sometimes taken of the body and sold, to extend its message and the pleasure of viewing it.[52] More discussion. Are these acts inexpressive and contentless? Are the pictures protected expression? Is a Black man's death made unreal by being photographed the way women's subordination is?[53] Suppose lynchings were done to make pictures of lynchings. Should their racist content protect them as political speech, since they do their harm through conveying a political ideology? Is *bigoted* incitement to murder closer to protected speech than plain old incitement to murder?[54] Does the lynching itself raise speech issues, since it is animated by a racist ideology? If the lynching includes rape, is it, too, potentially speech? A categorical no will not do here. Why, consistent with existing speech theory, are these activities not expressive? If expressive, why not protected?

Consider snuff pornography, in which women or children are killed to make a sex film. This is a film of a sexual murder in the process of being committed. Doing the murder is sex for those who do it. The climax is the moment of death. The intended consumer has a sexual experience watching it. Those who kill as and for sex are having sex through the murder; those who watch the film are having sex through watching the murder. A snuff film is not a discussion of the idea of sexual murder any more than the acts being filmed are. The film is not 'about' sexual murder; it sexualizes murder. Is your first concern what a snuff film *says* about women and sex or what it does? Now, why is rape different?

Child pornography is exclusively a medium of pictures and words. The Supreme Court has referred to it as 'pure speech'.[55] Civil libertarians and publishers argued to protect it as such.[56] Child pornography conveys very effectively the idea that children enjoy having sex with adults, the feeling that this is liberating for the child. Yet child pornography is prohibited as child abuse, based on the use of children to make it.[57] A recent Supreme Court case in passing extended this recognition of harm to other children downstream who are made to see and imitate the pictures.[58] Possessing and distributing such pictures is punishable by imprisonment consistent with the First Amendment, despite the fact that private reading is thereby restricted. Harm like this may be what the Supreme Court left itself open to recognizing when it said, in guaranteeing the right to possess obscenity in private, that 'compelling reasons may exist for overriding the right of the individual to possess' the prohibited materials.[59]

The point here is that sex pictures are legally considered sex acts, based on what, in my terms, is abuse due to the fact of inequality between children and adults. For seeing the pictures as tantamount to acts, how, other than that sexuality socially defines women, is inequality among adults different?

Now compare the lynching photograph and the snuff film with a *Penthouse* spread of December 1984 in which Asian women are trussed and hung.[60] One bound between her legs with a thick rope appears to be a child. All three express ideology. All had to be done to be made. All presumably convey something as well as provide entertainment. If used at work, this spread would create a hostile unequal working environment actionable under federal sex discrimination law.[61] But there is no law against a hostile unequal living environment, so everywhere else it is protected speech.

Not long after this issue of *Penthouse* appeared, a little Asian girl was found strung up and sexually molested in North Carolina, dead.[62] The murderer said he spent much of the day of the murder in an adult bookstore. Suppose he consumed the *Penthouse* and then went and killed the little girl. Such linear causality, an obsession of pornography's defenders, is not all that rare or difficult to prove. It is only one effect of pornography, but when one *has* that effect, is restricting those pictures 'thought control',[63] the judicial epithet used to invalidate our law against pornography? Would the girl's death be what *Penthouse* 'said'? If she was killed because of its 'content should it be protected?[64]

Should it matter: the evidence of the harm of such materials—from testimony of victims (called evidence, not anecdote, in court) to laboratory studies in which variables and predisposed men are controlled for, to social studies in which social reality is captured in all its messiness—shows that these materials change attitudes and impel behaviors in ways that are unique in their extent and devastating in their consequences. In human society, where no one does not live, the physical response to pornography is nearly a universal conditioned male reaction, whether they like or agree with what the materials say or not. There is a lot wider variation in men's conscious attitudes toward pornography than there is in their sexual responses to it.

There is no evidence that pornography does no harm; not even courts equivocate over its carnage anymore.[65] The new insult is that the potency of pornography *as idea* is said to be proven by the harm it does, so it must be protected as speech.[66] Having made real harm into the idea of harm, discrimination into defamation, courts tell us in essence that to the extent materials are defamatory, meaning they contain defamatory ideas, they are protected, even as they discriminate against women from objectification to murder.

'Every idea is an incitement', said Justice Holmes in a famous dissent in an early case on freedom of speech.[67] Whether or not this is true to the same degree for every idea, it has come to mean that every incitement to action that has an idea behind it—especially a big idea, and misogyny is a very big idea—is to that degree First Amendment protected territory. This doctrine was originally created to protect from suppression the speech of communists, thought by some to threaten the security of the US government. This experience is the crucible of the 'speech' doctrine, its formative trauma, the evil of suppression of dissent that First Amendment law, through coming to terms with this debacle, has been designed to avoid. This is where we got the idea that we must protect ideas regardless of the mischief they do in the world, where the First Amendment got its operative idea of what an 'idea' is.

Applying this paradigm for political speech to pornography requires placing, by analogy, sexually abused women relative to their abusers, in a position of power comparable to that of the US government relative to those who advocated its overthrow. This is bizarre, given that risk of harm is the issue. Women are far more likely to be harmed through pornography than the US government is to be overthrown by communists. Putting the pornographers in the posture of the excluded underdog, like communists, plays on the deep free speech tradition against laws that restrict criticizing the government. Need it be said, women are not the government? Pornography has to be done to women to be made; no government has to be overthrown to make communist speech. It is also interesting that whether or not forced sex is a good idea—pornography's so-called viewpoint on the subordination of women—is not supposed to be debatable to the same degree as is the organization of the economy. In theory, we have criminal laws against sexual abuse. We even have laws mandating sex equality.

Yet the First Amendment orthodoxy that came out of the communist cases is reflexively applied to pornography: if it is words and pictures, it expresses ideas. It *does* nothing. The only power to be feared as real is that of the government in restricting it. The speech is impotent. The analogy to communism has the realities reversed. Not only is pornography more than mere words, while the words of communism *are* only words. The power of pornography is more like the power of the state.[68] It is backed by power at least as great, at least as unchecked, and at least as legitimated. At this point, indeed, its power *is* the power of the state. State power protects it, silencing those who are hurt by it and making sure they can do nothing about it.

Law is only words. It has content, yet we do not analyze law as the mere expression of ideas. When we object to a law—say, one that restricts speech—we do not say we are offended by it. We are scared or threatened or endangered by it. We look to the consequences of the law's enforcement as an accomplished fact and to the utterance of legal words as tantamount to imposing their reality. This becomes too obvious to mention not only because the First Amendment does not protect government speech but because law is backed by power, so its words are seen as acts. But so is pornography: the power of men over women,[69] expressed through unequal sex, sanctioned both through and prior to state power. It makes no more sense to treat pornography as mere abstraction and representation than it does to treat law as simulation or fantasy. No one has suggested that our legal definition of pornography does what the pornography it describes in words does; nor that, if enacted in law, our ordinance would be only words.

As Andrea Dworkin has said, 'pornography is the law for women'.[70] Like law, pornography does what it says. That pornography is reality is what silenced women have not been permitted to *say* for hundreds of years. Failing to face this in its simplicity leaves one defending abstraction at the cost of principle, obscuring this emergency because it is not like other emergencies, defending an idea of an 'idea' while a practice of sexual abuse becomes a constitutional right. Until we face this, we will be left where Andrea Dworkin recognizes we are left at the end of *Intercourse*:[71] with a violated child alone on the bed—this one wondering if she is lucky to be alive.

Notes

1. Some of these facts are taken from years of confidential consultations with women who have been used in pornography; some are adapted from *People* v. *Burnham*, 222 Cal. Rptr. 630 (Ct. App. 1986), rev. denied, 22 May 1986, and media reports on it; and *Norberg* v. *Wynrib* [1992] 2 S.C.R. 224 (Can.).
2. Women used in pornography have provided the basis for the statements in these paragraphs over many years of work by me and my colleagues, including especially Andrea Dworkin, Therese Stanton, Evelina Giobbe, Susan Hunter, Margaret Baldwin, and Annie McCombs. Treatments of some of this damage are provided by Linda 'Lovelace' and Michael McGrady, *Ordeal* (1980) (her experience of being coerced to make *Deep Throat*), and, in fiction, by Kathryn Harrison, *Exposures* (1993) (experience of child model for sex pictures by her father). See also Collette Marie, 'The Coercion of Nudist Children', 3 *The ICONoclast* 1–6 (Spring 1991).
3. In the prosecution by Trish Crawford of South Carolina against her husband for marital rape, a thirty-minute videotape he took of the assault was shown. In it, Mr Crawford has intercourse with her and penetrates her with objects while her hands and legs are tied with rope and her mouth is gagged and eyes blinded with duct tape. He was acquitted on a consent defense. 'Acquittal of Husband Spurs Anger; Wife Accused of Raping Her', *Houston Chronicle*, 18 April 1992, sec. A, p. 3. The defendant testified he did not think his wife was serious when she said 'no'. Carolyn Pesce, 'Marital Rape Case Acquittal Fuels

Protest', *USA Today*, 21 April 1992, p. 3A. See also *State* v. *Jean*, 311 S.E.2d 266, 272—273 (N.C. 1984) (cross-examination of defendant on viewing pornographic movie five days after crime of rape charged, when movie showed the same kinds of sex acts charged, if error, was harmless).

4. As the defense lawyer in *Crawford* put it to the jury, as the tape described in note 3 above was played, 'Was that a cry of pain and torture? Or was that a cry of pleasure?' 'Marital Rape Acquittal Enrages Women's Groups', *Chicago Tribune*, 18 April 1992, p. 9C. This woman was clear she was being tortured. For the viewer who takes pleasure in her pain, however, the distinction between pain and pleasure does not exist. Her pain is his pleasure. This sexual sadism provides an incentive, even an epistemic basis, to impute pleasure to the victim as well. I believe this dynamic makes queries such as those by the defense lawyer successful in exonerating rapists.
5. In this setting, the only work regarded as part of the deconstruction school that I have encountered that makes me hesitate even slightly in this characterization is Jean-François Lyotard, 'The Differend, the Referent, and the Proper Name', 4 *diacritics* (Fall 1984). I read this work as an attack on the supposed difficulty of establishing that the Holocaust's gas chambers existed. It is, however, peculiar—and consistent with my critique here—that Lyotard does not mention that there are *Germans* who saw the gas chambers and survived to speak of their existence. His anatomy of silencing as a reality-disappearing device in its interconnection with the legal system is most useful, however. I am also unsure that this piece fits properly within deconstruction as a theoretical approach.
6. Andrea Dworkin's brilliant article on pornography infused new meaning into Woolf's phrase. Andrea Dworkin, 'Against the Male Flood: Censorship, Pornography, and Equality', 8 *Harvard Women's Law Journal* 1 (1985).
7. Diana E. H. Russell, *The Secret Trauma* (1986) and *Rape in Marriage* (1990); United States Merit Protection Board, *Sexual Harassment of Federal Workers: Is It A Problem?* (1981); *Sexual Harassment of Federal Workers: An Update* (1988); Majority Staff of US Senate Judiciary Committee, *Violence against Women: A Week in the Life of America* (1992).
8. For further discussion, see Andrea Dworkin, 'Woman-Hating Right and Left', in J. Raymond and D. Leidholdt (eds.), *The Sexual Liberals and the Attack on Feminism* (1990).
9. As to the state's position on pornography, *American Booksellers Ass'n* v. *Hudnut*, 771 F.2d 323 (7th Cir. 1985), aff'd, 475 U.S. 1001 (1986), makes explicit the protection of pornography that years of posturing and neglect under obscenity law left to interpretation.
10. See his opinion in *Hudnut*, 771 F.2d at 323.
11. Ronald Dworkin, 'Pornography, Feminism, and Liberty', *New York Review of Books*, 15 August 1991.
12. Richard A. Posner, *Sex and Reason* (1992); *Miller* v. *City of South Bend*, 904 F.2d 1081, 1089–1104 (7th Cir 1990) (Posner, J., concurring).
13. Edward DeGrazia, *Girls Lean Back Everywhere: The Law of Obscenity and the Assault on Genius* (1991).
14. I write about these issues in more detail in 'Pornography as Defamation and Discrimination', 71 *Boston University Law Review* 793 (1991).
15. *United States* v. *American Airlines. Inc..* 743 F.2d 1114 (5th Cir. 1984), cert.

dismissed, 474 U.S. 1001 (1985) ('highly verbal crime', 1121; 'Raise your goddamn . . .' and 'We can talk about any . . .' are both on 1116).

16. *Palmer* v. *Thompson*, 403 U.S. 217 (1971) (holding that closure by city of Jackson, Mississippi, of public swimming pools formerly available to 'whites only' did not violate equal protection clause of the Fourteenth Amendment because both Blacks and whites were denied access); *Jones* v. *Alfred H. Mayer Co.*, 392 U.S. 409 (1968) (prohibiting discriminatory sale or rental of property to 'whites only'); *Blow* v. *North Carolina*, 379 U.S. 684 (1965) (holding that restaurant serving 'whites only' violated Civil Rights Act of 1964); *Watson* v. *City of Memphis*, 373 U.S. 526(1963) (holding that city's operation of large percentage of publicly owned recreational facilities for 'whites only' due to delays in implementing desegregation violated the Fourteenth Amendment); see also *Hazelwood Sch. Dist.* v. *United States*, 433 U.S. 299, 304–305 n. 7 (1977) (stating that, in employment discrimination claim against school district, plaintiffs alleged that district's newspaper advertisement for teacher applicants specified 'white only'); *Pierson* v. *Ray*, 386 U.S. 547, 558 (1967) (holding that Black and white clergymen did not consent to their arrest by peacefully entering the 'White Only' designated waiting area of bus terminal).

17. *The Yellow Spot: The Outlawing of Half a Million Human Beings* 176–177 (1936) (photos of 'Jews not wanted' signs).

18. *Pittsburgh Press Co* v *Pittsburgh Comm'n on Human Relations*, 413 U.S. 376 379 (1973) ('help wanted—male'); *Alexander* v. *Yale Univ.*, 459 F. Supp. 1, 3–4 (D. Conn. 1977), aff'd, 631 F.2d 178 (2d Cir. 1984) (offer of 'A' grade for sexual compliance); *Stockett* v *Tolin*, 791 F. Supp. 1536, 1543 (S.D. Fla. 1992) ('F——me or you're fired'); *Hopkins* v. *Price Waterhouse*, 825 F.2d 458, 463 (D.C. Cir. 1987) ('walk more femininely . . .'); *Davis* v. *Passman*, 442 U.S. 228, 230 (1979)('. . . be a man').

19. *State* v. *Davidson*, 481 N.W.2d 51, 59 (Minn. 1992).

20. The law actually appears to permit the regulation of some forms of expression that manipulate the mind without its conscious awareness. Subliminal communications are flatly prohibited as 'deceptive' in the advertising of distilled spirits. 27 C.F.R. §5.65(h) (1992). The National Association of Broadcasters favors regulation of subliminal communication; its voluntary guidelines were invalidated on antitrust grounds, *United States* v. *National Ass'n of Broadcasters*, 536 F. Supp. 149 (D.D.C. 1982).

    The most evocative and advanced treatment of the issue occurs in *Vance* v. *Judas Priest*, 1990 WL 130920 (Nev. Dist. Ct. 24 Aug 1990). Two boys attempted suicide, one successfully, as a result, it was alleged, of messages embedded in a heavy metal recording. The court found the subliminals not to be protected by the First Amendment based on a right to be free of intrusive speech, because subliminal communications do not advance the purposes of free speech, and because of the listeners' right to privacy. The court also found no proximate cause existed between the lyrics and the suicides. NBC, CBS, and ABC all have policies prohibiting subliminal messages in ads, but I could find none regarding program content. See generally T. Bliss, 'Subliminal Projection: History and Analysis', 5 *Comment* 419, 422 (1983); Wilson Key, *Subliminal Seduction* (1972); Scot Silverglate, Comment, 'Subliminal Perception and the First Amendment: Yelling Fire in a Crowded Mind', 44 *University of Miami Law Review* 1243 (1990).

21. *Hudnut*, 771 F.2d at 328–329.
22. This does not mean that all masturbation material is pornography. Nor is this a definition; it is an empirical observation.
23. Aristotle, *Nicomachean Ethics*, as cited in Posner, *Sex and Reason* at 1.
24. 'Wenn der putz stegt, ligt der seykhel in drerd' is the best transliteration I could find, thanks to Alan Keiler.
25. *Schiro* v. *Clark*, 963 F.2d 962, 972 (7th Cir. 1992), petition for cert. filed (U.S. 5 Feb. 1993) (No. 92–7549).
26. *Hudnut*, 771 F.2d at 329.
27. Documentation of the harm of pornography in real life is contained in Public Hearings on Ordinances to Add Pornography as Discrimination against Women, Minneapolis City Council, Government Operations Committee (12 and 13 Dec. 1983); M. McManus (ed.), *Final Report of the Attorney General's Commission on Pornography* (1986); *Pornography and Prostitution in Canada: Report of the Special Committees on Pornography and Prostitution* (1985). See also Diana E. H. Russell, 'Pornography and Rape: A Causal Model', 9 *Political Psychology* 41 (1988); Gloria Cowan et al., 'Dominance and Inequality in X-Rated Videocassettes', 12 *Psychology of Women Quarterly* 299, 306–307 (1988); Park E. Dietz and Alan E. Sears, 'Pornography and Obscenity Sold in Adult Bookstores: A Survey of 5,132 Books, Magazines, and Films in Four American Cities', 21 *University of Michigan Journal of Law Reform* 7, 38–43 (1987–88) (documenting violence, bondage, sadomasochism, and gender differences in pornography); Neil M. Malamuth and Barry Spinner, 'A Longitudinal Content Analysis of Sexual Violence in the Best Selling Erotic Magazines', 16 *Journal of Sexual Research* 226–227 (1980) (documenting increases in violent sex in pornography).
28. In addition to the citations in the preceding note, my own five years of research on the making of pornography in cults and white supremacist organizations, for marketing by organized crime, informs this paragraph.
29. When women are coerced to perform for pornography, the resulting materials should clearly be actionable in spite of *Simon & Schuster, Inc.* v. *Members of the New York State Crime Victims Bd.*, 112 S. Ct. 501(1991), which invalidated a statutory financial restriction on books that were products of criminal activity. Most centrally, the crimes considered by the *Simon & Schuster* court were not committed so that they could be written about. The court also recognized that the state 'has an undisputed compelling interest in ensuring that criminals do not profit from their crimes', 510, which may be pursued by narrowly tailored means.
30. Under the recent decision holding a magazine publisher liable for a murder that resulted from an ad it ran, the consequential coercion produced by coerced pornography may be at least as 'foreseeable', especially if the coercion is visible in the materials. *Braun* v. *Soldier of Fortune Magazine, Inc.*, 968 F.2d 1110, 1118 (11th Cir. 1992) (negligence standard that ad '"on its face" would have alerted a reasonably prudent publisher that [it] "contained a clearly identifiable unreasonable risk that the offer . . . is one to commit a serious violent crime"' satisfies First Amendment).
31. J. L. Austin's *How to Do Things with Words* (1962) is the original enunciation of the theory of performative speech, which examines language for which 'the issuing of the utterance is the performing of an action—it is not normally

thought of as just saying something', at 6–7. While he does not confine himself to inequality, which is crucial to my argument here, neither does he generalize the performative to all speech, as have many speech act theorists who came after him. Austin is less an authority for my particular development of 'doing things with words' and more a foundational exploration of the view in language theory that some speech can be action.

32. For discussion, see Andrea Dworkin and Catharine A. MacKinnon, *Pornography and Civil Rights: A New Day for Women's Equality* (1988). The Model Ordinance, making pornography actionable as a civil rights violation, defines 'pornography' as 'the graphic sexually explicit subordination of women through pictures and/or words that also includes one or more of the following: (a) women are presented dehumanized as sexual objects, things, or commodities; or (b) women are presented as sexual objects who enjoy humiliation or pain; or (c) women are presented as sexual objects experiencing sexual pleasure in rape, incest, or other sexual assault; or (d) women are presented as sexual objects tied up or cut up or mutilated or bruised or physically hurt; or (e) women are presented in postures or positions of sexual submission, servility, or display; or (f) women's body parts—including but not limited to vaginas, breasts, or buttocks—are exhibited such that women are reduced to those parts; or (g) women are presented being penetrated by objects or animals; or (h) women are presented in scenarios of degradation, humiliation, injury, torture, shown as filthy or inferior, bleeding, bruised, or hurt in a context that makes these conditions sexual.' In this definition, the use of 'men, children, or transsexuals in the place of women' is also pornography.
33. Query whether all elements of speech are necessarily either 'content' or 'noncontent'.
34. *New York* v. *Ferber*, 458 U.S. 747, 763 (1982), cited in *R.A.V.* v. *City of St. Paul*, 112 S. Ct. 2538, 2543 (1992).
35. *Osborne* v. *Ohio*, 495 U.S. 103, 111 (1990) (use of child pornography by pedophiles may hurt children other than those in it).
36. Creel Froman, *Language and Power* 112 (1992).
37. *Olivia N.* v. *National Broadcasting Co.*, 141 Cal. Rptr. 511, 512 (1977), cert. denied sub nom. *Niemi* v. *National Broadcasting Co.*, 458 U.S. 1108 (1982) ('The complaint alleges that the assailants had seen the "artificial rape" scene' on television).
38. This more sophisticated version is illustrated by Susanne Kappeler, *The Pornography of Representation* (1986).
39. 'What matters for a legal system is what words *do*, not what they *say* . . .' Edward J. Bloustein, 'Holmes: His First Amendment Theory and His Pragmatist Bent', 40 *Rutgers Law Review* 283, 299 (1988).
40. *Personnel Administrator* v. *Feeney*, 442 U.S. 256 (1979); *Washington* v. *Davis*, 426 U.S. 229 (1976).
41. Postmodernism is premodern in the sense that it cannot grasp, or has forgotten, or is predicated on obscuring, this function of language in social hierarchy.
42. *Barnes* v. *Glen Theatre*, 111 S. Ct. 2456, 2466 n. 4 (1991) ('Nudity is *not* normally engaged in for the purpose of communicating an idea or an emotion'). But see *Schad* v. *Borough of Mt. Ephraim*, 452 U.S. 61, 66 (1981) (suggesting that nude dancing has some protection from regulation).

43. *Barnes* v. *Glen Theatre* was litigated below as *Miller* v. *City of South Bend*, 904 F.2d 1081, 1131 (7th Cir. 1990) ('At oral argument Miller's attorney admitted that this dancing communicated no idea or message').
44. Brief for Appellants at 5–6, *California* v. *LaRue* 409 U.S. 109 (1972) (No. 71–36) (in nude dancing establishment, oral copulation of women by customers, masturbation by customers, inserting money from customers into vagina, rubbing money on vaginal area, customers with rolled-up currency in mouths placing same in women's vaginas, customers using flashlights rented by licensees to better observe women's genitalia, customers placing dollar bills on bar and women attempting to squat and pick up bills with labia, women urinating in beer glasses and giving them back to customer, women sitting on bars and placing their legs around customers' heads, etc.). See also *Commonwealth* v. *Kocinski*, 414 N.E.2d 378 (Mass. App. Ct. 1981).
45. *Barnes*, 111 S. Ct. at 2468–71 (interest in preventing prostitution, sexual assault, and other attendant harms sufficient to support nude dancing provision). See also the extensive discussion of these harms in the dissenting opinion by Judge Coffey in *Miller*, 904 F.2d at 1104–20.
46. *Barnes*, 111 S. Ct. at 2458 (Rehnquist) and 2471 (Souter).
47. Ibid. at 2468.
48. These examples are discussed and documented in a brief by Burke Marshall and me, Brief Amicus Curiae of the National Black Women's Health Project, *R.A.V.* v. *City of St. Paul*, 112 S. Ct. 2538 (1992) (No. 90–7675).
49. *R.A.V.*, 112 S. Ct. at 2547.
50. Ibid. at 2569.
51. Andrea Dworkin and I discuss this in our *Pornography and Civil Rights: A New Day for Women's Equality* 60–6l (1988).
52. James R. McGovern, *Anatomy of a Lynching* 84 (1982).
53. An incident in Los Angeles in which a Black man was photographed being beaten by police who were acquitted in a criminal trial after repeated showings to the jury of a videotape of the assaults makes me think there is more to this than I thought. Two of the officers were later convicted in a civil trial.
54. A recent legal defense of the White Aryan Resistance, and its leaders Tom and John Metzger, connected with the murder of an African man in part through a leaflet organizing skinheads to kill Blacks in 'Aryan' race-destined territory, suggests this: because the murder was effectuated through a leaflet with a political ideology, it was not plain old advocacy to commit murder, it was *bigoted* advocacy to commit murder *in writing*—hence protected expression. See *Berhanu* v. *Metzger*, 119 Ore. App. 175, (No. CA A67833), Appellants' Opening Brief (29 Jan 1992). The defendants' conviction for wrongful death, conspiracy, and murder by agency, with damages, has been upheld over First Amendment challenge. *Berhanu* v. *Metzger*, 119 Ore. App. 175 (14 April 1993).
55. *Brockett* v. *Spokane Arcades, Inc.*, 472 U.S. 491, 503 n. 12 (1985), appears to refer to child pornography as an issue of 'pure speech rather than conduct'.
56. Brief on Behalf of American Booksellers Ass'n et al., *New York* v. *Ferber*, 458 U.S. 747(1982) (No. 81–55).
57. *Ferber*, 458 U.S. at 747.
58. *Osborne* v. *Ohio*, 495 U.S. 103, 111 (1990). This harm seems to have been lost sight of in the recent ruling in *United States* v. *X-Citement Video, Inc.*, 982 F.2d 1285 (9th Cir. 1992), in which the majority allows downstream vendors of

child pornography to use their lack of knowledge of a child's actual age as a defense. The dissent recognizes the harm to those who are 'hurt by the attitudes these materials foster'. *X-Citement Video*, 982 F.2d at 1293–94 n. 3 (Kozinski, J., dissenting).

59. *Stanley* v. *Georgia*, 394 U.S. 557, 568 n. 11 (1969).
60. 16 *Penthouse* 118 (December 1984).
61. *Robinson* v. *Jacksonville Shipyards, Inc.*, 760 F. Supp. 1486 (M.D. Fla. 1991).
62. George Fisher was convicted of the murder and attempted rape of Jean Kar-Har Fewel, an 8-year-old adopted Chinese girl found strangled to death hanging from a tree in 1985. Mr Fisher testified that he went to an adult bookstore on the day of the murder to watch movies. UPI, 20 August 1985.
63. *Hudnut* 771 F.2d at 328.
64. This is, in effect, what is permitted in *Herceg* v. *Hustler Magazine, Inc.*, 814 F.2d 1017 (5th Cir. 1987) (survivors of boy who died of autoerotic asphyxia may not recover against *Hustler*, which caused it).
65. *Hudnut*, 771 F.2d at 328–329.
66. Ibid. at 329–331.
67. *Gitlow* v. *New York*, 268 U.S. 652, 673 (1925) (Holmes, J., dissenting).
68. For a discussion of how 'pornographers are more like the police in police states', see Andrea Dworkin, 'Against the Male Flood', in *Letters from a War Zone* 264 (1988).
69. For an analysis of the place of pornography in male power, see Andrea Dworkin, *Pornography: Men Possessing Women* 13–47 (1979).
70. Andrea Dworkin has said this in many public speeches, including ones I attended in 1983 and 1984. The idea behind it was originally developed in her *Pornography: Men Possessing Women* at 48–100.
71. Andrea Dworkin, *Intercourse* 194 (1987).

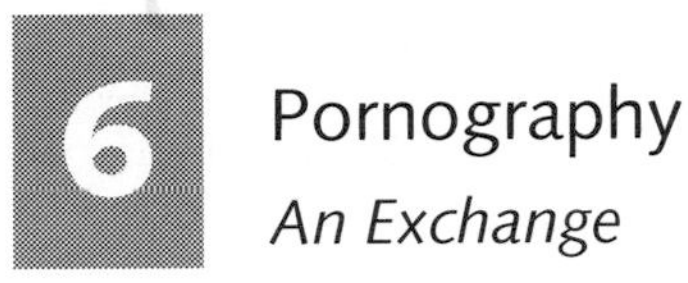

Pornography
An Exchange

Catharine A. MacKinnon/Ronald Dworkin

To the Editors:

This letter is not part of a dialogue over pornography or my book, *Only Words. NYR* consistently makes sure that its articles defend pornography and do not take its harm to women and children seriously. Dissent from this point of view is confined to letters which must focus on correcting the factual errors in the articles. This letter is no exception.

Even in this editorial context, Ronald Dworkin's review of my recent book [*NYR*. October 21, 1993] is startlingly incompetent, inconsistent, and ignorant.

It is appalling to read that the equality argument advanced in my book is a 'new argument'. In 1983, Andrea Dworkin and I advanced our equality approach to pornography through our ordinance allowing civil suits for sex discrimination by those who can prove harm through pornography. Since then, every argument we have advanced to support this initiative has been an equality argument. Every harm pornography does is a harm of inequality, and we have said so. Equality was the 'compelling state interest' urged in support of the Indianapolis ordinance. Equality was the central argument in writing of mine that Ronald Dworkin critized previously. Equality was Andrea Dworkin's argument against Ronald Dworkin's defense of pornography in a debate with him at Davis in the mid-1980s. She even read to him about equality from his work.

Are we to understand that it took him until now to hear it? This is one example of the 'silence' he has such trouble understanding. In it, nothing women say is real. Now, after a decade of respectfully repeating ourselves, it becomes clear that he has had no idea what we have been saying, hence no idea what he was talking about.

Maybe a decade from now he will figure out the argument that *is* new, or newly developed, in *Only Words*: the argument on pornography's status as 'speech' that pornography is what it does, not what it says. In light of this, Professor Dworkin's discussion of protecting 'views', 'ideas', 'opinions', and 'tastes' through protecting pornography is beside the point. We are talking about acts of discrimination: sex-based coercion, force, assault, and trafficking in sexual subordination. His discussion of the 'offensiveness' of pornography is equally irrelevant to its actual harms. The book repeatedly explains this. It is one thing to disagree on these points; it is another to miss them. To join issue, Professor Dworkin should now explain, instead of assume, how pornography really is about 'ideas', or how being discriminated against on the basis of sex really is just 'being offended'.

If his missing the point of the book is surprising, his misstatement of the Seventh Circuit's decision in *American Booksellers* v. *Hudnut*, which ruled on the Indianapolis version of our pornography ordinance, is shocking. Ronald Dworkin says that the Court 'assumed that pornography is a significant cause of sexual crime only for the sake of the argument it made' and cited other sources 'as support for the Court's own denial of any such demonstrated causal connection'. This is false.

The court said this, unedited emphasis-supplied:

Indianapolis justifies the ordinance on the ground that pornography affects thoughts. Men who see women depicted as subordinate are more likely to treat them so. Pornography is an aspect of dominance. It does not persuade people so much as change them. It works by socializing, by establishing the expected and the permissible. In this view pornography is not an idea; pornography is the injury.

There is much to this perspective. Beliefs are also facts. People often act in accordance with the images and patterns they find around them. People raised in a religion tend to accept the tenets of that religion, often without independent examination. People taught from birth that black people are fit only for slavery rarely rebelled against that creed: beliefs coupled with the self-interest of the masters established a social structure that inflicted great harm while enduring for centuries. Words and images act at the level of the subconscious before they persuade at the level of the conscious. Even the truth has little chance unless a statement fits within the framework of beliefs that may never have been subjected to rational study.

Therefore we accept the premises of this legislation. Depictions of subordination tend to perpetuate subordination. The subordinate status of women in turn leads to affront and lower pay at work, insult and injury at home, battery and rape on the streets. In the language of the legislature, '[p]ornography is central in creating and maintaining sex as a basis of discrimination. Pornography is a systematic practice of exploitation and subordination based on sex which differentially harms women. The bigotry and contempt it produces, with the acts of aggression it fosters, harm women's opportunity for equality and rights [of all kinds.]' [citation omitted]. Yet this simply demonstrates the power of pornography as speech. All of these unhappy effects depend on mental intermediation. Pornography affects how people see their world, their fellows, and social relations. If pornography is what pornography does, so is other speech. Hitler's orations affected how some Germans saw Jews.

This statement unambiguously 'accept[s]' what pornography is said to do, because there is 'much to' it. Its harms are observed to include sex crimes (rape) but are not confined to them, as sex inequality is not so confined.[1] The court could have said it accepted the harms of pornography 'only for purposes of argument'. It did not

Actually, the court misses Indianapolis's argument in the same way Professor Dworkin misses ours. Both Indianapolis and my book argue that what matters for law is how pornography affects behavior, not 'thoughts', the ordinance made some of that behavior, *and no thoughts*, actionable. Our argument is not that ideas and actions are causally connected, although they no doubt are. It is that pornography is factually connected in many ways to a whole array of tangible human injuries.

The court observes in a footnote that it is accepting the legislative resolution of a disputed empirical question. It could have found the empirical support for the legislation insufficient; it found to the contrary. It did not have to adopt the legislative view as its own; it did. There were no legislative findings on slavery or the Holocaust, yet the court's views on these subjects were presented to support its view on the parallel relation between those literatures of inequality and attendant harms.

In other words, far from denying a demonstrated causal connection between pornography and social harms, this court explicitly embraced one. It went on to say that the materials matter more than the people who are harmed through them. Criticizing this was my point in *Only Words*, one of many Professor Dworkin evades.

That the Seventh Circuit accepts that pornography causes harms as its own position is indisputably reasserted in a later case, involving no legislative review. In *Schiro* v. *Clark*, expert evidence supported the lower court's finding that Thomas Schiro, convicted of rape and murder, could not appreciate the wrongfulness of his acts, due to his extensive consumption of sadomasochistic pornography and snuff films.

Whether he can be executed turned in part on whether this conclusion can be drawn from this evidence.[2] The reviewing court, which included the author of *Hudnut*, faced a dilemma: having decided that pornography causes rapes but must be permitted, must it also permit the rapes pornography causes, because it causes them? The court stated that '*the recognition in Hudnut that pornography leads to violence against women* does not require Indiana to establish a defense of insanity by pornography' (emphasis added). It refused 'to tell Indiana that it can neither ban pornography nor hold criminally responsible persons who are encouraged to commit violent acts because of pornography!' To repeat: *Hudnut* held that pornography 'leads to' violence against women. *Schiro* recognized that persons like Schiro exist, who 'are encouraged to' commit violent acts because of pornography. Both are causal connections.

Professor Dworkin's review begins by conceding the gendered nature of pornography and then forgets it. Expressed concern for women is a figleaf behind which to write as if women do not exist. Reports from women's real lives are then trivialized as 'intended to shock'. Apparently Ronald Dworkin's life has shielded him from their reality. Maybe we can spread the privilege, so some day more women can feel incredulity rather than recognition when encountering these atrocities on a page.

Although his tone is formally respectful, he often demeans the book instead of coming to grips with it. 'Grim' is my view of the world, without discussion of whether the fun world 'we' presumably live in is real or for whom. Direct address to listeners and readers—my invitation that you imagine yourselves being abused like the women in the materials (which for many readers calls on memory, not imagination)—is 'rhetorical' stereotyping of 'all female readers'. Is it that unthinkable, Professor Dworkin, that I am talking to you?

When otherwise at a loss for a rock to throw, he questions the intellectual honesty of the author. On the Indianapolis ruling, I am 'disingenuous'. See above. Dismissing the book's main argument as 'intellectual sleight of hand' is as close as he gets to it. At the same time, he concedes much of it. In his view of equality, 'Sexists and bigots have no right to live in a community whose ideology of culture is even partially sexist or bigoted.' But nobody has a right to stop them? Search me.

It is absurd to have to publish, in the only space I am allowed here, columns of Judge Easterbrook's ruling on pornography's harms, in order to defend craft values on a point that is not even a matter of interpretation. It is also more than absurd. If this space were not wasted establishing the incontestable, we might have a real discussion. What would be the risk? It is time to consider that misrepresentation, shoddy scholarship, ignorance, and evasion are all pornography's defenders have to offer. It is past time to conclude that reviews like this pose as an exchange of ideas but are really whatever-it-takes defenses of an article of faith and a vested interest. It is beginning to look like one cannot face facts, address the real arguments, and still defend pornography. After a decade of recycled junk from liberals like Ronald Dworkin to conservatives like Judge Richard Posner, from kept writers in pornography magazines to scholars who should know better—a distance increasingly measurable in millimeters and microseconds—we wait. And women continue to be ground down.

Catharine A. MacKinnon
Berlin, Germany

Ronald Dworkin *replies*:

Professor MacKinnon says that my review of her book is incompetent, inconsistent, ignorant, appalling, shocking, rock-throwing junk, and that there is next to no difference between me and 'kept writers in pornography magazines'. This carpet bombing is aimed mainly at my two-sentence discussion, in a footnote, of the Seventh Circuit Court of Appeals decision in the *Hudnut* case, which declared unconstitutional an antipornography statute Catharine MacKinnon and Andrea Dworkin had drafted. I said that that court 'assumed that pornography is a significant cause of sexual crime only for the sake of the argument it made', and that it in fact denied that any such significant causal connection had been 'demonstrated'. MacKinnon sets out three paragraphs of Judge Easterbrook's opinion to show how inaccurate my report is, and adds that her quotation is 'unedited'. In fact, however, she omitted a crucial footnote, which he attached to the third sentence of the third paragraph she cites, qualifying particularly his remarks about the effect of pornography on sexual violence. Though she mentions the footnote later in her letter, she gives no sense of what it actually contains. Here is the omitted footnote in full (with emphasis added).

MacKinnon's article collects empirical work that supports this proposition. *The social science studies are very difficult to interpret, however, and they conflict.* Because much of the effect of speech comes through a process of socialization, it is difficult to measure incremental benefits and injuries caused by particular speech. Several psychologists have found, for example, that those who see violent, sexually explicit films tend to have more violent thoughts. *But how often does this lead to actual violence?* National commissions on obscenity here, in the United Kingdom, and in Canada *have found that it is not possible to demonstrate a direct link between obscenity and rape* or exhibitionism. The several opinions in Miller v. California discuss the US commission. See also Report of the Committee on Obscenity and Film Censorship 61–95 (Home Office, Her Majesty's Stationery Office, 1979); Special Committee on Pornography and Prostitution, 1 Pornography and Prostitution in Canada 71–73, 95–103 (Canadian Government Publishing Centre 1985). *In saying that we accept the finding that pornography as the ordinance defines it leads to unhappy consequences, we mean only that there is evidence to this effect, that this evidence is consistent with much human experience, and that as judges we must accept the legislative resolution of such disputed empirical questions.* See Gregg v. Georgia, 428 US 153, 184–87, 49 L. Ed. 2d 859, 96 S. Ct. 2909 (1976) (opinion of Stewart, Powell, and Stevens, J.J.).

When a court is asked to declare a statute unconstitutional, it defers to the findings of fact on which the legislature based the statute if the court thinks there is any evidence supporting those findings, even if in its view that evidence is inconclusive. The court is particularly likely to give the legislature the benefit of the doubt about the facts, in that way, when it decides that the statute would be unconstitutional even if the facts *were* as the legislature supposed. That is what Judge Easterbrook decided in the *Hudnut* case: he held that even if pornography does cause violence, it could do so only through 'mental intermediation', and the First Amendment, he said, forbids banning material because it might produce dangerous effects that way. His footnote is explicit in stating that he 'accepts' the legislature's findings out of deference, for the sake of the constitutional argument. But he says more: he questions the probative force of the only evidence for the finding that he mentions, and he cites a variety of prestigious reports to the contrary, all claiming that it is impossible to show a causal connection between obscenity and rape. It seems an understatement to conclude that he did not believe that such a connection had been 'demonstrated'.

MacKinnon, also refers to the later *Schiro* case in which the Seventh Circuit allowed Indiana to reject a killer's defense that he had been rendered insane by reading pornography. The *Schiro* court said that it would be inconsistent for the Seventh Circuit to insist, as it had the *Hudnut* decision, that Indiana could not ban pornography even if pornography did lead to violence, on the grounds that such violence would be mediated by intellectual processes, and then to forbid

Indiana to convict a killer who said that his intellectual processes had been destroyed by pornography. That argument, like the earlier *Hudnut* decision it described, 'recognizes' that pornography leads to violence only in the hypothetical sense made explicit in the footnote MacKinnon omitted.

She has other complaints: she is angry that I called one of the arguments in her book a new one. I did not mean, however, the very general argument she now mentions: that pornography should be banned because 'every harm pornography does is a harm of inequality'. It is indeed a familiar argument that pornography offends sexual equality by contributing to women's social, economic, and political subordination, and though MacKinnon says she is appalled that I have been unaware of that argument—she offers my failure to hear it as evidence that she herself has been 'silenced'—I have in fact discussed it at length in the *New York Review* ('Liberty and Pornography,' August 15, 1991: The Coming Battle Over Free Speech.' June 11, 1992) and elsewhere.

The argument I said I had not discussed is a much more specific constitutional thesis: that even if anti-pornography laws do offend the First Amendment's guarantee of free speech taken on its own, such laws should nevertheless be sustained because they protect rights that the Constitution also guarantees, through the equal protection clause of its Fourteenth Amendment. MacKinnon may mean that she has made that specific argument before; if so, I am sorry that I did not notice and consider it in an earlier article. But since I think, as I said, that the argument is a particularly bad one, I am unclear why she should be so upset that I did not. In any case, the *Hudnut* court seems to have been unaware of the constitutional argument as well: though Easterbrook referred to and discussed a wide range of both her and Andrea Dworkin's arguments, he neither mentioned nor addressed that one. I have no memory whatever, finally, of any such argument arising in the public discussion between Andrea Dworkin and myself.

It is more important that MacKinnon thinks I ignored the real point of her book, which, she says, is that pornography is not 'speech' because 'pornography is what it does, not what it says'. I did not ignore that claim. I did say that I could find no genuine argument in it—I still can't—but I tried. I reported her suggestion that a pornographic description of a rape is itself a kind of rape, which I said is silly, and her claim that pornography is 'reality' rather than speech because it produces erections and aids masturbation, which, as I said, seems an unsatisfactory basis on which to deny First Amendment protection.

She also demands that I defend my view that 'being discriminated against on the basis of sex' is just being 'offended'. But I said nothing even close to that: on the contrary, I said that distributing pornography, as distinct from using it to sexually harass, does not constitute sexual discrimination. She also demands that I defend the view that pornography is about 'ideas'. In fact, I took care explicitly to reject that view: I said that much pornography offers no ideas at all, and that it would be wrong to base a First Amendment claim on the view that it does. I added, however, that everyone has an equal right to contribute to what I called the 'moral environment'—even people whose tastes reflect no 'ideas' but only very offensive 'prejudices, life styles, and cultures'.

Her reaction to that claim is the most disturbing part of her letter. She refers to my statement that sexists and bigots have no right that laws and institutions be sexist or bigoted, even partially, in proportion to their numbers. She is astonished ('Search me') that, in that case, I can think that no one has a right to 'stop them'. I added, just after the passage she quotes, that 'In a genuinely egalitarian society, however, those views cannot be locked out, in advance, by criminal or civil law: they must instead be discredited by the disgust, outrage, and ridicule of other people.' MacKinnon is not satisfied: she has in mind a quicker, more chilling way of 'stopping them' than that.

She ends her letter, characteristically, by picturing me and her other critics as indifferent to the suffering of women. But many feminists, including several who wrote or spoke to me about my review, regret her single-minded concentration on lurid sex. They think that though it has predictably attracted much publicity, it tends to stereotype women as victims, and it takes attention from still urgent questions of economic, political, and professional equality. They deplore her alliances with right-wing groups that have produced, for example, a Canadian censorship law that, as many had warned, has been used by conservative moralists to ban gay and lesbian literature by well-known authors, a book on racial injustice by the black feminist scholar bell hooks, and, for a time, Andrea Dworkin's own feminist writing as well. Perhaps MacKinnon should reflect on these suggestions that the censorship issue is not so simple-minded, so transparently gender-against-gender, as she insists. She should stop calling names long enough to ask whether personal sensationalism, hyperbole, and bad arguments are really what the cause of sexual equality now needs.

Notes

1. Narrowing the harms of pornography from all forms of inequality to 'sex crime', and then demanding a showing of an exclusive linear causal relation between them—rather than, say, a powerful contribution, or an interactive relation—are standard ploys of pornography's apologists. This particular concept of causality is never argued for and is not required in law.
2. The US Supreme Court is reviewing this case now.

The Roar on the Other Side of Silence

Catharine A. MacKinnon

Women speak in public for the first time in history of the harms done to them through pornography in the hearings collected in this volume [*Ed's note*: 'This volume', here and throughout this chapter, refers to *In Harm's Way: The Pornography Civil Rights Hearing*, ed. Andrea Dworkin and Catharine A. MacKinnon (Harvard University Press, 1997)]. Their first-person accounts stand against the pervasive sexual violation of women and children that is allowed to be done in private and is not allowed to be criticized in public. Their publication, which comes almost fifteen years[1] after the first hearing was held, ends the exclusion from the public record of the information they contain on the way pornography works in social reality. Now ended is the censorship of these facts and voices from a debate on the social and cultural role of pornography that has gone on as if it could go on without them.

Until these hearings took place, pornography and its apologists largely set the terms of public discussion over pornography's role in social life. Public, available, effectively legal, pornography has stature: it is visible, credible, and legitimated. At the same time its influence and damaging effects are denied as nonexistent, indeterminate, or merely academic, contrary to all the evidence. Its victims have had no stature at all. The hearings changed the terms of this discussion by opening a space to speak for the real authorities on pornography: the casualties of its making and use. Against a background of claims that the victims and the harms done to them do not exist, must not be believed, and should not be given a legal hearing, the harms of

Catharine A. MacKinnon, 'The Roar on the Other Side of Silence', from *In Harm's Way: The Pornography Civil Rights Hearing*, ed. Andrea Dworkin and Catharine A. MacKinnon (Harvard University Press, 1997), 3–24, copyright © 1997 by Catharine A. MacKinnon and Andrea Dworkin, reprinted by permission of J. A. Christian Ltd. and the author.

pornography stood exposed and took shape as potential legal injuries. These hearings were the moment when the voices of those victimized through pornography broke the public surface. Their publication gives the public unmediated and unrestricted access to this direct evidence for the first time. The authority of their experience makes the harm of pornography undeniable: it harmed them.

In late 1983, legislators in Minneapolis initiated this process[2] by employing Andrea Dworkin and me to write a law for the city that we had conceived on pornography as a human rights violation. Other jurisdictions followed, including Indianapolis, Los Angeles County, and the Commonwealth of Massachusetts,[3] each seeking to adapt our civil rights approach to local concerns. All these laws recognized the concrete violations of civil rights done through pornography as practices of sex discrimination[4] and gave the survivors access to civil court for relief through a law they could use themselves. The hearings that resulted from the introduction of the legislation gave pornography's survivors a forum, an audience, and a concrete opportunity to affect their world. Grasping the real chance that rights might be given to them, seeing that their participation could make a difference to the conditions of their lives, these women and men became prepared to run the risks of this political expression. The consequences anticipated at that time included public humiliation and shame, shunning and ostracism, loss of employment, threats, harassment, and physical assault.

The act of introducing the antipornography civil rights ordinances into the legislative arena gave pornography's victims back some measure of the dignity and hope that the pornography, with its pervasive social and legal support, takes away. The ordinances, in formulating pornography's harms as human rights deprivations, captured a denigrated reality of women's experience in a legal form that affirmed that to be treated in these ways violates a human being; it does not simply reveal and define what a woman is. As ending these violations and holding their perpetrators accountable became imaginable for the first time, and women participated directly in making the rules that govern their lives, the disgrace of being socially female—fit only for sexual use, unfit for human life—was exposed as a pimp's invention. In these hearings, women were citizens.

The first-person testimony, contextualized by expert witnesses as representative rather than unique or isolated, documented the material harm pornography does in the real world, showing the view that pornography is harmless fantasy to be as false as it is clichéd.

Women used for sex so that pornography can be made of them against their will—from Linda 'Lovelace'[5] forced to fellate men so *Deep Throat* could be made to a young girl sold as sex to *Hustler's* 'Beaverhunt'[6] to Valerie Harper's face on another woman's naked body on a T-shirt[7]—refute the assumption promoted by the pornography industry that women are in pornography because they want to be there. The information provided by these witnesses also underlines the simplest fact of the visual materials: to be made, the acts in them had to be *done to someone.* A few who have escaped the sex factories describe the forms of force required.

Woman after woman used by consumers of pornography recounts its causal role in her sexual violation by a man close to her. A husband forces pornography on his wife and uses it to pressure her into sex acts she does not want.[8] A father threatens his children with pornography so they will keep silent about what he shows them is being done, audibly, to their mother at night.[9] A brother holds up pornography magazines as his friends gang-rape his sister, making her assume the poses in the materials, turning her as they turn the pages.[10] A woman's boyfriend becomes aroused by watching other women being used in pornography and forces sexual access.[11] A gay man inflicts the abusive sex learned through using pornography on his male lover, who tolerates it because he learned from pornography that a man's violence is the price of his love.[12]

Although intimate settings provide privileged access for these acts, such violations occur throughout social life. White male motorists, spewing racist bile, rape a Native American woman at a highway rest stop in reenactment of a pornographic video game.[13] Working men plaster women's crotches on the walls of workplaces.[14] Therapists force pornography on clients.[15] Pimps use pornography to train and trap child prostitutes.[16] Men who buy and use women and children for sex bring pornography to show those prostituted what the men want them to do.[17] Pornography is made of prostituted children to threaten them with exposure to keep them in prostitution.[18] Serial sexual murderers use pornography to prepare and impel them to rape and kill.[19]

Grounded in these realities, the ordinance that produced and resulted from the hearings provides civil access to court to prove the abuse and the role of pornography in it in each situation. The ordinance, with local variations, provides a cause of action to individuals who are coerced into pornography, forced to consume pornography, defamed by being used in pornography without consent, assaulted due to specific pornography, or subordinated as a member of a sex-based group through traffic in pornography as legally defined.[20] The chance to prove in court the harmful role of pornography in each situation is what pornography's victims have sought. This, to date, is what they have been denied.

The opponents of the civil rights laws against pornography are amply represented in the hearings. They did not openly defend pornography as such,[21] or address the harms the witnesses document even to deny them. They treat the survivors as if they are not there or do not matter. That those victimized by pornography are lying or expendable is the upshot of the First Amendment defense of pornography that the opponents do present, proceeding as if the 'speech' of violation matters over the violation of the violated. Some opponents adopt the view that factual disputes over the harm should not be resolved in court—in other words, that whatever harm may exist can be debated so long as the debate is endless, but the harm can never be stopped. As the Massachusetts hearing shows, the issue of whether pornography is harmful matters to pornography's defenders only as long as it is considered impossible to demonstrate that harm. Once it is judicially established that pornography does the harms made actionable in this law—as it was established in the litigation on the ordinance in 1985[22]—the ordinance's opponents lose interest in the question.

Addressed not at all by the opposition in the hearings is whether or not the practices of pornography made actionable by the ordinance are properly conceptualized as sex-based discrimination. Like the conclusion that pornography causes harm, the conclusion on the nature of that harm is based on evidence, on fact; these hearings provide those facts. As an analytic matter, although many people are shown to be victimized, actually and potentially, if even one women, man or child is victimized *because of their sex*, as a member of a group defined by sex, that person is discriminated against on the basis of sex; those who testified to their experiences in the hearings incontestably were hurt as members of their gender. Their specifically, differentially, and uncontestedly sex-based injuries ground the state's interest in equality that is vindicated by the ordinance.

The hearings show the ordinance in practice: it produced them. The hearings also present case after case of precisely the kinds of evidence the ordinance would introduce into court if it were enacted into law. These are the people who need to use it, who have nothing to use without it. The hearings empowered individuals to speak in public, provided a forum for them to confront their abusers, to prove their violations, and to secure accountability and relief, as the ordinance would in court. The hearings present witnesses to acts of abuse and injury—acts, not ideas, like those acts the ordinance would redress in court. In the hearings, the industry of exploitation and violence that produced these acts is connected inextricably with them, as it would also have to be in civil court proceedings. The hearings challenged the same concentration of nongovernmental power that the ordinance would challenge in court, empowering the government no more than the hearings did. The hearings used the legislative process for the ends to which it is given to citizens to use, as the ordinance would use the civil judicial process to its designed purposes of conflict resolution and rectification of injury. As the ordinance would in court, the hearings brought pornography out of a half-lit underground into the public light of day. The hearings freed previously suppressed speech. So would the ordinance. Neither the ordinance nor the hearings have anything in common with censorship.[23]

Until the publication of this volume, the public discussion of pornography has been impoverished and deprived by often inaccurate or incomplete reports of victims' accounts and experts' views.[24] Media reports of victims' testimony at the time of the hearings themselves were often cursory, distorted, or nonexistent. Some reports by journalists covering the Minneapolis hearings were rewritten by editors to conform the testimony to the story of pornography's harmlessness that they wanted told.[25] Of this process, one Minneapolis reporter assigned to cover those hearings told me, in reference to the reports she filed, 'I have never been so censored in my life.' Thus weakened, the victim testimony became easier to stigmatize as emotional and to dismiss as exceptional. Its representativeness has been further undermined by selective or misleading reports of expert testimony on scientific studies. This body of scholarship predicts that the precise kinds of consequences *will* happen from exposure to pornography that the survivors report *did* happen in their own experience. In making the whole record available, this book shows these two kinds of evidence documenting the same harm in two different ways.

This volume contributes other neglected or otherwise inaccessible information to the public discussion over the civil rights ordinance against pornography. For example, the allegation that opposing points of view were excluded from the hearings by the bills' proponents[26] is refuted by the hearings on their face. Opponent after opponent of the civil rights of women, mostly liberals, parade through these pages, testifying ad nauseam. The hearings also go some distance toward refuting the now ubiquitous fabrication that locates the engine of the civil rights antipornography ordinances in an 'unusual coalition of radical feminists and conservative women politicians'.[27] This invention originated in a false report in *The New York Times* that Charlee Hoyt, one of the bill's original sponsors in Minneapolis, opposed the Equal Rights Amendment. The *Times* published a correction affirming Hoyt's constant support of ERA, but the lie about the ordinance's alliance with the right stuck, always changing ground but always growing.[28] The same *Times* article stated that the Indianapolis ordinance was passed with 'the support of the Rev. Greg Dixon, a former Moral Majority official', who 'packed Council hearings to lobby for passage of the proposed ordinance'.[29] Neither Rev. Dixon nor his followers appear to have spoken at the Indianapolis hearings. Enough votes for passage (the bill passed 24 to 5) existed prior to the meeting at which these individuals sat in the audience. No one has said that Rev. Dixon or his group had any other contact with the process. Thus it was that the outcome of a legislative vote came to be attributed to the presence of some who came to watch as others cast it.

Taint through innuendo has substituted for fact and analysis in much reporting and discussion of the ordinance. As the hearings document, of all the sponsors of the bill in all the cities in which it has been introduced, only one—Beulah Coughenour of Indianapolis—has been conservative. Work on one bill with an independent individual is hardly an alliance with a political wing.[30] And exactly what is sinister about women uniting with women across conventional political lines against a form of abuse whose politics are sexual has remained unspecified by the critics.

The hearings correct such widely distorted facts simply by showing the sponsors and supporters of the ordinance in action, illustrating its progressive politics. The ordinance's two original sponsors in Minneapolis appear: Van White, a liberal Democratic African American man, and Charlee Hoyt, a liberal Republican white woman. (Sharon Sayles Belton, the Democratic African American woman who is now mayor of Minneapolis, sponsored the reintroduced ordinance after the first veto.) The grass-roots groups who inspired the Minneapolis ordinance by requesting help in their fight against pornographers' invasion of their neighborhoods testify in support of it. These same groups later supported the Indianapolis ordinance when it was challenged in court.[31] Battered women's groups, rape crisis center workers and advocates, organizations of survivors of sexual abuse in childhood, and groups of former prostitutes present unanimous evidence from their experience in favor of the ordinance. They, too, supported it against later legal challenge.[32] The large, ethnically diverse Los Angeles County Commission on Women that sponsored and supported the ordinance chaired the hearings there.

The progression of hearings reveals that opposition to the ordinance became better organized over time, its strategy refined. In the Los Angeles hearing on April 22, 1985, in which the pro-pimp lobby remained as always centered in the American Civil Liberties Union, the woman card was first played. There, a tiny, noisy elite of women who defend pornography professionally contrast with survivor after survivor whom they talk past and disregard—a division of a few women from all women subsequently magnified by a gleeful press. There, women's material interest in pornography was presented as divided: if it hurts some women other women love it, and stopping it hurts women more.[33] Women against women subsequently became the pornographers' tactic of choice, as if women's oppression by pornography had been argued to be biological, as if biological females saying they were not hurt by it undercut that case. This choice of strategy was revealed in the orchestration of the ordinance referendum battle in Cambridge, Massachusetts, in November 1985, in which the ordinance narrowly lost, and even more graphically in evidence in the Boston, Massachusetts, hearing of March 1992. In Boston, speaking almost entirely through female mouthpieces, the corporate interests of the entertainment industry came out of the woodwork for the first time weighing in on the side of the pornography industry, arraying abstraction after evasion after obfuscation after self-interested, profit-oriented rationalization against survivors' simple, direct accounts of the role of pornography in their abuse.[34] Much of the media persistently position women against women in their coverage, employing the pornographers' strategy in the way they report events and frame issues for public discussion. Corrective letters showing wide solidarity among women on the ordinance are routinely not published.[35]

These hearings took place in public and on the record. The witnesses, unless they say otherwise, were fully identified to the governmental bodies before whom they testified. Some of the consequences to them show why it has taken so long and has been so hard to make this information public, and prefigure the onslaught that followed. Some of those who spoke in Minneapolis were hounded and punished for what they said. One woman's testimony was published by *Penthouse Forum* without her knowledge or permission, selling her assault for sexual use. A copy of *Penthouse's* pages with 'We're going to get you, squaw' scrawled across it in red appeared in her mailbox. A dead rabbit appeared there a few days later; she was telephoned repeatedly by a man who appeared to be watching her in her home. Another witness was subsequently telephoned night after night at her unlisted telephone number: 'The calls are not simply harassing phone calls. It is like someone is reading something out of the pornography books . . . we can't get away from it.'[36] These are techniques of terror.

By bringing forward festering human pain that had been denied, the hearings unleashed an explosion of reports by women and men desperate for help. A local organizing group formed after the Minneapolis hearing was deluged with them. Women told 'about the time their boyfriend urinated on them while using pornography depicting "golden showers."'[37] Rape victims reported that 'their attacker took pictures during the rape and that she's afraid he is going to sell and distribute them'.[38] The group reported that 'we have received a call from a man in Fort Collins, Colorado, terrified because a group of men were holding him captive and making pornography with him. He has called and sent us the pornography in the hope that it could be used as evidence, that the whip lashes would prove that he was forced.'[39] Some groups held more hearings. The National Organization for Women hosted testimony on pornography across the nation.[40]

The Minneapolis hearings, circulated in photocopied transcript hand to hand, had a substantial impact on consciousness, politics, scholarship, theory, and policy.[41] At the federal level, the first explosion of publicity surrounding the Minneapolis hearings revived a long-moribund proposal for a new national commission on pornography. Attorney General William French Smith created the Attorney General's Commission on Obscenity and Pornography and selected its members. The prior Commission on Obscenity and Pornography in 1970, appointed by President Nixon, had exonerated 'obscenity' and 'erotica' of a role in 'crime', looking at no violent materials and looking for only violent effects.[42] The President's Commission heard from not a single direct victim—offended moralists are not victims—and considered only evidence from 'experts', meaning academics, on the question of harm. Understanding that asking the wrong questions of the wrong people might have produced the wrong answers, the Attorney General's Commission took extensive testimony from scores of survivors of all kinds of real abuse and investigated the effects of violent as well as nonviolent sexual materials. In other words, it investigated what those on the receiving end were in a position to know about the materials that are actually made and marketed by the pornography industry and consumed by its users. This commission was later named 'the Meese Commission' by a hostile press in order to discredit it by association with an almost universally despised man who did announce the inquiry's formation but did not originate it and did virtually nothing with its results.

The *Final Report* of the Attorney General's Commission, which repeatedly footnoted the Minneapolis hearings, substantially adopted the civil rights approach in its approach, findings, and recommendations. The report included an entire chapter on harm to 'performers'—of all survivors, the most ignored and, when noticed, blamed. It found that 'the harms at which the ordinance is aimed are real and the need for a remedy for those harms is pressing'.[43] It concluded that 'civil and other remedies ought to be available to those who have been in some way injured in the process of producing these materials'.[44] It endorsed a limited concept of civil remedies.[45] It found that the civil rights approach is the only legal tool suggested to the Commission which is specifically designed to provide direct relief to the victims of the injuries so exhaustively documented in our hearings throughout the country.'[46] The Commission also agreed that pornography, as made actionable in the ordinance, 'constitutes a practice of discrimination on the basis of sex'.[47] In an embrace of the ordinance's specific causes of action as well as its approach, the Commission recommended that Congress 'consider legislation affording protection to those individuals whose civil rights have been violated by the production or distribution of pornography . . . At minimum, claims could be provided against trafficking, coercion, forced viewing, defamation, and assault, reaching the industry as necessary to remedy these abuses.'[48] Unable to find constitutional legal definition of pornography that did not duplicate the existing obscenity definition, the Commission nonetheless found itself 'in substantial agreement with the motivations behind the ordinance, and with the goals it represents'.[49]

In the years soon following the Commission's Report, parts of the ordinance were introduced as bills in Congress. Senator Arlen Specter introduced a version of the ordinance's coercion provision as the Pornography Victims' Protection Act, making the coercion of an adult or the use of a child to make pornography civilly actionable.[50] Senator Mitch McConnell introduced a rendition of the ordinance's assault provision as the Pornography Victims' Compensation Act, creating a civil action for assault or murder caused by pornography.[51] Most stunningly, Congress in 1994 adopted the Violence Against Women Act, providing a federal civil remedy for gender-based acts of violence such as rape and battering.[52] In so doing, Congress made legally real its understanding that sexual violation is a practice of sex discrimination, the legal approach that the antipornography civil rights ordinance pioneered in legislative form.

More broadly, the exposure of pornography's harms has moved the ground under social theory across a wide range of issues. The place of sex in speech, including literature and art, and its role in social action has been thrown open to reconsideration, historically and in the present. The implications of visual and verbal presentation and representation for the creation and distribution of social power—the relation between the way people are imaged and imagined to the ways they are treated—are being rethought. The buying and selling of human flesh in the form of pornography has given scholarship on slavery a new dimension. More has been learned about the place of sexuality in ideology and about the importance of sexual pleasure to the exercise of dominant power. The hearings are fertile ground for analyzing the role of visceral belief in inequality and inferiority in practical systems of discrimination, and of the role of denial of inequality in maintaining that inequality. The cultural legitimation of sexual force, including permission for and exoneration of rape and transformation of sexual abuse into sexual pleasure and identity, is being newly interrogated. New human rights theories are being built to respond to the human rights violations unearthed. As events that have been hidden come to light, the formerly unseen appears to determine more and more of the seen. The repercussions for theory, the requisite changes in thinking on all levels of society, have only begun to be felt.

For those who survived pornography, the hearings were like coming up for air. Now the water has closed over their heads once again. The ordinance is not law anywhere. Mayor Donald Fraser of Minneapolis vetoed it twice after passage by two different city councils. Minneapolis has dithered and done nothing to this day. The Indianapolis ordinance was declared unconstitutional by the Court of Appeals for the Seventh Circuit in a decision that inverted First Amendment law, saying that the harm of pornography only proved the importance of protecting it as speech, and reduced equality rights, by comparison, to a constitutional nullity.[53] The U.S. Supreme Court summarily affirmed this result without hearing arguments, reading briefs, or issuing an opinion,[54] using a now largely obsolete legal device for upholding a ruling without expressing a view on its reasoning.[55] Although the Seventh Circuit decision is wrong in law,[56] and the summary affirmance of it need not necessarily bind subsequent courts, the ordinance passed in Bellingham, Washington, by public referendum was invalidated by a federal court there, citing the Indianapolis decision as controlling.[57] The Los Angeles ordinance was narrowly defeated, 3 to 2, in a vote delayed in order to be as inconspicuous as possible. The Massachusetts ordinance was maneuvered behind the scenes out of coming to a vote at all. Senators Specter and McConnell compromised their bills fundamentally.[58] Neither bill—for all the purported political expediency of their sponsors in gutting them as tools against the pornography industry—passed or even made it out of committee.

The victims have been betrayed. To adapt George Eliot's words, 'that roar which lies on the other side of silence'[59] about sexual violation in the ordinary lives of women was heard in these hearings. Now society knows what is being done to the victims and has decided to turn away, close its mind, and, 'well wadded with stupidity',[60] go back to masturbating to the violation of their human rights. The debate over pornography that was reconfigured by the survivors' testimony to make harm to women indispensable to the discussion has increasingly regressed to its old right/left morality/freedom rut, making sexual violence against women once again irrelevant and invisible.[61] Politicians are too cowed by the media even to introduce the bill. Truth be told, for survivor and expert both, it has become more difficult than it was before to speak out against pornography, as those in these hearings did. The consequences are now known to include professional shunning and blacklisting, attacks on employment and publishing, deprivation of research and grant funding, public demonization, litigation and threats of litigation, and physical assault.[62] The holy rage of the pornographers at being publicly exposed, legalized through ACLU lawyers at every bend in the road and accompanied by the relentless beat of media lies, has made aggression against pornography's critics normative and routine, fighting back unseemly, seemingly impossible. The silencing is intentional, and it is effective. In this atmosphere, few stand up and say what they know.

The concerted attacks on anyone who dares to give even a respectful hearing to the critique of pornography from this point of view has been reminiscent of the left's vicious treatment of so called 'premature anti-fascists' during the period of the Hitler–Stalin pact or of those who questioned Stalin including after the Moscow Trials. In the establishment today, support or at least tolerance for pornography, if slightly shaken, remains an article of faith among liberals and libertarians alike. The liberal establishment is its chief bastion but the right is actively complicit, its moralistic decency crusades and useless obscenity laws protecting pornography while pretending to stop it, contributing its share of judicial and other misogynists to the ranks of pornography's defenders, forever defending private concentrations of power and mistaking money for speech.

Against this united front, many a well-placed and secure professional, upon taking a rather obvious position against exploitation and abuse, or upon simply describing what is in the pornography or in the research on its effects, has been startled to be screamed at by formerly rational colleagues, savaged by hostile mail (sometimes widely electronically disseminated), defamed by attacks on professional competence, subjected to false rumors, ostracized instead of respected, libeled in and out of pornography, sued for speech by those who say they oppose suits for speech, and investigated by journalists and committees—not to mention blandishments of money from pornographers, eviction from homes, and threats against families. Most fold. With intellectuals intimidated, what chance do prostituted women and raped children have?

In the defense of pornography against the ordinance—the first effective threat to its existence—the outline of a distinctive power bloc has become discernible in the shadows of American politics. Cutting across left and right, uniting sectors of journalism, entertainment, and publishing with organized crime, sprawling into parts of the academy and the legal profession, this configuration has emerged to act as a concerted political force. Driven by sex and money, its power is largely hidden and institutionally without limit, Most of those who could credibly criticize it either become part of it or collaborate through silence. No political or legal organ is yet designed or equipped to counter it. Existing structural restraints on excess power—such as the government's checks and balances—are not designed to counter social combinations like this one. In western democracies, only governmental power is formally controlled, as if the government is the only entity that can cohere power or abuse it. Private in the sense of nongovernmental in origin, this bloc uses government (such as First Amendment adjudications) as just one tool, wielding less visibly against dissenters a clout similar to the government's clout in the McCarthy era.

Politicians who live and die by spin and image grovel before this machine. Law has been largely impotent in the face of it and lacks the will and resources to resist it. Indeed, law has largely been created by it, the reality perceptions entrenched through the machine's distinctively deployed weapons of sex, money, and reputation being largely indelible and impervious to contrary proof. Academic institutions are often found cowering before it and have ceded to it much of their role of credentialing the intelligentsia. Its concerted power defines what is taken as reality and aims to destroy those who challenge or deviate. Almost no one stands up to it. Those who testified in these hearings did.

One incident exposed the workings of this *de facto* machine accidentally. In 1986, a leaked memo from the public relations firm of Gray & Company proposed a press campaign for the Media Coalition, the group of trade publishers and distributors, including some pornographers, that is substantially funded by *Penthouse*[63] and was behind the litigation against the ordinance in Indianapolis and Bellingham. Gray & Company proposed to 'discredit the Commission on Pornography' and stop 'self-styled anti-pornography crusaders' from creating 'a climate of public hostility toward selected publications'.[64] They got the contract, which budgeted about a million dollars to pursue their recommended lines of attack. As reflected in the press this campaign produced, this planned onslaught focused on two items of disinformation contained in the proposal. The first is that there is no evidence that pornography does harm. In their euphemistic PR language, 'there is no factual or scientific basis for the exaggerated and unfounded allegations that sexually-oriented content in contemporary media is in any way a cause of violent or criminal behavior.'[65] The second is that the campaign to stop pornography 'is being orchestrated by a group of religious extremists'.[66] The mainstream media slavishly published *as news* the spewings of the groups fronting this strategy, establishing both lies as conventional wisdom.

The false statement that scientific evidence on the harmful effects of exposure to pornography is mixed or inconclusive is now repeated like a mantra, even in court. It has become the official story, the baseline, the pre-established position against which others are evaluated, the standard against which deviations must defend themselves, the common sense view that needs no source and has none, the canard that individuals widely believe as if they had done the research themselves. Few read the scholarly literature or believe they need to. No amount of evidence to the contrary—and evidence to the contrary is all there is—is credible against the simple reassertion of what was believed, without evidence, to begin with. Associating all work against pornography with widely reviled extremists of the religious and political right—without regard for the lack of factual basis for this guilt by association—is similarly impervious to contrary proof and produces a self-righteous witch-hunt mentality. Individuals strategically singled out as threatening to the financial health of Gray & Company's 'selected publications' are also used in pornography,[67] this cabal's ultimate weapon. Such attack-pornography potently and pervasively targets sexualized hostility at pornography's critics and destroys their status as credible speakers who have anything of value to say. The effect of lowering the human status of the critics can be relied upon to be discounted as having occurred by the norms of public discourse, which pervasively pretend that what is done in pornography occurs off stage in some twilight zone—coming from nowhere, meaning nothing, going noplace.

If this cabal acts in planned and organized ways at times, usually its common misogyny and attachment to pornography are themselves the conspiracy. The legitimate media act in their own perceived self-interest when they defend pornography, making common cause with mass sexual exploitation by calling pornography 'speech'. They seem to think that any restraint on pornography is a restraint on journalism. Their mistaken view that mainstream media and pornography are indistinguishable—the ordinance's definition of pornography distinguishes them, as does every pornography outlet in the world—pervasively distorts factual and legal reporting.[68] The resulting tilt is inescapable and uncorrectable; other than one's own experience to the contrary, which this process makes marginal, readers have no access to other information. That mainstream journalists tend to see their own power at stake in the legal treatment of pornography is particularly worth noting because they are not pornographers.

Sometimes the ax being ground is close to home, such as for journalists to whom Linda 'Lovelace' was pimped when in captivity.[69] Those who used her sexually have a specific stake in not believing that she was coerced to perform for the pornography film *Deep Throat*. They remain at large, mostly unidentified and writing. How often pornographer-manipulated news stories are concretely bought and planted can only be imagined, but how difficult can privileged access be for the pornographers and their point of view, given that they are often dealing with their own customers? Under these conditions, with access to information owned and controlled for content, with sex and money as potent motivators, the availability of unmediated original materials such as these hearings—these documents against the deluge—is as precious as it is rare.

You hold in your hands the samizdat of a resistance to a sexual fascism of everyday life—a regime so pervasive, so ordinary, so normalized, so established, so condoned, that there is no underground from which to fight it or in which to get away from it. The hearings are the only source on the way pornography concretely works in everyday life that has seen the public light of day. And they may be the last. Every day the pornography industry gets bigger and penetrates more deeply and broadly into social life, conditioning mass sexual responses to make fortunes for men and to end lives and life chances for women and children. Pornography's up-front surrogates swallow more public space daily, shaping standards of literature and art. The age of first pornography consumption is young, and the age of the average rapist is ever younger.[70] The acceptable level of sexual force climbs ever higher, women's real status drops ever lower. No law is effective against the industry, the materials, or the acts. Because the aggressors have won, it is hard to believe that they are wrong. When women can assert human rights against them, through a law they can use themselves, women will have a right to a place in the world.[71]

Notes

1. Everywoman published only the Minneapolis hearings, and those only in Britain, in 1988. *Pornography and Sexual Violence: Evidence of the Links* (Everywoman, 1988). Everywoman noted in its introduction, '[p]ublication of this material . . . is an historic event because strenuous efforts have been made . . . to persuade a publisher in the United States to make them publicly available. It has proved impossible to persuade any publisher, in the very country where pornography is itself protected as "freedom of speech," to risk any association with evidence about its harmful effects on society—and especially on women and children. This is one of many indications that in the United States, freedom of speech is available only to the assailants and not to the victims. The power and wealth of the pornography industry, and interconnections with 'respectable' publishing, distribution, and sales outlets, mean the power to censor those who do not participate, do not agree with what is being said, and seek to expose the harm they are doing' (p. 1).
2. As with all social movements, the process began substantially earlier with the women's movement as a whole, and more particularly with the feminist movement against pornography, 'Take Back the Night' demonstrations and rallies, Women Against Pornography in New York City, and formatively with Andrea Dworkin's pathbreaking *Pornography: Men Possessing Women* (G. P. Putnam's Sons, 1981).
3. The ordinance has been actively considered in many other jurisdictions in the United States and was introduced before legislative bodies in Germany, Sweden, and the Philippines. No Canadian legislature or court has considered the civil rights ordinance. The Supreme Court of Canada upheld Canada's pre-existing *criminal obscenity* law on the constitutional ground that porn-

ography harms women and equality. *R.* v. *Butler*, [1992] 1 S.C.R. 452 (S.C.C.). Widely circulated false reports of the role of *Butler* in customs seizures of gay and lesbian pornography in Canada, and an analysis of the contribution of the civil rights approach to pornography to promoting gay liberation, are discussed in Christopher N. Kendall, 'Gay Male Pornography after Little Sisters Book and Art Emporium: A Call for Gay Male Cooperation in the Struggle for Sex Equality', 12 *Wisconsin Women's Law Journal* 21 (1997).

4. We also worked with the cities and citizens of Bellingham, Washington, and Cambridge, Massachusetts, to pass these ordinances by referendum on direct vote of the people. The ordinance in Bellingham passed with 62% of the vote. The ordinance in Cambridge failed to pass but received 42% of the vote. A bastardized version was introduced in Suffolk County, New York, which we helped to defeat.
5. Testimony of Linda Marchiano, Minneapolis Hearings pp. 60–65.
6. Letter of Women Against Pornography, Minneapolis Hearings pp. 131–133.
7. Letter from Valerie Harper, Minneapolis Hearings pp. 140–142.
8. Testimony of R. M. M., Minneapolis Hearings, pp. 108–112.
9. Testimony of S. G., Minneapolis Hearings, pp. 145–147.
10. The details of this account were provided at the press conference on 25 July 1984, by the young woman whose statement appears on p. 265.
11. Testimony of N. C., Minneapolis Hearings, pp. 106–107.
12. Testimony of G. C., Minneapolis Hearings, pp. 107–108.
13. Testimony of Carole laFavor, Minneapolis Hearings, pp. 147–149.
14. Testimony of J. B., Minneapolis Hearings, pp. 121–124.
15. Minneapolis Exhibit 11, Letter of Marvin Lewis, p. 227.
16. Testimony of T. S., Minneapolis Hearings, pp. 114–120.
17. Ibid.
18. Ibid.
19. Minneapolis Exhibit 16, pp. 230–232.
20. The ordinances appear in the Appendices of *In Harm's Way*, ed. Dworkin and MacKinnon, beginning on p. 426.
21. Increasingly, since then, they do. *Sex Exposed: Sexuality and the Pornography Debates*. ed. Lynne Segal and Mary McIntosh (Virago Press, 1992); Nadine Strossen, *Defending Pornography: Free Speech, Sex, and the Fight for Women's Rights* (Scribner, 1995); Wendy McElroy, *XXX: A Woman's Right to Pornography (St Martin's Press, 1995).*
22. *American Booksellers* v *Hudnut*, 771 F.2d 323, 328 (7th Cir. 1985). 'Therefore we accept the premises of this legislation. Depictions of subordination tend to perpetuate surbordination. The subordinate status of women in turn leads to affront and lower pay at work, insult and injury at home, battery and rape on the streets.' See the Appendix of *In Harm's Way*, ed. Dworkin and MacKinnon, on pp. 465–482 for the full text of this opinion. Given that Judge Easterbrook strongly concludes that pornography as defined does the harms the ordinance makes actionable, some statements in its footnote 2 (see Ibid., p. 481) have generated confusion. Contrary to footnote 2, the empirical studies on the effects of exposure to pornography do not 'conflict'; the older studies have merely been superseded, as often happens when science progresses. The legislative record in turn did not 'conflict' either. The legislative record before the Seventh Circuit contained only empirical studies and

victims' testimony documenting harm. There were no empirical studies that showed no harm. Legal briefs before the Seventh Circuit by ordinance *did* contain in their arguments references to prior governmental bodies elsewhere that, based on the superseded empirical studies and no testimony by victims, had concluded that the empirical record on harm was divided. This, however, presented no conflict in the legislative facts of record. Further contrary to the suggestion implicit in footnote 2, no Court is constrained to conclude that a legislature's factual record adequately supports its legislation if that record is not strong enough. That is, there was no empirical conflict of legislative fact before the Seventh Circuit on the question of harm, and the Seventh Circuit was not compelled to find that Indianapolis was permitted to legislate on the basis of the facts it had.

23. The hearings also show some differences among the ordinances in specific localities, distinctions that have been previously obscured. Unlike the Minneapolis ordinance, the Indianapolis ordinance requires that violence be shown or done for the materials to be actionable (see *In Harm's Way* ed. Dworkin and MacKinnon, p. 444, defense to trafficking claim that materials are only subsection (6) of definition). The Massachusetts ordinance effectively limits its trafficking provision to visual materials (see Ibid., p. 460). Both of these features were thought by politicians to make the bills more acceptable to the ordinance's opposition, but they made no difference at all. The judge who invalidated the Indianapolis ordinance did not even notice that it was limited to violence, and the Massachusetts ordinance was just as politically untouchable as if it had also made words-only materials actionable.

24. Notable examples can be found in accounts of the Indianapolis hearings in Donald Alexander Downs, *The New Politics of Pornography* (University of Chicago Press, 1989) ('Downs'), which was not based on a transcript, but on a document footnoted by him as 'Administration Committee Notes'. Errors resulted. For example, Edward Donnersteins's appearance before the Council was not, as Downs asserts, a 'surprise move' (Downs, p. 123). It had been clearly announced before by Deborah Daniels. See Indianapolis Hearings, p. 283. Downs states further: 'As at Minneapolis, MacKinnon questioned Donnerstein, eliciting testimony on his research to support her legal points' (Downs, p. 123). I was not present when Donnerstein testified in Indianapolis. The ordinance's proponents did not manipulate these events, as Downs implies. Downs did. Presumably, the publication of these hearings makes distortions like these less possible. It should be noted that the official videotape on which the transcript of the Indianapolis hearings in this volume is based was incomplete when received. Attempts to locate sources for the hearings beyond the partial videotape proved fruitless. Asked for the source documents he referenced, Downs said he no longer had them (Letter of Donald A. Downs to author, 19 July 1996). John Wood and Sheila Seuss Kennedy, asked for written copies of their testimony, said they could not find them. The Records office at the City-County Council in Indianapolis said they keep official documents for seven years only, which is legally standard. Media sources who videotaped the hearings independently said they did not keep the tapes.

25. Altering the record to weaken the case on causality is illustrated by comparing two editions of the first national story *The New York Times* ran covering the

Minneapolis hearings. One included in its report of the testimony of R.M. her direct how-to causal sentence: 'When he convinced me to be bound, when he finally convinced me to do it, he read in a magazine how to tie the knots.' 'Minneapolis Rights Attack on Pornography Weighed', *The New York Times*, Sunday, 18 December 1983, p. 22. A different edition of *the same article*, headlined 'Minneapolis Asked to Attack Pornography as Rights Issue', omitted *only this sentence*, leaving the witness with only her testimony stating by simile a weaker relation between using pornography and his actions: 'My husband would read the pornography like it was a textbook', Sunday, 18 December 1983, p. 44.

26. For example, Wendy McElroy, *XXX: A Woman's Right to Pornography* (St Martin's Press, 1995) states: 'Dworkin and MacKinnon orchestrated the public hearings at which the ordinance was aired. They called only the witnesses they wished to hear from' (p. 92). In Minneapolis, Andrea Dworkin and I were hired as expert consultants to present relevant witnesses. As the transcript shows, we did not control who was called or who was allowed to speak. Everywhere, the hearings were public. Notably, Wendy McElroy was listed third of those who were to speak against the ordinance at the Los Angeles hearing, but she did not present herself to speak.
27. E. R. Shipp, 'A Feminist Offensive Against Exploitation', *The New York Times*, 10 June 1984, sec. 4, p. 2.
28. Minus the claim about Charlee Hoyt and plus many additional false or misleading details, essentially the same 'report' was recycled six months later in Lisa Duggan, 'Censorship in the Name of Feminism', *Village Voice*, 16 October 1984, p. 13, as if it were news.
29. *The New York Times*, note 27 above.
30. Beulah Coughenour was chosen by Mayor William Hudnut to shepherd the bill through the process largely on the basis of her political skills, which were exceptional. She also chaired the Administration Committee, through which the bill had to pass in order to be voted on by the City-County Council.
31. Brief of the Neighborhood Pornography Task Force, *Amicus Curiae*, in Support of Appellant, *American Booksellers* v. *Hudnut* (No. 84–3147), 771 F.2d 323 (7th Cir. 1985).
32. Brief *Amici Curiae* of Women Against Pornography et al., *American Booksellers Association, Inc.* v. *Hudnut* (Docket No. 84–3147), 771 F.2d 323 (7th Cir. 1985) (brief for groups including The Minnesota Coalition for Battered Women, 'a coalition of fifty-three local, regional, and state-wide organizations that provide services and advocacy to battered women and their families'); Brief of *Amici Curiae* Trudee Able-Peterson, WHISPER et al. in support of Defendant and Intervenor-Defendants, *Village Books* v. *City of Bellingham*, No. C88–1470D Memorandum and Order (D. Wash., Feb. 9, 1989) (unpublished) (brief of organizations of and for formerly prostituted women); Memorandum of *Amici Curiae* Institute for Youth Advocacy, Voices in Action, et al., *Village Books* v. *City of Bellingham*, No. C88–1470D Memorandum and Order (D. Wash., Feb. 9, 1989) (unpublished) (brief on harms of pornography to children).
33. That this was a concerted strategic decision is clear from the fact that the FACT brief, adopting this same tactic, was filed on April 8, 1985. See Nan D.

Hunter and Sylvia A. Law, Brief *Amici Curiae* of Feminist Anti-Censorship Taskforce, et al., 21 *University of Michigan Journal of Law Reform* 69 (1987/1988).

34. In contrast, many Hollywood actors, producers, and directors had actively lobbied for the passage of the Minneapolis ordinance, and some supported the Los Angeles one.
35. *Time* magazine, for one example, refused to publish the following letter signed by Gloria Steinem, Kate Millett, Alice Walker, Susan Brownmiller, Diana E. H. Russell, and Robin Morgan: 'The reasons feminists oppose pornography as a practice of sex discrimination [were] invisible in your story (*Sex-busters*, July 14, 1985). We oppose the harm pornography does to those who are coerced to make it, forced to consume it, defamed through involuntary appearances in it, assaulted because of it, and targeted for abuse and exploitation through its eight billion dollar a year traffic. When pornography's victims—mostly women and children—are believed, its harm is amply documented. Unlike the right wing's approaches, the civil rights approach to pornography was created to permit the injured access to court to try to prove that pornography *did* harm them in these ways. Inflicting such devastation on human beings is no one's civil liberty.' This unanimity was particularly remarkable in light of Kate Millett's signature on the FACT brief, although many who signed the FACT brief seem not to have read it.
36. Task Force Hearing on Ordinances to Add Pornography as Discrimination Against Women, June 7, 1984, p. 81 (Testimony of E.M.). This Task Force was set up by Mayor Fraser to look responsive after his second ordinance veto. Nothing came of it.
37. Task Force Hearings on Ordinances to Add Pornography as Discrimination Against Women, June 7, 1984, p. 45 (Testimony of Therese Stanton).
38. Ibid.
39. Ibid., p. 46.
40. NOW Hearings on Pornography, Materials on the Personal Testimony of NOW Activists on Pornography (Lois Reckitt, Twiss Butler, and Melanie Gilbert eds.) National Organization for Women, Inc., May 23, 1986. NOW also adopted a national resolution that pornography violates the civil rights of women and children and testified against pornography in Congress. NOW Resolution of June 1984 National Conference; Testimony of the National Organization for Women, presented by Judy Goldsmith, President, on the Impact of Pornography on Women before the Subcommittee on Juvenile Justice, Committee on the Judiciary (September 12, 1984). It has done little to nothing to implement this position since.
41. See, for example, Diana E. H. Russell, 'Pornography and Rape: A Causal Mode', 9 *Political Psychology* 1, 41–73 (1988); Gloria Cowan, Carole Lee, Daniella Levy, and Debra Snyder, 'Dominance and Inequality in X-Rated Videocassettes', 12 *Psychology of Women Quarterly* 299–311 (1988); Wendy Stock, 'The Effects of Pornography on Women', in Laura Lederer and Richard Delgado, eds., *The Price We Pay*, pp. 80–88 (Hill and Wang, 1995); James Check and Ted Guloien, 'Reported Proclivity for Coercive Sex Following Repeated Exposure to Sexually Violent Pornography, Nonviolent Dehumanizing Pornography, and Erotica', in D. Zillmann and J. Bryant, eds., *Pornography: Research Advances and Policy Considerations* (Erlbaum, 1989); E.

Sommers and James Check, 'An Empirical Investigation of the Role of Pornography in the Verbal and Physical Abuse of Women', 2 *Violence and Victims* 189–209 (1987); Catherine Itzin, ed., *Pornography: Women, Violence and Civil Liberties* (Oxford University Press, 1992); Andrea Dworkin, 'Against the Male Flood: Censorship, Pornography, and Equality', 8 *Harvard Women's Law Journal* 1 (1985); Catharine A. MacKinnon, *Only Words* (Harvard University Press, 1993).

42. Commission on Obscenity and Pornography, *The Report of the Commission on Obscenity and Pornography* (Government Printing Office, 1970).
43. Attorney General's Commission on Pornography, *Final Report* (U.S. Department of Justice, July 1986) (hereafter cited as *Final Report*) p. 393.
44. *Final Report*, p. 396. The Commission also said that no remedy could reach coerced materials that were not also legally obscene (p. 396)—an incoherent, unprincipled, and legally unsupported restriction on relief for proven injury.
45. *Final Report*. pp. 393–395.
46. *Final Report*, p. 749. New Zealand's *Pornography: Report of the Ministerial Committee of Inquiry* (January 1989) adopted the ordinance's definition of pornography for its own investigation, on p. 28, and called the ordinance 'a brilliant strategy for expunging pornography from the face of any society that might adopt it' (p. 152). It recommended that the Human Rights Commission Act be reviewed and 'that pornography be considered a practice of sex discrimination which can be expressly identified' by the Act (p. 155). The Human Rights Commission of New Zealand, before the Committee, recommended that the coercion, forcing, assault, and defamation provisions be added to the causes for complaint under the Act (p. 153).
47. *Final Report*, p. 756.
48. Ibid. Accordingly, Carole Vance's claim, in reference to Andrea Dworkin's and my work, that the Commission 'decisively rejected their remedies' and that 'the Commission's Report summarily rejected Minneapolis style ordinances' is false. Carole S. Vance, 'Negotiating Sex and Gender in the Attorney General's Commission on Pornography', in *Sex Exposed: Sexuality and the Pornography Debates*, ed. Lynne Segal and Mary McIntosh (Virago Press, 1992), p. 37. Her charge that we publicly misrepresented the Commission's results when we said it supported our approach—'Even more startling were MacKinnon's and Dworkin's statements to the press that the Commission "has recommended to Congress the civil rights legislation women have sought", p. 38—is defamatory as well as false.
49. *Final Report*, p. 393.
50. 98th Cong. 2d Sess., S13191–13193, S. 3063 (October 3, 1984) and S13838–S13839 (October 9, 1984); S. 1187 (1985), 99th Cong. 1st Sess., S6853–6855 Cong. Rec. (May 22, 1985). The bill proposed to 'allow victims of child pornography and adults who are coerced, intimidated, or fraudulently induced into posing or performing in pornography to institute Federal civil actions against producers and distributors'. S6853 Cong. Rec. (May 22, 1985).
51. Originally S. 1226, the McConnell bill gave a civil right of action to victims of sexual crimes against pornographers if the victims could prove that 'sexually explicit materials' influenced or incited the assault. 101st Cong. 1st Sess., S7281–S7283 Cong. Rec. (June 22, 1989). In 1991, as S. 1521, the bill addressed 'obscene materials and child pornography' instead. Its purpose was

to require that those who trafficked such material 'be jointly and severally liable for all damages resulting from any sexual offense that was foreseeably caused, in substantial part, by the sexual offender's exposure to the obscene material or child pornography'. S. 1521, 102d Cong. 1st Sess. (July 22, 1991), Sec. 2(b).

52. 108 Stat. 1796 (1994). In one early case, the performer La Toya Jackson sued her former husband under the VAWA for systematically beating her until she performed for *Playboy* and other pornography. Complaint *Jackson* v. *Gordon.* D. Nevada, Case No. CV S 00563 DWH (RJJ).
53. *American Booksellers* v. *Hudnut*, 771 F.2d 323 (7th Cir. 1985).
54. *Hudnut* v. *American Booksellers*, 106 S. Ct. 1172 (1986) (affirming without opinion). For the dissent see Appendix of *In Harm's Way*, ed. Dworkin and MacKinnon, p. 482.
55. Robert L. Stern, Eugent Gressman, Stephen M. Shapiro, and Kenneth S. Geller, *Supreme Court Practice*, 7th ed. (BNA, 1993), pp. 264–268.
56. In January 1984, Constitutional scholar Laurence Tribe wrote to Minneapolis City Council President Alice W. Rainville 'to express dissent and dismay at Mayor Donald Fraser's veto of your ordinance to define pornography as a violation of civil rights . . . While many hard questions of conflicting rights will face any court that confronts challenges to the ordinance, as drafted it rests on a rationale that closely parallels many previously accepted exceptions to justly stringent First Amendment guarantees. While remaining uncertain myself as to the ultimate outcome of a judicial test, I urge you not to allow an executive to prevent the courts from adjudicating what may eventually be found to be the first sensible approach to an area which has vexed some of the best legal minds for decades.' (Letter of Laurence Tribe to The Honourable Alice W. Rainville, January 8, 1984.) See also Catharine A. MacKinnon, *Only Words* (Harvard University Press, 1993); Cass R. Sunstein, 'Pornography and the First Amendment', 1986 *Duke L. J. 589* (1986) Frank I. Michelman, 'Conceptions of Democracy in American Constitutional Argument: The Case of Pornography Regulation', 56 *Tennessee Law Review* 291 (1989); Owen M. Fiss, 'Freedom and Feminism', 80 *The Georgetown Law Journal* 2041 (1992).
57. *Village Books et al.* v. *City of Bellingham*, C88-1470D (W.D. Wash, 1989).
58. Senator Specter, under intense pressure from liberals, exempted traffickers in coerced adult materials. Senator McConnell, under pressure from across the political spectrum, adopted the obscenity definition for the materials his bill covered. Senator Specter's bill thus left the material incentive for coercion into pornography squarely in place, permitting pornographers to coerce women into sex for pornography and run with the products and profits. He was told this. Senator McConnell's bill was rendered useless for victims because the legal definition of obscenity makes harm to victims irrelevant and is nearly impossible to prove. He was told this.
59. 'If we had a keen vision and feeling of all ordinary human life, it would be like hearing the grass grow and the squirrel's heart beat, and we should die of that roar which lies on the other side of silence. As it is, the quickest of us walk about well wadded with stupidity.' George Eliot, *Middlemarch* (Bantam Books, 1985 ed. [from 1874 ed.] p. 177.
60. Ibid.

61. See Catharine A. MacKinnon, 'Pornography Left and Right', 30 *Harvard Civil Rights-Civil Liberties Law Review* 143 (1995); Andrea Dworkin, 'Woman-Hating Right and Left', in *The Sexual Liberals and the Attack on Feminism*, ed. Dorchen Leidholt and Janice G. Raymond (Pergamon, 1990), p. 28.
62. To document specifically most instances of the treatment that forms the basis for this and the next paragraphs would further target those subjected to it. Below are just a few examples that can be mentioned.

    The Attorney General's Commission on Pornography was sued as a whole, and its members individually, on the basis of a letter sent by the Executive Director asking distributors of adult magazines whether they were selling pornography. *Penthouse International, Ltd* v. *Meese et al.*, 939 F.2d 1011 (1991). The fact that the case was thrown out on appeal as baseless did not prevent it from operating as an instrument of intimidation and silencing of the commissioners.

    Al Goldstein, editor of *SCREW*, a pornography magazine, sued Women Against Pornography and Frances Patai, an individual member of WAP, for libel for Patai's statement on WCBS-TV that *SCREW* 'champion[ed] abuse of children'. Goldstein said he did not champion or defend abuse of children. *Goldstein and Milky Way Productions, Inc. et al.* v. *Patai Women Against Pornography*, Summons and Complaint (Supreme Court of the State of New York, County of New York, October 10, 1984). The defendants produced extensive examples of eroticization of incest and other sexual use of children in *SCREW* magazine over time. Having seriously damaged those sued, the case was settled.

    Marty Rimm, undergraduate author of a sound and methodologically creative study, 'Marketing Pornography on the Information Superhighway', 83 *Georgetown Law Journal* 1849 (1995), described accurately the pornography that is available on computer networks and measured patterns of its actual use. He found the simple truth of pornography's content and use, for example, that the more violating the materials are to women, the more popular they are. Once some of his findings were given visibility and credibility in a *Time* magazine cover story, he was hounded, harassed, and probed by journalists and attacked in *Playboy*; excoriated as a censor and subjected to an intense rumor campaign of vilification on the Internet; likely deprived of a scholarship offer for graduate school at MIT; canceled before a Congressional committee, where he was to testify; and threatened with the loss of his degree by his sponsoring institution, Carnegie Mellon University, which convened a formal inquiry into bogus charges that went on for years, although he was eventually cleared of all the serious charges. His initially sought book proposal, an analysis of the approximately 85% of his data that was not discussed in the article, suddenly could not find a publisher. No lawyer could be found to defend his academic freedom.

    Shots were fired into the windows of the office of Organizing Against Pornography in Minneapolis when the ordinance was pending there.

    Andrea Dworkin and I have each been attacked in most of the ways described in this and subsequent paragraphs, and in others as well. Andrea Dworkin discusses some of her experiences in *Letters from a War Zone* (E. P Dutton, 1988).

    Exploring the attacks on Marrin Garbus, a well known defender of rights of free speech, for the sin of suing the press for a plaintiff in a libel case, *The New Yorker* said this: 'Robert Sack, who represents the *Wall Street Journal*, likens First Amendment law to a religion. "Switching sides," he concludes, "is close to apostasy,"' Reflecting the pressure brought on him, Garbus was also quoted as saying: 'I've told my colleagues within the First Amendment world that I would *never* take another plaintiff's case.' *The New Yorker* author commented, '[u]ndoubtedly, membership in the club does have its privileges . . .' Susie Linfeld, 'Exile on Centre Street', *The New Yorker*, March 11,1996, pp. 40, 42.

63. Susan B. Trento, *The Power House* (St Martin's Press, 1992), p. 192.
64. Letter from Steve Johnson to John M. Harrington, June 5, 1986, pp. 2, 1.
65. Ibid., p.4.
66. Ibid.
67. *Hustler* Magazine has often attacked critics of pornography in their 'Asshole of the Month' feature. Peggy Ault, Dorchen Leidholdt, and Andrea Dworkin sued them for libel. *Ault* v. *Hustler Magazine, Inc.*, 860 F.2d 877 (9th Cir. 1988); *Leidholdt* v. *L.F.P Inc.*, 860 F.2d 890 (9th Cir. 1988); *Dworkin* v. *Hustler Magazine Inc.*, 867 F.2d 1188 (9th Cit. 1989). All three cases were held legally insufficient before reaching the facts, holding in essence that pornography is unreal, hence not factual in nature, hence protected opinion. Both Gloria Steinem and Susan Brownmiller were used in pornography by *Hustler*. See Brief of *Amici Curiae* in Support of Plaintiff-Appellant, *Dworkin* v. *Hustler Magazine Inc.*, 867 F.2d 1188 (9th Cit. 1989) (App. No. 87–6393) (pornography of both women in appendix). Andrea Dworkin and I have been used in visual pornography.
68. This is particularly apparent in reports of rapes and sexual murders (in which the presence of pornography is usually just left out, particularly of national coverage), on child pornography, and on the technological frontiers of the pornographers' coveted new markets, such as computer networks.
69. Linda Lovelace and Mike McGrady, *Ordeal* (Citadel Press, 1980), pp. 177–179.
70. James V. P. Check and D. K. Maxwell, 'Pornography and Pro-Rape Attitudes in Children', paper delivered at 25th International Congress of Psychology, Brussels, July 19–24, 1992. Cheek and Maxwell found, in a survey of 276 grade 9 students in Canada, that 9 out of 10 boys and 6 out of 10 girls had viewed video pornography. The mean age of first exposure was just under 12 years of age. Boys who were frequent consumers of pornography and/or reported learning useful information about sex from pornography were more accepting of rape myths and violence against women. Forty-three percent of the boys in one or both of these categories agreed that it was 'at least maybe OK' to force a girl to have sexual intercourse 'if she gets him sexually excited'.

    Examination of the Department of Justice's *Uniform Crime Reports* from 1991 to 1995 shows a steady increase in the double digits in the number of arrests for sex crimes reportedly committed by perpetrators under 18 years of age up to 1993, then a small decrease thereafter. FBI, U.S. Department of Justice, *Uniform Crime Report for the United States*, 1991, 1992, 1993, 1994, 1995. Closer scrutiny of the affected groups, beyond simply reported crime, suggests that sexual assaults are increasingly being committed by younger and younger perpetrators. Melinda Henneberger, 'Now Sex and Violence Link at an Earlier Age', *The New York Times*, July 4, 1993, sec. 4, p. 6, col. 4; Claudia

Morain, 'When Children Molest Children', *San Francisco Chronicle*, May 4, 1994, p. F7. 'The "portrait" of the American sex offender increasingly "bears the face" of a juvenile." Sander Rothchild, 'Beyond Incarceration: Juvenile Sex Offender Treatment Programs Offer Youths a Second Chance', 4 *Journal of Law and Policy* 719 (1996). In the same publication, see a report of a 1992 study at the University of New Hampshire's Family Research Laboratory concluding that 'forty-one percent of sexual assaults on children ages 10 to 16 were done by other children', p. 720.

71. This passage was inspired by Louis Begley, 'At Age 12, A Life Begins', *New York Times Magazine*, May 7, 1995, p. 101: 'Hitler was dead and the 10 days of miracles had begun . . . finally I could believe the Germans had been wrong. I had not, after all, been marked at birth as unfit to live. My disgrace was not inside me; it was their invention. I had the right to a place in the world.'

8 Suffering and Speech

Andrea Dworkin

In these hearings—Minneapolis in 1983 to Massachusetts in 1992—women testify about being hurt in and by pornography. This hurt includes every kind of sexual exploitation and abuse. The hearings are road maps of injury, made graphic through the speech of those who had their legs spread, their hands tied, their mouths gagged. These hearings and the political organizing that went into creating them pushed silence off the women in these pages—they stood up and spoke. But while some legislators listened—and while other hurt women, still silent, hoped—society at large pretty much turned its back on the suffering caused by pornography and refused to consider honorable and equitable remedies. These hearings also contain all the familiar leftist arguments for pornography: it is free speech or free sexuality in a free marketplace of ideas. Only when women's bodies are being sold for profit do leftists claim to cherish the free market. The protectors of pornography have arguments and principles; the status quo supports the validity and legitimacy of their world view. Their arguments and principles help to continue pornography's current status as constitutionally protected commerce in women and maintain the colonialization of women's bodies for male pleasure.

Listening to the arguments for pornography is like listening to the refrain of a song one can sing in one's sleep. Listening to the victims, on the other hand, requires patience and rigor; it requires the courage to take in what they have to say—to feel even a tiny measure of what they have endured. Many women try to distance themselves from the shame and squalor of sexualized violation—and refuse to empathize

Andrea Dworkin, 'Suffering and Speech', from *In Harm's Way: The Pornography Civil Rights Hearing*, ed. Andrea Dworkin and Catharine A. MacKinnon (Harvard University Press, 1994), 25–38, reprinted by permission of Elaine Markson Literary Agency, Inc.

with hurt women. They especially do not want the hurt to be public; they reject what they consider a politics of victimization. In reality, they are rejecting the facts of women's lives, often including their own, and a politics of resistance to male power over women.

I come from a generation of women who did not have feminism. I was born in 1946 and graduated from high school in 1964. Women were invisible in history and culture, literature and politics, art and athletics. The best way to see a woman protagonist would have been to go to a play by Euripides. After the Greeks, it was all downhill. I found myself on the political Left because of the issues I cared about as a child: prejudice against blacks, including de jure segregation in the South and apartheid in South Africa; abortion and contraception, both of which were then criminal in the United States; anti-Semitism, from pogrom to Holocaust, all of which my family, mostly dead, had experienced; the rights of the working man, because my father, who was pro-union, worked in a post office as well as being a teacher; literacy and access to books; poverty; peace in the face of nuclear threat and the Cold War; and I liked Lenny Bruce, Bessie Smith, and jazz. My concerns had to do with human suffering—I was against it—and social fairness—I was for it. This may sound simplistic, but concentrating on suffering and fairness is an exacting and difficult discipline. For me, these were urgent and troubling issues of conscience, not ideology. I never took a stand based on what is now called theory, although I did read Marx and Engels, Bakunin, Kropotkin, Prudhomme, Henry David Thoreau, and even Ernesto Che Guevara's *Guerilla Warfare*, which, in high school, along with *Catcher in the Rye*, I studied and adored. There weren't any mountains where I lived in New Jersey, but I practiced possible assault strategies on the first shopping mall built in the United States, just blocks from my parents' home. My understanding of politics has always been concrete: humans are being hurt; here are actions that must be taken and institutions that must be changed. And I read to learn: more about suffering, more about fairness. As with many of my generation, maybe all, the Vietnam War was the defining event of my young adult life. I was against it. I fought against it from 1965, when I was arrested at a sit-in at the United States Mission to the United Nations, until April 1975 when it ended.

It has been a devastation to me to see the US Left's disregard for women and women's rights over the last twenty-five years: a nearly absolute indifference to our suffering and an unapologetic disdain for what is fair. In the 1960s many women my age lived as militant left-wing radicals or flower children or both; but by 1970 some began to apply to women the standards of justice applied to other disempowered groups. On the Left women were used as menial labor, and our sexual availability was taken for granted. Fighting for others, some of us learned to fight for ourselves. Radical feminism emerged from the Left and brought left-wing values of equality to women. The Left opposed feminists every step of the way—and not just because the boys were losing cheap labor and cheap lays. They were blind to injustice against women: injustice that had their names on it. The Left especially opposed emerging consciousness and activism regarding rape, wife-abuse, incest, pornography, and prostitution. In the early 1970s, rape became a cutting-edge issue. The organized Left opposed prosecuting rapists without fear or favor because bogus charges of rape had been used to persecute black men. Convicting white men who raped did not seem to the men on the Left a fair move—one that would change everyone's perception of rape and of black men. Redefining rape from the point of view of the victims was taken to be vindictive and mean. Men of the Left wanted female voices on rape silenced. In the mid-1970s, battery became a cutting-edge issue. Left-wing lawyers conjured up the specter of the 'knock on the door', police-state entry into the home that is, after all, a man's castle. They wanted the voices of beaten women and feminist advocates silenced. Rather than face the suffering of the victims, they became militant on the due-process rights of the perpetrators. A few years later, incest became a cutting-edge issue. The Left denied its existence while protecting the sexualization of children under the rubric of free sexuality for children. The Left simply denied the harm done to children by pedophiles, rapists, sadists, and pornographers, any of whom might be strangers or acquaintances or family. Efforts to protect children from sexual abuse and exploitation were characterized as a tyranny of the repressed. The Left wanted the voices of adult survivors silenced and refused to listen to child victims without a mountain of independent corroboration. In the late 1970s, pornography became a cutting-edge issue. The Left took the position that pornography was liberated sexuality and that those opposing it were right-wing collaborators. A free-speech absolutism, which in earlier years the Left abhorred with respect to racism, became the Left's über-principle. When prostitution and the trafficking in women globally became cutting-edge issues in the mid-1980s, the Left suddenly honored money, contracts, and exploited labor—as if it were the dream of all girls to suck cocks for a few bucks.

This chronology of issues is only approximate, because victims, survivors, and organizers worked on all these issues (always with opposition from the Left) before the larger public became aware of them. For instance, the first antipornography demonstration by feminists was in 1970 in New York City: a sit-in to denounce both the low pay of women workers at Grove Press and its publishing of pornography. Barney Rossett, owner of Grove, condemned the sit-in as a CIA plot. The charge of right-wing collaboration was born then. Earlier, in 1968 and 1969, there had been protests against the Miss America Pageant: protests against objectifying and dehumanizing women through sexual voyeurism. In the public's perception, one issue followed on the heels of another, often supplanting attention paid to the prior agitation; but for feminists who worked against violence against women, the 1970s and 1980s were two decades of constantly expanding knowledge, all related through speak-outs, consciousness-raising, books, conferences, demonstrations, marches, civil disobedience, lobbying, drafting legislation, and building women's studies departments. It started with rape, what is now called 'stranger rape'. But once women began to understand rape, to unravel the lies about it (legal and vulgar), each of the other issues began to show through what had been a lead barrier of obfuscation, denial, indifference, and outright cruelty. These issues were all connected, intertwined; in any given woman's life, they intersected in complex ways.

The Left has pretty much failed in its efforts to block feminist work against rape, wife-abuse, and incest, but it has been more successful in protecting pornography and prostitution. Every conceivable effort has been made to silence women who have been hurt in or by pornography: they are slandered, stigmatized, stalked, and shunned. Similarly, survivors of prostitution are expected to disappear into that thin gray line between night and day, not living or dead: touched too much inside; dirty vaginas, dirty mouths; not citizens, not like us, not of us; nothing to say. The men who rape or batter or incestuously rape or sexually abuse children or make pornography out of women and children or use pornography made of women or children or use prostitutes or pimp prostitutes always have something to say. On the Left, these men are deemed to have ideas; their experience is respected—the more low-down, dirty, or violent, the better; they are crowned as liberators, rhetorically worshiped as freedom-fighters—each woman or girl used (plugged or boned or whatever the current hostile slang is) representing a triumph over repression or suppression or oppression; in fact, a triumph of expression.

In addition to romanticizing forced sex and celebrating sexual exploitation, the Left has joined the Right in defending the culture of dead white men: protecting it from criticism or change; keeping it inviolate, immune from contamination by creative persons not dead or white or male. The culture of dead white men, built on the bodies of silenced women and colonialized people of color, has become a weapon to keep living women of all races silent. Like a private club that keeps out all but an elite few, art and books especially are used to tell the emerging women—emerging not only from silence but often enough from hell—that they are not good enough or important enough or worthy enough to be listened to. The proof of their insignificance is in their suffering: having been raped or beaten or prostituted. Was Aristotle? Was Descartes? Why listen to women who are more pleasing laid out flat, legs spread, than standing up, talking back, talking real? Why should the men of liberation interrupt the liberatory act itself to listen to the person whose hole he was sticking it in? And if I were to say that hole is not empty space waiting to be filled by anyone or anything, what would my authority be? How do I know? But he knows—every 'he' knows.

The books I read growing up—the books of dead white men, or near dead, the men living but remote by virtue of their own presumed superiority to women—did not, could not, tell me about the suffering of women or what it would take to make society fair for women. I read the men of conscience—but Camus did not consider these questions, nor did Sartre or Whitman or Shelley or Lord Byron. I read the men of suffering—Dostoevsky, Proust, Rimbaud—but they were silent on the suffering of women. The things I wanted in life were in the realm of men, of culture: to write books, to be politically engaged; to strategize against injustice, to expose it; to break down institutions that supported suffering—laws, manners, habits, threat of force or threat of the mob or threat of prison or threat of exile. I simply did not understand that girls in my generation were excluded by definition from doing virtually everything I wanted to do. The exclusion was egregious; but so was the consequence of not identifying the excluded group by name—women. I empathized with every group I knew to be excluded and I knew them by name: blacks, the poor, exploited workers. But men were the real people; women did not exist in consciousness. Men were actors on the stage of history, doers in the culture of intellect and creativity. Women were absent; and it is impossible to empathize with a vacuum, a blank space, a nonentity. There was no injustice in this invisibility; it was the nature of women to be absent from action.

There was no political conception that women were excluded, thus disenfranchised, socially stigmatized, politically powerless—only that women had a different, opposite function to men, a preordained, predetermined purpose that precluded heroism and originality. History, culture, justice were not our province; romance was, marriage was, babies were. In truth, one's body got touched and pushed into and hit and knocked around by men who had a birthright to invade using force, which was taken to be a measure of desire: and one rooted for the invader, the action hero, and disavowed her, the culpable victim. Wanting to be the hero, a girl did not recognize rape as rape even when it happened: she'd stumble around hurt and confused, trying to forget. Wanting to be human, even when one was pushed down and pushed over and drilled into, one did not recognize the generic nature of the event. Any such recognition would strip one's life of dignity and individuality; one would lose all credibility, even in one's own mind. Wanting to love, even when treated with contempt wrapped in seduction and condescension, one could not draw a line, even around one's own body, because he, not she, was the significant person, the one who acted, the line drawer: the real person. Girls wanted so much, not knowing they wanted the impossible: to move in a real world of action and accomplishment; to be someone individual and unique; to act on one's own feelings, not to have to wait passively until a boy felt something so that one might react—he turns on the switch and then the current flows; which switch will he flick? One had appetites and ambitions, talents and desires, capacities and potential, drive and vision, questions and curiosity. Almost inevitably in my generation, girls were raped in response to assertions of self: being in a proscribed place; being alone; being outside; being inside; showing affection or interest or delight; asserting ambition—intellectual, creative, athletic: every act was a provocation, and eventually a man punished one for wanting either something or anything.

It was the biblical god of the Old Testament who said that knowledge and sex were synonyms and made knowledge a male domain: he knew her. She knew nothing and ate the apple from the Tree of Knowledge because she was pliable and weak; she got expelled from the Garden, her home, and got pregnant and multiplied, her labor painful and bloody to punish her for daring to want to know, or for daring to act—to pick an apple. There is no divinely inspired paradigm for a woman's wanting to know without her also deserving and getting punishment: not, at least, in the Judeo-Christian world. The punishment is against her body: taking it, using it, entering it, causing her pain, her will irrelevant. The punisher has power and gets pleasure, his recompense for being mortal. The girl, erased and mute in the culture originating in that old book, increasingly becomes invisible and silent to herself. The ambitions die. The dreams die. The adventurer, the explorer, the creator in her dies. She becomes whatever her body means to men. Her mind is hurt by rape and other physical assault to her body; it fades and shrinks and seeks silence as refuge; it becomes the prison cell inside her. Rape and physical assault damage the mind; and rape is concrete and consistent, mandated by the man's ownership of the woman and by her separate destiny, her bloody, painful destiny. Every invasion of the body is marked in the brain: contusions, abrasions, cuts, swellings, bleeding, mutilation, breaking, burning. Each capacity of the brain—memory, imagination, intellect, creation, consciousness itself—is distressed and deformed, distorted by the sexualized physical injuries that girls and women sustain. No matter how much we are undressed, the shadow of unexplained, undeserved pain covers us with shame and despair. All around us there are other women, seemingly not hurt, making small talk, acting normal, which means happy, not discontent, certainly not devastated. Girls are still being socialized not to identify with—feel empathy for—other females: she got hurt because she did x, y, z—I didn't, so I didn't get hurt; she's at fault, I'm not; the punishment fits her crime; blame her, exonerate him. This continuing, culturally applauded socialization of women not to empathize with other women is a malignant part of the culture of men, dead white ones or not. Women are perceived to be appalling failures when we are sad. Women are pathetic when we are angry. Women are ridiculous when we are militant. Women are unpleasant when we are bitter, no matter what the cause. Women are deranged when women want justice. Women are man-haters when women want accountability and respect from men. Women are trash when women let men do what men want. Women are shrews or puritans when we do not.

We learn—still, now, despite the gains of feminism—not to call attention to ourselves, only to the signets of our conformity: the sexualized conventions of grooming. We cover over being the victims of sexual abuse, because otherwise we are exposed in poses and positions and with bruises that excite some men or many men or nearly all men or the next man. Each abuser makes his cut, adds his mark, his smell, his ejaculate, his contempt, his destruction, to the social identity of a woman exposed. She is in the male mind—the minds of men—as the spread-out thing, or the bruised and brazen thing, or the serially fucked thing. She's rarely more than a picture in his mind anyway: spread ejaculate on her and she's a dirtier picture.

In 1972 I came back to the United States after five years in Amsterdam, four of which I spent doing time as the battered wife of a tormenter, a torturer even Amnesty International would hesitate to approach. In the year before I came back—a year of being stalked, a year of running, hiding, being homeless, having nothing—I began to ask questions about women: why women were treated with contempt, violence; why no one cared or intervened or helped even a little. When I was battered, virtually every person whom I asked for help the many times I tried unsuccessfully to run away told me I provoked the violence, that it was my fault, that I liked it (even though I was running from it). My friends were all leftists who cared about human rights—about suffering and fairness. Only one was honest when I asked her why she wouldn't help me: I'm afraid he'll hurt me, she said. Only feminists did not back off; only feminists cared about how badly I had been hurt; only feminists did not think that whatever he, the mad dog, did, I deserved or craved—or that it was his right.

Back in the United States in November 1972, I started working with antiwar groups again. I found my former allies indifferent to violence against women—and these were mostly pacifists. Organizationally, Left groups embraced the idea of 'strong chicks' (in the parlance of the time) but repudiated a politics of anathematizing violence against women. Feminists in the United States had been organizing speak-outs and consciousness-raising groups since at least 1970; rape had emerged as a political issue. The Left ignored, trivialized, and opposed the new movement; and feminists did the work of creating a real political home for women, a social place out in the open in which the suffering of women counted and fairness toward women was a goal of social policy, not just noblesse oblige on the part of individual men.

The accomplishment of the women's movement in this regard was staggering. Silence—a heavy tombstone over each woman's hurt body and torn heart—was broken; one could hear the concrete crack, splintering, breaking open, crevices becoming gorges. Women talked: this happened to me. The stories were similar even as the women were different. The rapes were similar even as the rapists were different. The devaluing through insult and overbearing arrogance and vulgar assumptions of an innate superiority was the same, no matter what the social or economic status of the woman appeared to be. The rapists were men who crawled through locked windows and skylights or emerged at night from dark bushes or alleys; the rapists were teachers and neighbors and friends; the rapists were daddy or daddy's best buddy or step-daddy or uncle or brother or brother's best friend. Only the victims were able to articulate the elements of the crime. Only the victims knew who the rapist was, what he said, what he did, how he did it, and what it meant: what the act expressed. (Rape is a very expressive act.) US laws on rape, originating in English common law, made assumptions about women that disguised and protected both rape and the rapist. Those laws assumed that women would lie: accusations of rape were construed to be vengeful lies by an angry slut or spurned lover. Rape itself was seen as a crime against men if it was seen as a crime at all: a husband was injured in his conjugal rights if his wife—loyal and not adulterous—was violated; a father's rights over his unmarried virgin daughter became worthless when she was ruined and despoiled. The crime was not against the rape victim but against her male owner. If the male owner raped her, it was not rape. Only when women said what happened to them when they were forced was rape properly defined, understood, and prosecuted.

The Left and the Right have consistently had different positions on rape; but neither has acknowledged rape from the point of view of the women who experienced it. Both the Left and the Right denounced rape with varying degrees of outrage, but the Left saw most rape as free sex saturated with desire and the Right characterized rape as deviant and rare. Rape in marriage was legal; this was not an issue for Left or Right. The Left, which wanted to bring down power, hierarchies, and despotism, did not have a problem with forced sex—with its gender-based power, hierarchy, or despotism. I left the Left, although, really, the Left left the Left by betraying women, who were suffering and needed fairness in law, social policy, money, culture, speech, media, politics, and governance. The Left moved rightward when it abandoned women to rape, battery, incest, pornography, and prostitution. As with many women, for me equality became the heart of a living political quest to end the suffering caused by sexual abuse and exploitation through finding fairness. In betraying women, the Left sold itself out; and it is correct to say, I think, that the demands of feminism have caused a political realignment in the United States in which the recognized political continuum moves from Right to further Right to armed and murderous Right. Far to the left, off the mainstream continuum—at least as currently articulated in popular discourse—are women whose politics are animated by a commitment to listening to those who have been hurt and finding remedies that are fair.

The fact is that the speech of the socially worthless, the sexually stigmatized, is hard to hear even when the victims shout. Rapists and pimps talk louder, their speech amplified by the money behind the words they use. Rapists and pimps, representing the interests of normal men, some of whom rape, some of whom buy, seem to have the law of gravity on their side: they reify the status quo, which is what gives them credibility, legitimacy, and authority. They sound coherent. No matter what lie they tell, it passes for truth, because the hatred of women underlying the lie is an accepted hatred, a shared and unchallenged set of prejudiced assumptions. The woman who has been raped or pimped has to convince a hearer to listen because she counts. But she does not count unless she can make herself count, unless she can change the direction of gravity—turn the status quo, even momentarily, not just upside down but also inside out. She needs the women's movement; she needs courage; she needs stubbornness; she needs to want justice. It is fine for her to hate those who ripped into her if hate keeps her willing to talk, unwilling to let silence bury her again. She must dare to remember what she prefers to forget; and then she must stand fast on the sickening memory, which tries to drown her. She must stand right there. Any healed wound she must reopen, must tear away scar tissue and scabs to see what's underneath: ripping off her own skin, she sees the color of her own blood. She has to use her body to remember and he's on her and in her again; and this she must endure in order to speak. She has to be able to relive pain and humiliation: however shy, however modest, however unhappy to do so, she has to articulate violation, communicate dread, explicate sadism, remember the hate he had for her, which motivated him, and not die from that hate or the memory of it. Then he—rapist or pimp or buyer—says something, anything, and she is drowning again, back under, invisible, silent, worthless, except for whatever he gets out of her—pleasure or power or money. He always has a revered principle on which to hang his prick: free speech or free sex in the free market.

He has a constitutional right to express himself, and if his art requires that she be the canvas, so what? If he's an engraver and her skin is his surface, so what? If he wants to sculpt her to death or twist her body until it breaks where he turns her, so what? He's a citizen; she's a cunt. The Constitution protects him. All's right with the world.

Then there is the right to sex, which is implicitly his, since he gets what he wants: law, justice, honor, and feminist agitation notwithstanding. If it gives him sexual pleasure, getting in his way is mean and petty. If it hurts her, so what? If it insults or dehumanizes her, so what? If—in order for her to be available—she needs to be fucked as a child, trained, seasoned, so what? And if she screams, and he gets off on it, so what? If she tears—her rectum, her vagina, her throat—and he likes it, so what? If she bleeds—well, bitches bleed; so what?

The free market is where she is bartered, bought, and sold. It is often euphemistically called a marketplace of ideas, but only his ideas have value, especially his ideas, put into practice, of how to sell her. She is meat in his marketplace; he is the butcher who wields the knife to get the right cut; and he communicates through the cutting, then the display of the body parts. She is worth more in pieces than she ever was whole. The pimps' motive is twofold: money and pleasure. The user does what he wants, calls it what he likes. Everyone wants to be him—to be the user, not the used. This is a political point: what once was the Left wants to be the user, does not want to be anywhere but on top of the used; and some so-called feminists want to be the user, not to be under, not to be the condemned, the injured. Each time a victim is looked at, a man gets hard; the brave 'women-aren't-victims' girls want to be allies of the users, not of the used. It was ignorance to disassociate oneself from the raped before raped women articulated what rape is and means; it is malice, cowardice, and venality to disassociate oneself from the raped now—after the raped have made rape socially real. The same is true for battery, incest, prostitution; the same for pornography, made from the raw material of women's bodies, used against women's bodies, the production and the use designed to control, dehumanize, humiliate, injure, and subordinate: push down, push under, make lower, make less, render inferior.

I am asking you to listen in these hearings to those who have been hurt—and to care. I have always thought that conscience meant bearing witness to injustice and standing with the powerless. I still think that. I have always thought that equality meant an antagonism to exploiters. I still think that. I used to think that the Left was the side that valued those dehumanized by hate. I don't think that anymore—unless feminists fighting pornography and the global trafficking in women are the remnant, the last living leftists: facing the new millennium in opposition to the biggest trafficking in human beings this planet has yet seen. All the power is on the other side: all the money, media, current law, unexamined assumptions about speech, sex, women; all the fetishized sex that depends on dominance and submission as a dynamic and the objectification of women as a fundamental element of pleasure. There is nothing wrong with selling objects, generally speaking, provided the labor of human beings is not exploited to make the desired profit; but it is always and without exception a vicious practice to buy and sell human beings, which we are—which women are—no matter how used or raped or prostituted or incested or beaten we have been; no matter how shamed or humiliated by the overt sadism of some and the brutal indifference of the rest. You need to listen. You need to know. You need to care about the suffering pornography causes and be willing to decide what is fair.

Part II. Questioning Moralism

9 Not a Moral Issue

Catharine A. MacKinnon

> Pornosec, the subsection of the Fiction Department which turned out cheap pornography for distribution among the proles . . . nicknamed Muck House by the people who worked in it . . . produce[d] booklets in sealed packets with titles like *Spanking Stories* or *One Night in a Girls' School*, to be bought furtively by proletarian youths who were under the impression that they were buying something illegal.
>
> (George Orwell, *Nineteen Eighty-four* (1949))

A critique of pornography[1] is to feminism what its defense is to male supremacy. Central to the institutionalization of male dominance, pornography cannot be reformed or suppressed or banned. It can only be changed. The legal doctrine of obscenity, the state's closest approximation to addressing the pornography question, has made the First Amendment[2] into a barrier to this process. This is partly because the pornographers' lawyers have persuasively presented First Amendment absolutism,[3] their advocacy position, as a legal fact, which it never has been. But they have gotten away with this (to the extent they have) in part because the abstractness of obscenity as a concept, situated within an equally abstract approach to freedom of speech embodied in First Amendment doctrine, has made the

Catharine A. MacKinnon, 'Not a Moral Issue', from *Feminism Unmodified: Discourse on Life and Law*, Catharine A. MacKinnon (Harvard University Press, 1987), 146–62, copyright © by the President and Fellows of Harvard College, reprinted by permission of J. A. Christian Ltd. and the author. This speech was originally delivered to the Morality Colloquium, University of Minnesota, Feb. 23, 1983. These ideas were also discussed at the National Conference on Women and the Law, Apr. 4, 1983, and at the Conference on Media Violence and Pornography, Ontario Institute for Studies in Education, Feb. 4, 1984. The title is a play on 'Not a Love Story', a 1983 anti-pornography film by the Canadian Film Board.

indistinguishability of the pornographers' speech from everyone else's speech, their freedom from our freedom, appear credible, appealing, necessary, inevitable, *principled*.[4] To expose the absence of a critique of gender[5] in this area of law is to expose both the enforced silence of women and the limits of liberalism.

This brief preliminary commentary focuses on the obscenity standard in order to explore some of the larger implications of a feminist critique of pornography for First Amendment theory. This is the argument. Obscenity law is concerned with morality, specifically morals from the male point of view, meaning the standpoint of male dominance. The feminist critique of pornography is politics, specifically politics from women's point of view meaning the standpoint of the subordination of women to men.[6] Morality here means good and evil; politics means power and powerlessness. Obscenity is a moral idea; pornography is a political practice. Obscenity is abstract; pornography is concrete. The two concepts represent two entirely different things. Nudity, explicitness, excess of candor, arousal or excitement, prurience, unnaturalness—these qualities bother obscenity law when sex is depicted or portrayed. Abortion, birth control information, and treatments for 'restoring sexual virility' (whose, do you suppose?) have also been included.[7] Sex forced on real women so that it can be sold at a profit to be forced on other real women; women's bodies trussed and maimed and raped and made into things to be hurt and obtained and accessed, and this presented as the nature of women; the coercion that is visible and the coercion that has become invisible—this and more bothers feminists about pornography. Obscenity as such probably does little harm,[8] pornography causes attitudes and behaviors of violence and discrimination that define the treatment and status of half of the population.[9] To make the legal and philosophical consequences of this distinction clear, I will describe the feminist critique of pornography, criticize the law of obscenity in terms of it, then discuss the criticism that pornography 'dehumanizes' women to distinguish the male morality of liberalism and obscenity law from a feminist political critique of pornography.[10]

This inquiry is part of a larger project that attempts to account for gender inequality in the socially constructed relationship between power—the political—on the one hand and the knowledge of truth and reality—the epistemological—on the other.[11] For example, the candid description Justice Stewart once offered of his obscenity standard, 'I know it when I see it',[12] becomes even more revealing than it is usually understood to be if taken as a statement that connects epistemology with power. If I ask, from the point of view of women's experience, does he know what I know when I see what I see, I find that I doubt it, given what's on the newsstands. How does his point of view keep what is there, there? To liberal critics, his admission exposed the obscenity standard's relativity, its partiality, its insufficient abstractness. Not to be emptily universal, to leave your concreteness showing, is a sin among men. Their problem with Justice Stewart's formulation is that it implies that anything, capriciously, could be suppressed. They are only right by half. My problem is more the other half: the meaning of what his view permits, which, as it turns out, is anything but capricious. In fact, it is entirely systematic and determinate. To me, his statement is precisely descriptively accurate; its candor is why it has drawn so much criticism.[13] Justice Stewart got in so much trouble because he said out loud what is actually done all the time; in so doing, he both *did it* and gave it the stature of doctrine, even if only dictum. That is, the obscenity standard—in this it is not unique—*is* built on what the male standpoint sees. My point is: *so is pornography.* In this way the law of obscenity reproduces the pornographic point of view on women on the level of Constitutional jurisprudence.

Pornography, in the feminist view, is a form of forced sex, a practice of sexual politics, an institution of gender inequality. In this perspective, pornography is not harmless fantasy or a corrupt and confused misrepresentation of an otherwise natural and healthy sexuality. Along with the rape and prostitution in which it participates, pornography institutionalizes the sexuality of male supremacy, which fuses the erotization of dominance and submission with the social construction of male and female.[14] Gender is sexual. Pornography constitutes the meaning of that sexuality. Men treat women as who they see women as being. Pornography constructs who that is. Men's power over women means that the way men see women defines who women can be. Pornography is that way.

In pornography, women desire dispossession and cruelty. Men, permitted to put words (and other things) in women's mouths, create scenes in which women desperately want to be bound, battered, tortured, humiliated, and killed. Or merely taken and used. This is erotic to the male point of view. Subjection itself, with self-determination ecstatically relinquished, is the content of women's sexual desire and desirability. Women are there to be violated and possessed, men to violate and possess them, either on screen or by camera or pen, on behalf of the viewer.

One can be for or against this pornography without getting beyond liberalism. The critical yet formally liberal view of Susan Griffin, for example, conceptualizes eroticism as natural and healthy but corrupted and confused by 'the pornographic mind'.[15] Pornography distorts Eros, which preexists and persists, despite male culture's pornographic 'revenge' upon it. Eros is, unaccountably, *still there.* Pornography mis-takes it, mis-images it, mis-represents it. There is no critique of *reality* here, only objections to how it is seen; no critique of that reality that pornography imposes on women's real lives, those lives that are so seamlessly *consistent* with the pornography that pornography can be credibly defended by saying it is only a mirror of reality.

Contrast this view with the feminist analysis of Andrea Dworkin, in which sexuality itself is a social construct, gendered to the ground. Male dominance here is not an artificial overlay upon an underlying inalterable substratum of uncorrupted essential sexual being. Sexuality free of male dominance will require *change*, not reconceptualization, transcendence, or excavation. Pornography is not imagery in some relation to a reality elsewhere constructed. It is not a distortion, reflection, projection, expression, fantasy, representation, or symbol either. It is sexual reality. Dworkin's *Pornography: Men Possessing Women*[16] presents a sexual theory of gender inequality of which pornography is a core constitutive practice. The way pornography produces its meaning constructs and defines men and women as such. Gender is what gender means.[17] It has no basis in anything other than the social reality its hegemony constructs. The process that gives sexuality its male supremacist meaning is therefore the process through which gender inequality becomes socially real.

In this analysis the liberal defense of pornography as human sexual liberation, as derepression—whether by feminists, lawyers, or neo-Freudians[18]—is a defense not only of force and sexual terrorism, but of the subordination of women. Sexual liberation in the liberal sense frees male sexual aggression in the feminist sense. What looks like love and romance in the liberal view looks a lot like hatred and torture in the feminist view. Pleasure and eroticism become violation. Desire appears as lust for dominance and submission. The vulnerability of women's projected sexual availability—that acting we are allowed: asking to be acted upon—is victimization. Play conforms to scripted roles, fantasy expresses ideology—is not exempt from it—and admiration of natural physical beauty become objectification.

The experience of the (overwhelmingly) male audiences who

consume pornography[19] is therefore not fantasy or simulation or catharsis[20] but sexual reality: the level of reality on which sex itself largely operates. To understand this, one does not have to notice that pornography models are real women to whom something real is being done,[21] nor does one have to inquire into the systematic infliction of pornographic sexuality upon women,[22] although it helps. The aesthetic of pornography itself, the *way* it provides what those who consume it want, is itself the evidence. When uncensored explicit—that is, the most pornographic—pornography tells all, all means what a distanced detached observer would report about who did what to whom. This is the turn-on. Why does observing sex objectively presented cause the male viewer to experience his own sexuality? Because his eroticism is, socially, a watched thing.

If objectivity is the epistemological stance of which objectification is the social process,[23] the way a perceptual posture is embodied as a social form of power, the most sexually potent depictions and descriptions *would* be the most objective blow-by-blow re-presentations. Pornography participates in its audience's eroticism because it creates an accessible sexual object, the possession and consumption of which *is* male sexuality, to be consumed and possessed as which *is* female sexuality. In this sense, sex in life is no less mediated than it is in art. Men *have sex* with their *image* of a woman. Escalating explicitness, 'exceeding the bounds of candor',[24] is the aesthetic of pornography not because the materials depict objectified sex but because they create the experience of a sexuality that is itself objectified. It is not that life and art imitate each other; in sexuality they *are* each other.

The law of obscenity,[25] the state's primary approach[26] to its version of the pornography question, has literally nothing in common with this feminist critique. Their obscenity is not our pornography. One commentator has said, 'Obscenity is not suppressed primarily for the protection of others. Much of it is suppressed for the purity of the "community." Obscenity, at bottom, is not a crime. Obscenity is a sin.'[27] This is, on one level, literally accurate. Men are turned on by obscenity, including its suppression, the same way they are by sin. Animated by morality from the male standpoint, in which violation—of women and rules—is eroticized, obscenity law can be seen to proceed according to the interest of male power, robed in gender-neutral good and evil.

Morality in its specifically liberal form (although, as with most dimensions of male dominance, the distinction between left and right is more formal than substantive) revolves around a set of parallel distinctions that can be consistently traced through obscenity law. Even though the approach this law takes to the problem it envisions has shifted over time, its fundamental norms remain consistent: public is opposed to private, in parallel with ethics and morality, and factual is opposed to valued determinations. Under male supremacy, these distinctions are gender-based: female is private, moral, valued, subjective; male is public, ethical, factual, objective.[28] If such gendered concepts are constructs of the male experience, imposed from the male standpoint on society as a whole, liberal morality expresses male supremacist politics. That is, discourse conducted in terms of good and evil that does not expose the gendered foundations of these concepts proceeds oblivious to—and serves to disguise—the position of power that underlies, and is furthered by, that discourse.

For example, obscenity law proposes to control what and how sex can be publicly shown. In practice, its standard centers upon the same features feminism identifies as key to male sexuality: the erect penis and penetration.[29] Historically, obscenity law was vexed by restricting such portrayals while protecting great literature. (Nobody considered protecting women.) Having solved this by exempting works of perceived value from obscenity restrictions,[30] the subsequent relaxation—some might say collapse—of obscenity restrictions in the last decade reveals a significant shift. The old private rules have become the new public rules. The old law governing pornography was that it would be publicly repudiated while being privately consumed and actualized: do anything to women with impunity in private behind a veil of public denial and civility. Now pornography is publicly celebrated.[31] This victory for Freudian derepression theory probably did not alter the actual treatment of women all that much. Women were sex and still are sex. Greater efforts of brutality have become necessary to eroticize the tabooed—each taboo being a hierarchy in disguise—since the frontier of the tabooed keeps vanishing as one crosses it. Put another way, more and more violence has become necessary to keep the progressively desensitized consumer aroused to the illusion that sex is (and he is) daring and dangerous. Making sex with the powerless 'not allowed' is a way of defining 'getting it' as an act of power, an assertion of hierarchy. In addition, pornography has become ubiquitous. Sexual terrorism has become democratized. Crucially, pornography has become truly available to women for the first time in history. Show me an atrocity to women, I'll show it to you eroticized in the pornography. This central mechanism of sexual subordination, this means of systematizing the definition of women as a sexual class, has now become available to its victims for scrutiny and analysis as an open public system, not just as a private secret abuse.[32] Hopefully, this was a mistake.

Reexamining the law of obscenity in light of the feminist critique of pornography that has become possible, it becomes clear that male morality sees as good that which maintains its power and sees as evil that which undermines or qualifies it or questions its absoluteness. Differences in the law over time—such as the liberalization of obscenity doctrine—reflect either changes in the group of men in power or shifts in their perceptions of the best strategy for maintaining male supremacy—probably some of both. But it must be made to work. The outcome, descriptively analyzed, is that obscenity law prohibits what it sees as immoral, which from a feminist standpoint tends to be relatively harmless, while protecting what it sees as moral, which from a feminist standpoint is often that which is damaging to women. So it, too, is politics, only covertly so. What male morality finds evil, meaning threatening to its power, feminist politics tends to find comparatively harmless. What feminist politics identifies as central in our subordination—the erotization of dominance and submission—male morality tends to find comparatively harmless or defends as affirmatively valuable, hence protected speech.

In 1973 obscenity under law came to mean that which '"the average person applying contemporary community standards" would find that, . . . taken as a whole, appeals to the prurient interest . . . [which] depicts or describes, in a patently offensive way, sexual conduct specifically defined by the applicable state law; and [which], taken as a whole, lacks serious literary, artistic, political, or scientific value'.[33] Feminism doubts whether the average person, gender-neutral, exists; has more questions about the content and process of definition of community standards than about deviations from them; wonders why prurience counts but powerlessness doesn't; why sensibilities are better protected from offense than women are from exploitation; defines sexuality, hence its violation and expropriation, more broadly than does any state law and wonders why a body of law that can't in practice tell rape from intercourse should be entrusted with telling pornography from anything less. The law of obscenity says that intercourse on street corners is not legitimized by the fact that the persons are 'simultaneously engaged in a valid political dialogue'.[34] But, in a feminist light, one sees that the requirement that a work be considered 'as a whole' legitimizes something very like that on the level of publications like *Playboy*.[35] Experimental evidence is beginning to support what victims have long known: legitimate settings diminish the injury perceived as done to the women whose trivialization and objectification it contextualizes.[36] Besides, if a woman is subjected, why should it matter that the work has other value?[37] Perhaps what redeems a work's value among men *enhances* its injury to women. Existing standards of literature, art, science, and politics are, in feminist light, remarkably consonant with pornography's mode, meaning, and message. Finally and foremost, a feminist approach reveals that although the content and dynamic of pornography are about women—about the sexuality of women, about women as sexuality—in the same way that the vast majority of 'obscenities' refer specifically to women's bodies, our invisibility has been such that the law of obscenity has *never even considered pornography a women's issue.*[38]

To appeal to 'prurient interest'[39] means, I believe, to give a man an erection. Men are scared to make it possible for some men to tell other men what they can and cannot have sexual access to because men have power. If you don't let them have theirs, they might not let you have yours. This is why the *indefinability* of pornography, all the 'one man's this is another man's that',[40] is so central to pornography's *definition.* It is not because they are such great liberals, but because some men might be able to do to them whatever they can do to those other men, and this is more why the liberal principle is what it is. Because the fought-over are invisible in this, it obscures the fact that the fight over a definition of obscenity is a fight among men over the best means to guarantee male power as a system. The question is, whose sexual practices threaten this system that can afford to be sacrificed to its maintenance for the rest? Public sexual access by men to anything other than women is less likely to be protected speech. This is not to say that male sexual access to anything—children, other men, women with women, objects, animals—is not the real system. The issue is *how public* that system will be; the obscenity laws, their definition and patterns of enforcement, have a major role in regulating that. The bind of the 'prurient interest' standard here is that, to find it as a fact, someone has to admit that they are sexually aroused by the materials,[41] but male sexual arousal signals the importance of protecting them. They put themselves in this bind and then wonder why they cannot agree. Sometimes I think that what is ultimately found obscene is what does *not* turn on the Supreme Court, or what revolts them more, which is rare, since revulsion is eroticized; sometimes I think that what is obscene is what turns on those men the men in power think they can afford to ignore; sometimes I think that part of it is that what looks obscene to them is what makes them see themselves as potential targets of male sexual aggression, even if only momentarily; sometimes I think that the real issue is how male sexuality is presented, so that anything can be done to a woman, but obscenity is sex that makes male sexuality look bad.[42]

The difficulties courts have in framing workable standards to separate 'prurient' from other sexual interest, commercial exploitation from art or advertising, sexual speech from sexual conduct, and obscenity from great literature make the feminist point. These lines have proven elusive in law because they do not exist in life. Commercial sex resembles art because both exploit women's sexuality. The liberal's slippery slope is the feminist totality. Whatever obscenity may do, pornography converges with more conventionally acceptable depictions and descriptions just as rape converges with intercourse because both express the same power relation. Just as it is difficult to distinguish literature or art against a background, a standard, of objectification, it is difficult to discern sexual freedom against a background, a standard, of sexual coercion. This does not mean it cannot be done. It means that legal standards will be practically unenforceable, will reproduce this problem rather than solve it, until they address its fundamental issue—gender inequality—directly.

To define the pornographic as the 'patently offensive' further misconstrues its harm. Pornography is not bad manners or poor choice of audience; obscenity is. Pornography is also not an idea; obscenity is. The legal fiction whereby the obscene is 'not speech'[43] has deceived few; it *has* effectively avoided the need to adjudicate pornography's social etiology. But obscenity law got one thing right: pornography is more actlike than thoughtlike. The fact that pornography, in a feminist view, furthers the idea of the sexual inferiority of women, a political idea, does not make the pornography itself a political idea. That one can express the idea a practice embodies does not make that practice into an idea. Pornography is not an idea any more than segregation is an idea, although both institutionalize the idea of the inferiority of one group to another. The law considers obscenity deviant, antisocial. If it causes harm, it causes antisocial acts, acts against the social order.[44] In a feminist perspective, pornography is the essence of a sexist social order, its quintessential social act.

If pornography is an act of male supremacy, its harm is the harm of male supremacy made difficult to see because of its pervasiveness, potency, and success in making the world a pornographic place. Specifically, the harm cannot be discerned from the objective standpoint because it *is* so much of 'what is'. Women live in the world pornography creates. We live its lie as reality. As Naomi Scheman has said, 'Lies are what we have lived, not just what we have told, and no story about correspondence to what is real will enable us to distinguish the truth from the lie.'[45] So the issue is not whether pornography is harmful, but how the harm of pornography is to become visible. As compared with what? To the extent pornography succeeds in constructing social reality, it becomes *invisible as harm.* Any perception of the success, therefore the harm, of pornography, I will argue, is precluded by liberalism and so has been defined out of the customary approach taken to, and dominant values underlying, the First Amendment.

The theory of the First Amendment under which most pornography is protected from governmental restriction proceeds from liberal assumptions[46] that do not apply to the situation of women. First Amendment theory, like virtually all liberal legal theory, presumes the validity of the distinction between public and private: the 'role of law [is] to mark and guard the line between the sphere of social power, organized in the form of the state, and the area of private right'.[47] On this basis, courts distinguish between obscenity in public (which can be regulated, even if some attempts founder, seemingly in part *because* the presentations are public)[48] and the private possession of obscenity in the home.[49] The problem is that not only the public but also the private *is* a 'sphere of social power' of sexism. On paper and in life pornography is thrust upon unwilling women in their homes.[50] The distinction between public and private does not cut the same for women as for men.[51] It is men's right to inflict pornography upon women in private that is protected.

The liberal theory underlying First Amendment law further believes that free speech, including pornography, helps discover truth. Censorship restricts society to partial truths. So why are we now—with more pornography available than ever before—buried in all these lies? Laissez faire might be an adequate theory of the social preconditions for knowledge in a nonhierarchical society. But in a society of gender inequality, the speech of the powerful impresses its view upon the world, concealing the truth of powerlessness under that despairing acquiescence that provides the appearance of consent and makes protest inaudible as well as rare. Pornography can invent women because it has the power to make its vision into reality, which then passes, objectively, for truth. So while the First Amendment supports pornography, believing that consensus and progress are facilitated by allowing all views, however divergent and unorthodox, it fails to notice that pornography (like the racism, in which I include anti-Semitism, of the Nazis and the Klan) is not at all divergent or unorthodox. It is the ruling ideology. Feminism, the dissenting view, is suppressed by pornography. Thus, while defenders of pornography argue that allowing all speech, including pornography, frees the mind to fulfill itself, pornography freely enslaves women's minds and bodies inseparably, normalizing the terror that enforces silence from women's point of view.

To liberals, speech must never be sacrificed for other social goals.[52] But liberalism has never understood that the free speech of men silences the free speech of women. It is the same social goal, just other *people*. This is what a real inequality, a real conflict, a real disparity in social power looks like. The law of the First Amendment comprehends that freedom of expression, in the abstract, is a system, but it fails to comprehend that sexism (and racism), *in the concrete*, are also systems. That pornography chills women's expression is difficult to demonstrate empirically because silence is not eloquent. Yet on no more of the same kind of evidence, the argument that suppressing pornography might chill legitimate speech has supported its protection.

First Amendment logic, like nearly all legal reasoning, has difficulty grasping harm that is not linearly caused in the 'John hit Mary' sense. The idea is that words or pictures can be harmful only if they produce harm in a form that is considered an action. Words work in the province of attitudes, actions in the realm of behavior. Words cannot constitute harm in themselves—never mind libel, invasion of privacy, blackmail, bribery, conspiracy or most sexual harassment. But which is saying 'kill' to a trained guard dog, a word or an act? Which is its training? How about a sign that reads 'Whites only'? Is that the idea or the practice of segregation? Is a woman raped by an attitude or a behavior? Which is sexual arousal? Notice that the specific idea of causality used in obscenity law dates from around the time that it was first 'proved' that it is impossible to prove that pornography causes harm.[53] Instead of the more complex causality implicit in the above examples, the view became that pornography must cause harm the way negligence causes car accidents or its effects are not cognizable as harm. The trouble with this individuated, atomistic, linear, isolated, tortlike—in a word, positivistic—conception of injury is that the way pornography targets and defines women for abuse and discrimination does not work like this. It does hurt individuals, not *as* individuals in a one-at-a-time sense, but as members of the group 'women'. Harm is caused to one individual woman rather than another essentially the way one number rather than another is caused in roulette. But on a group basis, as women, the selection process is absolutely selective and systematic. Its causality is essentially collective and totalistic and contextual. To reassert atomistic linear causality as a sine qua non of injury—you cannot be harmed unless you are harmed through this etiology—is to refuse to respond to the true nature of this specific kind of harm. Such a refusal calls for explanation. Morton Horowitz says that the issue of causality in tort law is 'one of the pivotal ideas in a system of legal thought that sought to separate private law from politics and to insulate the legal system from the threat of redistribution'.[54] Perhaps causality in the pornography issue is an attempt to privatize the injury pornography does to women in order to insulate the same system from the threat of gender equality, also a form of redistribution.

Women are known to be brutally coerced into pornographic performances.[55] But so far it is only with children, usually male children, that courts consider that the speech of pornographers was once someone else's *life*.[56] Courts and commissions and legislatures and researchers have searched and re-searched, largely in vain, for the injury of pornography in the mind of the (male) consumer or in 'society', or in empirical correlations between variations in levels of 'antisocial' acts and liberalization in obscenity laws.[57] Speech can be regulated 'in the interests of unwilling viewers, captive audiences, young children, and beleaguered neighborhoods',[58] but the normal level of sexual force—force that is not seen as force because it is inflicted on women and called sex—has never been a policy issue. Until the last few years experimental research never approached the question of whether pornographic stimuli might support *sexual* aggression against women[59] or whether violence might be sexually stimulating or have sexual sequelae.[60] Only in the last few months have laboratory researchers begun to learn the consequences for women of so-called consensual sexual depictions that show normal dominance and submission.[61] We still don't have this kind of data on the impact of female-only nudity or of depictions of specific acts like penetration or even of mutual sex in a social context of gender inequality.

The most basic assumption underlying First Amendment adjudication is that, socially, speech is free. The First Amendment says, 'Congress shall not abridge *the freedom of speech*.' Free speech exists. The problem for government is to avoid constraining that which, if unconstrained by government, *is* free. This tends to presuppose that whole segments of the population are not systematically silenced *socially*, prior to government action. The place of pornography in the inequality of the sexes makes such a presupposition untenable and makes any approach to *our* freedom of expression so based worse than useless. For women, the urgent issue of freedom of speech is not primarily the avoidance of state intervention as such, but finding an affirmative means to get access to speech for those to whom it has been denied.

Beyond offensiveness or prurience, to say that pornography is 'dehumanizing' is an attempt to articulate its harm. But 'human being' is a social concept with many possible meanings. Here I will criticize some liberal moral meanings of personhood through a feminist political analysis of what pornography does to women, showing how the inadequacy of the liberal dehumanization critique reflects the inadequacy of its concept of person. In a feminist perspective, pornography dehumanizes women in a culturally specific and empirically descriptive—not liberal moral—sense. Pornography dispossesses women of the power of which, in the same act, it possesses men: the power of sexual, hence gender, definition. Perhaps a human being, for gender purposes, is someone who controls the social definition of sexuality.

A person, in one Kantian view, is a free and rational agent whose existence is an end in itself, as opposed to instrumental.[62] In pornography women exist to the *end* of male pleasure. Kant sees human as characterized by universal abstract rationality, with no component of individual or group differences, and as a 'bundle of rights'.[63] Pornography purports to define what a woman *is*. It does this on a group basis, including when it raises individual qualities to sexual stereotypes, as in the strategy of *Playboy's* 'Playmate of the Month'. I also think that pornography derives much of its sexual power, as well as part of its justification, from the implicit assumption that the Kantian notion of person actually describes the condition of women in this society. According to that assumption, if we are there, we are freely and rationally there, when the fact is that women—in pornography and in part because of pornography—have no such rights.

Other views of the person include one of Wittgenstein's, who says that the best picture of the human soul is the human body.[64] I guess this depends upon what picture of the human body you have in mind. Marx's work offers various concepts of personhood deducible from his critique of various forms of productive organization. A person is defined by whatever material conditions the society values; in a bourgeois society, a person might be a property owner.[65] The problem here is that women *are* the property that constitutes the personhood, the masculinity, of men under capitalism. Thinking further in marxian theoretical terms, I have wondered whether women in pornography are more properly conceived as fetishes or objects. Does pornography more attribute lifelikeness to that which is dead, as in fetishism—or make deathlike that which is alive—as in objectification? I guess it depends upon whether, socially speaking, women are more alive than dead.

In Hume's concept of a person as a bundle or collection of sense perceptions, such that the feeling of self-identity over time is a persistent illusion,[66] we finally have a view of the human that coincides with the view of women in pornography. That is, the empiricist view of person is the pornographic view of women. No critique of dominance or subjection, certainly not of objectification, can be grounded in a vision of reality in which all sense perceptions are just sense perceptions. This is one way an objectivist epistemology supports the unequal holding and wielding of power in a society in which the persistent illusion of selfhood of one half of the population is materially supported and maintained at the expense of the other half. What I'm saying is that those who are socially allowed a self are also allowed the luxury of postulating its illusoriness and having that called a philosophical position. Whatever self they ineluctably have, they don't lose by saying it is an illusion. Even if it is not particularly explanatory, such male ideology, if taken as such, is often highly descriptive. Thus Hume defines the human in the same terms feminism uses to define women's dehumanization: for women in pornography, the self is, precisely, a persistent illusion.

Contemporary ordinary language philosopher Bernard Williams says 'person' ordinarily means things like valuing self-respect and feeling pain.[67] How self is defined, what respect attaches to, stimuli of pleasure and to an extent stimuli and thresholds of pain, are cultural variables. Women in pornography are turned on by being put down and feel pain as pleasure. We want it; we beg for it; we get it. To argue that this is dehumanizing need not mean to take respect as an ahistorical absolute or to treat the social meaning of pain as invariant or uniformly negative. Rather, it is to argue that it is the acceptance of the social definition of these values—the acceptance of self-respect and the avoidance of pain as values—that permits the erotization of their negative—debasement and torture—in pornography. It is only to the extent that each of these values is *accepted as human* that their negation becomes a quality of, and is eroticized in and as, woman. Only when self-respect is accepted as human does debasement become sexy and female; only when the avoidance of pain is accepted as human does torture become sexy and female. In this way, women's sexuality as expressed in pornography precisely negates her status as human. But there is more: exactly what is defined as degrading to a human being, *however* that is socially defined, is exactly what is sexually arousing to the male point of view in pornography, just as the one to whom it is done is the girl regardless of sex. In this way, it is specifically women whom pornography identifies with and by sexuality, as the erotic is equated with the dehumanizing.

To define the pornographic as that which is violent, not sexual, as liberal moral analyses tend to, is to trivialize and evade the essence of this critique, while seeming to express it. As with rape, where the issue is not the presence or absence of force but what sex *is* as distinct from coercion,[68] the question for pornography is what eroticism *is* as distinct from the subordination of women. This is not a rhetorical question. Under male dominance, whatever sexually arouses a man is sex. In pornography the violence *is* the sex. The inequality is the sex. Pornography does not work sexually without hierarchy. If there is no inequality, no violation, no dominance, no force, there is no sexual arousal.[69] Obscenity law does the pornographers a real favor by clouding this, pornography's central dynamic, under the coy gender-neutral abstraction of 'prurient interest'. Obscenity law also adds the attraction of state prohibition, a tool of dominance, to whatever the law of obscenity is seen to encompass.

Calling rape and pornography violent, not sexual, the banner of much antirape and antipornography organizing,[70] is an attempt to protest that women do not find rape pleasurable or pornography stimulating while avoiding claiming this rejection as *women's* point of view. The concession to the objective stance, the attempt to achieve credibility by covering up the specificity of one's viewpoint, not only abstracts from our experience, it lies about it. Women and men know men find rape sexual and pornography erotic. It therefore *is*. We also know that sexuality is commonly violent without being any the less sexual. To deny this sets up the situation so that when women are aroused by sexual violation, meaning we experience it *as* our sexuality, the feminist analysis is seen to be contradicted. But it is not contradicted, it is *proved*. The male supremacist definition of female sexuality as lust for self-annihilation has won. It would be surprising, feminist analysis would be wrong, and sexism would be trivial, if this were merely exceptional. (One might ask at this point, not why some women embrace explicit sadomasochism, but why any women do not.) To reject forced sex in the name of women's point of view requires an account of women's experience of being violated by the same acts both sexes have learned as natural and fulfilling and erotic, since no critique, no alternatives, and few transgressions have been permitted.

The depersonalization critique, with the 'violence not sex' critique, exposes pornography's double standard but does not attack the masculinity of the standards for personhood and for sex that pornography sets. The critiques are thus useful, to some extent deconstructive, but beg the deeper questions of the place of pornography in sexuality and of sexuality in the construction of women's definition and status, because they act as if women can be 'persons' by interpretation, as if the concept is not, in every socially real way, defined by and in terms of and reserved for men and as if sexuality is not itself a construct of male power. To do this is to act as if pornography did not exist or were impotent. Deeper than the personhood question or the violence question is the question of the mechanism of social causation by which pornography *constructs* women and sex, defines what 'woman' means and what sexuality is, in terms of each other.

The law of obscenity at times says that sexual expression is only talk, therefore cannot be intrinsically harmful. Yet somehow pornographic talk is vital to protect. If pornography is a practice of the ideology[71] of gender inequality, and gender *is an ideology*, if pornography is sex and gender is sexual, the question of the relation between pornography and life is nothing less than the question of the dynamic of the subordination of women to men. It 'objectification . . . is never trivial',[72] girls *are* ruined by books.[73] To comprehend this process will require an entirely new theory of social causality—of ideology in life, of the dynamic of mind and body in social power—that connects point of view with politics. The development of such an analysis has been stymied equally by fear of repressive state use of any critique of any form of expression, by the power of pornography to create women in its image of use, and by the power of pornographers to create a climate hostile to inquiry into their power and profits.

I said all that in order to say this: the law of obscenity has the same surface theme and the same underlying theme as pornography itself. Superficially both involve morality: rules made and transgressed for purposes of sexual arousal. Actually, both are about power, about the equation between the erotic and the control of women by men: *women* made and transgressed for purposes of sexual arousal. It seems essential to the kick of pornography that it be to some degree against the rules, but it is never truly unavailable or truly illegitimate. Thus obscenity law, like the law of rape, preserves the value of, without restricting the ability to get, that which it purports to both devalue and to prohibit. Obscenity law helps keep pornography sexy by putting state power—force, hierarchy—behind its purported prohibition on what men can have sexual access to. The law of obscenity is to pornography as pornography is to sex: a map that purports to be a mirror, a legitimization and authorization and set of directions and guiding controls that project themselves onto social reality while claiming merely to reflect the image of what is already there. Pornography presents itself as fantasy or illusion or idea, which can be good or bad as it is accurate or inaccurate, while it actually, *hence accurately*, distributes power. Liberal morality cannot deal with illusions that *constitute* reality because its theory of reality, lacking a substantive critique of the distribution of social power, cannot get behind the empirical world, truth by correspondence. On the surface, both pornography and the law of obscenity are about sex. In fact, it is the status of women that is at stake.

Notes

Many of the ideas in this essay were developed and refined in close collaboration with Andrea Dworkin. It is difficult at times to distinguish the contribution of each of us to a body of work that—through shared teaching, writing, speaking, organizing, and political action on every level—has been created together. I have tried to credit specific contributions that I am aware are distinctly hers. This text is mine; she does not necessarily agree with everything in it.

1. This speech as a whole is intended to communicate what I mean by pornography. The key work on the subject is Andrea Dworkin, *Pornography: Men Possessing Women* (1981). No definition can convey the meaning of a word as well as its use in context can. However, what Andrea Dworkin and I mean by pornography is rather well captured in our legal definition: 'Pornography is the graphic sexually explicit subordination of women, whether in pictures or in words, that also includes one or more of the following: (i) women are presented dehumanized as sexual objects, things or commodities; or (ii) women are presented as sexual objects who enjoy pain or humiliation; or (iii) women are presented as sexual objects who experience sexual pleasure in being raped; or (iv) women are presented as sexual objects tied up or cut up or mutilated or bruised or physically hurt; or (v) women are presented in postures of sexual submission, servility or display; or (vi) women's body parts—including but not limited to vaginas, breasts, and buttocks—are exhibited,

such that women are reduced to those parts; or (vii) women are presented as whores by nature; or (viii) women are presented being penetrated by objects or animals; or (ix) women are presented in scenarios of degradation, injury, torture, shown as filthy or inferior, bleeding, bruised, or hurt in a context that makes these conditions sexual.' Pornography also includes 'the use of men, children or transsexuals in the place of women'. Pornography, thus defined, is discrimination on the basis of sex and, as such, a civil rights violation. This definition is a slightly modified version of the one passed by the Minneapolis City Council on 30 December 1983. Minneapolis, Minn., Ordinance amending tit. 7, chs. 139 and 141, Minneapolis Code of Ordinances Relating to Civil Rights (30 Dec. 1983). The ordinance was vetoed by the mayor, reintroduced, passed again, and vetoed again in 1984. See 'Francis Biddle's Sister', in Catharine A. MacKinnon, *Feminism Unmodified: Discourses on Life and Law* (1987), for subsequent developments.

2. 'Congress shall make no law . . . abridging the freedom of speech, or of the press . . .' US Const. amend. I.
3. Justice Black, at times joined by Justice Douglas, took the position that the Bill of Rights, including the First Amendment, was 'absolute'. Hugo Black, 'The Bill of Rights', 35 *New York University Law Review* 865, 867 (1960): Edmund Cahn, 'Justice Black and First Amendment "Absolutes": A Public Interview', 37 *New York University Law Review* 549 (1962). For a discussion, see Harry Kalven, 'Upon Rereading Mr. Justice Black on the First Amendment', 14 *UCLA Law Review* 428 (1967). For one exchange in the controversy surrounding the 'absolute' approach to the First Amendment, as opposed to the 'balancing' approach, see e.g. W. Mendelson, 'On the Meaning of the First Amendment: Absolutes in the Balance', 50 *California Law Review* 821 (1962); L. Frantz, 'The First Amendment in the Balance', 71 *Yale Law Journal* 1424 (1962); Frantz, 'Is the First Amendment Law?—A Reply to Professor Mendelson', 51 *California Law Review* 729 (1963); Mendelson, 'The First Amendment and the Judicial Process: A Reply to Mr. Frantz', 17 *Vanderbilt Law Review* 479 (1964). In the pornography context, see e.g. *Roth* v. *United States*, 354 U.S. 476, 514 (1957) (Douglas, J., joined by Black, J., dissenting); *Smith* v. *California*, 361 U.S. 147, 155 (1959) (Black, J., concurring); *Miller* v *California*, 413 U.S. 15, 37 (1973) (Douglas, J., dissenting). The purpose of this discourse is not to present a critique of absolutism as such, but rather to identify and criticize some widely and deeply shared implicit beliefs that underlie both the absolutist view and the more mainstream flexible approaches.
4. The history of obscenity law can be read as a failed attempt to make this separation, with the failure becoming ever more apparent from the *Redrup* decision forward. *Redrup* v. *New York*, 386 U.S. 767 (1967). For a summary of cases exemplifying such a trend, see the dissent by Justice Brennan in *Paris Adult Theatre I* v. *Slaton*, 413 U.S. 49, 73 (1973).
5. Much has been made of the distinction between sex and gender. Sex is thought the more biological, gender the more social. The relation of sexuality to each varies. See e.g. Robert Stoller, *Sex and Gender* 9–10 (1974). Since I think that the importance of biology to the condition of women is the social meaning attributed to it, biology *is* its social meaning for purposes of analyzing the inequality of the sexes, a political condition. I therefore tend to use sex and gender relatively interchangeably.

6. The sense in which I mean women's perspective as different from men's is like that of Virginia Woolf's reference to 'the difference of view, the difference of standard' in her 'George Eliot', 1 *Collected Essays* 204 (1966). Neither of us uses the notion of a gender difference to refer to something biological or natural or transcendental or existential. Perspective parallels standards because the social experience of gender is confined by gender. See Catharine A. MacKinnon, *Sexual Harassment of Working Women* 107–41 (1979), and the articles mentioned in note 11, below; Virginia Woolf, *Three Guineas* (1938); see also Andrea Dworkin, 'The Root Cause', in *Our Blood: Essays and Discourses on Sexual Politics* 96 (1976). I do not refer to the gender difference here descriptively, leaving its roots and implications unspecified, so they could be biological, existential, transcendental, in any sense inherent, or social but necessary. I mean 'point of view' as a view, hence a standard, that is imposed on women by force of sex inequality, which is a political condition. 'Male', which is an adjective here, is a social and political concept, not a biological attribute; it is a status socially conferred upon a person because of a condition of birth. As I use 'male', it has nothing whatever to do with inherency, preexistence, nature, inevitability, or body as such. Because it is in the interest of men to be male in the system we live under (male being powerful as well as human), they seldom question its rewards or even see it as a status at all.
7. Criminal Code, Can. Rev. Stat. chap. c-34, § 159(2)(c) and (d) (1970). *People* v. *Sanger*, 222 N.Y. 192, 118 N.E. 637 (1918).
8. *The Report of the Commission on Obscenity and Pornography* (1970) (majority report). The accuracy of the commission's findings is called into question by: (1) widespread criticism of the commission's methodology from a variety of perspectives, e.g. L. Sunderland, *Obscenity—The Court, the Congress and the President's Commission* (1975); Edward Donnerstein, 'Pornography Commission Revisited: Aggression—Erotica and Violence against Women', 39 *Journal of Personality and Social Psychology* 269 (1980); Ann Garry, 'Pornography and Respect for Women', 4 *Social Theory and Practice* 395 (Summer 1978); Irene Diamond, 'Pornography and Repression', 5 *Signs: A Journal of Women in Culture and Society* 686 (1980); Victor Cline, 'Another View: Pornography Effects, the State of the Art', in *Where Do You Draw the Line?* (V. B. Cline ed. 1974); Pauline Bart and Margaret Jozsa, 'Dirty Books, Dirty Films, and Dirty Data', in *Take Back the Night: Women on Pornography* 204 (Laura Lederer ed. 1982); (2) the commission's tendency to minimize the significance of its own findings, e.g. those by Donald Mosher on the differential effects of exposure by gender; and (3) the design of the commission's research. The commission did not focus on questions about gender, did its best to eliminate 'violence' from its materials (so as not to overlap with the Violence Commission), and propounded unscientific theories such as Puritan guilt to explain women's negative responses to the materials.

   Further, scientific causality is unnecessary to legally validate an obscenity regulation: 'But, it is argued, there is no scientific data which conclusively demonstrate that exposure to obscene materials adversely affects men and women or their society. It is [urged] that, absent such a demonstration, any kind of state regulation is "impermissible." *We reject this argument.* It is not for us to resolve empirical uncertainties underlying state legislation, save in the exceptional case where that legislation plainly impinges upon rights protected by the Constitution itself . . . Although there is no conclusive proof of a connection between antisocial behavior and obscene material, the legislature of Georgia could quite reasonably determine that such a connection does or might exist.' *Paris Adult Theatre I* v. *Slaton*, 413 U.S. 49, 60–61 (1973) (Burger, J., for the majority) (emphasis added); see also *Roth* v. *US*, 354 U.S. 476, 501 (1957).

9. Some of the harm of pornography to women, as defined in note 1 above, and as discussed in this talk, has been documented in empirical studies. Recent studies have found that exposure to pornography increases the willingness of normal men to aggress against women under laboratory conditions; makes both women and men substantially less able to perceive accounts of rape as accounts of rape; makes normal men more closely resemble convicted rapists psychologically; increases attitudinal measures that are known to correlate with rape, such as hostility toward women, propensity to rape, condoning rape, and predictions that one would rape or force sex on a woman if one knew one would not get caught; and produces other attitude changes in men, such as increasing the extent of their trivialization, dehumanization, and objectification of women. Diana E. H. Russell, 'Pornography and Violence: What Does the New Research Say?' in Lederer, note 8 above, at 216; Neil M. Malamuth and Edward Donnerstein (eds.), *Pornography and Sexual Aggression* (1984); Dolph Zillman, *The Connection between Sex and Aggression* (1984); J. V. P. Check, N. Malamuth, and R. Stille, 'Hostility to Women Scale' (1983) (unpublished manuscript); Edward Donnerstein, 'Pornography: Its Effects on Violence against Women', in Malamuth and Donnerstein (eds.), *Pornography and Sexual Aggression* (1984); Neil M. Malamuth and J. V P. Check, 'The Effects of Mass Media Exposure on Acceptance of Violence against Women: A Field Experiment', 15 *Journal of Research in Personality* 436 (1981); Neil M. Malamuth, 'Rape Proclivities among Males', 37 *Journal of Social Issues* 138 (1981); Neil M. Malamuth and Barry Spinner, 'A Longitudinal Content Analysis of Sexual Violence in the Best-Selling Erotic Magazines', 16 *Journal of Sex Research* 226 (1980); Mosher, 'Sex Callousness Towards Women', in 8 *Technical Report of the Commission on Obscenity and Pornography* 313 (1971); Dolph Zillman and J. Bryant, 'Effects of Massive Exposure to Pornography', in Malamuth and Donnerstein (eds.), *Pornography and Sexual Aggression* (1984).

10. The following are illustrative, not exhaustive, of the body of work I term the 'feminist critique of pornography'. Andrea Dworkin, note 1 above; Dorchen Leidholdt, 'Where Pornography Meets Fascism', *Win*, 15 Mar. 1983, at 18; George Steiner, 'Night Words', in *The Case Against Pornography* 227 (D. Holbrook ed. 1973); Susan Brownmiller, *Against Our Will: Men, Women and Rape* 394 (1975); Robin Morgan, 'Pornography and Rape: Theory and Practice', in *Going Too Far* 165 (Robin Morgan ed. 1977); Kathleen Barry, *Female Sexual Slavery* (1979); *Against Sado-Masochism: A Radical Feminist Analysis* (R. R. Linden, D. R. Pagano, D. E. H. Russell, and S. L. Star eds. 1982), especially chapters by Ti-Grace Atkinson, Judy Butler, Andrea Dworkin, Alice Walker, John Stoltenberg, Audre Lorde, and Susan Leigh Star; Alice Walker, 'Coming Apart', in Lederer, *Take Back the Night*, note 8 above, and other articles in that volume with the exception of the legal ones; Gore Vidal, 'Women's Liberation Meets the Miller–Mailer–Manson Man', in *Homage to Daniel Shays: Collected*

Essays 1952–1972 389 (1972); Linda Lovelace and Michael McGrady, *Ordeal* (1980). Works basic to the perspective taken here are Kate Millett, *Sexual Politics* (1969) and Florence Rush, *The Best-Kept Secret: Sexual Abuse of Children* (1980). 'Violent Pornography: Degradation of Women versus Right of Free Speech', 8 *New York University Review of Law and Social Change* 181(1978) contains both feminist and nonfeminist arguments.

11. For more extensive discussions of this subject, see my prior work, especially 'Feminism, Marxism, Method and the State: An Agenda for Theory', 7 *Signs: Journal of Women in Culture and Society* 515 (1982) (hereinafter cited as Signs I); 'Feminism, Marxism, Method and the State: Toward Feminist Jurisprudence', 8 *Signs: Journal of Women in Culture and Society* 635 (1983) (hereinafter cited as *Signs* II).
12. *Jacobellis* v. *Ohio*, 378 U.S. 184, 197 (1964) (Stewart, J., concurring).
13. Justice Stewart is said to have complained that this single line was more quoted and remembered than anything else he ever said.
14. *See Signs* I, note 11 above.
15. Susan Griffin, *Pornography and Silence: Culture's Revenge Against Nature* 2–4, 251–65 (1981).
16. Dworkin, note 1 above.
17. See also Dworkin, note 6 above.
18. The position that pornography is sex—that whatever you think of sex you think of pornography—underlies nearly every treatment of the subject. In particular, nearly every nonfeminist treatment proceeds on the implicit or explicit assumption, argument, criticism, or suspicion that pornography is sexually liberating in some way, a position unifying an otherwise diverse literature. See e.g. D. H. Lawrence, 'Pornography and Obscenity', in his *Sex, Literature and Censorship* 64 (1959); Hugh Hefner, 'The Playboy Philosophy', *Playboy*, December 1962, at 73, and *Playboy*, February 1963, at 43; Henry Miller, 'Obscenity and the Law of Reflection', in his *Remember to Remember* 274, 286 (1947); Deirdre English, 'The Politics of Porn: Can Feminists Walk the Line?' *Mother Jones*, Apr. 1980, at 20; Jean Bethke Elshtain, 'The Victim Syndrome: A Troubling Turn in Feminism', *The Progressive*, June 1982, at 42. To choose an example at random: 'In opposition to the Victorian view that narrowly defines proper sexual function in a rigid way that is analogous to ideas of excremental regularity and moderation, pornography builds a model of plastic variety and joyful excess in sexuality. In opposition to the sorrowing Catholic dismissal of sexuality as an unfortunate and spiritually superficial concomitant of propagation, pornography affords the alternative idea of the independent status of sexuality as a profound and shattering ecstasy.' David Richards, 'Free Speech and Obscenity Law: Toward a Moral Theory of the First Amendment', 123 *University of Pennsylvania Law Review* 45, 81 (1974) (footnotes omitted). See also F. Schauer, 'Response: Pornography and the First Amendment', 40 *University of Pittsburgh Law Review* 605, 616 (1979).
19. Spending time around adult bookstores, attending pornographic movies, and talking with pornographers (who, like all smart pimps, do some form of market research), as well as analyzing the pornography itself in sex gender terms, all confirm that pornography is for men. That women may attend or otherwise consume it does not make it any less for men, any more than the observation that mostly men consume pornography means that pornography

does not harm women. See Martha Langelan, 'The Political Economy of Pornography', *Aegis: Magazine on Ending Violence against Women*, Autumn 1981, at 5; J. Cook, 'The X-Rated Economy', *Forbes*, 18 Sept. 1978, at 60. Personal observation reveals that most women tend to avoid pornography as much as possible—which is not very much, as it turns out.

20. The 'fantasy' and 'catharsis' hypotheses, together, assert that pornography cathects sexuality on the level of fantasy fulfillment. The work of Edward Donnerstein, particularly, shows that the opposite is true. The more pornography is viewed, the *more* pornography—and the more brutal pornography—is both wanted and required for sexual arousal. What occurs is not catharsis, but desensitization, requiring progressively more potent stimulation. See works cited note 9 above; Murray Straus, 'Leveling, Civility, and Violence in the Family', 36 *Journal of Marriage & The Family* 13 (1974).
21. Lovelace and McGrady, note 10 above, provide an account by one coerced pornography model. See also Andrea Dworkin, 'Pornography's "Exquisite Volunteers"', *Ms.*, March 1981, at 65.
22. However, for one such inquiry, see Russell, note 9 above, at 228: a random sample of 930 San Francisco households found that 10 per cent of women had at least once 'been upset by anyone trying to get you to do what they'd seen in pornographic pictures, movies or books'. Obviously, this figure could only include those who knew that pornography was the source of the sex, so this finding is conservative. See also Diana E. H. Russell, *Rape in Marriage* 27–41 (1983) (discussing the data base). The hearings Andrea and I held for the Minneapolis City Council on the ordinance cited in note 1 produced many accounts of the use of pornography to force sex on women and children. *Public Hearings on Ordinances to Add Pornography as Discrimination against Women*, Committee on Government Operations, City Council, Minneapolis, Minn., 12–13 Dec. 1983 (hereinafter cited as *Hearings*).
23. See *Signs* I; see also Susan Sontag, 'The Pornographic Imagination', 34 *Partisan Review* 181 (1977).
24. 'Explicitness' of accounts is a central issue in both obscenity adjudications and audience access standards adopted voluntarily by self-regulated industries or by boards of censor. See e.g. *Grove Press* v. *Christenberry*, 175 F. Supp. 488, 489 (S.D.N.Y. 1959) (discussion of 'candor' and 'realism'); *Grove Press* v. *Christenberry*, 276 F.2d 433, 438 (2d Cir. 1960) ('directness'); *Mitchum* v. *State*, 251 So.2d 298, 302 (Fla. Dist. Ct. App. 1971) ('show it all'); *Kaplan* v. *California*, 413 U.S. 115, 118 (1973). How *much* sex the depiction shows is implicitly thereby correlated with how *sexual* (that is, how sexually arousing to the male) the material is. See e.g. *Memoirs* v. *Massachusetts*, 383 U.S. 413, 460 (1966) (White, J., dissenting); Richard Heffner, 'What G, PG, R and X Really Means', 126 *Cong. Rec.* 172 (daily ed. 8 Dec. 1980); *Report of the Committee on Obscenity and Film Censorship* (the Williams Report) (1981). Andrea Dworkin brilliantly gives the reader the experience of this aesthetic in her account of the pornography. Dworkin, note 1 above, at 25–47.
25. To the body of law ably encompassed and footnoted by William Lockhart and Robert McClure, 'Literature, the Law of Obscenity and the Constitution', 38 *Minnesota Law Review* 295 (1954) and 'Censorship of Obscenity', 45 *Minnesota Law Review* 5 (1960), I add only the most important cases since then: *Stanley* v. *Georgia*, 394 U.S. 557 (1969); *US* v. *Reidel*, 402 U.S. 351 (1970); *Miller*

v. *California*, 413 U.S. 15 (1973); *Paris Adult Theatre I* v *Slaton*, 413 U.S. 49 (1973); *Hamling* v. *US*, 418 U.S. 87 (1973); *Jenkins* v. *Georgia*, 418 U.S. 153 (1973); *US* v. *12 200-Ft. Reels of Super 8mm Film*, 413 U.S. 123 (1973); *Erznoznik* v. *City of Jacksonville*, 422 U.S. 205 (1975); *Splawn* v. *California*, 431 U.S. 595 (1976); *Ward* v. *Illinois*, 431 U.S. 767 (1976); *Lovisi* v. *Slayton*, 539 F.2d 349 (4th Cir. 1976). See also *New York* v. *Ferber*, 458 U.S. 747 (1982).

26. For a discussion of the role of the law of privacy in supporting the existence of pornography, see Ruth Colker, 'Pornography and Privacy: Towards the Development of a Group Based Theory for Sex Based Intrusions of Privacy', 1 *Law and Inequality: A Journal of Theory and Practice* 191 (1983).
27. Louis Henkin, 'Morals and the Constitution: The Sin of Obscenity', 63 *Columbia Law Review* 391, 395 (1963).
28. These parallels are discussed more fully in *Signs* II. It may seem odd to denominate 'moral' as *female* here, since this article discusses male morality. Under male supremacy, men define things; I am describing that. Men define women *as* 'moral'. This is the male view of women. My analysis, a feminist critique of the male standpoint, terms 'moral' the concept that pornography is about good and evil. This is *my* analysis of *them*, as contrasted with their attributions to women.
29. A reading of case law supports the reports in Robert Woodward and Scott Armstrong, *The Brethren* 194 (1979), to the effect that this is a 'bottom line' criterion for at least some justices. The interesting question becomes why the tactics of male supremacy would change from keeping the penis hidden, covertly glorified, to having it everywhere on display, overtly glorified. This suggests at least that a major shift from private terrorism to public terrorism has occurred. What used to be perceived as a danger to male power, the exposure of the penis, has now become a strategy in maintaining it.
30. One possible reading of Lockhart and McClure, note 25 above, is that this was their agenda, and that their approach was substantially adopted in the third prong of the *Miller* doctrine. For the law's leading attempt to grapple with this issue, see *Memoirs* v. *Massachusetts*, 383 U.S. 413 (1966), *overruled in part*, *Miller* v. *California*, 413 U.S. 15 (1973). See also *US* v. *Ulysses*, 5 F. Supp. 182 (S.D.N.Y. 1933), *aff'd* 72 F.2d 705 (2d Cir. 1934).
31. Andrea Dworkin and I developed this analysis in our class 'Pornography' at the University of Minnesota Law School, Fall 1983. See also Dworkin, 'Why So-Called Radical Men Love and Need Pornography', in Lederer, note 8 above, at 141 (the issue of pornography is an issue of sexual access to women, hence involves a fight among men).
32. Those termed 'fathers' and 'sons' in Dworkin's article, note 31 above, we came to call 'the old boys', whose strategy for male dominance involves keeping pornography and the abuse of women private, and 'the new boys', whose strategy for male dominance involves making pornography and the abuse of women public. In my view Freud and the popularization of his derepression hypothesis figure centrally in 'the new boys'' approach and success. To conclude, as some have, that women have benefited from the public availability of pornography and hence should be grateful for and have a stake in its continuing availability is to say that the merits of open condoned oppression relative to covert condoned oppression warrant its continuation. This reasoning obscures the possibility of *ending* the oppression. The benefit of pornography's

open availability, it seems to me, is that women can know who and what we are dealing with in order to end it. How, is the question.

33. *Miller* v. *California*, 413 U.S. 15, 24 (1973).
34. *Paris Adult Theatre I* v. *Slaton*, 413 U.S. 49, 67 (1973). See also *Miller* v. *California*, 413 U.S. 15, 25 n.7 ('A quotation from Voltaire in the flyleaf of a book will not constitutionally redeem an otherwise obscene publication,' quoting *Kois* v. *Wisconsin*, 408 U.S. 229, 231 [1972]).
35. *Penthouse International* v. *McAuliffe*, 610 F.2d 1353, 1362–73 (5th Cir. 1980). For a study in enforcement, see *Coble* v. *City of Birmingham*, 389 So.2d 527 (Ala. Ct. App. 1980).
36. Malamuth and Spinner, note 9 above (' . . . the portrayal of sexual aggression within such "legitimate" magazines as *Playboy* and *Penthouse* may have a greater impact than similar portrayals in hard-core pornography'); Neil M. Malamuth and Edward Donnerstein, 'The Effects of Aggressive-Pornographic Mass Media Stimuli', 15 *Advances in Experimental Social Psychology* 103, 130 (1982).
37. Some courts, under the obscenity rubric, seem to have understood that the quality of artistry does not undo the damage. *People* v. *Mature Enterprises*, 343 N.Y.S.2d 911, 925 n.14 (N.Y. Sup. 1973) ('This court will not adopt a rule of law which states that obscenity is suppressible but that well-written or technically well produced obscenity is not,' quoting, in part, *People* v. *Fritch*, 13 N.Y.2d 119, 126, 243 N.Y.S.2d 1, 7, 192 N.E.2d 713 [1963]). More to the point of my argument here is Justice O'Connor's observation that '[t]he compelling interests identified in today's opinion . . . suggest that the Constitution might in fact permit New York to ban knowing distribution of works depicting minors engaged in explicit sexual conduct, regardless of the social value of the depictions. For example, a 12-year-old child photographed while masturbating surely suffers the same psychological harm whether the community labels the photograph "edifying" or "tasteless". The audience's appreciation of the depiction is simply irrelevant to New York's asserted interest in protecting children from psychological, emotional, and mental harm.' *New York* v. *Ferber*, 458 U.S. 747, 774–75 (1982) (concurring). Put another way, how does it make a harmed child *not harmed* that what was produced by harming him is great art?
38. Women typically get mentioned in obscenity law only in the phrase, 'women and men', used as a synonym for 'people.' At the same time, exactly who the victim of pornography is, has long been a great mystery. The few references to 'exploitation' in obscenity litigation do not evoke a woman victim. For example, one reference to 'a system of commercial exploitation of people with sadomasochistic sexual aberrations' concerned the customers of women dominatrixes, all of whom were men. *State* v. *Von Cleef*, 102 N.J. Super. 104, 245 A.2d 495, 505 (1968). The children at issue in *Ferber* were boys. Similarly, Justice Frankfurter invoked the 'sordid exploitation of man's nature and impulses' in discussing his conception of pornography in *Kingsley Pictures Corp.* v. *Regents*, 360 U.S. 684, 692 (1958).
39. *Miller* v. *California*, 413 U.S. 15, 24 (1973).
40. See e.g. *Miller* v. *California*, id. at 40–41 (Douglas, J., dissenting) ('What shocks me may be sustenance for my neighbors'); *US* v. *12 200-Ft. Reels of Super 8mm Film*, 413 U.S. 123, 137 (1972) (Douglas, J., dissenting) ('[W]hat may be trash to me may be prized by others'); *Cohen* v. *California*, 403 U.S. 15, 25

(1970) (Harlan, J.) ('One man's vulgarity is another's lyric'); *Winters* v. *New York*, 333 U.S. 507, 510 (1947) ('What is one man's amusement, teaches another's doctrine'); Lawrence, note 18 above, at 195 ('What is pornography to one man is the laughter of genius to another'); *Ginzburg* v. *United States*, 383 U.S. 463, 489 (1966) (Douglas, J., dissenting) ('Some like Chopin, others like "rock and roll"'). As one man, the pimp who forced Linda Lovelace into pornography, said to another: 'I don't tell you how to write your column. Don't tell me how to treat my broads.' (Quoted in Gloria Steinem, 'The Real Linda Lovelace,' in *Outrageous Acts and Everyday Rebellions* 243, 252 [1983].)

41. For the resolution of this issue for nonconventional sexuality, see *Mishkin* v. *New York*, 383 U.S. 502, 508 (1966).
42. None of this is intended as a comment about the personal sexuality or principles of any judicial individual; it is rather a series of analytic observations that emerge from a feminist attempt to interpret the deep social structure of a vast body of case law on the basis of a critique of gender. Further research should systematically analyze the contents of the pornography involved in the cases. For instance, with respect to the last hypothesis in the text above, is it just chance that the first film to be found obscene by a state supreme court depicts male masturbation? *Landau* v. *Fording* 245 C. A.2d 820, 54 Cal. Rptr. 177 (1966). Given the ubiquity of the infantilization of women and the sexualization of little girls, would *Ferber* have been decided the same way if it had shown 12-year-old girls masturbating? Did works like *Lady Chatterley's Lover* and *Tropic of Cancer* get in trouble because male sexuality is depicted in a way that men think is dangerous for women and children to see?
43. *Roth* v. *US*, 354 U.S. 476 (1957), but cf. *Stanley* v. *Georgia*, 394 U.S. 557 (1969), in which the right to private possession of obscene materials is protected as a First Amendment *speech* right. See 67 *Landmark Briefs and Arguments of the Supreme Court of the United States: Constitutional Law* 850 (P. Kurland and G. Casper eds. 1975).
44. e.g. *The Report of the Commission on Obscenity and Pornography*, note 8 above, at 1, charges the commission to study '[t]he effect of obscenity and pornography upon the public and particularly minors and its relation to crime and other antisocial behavior'.
45. Naomi Scheman, 'Making It All Up', transcript of speech, January 1982, at 7.
46. This body of work is usually taken to be diverse. Thomas I. Emerson, *Toward a General Theory of the First Amendment* (1966); Emerson, *The System of Freedom of Expression* (1970); Alexander Meiklejohn, *Free Speech and Its Relation to Self-Government* (1948); *Whitney* v. *California*, 274 U.S. 357, 375 (1927) (Brandeis, J., concurring, joined by Holmes, J.), T. Scanlon, 'A Theory of Free Expression', 1 *Philosophy and Public Affairs* 204 (1972); John Hart Ely, 'Flag Desecration: A Case Study in the Roles of Categorization and Balancing in First Amendment Analysis', 88 *Harvard Law Review* 1482 (1975); Zechariah Chafee, *Free Speech in the United States* 245 (1948). This literature is ably summarized and anatomized by Ed Baker, who proposes an interpretative theory that goes far toward responding to my objections here, without really altering the basic assumptions I criticize. See C. F. Baker, 'Scope of the First Amendment Freedom of Speech', 25 *UCLA Law Review* 964 (1978) and 'The Process of Change and the Liberty Theory of the First Amendment', 55 *Southern California Law Review* 293 (1982).

47. Emerson, *Toward a General Theory of the First Amendment*, note 46 above, at 28.
48. See *Erznoznik* v. *City of Jacksonville*, 422 U.S. 205 (1975); *Breard* v. *Alexandria*, 341 U.S. 622, 641–45 (1951); *Kovacs* v. *Cooper*, 336 U.S. 77, 87–89 (1949).
49. *Stanley* v. *Georgia*, 394 U.S. 557 (1969).
50. See Walker, 'Coming Apart', in Lederer, note 8 above, at 85; Russell, note 9 above; *Hearings*. Cf. *Paris Adult Theatre I* v. *Slaton*, 413 U.S. 49, 71 (1973) (Douglas, J., dissenting) ('[In] a life that has not been short, I have yet to be trapped into seeing or reading something that would offend me'). He probably hadn't.
51. See 'Privacy v. Equality' in MacKinnon, *Feminism Unmodified*, for a fuller discussion of this point.
52. Emerson, *Toward a General Theory of the First Amendment*, note 46 above, at 16–25. See also Emerson, *The System of Freedom of Expression*, note 46 above, at 17.
53. The essentially scientific notion of causality did not *first* appear in this law at this time, however. See e.g. *US* v. *Roth*, 237 F.2d 796, 812–17 (2d Cir. 1956) (Frank, J., concurring) ('According to Judge Bok, an obscenity statute may be validly enforced when there is proof of a causal relation between a particular book and undesirable conduct. Almost surely, such proof cannot ever be adduced.' Id., 826 n. 70).

    Werner Heisenberg, criticizing old ideas of atomic physics in light of Einstein's theory of relativity, states what conditions must exist for a causal relation to make sense: 'To coordinate a definite cause to a definite effect has sense only when both can be observed without introducing a foreign element disturbing their interrelation. The law of causality, because of its very nature, can only be defined for isolated systems.' Werner Heisenberg, *The Physical Principles of the Quantum Theory* 63 (1930). Among the influences that disturb the isolation of systems are observers. Underlying the adoption of a causality standard in obscenity law is a rather hasty analogy between the regularities of physical and of social systems, an analogy that has seldom been explicitly justified or even updated as the physical sciences have questioned their own epistemological foundations. This kind of scientific causality may not be readily susceptible to measurement in social systems for the simple reason that social systems are not isolated systems; experimental research (which is where it *has* been shown that pornography causes harm) can only minimize the influence of what will always be 'foreign elements'. Pornography and harm may not be two definite events anyway; perhaps pornography *is* a harm. Moreover, if the effects of pornography are systematic, they may not be isolable from the system in which they exist. This would not mean that no harm exists. Rather, it would mean that because the harm is so pervasive, it cannot be sufficiently isolated to be *perceived* as existing according to this causal model. In other words, if pornography is seen as harmful only if it causes harm by this model, and if it exists socially only in ways that cannot be isolated from society itself, its harm will not be perceived to exist. I think this describes the conceptual situation in which we find ourselves.
54. Morton Horowitz, 'The Doctrine of Objective Causation', in *The Politics of Law* 201 (David Kairys ed. 1982). The pervasiveness of the objectification of women has been treated as a reason why pandering should not be consti-

tutionally restricted: 'The advertisements of our best magazines are chock-full of thighs, ankles, calves, bosoms, eyes, and hair, to draw the potential buyer's attention to lotions, tires, food, liquor, clothing, autos, and even in insurance policies. '*Ginzburg* v. *US*, 383 U.S. 463, 482 (1966) (Douglas, J., dissenting). Justice Douglas thereby illustrated, apparently without noticing, that *somebody* knows that associating sex, that is, women's bodies, with things causes people to *act* on that association.

55. See Lovelace and McGrady, note 10 above.
56. Two boys masturbating with no showing of explicit force demonstrates the harm of child pornography in *New York* v. *Ferber*, 458 U.S. 747 (1982), while shoving money up a woman's vagina, among other acts, raises serious questions of 'regulation of "conduct" having a communicative element' in live sex adjudications, *California* v. *LaRue*, 409 U.S. 109, 113 (1972) (live sex can be regulated by a state in connection with serving alcoholic beverages). 'Snuff' films, in which a woman is actually murdered to produce a film for sexual entertainment, are known to exist. *People* v. *Douglas and Hernandez*, Felony Complaint No. NF8300382, Municipal Court, North Judicial District, Orange County, Calif., 5 Aug. 1983, alleges the murder of two young girls to make a pornographic film. Hernandez turned state's evidence; Douglas was convicted of first-degree murder in November 1984. No snuff film was found. (Conversation with Tony Rackackaus, district attorney, 3 Sept. 1986.)
57. Both Griffin, note 15 above, and the oldest Anglo-Saxon obscenity cases locate the harm of pornography in the mind of the consumer. See e.g. *Regina* v. *Hicklin*, 3 L.R-Q.B. 360, 371 (1868) ('tendency . . . to deprave and corrupt those whose minds are open to such immoral influences and into whose hands a publication of this sort may fall'). The data of John Court and Berl Kutchinsky, both correlational, reach contrary conclusions on the relation of pornography's availability to crime statistics. Kutchinsky, 'Towards an Explanation of the Decrease in Registered Sex Crimes in Copenhagen', 7 *Technical Report of the Commission on Obscenity and Pornography* 263 (1971); Kutchinsky, 'The Effect of Easy Availability of Pornography on the Incidence of Sex Crimes: The Danish Experience', 29 *Journal of Social Issues* 163 (1973); cf. Court, 'Pornography and Sex Crimes: A Re-Evaluation in the Light of Recent Trends around the World', 5 *International Journal of Criminology and Penology* 129 (1977). More recent investigations into correlations focused on rape in the United States have reached still other conclusions. Larry Baron and Murray Straus have found a strong correlation between state-to-state variations in the rate of reported rape and the aggregate circulation rate of popular men's sex magazines, including *Playboy* and *Hustler*. 'Sexual Stratification, Pornography, and Rape', Family Research Laboratory and Department of Sociology, University of New Hampshire, Durham, N.H., 18 Nov. 1983 (manuscript). The authors conclude that 'the findings suggest that the combination of a society which is characterized by a struggle to secure equal rights for women, by a high readership of sex magazines which depict women in ways which may legitimize violence, and by a context in which there is a high level of non-sexual violence, constitutes a mix of societal characteristics which precipitate rape' at 16. See also the 'Williams Report', note 24 above, and the opinions of Justice Harlan on the injury to 'society' as a permissible basis for

legislative judgments in this area. *Roth* v. *US*, 354 U.S. 476, 501–02 (1957) (concurring in companion case, *Alberts* v. *California*).

58. Laurence Tribe, *American Constitutional Law* 662 (1978).
59. I am conceiving rape as *sexual* aggression. On the connection between pornography and rape, see Neil M. Malamuth, 'Rape Proclivity among Men', 37 *Journal of Social Issues* 138 (1981); Neil M. Malamuth, 'Rape Fantasies as a Function of Exposure to Violent Sexual Stimuli', 10 *Archives of Sexual Behavior* 33 (1981); Scott Haber and Seymour Feshbach, 'Testing Hypotheses Regarding Rape: Exposure to Sexual Violence, Sex Differences, and the "Normality" of Rapists', 14 *Journal of Research in Personality* 121 (1980); Maggie Heim and Seymour Feshbach, 'Sexual Responsiveness of College Students to Rape Depictions: Inhibitory and Disinhibitory Effects', 38 *Journal of Personality and Social Psychology* 399 (1980). See also works by Malamuth, note 9 above. Of course, there are difficulties in measuring rape as a direct consequence of laboratory experiments, difficulties that have led researchers to substitute other measures of willingness to aggress, such as electric shocks.
60. Apparently, it may be impossible to *make* a film for experimental purposes that portrays violence or aggression by a man against a woman that a substantial number of male experimental subjects do not perceive as sexual. See *Hearings*, at 31 (testimony of Edward Donnerstein).
61. See works of Zillman, note 9 above.
62. Immanuel Kant, *Fundamental Principles of the Metaphysics of Morals* (T. Abbott trans. 1969); Arthur Danto, 'Persons', in 6 *Encyclopedia of Philosophy* 10 (P. Edwards ed. 1967); Margaret Radin, 'Property and Personhood', 34 *Stanford Law Review* 957 (1982).
63. See Kant, note 62 above; Danto, note 62 above; Radin, note 62 above. See also the 'original position' of John Rawls, *A Theory of Justice* (1971), and Rawls, 'Kantian Constructivism in Moral Theory', *Journal of Philosophy* 515, 533–35 (1980).
64. Ludwig Wittgenstein, *Philosophical Investigations* 178 (G. Anscombe trans. 3d ed. 1958).
65. Karl Marx's critique of capitalist society is epitomized in *Capital* chap. 1 (1867). His concept of the 'fetishism of commodities' in which 'relations between men [assume], *in their eyes*, the fantastic form of a relation between things' (emphasis added) is presented in the 1970 edition at 72.
66. David Hume, 'Of Personal Identity', in *A Treatise of Human Nature* bk. I, pt. IV, § VI (1888).
67. Bernard Williams, 'Are Persons Bodies? Personal Identity and Individualization' and 'Bodily Continuity and Personal Identity', in his *Problems of the Self* 1, 64 (1973). Bernard Williams was principal author of the 'Williams Report', note 24 above, Britain's equivalent of the US Commission on Obscenity and Pornography, in which none of his values of 'persons' were noticed lacking in, or women deprived of them by, pornography.
68. See *Signs* I and II.
69. I have come to this conclusion from my analysis of all the empirical data available to date, the pornography itself, and personal observations.
70. Brownmiller, note 10 above, is widely considered to present the view that rape is an act of violence, not sex. Women Against Pornography, a New York based antipornography group, has argued that pornography is violence against

women, not sex. This has been almost universally taken as *the* feminist position on the issue. For an indication of possible change, see 4 *NCASA News* 19–21 (May 1984).

71. This, again, does not mean that it is an *idea.* A new theory of ideology, prefigured in Dworkin, note 1 above, will be needed to conceptualize the role of pornography in constructing the condition of women.
72. Dworkin, note 1 above, at 115.
73. 'Echoing Macaulay, "Jimmy" Walker remarked that he had never heard of a woman seduced by a book.' *US* v. *Roth*, 237 F.2d 796, 812 (1956) (appendix to concurrence of Frank, J.) What is classically called seduction, I expect feminists might interpret as rape or forced sex.

10 The Mirror of Pornography

Wendy Brown

> Too much freedom seems to change into nothing but too much slavery, both for private man and the city. Well then, tyranny is probably established out of no other regime than democracy, I suppose—the greatest and most savage slavery out of the extreme of freedom.
>
> ('Socrates,' in *Plato's Republic*)

> To lead a life soaked in the passionate consciousness of one's gender at every single moment, to will to be a sex with a vengeance—these are impossibilities, and far from the aims of feminism.
>
> (Denise Riley, '*Am I That Name?*')

This effort to apprehend the *rhetorical* power of Catharine MacKinnon's social theory of gender is compelled by an aim that exceeds critique of her depiction of women as always and only sexually violable, her pornography politics, or her arguments about the First Amendment. Insofar as MacKinnon's work has extraordinary political purchase, this essay seeks to discern something of the composition and constituency of this power in her theoretical project. How and why does MacKinnon's complicatedly radical political analysis and voice acquire such hold? And what are the possibilities that other feminisms could rival such power with analyses more multivalent in their representation of gender subordination and gender construction, more attentive to the race and class of gender, more compatible with the rich diversity of female sexual experience, more complex in their representations of sexuality and sexual power, more extravagant and democratic in their political vision? In other words, while MacKinnon might be 'wrong'

Wendy Brown, 'The Mirror of Pornography', from *States of Injury: Power and Freedom in Late Modernity*, Wendy Brown (Princeton University Press, 1995), 7–95, about Marxism, gender, sexuality, power, the state, or the relation between freedom and equality, those issues are of less concern here than the potent order of 'truth' she produces. How did MacKinnon so successfully deploy a militant feminism during the 1980s, a decade markedly unsympathetic to all militancies to the left of center?

Whether developing antipornography ordinances in midwestern cities and, more recently, Canada, or articulating an analysis of sexual harassment on the MacNeil/Lehrer News Hour, Catharine MacKinnon has been taken up and taken seriously by those in mainstream judicial and media institutions as well as in august corners of academe, an unusual phenomenon in any event and certainly rare for a feminist who is no liberal. Featured in fall 1991 as the cover story of the *New York Times* magazine, she was anointed in the same season by philosopher Richard Rorty as the new prophet of our age. Named NBC 'person of the week' during the Hill–Thomas hearings, shortly after which she delivered the prestigious Gauss Lectures at Princeton University, she has also appeared frequently in other commercial media venues to discuss issues ranging from pornography and sexual harassment to hate speech.

While MacKinnon has made an unusual splash in the mainstream, her following among radical feminists is equally significant. The unquestioned theoretical lodestar of the feminist antipornography movement, she is an important figure in the rapidly developing field of feminist jurisprudence, and her rhetorical persuasiveness also shows its measure on ordinary undergraduates: young women and men across political and sexual orientations, racial and class formations, find themselves compelled, disturbed, and convinced by her work.

Anyone who has seen or heard MacKinnon knows that she is extremely smart, articulate, charismatic, and a master of an oratorical style in which righteous rage is alloyed with icy rationality, hammering empiricism, and a beseeching feminine anguish—all of which must be mentioned in an analysis that purports to account for her power and purchase in American politics, the law school classroom, and the feminist activist community. However, without diminishing the importance of these elements, nor the sheer brilliance and deftness of some of her arguments, I want to ask a different set of questions about MacKinnon's political hold, questions concerned with the logical and narrative structures of her prose, with rhetorical strategies and contemporary political resonances in her writing.

To some degree, discerning MacKinnon's analytic potency entails debunking the putative radicalism of MacKinnon's work. It involves exploring the ways in which MacKinnon's formulation of gender, notwithstanding its flirtations with social construction and its concern to supplant arguments from difference with arguments from inequality, closely echoes the universalizing, transcultural, and transhistorical arguments about the sexual order of things proffered by orthodox political conservatives. But elaborating the purchase of her arguments is not only a matter of locating the conservative body beneath the radical attire. Indeed, MacKinnon's complex residual attachments to Marxism and to monological, structural analyses of oppression also produce a set of questions about the rhetorical powers of certain kinds of logical and narrative structures. Here, the problem for which a study of MacKinnon's work provides only an occasion could be put this way: Can a radical postfoundationalist feminist political discourse about women, sexuality, and the law—with its necessarily partial logics and provisional truths, situated knowledges, fluid subjects, and decentered sovereignty—work to claim power, or to contest hegemonic power, to the degree that MacKinnon's discourse does? Or do the commitments of postfoundationalist feminist analysis condemn it to a certain political marginalization, to permanent gadfly status, to a philosopher's self-consolation that she is on the side of 'truth' rather than power? In the domain of late modern political life, and especially the domain of the law, can political-theoretical strategies of subversion, displacement, proliferation, and resignification compare or compete with the kinds of systematic and ontological claims MacKinnon makes about the condition of women and the good for women? And is any answer we might venture to this question specific to the resonant range of the contemporary discursive field into which these claims are inserted, a field that remains formally dominated by a modernist political idiom? Or might we venture some more quasi-transcendental postulates about the powers of systematic analytical structures and syllogistic logical forms, about the ways in which (scientistic) modes of analysis that totalize, reduce, systematize, and close achieve their superior power effects precisely through such discursive violence and can effectively ignore or dominate 'postmodern' incursions because of this greater violence? While these are not questions to be fully answered here, they frame and animate this investigation of the rhetorical structure of MacKinnon's work.

> Sexuality is to feminism what work is to Marxism.
>
> (Catharine MacKinnon, *Toward a Feminist Theory of the State*)

MacKinnon's social theory of gender is an adaptation of Marxism, which, somewhat paradoxically, it intends both to parallel and displace.[1] Paralleling the systemic and totalizing explanatory logic of the realm of production and the materiality of labor in explaining and criticizing class society, MacKinnon develops an analogical account of sexuality and gender. Yet by simultaneously displacing the Marxist emphasis on the primacy of class, and of economics, as the constructing and positioning feature of women and men, MacKinnon identifies Marxism as a partial rather than inclusive social theory and positions feminism as that which can 'turn marxism inside out and on its head'.[2] Her desire to match and displace Marxism's systematicity is captured in the following statement:

> Feminism has not been perceived as having a method, or even a central argument. It has been perceived [by whom?] not as a systematic analysis but as a loose collection of complaints and issues that, taken together, describe rather than explain the misfortunes of the female sex. The challenge is to demonstrate that feminism systematically converges upon a central explanation of sex inequality through an approach distinctive to its subject yet applicable to the whole of social life, including class.[3]

MacKinnon's social theory of gender rests upon a crucial conceptual identification and a crucial conceptual equivalence: it depends upon an identity—not merely a relation—between sexuality and gender, and an equivalence—not merely an analogy—between the capital–labor relation in Marxism and the male–female relation in feminism. For Marx, the organization of production expressed by the capital–labor relation *is* the material of class in capitalism; for MacKinnon, the organization of sexuality expressed in the male–female relation *is* the material of gender in male dominance. Sexuality is the stuff of gender *because* labor is the stuff of class, and class is like gender—both are relations of dominance and subordination rooted in fundamental social processes, sexual activity and production respectively. Thus the organization of desire is to gender as the organization of labor is to class—fully constitutive but masked in the ideologically naturalized form that legitimates the regime. If sexuality signifies the organization of human desire and labor signifies the organization of human productive power, the former makes gender and the latter makes class: together they make history, the social world, ideology, the state, and the individual. 'As the organized appropriation of the work of some for the benefit of others defines a class, workers, the organized expropriation of the sexuality of some for the use of others defines the sex, woman.'[4]

In MacKinnon's account, the sexiness of the social process she calls desire closes a loop in gender formation that is not closed in Marx's account of class formation. If gender is a relation of domination and subordination in male dominant societies, and gender is constituted by sexuality, then, argues MacKinnon, sexuality in such societies *is* the eroticization of dominance and submission.[5] Thus, female sexuality is not only expropriated by men (as labor is expropriated by capital), heterosexual desire itself constitutes, insofar as it eroticizes, gender subordination by eroticizing dominance and submission as gendered positions. Sexuality in male dominant societies *is* the eroticization of male dominance, an eroticization that *produces* gender as this dominance, a gendering that *reproduces* the erotics of this dominance. Thus, 'feminism is a theory of how the eroticization of dominance and submission creates gender, creates woman and man in the social form in which we know them.'[6] For MacKinnon, if sex is to gender what work is to class—only more so, because the sexiness of sex eroticizes gender inequality and does not simply coercively or ideologically enforce it—then every feminist issue, every injustice and injury suffered by women, devolves upon sexuality: the construction of femininity is the making of female vulnerability and violation as womanhood; the construction of female economic dependence is sexual availability to men; incest, sexual harassment, rape, and prostitution are all modes of sexual subordination; women's lack of authoritative speech is women's always already sexually violated condition.[7]

However, it is pornography that MacKinnon isolates as the most potent and tangible vehicle of women's subordination in contemporary culture. Neither a 'harmless fantasy nor a corrupt and confused misrepresentation of an otherwise natural and healthy sexual situation', pornography 'institutionalizes the sexuality of male supremacy, fusing the erotization of dominance and submission with the social construction of male and female'.[8] For MacKinnon, pornography is the distillate of gender relations in male dominant regimes, not merely an expression but the legitimating institution of male dominance:

> Pornography, in the feminist view, is a form of forced sex, a practice of sexual politics, an institution of gender inequality. In this perspective, pornography is not harmless fantasy or a corrupt and confused misrepresentation of an otherwise natural and healthy sexuality. Along with the rape and prostitution in which it participates, pornography institutionalizes the sexuality of male supremacy, which fuses the eroticization of dominance and submission with the social construction of male and female. Gender is sexual. Pornography constitutes the meaning of that sexuality. Men treat women as who they see

women as being. Pornography constructs who that is. Men's power over women means that the way men see women defines who women can be. Pornography is that way.[9]

Although MacKinnon never says so explicitly, pornography presumably is to male dominance as, for Marx, liberalism is to capitalism—something institutionally securing, discursively naturalizing, ideologically obscuring, and historically perpetrating the power of the dominant.

There are any number of questions to be raised about MacKinnon's effort to install gender and sexuality into categories and dynamics used to explain the making of class through labor. We might begin by wondering at her failure to develop a specific theory of sexuality and gender—as opposed to adapting a theory of work and class for this project. If sex is to gender what work is to class, then presumably a theory of sexuality, rather than a theory of work applied to sex, is required for a feminist critique and theory of emancipation. Moreover, given the importance to Marx's theory of class of the capacity to generate a surplus—and hence to produce surplus value and to support the revolutionary aim dependent on the possibility of collectivizing work and collectively sharing in the benefits of such surplus generativity—and given the absence of this element in the power(s) constitutive of gender or organizing desire, we might also wonder about the fit of a Marxist theory of class to a theory of gender based on sexuality. Even if it were granted that a single social relation, called sexuality, produced gender, would it therefore be eligible for a theoretical apparatus designed to apprehend class? And what if sexuality is not reducible to a single social relation but is itself a complex nonschema of discourses and economies, which are constitutive not only of the semiotics of gender but of race and class formations? What if gender generally and women's subordination in particular do not devolve on a single social relation but have manifold sites and sources of production and reproduction—for example, in discourses organizing motherhood, race, philosophical truth, citizenship, class, heterosexuality, war, science, and so forth? Does sexuality's inability to be systematized and the lack of a single mechanism on which gender turns make gender subordination less real than class distinctions, or sexual violation less injurious than exploited labor? Or does it instead make gender less conducive to a monological theoretical form and unified political practice? In this regard, might MacKinnon's anxiety about supplying feminism with a systematicity, with a single logic, mechanism, and explanatory principle, betoken a distinctly late modernist (as well as phallogocentric) anxiety about what constitutes the real and the potent?

Insofar as MacKinnon's Marxism is intended to be less doctrinal than methodological, it gives the illusion of being surgically reconfigured to fit its subject and thus to elide one of MacKinnon's chief anxieties—namely, that the intercourse of Marxism and feminism will inevitably subordinate the latter.[10] However, MacKinnon's adoption of Marxism as method and worldview may ultimately constitute problems more insidious for feminism than did more patently limited efforts to assimilate feminist concerns to an unreconstructed Marxist lexicon, efforts that revealed the character of women's work (caretaking and service), domain of injury (bodily, private, subjective), consciousness (always exceeding a relation to the mode of production), and social location (isolated, private) to make it a poor candidate for intelligent apprehension within terms such as 'production of surplus value' or 'history of class struggle'. In MacKinnon's own words, the abiding significance and value of Marxist theory pertains to its critical analysis of 'society's dynamic laws of motion in their totality, materiality, and historicity, combining determinacy with agency, thought with situation, complexly based on interest.'[11] In other words, MacKinnon intends to appropriate from Marxist theory not its categories, its theory of history, nor even its historical approach to social life, but an extract from its *science* of domination. Indeed, hers is a strikingly nonhistorical and nondialectical account of antagonistic social dynamics constitutive of an apprehensible social totality. In this MacKinnon not only takes over but exaggerates Marxism's totalizing constructions of social life—including and especially its reduction of subjects and subjectivity to subject *positions*—and its ontological generalization of historically specific subject production (about which more shortly).

MacKinnon's conceptual equivalent between the absolute domination of capital and the absolute domination of men—'as many work and few gain . . . some fuck and others get fucked'[12]—de-essentializes gender, by making it fully a production of power. At the same time, this conceptual equivalent unifies and universalizes gender by dehistoricizing it; by divesting it of any greater specifiability through class, age, sexuality, race, or culture; by exhaustively identifying it with respectively dominant and subordinate social positions; and by making gender fully a function of such positions, giving it no plasticity, complex and diverse interiors, variability, or domain of invention. In this replacement of mystified political subjects with reified ones, in this subversion of denaturalizing analytic strategies with dehistoricizing and totalizing ones, MacKinnon is operating both within and outside a Marxist framework. She is repeating a certain Marxist limitation but repeating it with a difference that, as we shall see, intensifies the force of the limitation.

First, what is she repeating? By Baudrillard as well as Arendt, we are reminded that Marx's powerful analytic critique of nineteenth century political economy may have been less Archimedean with respect to its specific historical context than Marx had imagined or than his followers ordinarily acknowledge. In Baudrillard's analysis, Marx was so steeped in the milieu of capitalist political economy that he rendered its cultural productions and effects in a vein more ontological than historical and thus reified the *activity* of the nineteenth-century proletarian as an eternal verity of man and the *culture* of nineteenth-century European industrialization as the soul of history. In Baudrillard's reading, the mid-nineteenth-century resolution of industrializing European societies into two great oppositional classes led Marx to regard history as fully constituted by class struggle and labor as fully constitutive of man. This is Baudrillard:

> If on the one hand Marx is interested in the later fate of the labor power objectified in the production process as abstract social labor[,] . . . Marxist theory, on the other hand, never challenges human capacity of production[,] . . . this productive potential of every man in every society 'of transforming his environment into ends useful for the individual or society.' . . . Criticism and history are strangely arrested before this anthropological postulate: a curious fate for a Marxist concept. . . . Radical in its *logical* analysis of capital, Marxist theory nonetheless maintains an *anthropological* consensus with the options of Western rationalism in its definitive form acquired in eighteenth-century bourgeois thought.[13]

'Overwhelmed', as Hannah Arendt puts the matter, 'by the unprecedented actual productivity of Western mankind [in the modern age],' Marx deduces 'man' from this epoch and thus dehistoricizes the relative valences of political economy and its components—labor, labor power, and relations of production—even while treating the development of specific modes of production as a problem of dialectics and history.[14] 'But,' as Baudrillard reminds us, 'differentiating modes of production renders unchallengeable the evidence of production as the determinant instance. It generalizes the economic mode of rationality over the entire expanse of human history, as the generic mode of human becoming.' Thus, failing to grasp his critical ontology of man the producer as itself historically produced, Marx posits a *homo faber* who mirrors rather than criticizes the age of political economy—'the abstract and generalized development of productivity (the developed form of political economy) is what makes *the concept of production* itself appear as man's movement and generic.'[15] Production as the determinant instance, Baudrillard argues,

> circumscribes the entire history of man in a gigantic simulation model. It tries somehow to turn against the order of capital by using as an analytic instrument the most subtle ideological phantasm that capital has itself elaborated. Is this a 'dialectical' reversal? Isn't the system pursuing its dialectic of universal reproduction here? If one hypothesizes that *there has never been and will never be anything but the single mode of production ruled by capitalist political economy*—a concept that makes sense only in relation to the economic formation that produced it (indeed, to the theory that analyzes this economic formation)—then even the 'dialectical' generalization of this concept is merely the *ideological* universalization [the mirror] of this system's postulates.[16]

Just as Baudrillard suggests that Marx 'generalizes the economic mode of rationality over the entire expanse of human history, as the generic mode of human becoming,' so MacKinnon's thesis that sexuality is fully constitutive of gender, and that heterosexuality is gender's male dominant form, also 'generalizes the [pornographic heterosexual sexual] mode of rationality over the entire expanse of human history, as the generic mode of [gender] becoming'. As Marx's 'discovery' that economic production is the ontological ground of humanity mirrors the age in which it occurred, MacKinnon's thesis mirrors a hyperbolic expression of gender as sexuality in the late twentieth-century United States and reveals the extent to which construction and regulation of gender by a panoply of discourses, activities, and distinctions other than sexuality have been sharply eroded and destabilized. These would include the privatization and pervasive feminization of reproductive work; a gendered division of labor predicated on the exchange between household labor and socialized production; gendered religions, political, and civic codes; and other sharply gendered spheres of activity and social norms—in short, all elements of the construction of gender that are institutionalized, hence enforced, elsewhere than through the organization of desire. The destabilization of these other domains of the production and regulation of gender lead not only MacKinnon but feminist theorists putatively quite different from her—those theorizing gender as performativity vis-à-vis heterosexual norms, for example—to read gender as almost wholly constituted by the (heterosexual) organization of *desire.*[17]

While a clearly delineated and complexly arrayed sexual division of labor may have constituted regimes of gender—gendered social locations, productions of subjectivity, and mechanisms of subordination—more profoundly in other times and places, the culturally normative heterosexual organization of desire, including its pornographic commercial expression, emerges most fiercely inscribed in our own.[18] Moreover, as in Baudrillard's reading 'the system of political economy does not produce only the individual as labor power that is sold and exchanged . . . [but] the very conception of labor power as the fundamental human potential', the pornographic sexual order, of which MacKinnon's theory is a mirror, does not produce only women as sexuality but the very conception of sexuality as the fundamental feature of gender. In Baudrillard's elaboration:

> More deeply than in the fiction of individuals freely selling their labor power in the market, the system is rooted in the identification of individuals with their labor power and with their acts of 'transforming nature according to human ends.' In a word, man is not only quantitatively exploited as a productive force by the *system* of capitalist political economy, but is also metaphysically overdetermined as a producer by the *code* of political economy. In the last instance, the system rationalizes its power here. *And in this Marxism assists the cunning of capital.*[19]

I am suggesting that MacKinnon's theory of gender as fully constituted by sexuality and of pornography as the ultimate expression of male dominance is itself historically produced by, on the one hand, the erosion of other sites of gender production and gender effects, and on the other, the profusion, proliferation, and radical deprivatization and diffusion of sexuality in the late twentieth century. The phenomenon Marcuse called repressive desublimation, which Foucault reconceived as the production of a specific regime of sexuality, is what we might call the pornographic age that MacKinnon's theory 'mirrors' rather than historically or analytically decodes. So, too, does her social theory of gender mirror rather than deconstruct the *subjects* of heterosexual male pornography—both the male consumer and the female model subjects that, we may speculate, function largely (and futilely) to shore up or stabilize a sexual/gender dominance itself destabilized by the erosions of other elements of gender subordination in the late twentieth century.

In other words, if not only gendered divisions of labor and activity, but a regime of sexual binarism—heterosexuality—itself is decentered by the political-economic-cultural forces of late modernity, then MacKinnon's theory of gender unwittingly consolidates gender out of symptoms of a crisis moment in male dominance. In this way, MacKinnon formulates as the deep, universal, and transhistorical structure of gender what is really a hyperpornographic expression: indeed, it marks the crisis attendant upon the transmutation from overdetermined gender dualism and gender subordination (here underspecified) to a present and future characterized by the erosion of compulsory heterosexuality itself is constitutive of everyday gender constructions.[20]

MacKinnon's move to read gender off of pornography, her construction of a social theory of gender that mirrors heterosexual male pornography, not only convenes a pervasively, totally, and singly determined gendered subject, it encodes the pornographic age as the truth rather than the hyperbole of gender production: it fails to read the $10 billion a year porn industry as a 'state of emergency' (as Nietzsche spoke of the hyperrationality of classical Greek philosophy) of a male dominant heterosexual regime.[21] Moreover, her move to read pornography as the literal and essential representation of gendered heterosexuality precisely identifies the pornographic male consumer and pornographic female subject as ontologically male and female. In arguing that 'pornography literally means what it says',[22] MacKinnon not only begs questions about the workings of representation and fantasy, of hermeneutics and interpellation, she ontologizes pornography *as* gender. In short, MacKinnon's theory of gender mirrors the straight male pornography it means to criticize, a mirroring that manifests in a number of ways.

First, in MacKinnon's theory of gender as in the heterosexual male porn she analyzes, the subject positions of male and female are depicted as relentlessly dualistic and absolute, figured literally, not metaphorically or qualifiedly, as subject and object, person and thing, dominant and subordinate: or, as Drucilla Cornell puts it in *Beyond Accommodation*, 'fuckor and fuckee'.[23]

Second, in MacKinnon's theory of gender as in the heterosexual male porn she analyzes, the subject positions of male and female are formed only and totally by sexuality. Not only does gender lack other constituents, but the making of gender is not seen to vary substantively across other formations and vectors of power—for example, race—except insofar as these differences are expressed sexually. Sexuality may be racialized, racial subordination may be sexualized; but differences among women dissolve when sexuality is grasped as the universal axis of subordination. In this metaphysical overdetermination of gender as sexual, MacKinnon assists in the cunning of pornography. (Recall Baudrillard's argument that Marxism assists in the cunning of capital in its complicity with the metaphysical overdetermination of man as a producer by the code of political economy.)

Third, in MacKinnon's theory as in the heterosexual male porn she analyzes, the sexual subject positions of male and female are also made one with the *subjectivity* of male and female, with the consequence that male and female subjectivities are totalized, dichotomized, and pervasively sexualized. This is MacKinnon:

> [A] woman is a being who identifies and is identified as one whose sexuality exists for someone else, who is socially male. What is termed women's sexuality is the capacity to arouse desire in that someone. Considering women's sexuality in this way forces confrontation with whether there is, in the possessive sense of 'women's', any such thing. Is women's sexuality its absence?[24]

If gender is sexuality as it appears in heterosexual male pornography, then not only female sexuality but the totality of female consciousness consist solely of what men (now also unified as a consumer subject) require. Thus, MacKinnon concludes, 'if women are socially defined such that female sexuality cannot be lived or spoken or felt or even somatically sensed apart from its enforced definition, then there is no such thing as a woman as such; there are only walking embodiments of men's projected needs.'[25] Of course, this evacuation of female subjectivity of any element not transparent on the pornographic page renders any emancipatory project nearly impossible. MacKinnon is no more able to answer her own question about consciousness—'how can woman, "thingified in the head", complicit in the body, see her condition as such?'[26]—than she is able to imagine the making of a feminist female sexual future.

Fourth, in MacKinnon's theory as in the pornography she analyzes, heterosexuality is the past, present, and eternal future of gender. If gender is sexuality, sexuality is always gendered and women are sex for men, then, for example, lesbian sexuality either doesn't exist, is sex for men, or imitates heterosexuality—all of which are indeed tropes of lesbian representation in straight male porn as well as MacKinnon's account of lesbianism: 'If being for another is women's sexual construction, it can be no more escaped by . . . men's temporary concrete absence, than it can be eliminated . . . by sexual permissiveness, which, in this context, looks like women emulating male roles.'[27] And, 'lesbian sex, simply as sex between women, given a social definition of gender and sexuality, does not by definition transcend the erotization of dominance and submission and their social equation with masculinity and femininity.'[28]

Finally, and here the ground is more speculative, MacKinnon's social theory of gender mirrors pornography in its prose structure and rhetorical effect, in a fashion similar to what Baudrillard identified as Marxism's mirroring of the *code* of political economy. The pornographic rhetorical structure of MacKinnon's writing and speech would appear to inhere in the insistent and pounding quality of her prose: in the rhythmic pulses of her simple subject-verb-object sentences in which a single point is incessantly reiterated, reworked, driven, and thrust at its audience; in an overburdened syllogistic structure, which makes the syllogistic logic more proliferative, intoxicating, overstimulating, agitated, and less contestable; in the literalism and force of her abstract claims—'pornography is that way'—which simultaneously structure the scene and permit any (man) his own imaginative entry into the scene; in the use of simple, active verbs, hyperbolic adverbs, and strategically deployed sentence fragments; in the slippage between representation and action; in the direct and personalized form of address; in the repeated insistence on gender, sexuality, and representation as 'the real'; and in the personification and activation of things or concepts. Consider:

> In pornography, women desire dispossession and cruelty. Men, permitted to put words (and other things) in women's mouths, create scenes in which women desperately want to be bound, battered, tortured, humiliated, and killed. Or merely taken and used. This is erotic to the male point of view. Subjection itself is the content of women's sexual desire and desirability. Women are there to be violated and possessed, men to violate and possess them, either on screen or by camera or pen, on behalf of the viewer.[29]

Listen again:

> What looks like love and romance in the liberal view looks a lot like hatred and torture in the feminist view. Pleasure and eroticism become violation. Desire appears as lust for dominance and submission. The vulnerability of women's projected sexual availability—that acting we are allowed; asking to be acted upon [a brief lingering, a tease, before returning to . . .] is victimization. Play conforms to scripted roles, fantasy expresses ideology[,] . . . and admiration of natural physical beauty becomes objectification.[30]

I am suggesting that MacKinnon repeats one of Marxism's most problematic but also most rhetorically compelling features: the stylistic mirroring of its subject of critique. MacKinnon's analysis acquires much of its potency from the cultural resonance it strikes, the libidinal excitation it incites, the pornographic guilt it taps and reworks—all under the sign of radical critique. This is a slightly different claim from Drucilla Cornell's bold suggestion that MacKinnon 'fucks her audience', yet it also converges with that view: MacKinnon's theory of gender transpires within a pornographic genre, suspending us in a complex pornographic experience in which MacKinnon is both purveyor and object of desire and her analysis is proffered as substitute for the sex she abuses us for wanting. This substitution itself participates in a pornographic chain; pornography *as* substitute for sex and the endless substitutability of all the parties to pornography are mirrored in MacKinnon's insistence on sexual equality as substitute for sexual pleasure and the endless substitutability of all parties to the figure of male and female in the regime of masculine dominance. MacKinnon's analysis takes part as well in the pornographic chain of prohibition and transgression: as pornography is premised upon desire constructed out of prohibition and must therefore continually reestablish the prohibitions it purports to undo through transgression, MacKinnon's analysis participates in this project by proliferating prohibitions, speaking transgressively, working our desire into a political opposition to itself. If she assists in this way in the 'cunning of pornography', perhaps literally abetting its production, her rhetoric also mirrors pornographic strategy insofar as she marks repeatedly the prohibitions against her work, its transgressiveness, and its unspeakability, even as she persists in it. And as with pornography, this economy of transgression and prohibition is a closed one: as the sexiness of porn lies in its temporal repetitiveness and spatial sequestering, the power of MacKinnon's analysis is bound to its oft-noted theoretical closures and political foreclosures. 'There's no way out' is among students' most frequent responses to her work.

In short, in its rehearsal of a powerful underground (pornographic) code of gender and sexuality, reinscribing and exploiting the power of this code even while denouncing its contents, MacKinnon's theory permits easy cultural identification and recognition, giving her 'radicalism' a seductively familiar rather than threatening resonance and cultural location. In this way, her putative radicalism simultaneously sustains the pleasure of the familiar, the pleasure of the illicit, the pleasure of moralizing against the illicit, and the comforts of conservatism—gender is eternal and sexual pleasure is opprobrious—in an era of despair about substantive political transformation.

While the potency of MacKinnon's analysis is drawn in part from the Marxist method she seeks to appropriate for feminism, she also intensifies one of its more problematic tendencies by shearing it of history, dialectics, and a dynamic of change. For Marx, the resolution of society into 'two great classes directly facing each other' is a historical achievement—'complete' only in the mid-nineteenth century.[31] (This 'completion' turned out to be, as I am arguing hyperheterosexual gendering is, a fairly brief moment in the history of capitalism, a dualistic social formation that was probably unraveling even as Marx wrote, to be reconfigured by the rise of the middle class, corporate capital, the decline of the bourgeoisie, and so forth.) Moreover, as a historical process structured by the inherent contradiction of class domination and exploitation, capitalism produces in the proletariat not merely a class that serves the needs of capital but also 'its own gravedigger'.[32]

By contrast, MacKinnon's utterly static account of sexual antagonism, conjoined with a Marxist view of the socially pervasive quality of this antagonism—its function as a structure of domination rather than mere or random 'interest'—theoretically forecloses both the mechanism and trajectory of political transformation proffered by Marxist theory, namely, the movement of history according to struggle conditioned by systemic contradictions. So also does she foreclose one of the transformative possibilities held out by Marxism, by refusing to vest the class of women with the kind of power Marx vested in the proletariat: anxious not to sentimentalize femininity or female sexual power, she eliminates the very dynamic of social change on which Marx counted for emancipatory praxis, namely, that the class that is 'in but not of society' harbors all of the productive force but none of the social or political power of society.[33] In Marx's account, 'for the oppressed class to be able to emancipate itself, it is necessary that the productive powers already acquired and the existing social relations should no longer be capable of existing side by side.'[34] But unlike the contradictions of capital, sexism for MacKinnon is 'metaphysically nearly perfect' and utterly static—without a history or a dynamic of transformation to open a different future.[35] Moreover, while labor is exploited for profit and is exploitable because of its capacity to generate a surplus, sexuality lacks such a dimension; thus the *raison d'être* of sexism would seem to recur, darkly, to the intrinsic pleasures of male sexual dominance.

This evisceration of history, generativity, and dialectics from Marxism transforms it from radical political theory into an implicitly positivist, conservative project. The very meaning of a radical critique is transformed when there is no historical prospect of redressing the critique, when there is no social dynamic, and when the power deployed by the dominant class is not retrievable by the subordinate class because it never belonged to the latter and, indeed, is foreign to it. Prospects for radical social change evaporate when the oppressed class is only derivative of the dominant class, when it has no cultural meaning or existence other than this derivation, and when the oppressed have no inner resources for the development of consciousness or agency, precisely because they have been produced subjectively, and not only positioned, by dominant power. Whereas Marx distinguished between the conditions in which the proletarian found himself and his potential consciousness of his situation as being in contradiction with the dominant ideology—indeed, Marx counted on the contradictions between material conditions, proletarian consciousness, and dominant ideology for revolutionary possibility—MacKinnon's formulation of the organization of sexuality as the organization of gender erases this distinction. Male dominance does not simply organize a class to serve it but, in producing a class whose identity is 'to be for men', makes a class whose subjectivity is its social position and vice versa.

In this regard, MacKinnon is not, as she suggests, merely methodologically post-Marxist but historically post-Marxist; in fact, she is posthistorical. She is a Marxist for whom history either never existed or never mattered, for whom the past has been erased and the future is an abyss, but for whom what Marx called the weight of the nightmare of dead generations on the brains of the living is incalculably heavy. As a total analysis of a social totality, a Marxism voided of historical struggle, contingency, and variation, as well as of prospects of change from within, is precisely totalitarianism. Indeed, a 'Communist Manifesto' written without history or historical reason, without dialectics, without a dynamic of change, would not only transform in tone from exhilarating to depressing, but would become an argument for the condition it describes as being in the nature of things; capitalist domination would appear rooted in a will to dominate combined with the intrinsic power to dominate, and its 'victims' would thus appear to be in need of protection rather than emancipation. Not surprisingly, sexual emancipation is what MacKinnon is always insisting women do not need more of.

In other words, theory in a Marxist modality without history and without dialectics is conservative insofar as it becomes hermeneutically and ontologically positivist—the condition it describes loses its historically contingent and socially dynamic character. A different past never existed and the future contains no openings, no promises. I want to suggest that this core of MacKinnon's theory speaks directly to the anxieties of an age in the throes of a theoretical and political crisis about the end of history, an era defined by lost faith in progressivist or teleological movement in history. Indeed, in gutting Marxist social theory of historical laws of development and dynamics of change, MacKinnon's analysis converges with certain poststructural critiques of Marxist historiography, dialectics, and logics of systemic contradictions, critiques that figure all of these as part of Marx's uncritical and problematic assumption of Enlightenment premises.

This 'end of history' phenomenon—articulated in one domain by contemporary theoretical challenges to progressivist historiography, in another by both the global collapse of socialist aspirations and the retrenchment of liberal-democratic promises of social improvement—breeds for many an ensemble of anxious questions about political identity, strategy, possibility, and future. For what the combination of theoretical critiques and apparent political refutations of progressivist historiography appears to configure is an unrelieved past, present, and future of domination: precisely what is articulated in MacKinnon's totalizing, circular theory of masculinist power and female subordination. Thus, not only MacKinnon's depiction of women as relentlessly victimized by their gendered construction but also the character of her political interventions—her insistence on the need to insulate us from the worst abuses of such domination not through emancipatory strategies but by curtailing and regulating sexuality, speech, and so forth—betoken radical despair in the face of this moment in history. With the lost promise of forward movement, when substantive political freedom no longer seems possible or even intelligible, the best we might hope for is some minor relief from domination's excess. Not freedom but censorship; not First Amendment guarantees but more rights to sue for damages; not risky experiments with resignification and emancipation but more police, more regulation, better dead-bolt locks on the doors.

But to note how MacKinnon's account has elements of convergence with late modern theoretical critiques and global political developments is not to say they all amount to the same thing. Indeed, MacKinnon's postulations of a social totality, of a single socially pervasive dualism structuring that totality, and of that dualism relentlessly and universally governing the production of all subjects—these are at odds with poststructuralist insights about the character of multiply constructed social orders and social subjects who bear some capacity for subversive resignification. Where much contemporary theory and many contemporary political developments cast into question—that is, deconstruct and destabilize—the categories of subject, identity, and society so central to modern and more specifically liberal societies, MacKinnon resurrects, restores, and reworks these categories. In her account, there are men and women, dominators and dominated, exploiters and exploited, social systems and social wholes. Thus, MacKinnon gives us the comfort of recognizing ourselves in modernist terms, even as she exploits a growing popular and academic sentiment that we have no modernist future.

From this perspective, it would appear that the very structure and categories of her theory—its tautological and totalizing dimensions, its dualisms and absolutes, its strange syllogisms and forced equivalences—articulate a profound late modern anxiety, channeling it into a certain militance while doing nothing to resolve its constituents. Thus the rhetorical force of MacKinnon's theory of gender may inhere as much in its homological refiguring of a late modern political despair as in its pornographic cadences, and perhaps especially in the potentially fascistic interplay of manipulated despair and libidinal arousal.

Notes

1. Early in *Toward a Feminist Theory of the State* (Cambridge, Mass. Harvard University Press, 1989). MacKinnon refers to Marxism and feminism as two social theories of power, defining and tracking two 'basic social processes' (p. 4). However, when she is engaged in a critical analysis of Marxist method for feminism, she refers to feminism as 'stand[ing] in relation to marxism as marxism does to classical political economy: its final conclusion and ultimate critique' (p. 125).
2. Ibid., p. 125.
3. Ibid., p. 108.
4. Ibid., p. 3. One can begin to discern here a number of problems with the parallel MacKinnon is attempting to establish between work and sex, class and gender. Sexuality, which MacKinnon defines at times as the organization of desire—leaving open an ensemble of questions about the ontological status of desire—and at other times as 'whatever a given society eroticizes'—leaving open questions about the ontological status of society and the erotic—is the 'linchpin of gender inequality' because sexuality is a form of power, indeed, the form of power that creates gender. Marx, of course, rooted his argument

about labor as power in labor's generativity—its capacity to produce a surplus that could be commodified as labor power, appropriated as surplus value, and congealed as capital. While MacKinnon posits the 'organized expropriation of the sexuality of some for the use of others' as defining the sex, woman, and posits 'gender and family as its congealed forms' (*Toward a Feminist Theory of the State*, pp. 3–4), she never quite specifies how—through what generativity—the political economy of sexuality is orchestrated. Thus, where Marx's argument is logical (dialectical) and developmental (progressive), MacKinnon's is tautological (circular) and static (rooted in equivalents and syllogisms). As will become clear in the last portion of this chapter, this has political implications that exceed the mere irritant of its analytic incoherence.

5. Ibid., p. 113.
6. *Feminism Unmodified: Discourses on Life and Law* (Cambridge, Mass. Harvard University Press, 1987), p. 50.
7. *Toward a Feminist Theory of the State*, pp. 109–12.
8. *Feminism Unmodified*, p. 172.
9. Ibid., p. 148.
10. 'Underlying marxist attempts to accommodate or respond to feminism, including most socialist-feminist theories, is one of three approaches: equate and collapse, derive and subordinate, and substitute contradictions' (*Toward a Feminist Theory of the State*, p. 60).
11. Ibid., p. 39.
12. Ibid., p. 4.
13. 'The Mirror of Production', in *Selected Writings*, ed. Mark Poster (Stanford, Calif. Stanford University Press, 1988), pp. 104–5.
14. *The Human Condition* (Chicago: University of Chicago Press, 1958). p. 87.
15. 'Mirror of Production', pp. 105, 104.
16. Ibid., p. 105.
17. Baudrillard himself mentions psychoanalytic categories as taking flight from the history that produces them—'What we have said about the Marxist concepts holds for the unconscious, repression, Oedipus complex, etc. as well' ('Mirror of Production', p. 113)—but it is not a point that he develops. Moreover, Baudrillard implies that the problem with the psychoanalytic concepts is their complicity with the Marxist economic one. My point, which could not be Baudrillard's, given his inattention to the construction of gender, is that their dehistoricized character is linked to the naturalized constituents of gender.
18. This is, crucially, a different argument from Hegel's argument about the relation of philosophy to history in which the 'owl of Minerva flies at dusk', For I am suggesting that the reduction of gender construction and regulation to heterosexual sexual orders is a historical process of our time, not that MacKinnon is only retrospectively grasping what held together an order now unraveling. Yet I also want to make the second argument: Evidence of the unraveling of the heterosexual gender regime is everywhere in popular culture, from Madonna and Michael Jackson to Ronald Reagan's possibly queer son and PeeWee Herman. In short, MacKinnon is theorizing a very peculiar historical moment, as Marx did when he described 'society as a whole as more and more splitting up into two great hostile camps, into two great classes directly facing each other' (*Manifesto of the Communist Party*, in *The Marx–Engels Reader*, 2d ed., ed. R. C. Tucker (New York: Norton, 1978), p. 474).

19. 'Mirror of Production', p. 104.
20. MacKinnon herself glimpses this: '[I]f you understand that pornography literally means what it says, you might conclude that sexuality has become the fascism of contemporary America and we are moving into the last days of Weimar' (*Feminism Unmodified*, p. 15).
21. Nietzsche, *Twilight of the Idols*, in *The Portable Nietzsche*, ed. W. Kaufmann (New York: Viking. 1954). Nietzsche argues that the hyperrationality of the Greeks should be read as a symptom: 'The fanaticism with which all Greek reflection throws itself upon rationality betrays a desperate situation; there was danger, there was but one choice: either to perish or—to be *absurdly rational*' (p. 478).
22. *Feminism Unmodified*, p. 15.
23. *Beyond Accommodation: Ethical Feminism, Deconstruction, and the Law* (New York: Routledge, 1991), p. 119.
24. *Toward a Feminist Theory of the State*, p. 118.
25. Ibid., p.119.
26. Ibid., p. 124.
27. Ibid., p. 118.
28. Ibid., p. 119. In 'Does Sexuality Have a History?' (*Discourses of Sexuality: From Aristotle to AIDS*, ed. Domna Stanton (Ann Arbor: University of Michigan Press, 1992)), MacKinnon comments further on lesbian sexuality, but not in ways that are either analytically compelling or politically consistent. Here is a sample: 'Women and men are still women and men in the world, even when they are gay or lesbian. That makes lesbian women distinctively subordinated within a subordinate group, women, and gay men distinctively subordinated within a dominant group, men.

    Heterosexuality is constructed around gender, as the dominant paradigm of sex; homosexuality is constructed around gender, as the subordinated paradigm of sex. Both are deeply invested in gender, if in different ways' (p. 135).
29. *Feminism Unmodified*, p. 148.
30. Ibid., p. 149.
31. *Communist Manifesto*, p. 474.
32. Ibid., p. 483.
33. See Drucilla Cornell's critique of MacKinnon, in which she argues that 'the feminine' is not reducible to what women are made to be for men: 'Put very simply, MacKinnon's central error is to reduce feminine "reality" to the sexualized object we are for *them* by *identifying* the feminine totally with the "real world" as it is seen and constructed through the male gaze' (*Beyond Accommodation*, p. 130). Cornell seeks to avoid MacKinnon's totalization, on the one side, and an essentialized femininity, on the other, by mobilizing a 'feminine imaginary' that is productive even as it is without specific content (see *Beyond Accommodation*, p. 17).
34. 'The Poverty of Philosophy', in *Marx–Engels Reader*, p. 218.
35. *Toward a Feminist Theory of the State*, p. 115.

11 The 2 Live Crew Controversy

Kimberle Crenshaw

In June 1990, the members of 2 Live Crew were arrested and charged under a Florida obscenity statute for their performance in an adults-only club in Hollywood, Florida. The arrests came just two days after a federal court judge ruled that the sexually explicit lyrics in 2 Live Crew's album, As Nasty As They Wanna Be,[1] were obscene.[2] Although the members of 2 Live Crew were eventually acquitted of charges stemming from the live performance, the federal court determination that Nasty is obscene still stands. This obscenity judgment, along with the arrests and subsequent trial, prompted an intense public controversy about rap music, a controversy that merged with a broader debate about the representation of sex and violence in popular music, about cultural diversity, and about the meaning of freedom of expression.

Two positions dominated the debate over 2 Live Crew. Writing in *Newsweek*, political columnist George Will staked out a case for the prosecution.[3] Will argued that Nasty was misogynistic filth and characterized 2 Live Crew's performance as a profoundly repugnant 'combination of extreme infantilism and menace' that objectified Black women and represented them as suitable targets of sexual violence.[4] The most prominent defense of 2 Live Crew was advanced by Henry Louis Gates, Jr., Harvard professor and expert on African-American literature. In a *New York Times* op-ed piece and in testimony at the criminal trial, Gates contended that 2 Live Crew's members were important artists operating within and inventively elaborating upon distinctively African-American forms of cultural expression.[5] According to Gates, the characteristic exaggeration featured in 2 Live Crew's lyrics served a political end: to explode popular racist stereotypes in a

Kimberle Crenshaw, edited extract from 'The 2 Live Crew Controversy' *Stanford Law Review*, 1241 (1993) 20–52, reprinted by permission of the author and the publisher via Copyright Clearance Center, Inc.

comically extreme form.[6] Where Will saw a misogynistic assault on Black women by social degenerates, Gates found a form of 'sexual carnivalesque' with the promise to free us from the pathologies of racism.[7]

Unlike Gates, there are many who do not simply 'bust out laughing' upon first hearing 2 Live Crew.[8] One does a disservice to the issue to describe the images of women in Nasty as simply 'sexually explicit'.[9] Listening to Nasty, we hear about 'cunts' being 'fucked' until backbones are cracked, 'asses' being 'busted', 'dicks' rammed down throats, and semen splattered across faces. Black women are 'cunts', 'bitches', and all-purpose 'hos'.[10]

This is no mere braggadocio. Those who are concerned about high rates of gender violence in our communities must be troubled by the possible connections between these images and the tolerance for violence against women. Children and teenagers are listening to this music, and one cannot but be concerned that the range of acceptable behavior is being broadened by the constant propagation of misogynistic imagery. One must worry as well about young Black women who, like young men, are learning that their value lies between their legs. But the sexual value of women, unlike that of men, is a depletable commodity; boys become men by expanding theirs, while girls become whores.

Nasty is misogynist, and an intersectional analysis of the case against 2 Live Crew should not depart from a full acknowledgement of that misogyny. But such an analysis must also consider whether an exclusive focus on issues of gender risks overlooking aspects of the prosecution of 2 Live Crew that raise serious questions of racism.

THE OBSCENITY PROSECUTION OF 2 LIVE CREW

An initial problem with the obscenity prosecution of 2 Live Crew was its apparent selectivity.[11] Even the most superficial comparison between 2 Live Crew and other mass-marketed sexual representations suggests the likelihood that race played some role in distinguishing 2 Live Crew as the first group ever to be prosecuted for obscenity in connection with a musical recording, and one of a handful of recording artists to be prosecuted for a live performance. Recent controversies about sexism, racism, and violence in popular culture point to a vast range of expression that might have provided targets for censorship, but was left untouched. Madonna has acted out masturbation, portrayed the seduction of a priest, and insinuated group sex on stage,[12] but she has never been prosecuted for obscenity. While 2 Live Crew was performing in Hollywood, Florida, Andrew Dice Clay's recordings were being sold in stores and he was performing nationwide on HBO. Well-known for his racist 'humor', Clay is also comparable to 2 Live Crew in sexual explicitness and misogyny. In his show, for example, Clay offers, 'Eenie, meenie, minee, mo / Suck my [expletive] and swallow slow', and 'Lose the bra, bitch'.[13] Moreover, graphic sexual images—many of them violent—were widely available in Broward County where the performance and trial took place. According to the testimony of a Broward County vice detective, 'nude dance shows and adult bookstores are scattered throughout the county where 2 Live Crew performed.'[14] Given the availability of other forms of sexually explicit 'entertainment' in Broward County, Florida, one might wonder how 2 Live Crew could have been seen as uniquely obscene by the lights of the 'community standards' of the county.[15] After all, patrons of certain Broward County clubs 'can see women dancing with at least their breasts exposed', and bookstore patrons can 'view and purchase films and magazines that depict vaginal, oral and anal sex, homosexual sex and group sex'.[16] In arriving at its finding of obscenity, the court placed little weight on the available range of films, magazines, and live shows as evidence of the community's sensibilities. Instead, the court apparently accepted the sheriff's testimony that the decision to single out Nasty was based on the number of complaints against 2 Live Crew 'communicated by telephone calls, anonymous messages, or letters to the police'.[17]

Evidence of this popular outcry was never substantiated. But even if it were, the case for selectivity would remain.[18] The history of social repression of Black male sexuality is long, often violent, and all too famillar.[19] Negative reactions to the sexual conduct of Black men have traditionally had racist overtones, especially where that conduct threatens to 'cross over' into the mainstream community.[20] So even if the decision to prosecute did reflect a widespread community perception of the purely prurient character of 2 Live Crew's music, that perception itself might reflect an established pattern of vigilante attitudes directed toward the sexual expression of Black men.[21] In short, the appeal to community standards does not undercut a concern about racism; rather, it underscores that concern.

A second troubling dimension of the case brought against 2 Live Crew was the court's apparent disregard for the culturally rooted aspects of 2 Live Crew's music. Such disregard was essential to a finding of obscenity given the third prong of the Miller test requiring that material judged obscene must, taken as a whole, lack literary, artistic, or political value.[22] 2 Live Crew argued that this criterion of the Miller test was not met in the case of Nasty since the recording exemplified such African-American cultural modes as 'playing the dozens', 'call and response', and 'signifying'.[23] The court denied each of the group's claims of cultural specificity, recharacterizing in more generic terms what 2 Live Crew contended was distinctly African American. According to the court, 'playing the dozens' is 'commonly seen in adolescents, especially boys, of all ages'; 'boasting' appears to be 'part of the universal human condition'; and the cultural origins of 'call and response'—featured in a song on Nasty about fellatio in which competing groups chanted 'less filling' and 'tastes great'—were to be found in a Miller beer commercial, not in African-American cultural tradition.[24] The possibility that the Miller beer commercial may have itself evolved from an African-American cultural tradition was apparently lost on the court.

In disregarding the arguments made on behalf of 2 Live Crew, the court denied that the form and style of Nasty and, by implication, rap music in general had any artistic merit. This disturbing dismissal of the cultural attributes of rap and the effort to universalize African-American modes of expression are a form of colorblindness that presumes to level all significant racial and ethnic differences in order to pass judgment on intergroup conflicts. The court's analysis here also manifests a frequently encountered strategy of cultural appropriation. African-American contributions that have been accepted by the mainstream culture are eventually absorbed as simply 'American' or found to be 'universal'. Other modes associated with African-American culture that resist absorption remain distinctive and are either neglected or dismissed as 'deviant'.

The court apparently rejected as well the possibility that even the most misogynistic rap may have political value as a discourse of resistance. The element of resistance found in some rap is in making people uncomfortable, thereby challenging received habits of thought and action. Such challenges are potentially political, as are more subversive attempts to contest traditional rules by becoming what is most feared.[25] Against a historical backdrop in which the Black male as social outlaw is a prominent theme, 'gangsta' rap' might be taken as a rejection of a conciliatory stance aimed at undermining fear through reassurance, in favor of a more subversive form of opposition that attempts to challenge the rules precisely by becoming the very social outlaw that society fears and attempts to proscribe. Rap representations celebrating an aggressive Black male sexuality can be easily construed as discomforting and oppositional. Not only does reading rap in this way preclude a finding that Nasty lacks political value, it also defeats the court's assumption that the group's intent was to appeal solely to prurient interests. To be sure, these considerations carry greater force in the case of other rap artists, such as N.W.A., Too Short, Ice Cube, and The Geto Boys, all of whose standard fare includes depictions of violent assault, rape, rape-murder, and mutilation.[26] In fact, had these other groups been targeted rather than the comparatively less offensive 2 Live Crew, they might have successfully defeated prosecution. The graphic violence in their representations militate against a finding of obscenity by suggesting an intent not to appeal to prurient interests but instead to more expressly political ones. So long as violence is seen as distinct from sexuality, the prurient interest requirement may provide a shield for the more violent rap artists. However, even this somewhat formalistic dichotomy may provide little solace to such rap artists given the historical linkages that have been made between Black male sexuality and violence. Indeed, it has been the specter of violence that surrounds images of Black male sexuality that presented 2 Live Crew as an acceptable target of an obscenity prosecution in a field that included Andrew Dice Clay and countless others.

The point here is not that the distinction between sex and violence should be rigorously maintained in determining what is obscene or, more specifically, that rap artists whose standard fare is more violent ought to be protected. To the contrary, these more violent groups should be much more troubling than 2 Live Crew. My point instead is to suggest that obscenity prosecutions of rap artists do nothing to protect the interests of those most directly implicated in rap—Black women. On the one hand, prevailing notions of obscenity separate out sexuality from violence, which has the effect of shielding the more violently misogynistic groups from prosecution; on the other, historical linkages between images of Black male sexuality and violence permit the singling out of 'lightweight' rappers for prosecution among all other purveyors of explicit sexual imagery.

ADDRESSING THE INTERSECTIONALITY

Although Black women's interests were quite obviously irrelevant in the 2 Live Crew obscenity judgment, their images figured prominently in the public case supporting the prosecution. George Will's *Newsweek* essay provides a striking example of how Black women's bodies were appropriated and deployed in the broader attack against 2 Live Crew. Commenting on 'America's Slide into the Sewers', Will laments that

> America today is capable of terrific intolerance about smoking, or toxic waste that threatens trout. But only a deeply confused society is more concerned about protecting lungs than minds, trout than black women. We legislate against smoking in restaurants; singing 'Me So Horny' is a constitutional right. Secondary smoke is carcinogenic; celebration of torn vaginas is 'mere words'.[27]

Lest one be misled into thinking that Will has become an ally of Black women, Will's real concern is suggested by his repeated references to the Central Park jogger assault. Will writes, 'Her face was so disfigured a friend took 15 minutes to identify her. "I recognized her ring." Do you recognize the relevance of 2 Live Crew?'[28] While the connection between the threat of 2 Live Crew and the image of the Black male rapist was suggested subtly in the public debate, it is blatant throughout Will's discussion. Indeed, it bids to be the central theme of the essay. 'Fact: Some members of a particular age and societal cohort—the one making 2 Live Crew rich—stomped and raped the jogger to the razor edge of death, for the fun of it'.[29] Will directly indicts 2 Live Crew in the Central Park jogger rape through a fictional dialogue between himself and the defendants. Responding to one defendant's alleged confession that the rape was fun, Will asks, 'Where can you get the idea that sexual violence against women is fun? From a music store, through Walkman earphones, from boom boxes blaring forth the rap lyrics of 2 Live Crew'.[30] Since the rapists were young Black males and Nasty presents Black men celebrating sexual violence, 2 Live Crew was in Central Park that night, providing the underlying accompaniment to a vicious assault. Ironically, Will rejected precisely this kind of argument in the context of racist speech on the ground that efforts to link racist speech to racist violence presume that those who hear racist speech will mindlessly act on what they hear.[31] Apparently, the certain 'social cohort' that produces and consumes racist speech is fundamentally different from the one that produces and consumes rap music.

Will invokes Black women—twice—as victims of this music. But if he were really concerned with the threat of 2 Live Crew to Black women, why does the Central Park jogger figure so prominently in his argument? Why not the Black woman in Brooklyn who was gang-raped and then thrown down an airshaft? In fact, Will fails even to mention Black victims of sexual violence, which suggests that Black women simply function for Will as stand-ins for white women. Will's use of the Black female body to press the case against 2 Live Crew recalls the strategy of the prosecutor in Richard Wright's novel *Native Son*. Bigger Thomas, Wright's Black male protagonist, is on trial for killing Mary Dalton, a white woman. Because Bigger burned her body, it cannot be established whether Bigger had sexually assaulted her, so the prosecutor brings in the body of Bessie, a Black woman raped by Bigger and left to die, in order to establish that Bigger had raped Mary Dalton.[32]

These considerations about selectivity, about the denial of cultural specificity, and about the manipulation of Black women's bodies convince me that race played a significant, if not determining, role in the shaping of the case against 2 Live Crew. While using antisexist rhetoric to suggest a concern for women, the attack on 2 Live Crew simultaneously endorses traditional readings of Black male sexuality. The fact that the objects of these violent sexual images are Black women becomes irrelevant in the representation of the threat in terms of the Black rapist/white victim dyad. The Black male becomes the agent of sexual violence and the white community becomes his potential victim. The subtext of the 2 Live Crew prosecution thus becomes a re-reading of the sexualized racial politics of the past.

While concerns about racism fuel my opposition to the obscenity prosecution of 2 Live Crew, the uncritical support for, and indeed celebration of, 2 Live Crew by other opponents of the prosecution is extremely troubling as well. If the rhetoric of antisexism provided an occasion for racism, so, too, the rhetoric of antiracism provided an occasion for defending the misogyny of 2 Live Crew. That defense took two forms, one political, the other cultural, both advanced prominently by Henry Louis Gates. Gates's political defense argues that 2 Live Crew advances the antiracist agenda by exaggerating stereotypes of Black male sexuality 'to show how ridiculous [they] are'.[33] The defense contends that by highlighting to the extreme the sexism, misogyny, and violence stereotypically associated with Black male sexuality, 2 Live Crew represents a postmodern effort to 'liberate' us from the racism that perpetuates these stereotypes.[34]

Gates is right to contend that the reactions of Will and others confirm that the racial stereotypes still exist, but even if 2 Live Crew intended to explode these stereotypes, their strategy was misguided. Certainly, the group wholly miscalculated the reaction of their white audience, as Will's polemic amply illustrates. Rather than exploding stereotypes, as Gates suggests, 2 Live Crew, it seems most reasonable to argue, was simply (and unsuccessfully) trying to be funny. After all, trading in sexual stereotypes has long been a means to a cheap laugh, and Gates's cultural defense of 2 Live Crew recognizes as much in arguing the identification of the group with a distinctly African-American cultural tradition of the 'dozens' and other forms of verbal boasting, raunchy jokes, and insinuations of sexual prowess, all of which were meant to be laughed at and to gain for the speaker respect for his word wizardry, and not to disrupt conventional myths of Black sexuality.[35] Gates's cultural defense of 2 Live Crew, however, recalls similar efforts on behalf of racist humor, which has sometimes been defended as antiracist—an effort to poke fun at or to show the ridiculousness of racism. More simply, racist humor has often been excused as 'just joking'—even racially motivated assaults have been defended as simple pranks. Thus the racism of an Andrew Dice Clay could be defended in either mode as an attempt to explode racist stereotypes or as simple humor not meant to be taken seriously. Implicit in these defenses is the assumption that racist representations are injurious only if they are intended to injure, or to be taken literally, or are devoid of some other nonracist objective. It is highly unlikely that this rationale would be accepted by Blacks as a persuasive defense of Andrew Dice Clay. Indeed, the Black community's historical and ongoing criticism of such humor suggests widespread rejection of these arguments.

The claim that a representation is meant simply as a joke may be true, but the joke functions as humor within a specific social context in which it frequently reinforces patterns of social power. Though racial humor may sometimes be intended to ridicule racism, the close relationship between the stereotypes and the prevailing images of marginalized people complicates this strategy. And certainly, the humorist's positioning vis-à-vis a targeted group colors how the group interprets a potentially derisive stereotype or gesture. Although one could argue that Black comedians have broader license to market stereotypically racist images, that argument has no force here. 2 Live Crew cannot claim an in-group privilege to perpetuate misogynist humor against Black women: the members of 2 Live Crew are not

Black women, and more importantly, they enjoy a power relationship over them.

Humor in which women are objectified as packages of bodily parts to serve whatever male-bonding/male-competition needs men please subordinates women in much the same way that racist humor subordinates African Americans. Claims that incidences of such humor are just jokes and are not meant to injure or to be taken literally do little to blunt their demeaning quality—nor, for that matter, does the fact that the jokes are told within an intragroup cultural tradition.

The notion that sexism can serve antiracist ends has proponents ranging from Eldridge Cleaver[36] to Shahrazad Ali,[37] all of whom seem to expect Black women to serve as vehicles for the achievement of a 'liberation' that functions to perpetuate their own subordination.[38] Claims of cultural specificity similarly fail to justify toleration of misogyny.[39] While the cultural defense of 2 Live Crew has the virtue of recognizing merit in a form of music common to the Black community, something George Will and the court that convicted 2 Live Crew were all too glib in dismissing, it does not eliminate the need to question both the sexism within the tradition it defends and the objectives to which the tradition has been pressed. The fact that playing the dozens, say, is rooted in the Black cultural tradition, or that themes represented by mythic folk heroes such as 'Stackolee' are African American does not settle the question of whether such practices oppress Black women.[40] Whether these practices are a distinctive part of the African American cultural tradition is decidedly beside the point. The real question is how subordinating aspects of these practices play out in the lives of people in the community, people who share the benefits as well as the burdens of a common culture. With regard to 2 Live Crew, while it may be true that the Black community has accepted the cultural forms that have evolved into rap, that acceptance should not preclude discussion of whether the misogyny within rap is itself acceptable.

With respect to Gates's political and cultural defenses of 2 Live Crew, then, little turns on whether the 'word play' performed by the Crew is a postmodern challenge to racist sexual mythology or simply an internal group practice that crossed over into mainstream America. Both defenses are problematic because they require Black women to accept misogyny and its attendant disrespect and exploitation in the service of some broader group objective, whether it be pursuing an antiracist political agenda or maintaining the cultural integrity of the

Black community. Neither objective obligates Black women to tolerate such misogyny.

Likewise, the superficial efforts of the anti-2 Live Crew movement to link the prosecution of the Crew to the victimization of Black women had little to do with Black women's lives. Those who deployed Black women in the service of condemning 2 Live Crew's misogynist representations did not do so in the interest of empowering Black women; rather, they had other interests in mind, the pursuit of which was racially subordinating. The implication here is not that Black feminists should stand in solidarity with the supporters of 2 Live Crew. The spirited defense of 2 Live Crew was no more about defending the entire Black community than the prosecution was about defending Black women. After all, Black women whose very assault is the subject of the representation can hardly regard the right to be represented as bitches and whores as essential to their interest. Instead, the defense primarily functions to protect 2 Live Crew's prerogative to be as misogynistic as they want to be.[41]

Within the African-American political community, Black women will have to make it clear that patriarchy is a critical issue that negatively affects the lives not only of Black women, but of Black men as well. Doing so would help reshape traditional practices so that evidence of racism would not constitute sufficient justification for uncritical rallying around misogynistic politics and patriarchal values. Although collective opposition to racist practice has been and continues to be crucially important in protecting Black interests, an empowered Black feminist sensibility would require that the terms of unity no longer reflect priorities premised upon the continued marginalization of Black women.

CONCLUSION

This article has presented intersectionality as a way of framing the various interactions of race and gender in the context of violence against women of color. Yet intersectionality might be more broadly useful as a way of mediating the tension between assertions of multiple identity and the ongoing necessity of group politics. It is helpful in this regard to distinguish intersectionality from the closely related perspective of antiessentialism, from which women of color have critically engaged white feminism for the absence of women of color on the one hand, and for speaking for women of color on the other. One rendition of this antiessentialist critique—that feminism essentializes the category woman—owes a great deal to the postmodernist idea that categories we consider natural or merely representational are actually socially constructed in a linguistic economy of difference.[42] While the descriptive project of postmodernism of questioning the ways in which meaning is socially constructed is generally sound, this critique sometimes misreads the meaning of social construction and distorts its political relevance.

One version of antiessentialism, embodying what might be called the vulgarized social construction thesis, is that since all categories are socially constructed, there is no such thing as, say, Blacks or women, and thus it makes no sense to continue reproducing those categories by organizing around them.[43] Even the Supreme Court has gotten into this act. In *Metro Broadcasting, Inc.* v. *FCC*,[44] the Court conservatives, in rhetoric that oozes vulgar constructionist smugness, proclaimed that any set-aside designed to increase the voices of minorities on the air waves was itself based on a racist assumption that skin color is in some way connected to the likely content of one's broadcast.[45]

But to say that a category such as race or gender is socially constructed is not to say that that category has no significance in our world. On the contrary, a large and continuing project for subordinated people—and indeed, one of the projects for which postmodern theories have been very helpful—is thinking about the way power has clustered around certain categories and is exercised against others. This project attempts to unveil the processes of subordination and the various ways those processes are experienced by people who are subordinated and people who are privileged by them. It is, then, a project that presumes that categories have meaning and consequences. And this project's most pressing problem, in many if not most cases, is not the existence of the categories, but rather the particular values attached to them and the way those values foster and create social hierarchies.

This is not to deny that the process of categorization is itself an exercise of power, but the story is much more complicated and nuanced than that. First, the process of categorizing—or, in identity terms, naming—is not unilateral. Subordinated people can and do participate, sometimes even subverting the naming process in empowering ways. One need only think about the historical subversion of the category 'Black' or the current transformation of 'queer' to understand that categorization is not a one-way street. Clearly, there is unequal power, but there is nonetheless some degree of agency that people can and do exert in the politics of naming. And it is important to note that identity continues to be a site of resistance for members of different subordinated groups. We all can recognize the distinction between the claims 'I am Black' and the claim 'I am a person who happens to be Black.' 'I am Black' takes the socially imposed identity and empowers it as an anchor of subjectivity. 'I am Black' becomes not simply a statement of resistance but also a positive discourse of self-identification, intimately linked to celebratory statements like the Black nationalist 'Black is beautiful.' 'I am a person who happens to be Black,' on the other hand, achieves self-identification by straining for a certain universality (in effect, 'I am first a person') and for a concomitant dismissal of the imposed category ('Black') as contingent, circumstantial, nondeterminant. There is truth in both characterizations, of course, but they function quite differently depending on the political context. At this point in history, a strong case can be made that the most critical resistance strategy for disempowered groups is to occupy and defend a politics of social location rather than to vacate and destroy it.

Vulgar constructionism thus distorts the possibilities for meaningful identity politics by conflating at least two separate but closely linked manifestations of power. One is the power exercised simply through the process of categorization; the other, the power to cause that categorization to have social and material consequences. While the former power facilitates the latter, the political implications of challenging one over the other matter greatly. We can look at debates over racial subordination throughout history and see that in each instance, there was a possibility of challenging either the construction of identity or the system of subordination based on that identity. Consider, for example, the segregation system in *Plessy* v. *Ferguson.*[46] At issue were multiple dimensions of domination, including categorization, the sign of race, and the subordination of those so labeled. There were at least two targets for Plessy to challenge: the construction of identity ('What is a Black?'), and the system of subordination based on that identity ('Can Blacks and whites sit together on a train?'). Plessy actually made both arguments, one against the coherence of race as a category, the other against the subordination of those deemed to be Black. In his attack on the former, Plessy argued that the segregation statute's application to him, given his mixed race status, was inappropriate. The Court refused to see this as an attack on the coherence of the race system and instead responded in a way that simply reproduced the Black/white dichotomy that Plessy was challenging. As we know, Plessy's challenge to the segregation system was not successful either. In evaluating various resistance strategies today, it is useful to ask which of Plessy's challenges would have been best for him to have won—the challenge against the coherence of the racial categorization system or the challenge to the practice of segregation?

The same question can be posed for *Brown* v. *Board of Education.*[47] Which of two possible arguments was politically more empowering—that segregation was unconstitutional because the racial categorization system on which it was based was incoherent, or that segregation was unconstitutional because it was injurious to Black children and oppressive to their communities? While it might strike some as a difficult question, for the most part, the dimension of racial domination that has been most vexing to African Americans has not been the social categorization as such, but the myriad ways in which those of us so defined have been systematically subordinated. With particular regard to problems confronting women of color, when identity politics fail us, as they frequently do, it is not primarily because those politics take as natural certain categories that are socially constructed but rather because the descriptive content of those categories and the narratives on which they are based have privileged some experiences and excluded others.

Along these lines, consider the Clarence Thomas/Anita Hill controversy. During the Senate hearings for the confirmation of Clarence Thomas to the Supreme Court, Anita Hill, in bringing allegations of sexual harassment against Thomas, was rhetorically disempowered in part because she fell between the dominant interpretations of feminism and antiracism. Caught between the competing narrative tropes of rape (advanced by feminists) on the one hand and lynching (advanced by Thomas and his antiracist supporters) on the other, the race and gender dimensions of her position could not be told. This dilemma could be described as the consequence of antiracism's essentializing Blackness and feminism's essentializing womanhood. But recognizing as much does not take us far enough, for the problem is not simply linguistic or philosophical in nature. It is specifically political: the narratives of gender are based on the experience of white, middle-class women, and the narratives of race are based on the experience of Black men. The solution does not merely entail arguing for the multiplicity of identities or challenging essentialism generally. Instead, in Hill's case, for example, it would have been necessary to assert those crucial aspects of her location that were erased, even by many of her advocates—that is, to state what difference her difference made.

If, as this analysis asserts, history and context determine the utility of identity politics, how then do we understand identity politics today, especially in light of our recognition of multiple dimensions of identity? More specifically, what does it mean to argue that gender identities have been obscured in antiracist discourses, just as race identities have been obscured in feminist discourses? Does that mean we cannot talk about identity? Or instead, that any discourse about identity has to acknowledge how our identities are constructed through the intersection of multiple dimensions? A beginning response to these questions requires that we first recognize that the organized identity groups in which we find ourselves in are in fact coalitions, or at least potential coalitions waiting to be formed.

In the context of antiracism, recognizing the ways in which the intersectional experiences of women of color are marginalized in prevailing conceptions of identity politics does not require that we give up attempts to organize as communities of color. Rather, intersectionality provides a basis for reconceptualizing race as a coalition between men and women of color. For example, in the area of rape, intersectionality provides a way of explaining why women of color have to abandon the general argument that the interests of the community require the suppression of any confrontation around intraracial rape. Intersectionality may provide the means for dealing with other marginalizations as well. For example, race can also be a coalition of straight and gay people of color, and thus serve as a basis for critique of churches and other cultural institutions that reproduce heterosexism.

With identity thus reconceptualized, it may be easier to understand the need for and to summon the courage to challenge groups that are after all, in one sense, 'home' to us, in the name of the parts of us that are not made at home. This takes a great deal of energy and arouses intense anxiety. The most one could expect is that we will dare to speak against internal exclusions and marginalizations, that we might call attention to how the identity of 'the group' has been centered on the intersectional identities of a few. Recognizing that identity politics takes place at the site where categories intersect thus seems more fruitful than challenging the possibility of talking about categories at all. Through an awareness of intersectionality, we can better acknowledge and ground the differences among us and negotiate the means by which these differences will find expression in constructing group politics.

Notes

1. 2 Live Crew, As Nasty As They Wanna Be (Luke Records 1989).
2. In June 1990, a federal judge ruled that 2 Live Crew's lyrics referring to sodomy and sexual intercourse were obscene. *Skywalker Records, Inc.* v. *Navarro*, 739 F.Supp. 578, 596 (S.D.Fla. 1990). The court held that the recording appealed to the prurient interest, was patently offensive as defined by state law, and taken as a whole, lacked serious literary, artistic or political value. Id. at 591–96. However, the court also held that the sheriff's office had subjected the recording to unconstitutional prior restraint and consequently granted 2 Live Crew permanent injunctive relief. Id. at 596–604. Two days after the judge declared the recording obscene, 2 Live Crew members were charged with giving an obscene performance at a club in Hollywood, Florida. 'Experts Defend Live Crew Lyrics', UPI, Oct. 19, 1990. Deputy sheriffs also arrested Charles Freeman, a merchant who was selling copies of the Nasty recording. See Gene Santoro, 'How 2 B Nasty', *Nation*, July 2, 1990, at 4. The 11th Circuit reversed the conviction, *Luke Records, Inc.* v. *Navarro*, 960 F.2d 134 (11th Cir.1992).
3. George F. Will, 'America's Slide into the Sewer', *Newsweek*, July 30, 1990, at 64.
4. Id.
5. Henry Louis Gates, '2 Live Crew, Decoded', *N.Y. Times*, June 19, 1990, at A23. Professor Gates, who testified on behalf of 2 Live Crew in the criminal proceeding stemming from their live performance, pointed out that the members of 2 Live Crew were expressing themselves in coded messages, and were engaging in parody. 'For centuries, African-Americans have been forced to develop coded ways of communicating to protect them from danger. Allegories and double meanings, words redefined to mean their opposites . . . have enabled blacks to share messages only the initiated understood.' Id. Similarly, parody is a component of 'the street tradition called "signifying" or "playing the dozens," which has generally been risque, and where the best signifier or "rapper" is the one who invents the most extravagant images, the biggest "lies," as the culture says.' Id.
6. Testifying during 2 Live Crew's prosecution for obscenity, Gates argued that, '[o]ne of the brilliant things about these four songs is they embrace that stereotype [of blacks having overly large sexual organs and being hypersexed individuals]. They name it and they explode it. You can have no reaction but to bust out laughing. The fact that they're being sung by four virile young black men is inescapable to the audience.' Laura Parker, 'Rap Lyrics Likened to Literature; Witness in 2 Live Crew Trial Cites Art, Parody, Precedents,' *Wash. Post*, Oct. 20, 1990, at Dl.
7. Compare Gates, note 5 above (labeling 2 Live Crew's braggadocio as 'sexual carnivalesque') with Will, note 3 above (characterizing 2 Live Crew as 'lower animals').
8. See note 6 above.
9. Although I have elected to print some of the actual language from Nasty, much of the debate about this case has proceeded without any specific discussion of the lyrics. There are reasons one might avoid repeating such sexually explicit material. Among the more compelling ones is the concern that presenting lyrics outside of their fuller musical context hampers a complex

understanding and appreciation of the art form of rap itself. Doing so also essentializes one dimension of the art work—its lyrics—to stand for the whole. Finally, focusing on the production of a single group may contribute to the impression that that group—here, 2 Live Crew—fairly represents all rappers.

Recognizing these risks, I believe that it is nonetheless important to incorporate excerpts from the Crew's lyrics into this analysis. Not only are the lyrics legally relevant in any substantive discussion of the obscenity prosecution, but also their inclusion here serves to reveal the depth of misogyny many African-American women must grapple with in order to defend 2 Live Crew. This is particularly true for African-American women who have been sexually abused by men in their lives. Of course, it is also the case that many African-American women who are troubled by the sexual degradation of Black women in some rap music can and do enjoy rap music generally.

10. See generally 2 Live Crew, note 1 above; N.W.A., Straight Outta Compton (Priority Records, Inc. 1988); N.W.A., N.W.A. & The Posse (Priority Records, Inc. 1989).
11. There is considerable support for the assertion that prosecution of 2 Live Crew and other rap groups is a manifestation of selective repression of Black expression which is no more racist or sexist than expression by non-Black groups. The most flagrant example is Geffen Records' decision not to distribute an album by the rap act, the Geto Boys. Geffen explained that 'the extent to which The Geto Boys album glamorizes and possibly endorses violence, racism, and misogyny compels us to encourage Def American (the group's label) to select a distributor with a greater affinity for this musical expression'. Greg Ket, 'No Sale, Citing Explicit Lyrics, Distributor Backs Away From Geto Boys Album', *Chicago Trib.*, Sept. 13, 1990, § 5, at 9. Geffen apparently has a greater affinity for the likes of Andrew Dice Clay and Guns 'N Roses, non-Black acts which have come under fire for racist and sexist comments. Despite criticism of Guns 'N Roses for lyrics which include 'niggers' and Clay's 'joke' about Native Americans (see note 13 below), Geffen continued to distribute their recordings. Id.
12. See Derrick Z. Jackson, 'Why Must Only Rappers Take the Rap?', *Boston Globe*, June 17, 1990, at A17.
13. Id. at A20. Not only does Clay exhibit sexism comparable to, if not greater than, that of 2 Live Crew, he also intensifies the level of hatred by flaunting racism: 'Indians, bright people, huh? They're still livin' in [expletive] tepees. They deserved it. They're dumb as [expletive].' Id. (quoting Clay).

    One commentator asked, 'What separates Andrew Dice Clay and 2 Live Crew? Answer: Foul-mouthed Andrew Dice Clay is being chased by the producers of "Saturday Night Live." Foul-mouthed 2 Live Crew are being chased by the police.' Id. at A17. When Clay did appear on Saturday Night Live, a controversy was sparked because cast member Nora Dunn and musical guest Sinead O'Connor refused to appear. Jean Seligmann, 'Dicey Problem,' *Newsweek*, May 21, 1990, at 95.
14. Jane Sutton, Untitled, 2 Live Crew, UPI, Oct.18, 1990.
15. Prosecuting 2 Live Crew but not Clay might be justified by the argument that there is a distinction between 'obscenity', defined as expressions of prurient interests, and 'pornography' or 'racist speech', defined as expressions of

misogyny and race hatred, respectively. 2 Live Crew's prurient expressions could be prosecuted as constitutionally unprotected obscenity while Clay's protected racist and misogynistic expressions could not. Such a distinction has been subjected to critical analysis. See Catharine A. MacKinnon, 'Not A Moral Issue', 2 *Yale L. & Pol'y Rev.* 321 (1984). The distinction does not explain why other expressions which appeal more directly to 'prurient interests' are not prosecuted. Further, 2 Live Crew's prurient appeal is produced, at least in part, through the degradation of women. Accordingly, there can be no compelling distinction between the appeal Clay makes and that of 2 Live Crew.

16. Sutton, note 14 above.
17. *Skywalker Records, Inc.* v. *Navarro*, 739 F.Supp. 578, 589 (S.D.Fla 1990). The court rejected the defendants' argument that 'admission of other sexually explicit works' is entitled to great weight in determining community standards and held that 'this type of evidence does not even have to be considered even if the comparable works have been found to be nonobscene'. Id. (citing *Hamling* v. *United States*, 418 U.S. 82, 126–27 (1974)). Although the court gave 'some weight' to sexually explict writings in books and magazines, Eddie Murphy's audio tape of Raw, and Andrew Dice Clay's tape recording, it did not explain why these verbal messages 'analogous to the format in the Nasty recording' were not obscene as well. Id.
18. One report suggested that the complaint came from a lawyer, Jack Thompson. Thompson has continued his campaign, expanding his net to include rap artists The Geto Boys and Too Short. Sara Rimer, 'Obscenity or Art? Trial on Rap Lyrics Opens', *N.Y. Times*, Oct. 17, 1990, at Al. Despite the appearance of selective enforcement, it is doubtful that any court would be persuaded that the requisite racial motivation was proved. Even evidence of racial disparity in the heaviest of criminal penalties—the death sentence—is insufficient to warrant relief absent of specific evidence of discrimination in the defendant's case. See *McClesky*. v. *Kemp*, 481 U.S. 279 (1987).
19. See 43 *Stanford Law Review*, 2141 (1993), notes 101–104 and accompanying text.
20. Some critics speculate that the prosecution of 2 Live Crew has less to do with obscenity than with the traditional policing of Black males, especially as it relates to sexuality. Questioning whether 2 Live Crew is more obscene than Andrew Dice Clay, Gates states, 'Clearly, this rap group is seen as more threatening than others that are just as sexually explicit. Can this be completely unrelated to the specter of the young black male as a figure of sexual and social disruption, the very stereotypes that 2 Live Crew seems determined to undermine?' Gates, note 5 above. Clarence Page makes a similar point, speculating that '2 Live Crew has become the scapegoat for widespread frustration shared by many blacks and whites over a broad range of social problems that seem to have gotten out of control.' Clarence Page, 'Culture, Taste and Standard-Setting,' *Chicago Trib.*, Oct. 7, 1990, § 4, at 3. Page implies, however, that this explanation is something more than or different from racism. 'Could it be (drumroll, please) racism? Or could it be fear?' Id. (emphasis added). Page's definition of racism apparently does not include the possibility that it is racist to attach one's societal fears and discomforts to a subordinated and highly stigmatized 'other'. In other words, scapegoating, at least in this coun-

try, has traditionally been, and still is, considered racist, whatever the source of the fear.

21. Even in the current era, this vigilantism is sometimes tragically expressed. Yusef Hawkins became a victim of it in New York on August 23, 1989, when he was killed by a mob of white men who believed themselves to be protecting 'their' women from being taken by Black men. UPI, May 18, 1990, Jesse Jackson called Hawkins's slaying a 'racially and sexually motivated lynching' and compared it to the 1955 murder of black Mississippi youth Emmett Till, who was killed by men who thought he whistled at a white woman. Id. Even those who denied the racial overtones of Hawkins's murder produced alternative explanations that were part of the same historical narrative. Articles about the Hawkins incident focused on Gina Feliciano as the cause of the incident, attacking her credibility. See, e.g., Lorrin Anderson, 'Cracks in the Mosaic', *Nat'l Rev.*, June 25, 1990, at 36. 'Gina instigated the trouble . . . . Gina used drugs and apparently still does. She dropped out of a rehabilitation program before testifying for the prosecution at trial' and was later picked up by the police and 'charged with possession of cocaine—15 vials of crack fell out of her purse, police said, and she had a crack pipe in her bra.' Id. at 37. At trial, defense attorney Stephen Murphy claimed that Feliciano 'lied, . . . perjured herself . . . . She divides, polarizes eight million people . . . . It's despicable what she did, making this a racial incident.' Id. (quoting Murphy). But feminists attacked the 'scapegoating' of Feliciano, one stating, 'Not only are women the victims of male violence, they're blamed for it.' Alexis Jetter, 'Protesters Blast Scapegoat Tactics', *Newsday*, Apr. 3, 1990, at 29 (quoting Francoise Jacobsohn, president of the New York chapter of the National Organization for Women). According to Merle Hoffinan, founder of the New York Pro-Choice Coalition, 'Gina's personal life has nothing to do with the crime, . . . [b]ut rest assured, they'll go into her sexual history. . . . It's all part of the "she made me do it" idea.' Id. (quoting Hoffman). And New York columnist Ilene Barth observed that 'Gender . . . has a role in New York's race war. Fingers were pointed in Bensonhurst last week at a teenage girl . . . [who] never harmed anyone . . . . Word of her invitation offended local studs, sprouting macho-freaks determined to own local turf and the young females in their ethnic group. . . . [W]omen have not made the headlines as part of marauding bands intent on racial assault. But they number among their victims.' Ilene Barth, 'Let the Women of Bensonhurst Lead Us in a Prayer Vigil', *Newsday*, Sept. 3, 1989, at 10.

22. The Supreme Court articulated its standard for obscenity in *Miller* v. *California*, 413 U.S. 15 (1973), reh'g denied, 414 U.S. 881 (1973). The Court held that the basic guidelines for the trier of fact were (a) 'whether the "average person, applying contemporary community standards" would find that the work, taken as a whole, appeals to the prurient interest'; (b) 'whether the work depicts or describes, in a patently offensive way, sexual conduct specifically defined by the applicable state law'; and (c) 'whether the work, taken as a whole, lacks serious literary, artistic, political, or scientific value.' Id. at 24 (citations omitted).

23. See Gates, note 5 above.

24. *Skywalker Records, Inc.* v. *Navarro*, 739 F.Supp. 578, 595 (S.D.Fla. 1990). The commercial appropriation of rap is readily apparent in pop culture. Soft drink

and fast food commercials now feature rap even though the style is sometimes presented without its racial/cultural face. Dancing McDonald's french fries and the Pillsbury Doughboy have gotten into the rap act. The crossover of rap is not the problem; instead, it is the tendency, represented in Skywalker, to reject the cultural origins of language and practices which are disturbing. This is part of an overall pattern of cultural appropriation that pre-dates the rap controversy. Most starkly illustrated in music and dance, cultural trailblazers like Little Richard and James Brown have been squeezed out of their place in popular consciousness to make room for Elvis Presley, Mick Jagger, and others. The meteoric rise of white rapper Vanilla Ice is a contemporary example.

25. Gates argues that 2 Live Crew is undermining the 'specter of the young black male as a figure of sexual and social disruption'. Gates, note 5 above. Faced with 'racist stereotypes about black sexuality', he explains, 'you can do one of two things: you can disavow them or explode them with exaggeration.' Id. 2 Live Crew, Gates suggests, has chosen to burst the myth by parodying exaggerations of the 'oversexed black female and male'. Id.
26. Other rap acts that have been singled out for their violent lyrics include Ice Cube, The Geto Boys, and Too Short. See, e.g., Ice Cube, Kill At Will (Gangsta Boogie Music (ASCAP)/UJAMA Music, Inc. 1990); Geto Boys, The Geto Boys (N-The-Water Music, Inc. (ASCAP) 1989); Too Short, Short Dog's In the House (RCA Records 1990). Not all rap lyrics are misogynist. Moreover, even misogynist acts also express a political world view. The differences among rap groups and the artistic value of the medium is sometimes overlooked by mainstream critics. See, e.g., Jerry Adler, 'The Rap Attitude', *Newsweek*, Mar. 19, 1990, at 56, 57 (labeling rap as a 'bombastic, self-aggrandizing' by-product of the growing 'Culture of Attitude'). Adler's treatment of rap set off a storm of responses. See, e.g., Patrick Goldstein, 'Pop Eye: Rappers Don't Have Time For Newsweek's Attitude', *L.A. Times*, Mar. 25, 1990, at 90 (Magazine). Said Russell Simmons, chairman of Def-Jam Records, rap's most successful label, 'Surely the moral outrage in [Adler's] piece would be better applied to contemporary American crises in health care, education, homelessness . . . . Blaming the victims—in this case America's black working class and underclass—is never a very useful approach to problem-solving.' Id. (quoting Simmons).
27. See Will, note 3 above.
28. Id.
29. Id.
30. Id.
31. See George F. Will, 'On Campuses, Liberals Would Gag Free Speech', *Newsday*, Nov. 6, 1989, at 62.
32. Richard Wright, *Native Son*, 305–8 (Perennial Library ed. 1989) (1940). Wright wrote, 'Though he had killed a black girl and a white girl, he knew that it would be for the death of the white girl that he would be punished. The black girl was merely "evidence." And under it all he knew that white people did not really care about Bessie's being killed. White people never searched for Negroes who killed other Negroes.' Id. at 306–07.
33. Gates, note 5 above. Gates's defense of 2 Live Crew portrayed the group as engaging in postmodern guerrilla warfare against racist sterotypes of Black sexuality. Says Gates, '2 Live Crew's music exaggerates stereotypes of black

men and women to show how ridiculous those portrayals are. One of the brilliant things about these songs is that they embrace the stereotypes . . . . It's ridiculous. That's why we laugh about them. That is one of the things I noticed in the audience's reaction. There is no undertone of violence. There's laughter, there's joy.' Id. Gates repeats the celebratory theme elsewhere, linking 2 Live Crew to Eddie Murphy and other Black male performers because they're saying all the things that we couldn't say even in the 1960s about our own excesses, things we could only whisper in dark rooms. They're saying we're going to explode all these sacred cows. It's fascinating, and it's upsetting everybody—not just white people but black people. But it's a liberating moment. John Pareles, 'An Album is Judged Obscene; Rap: Slick, Violent, Nasty and, Maybe Hopeful', *N.Y. Times*, June 17, 1990, at 1 (quoting Gates). For a cogent intersectional analysis of Eddie Murphy's popular appeal, see Herman Beavers, 'The Cool Pose: Intersectionality, Masculinity and Quiescence in the Comedy and Films of Richard Pryor and Eddie Murphy' (unpublished manuscript) (on file with the *Stanford Law Review*).

34. Gates and others who defend 2 Live Crew as postmodern comic heroes tend to dismiss or downplay the misogyny represented in their rap. Said Gates, 'Their sexism is so flagrant, however, that it almost cancels itself out in a hyperbolic war between the sexes.' Gates, note 5 above.
35. See note 5 above.
36. See 43 *Stanford Law Review*, 1241 (1993), note 47.
37. See ibid., notes 37–42 and accompanying text.
38. Gates occasionally claims that both Black male and Black female images are exploded by 2 Live Crew. Even if Gates's view holds true for Black male images, the strategy does not work—and was not meant to work—for Black women. Black women are not the actors in 2 Live Crew's strategy; they are acted upon. To challenge the images of Black women, Black women themselves would have to embrace them, not simply permit Black men to 'act out' on them. The only Black female rap groups that might conceivably claim such a strategy are Bytches With Problems and Hoes With Attitudes. Yet, having listened to the music of these Black female rap groups, I am not sure that exploding racist images is either their intent or effect. This is not to say, of course, that all Black female rap is without its strategies of resistance. See note 42 below.
39. It is interesting that whether those judging the 2 Live Crew case came out for or against, all seemed to reject the notion that race has anything to do with their analysis. See *Skywalker Records, Inc.* v. *Navarro*, 739 F.Supp. 578, 594–96 (S.D. Fla 1990) (rejecting defense contention that 2 Live Crew's Nasty had artistic value as Black cultural expression); see also Sara Rimer, 'Rap Band Members Found Not Guilty in Obscenity Trial', *N.Y. Times*, Oct. 21, 1990, at A 30 ('Jurors said they did not agree with the defense's assertion that the 2 Live Crew's music had to be understood in the context of black culture. They said they thought race had nothing to do with it.'). Clarence Page also rejects the argument that 2 Live Crew's Nasty must be valued as Black cultural expression: 'I don't think 2 Live Crew can be said to represent black culture any more than, say, Andrew Dice Clay can be said to represent white culture. Rather, I think both represent a lack of culture.' See Page, note 20 above.
40. Gay men are also targets of homophobic humor that might be defended as

culturally specific. Consider the homophobic humor of such comedians as Eddie Murphy, Arsenio Hall, and Damon Wayans and David Alan Grier, the two actors who currently portray Black gay men on the television show In Living Color. Critics have linked these homophobic representations of Black gay men to patterns of subordination within the Black community. Black gay filmmaker Marlon Riggs has argued that such caricatures discredit Black gay men's claim to Black manhood, presenting them as 'game for play, to be used, joked about, put down, beaten, slapped, and bashed, not just by illiterate homophobic thugs in the night, but by black American culture's best and brightest'. Marlon Riggs, 'Black Macho Revisited: Reflections of a SNAP! Queen', in *Brother to Brother: New Writings by Black Gay Men* 253, 254 (Essex Hemphill ed. 1991); see also Blair Fell, 'Gayface/Blackface: Parallels of Oppression', *NYQ*, Apr. 5, 1992, at 32 (drawing parallels between gayface and blackface and arguing that 'gayfaced contemporary comedy . . . serves as a tool to soothe the guilty consciences and perpetuate the injustices of gay-bashing America. After all, laughing at something barely human is easier than dealing with flying bullets, split skulls, dying bodies and demands for civil rights.').

41. Although much of the sexism that is voiced in rap pervades the industry, Black female rappers have gained a foothold and have undertaken various strategies of resistance. For some, their very presence in rap challenges prevailing assumptions that rap is a Black male tradition. See Tricia Rose, 'One Queen, One Tribe, One Destiny', *Village Voice Rock & Roll Quarterly*, Spring 1990, at 10 (profiling Queen Latifah, widely regarded as one of the best female rappers). Although Latifah has eschewed the head-on approach, her rap and videos are often women-centered, as exemplified by her single, 'Ladies First'. Queen Latifah, All Hail the Queen (Tommy Boy 1989). The 'Ladies First' video featured other female rappers, 'showing a depth of women's solidarity never seen before'. Rose, op cit., at 16. Rappers like Yo-Yo, 'hip-hop's first self-proclaimed feminist activist', take a more confrontational line; for example, Yo-Yo duels directly with rapper Ice Cube in 'It's a Man's World'. Joan Morgan, 'Throw the "F"', *Village Voice*, June 11, 1991, at 75.

Some female rappers, such as Bytches With Problems, have attempted to subvert the categories of bitches and whores by taking on the appellations and infusing them with power. As Joan Morgan observes, 'It's common practice for oppressed peoples to neutralize terms of disparagement by adopting and redefining them. Lyndah McCaskill and Tanisha Michelle Morgan's decision to define bitch "as a strong woman who doesn't take crap from anyone, male or female" and to encourage women to "wear the title as a badge of honor and keep getting yours" does not differ significantly from blacks opting to use the word nigger or gays embracing queer.' Id. However in the case of the Bytches, Joan Morgan ultimately found the attempt unsuccessful, in part because the subversion operated merely as an exception for the few ('Lynda and Tanisha Michelle are the only B-Y-T-C-H's here; all the other women they speak about, including the menstrual accident, the woman whose boyfriend Lyndah screws, and anyone else who doesn't like their style, are B-I-T-C-H's in the very male sense of the word') and because ultimately, their world view serves to reinscribe male power. Said Morgan, 'It's a tired female rendition of age-old sexist, patriarchal thinking: the power is in the pistol or the penis.' Id.

42. I follow the practice of others in linking antiessentialism to postmodernism. See generally Linda Nicholson, *Feminism/Postmodernism* (1990).
43. I do not mean to imply that all theorists who have made antiessentialist critiques have lasped into vulgar constructionism. Indeed, antiessentialists avoid making these troubling moves and would no doubt be receptive to much of the critique set forth herein. I use the term vulgar constructionism to distinguish between those antiessentialist critiques that leave room for identity politics and those that do not.
44. 110 S.Ct. 2997 (1990).
45. 'The FCC's choice to employ a racial criterion embodies the related notions that a particular and distinct viewpoint inheres in certain racial groups and that a particular applicant, by virtue of racc or ethnicity alone, is more valued than other applicants because the applicant is 'likely to provide [that] distinct perspective'. The policies directly equate race with belief and behavior, for they establish race as a necessary and sufficient condition of securing the preference. . . . The policies impermissibly value individuals because they presume that persons think in a manner associated with their race.' Id. at 3037 (O'Connor, J., joined by Rehnquist, C.J., and Scalia and Kennedy, J.J., dissenting) (internal citations omitted).
46. 163 U.S. 537 (1896).
47. 397 U.S. 483 (1954).

12

On the Question of Pornography and Sexual Violence

Moving Beyond Cause and Effect

Deborah Cameron and Elizabeth Frazer

What is to be done about pornography? Whenever feminists raise this question—and they have raised it insistently, on both sides of the Atlantic—one particular issue can be counted on to dominate discussion. That issue is: does pornography actually have significant effects in terms of causing violent and misogynistic behaviour? Can we, in other words, establish a firm relationship between the sphere of representation where pornography is located, and the sphere of action in which specific individuals harm other individuals? Any feminist who objects to pornography is immediately challenged to demonstrate such a causal relationship; anyone who doubts that the relationship exists is under pressure to concede that pornography is not a problem. The entire agenda for debate is drawn up in terms of this question.

The purpose of this chapter is to show what is wrong with framing the pornography issue in this way, and to suggest how feminists can move beyond simplistic notions of cause and effect without conceding the argument altogether. Arguments that pornography 'causes' violent acts are, indeed, inadequate. But the conclusion that therefore we should not be concerned about pornography at all is equally unjustified. Representation and action may not be related in a chain of cause and effect, but one can nevertheless discover important and complex connections between them—connections which imply that feminists should indeed concern themselves with the forms of representation that exist in our culture.

Deborah Cameron and Elizabeth Frazer, from 'On the Question of Pornography and Sexual Violence: Moving Beyond Cause and Effect', edited extract from *Pornography: Woman, Violence, and Civil Liberties*, ed. Catherine Itzin (Oxford University Press, 1994), 395–71, reprinted by permission of the author and the publisher.

The specific case with which we will be concerned here is sexual murder, an extreme form of violence whose catastrophic effects are impossible to deny or minimize; we believe, however, that our analysis can just as well be applied to less extreme instances. By examining the role that representations (primarily, but not exclusively, pornographic representations) play in the lives of sexual killers and in the cultures to which they belong, we hope to indicate new directions for the argument, producing a critique of pornography that does not depend on proving a specifically *causal* link with violence.

PORNOGRAPHY AND MURDER: CAUSE AND EFFECT?

More than any other form of sexual violence, sadistic sexual murder—killing in order to obtain sexual gratification—produces widespread unease about the health of the culture in which it occurs. Ever since the Jack the Ripper murders in 1888, one predictable response to this type of crime has been to ask what is wrong with the modern world that it has such people in it? And in addressing that question it has long been customary to cite the pervasiveness of pornography as a sign—perhaps even a cause—of social and sexual malaise.

This particular line of argument used to be associated with conservatives who saw sex-crime as indicative of a 'decline in moral values'. In recent years, though, it has also been deployed by a progressive and radical movement, namely feminism. It needs to be emphasized, of course, that the feminist and the conservative differ in their diagnoses of our moral ills as well as in the treatment they prescribe. Whereas conservatives criticize almost all expressions of sexuality as immoral and recommend a return to traditional religious and family values, feminist analysis criticizes instead the oppressive and misogynistic forms such expressions typically take in male-dominated culture. Stressing the pervasiveness of misogyny through time—that is, denying that we are witnessing a moral decline—feminists identify religion and the family as part of the problem.

From these otherwise opposed perspectives, however, there is some common support for the idea that pornography 'causes' sexual violence. This is the argument we want to take issue with here. For although we agree with the feminist contention that pornography is (1) oppressive and misogynistic and (2) connected with sexual violence, we do not believe that the idea of representations causing or leading to acts such as sexual murder is either theoretically compelling or politically progressive.

We want to rehearse the arguments for this position at greater length than we were able to do in our extended analysis of the phenomenon of sexual killing, *The Lust to Kill*.[1] It is worth elaborating on the position we sketch there if only because it is relatively unusual, differing in crucial respects from the two most familiar feminist positions on pornography and sexual violence: to put it very briefly, we disagree *both* with those anti-porn feminists who see a connection between pornography and violence, but analyse it only in causal terms, *and* with those feminists who have been critical of causal arguments, but who basically do not believe that there is any significant connection to be made between representation and action.

Causal Models and the Case of Ted Bundy

The issue of pornography and its alleged role in sexual murder has recently come to the attention of the public once again following the confession of US serial killer Ted Bundy immediately prior to his execution early in 1989. In his final account of himself, Bundy placed great emphasis on the role of pornography in his career as a sexual murderer. He represented himself as an obsessive consumer of increasingly sadistic material, and implied that pornography had been formative of desires which he was ultimately driven to act out in real life. He began with 'milder' forms of deviant behaviour, such as 'peeping Tom' activities, and worked his way up to repeated acts of killing.

Ted Bundy's story postulates some kind of cause and effect relation between what he read and what he did. It draws on certain familiar ideas: that images of torture, rape and murder engender (at least in some people) a compulsion to go out and do likewise; and that there is a progression—its course somehow inexorable—from less to more harmful fantasies and, by association, behaviours.

We may label these ideas about how porn affects its users the COPYCAT MODEL—you see it, then (therefore?) you do it—and the ADDICTION MODEL—initially erotic stimulation is obtained from relatively 'mild' forms of representation, but as the habit becomes established, it requires a stronger stimulus to achieve the same effect, and eventually representation itself is no longer strong enough, so that the user is impelled to act out the stimulus.

If these models are familiar, it is feminism which has made them so. For example, the copycat model is implicit in part of one of the best-known pieces of feminist writing/action against pornography: the Minneapolis ordinance devised by Andrea Dworkin and Catharine MacKinnon.[2] Among other things, the ordinance provides for victims of sexual violence to sue producers of pornography on the grounds that their product directly inspired an assault.

Let us hasten to point out the uselessness of denying that some incidents of sexual violence do indeed re-enact specific scenarios from pornographic texts with a literalness that might justify the epithet 'copycat'. At the hearings which took place in Minneapolis while the ordinance was being debated, witnesses testified to such incidents.[3] The question we raise is not whether copycat incidents occur, but whether they should be treated as paradigmatic of the general relationship between pornography and sexual violence, or whether they should be analysed as a special case. If they are paradigmatic then they provide very strong evidence for a causal model (and the adherents of causal models evidently do interpret them in this way). But we shall argue later that if we treat copycat incidents as paradigmatic we leave most incidents unexplained; that even in the case of clear copycat incidents the causal model is over-deterministic; and that copycat incidents can be explained satisfactorily without treating them as paradigmatic.

The addiction model is perhaps less familiar, though it is often an implicit accompaniment to the copycat model. Lately, though, it seems to have been gaining ground in its own right; we are hearing more and more about it, especially from women and men who wish to stress the damage pornography does to *men*.[4] We label it the addiction model (and note that the word *addiction* is used explicitly by the writers we are talking about) because it trades on an analogy between the use of pornography and the use of drugs (alcohol, tobacco, narcotics, etc.): all these habits are seen as harmful both to those who indulge in them—the 'addicts'—and to the community which must cope with the anti-social behaviour they engender. Although addiction is viewed as a social problem, there is a new emphasis on the individual within this model; the addict himself can be viewed as a victim whose weakness or inadequacy is exploited by the unscrupulous. We should not be surprised, then, that men find this model appealing when applied to their use of pornography; but we might do well to be suspicious of its depoliticizing implications (since the collective power of men and the institutionalized nature of sexual violence against women are nowhere at issue in this account).

The politics of the addiction account will be examined in more detail below; meanwhile, though, let us go back to the case of Ted Bundy, who characterized himself as both copycat and junkie.

A serial sexual murderer like Bundy stretches the addiction model to its limits; here we have a habit that got totally out of control. Just as smoking a joint is sometimes depicted as the first step on a slippery slope that leads to the shooting gallery, so in Bundy's case the addiction model posits that looking at pornographic representations was the first step on the long road which led to repeated and brutal killing. Once 'hooked', he could not stop: he was compelled to increase the 'dose' to the point where his behaviour became almost unimaginably destructive.

How compelling is this account? In a society currently obsessed with the 'drug problem' it is a way of understanding deviant behaviour that carries a powerful resonance; it commands instant understanding and, given that it is a medical model, the respect accorded to scientific truths. This might be one reason why feminists find it convenient: we have very often been obliged to describe the oppression of women in terms of other, more familiar social evils in order to be understood and, beyond that, taken seriously. But what has to be remembered is that when we explain one thing in terms of another we are constructing an essentially metaphorical account. The notion of addiction to pornography is a metaphor; the mechanisms of physiological dependence that characterize, say, cocaine addiction are not directly paralleled in someone who feels a compulsion to look at porn. Feminists are usually very cautious in using 'biological' analogies which imply that aspects of sexuality are 'natural', rather than constructed or indeed chosen: it is therefore necessary to consider very carefully how apt this particular metaphor is.

Nor should we be swayed in this by the fact that Ted Bundy himself thought the metaphor apt. We make this point because it is tempting to believe that Bundy's own endorsement constitutes the strongest possible evidence for the model and for causal explanations in general. From his disinterested position as a complete misogynist, Bundy has confirmed what feminists have been saying for years, i.e. that using pornography can lead to the commission of sexual crimes. Before we turn to the theoretical shortcomings of this argument generally, it is worth pointing out why we should be wary of treating what sex murderers say about themselves as unproblematically true, even when it seems to coincide with our own analysis.

Just after Bundy's execution, a feminist friend expressed the opinion that his confession, with its support for the idea of pornography as a cause of sex crime, would not be taken seriously by our generally misogynistic culture. She contrasted this apathy with the attention paid to less 'feminist' accounts produced by murderers: 'If he'd blamed it all on his mother,' she remarked, 'everyone would have believed him.' This is a revealing comment (and doubtless, an accurate prediction). But what it reveals is not that either the misogynistic, mother-blaming account of sex murder or the 'feminist', porn-blaming account is the truth of the matter; rather, it reveals that the discourse of explanation on this subject is highly contested and profoundly ideological.

Where does a sex killer's account of himself come from? Not, we suggest, from some privileged personal insight, but from a finite repertoire of cultural clichés which the murderer, like everyone else, has come across in case histories, pop-psychology, newspapers, films and ordinary gossip with family, friends and workmates. At any given time the clichés available are a heterogeneous and contradictory collection; some may carry more authority than others (for instance, we no longer think much of a killer who tells us he was possessed by the devil, though traces of this ancient supernatural account can be seen in the tabloid label 'fiend' used for sex murderers); new clichés may enter the repertoire, challenging or providing alternatives to the existing explanations. Porn-blaming is a recent example.

Let us examine how cultural clichés work by examining one that feminists are in no danger of confusing with 'the truth': the mother-blaming explanation of sexual murder. The idea that sexual killers are revenging themselves on dominating or inadequate mothers is a relatively recent cliché. Although it was found in expert discourse (i.e. forensic psychiatry, criminology) much earlier—its source, in fact, is psychoanalytic theory—it entered popular awareness only in the 1950s and 1960s, by way of cultural products like the Hitchcock movie *Psycho*. At this point, not untypically, the popularized version 'fed back' into expert pronouncements in a circular, reinforcing process. Police in the Boston Strangler case in the 1960s announced that they were looking for someone like Norman Bates, the mother-fixated character in *Psycho*.[5] The actual strangler, Albert DeSalvo, in fact bore little resemblance to this stereotype. But the perception of sexual murder as a consequence of pathological mother–son relations persisted, and during the 1970s became a theme in the testimony of some real-life killers (a striking example is Edmund Kemper, the 'Co-ed Killer' of Santa Cruz)[6]—whereupon it re-entered expert discourse in case-history form. The circle was completed once again.

By the time of Ted Bundy's confession in 1989, a new account had become culturally available: the porn-blaming explanation. This one entered popular awareness in a relatively unusual way, through organized political activity on the part of feminists during the 1970s. It did not replace earlier accounts like the mother-blaming explanation (or any number of other clichés, from the oversexed 'Beast' to the 'split personality' to the 'psychopath'), but it achieved sufficient status in the culture that Ted Bundy could invoke it where Ed Kemper (for example) could not.

That sexual offenders other than murderers use cultural clichés to construct their accounts of themselves is attested by the sociologists Diana Scully and Joseph Marolla who interviewed convicted rapists and found recurring, culturally familiar themes in their narratives.[7] Scully and Marolla call these clichés 'vocabularies of motive' and suggest that rapists use them in order to justify their behaviour and 'negotiate a non-deviant identity' for themselves.

In the case of murderers, of course, the goal is more likely to be negotiating a *deviant* identity. It is hardly surprising to find Kenneth Bianchi, one of the 'Hillside Stranglers', claiming a multiple personality—or Ted Bundy himself asserting, as he did for a number of years, that his murders had been committed by an 'entity' inside him—when one considers that, in a murder trial, convincing the court that you are incompetent or insane may be literally a matter of life and death. But for the purposes of the argument here it does not matter whether murderers have cynical and self-interested motives in offering their stereotypical accounts, or whether they sincerely believe those accounts to be true. The crucial point is that the accounts *come from the culture*. If they did not, they would make no sense, either to the murderer or to those he seeks to convince.

When Ted Bundy tells us he was corrupted by pornography, we need to ask not whether he is lying but where he got the story. It is unsatisfactory to accept Bundy's account while rejecting Kemper's just because one is misogynist while the other appears to be feminist. Instead, we must treat both accounts *as accounts*, that is, as discourse, subjecting them to further analysis and scrutiny. This is what we intend to do with the pornography-blaming explanation of sexual murder.

Before we turn to this central part of our argument, though, we want to return to a point we mentioned earlier regarding the politics of the explanation. In the discussion of cultural clichés we observed that murderers' accounts have a place within the judicial process in which their fates are decided, and this is something which feminists cannot afford to overlook.

The Politics of Addiction

Most court cases involving sexual murder do not revolve round the question of 'whodunnit'; there is usually, by this stage, agreement that the accused man did indeed commit the acts of which he stands accused. What is at issue is usually whether or not he should be held fully responsible for those acts. The accused and his counsel construct an account of the crimes in the hope of establishing a defence of what in English law is called 'diminished responsibility'. If such a defence succeeds, the offence is reduced from murder to manslaughter and the offender becomes a candidate for treatment rather than retributive punishment. (In most states of the USA, a crucial issue is whether the death penalty can be invoked.)

Feminists would presumably be reluctant to punish the mentally ill, and would therefore not object to this sort of defence *per se*. But in far too many cases, as a number of feminist scholars have demonstrated, diminished responsibility defences and their equivalents in other legal systems succeed although the grounds are flimsy and the underlying rationale systematically sexist. For instance, in several recent cases of wife-killing, the alleged infidelity or promiscuity or 'nagging' of the victim has been grounds for reducing the offence to manslaughter.[8] Sexually violent men have been defended on grounds of provocation, especially when their victims were prostitutes but even when they were children.[9] It thus appears that attributions of responsibility, however thickly cloaked in expert discourse, are fundamentally ideological and sexist in their operation. Their overall effect is to condone violence against women by repeatedly failing to punish its perpetrators.

If feminists follow through with the logic of the addiction model, they risk adding to an already depressing catalogue of defences and excuses. The truly novel thing about porn-blaming explanations may turn out to be that a feminist, as opposed to misogynist, account is being co-opted for use in the interests of violent men and against those of women.

The addiction model has political implications over and above its possible judicial uses, however. The central metaphor of drug addiction carries strong connotations of abnormality and deviance of the individual addict: drug abusers are seen as personally or socially inadequate—in some more liberal accounts, as disadvantaged and in need of help. Feminists have spent around twenty years attempting to combat the notion that sexual violence is the province of the pathological individual, arguing instead that it is structural and systemic, arising from gender hierarchy and conflict (which it also helps to maintain by intimidating women collectively). The addiction metaphor undermines that analysis, taking us back to abnormal individuals, and evacuating sexual politics from the account. Why it should be men and not women who (1) become 'addicts' and/or (2) turn to violence as a consequence of addiction remains totally mysterious in this individualized model. Surely we can agree to locate murderers at an extreme of male violence without completely losing sight of the wider social and political context: men as a group derive benefits from the institutionalized control of women, in which violence plays a major role.

BEYOND CAUSE AND EFFECT

It will not have gone unnoticed that so far we have put forward no sustained argument against causal explanations linking pornography to sexual violence; rather we have been trying to cast doubt on some of the arguments advanced in support of such explanations. But if a sex killer's endorsement of a particular explanation does not make it true, it does not necessarily make it false either. Nor is an argument automatically false just because its political implications are unpalatable. Surely the fact that Ted Bundy read pornography and attached significance to it calls for comment from a feminist?

We fully accept each of these points, and will respond to them by doing two things. First, we will put forward a general argument against causal accounts of human action. Second, we will try to construct an alternative model of the connections between pornography and sexual violence.

What Is Wrong with Causal Explanations?

The central objection we have to causal explanations of the relationship beween pornography and sexual violence can be stated very simply: causal accounts are completely inappropriate to explain any kind of human behaviour. Indeed, that very common term, human behaviour, has a certain misleading quality. Animals 'behave', impelled by instinct or simple stimuli; inanimate objects can (metaphorically) be said to 'behave', impelled by physical forces. Human beings, however, *act*.

The notion of cause is most appropriate in the physical sciences. For example, if we understand the forces acting upon them—things like gravity and inertia—and we know their physical specifications (mass, weight, etc.)—we can accurately predict the motion of two billiard balls colliding on a flat surface. The balls' 'behaviour' is determined by the laws of physics.

Humans are not like billiard balls—or indeed like animals, whose behaviour can be described in terms of a stimulus–response model. Humans have the capacity for symbolization and language, which enables us—and perhaps even obliges us—to impose meaning on the stimuli we encounter, and to respond in ways which also carry meaning. Human 'behaviour', therefore, is not determined by laws analogous to those of physics. It is not deterministically 'caused'. It needs to be explained in a different way, by interpretation of what it means and elucidation of the beliefs or understandings that make it possible and intelligible.

At this point, a sceptic might well raise two questions. First of all, is not sexual behaviour an exception to this rule? Sex is surely part of our 'natural', animal endowment, an instinctive rather than a cultural phenomenon, and therefore susceptible to less complex explanations. To this we would reply, using a formulation feminists are familiar with, that there is a conceptual distinction to be made between sex, which is a biological phenomenon, and sexuality, which is a social or cultural construct. Sexuality reflects human consciousness and the ability to impose meaning on basic bodily experience. It has to do not with instinctual need but with desire; and that the forms of desire are cultural rather than natural can be appreciated if one considers the extraordinary variety of sexual practice attested by historians, anthropologists and so on (not to speak of the blatant artificiality of many human sexual conventions: do animals wear black stockings?). In human culture sex is always overlaid with sexuality; more generally, biological phenomena (the emotions, pain, the cycle of birth, maturation and death) are always overlaid with cultural discourse.

Secondly, our sceptic might object that the actions of sex murderers are also exceptional, since they are too bizarre for us to be able to say what understandings make them 'possible and intelligible'. For most people, indeed, the acts of a sex murderer are impossible and unintelligible. But a moment's reflection will show this to be false. Of course not all of us share Ted Bundy's desires; but we are perfectly able to interpret them. We have a category for people like Bundy ('serial sexual killer') and a number of accounts are available to us to make sense of his actions (namely the cultural clichés discussed above). However repellent Bundy's acts, however distant his desires from our own, they are intelligible to us. They do not strike us as pointless and uninterpretable in the way the actions of, say, a severely autistic individual might seem pointless and uninterpretable. The difference between Ted Bundy and the autistic person is the difference between having a language (i.e. a set of socially shared meanings) and not having one. The autistic person's actions defy interpretation because only they have access to the code.

The code of sexual murder was once as uninterpretable as autistic behaviour—in some cultures, it still would be. As recently as 1888, the year of Jack the Ripper, people were at a loss to understand the motivation of someone who murdered and disembowelled prostitutes. It was seriously suggested that the killer wanted to sell his victims' reproductive organs to anatomists for profit; or that he was trying, in a grotesque way, to draw attention to the scandal of slum housing in London.[10] Nowadays we would immediately respond to a comparable set of killings by invoking the category of sexual murder. This account was given by some commentators in 1888, but it had to compete with other explanations (whereas today it would be the obvious, preferred account). And what this shows is that a certain interpretation or discourse has entered the culture and become familiar in the space of a hundred years.

The question we need to ask, then, is where that discourse came from, why it arose at the specific time and in the particular place it did, how it spread and developed subsequently and so on. These would be important questions because, from the kind of perspective advocated here, it is precisely the emergence of a discourse making sexual murder 'possible and intelligible' which creates the conditions for sexual murder to exist on the scale it now does: no longer as an isolated, random aberration but as a culturally meaningful act which an individual might consciously choose to perform.

We may sum up the argument so far by asserting that sexual murder is not a piece of abnormal sexual behaviour determined by innate drives, but a cultural category with a social significance. Sex killers are not responding unthinkingly or involuntarily to a stimulus, they are adopting a role which exists in the culture, as recognizable and intelligible to us (albeit not as acceptable) as the role of 'artist' or 'feminist' or 'hippie'.

What of pornography? Feminist proponents of the copycat and addiction models may be espousing a causal account, but it is not guilty of the biological determinism that pervades many so-called 'scientific' explanations (e.g. the account of sexual deviance which postulates excessive levels of testosterone in offenders). Rather, the 'cause' here is social conditioning through exposure to sadistic representations. And is this not a somewhat different, less objectionable version of the causal model?

The answer, in our view, is ultimately no. This 'social' account too is inadequate because it leaves out the crucial area of interpretation of meaning. The whole idea of conditioning—addiction is simply an extreme form of conditioning—implies a gradual process over which the subject has no control, and in which he does not actively engage (it is done to him, it determines his subsequent behaviour). Here it seems to us there is an implicit behaviouristic (stimulus–response) model in operation. It is taken for granted, for instance, that the addict's compulsion is fuelled by need and not desire, his initial arousal when looking at pornography is rooted somehow in natural/biological responses. At the point where need erupts into action, the behaviourism becomes explicit.

But if once again we compare the use of pornography with the use of narcotics—a comparison to which the addiction model directs us—this account seems less than compelling. A person does not have to interpret a line of cocaine in order to feel certain effects when it enters the bloodstream. S/he does have to interpret the picture of a dead and mutilated female body, along fairly narrow and conventional lines, in order to find it erotic. When someone looks or reads, they are constantly engaging, interacting with the text to produce meaning from it. The meaning is not magically, inherently 'there' in the pictures or the words: the reader has to make it. The text does not independently have effects on readers or compel them to act in particular ways, as if they were passive and unreflecting objects. They are subjects, creators of meaning; the pornographic scenario must always be mediated by their imagination. (This, incidentally, is why pornography calls forth such a variety of responses; why not only individuals, but groups derive such different meanings from it.)

Violent sexual acts, for example murders, are also works of the imagination before they are public events. Both common sense and the testimony of convicted rapists and killers suggest that these acts are conceived, planned, acted out in the imagination, in a way that is active, creative and conscious.[11] To speak of such acts as being 'caused' in the way a virus causes disease, gravity causes objects to fall or a bell caused Pavlov's famous dogs to salivate is to misunderstand their essence, their motivation, the very thing that makes them exciting and desired: in short, it is to overlook their *meaning*.

What, then, is the meaning of sexual murder for the cultures which recognize it and the men who engage in it? Let us answer this question by giving a brief account of the emergence of sex killing (drawn from Cameron and Frazer, 1987). This involves talking mainly about the forms of discourse which made sex murder 'possible and intelligible' (and continue to do so); our focus on discourse, representation, will lead into a more specific discussion of this chapter's main topic, pornography.

. . .

CONCLUSION

In analysing sexual violence and its links to cultural forms such as pornography, we overlook at our peril the pre-eminent role of imaginative mediation and the creation of meaning. All humans are endowed with the capacity and perhaps the need to interpret and represent their actions, their lives; our possession of consciousness, language and culture ensure that we will impose meaning on even the most fundamental bodily experience. That is not, in itself, problematic. But it does mean we need to move beyond causal accounts of human actions, and look instead at the resources humans bring to their interpretations and representations, the meanings which shape their desires and constrain the stories they can imagine for themselves. For we are clearly not free to imagine just anything; we work both with and against the grain of the cultural meanings we inherit.

In the sphere of sexuality, pornography is a significant source of ideas and narratives. It transmits to those who use it—primarily men but also women—notions of transcendence and mastery as intrinsic to sexual pleasure. These ideas are not taken up only by those who become rapists and killers. On the contrary, they pervade our everyday, unremarkable sexual encounters as surely as they do the grotesque acts of Ted Bundy and his ilk.

In the case of sex murderers (as in many other cases), the extreme, what is perceived as abnormal and deviant, throws light on the normal (of which it turns out to be a version). If we as feminists want to do something about sexual violence, it is precisely the normal and normative sexual practice of our culture that we must change. That means, among other things, that we must be critical of pornography and the other discourses which inform sexual practice, using our imagination to shape alternatives to the pleasures of transcendence and the thrills of transgression. In fact, feminists have been doing this for more than twenty years. But the recent focus of so many writers on causal models of sexual violence (which often imply that the problem is non-normal individuals and extreme sexual practices) is, at least in our view, a retreat from that radical politics of sexuality.

Notes

1. See Deborah Cameron and Elizabeth Frazer, *The Lust to Kill: A Feminist Investigation of Sexual Murder* (Cambridge: Polity Press, 1987).
2. For an account, see Catharine MacKinnon, *Feminism Unmodified: Discourses on Life and Law* (Cambridge, Mass. and London: Harvard University Press, 1987), ch. 14.
3. Cf. *Pornography and Violence: Evidence of the Links* (Minneapolis Hearings) (London: Everywoman, 1988); MacKinnon, op. cit., pp. 184–6.
4. The discourse of 'addiction' can be found in a number of very different sources, ranging from right-wing polemics (as in the Bundy case) through clinical materials used by those who counsel sex offenders to feminist critiques of socially-constructed dependence on various types of stimulus (drugs, alcohol, cigarettes, TV) induced by people's increasing alienation within patriarchal and capitalist cultures (see e.g. Sweet, in Catherine Itzin (ed.), *Pornography: Women, Violence, and Civil Liberties* (Oxford: Oxford University Press), ch. 10.
5. Gerold Frank, *The Boston Strangler* (London: Pan, 1967); also discussion in J. Caputi, *The Age of Sex Crime* (London: Women's Press, 1988).
6. For discussion of Edmund Kemper, see Cameron and Frazer, op. cit.
7. Diana Scully and Joseph Marolla, cited in L. Kelly, *Surviving Sexual Violence* (Cambridge: Polity Press, 1989), p. 47.
8. Cameron and Frazer, op. cit., p. 14 note.
9. S. Edwards, quoted in Kelly, op. cit., p. 224 note 61.
10. Cameron and Frazer, op. cit., p. 125.
11. A pertinent example here is the case of Ronald Frank Cooper, discussed in Cameron and Frazer, op. cit., pp. xiii–xiv.

13 The Politics of Postmodern Feminism

Lessons from the Anti-Pornography Campaign

Mary Joe Frug

A particular phase of the legal anti-pornography campaign is dead in the water. The ordinance which Catharine MacKinnon and Andrea Dworkin initially authored and then vigorously promoted in Minneapolis, Indianapolis, Cambridge, and other cities would have made pornography a form of discrimination against women. It would have permitted women to bring civil actions against those who produce, make, distribute, or sell pornography, which the ordinance generally defined as 'the graphic sexually explicit subordination of women, whether in pictures or in words'.[1] It would have provided civil remedies for the harm that pornography causes. But the Supreme Court's summary affirmance of the Seventh Circuit's decision holding the ordinance unconstitutional has rendered continued efforts to enact this particular ordinance very problematic. The campaign to enact the MacKinnon/Dworkin ordinance may, however, offer lessons for other feminist political projects.

The ordinance campaign fascinates me. As a political event involving the community of feminist lawyers it was a dazzling success and an appalling disaster. It politicized feminist lawyers, by engaging many of us in the practicalities of a grass-roots legislative reform effort which was widely publicized and electrifyingly controversial. But it also politicized us by brutally and bitterly fracturing our community. Catharine MacKinnon, in particular, put a high price on feminist opposition to her campaign. In a chapter chillingly entitled 'On Collaboration', from her book *Feminism Unmodified*, she charged, with an emotional intensity which also characterized other campaign participants, that 'women who defend the pornographers are

Mary Joe Frug, an extract from 'The Politics of Postmodern Feminism: Lessons from the Anti-Pornography Campaign', from *Postmodern Legal Feminism*, Mary Joe Frug (Routledge (NY), 1992), 145–53, reprinted with permission of Taylor and Francis/Routledge Inc. and Professor G. Frug.

defending a source of their relatively high position among women under male supremacy, keeping all women, including them, an inferior class on the basis of sex, enforced by sexual force.'[2]

'I really want you to stop your lies and misrepresentations of our position,' she continued, 'I want you to stop claiming that your liberalism, with its elitism, and your Freudianism, with its sexualized misogyny, has anything in common with feminism.'[3]

For reasons I will soon make clear, I don't particularly regret the anti-pornography ordinance defeat. But like the architects of the ordinance I too believe in using law to oppose the oppression of women. Indeed, the apparent jeopardy of *Roe* v. *Wade*[4] makes me especially cognizant at this moment that retaining the legalization of abortion may soon become a pressing project requiring astute political skills among feminists forced to seek legislative reform all across the United States. I hope, therefore, that closely examining the ordinance campaign, as a salient incident in the politics of legal feminism, will advance the prospects of an abortion reform effort that the Supreme Court might thrust upon us, as well as the prospects of other future feminist legal projects.

I want to make two points about the campaign. First, I intend to challenge the somewhat familiar criticisms of the campaign by suggesting that some of the campaign's weaknesses can also be understood as political strengths, strengths which might be adapted and deployed in other efforts. That is, my claim will be that the conventional failures of the campaign also constituted the campaign's successes.

Second, I will outline what I think is a new critique of the ordinance campaign. Shamelessly relying on the advantages of hindsight, I will argue that the ordinance proponents were fatally reluctant to apply the theory underlying the campaign to their own efforts. Having brilliantly identified the subordination of women by sex as a lynchpin of women's oppression, the ordinance proponents relentlessly perpetuated the dichotomy of gender in the style of their rhetoric, in the content of their arguments, and in the absolutism of the ordinance's structure, which would have rigidly divided pornographic material into two opposing categories—actionable or unactionable. My claim will be that the greatest strength of the anti-pornography ordinance campaign was also its greatest weakness. Having identified pornography as a cultural practice importantly implicated in the problem of women's condition, the ordinance advocates sought unsuccessfully to use law reform to destroy pornography. I now seek to turn this failure to some profit, by using an analysis of their campaign as an opportunity to deconstruct pornography. The interesting and perhaps troubling question that underlies my own position, however, is what effect this deconstruction would have had on the ordinance campaign.

A word of caution before I proceed. Each of us is likely to have a relatively concrete, relatively firm understanding of what we consider pornography, but we probably disagree about the components of a common conception. When I was 12, pornography meant a few pages in my parents' copy of *From Here to Eternity*[5] and a few words, like 'coitis', and 'fornicate', thrillingly available in my own dictionary. My personal definition now is more far ranging, but I do not know how widely shared it is.

Two Meese Commission guys recently published a survey in the *Michigan Journal of Law Reform* which comically purports to describe the character of 'adults only' pornography currently sold in the United States.[6] The survey classifies the cover photos of books, magazines, and films sold in 'adults only' bookstores, in four cities. Because the investigation is limited to 'adults only' stores, the survey does not include material which I consider part of the pornographic genre. Examples of omitted material I would include are: formula romances; science fiction and comics which feature sexually explicit material; lesbian and gay erotica which is too pretentious for 'adults only' bookstores; the dark, serious literature of sex and violence characterized by books like *The Story of O*[7] and Georges Bataille's *Story of the Eye*:[8] and portions of material found in many women's glossy magazines. I am not going to try to solve the problem of confusion which the term 'pornography' generates in listeners by contriving a general, abstract definition which many of you would probably dislike. I simply want to assert that what constitutes pornography is usually a charged and unexplored question in any discussion involving pornography.

CONVENTIONAL FAILURES REINTERPRETED: THE STRENGTHS OF THE ORDINANCE CAMPAIGN

A familiar criticism of the ordinance campaign is the charge that it produced an alliance between ordinance advocates and non-feminist conservatives. Many feminists during the campaign voiced concern that conservative support for the ordinance indicated their intention to turn the ordinance against material that is offensive only because it describes or depicts 'untraditional' sexuality. Because conservatives have considered the use of birth control devices and sexual activities such as cunnilingus 'untraditional sexual practices', ordinance opponents feared that the ordinance campaign might lead to repressing sexual freedom rather than to preventing sexual oppression.

The conservative alliance might not have occurred had the ordinance advocates been clearer, narrower, and more consistent in their explanation of what constituted pornography. The advocates repeatedly attempted to reassure wary feminists that the ordinance did not need to function to impose an orthodox, traditional form of sexuality on anyone. However, the general definition of pornography as 'the graphic sexually explicit subordination of women, whether in pictures or in words'[9] was broad enough to encourage the Vanilla-Sex Gestapo that they could get with the ordinance program.

I claim the conservative alliance was a virtue of the ordinance campaign because of its role in extending the ordinance debate beyond predictable feminist constituencies. In contrast to the typically narrow circle, for example, which has exhibited interest in radical legislative reforms related to the anti-family structure of the labor market, the ordinance campaign boldly and successfully engaged non-feminist political camps. Conservative support for the ordinance undoubtedly posed troublesome management issues for the feminists supporting the ordinance. However, a broad theater of political involvement was obviously vital to the ordinance campaign, and similarly broad coalitions will also be important to the success of other feminist law reform projects.

I acknowledge that extending feminist issues beyond familiar constituencies occurred in the ordinance campaign at the cost of feminist unity. My claim is that breaching this unity is a necessary component of feminist efforts against women's oppressions.

The broad definition of pornography adopted by the ordinance advocates radically challenged a fundamental premise of post-Freudian, Lacanian theories of self, the premise that domination and subordination are an inevitable aspect of interpersonal relations. Ordinance advocates assume that by eliminating *depictions* of sexual domination, *sexual domination* could be dealt a fatal blow. In contrast, ordinance opponents believed that domination and subordination constitute a psychological structure that does not depend on the pornography industry and that *need not* depend on gender division for its existence.

This dispute involves a profound question about the nature of the self. It is not surprising that people disagree about this issue; it is not surprising that women—indeed, that feminists—disagree about this issue. Although powerful, broad, and coherent political community is critical to feminist law reform projects, I believe it is a mistake to fear or avoid or condemn differences among feminists as we pursue these projects. Accepting and exploring our differences, in my view, is a critical component of challenging the ideology of gender difference, which includes the assumption that there is a feminine essence which unalterably unites women, binding us together under the generic category 'woman'.

A second criticism which has been leveled against the ordinance campaign is that it distracted feminists from other work more important to the women's movement. Ordinance advocates argued that pornography triggers massive physical violence against women; they claimed that by sexualizing domination and subordination, pornography functions to consign all women to unequal social and economic status on account of their sex; and they asserted that as an eight billion dollar industry, pornography economically exploits the women who participate in its production and drains substantial resources away from other, more significant purposes. In making their criticism that the ordinance campaign was a fruitless diversion, ordinance opponents disputed all these claims.

Opponents claimed that the data causally linking pornography to violence against women was insubstantial, unconvincing, and predicated on a simplistic and unpersuasive theory of causation. They disputed the claim that regulating pornography could have much effect on the subordination of women, arguing, as I have suggested above, that this subordination is not rooted in pornography. Indeed, some feminists claimed that pornography usefully functions in certain cases to channel and subdue troubling fantasies. The opponents were skeptical that bringing down the pornography industry would make eight billion dollars available for women's causes, and they were critical of the costs of pursuing the ordinance campaign.

In contrast to the ordinance opponents, but for different reasons, I believe that concentrating so much effort, energy, expertise, and even money on the anti-pornography issue simplified and thereby facilitated feminist political organizing, much the same way single-issue campaigning often constitutes an organizational advantage in electoral politics. Political success is predictably correlated with coordinating and consolidating efforts.

I also believe the theoretical claim that the subordination of women is rooted in sex is a message that will significantly benefit the feminist movement. This claim radically challenges the traditional focus of feminist concerns. It legitimates pornography as an appropriate field for struggle, analysis, and interpretation. It challenges the traditional feminist agenda of appropriate strategies for contesting the oppression of women. Whatever skirmishes or battles we may have lost because of the anti-pornography diversion will be worth the challenge to conventional attitudes which the theoretical innovations of the movement facilitated. I attribute the exposure and discussion that occurred about this theory to the choice of pornography as the theory's practical target. This suggests to me an important political lesson for feminists. Issue choice affects our political potential, and legislative reform efforts produce political capital beyond the passage or defeat of legislation.

The last criticism of the ordinance campaign I will mention may be less familiar, but I will raise it because of how disappointed I was when the ordinance campaign came to my town in the form of model or boiler plate legislation. By preventing feminists outside the circle of those who originally worked with MacKinnon and Dworkin from having a voice in the structure and scope of their local ordinances, the architects of the ordinance lost the organizing potential and the consciousness-raising benefits that would have inured from wider drafting participation. Moreover, broader drafting consultation, or experimenting in different cities with different ordinances, might have revealed that some of the model legislation provisions were miscalculations, mistakes that could have been corrected as the campaign moved from town to town.

Despite the criticism that using model legislation warrants, I realize that model legislation facilitates publicity and supports scholarship and efficient legal defense work, all of which strengthen local campaigns to enact feminist reform projects. Moreover, the ordinance campaign overall was remarkable for its broadly participatory character. The campaign heavily relied on indigenous, newly formed groups of concerned individuals in each of the targeted towns, and the ordinance utilized the strategy of allowing the victims of pornography to institute claims on their own behalf against pornographers. By eschewing city or state attorneys, the ordinance functioned to empower women. This strategy too could be adaptable and important in other feminist projects.

DESTROYING PORNOGRAPHY OR DECONSTRUCTING IT

I now turn to my claim that the ordinance campaign's greatest strength was also its greatest weakness, my claim that the advocates should have sought to deconstruct pornography rather than single-mindedly seeking to destroy it.

The ordinance campaign's most significant contribution to feminism was its pursuit of Catharine MacKinnon's theoretical insight that the oppression of women occurs through sexual subordination. The anti-pornography campaign allowed MacKinnon and others to dramatize what this theory means in practice, through its focus on a complex cultural phenomenon which is exclusively devoted to sex, a cultural practice consumed with depictions of what 'the oppression of women through sexual subordination' means. In pornography, women get fucked.

Now, women get 'fucked' in the workplace, too, where we do 'women's work' for 'women's wages', working for male bosses and working on male schedules. We get assigned to this inferior work track because we are identifiable by our sex. In addition, our past and present economic, social, and physical subordination makes us vulnerable to physical abuse at work, on the way there, and on the way back. We are raped at work or on route to work because of our sex, because we are cunts.

But the moment I say women get 'fucked' in the workplace, the clarity of the relationship between women's oppression and sex is jeopardized. 'Women's work' is a complicated construction; its origin and perpetuation depend on many factors in addition to misogyny. Pornography is a much cleaner site for demonstrating the practice of the theoretical insight; pornography is about women getting fucked.

I hasten to acknowledge here that pornography is also about violence against women, and that ordinance advocates sought to attack pornography in order to prevent women who participate in its production from being harmed and in order to prevent other women from being harmed by the imitative reactions of pornography users. But the ordinance campaign was not restricted to preventing these two forms of harm.

Ordinance advocates also attacked pornography in order to oppose the sexualization of hierarchy and the objectification of women. They understood the ordinance as more than a good example of the truth of feminist theory in practice. They believed that destroying pornography would lead to the end of women's oppression on account of sex. They believed that destroying this particular depiction of women's oppression would change the experience of women's oppression in its many manifestations. I believe this was a fatal miscalculation.

If women's oppression occurs through sex, then in order to end women's oppression in its many manifestations, the way people think and talk and act about sex must be changed. The ordinance campaign was not well organized to change how people think and talk and act about sex. Rather, the ordinance advocates relentlessly utilized and exploited traditional ideas and language regarding sex in all aspects of the campaign.

Let me give just a few examples.

First, the language and rhetorical style of campaign advocacy were characterized by stereotypically masculine attributes. The language and style were militant, authoritative, and riddled with the easy obscenities typical of male talk. (I've done a little male talk myself in this section.) This style was impressively successful—the advocates were powerful campaigners; but the use of additional, less masculine rhetorical styles, which can also be persuasive and moving, would have made the ordinance campaign less gendered.

The campaign also seemed gendered because the arguments of campaign advocates were typically structured by hierarchical dichotomies. Thus, advocates reduced arguments against the ordinance to dismissive epithets: they were 'anti-feminist' or 'individualistic'. Similarly, advocates oversimplified the character of pornography, suggestively referring only to rip and slash material in their discussions rather than acknowledging the complex character of the pornographic genre. Like the style of their rhetoric, the content of their arguments was stirring; it was arousing. But like the ideology of gender, which rigidly divides the world into two sexes, the campaign argument was premised on an assumption that its listeners were divisible into only two camps—those who were pro-woman, and, therefore, pro-ordinance, or those who weren't.

I believe a less dichotomized approach to the problem of the oppression of women by sex would have been more likely to change the way we think and act about sex. By falsely simplifying the content of the pornography genre, the advocates overlooked the way in which some workers within the genre already thematically challenge the subordination of women by sex. Not all pornography is simply about women being fucked. There are some pornographic works in which women fuck, for example; some works in which the objectification of the orgasming penis is not repeatedly depicted and valorized; and many works in which the subjectivity of a female character is a dominant and successful thematic concern. These works do not depict what the ordinance advocates suggested pornography 'is'.

The ordinance advocates falsely simplified user responses to pornography, assuming in most of their arguments that pornography users mechanistically identify with same-sex characters and mechanistically seek to reproduce pornography scenes in their own lives. This singular reaction does not characterize reader responses to non-pornographic literature or viewer responses to non-pornographic films. Although many individuals may use pornography for sex instruction, it also seems likely that others use pornography as an implement of fantasy, seeking through their reading or viewing to escape lives characterized by chastity, by routinized sex, or by genderized sex. They may also use pornography to transform their lives by a more complicated reaction than simple imitation.

Users would not be interested in or sexually aroused by many forms of pornography if they reacted only by identifying with same-sex characters. Works like sexually explicit formula romances, for example, in which a woman is the principal sexual subject, would most likely be sexually arousing to a male user only if he identified with the female heroine, thereby relinquishing his sex-stereotyped desires to fuck and fantasizing himself instead as fuckee. Similarly, the appeal of lesbian and gay pornography seems to depend on more than mechanistic same-sex identification, in that users must select differences other than biological sex to identify with particular characters.

I hope I am not misunderstood here. I do not want to be understood as a pornography apologist, for I believe that the proliferation and character of the pornography genre is one of the most complicated cultural events of our time, an event whose meanings are still quite indeterminate.

I also do not want to be understood as anti-feminist. The polarization of the feminist legal community during the ordinance campaign was terrifying to me; I understand the instinct to condemn the opposition that caused such division among friends and colleagues. However, I believe the divisions the campaign produced among feminists constituted an important challenge to the polarization of the world by gender. The closing lesson I want to draw from the anti-pornography campaign about feminist organization is the observation that exploring, pursuing, and accepting differences among women and differences among sexual practices is necessary to challenge the oppression of women by sex. Only when sex means more than male or female, only when the word 'woman' cannot be coherently understood, will oppression by sex be fatally undermined.

Notes

1. *American Booksellers Ass'n* v. *Hudnut*, 771 F.2d 323, 324 (7th Cir. 1985), aff'd, 475 U.S. 1001 (1986) (quoting Indeanapolis, Ind. Code § 16-3[q] [1984]).
2. Catharine MacKinnon, *Feminism Unmodified: Discourses on Life and Law* (Boston: Harvard University Press, 1987), at 205.
3. Id.
4. 410 U.S. 111 (1973).
5. James Jones, *From Here to Eternity* (1951).
6. See Park Elliott Dietz and Alan E. Sears,'Pornography and Obscenity Sold in "Adult Bookstores": A survey of 5132 Books, Magazines, and Films in Four American Cities', 21 Mich. J. L. Ref. 7, 10–11 (1987–88).
7. Pauline Réage, *The Story of O* (Sabine d'Estreé trans. 1965).
8. Georges Bataille, *Histoire de L'Oeil* (1967).
9. *American Booksellers Ass'n* v. *Hudnut*, 771 F.2d at 324 (7th Cir. 1985), aff'd, 475 U.S. 1001 (1986) (quoting Indianapolis, Ind. Code § 16–3[q] [1984]).

'It's Merely Designed for Sexual Arousal':* Interrogating the Indefensibility of Lesbian Smut

Becki L. Ross

> Good women . . . possess no language and no terminology, either for their feelings or their anatomy.
>
> (Dr Howard Kelly, 1913)

> Our pictures felt like proof that our reality could be altered, that the world we lived in and were part of was not the only world, and that within our imaginations dwelt another reality that was mysterious and potent. For me this reality included the possibility of women together, and signified that beneath the outer trappings of our everyday masks and costumes there existed a body that hungered and thirsted for freedom. That beneath the artifice there existed another 'self,' another, more authentic body—in my case, a lesbian body that was struggling to name itself by imagining and then imaging its own unspeakable yearnings.
>
> (Susan Stewart, 1994)

On 2 April 1992, Constable Patricia McVicar, a female member of Project P, the joint OPP/Metro Toronto Police anti-pornography squad, seized *Bad Attitude* (1991)—a 'lesbian erotic fiction' magazine (published bimonthly in Cambridge, Massachusetts) from Toronto's Glad Day Bookshop. Outfitted in plain clothes, undercover officer McVicar targeted *Bad Attitude* because 'the magazine contained sexually explicit materials with bondage and violence . . . that were degrading and obscene and not what Canadians would abide other

Becki L. Ross, 'It's Merely Designed for Sexual Arousal: Interrogating the Indefensibility of Lesbian Smut', from *Bad Attitudes on Trial: Pornography, Feminism and the Butler Decision*, Becki L. Ross (University of Toronto Press, 1997), 152–68, reprinted by permission of the publisher.

* This summary statement was made by Crown Attorney Charles Granek as part of his final argument in the *R.* v. *Scythes* obscenity trial, 18 December 1992.

Canadians seeing.'[1] Almost a month later, on 30 April 1992, McVicar charged John Scythes, owner of Glad Day Bookshop—the city's lesbian and gay bookstore—and manager Tom Ivison with possession and distribution of obscene material. Seven months later, in December 1992, the case was heard in the Ontario Court (Provincial Division). It marked the second 'lesbian pornography' trial in Canadian history—the first, involving the lesbian pulp novel *Women's Barracks*, was held in Ottawa in 1952 (Adams 1993: 21).

On 16 February 1993, Judge Claude Paris found the accused, Scythes and Ivison, guilty of the possession and sale of *Bad Attitude* (specifically, the story 'Wunna My Fantasies') because of its combination of sex and violence. Referencing the Supreme Court's decision on *R.* v. *Butler* (1992) Paris J. ruled in favour of 'protecting' the general public from lesbian material that would 'predispose individuals to anti-social behaviour' (*R.* v. *Scythes* 1993: 3). He convicted Scythes and Ivison of violating section 163(8) of the Canadian Criminal Code, and fined the store two hundred dollars. In moral tones suggestive of nineteenth century social-purity reform, Paris advised the criminals to refrain from selling the magazine in the future.

In this chapter, I explore the vulnerability of lesbian-made images, in particular s/m images, to legal judgments governed by the Canadian Supreme Court's *Butler* decision. Having been called upon as an expert witness to testify in the *R.* v. *Scythes* case, I draw from the Ontario Provincial court transcripts and the judge's ruling. Specifically, I examine the legal privileging of a school of social-science research that delivered certainty in the stunning absence of empirical evidence. And I counterpose this privileging to my (futile and failed) efforts as an expert witness to explicate and contextualize the specificities, nuances, and complexities of lesbian s/m fantasy, alongside the sociopolitical meanings it engenders within lesbian s/m subcultures. Rather than attribute my experience of futility and failure to 'poor performance', I argue that my refusal to interpret lesbian s/m as 'harmful to women' was simply unintelligible to gatekeepers of obscenity law in Canada. It seems clear to me in retrospect that the battle to defend *Bad Attitude* was lost before it began.

I maintain that the obscenity charge and eventual conviction against Glad Day Bookshop in 1993 are indicative of the makings of a moral panic reminiscent of anti-VD campaigns, postwar purges of homosexuals from the Canadian civil service, and the citizens' lobby to ban romance literature and crime comics in the 1940s and 1950s.[2] Paradoxically, the current moral panic has been met by independent producers of lesbian/queer pornography in Canada whose counter-hegemonic volleys I survey at the end of this chapter. In all, the case of *R.* v. *Scythes* invites me to examine how competing knowledge claims about sexuality, morality, and the zone of fantasy are bound up in operations of power. Empirically knowable, these operations of power do not function in the mode of repression and negation: they mark, in Michel Foucault's terms, an incitement to speak about and administer sex (Foucault 1980: 11, 24) Indeed *R.* v. *Scythes* reveals mechanisms by which so-called 'crimes against nature' continue to be speechified and regulated in the late twentieth century (ibid. 32).

Social-Scientific 'Truths' about Lesbian Pornography

To lead off discussion of the magazine *Bad Attitude* in *R.* v. *Scythes*, American psychologist Neil Malamuth was called as an expert witness by the prosecution to outline the media effects of pornography on human attitudes and behaviour. A professor of communication and psychology at the University of Michigan, Malamuth has built his reputation as one of a handful of social-science experts proclaiming and defending a causal link between (heterosexual) pornography and violence against women. He was invited by the prosecution *because* his clinical research indicates this link, despite the acknowledged inconclusivity of 'effects studies' as a whole. In fact, Malamuth's work in large part supplied the 'scientific' foundation for the *Butler* decision, and it appears as the 'Truth' about pornography in the factums submitted by the Attorney General of Manitoba, Attorney General of Canada, and the Group Against Pornography (see Gotell, 1997). And his previous engagement as a consultant for the prosecution in two Canada Customs cases involving lesbian and gay materials only served to enhance his expert status.

During the Crown's process of establishing Malamuth's credentials before Judge Paris, defence counsel Clare Barclay intervened to argue that Malamuth had never made the effects of lesbian/gay images a focus of his research, therefore he should be disqualified as an expert on lesbian pornography. Barclay was overruled by Judge Paris, who agreed to accept Malamuth as an expert on communications, psychology, and laboratory-based analyses of (heterosexual) pornography. Explaining his rationale for accepting Malamuth (in ways that foreshadow his final decision), Judge Paris added that he did not feel that 'there was a need to make a distinction between [representations of] heterosexual sex and homosexual sex.' Much later, I ruefully noted that Malamuth's obvious lack of expertise in no way undermined or delegitimized his efforts to render an objective, positivist interpretation of the 'offending' lesbian material. In fact, because Judge Paris accepted Malamuth's contentions before he had even spoken in the trial, I'm left to wonder why it was necessary for him to testify at all.

Over the course of his testimony, Malamuth flatly repeated that he had never studied lesbian and gay erotic material made specifically for members of the lesbian, gay, and bisexual community (Malamuth 1992: 17). Yet to reassure the Crown and the judge of his social-scientific expertise, he pointed to *Bad Attitude* and argued: 'It's very difficult to tell the difference between these [lesbian] materials and heterosexual materials . . . One could go through the [lesbian] stories and change three or four words saying it's a woman and a man . . . Chang[ing] 'she' into 'he' and there would be no difference . . . From the perspective of the effects on the public, I think that basic mechanisms and processes are likely to be very similar' (ibid. 18).

Malamuth was asked by the Crown to speculate on the negative effects of lesbian s/m fantasy on readers of *Bad Attitude*. (Here we can see the Crown's unchallenged assumptions at work: a. there *are* effects, and b. they are, matter-of-factly, negative and harmful.) In his content analysis Malamuth stated that the magazine contained 'acts that appear to be designed to humiliate', images of 'subservience of one person to another', 'elements of pain and suffering', 'the depiction of humiliation and demeaning terms', the 'lowering of rank', and 'references to participants as animals' (Malamuth 1992: 32, 35–6). According to his 'expert' opinion, *Bad Attitude* 'portrays unequal power relations as being sexy, as being arousing'(ibid. 44). Malamuth repeated several times that lesbian imagery like *Bad Attitude* relied on themes that were derivative of heterosexual materials: he said that if images like those in *Bad Attitude* appeared in a heterosexual magazine they 'would draw tremendous fire from the feminist community' (ibid. 49). Using the rhetorical technique of analogy Malamuth argued that 'there was an amazing similarity [between the seized copy of *Bad Attitude*] and sadomasochistic materials in the heterosexual community' (ibid. 36). He added that upon considering sadomasochistic portrayals, the consent that may appear in the depictions is 'really not a particularly relevant issue' (ibid. 41). To conclude, Malamuth predicted the harmful effects of *Bad Attitude* on the attitudes and behaviours of some lesbians and gays as well as some heterosexual readers (ibid. 46–9). When I analyse his testimony, I find that Malamuth did not define the terms humiliation and subservience; he did not produce empirical evidence of heterosexual s/m to verify his analogy (which I argue is unverifiable); he had no evidence of actual harm that flowed from exposure to *Bad Attitude*; and he roundly dismissed the crucial lever of consent in a self-consciously Butlerian flourish.

University of Toronto psychologist Jonathon Freedman, in later testifying for the defence, disputed Malamuth's claims on methodological grounds. He warned against simplistic extrapolation from studies of heterosexual, non-consensual pornography on film/TV to homosexual print material such as *Bad Attitude.* As Freedman explained, 'Malamuth took research done on the attitudes of straight men to what he called violent, degrading pornography, and he generalized the results to images of consensual sex between women . . . But [in *Bad Attitude*], the whole meaning, context and significance of the images has changed' (Freedman 1992: 39–44). Freedman added that because there are no scientific definitions of 'degradation' and 'humiliation', Malamuth's application of these terms to *Bad Attitude* reveals his subjective, non-scientific interpretation (ibid. 36).

DELIVERING COUNTER-TRUTHS

On 15 December 1992, in a third-floor, church-like room at Old City Hall, now the Ontario Court (Provincial Division), I took the stand to defend *Bad Attitude.* Briefed only two days before I appeared on the stand, I became part of the 'Defence Team' headed up by counsel Clare Barclay. I suspect that I was enlisted by Barclay and Glad Day Bookshop because I am a long-time anti-censorship activist—a former member of the Canadian Committee Against Customs Censorship, a former editor of *Rites*, a gay/lesbian liberation magazine, and a member of Censor-stop, a Toronto-based anti-censorship organization. I hold a Ph.D. in sociology with a specialization in feminist theory and lesbian/gay studies. Unlike Malamuth, at the time of the trial I did not hold a full-time university post: I was under-employed at the University of Toronto teaching one course a term. On the stand, I was immediately subjected to a two-hour attack by the Crown, who strove to discredit my scholarly qualifications and drastically narrow the purview of my testimony. Finally, I was sworn in as an expert witness on lesbian sexuality, culture, and community. Except for brief appearances by law student Suzanne Jarvie and lesbian photographer Jennifer Gillmor, I was the only other woman to testify.

Dire financial constraints meant that John Scythes, owner of Glad Day Bookshop, was unable to call additional witnesses such as Carole Vance, Pat Califia, Dorothy Allison, and Gayle Rubin—well-known American writers and academics who have argued vehemently against state censorship of feminist and lesbian/gay materials for twenty years, in some cases as lesbian s/m participants themselves. It is likely that most of these women would have agreed to testify had there been money, but it is not clear what impact they might have had. It is significant that in the 1994 challenge by Little Sister's bookstore to seizures of lesbian and gay materials by Canada Customs, the Crown decided to forgo cross-examination of almost all the writers and artists in what appeared to be a move to convey their perceived irrelevance (Fuller and Blackley 1995: 60)

I felt intense pressure *to perform* feminist pro-pornography analysis in ways that did its pioneering proponents justice, and in ways that convinced Judge Paris that the Supreme Court justices in *R.* v. *Butler* were wrong. And as the *Bad Attitude* trial progressed, I felt acutely uneasy about my role as a speaker *for* members of lesbian s/m communities. I am connected to these communities, but I am not an active member of them. Indeed, I remain steadfastly critical of the fact that no lesbian s/m aficionados were called forth in *R* v. *Scythes* to instruct the judge on the subtleties of s/m fantasy from their own standpoints.

Before my testimony, during the process of 'qualification', Crown Attorney Charles Granek repeatedly tried to discredit me as a defender of child pornography and intergenerational sex. He insinuated that I was someone with an appetite for 'kiddie porn' by pointing to my support for *The Body Politic* newspaper's right to publish the controversial 'Men Loving Boys Loving Men' feature in 1977 (the paper was charged with obscenity and eventually acquitted in 1983). 'Youth pornography' has become a favourite target of police and politicians of all ideological stripes and one that was recently and hastily codified in the punishing youth pornography law, Bill C–128 (see Bell 1997). This is not to say that issues of incest and the abuse of power by adults over children/youth are unimportant. Rather, it is my view that the stubborn and never-substantiated equation of gays and lesbians with child molestation motivated the Crown's line of questioning, and was deployed to intimidate me. It is noteworthy that there is absolutely no mention of cross-generational sex in the seized copy of *Bad Attitude*.

So, though Granek seemed off topic, I later realized that he highlighted my research/writing on obscenity law to establish for the judge my 'biased', subjective, and value-laden, anti-censorship stance. Importantly, neither Crown nor defence pigeonholed psychologist Neil Malamuth's bias as pro-censorship. In fact, the opposite occurred: his stance as an 'objective' and 'value free' scientist was incontrovertible. As the trial unfolded, it became crystal clear to me: I was partisan, Malamuth was neutral; Malamuth was the expert, I was the exhibit[3] (see Valverde 1996: 213).

On the stand, almost sixty-five years after Radclyffe Hall's classic lesbian romance *The Well of Loneliness* was banned and burned in England and named 'a moral pestilence' and a 'vile poison', I argued passionately for the historical and contemporary significance of lesbian-specific images (sexual and non-sexual) in a culture that institutionalizes, privileges, and mandates compulsory and compulsive heterosexuality. I battled to situate the seized issue of *Bad Attitude* on a spectrum of lesbian-produced images alongside the *Dyke Sex Calender* (1990), the San Francisco lesbian porn magazine *On Our Backs*, the British *Quim*, *Getting Wet: Tales of Lesbian Seduction* by the Women's Press (1993), and the writings of Susie Sexpert (Bright 1990, 1992), Joan Nestle (1987), Jewelle Gomez (1987), and Carolyn Gammon (1992). While naming these works in court, I remember the rueful feeling that each of these works was at risk of falling under the censuring gaze of the OPP/Metro Toronto anti-pornography squad. I then sensed that none of them was safe if they could be named and fingered by law enforcers.

INSIDE LESBIAN IMAGERY

Consistent with anti-porn feminists who have historically identified s/m as the 'epicentre of harm', during the *Bad Attitude* trial the Crown (and the judge) relentlessly centred and recentred sadomasochism as evil incarnate.[4] On the stand, I maintained that lesbian-made sexual imagery, including s/m imagery, articulates particular social meanings and is received by intended lesbian audiences and performers in very specific ways. For example, in issues of *Bad Attitude* and *On Our Backs*, in Pat Califia's *Macho Sluts* (1988), Carol Allen and Rosamund Elwin's *Getting Wet* (1993), Karen Barber's *Bushfire* (1991), and Lady Winston's collection, *The Leading Edge* (1987), the stories involve openly lesbian characters in varied settings. Barber situates her sexual and romantic encounters at an art gallery, at a downtown delicatessen, and in the construction trade. *The Leading Edge* delivers a wealth of polymorphously perverse lesbian sexcapades designed to entertain, to educate, and to honour the pussy. In her contribution, Jewelle Gomez skilfully depicts lusty sex between two women: one African American and one white (Gomez 1987: 161–71).

Photographs in lesbian-published magazines depict sex between women who are focused on, and engaged in, sex with each other; their mutual pleasure is of paramount concern. The photographic camera angles, lighting, cropping, positioning, and framing, combined with the lesbian-directed narratives, are all constructed to enhance a lesbian reader/viewer's enjoyment of, and vicarious participation in, the fantasy scenes. The narratives and pictures are made sense of by skilled members of lesbian leather and s/m subcultures who are intimately familiar with the expressed codes, techniques, etiquette, cues, argot, and rule-governed practices. Hence, as I described in detail to the court, the material context in which the images are produced and consumed is of utmost significance. Lesbian-made s/m images inscribe codes specific to lesbian s/m practice: role-playing and the exchange of power, confession, attention to rules and restrictions, staged sexual scenes, costume, drama, and ritual. To me, the contemporary images seem to draw inspiration from nineteenth-century French, German, and British s/m photographs (captured lovingly in the coffee-table collection *Jeux de dame cruelles, 1850–1960*) that feature women dressed as maids, school marms, nurses, school girls, or harlots spanking, gagging, biting, paddling, and whipping each other with gusto (Nazarieff 1988).

Queer theorist Judith Butler argues that 'Femininity is not the product of a choice, but the forcible citation of a norm, one whose complex historicity is indissociable from relations of discipline, regulation, punishment' (Butler 1993: 23). Lesbian s/m fantasy, which is often inflected with butch/femme signs, exposes the naturalized status of femininity (and masculinity) in ways that disrupt the power of heterosexualizing law. Indeed, I argue that portrayals of s/m in *Bad Attitude* enact the theatrical agency of queer performativity, the campy dramatization of leathered queerness that opens up spaces between the norms that regulate gender and sexuality.[5] In effect, we might say that elements of lesbian s/m send up or satirize conventional sexual and gender stereotypes and at the same time borrow from historical traditions of gay camp (Bergman 1993; Newton 1993). The s/m models perform, as do camp artists, for an audience – in this case, readers.[6] When I analyse lesbian s/m porn, I note the use of artifice, role-playing, masquerade, flamboyance, and exhibitionist abandon. In part, the camp of lesbian s/m emerges out of the incongruity between conventional images of suitable, rewarded femininity and distinctly anti-feminine images of bad girls decked out in combinations of leather corsets, dog collars, harnesses and silicon dildos, wrist bands, motorcycle boots, nipple rings, tit clamps, and chains. It seems to me that, contrary to Malamuth's claims, lesbian s/m self consciously trades in (and re-makes) conventions of gay male s/m much more than it mimics conventions of heterosexual s/m images.[7] Whether dominant or submissive or both, lesbian s/m players subvert the purportedly *natural* sexual submissiveness of women towards men. As such, lesbian s/m offers an intriguing exploration of the very signs of 'male' and 'female' (Creet 1991b: 33).

As part of my testimony I explained how in lesbian s/m fantasy, the 'bottom' actually 'runs the fuck'—a fact that throws into chaos the legally codified (yet highly subjective) notions of 'harm' and 'degradation' enacted via (male) dominance and (female) submission. By orchestrating the sexual encounter, the bottom disrupts popular conceptions that she is passive, subjugated, and exploited.[8] The objective of the top is to provide her bottom with sexual pleasure. As such, the top's own sexual needs/desires are dependent on the pleasure experienced by the bottom, and may even be sacrificed in the process of pleasure giving.[9]

In sharp opposition to Neil Malamuth's equation of s/m with degradation and humiliation, American lesbian feminist writer Pat Califia explains that '[s/m] participants are enhancing their sexual pleasure, not damaging or imprisoning one another' (Califia 1981: 31). And she adds that even if scenes are acted out, there is no necessary correlation between the roles women assume in s/m sex and how women behave in their ordinary, everyday worlds. During the trial, I recall thinking that my Califia-informed explanations would only confirm my 'prurient interest' in lesbian s/m porn to Crown and judge, and unveil yet another dimension of my 'subjective', hence problematic, approach. Moreover, I remember wanting to add how lesbians and gay men of colour have intitiated challenges to the racism and anti-Semitism inscribed in some s/m imagery (see below). But for me delivering testimony in courtroom 3-A, there seemed to be absolutely no opportunity to discuss or engage such an important issue.

READING TRISH THOMAS

During my testimony, I was asked to give a detailed reading of 'Wunna My Fantasies', written by California based lesbian writer Trish Thomas and published in *Bad Attitude* (Thomas 1991: 25–9). It features fully consensual sex-play between two fictional lesbian characters. The narrator imagines herself in s/m gear (leather, nose-ring, chains, etc.) inside a locker room; she approaches the other woman from behind, blindfolds, handcuffs, and then has sex with her. The author Trish Thomas, as I've since discovered through interviewing her for *X-tra!* magazine in 1993, is a 37-year-old grandmother, a shy butch who lives in San Francisco, has s/m sex with women she's in love with, and is not an active member of the public s/m community (Ross 1993: 27). Thomas contextualized 'Wunna My Fantasies', a story she wrote in 1986: 'It's about a girl I had a class with at San Francisco State and she would pick me up every Wednesday night and take me to class—'Incarcerated Women' taught by Angela Davis. I had a major crush on this girl, and it was a masturbation fantasy for me for months, and finally I decided to write it down.' Thomas continues, 'I would have loved to tell the Judge that the woman who inspired the story read it, was flattered and wanted a copy to act out the scene with her dominatrix girlfriend. But I think he would have regarded me as a monster pervert.' On the witness stand, I interpreted Thomas's story 'Wunna My Fantasies' as one of sexual play and role reversal where the aggressor is left unattended in the end while her prey engineers her own orgasm, watching herself come in the mirror. The fantasy story, printed in *Bad Attitude* in italics to designate its dream-like character, ends like this:

> *She crawls all the way out of the shower stall and across the wet tile floor, with my hand still in her pussy up to my forearm, until we're over in front of the mirror. I wipe the steam off the glass with the sleeve of my jacket so we can see ourselves. She watches my arm pump into her pussy. And I watch her. And she's checking me out, watching her. Then she grins this wicked grin and pulls herself up off her elbows until she's kneeling straight up with her arms over her head. She pushes her body flat out against the mirror. Still pushing her cunt down onto my fist, she watches her nipples graze the nipples of the woman in the mirror who is herself. Oh man, she's fucking herself. The fucking bitch is fucking herself!*
>
> (Thomas 1991: 29).

Indeed, the bottom—the woman who is pursued in the shower stall—is wearing a nipple ring, which signifies her membership in the s/m subculture. In this fantasy sequence, she is hardly, as the Crown insisted, an innocent, unsuspecting victim. If Thomas's intent was to portray (and legitimize) a rape, she would not have included numerous references to improving the comfort level of the woman pursued, nor details of how 'the pursuee' happily participates in the exchange by 'spreading her legs wide', 'letting out moans', and 'wrapping her legs' around her captor (ibid. 25–7). Nor would she be troubled to observe safer-sex practices that accompany the fisting—an act both players plainly enjoy. The top in 'Wunna My Fantasies' is vested with eroticized mastery and yet her open respect for guidance from her 'prey' dispels the enactment of traditional patriarchal authority. Like a dog with a bone, the Crown repeatedly cited decontextualized snippets of description in order to demonstrate what he argued was the narrative's essentially coercive, brutal, and non-consensual thrust.

By contrast, I argued that the consent established between the two female characters in 'Wunna My Fantasies' (and in lesbian s/m literature in general) is the motor that drives the story. Here, consent is the fundamental principle upon which the entire encounter is premised (though why questions of consent *in fiction* are so legally problematic warrants further attention). Rather than making the sexual materials 'more obscene' or 'more violent', as the *Butler* decision confirms (and as Judge Paris upheld in his verdict in *R* v. *Scythes*), the practice of consent guarantees mutuality, communication, and collaboration. Lesbian s/m sex involves a negotiation process between sexual partners whereby certain words are agreed upon and then used to set limits. Jasmine Sterling, publisher of *Bad Attitude* magazine, asserts: 'I write about how you use "safe words," which are mutually agreed-upon words that mean to slow down or stop a scene. I feel I'm empowering women, not promoting violence against them' (Toobin 1994: 74). Indeed, without consent the interaction cannot proceed (or it does and becomes something else, like rape, which is an indictable offence). Moreover, given feminists' longstanding concern for the methods used to produce commercial pornography, it is significant that the photographed models in 'Wunna My Fantasies' were not coerced to participate in the staged scenario—one is the author, Thomas herself and, her partner, Trashina, volunteered.

In court defending her photographs published in *Bad Attitude*, Toronto artist Jennifer Gillmor testified that her model, 'who has an exhibitionist nature', came up with the ideas for the images herself

and, in advance of publication, signed model release forms to formalize her consent and to ensure that she was over 18 years of age (Gillmor 1992: 16). One of Gillmor's three photos in the seized copy of *Bad Attitude* features her model—a young, white woman in a merry widow and garter belt, lashed with heavy ropes to a cross and tombstone, Christ-like, in a graveyard (Figure 1). This is the image that Neil Malamuth described as similar to sexually violent heterosexual pornography (Malamuth 1992: 34). In another photo the same model appears decked out in full top regalia. Gillmor explained: 'She likes to switch roles. On the cross she's submissive. Here, she's wearing a black leather motorcyle cap and black leather motorcycle chaps, a belt buckle that she designed from a piece of the motorcycle's gas tank (Figure 2), some hockey equipment, armour really, painted black. She has studded leather cuffs that go from her wrist to her elbow. She's wearing black leather boots, a G-string, and she's carrying a whip that she made entirely for show purposes—it's made out of bathtub chain' (Gillmor 1992: 17–18).

During cross-examination, the Crown pounced on Gillmor's defensive allusion to the whip as a fake, a prop (Granek 1992a: 22). He questioned why she felt the need to emphasize that the whip was not functional, not a real whip. When Gillmor responded that 'the idea is not to hurt people', the Crown pushed her to admit her discomfort with whipping, a tactic that succeeded in bolstering his anti-s/m agenda and in deflecting attention away from the more germane issues of fantasy, representation, and consent.

To date there have been no empirical studies proving the causal link between lesbian (or gay male) s/m images and violence against women. (Though, importantly, the *Butler* decision states that actual proof of harm is unnecessary.) In factums submitted to Supreme Court judges in *R.* v. *Butler*, the Attorney General of Manitoba, the Attorney General of Canada, and the feminist Group Against Pornography (GAP) conclude that, even without evidence, it is reasonable to conclude that significant harms flow from obscene materials (see Gotell, 1997). Not one lesbian, to my knowledge, has ever proclaimed in a court of law that lesbian s/m erotica is degrading, humiliating, and dehumanizing or that it is responsible for her experience of abuse. Furthermore, there is no conclusive evidence, following from the *Butler* decision, that 'harm would flow from exposure' to lesbian s/m materials. Nor is there socia-scientific research to determine what 'the community would tolerate others being exposed to' vis-a-vis lesbian sexual depictions. Interestingly, when I raised issues of the inconclusive research during my testimony, Crown Attorney Charles Granek

retorted: 'There's no proven causal linkage between smoking and cancer, but they're correlated' (Ross 1992: 63). In retrospect, I might have rebuffed Granek by using the correlation 'Silence = Death' devised by AIDS activists to capsulize my analysis of the effects of state sexual censorship.

Testifying in the case of *Little Sister's Book and Art Imporium* v. *B.C. Minister of Justice* in late 1994, pscyhologist and well-known 'media effects expert' William Marshall acknowledged that exposure to violent (heterosexual) pornography is not a correlate of sexual aggression against women in natural settings (rather than laboratory experiments) (cited in Fuller and Blackley 1995: 115). He also testified that exposure to pornography did not result in demonstrable negative changes in the motions, attitudes, and behaviours of Canada Customs officials. Americans Marcia Pally and Nadine Strossen have independently concluded, upon assessing the literature, that there is no credible evidence corroborating a causal link between exposure to sexually explicit material and violent behaviour (Pally 1994; Strossen 1995). Strossen cites studies that show the *inverse*: a rise in the availability of sexual material correlates to advances in the availability of education on gender equality and sex-positive curricula in schools, along with the unacceptability of sex-related violence (Strossen 1995). Upon reviewing the psychological literature on pornography and harm, British researcher Lynne Segal urges feminists and supporters to abandon the search for some spurious link between men's violence against women and pornography, however defined (Segal 1993: 5–21). Those who trumpet a definitive causal relationship are too (desperately) invested in their own moral agenda to ever probe why they cleave like barnacles to such an untenable 'fact' in the first place. Now when I read the *Butler* decision, I see that the glide from indeterminate empirical evidence to 'reasoned apprehension of harm' amounts to little more than an elaborate, sorcerous hoax.

LEZZIE SPREADS IN MAINSTREAM PORN

Like Jennifer Gillmor, in my testimony I strove to stress the particularities of lesbian-produced sexual texts in part through illustrating what they are not. I presented Judge Paris with the photo series 'Stream of Cuntiousness' in *Hustler* magazine (*Hustler* 1990: 36–41). Though this 'lesbian spread' features two women, it illustrates the photographic, compositional, and ideological conventions intrinsic to hetero-sexual pornography: masculinist fetishization of hypercaricatured femininity—large, pouty lips, large breasts, lots of facial make-up, most often white-skinned but sun-bronzed and oiled bodies, long fingernails and nail polish, big, lacquered hair, stiletto heels, colour-enhanced pussys, and so on. In these photographs (which signify a random but highly representative sampling) two white faux-dykes are splayed out across rocks in the middle of a swift-running stream. In the 'Nicki and Bronson: Aquavelvet' spread in *Hustler's* September 1993 issue, two white 'lesbians', one blonde, one brunette, cavort on the deck of a sun-drenched power boat (*Hustler* 1993: 96–104). Each photo (which likely cost more to produce than an entire year of *Bad Attitude*) is painstakingly constructed to embrace the male reader— in other words, 'Lesbianism as (heterosexual) Foreplay 101' or girl + girl = straight male titillation.[10] The processes of construction reveal how pornography as vehicle of fantasy is not reality. Through lighting, shading, framing, cropping, texturing, colouring, and so on, the intended male reader is invited to enter and master the scene—that is, to dominate the two women, thereby 'doubling his pleasure'. The women are typically painted as primed for heterosexual intercourse initiated and controlled by men; they appear as overburdened signs of male lust, male sexual appetites and obsessions, not as sexually self-defining subjects.

In contrast to lesbian-produced imagery, the women pictured in 'lesbian spreads' do not attend to each other: they stare out coyly at a male voyeur and their bodies are positioned to maximize both his arousal and their own submission to his needs.. They exist on the page to service men. The women tend to be almost identical in shape, size, age, and colour (no butch/femme codes here), and I have yet to see any evidence of safe-sex practice—a regular component of lesbian sexual imagery. (Indeed, the absence of latex suggests the absence of sex altogether.) Lesbianism itself, and more specifically (hot) lesbian sex, is of no or little interest to *Hustler* publisher Larry Flynt. Indeed, in numerous spots throughout *Hustler*, *Forum*, and *Penthouse*, lesbianism is lampooned and trivialized, rendered toxic and dangerous, in keeping with the magazines' deeply heterosexist and homophobic thrust. 'Real' lesbians routinely appear in cartoons as overweight, bra-less, badly dressed, and villainous sex freaks with bad haircuts lecherously seeking to poke cute, unsuspecting blondes in the ass with their deluxe dildos. This is not to say that lesbians (and non-lesbian women) never find straight lezzie spreads arousing or educational. Clearly some do, though lack of alternatives, especially in smaller communities, often determines their choices.

I contend that if the erotic/educational needs of lesbian readers were met by the 'lesbian spreads' in *Penthouse*, *Forum*, and *Hustler*, there would be no desire for, hence no consumers of, lesbian-produced images. If the two were ostensibly interchangeable, why not opt for the vastly easier to find super-slick hetero-spreads? As I observed in court, in terms of the relations of production, lesbian stories/images in *Bad Attitude*, *Girlfriends*, *Lezzie Smut*, *Lickerish*, and *Quim* are nested in a publishing environment whereby lesbian and feminist issues are addressed, be it safe-sex and HIV/AIDS prevention, the threat of gay bashing, the need for pay equity, the power of anti-racist praxis, spousal benefits, access to effective and non stigmatized artificial insemination, and affordable child care. The seized issue of *Bad Attitude* sports an editorial statement about the rise in street violence directed at lesbians and provides a series of phone lines for women in the Boston, Massachusetts, area (*Bad Attitude* 1991*b*: 2). Furthermore, without making a claim for the ultimate 'truth' or 'authentic' power of lesbian-made pornography to reveal the essence of lesbian sex, the stories and pictures unambiguously intend a lesbian and bisexual audience through the foregrounding of women's sexual desires and tastes. This context differs dramatically from the sexist, heterosexist, and often racist environment that frames 'lesbian spreads' in *Hustler*, *Forum*, and *Penthouse*. In these magazines, the figuring of 'lesbians' to attract and accommodate the male gaze confirms age-old myths of the gargantuan, ever-ready sapphic appetite best satisfied by a horny, straight he-man.

It is important to recognize that in lesbian-made erotica, including s/m imagery, the protagonists are women, hence the gender-based inequities that pervade commercial pornography (and society in general) are neither represented nor reinforced. Indeed, 'she' is not a 'he'. The economic, physical, and cultural power of men over women that is objectified and sexualized in much (though not all) heterosexual pornography, is not and cannot be accomplished in lesbian sexual imagery because straight men are either absent from, or insignificant to, the scene. Men, almost always gay men, might appear, as they do in Pat Califia's story, 'The Surprise Party', but their pleasure is secondary to the pleasure sought and found by the female characters (Califia 1988: 211–42).

To me, it is the unique sexual dynamic between two women captured in lesbian porn that constitutes the turn-on. In my opinion, and in my experience, the most arousing images involve the eroticization of sexual tension or difference (butch/femme, top/bottom), which may be positively complicated by age, race, and/or class difference, *in the context of gender sameness*. (There were a number of surreal moments during my testimony in *R.* v. *Scythes*: one involved my need to clarify for Crown and judge that a photograph of a butch/femme couple was of two women, not a man and a woman.) Pat Califia's short story 'Jessie,' first published in 1981, remains for me one of the hottest pieces of lesbian porn ever written. It was a 'breakthrough' for her, and is reprinted in the state-confiscated *Macho Sluts* (Califia 1988: 28–62).[11] The narrative has violent, rough elements; Califia plays with power, objectification, humiliation, and sexual want. 'Jessie' is not about wholesome, respectable love-making, and this both unnerves me and quickens my lust.

MADONNA'S *SEX*: PUTTING QUEER SEX OUT THERE?

In today's postmodern, mishmashed world of cross-referenced and borrowed image-making, gay and lesbian images are customarily appropriated, commodified, and sold back to us by astute entrepreneurs. It is worth noting that these images (some of which are silly, ironic spoofs) never seem to incite the wrath of police, crown attorneys, and judges. American First Lady Hilary Clinton appeared as a leather s/m dominatrix, crop in hand, smiling on the cover of *Spy* magazine in February 1993. In an image that oozed butch/femme and s/m overtones, scantily clad Cindy Crawford was pictured shaving a mannish and blissed-out k.d. lang in *Vanity Fair*, August 1993. During the *R.* v. *Scythes* trial, law student Suzanne Jarvie introduced Helmut Newton's photo spread in *Vogue* magazine (September 1992) entitled 'Chain Reactions' (incidentally, the name of a lesbian s/m sex club in London, England). Jarvie drew attention to sexual poses of the female models and the lesbian s/m codes incorporated into the spread—leather, chains, whips, harnesses, and dog collars. Though Judge Paris refused to acknowledge the context in which *Bad Attitude* and other lesbian-made porn is produced and received, he intervened to assert that *Vogue* was a *fashion magazine*, one his daughters read at home (Jarvie 1992: 25). In spite of evidence that both magazines deploy the signs of s/m fantasy, the judge elected to ignore the blurring of fictional genres. In my opinion, his intimation that *Vogue* was nothing like the nasty lesbian smut on trial reveals his desire to confirm fashion discourse as purely pornography-free, and pornographic discourse, that is *Bad Attitude*, as both unfashionable and unfit for home browsing.

A provocative example of trafficking in lesbian images from a non-lesbian standpoint is Madonna's controversial book, *Sex* (1992).[12] In *R.* v. *Scythes*, defence counsel Clare Barclay introduced *Sex* as a principal exhibit. Examined on the witness stand by Barclay about the form and content of *Sex*, I pointed out that, ironically, *Sex* contains more graphic and controversial images and references to whipping, bondage, watersports, hot-wax dripping, slapping, paddling, bestiality, intergenerational sex, tattooing, humiliation, group sex, and so on, than does *Bad Attitude*. The first ten pages of the over-sized collection are devoted to images of Madonna being sexually serviced by two New York lesbian s/m specialists, both bald and pierced, one with a Star of David tattooed on her back. Dita, Madonna's 'nom de tart', is depicted bound to a chair and gagged. One s/m dyke stretches Dita's hands high in the air above her head, while the other lays a switchblade against her barely concealed crotch. Other scenes place Dita in the role of leather dominatrix expertly snapping a cat-'o-nine-tails on the shiny, black vinyl butt of her kneeling female captive; in another, she's adorned in ripped school-girl garb in the company of two men who appear about to rape her on the gymnasium floor. Most of *Sex's* images match descriptions of obscenity detailed in Memorandum D9 1–1, the obscenity guidelines that govern the importation of materials at the Canada/United States border.[13]

Chock-full of pirated queer content, *Sex* resided atop the *New York Times* best-seller list for over four months. Yet it has not escaped queer tongue-lashing. Photographer Susan Stewart of 'Kiss & Tell' delivers a stinging critique: 'In *Sex*, Madonna's "blonde ambition" drapes itself over the dangerous transgressive sexuality of two radical leather dykes, titillating straight sensibilities with an indrawn breath, a momentary suspension of safety and its attendant adrenalin-rush value, at the same time underscoring the certainty that this experience is a mere throwaway exchange.' In the cheeky reader *Madonnarama* (1993), Pat Califia complains about 'somebody who has not paid her dues using my community as a series of bizarre backdrops for a photo shoot' (Califia 1993: 177). And gay critics Douglas Crimp and Michael Warner add that 'everything about *Sex* is made possible by Madonna's celebrity, and her celebrity is constructed, in however complex a way, as *heterosexual.* She can be as queer as she wants to, but only because we know she's not' (their emphasis) (Crimp and Warner 1993: 93).

Notwithstanding queer annoyance, *Sex* has sold thousands and thousands of copies internationally. In Canada and Quebec it sells for $60.00 a pop (+ GST and PST), and many public libraries stock it. In late 1995 three years after the court case, gay journalist Bill Richardson wrote that the four copies of *Sex* in Vancouver's public library system collectively bear the weight of 1,020 outstanding reserves (Richardson 1995: 17). *Sex* has not, to my knowledge, been subject to obscenity charges of any kind. *Sex's* metal covers serve as a bullet-proof, anti-cop shield held smugly by the multinational dynasty Time-Warner and its stable of crackerjack entertainment lawyers. As is common practice amongst media magnates, Time-Warner sought and obtained pre-clearance for *Sex* from Canada Customs. Lawyer Brian Blugerman of the prestigious Canadian firm Osler, Hoskin & Harcourt was hired to instruct customs officials on how to interpret *Sex*: 'Since there was no penetration we could say it was just violence, no sex. Violence alone is OK under Butler' (cited in Toobin 1994: 76). Blugerman notes that in order to pre-empt a censorious strike at the border they could have used the 'internal necessities test' or 'artistic defence', but they didn't need to. Two years later, at the trial of *Little Sister's Book and Art Emporium* v. *B. C. Minister of Justice* (1994), the bookstore's lawyer, Joseph Arvay, cross-examined Linda Murphy about her professional evaluation of Madonna's *Sex.* Murphy, the director of the Prohibited Importations Directorate in Ottawa, confessed that there was no written version of her own unit's decision to permit the sale of *Sex* in Canada. Journalists Fuller and Blackley report: 'Murphy was unable to provide either a credible or consistent accounting for *Sex's* innocence. Murphy agreed that many of the images seemed to involve the "undue exploitation of sex," yet she was frequently evasive' (Fuller and Blackley 1995: 125). Evidently, the safe passage of *Sex* across the U.S./Canada border was eased by the twin lubricants of money and power; the publishers of *Bad Attititude* had no such 'luck'.

Certainly the dazzling production values of *Sex* and its embeddedness in the legitimizing discourses of high art and fashion photography aid in securing its virtual inviolability. And *Sex* is protected by and marketed through Madonna's status as international pop icon. (As a femme I find that neither the shots of Madonna-the-heterosex-kitten nor of Madonna-the-object-of-leather-dyke-attention pass my wet test. But there is one very hot image of Madonna from behind affecting a Jimmy Dean-like pose, standing in a door frame, cockily and sweetly butch, that I quite like.)

During the *Bad Attitude* hearing, Crown Attorney Charles Granek dismissed *Sex* as Madonna's 'cynical marketing ploy', a shrewd manoeuvre to increase sales of her album, 'Erotica' (Granek 1992*b*: 67). In ways exemplary of the adversarial nature of criminal trial proceedings, he then attempted to pressure me into agreeing that the elimination of certain 'shocking and graphic' images in *Sex* would not compromise the book's integrity. Granek pressed me to assume the role of censor, slicing up and chopping out those images in *Sex* that he had already decided were obscene and harmful. Granek also, ineffectually, attempted to elicit my agreement with his assertion that people only rushed out to purchase *Sex* because they were (mindlessly) curious about Madonna and her celebrity status (which, extending Granek's logic, cancelled out any prurient or 'dirty' rationale for buying the book) (ibid. 68, 71–4). In other words, Granek sought to undermine our analysis of *Sex* by insinuating that people were bamboozled by their own foolishiness and by excessive media hype; they were duped into lining Madonna's pockets either because they were stupid or they wanted to buy art, *not because they wanted to get off*.

Annoyed by the Crown's incessant efforts to manipulate and trap me, Clare Barclay and I argued that the commercial success of Madonna's *Sex* signified a decisive shift in community standards. (Because I was disallowed as an expert on community standards, this argument carried little weight.) Most notably, the book has never been proved responsible for inciting 'harm to women' or 'anti-social behaviour,' nor has it been prevented from travelling freely across the Canada/U.S. border. In the end, Judge Paris dismissed our exhibit, *Sex*, and all of our attendant arguments regarding changes in community standards evidenced by the book's mass dissemination and popular appeal, as unpersuasive. Here he was aided by the Crown Attorney, Granek, who stressed in his summation that because *Sex* is sold in a sealed package, the community cannot look at or read it before they buy it; therefore, it is an unreliable indicator of liberalizing community standards (Granek 1992*c*: 48). Moreover, Cranek added that Madonna's book *Sex* 'can be distinguished on the very ground of an artistic defense' while *Bad Attitude* was 'merely a document designed for sexual arousal,' hence any comparison or analogy drawn between the two was necessarily specious (ibid. 50). In so doing, he activated a fundamental premise undergirding the *Butler* decision as identified by legal theorist Brenda Cossman: 'Art cannot be sex for sex's sake. By definition, sex is not art' (see Cossman, 1997).

Lesbian pornography produced by and for lesbians has little commercial currency or public profile: in North America there are fewer than eight lesbian magazines that contain explicit sex, and there are approximately forty sexually explicit lesbian-produced videos that are poorly distributed in Canada and the United States. *Bad Attitude* is a low-budget, bimonthly magazine that sells less than two hundred copies an issue across Canada at self-identified lesbian and gay bookstores. The owner and editor of the magazine, Jasmine Sterling, explains: 'We call it *Bad Attitude* because society says that a woman who takes charge of her own sexuality has a bad attitude, and that's what the magazine is about—women taking charge' (cited in Toobin 1994: 74). At $8.95, *Bad Attitude* is not glossy, the reproduction of images is poor, and the text is littered with typos and grammatical errors. In spite of these shortcomings, I explained to Judge Paris during the *R.* v. *Scythes* trial that seekers of lesbian-made pornography had a very difficult time finding *Bad Attitude*, and that Glad Day Bookshop rarely received or sold more than twenty copies per issue. (Interviewed after the *R.* v. *Scythes* case publisher Jasmine Sterling reported that she used to send fifty copies to bookstores in Canada, but that she had stopped doing it because it wasn't worth the hassle; cited in Toobin 1994: 74.) This situation is in contrast to the millions of male consumers who first encounter and form impressions of 'lesbians' in heterosexual porn. I argued that stories/images in *Bad Attitude* (as well as in *On Our Backs*, *Quim*, and *Deneuve*) typically incorporate safe-sex practice, including latex gloves, condoms on penises, dildoes, and vibrators, and safe-sex information. The more I struggled to establish the cultural and political import of lesbian texts that intend lesbian arousal, the more the judge seemed impatient, bored, and exasperated.

DISCIPLINED AND PUNISHED

Because I attempted to contextualize *Bad Attitude*, because I refused to provide the court with the 'exact size of the lesbian s/m subcommunity' in Toronto, and because I (on occasion) hesitated to give yes and no answers, I was scolded by judge and Crown for being uncooperative and given to 'hearsay' (Ross 1992: 18) Because I was unable to 'count' s/m lesbians or to admit to their 'fringe status', my knowledge was not interpreted by the Crown (and judge) as objective social science—my analysis ran counter to the structuring of obscenity law. Though trained as a social scientist, I had no genuinely positivist claims of my own to announce. Unlike Malamuth, I had not conducted experimental research in laboratories, hence I could not generalize from 'hard data' and statistically significant findings. The Crown and judge wanted me to solidify the lesbian s/m subculture as a constitutive group that was mathematically measurable. They sought numbers and certainty and 'solid facts'. As legal scholar Carol Smart argues, 'legal arguments . . . that present simple, certain and authoritative pictures of social reality are likely to be privileged within legal discourse' (Smart 1989: 71). Ironically, Malamuth himself had no 'facts' to disclose; however, his authority had been pre-established and needed no further justification.

The Crown urged me to pin down the particulars of lesbian s/m identity; I endeavoured to elucidate the unsolicited layers of s/m discourse. I argued that s/m cannot be easily and neatly packaged: there is tremendous variability of s/m fantasy and action. Elements of s/m enter the lives and imaginations of many women (lesbian and non-lesbian), which makes the quantification of a 'lesbian s/m subculture' impossible. In all, my postmodern insistence that pornography has many meanings, that sexual expression (including s/m) can promote self-fulfilment and alternative sexualities, and that feminists are deeply divided on issues of representation damaged my worthiness and credibility in court. Try as I could, I was unable to argue for the *specificity* of lesbian s/m fantasy, and at the same time underscore the *fluidity* of sexual desire, and be understood. In other words, I was committed to defending *Bad Attitude* as one product of lesbian sexual dissent, *and* I remember wanting to normalize a blurring of s/m-non-s/m boundaries as a way of flipping the hegemonic caricature of s/m on its head. Like American feminist historian Alice Kessler-Harris in her testimony against the gendered discriminatory practices of Sears in the mid-1980s, I learned that developing subtle distinctions and negotiating fine points of interpretation are skills that must be abandoned in the courtroom (Kessler-Harris 1987: 61). And like Kessler-Harris, when I responded to the Crown's questions by underlining the import of nuance and diversity, my answers were often demeaned (ibid. 61–2). Judge Paris warned me that my attitude was corroding my credibility and the helpfulness of my testimony (Ross 1992: 70). He disciplined me several times over the course of my testimony much as a dominatrix would punish her 'prey'. When I string these occasions of punishment and humiliation together, I find ineluctable, ironic confirmation of the trial itself as ritualized s/m theatre.

Lesbian Invisibility in Court and out

Outside of my testimony, over the course of almost thirty hours of examination and cross examination, the word 'lesbian' was only mentioned sporadically. Almost two full days were spent debating the responses of white, American, college-educated males to non-consensual images of rape and coercion. The freedom, privilege, and power to make sense of, to comment on, and to judge lesbian s/m fantasy were rolled around like marbles in the hands of white, heterosexual male experts—judge, Crown and witnesses. Even psychologist Jonathon Freedman, in an otherwise superb denunciation of Neil Malamuth and the entire 'porn causes violence' school of media analysis, referred to the image of lesbian fisting in *Bad Attitude* as 'disgusting' (Freedman 1992: 40). Artist Ellen Flanders attended the trial: 'They had these men discussing in a very clinical way what was going on in [the *Bad Attitude*] images, and that was the only time they discussed anything about lesbianism. And they didn't know what they were talking about [laughing]. And I found that incredible: here they were, the supposed experts, the judge and the Crown, discussing fisting and they had no idea what they were talking about' (Flanders 1993: 9). Revealing his profound knowledge of, and sensitivity to lesbians, the Crown Attorney, Charles Granek, used his summation to pontificate: '[We know] that the sadomasochistic group is only one fraction of the lesbian community itself. To suggest, therefore, that lesbians on the whole are discriminated against if we are to ban material like *Bad Attitude* is insulting to that very community' (Granek 1992*c*: 32). He continued by insisting that the trial was not about lesbians; it was about 'the sadomasochistic community of either sex and of any sexual orientation', a community 'whose rights are, thankfully, not protected by the Canadian Charter of Rights and Freedoms' (ibid. 32–3). When I read the court transcript now, I am sickened by what I interpret to be the Crown's smug separation of good lesbians/bad lesbians and his declaration of the subhuman status of s/m practitioners. I bristle at Granek's highfalutin' inference that he knows what is best for 'the lesbian community'. Indeed, it was the startling invisibility of LESBIAN at a lesbian porn trial that I and others experienced bodily and intellectually as most incredible, angering, and insanity-making.

In his summation, Granek also stated baldly that because *Bad Attitude* was indisputably 'dirt for dirt's sake', my extralegal interpretation of the lesbian text '[flew] in the face of common sense and ought to be disregarded' (Granek 1992*c*: 44). In other words, my knowledge of lesbian sexuality and culture was nothing but anecdotal, confessional, and impressionistic non-sense; it was, in short, dispensable. I now see that it was the law, specifically *Butler*, that had discursive monopoly over 'common sense'. My active, sociological disloyalty to *Butler's* sovereignty placed me in a position of major strategic disadvantage on the terrain of law. By contrast, Malamuth's testimony—a clever incantation of *Butler's* internal logic and coherence—functioned as a polished mirror for the law's narcissistic contemplation of itself (Valverde 1996: 202). I suspect that from the standpoint of the prosecutorial team, my challenge marked a churlish affront to hegemonic conceptions of s/m porn as *the* trope of brutality, depravity, cruelty, and the exploitation of women. In *Butler*, s/m porn lurks between the lines as the unspoken, consummate apex of 'degradation' and 'dehumanization'. To date across Canada and the United States, the only s/m depictions successfully defended in legal arenas—Robert Mapplethorpe's photographic retrospective 'The Perfect Moment'—have been defended as art based on 'expert' ideas of art (see Lang 1995).[14] In a Toronto court in December 1992, the Crown Attorney, Charles Granek, argued that *Bad Attitude* could not be exculpated on grounds of artistic merit or intent (Granek 1992*c*: 56-7).

In the end, Judge Paris, the 'trier of fact', made a ruling on one issue of the 'lesbian erotic fiction' magazine *Bad Attitude* based primarily on Malamuth's use of extrapolation in the place of scientific evidence. He did not reference the discourses of religion, psychiatry, or biology—discourses that have historically been integral to the pathologization of homosexuality.[15] He did not need to. In his official ruling Judge Paris maintained that by substituting a man for the 'sexually aggressive' woman in the story 'Wunna My Fantasies', the criminally violent character of the scene is fully revealed (*Scythes* 1993: 5). By crafty sleight of hand, Paris-the-magician transformed one (paper) expression of consensual female homoerotic desire into a (live) non-consensual heterosexual 'rape' and in so doing obliterated the radical specificity of the lesbian imagery/text. Here, the inadmissability of lesbians and lesbian sexual images was legally secured. At the same time, Judge Paris disallowed the reality that in commercial heterosexual s/m, the men are most often submissive, not the women.[16]

Unable or unwilling to interpret lesbian s/m imagery from inside the interpretive frame that I and others built over the course of the trial, Judge Paris drained the lesbian-specific images of content and context. In superimposing a heterosexual template, he was aided by expert witness Neil Malamuth's 'scientific' postulation that it was possible to generalize and universalize from research findings based on exclusively heterosexual male samples.[17] Indeed, Malamuth's inference provides graphic substantiation of Stanley Fish's perception that 'the law wants social science to tell it that a new problem or social experience can be properly and fairly managed by being construed as analagous to something else' (Fish 1989: chap. 17). To Judge Paris, once the original lesbian image was remade into a heterosexual exchange between a man and a woman, it became instantly intelligible. (Ironically, in their factum to the Supreme Court on *Butler*, LEAF's lawyers recommended the substitution of an 'abused' woman-as-bottom for an 'abused' gay man-as-bottom in gay male porn in order to 'teach' judges about the coercion and violence inscribed in heterosexual pornography.) The gender of the female actors/models in lesbian-made sexual imagery is fundamentally relevant and defies the mental practice of substitution or translation. A reading that denies gender relevancy irreparably ruptures the integrity and intention of lesbian texts made explicitly for lesbian viewers/readers, and the particular context/s in which the work is received. In so doing, it discounts the radical specificity of a lesbian sub-genre that exists outside of, heterosexual male imaging of lesbian sex.

To me, there is no question that Judge Paris's decision is shot through with heterosexist and homophobic assumptions and double standards. Never has it been more clear to me that the relevances of anti-violence and anti-porn discourse are contingent on the sexist and heterocentric suspension, if not the disavowal, of women's self-defined pleasure. In the face of massive resources marshalled to extinguish the 'lesbian threat'—the legal profession, the judiciary, and the police—I am certain that I could find no better evidence of the *instability* of normative heterosexuality. Indeed, the legal judgment rendering *Bad Attitude* 'obscene' seems to substantiate Diana Fuss's eloquent argument that 'heterosexuality secures its ontological boundaries by protecting itself from what it sees as the continual predatory intrusion of its diseased other, homosexuality' (Fuss 1989: 2).

RE-INVOKING SOCIAL-PURITY DISCOURSE IN THE LATE TWENTIETH CENTURY

The categories of degradation, dehumanization, and harm used repeatedly by the Crown during the *Bad Attitude* case (and enshrined in *Butler*) bespeak a persisting concentration on female victimization that centres around women's sexual danger, guilt, shame, and fear. (For much of the *Bad Attitude* trial, the Crown clutched the feminist anthology *Against Sadomasochism* [Linden et al. 1982] to his chest.) Importantly, the construct of female sexual degradation was pivotal to the rhetoric of English Canadian moral reformers in the early 1900s: the National Council of Women (NCW), the Women's Christian Temperance Union's Department of Purity in Literature, Art and Fashion, and the Methodist Department of Temperance and Moral Reform—all of whom lobbied for obscenity legislation and greater legal/sexual/moral protection for women and children. And as historian Mary Louise Adams has discovered, in the early 1950s women took the leadership role in urging state censorship of crime comics and pulp fiction that they believed were destined to corrupt morally impressionable young people (Adams 1994). As the Congress of Canadian Women put it in 1952, 'The mass production and distribution of sensational novels depicting lewd, repulsive and perverted behaviour of the characters as a normal way of life has superceded all other worthwhile publications offered for sale in Canadian stores. Men and women are portrayed as monsters of perversion and the women pictured as Lesbians and modern Messalinas. Added to this is the continuous suggestion that crime and perversion is normal' (Congress of Canadian Women 1952: 149). The continuity between the early and late twentieth centuries seems to be the maternal, and later cultural feminist, fixing of certain norms of femininity and masculinity as natural, unchanging, and essentially rooted in binary opposites: the female is morally superior and in need of rescue from the oversexed, uncontrollably lustful and inherently violent male. Today, given the structuring of woman-as-object-to-be-violated-by-man in pro-censorship feminist, conservative, and legal discourse, woman as sexual subject becomes an oxymoron. Once the paradox becomes inscribed in a law that animates police and court action, how then is it possible to tell different stories?

In his final decision, Judge Paris concluded that 'Wunna My Fantasies' 'blew all the whistles and rang all the bells' (*Scythes* 1993: 4). Clearly, he did not read Trish Thomas's story 'Wunna My Fantasies' as fantasy—a work of the imagination, a symbolic representation. He read it literally as real, actual abuse meted out by an attacker on her victim. Accepting *Butler's* premise that porn is believed by the Canadian public to cause harm, and that consent 'cannot save materials' deemed to be degrading to women, the judge ruled that it is now a felony to fantasize participating in a lesbian s/m sexual act.

I communicated to Judge Paris that lesbian s/m imagery plays a crucial role in the formation of lesbian s/m identities, networks, and subcultures. I argued that isolating s/m (and anal penetration in gay porn) as punishable depictions strips them from the larger political context of resistance and self-definition by marginalized communities. My elaboration of these themes in court was, in the end, entirely disregarded by Judge Paris. In his final judgment he explained that 'The community tolerance test is blind to sexual orientation. Its only focus is the potential harm to the public' (*Scythes* 1993: 4). Defence counsel Clare Barclay had anticipated this tack, and used her summation to caution that 'The community standards test should not be whether a heterosexual majority is willing to tolerate others being exposed to lesbian or gay sexually explicit imagery, for it is the community as a whole which must be the arbiter' (Barclay 1992: 12). Barclay bravely argued that the exclusion of lesbian and gay Canadians from determinations of community standards would mean discrimination on the basis of sexual orientation. She added that such exclusion would violate section 15 of the Canadian Charter of Rights and Freedoms, and would be unconstitutional. Barclay then reviewed case law on sexual orientation as evidence that 'community understanding and tolerance of lesbian and gay sexuality has increased immensely' (ibid. 17). Finally, she reintroduced Madonna's *Sex* as evidence of what communities do tolerate in the 1990s, and she reiterated the necessity of evaluating lesbian images in the contexts within which they are produced and disseminated.

In his six-page ruling, Judge Paris conceded a point to Barclay in his willingness to recognize 'the rights of sexual minorities to communicate publicly on the subject that binds them together' (*Scythes* 1993: 4). And then he delivered his view that, in this case, curtailing these rights was justified 'in the public interest' (ibid.). To me, his decision suggests that lesbian producers and consumers of *Bad Attitude* (and queers in general) are not members of the 'public', hence their (subhuman) views on community standards do not count, need never matter, and are not officially registrable.[18] Indeed, it seems a short slide from the erasure of lesbian pornographic images to Eve Sedgwick's sobering apprehension of 'an overarching, hygienic Western fantasy of a world without any homosexuals in it' (Sedgwick 1990: 42).

The moral standpoint that governed both the police raid on Glad Day Bookshop and the judge's conviction of obscenity is legally codified in the *Butler* decision. By deploying *Butler*, Judge Paris consigned lesbian-made images to the private sphere hidden from view, in Linda Williams's terms, 'off the scene of representation' (Williams 1990: 2). Thus, lesbian-made depictions remain dirty and forbidden while straight male publishers circulate often sexist and racist images that are one-dimensional distortions worked up from inside male fantasy, or sanitized, sugared versions sold via fashion, art, and entertainment magazines. In other words, *R.* v. *Scythes* shows that a double standard falsely separates respectable from ignominious lesbian images, and heterosexualized from lesbianized female bodies.

Rather than promote (or legislate) women's equality, I argue that the decision made by Judge Paris re-encodes late nineteenth-century social-purity definitions of women as sexually passive objects in need of manly protection (see Backhouse 1991; Mitchinson 1991; Valverde 1991). As such, this ruling is not simply or merely about lesbians or more pointedly, 'nasty s/m perverts'. It is about patriach preoccupation with re-making good/bad, moral/immoral, madonna/whore, and male/female in ways that re-demarcate boundaries of hegemonic heterosexual norms and reassign what is 'properly' public and private. Arguably, the overt challenge made by lesbian s/m porn to commonsense roles of male dominance and female submission unnerved the Crown and judge. In my opinion, it is possible that the images in *Bad Attitude* (particularly those of fisting) threatened their sense of masculine prowess in part through obstructing their ability to enter and control the pornographic scene. Indeed, portrayals of sexually self-sufficient lesbians may shake heterosexual men's sense of entitlement to power over women in general—not only sexually, but economically, politically, and culturally.

The decision made in *R.* v. *Scythes* is not without serious implications. We know that the censorship of *Bad Attitude* and the ongoing Canada Customs seizure of lesbian and gay images denies access to valuable information and it relegates much-needed knowledge to a largely unavailable, unreliable underground (Jones 1993; Fuller and Blackley 1995). Removing lesbian sexual depictions, s/m and non-s/m, from circulation creates an open wound that harms the much broader ecosystem of lesbian/gay cultural production and consumption. Among queers, especially those fearful of exposure, printed materials are highly prized and defended because the practice of reading is safer than going to an outwardly visible gay/lesbian bar, a theatre, or Pride Day. Materials about sex and sexual fantasy are especially significant for lesbians and gays who live in small towns and remote areas far from large urban centres. Without access to meaningful images, sexual and non-sexual, lesbians and gay men are consigned to speechlessness, invisibility, and internalized homophobia. We are told that lust is something to be ashamed of, to apologize for, and we are punished for stepping out of line. We are denied knowledge of the breadth and diversity of queerness manifested in different body shapes, cultures, races, ethnicities, ages, abilities, and sexual tastes. This does not mean that we are left with nothing; some queer cultural workers interpret censorship law as an invitation to get busy (see below). However, in the case of *R.* v. *Scythes*, the single-minded containment of lesbian sexual discourse suggests that queer-made images and the queer bodies they document are terrifying, dangerous, and polluted.

AMBIVALENCES

Over the course of the *Bad Attitude* trial, the number of lesbian, feminist, and pro-feminst supporters in the courtroom averaged ten a day.[19] Gay men routinely outnumbered lesbians. Only a handful of anti-censorship advocates were present on the final day as Charles Granek and Clare Barclay offered their final submissions. I suspect that the low attendance at the trial reflected a series of factors: (a) the low profile of the case in the local, national, and even alternative press, (b) the limited resources that Glad Day Bookshop had to finance the defence, and (c) the persisting ambivalence vis-à-vis pornography (defined here as sexually explicit materials) expressed by many lesbians and feminists, compounded by age-old skirmishes between feminists, lesbians, and gay men over sexual politics (see Ross 1993). Indeed, after more than fifteen years of intermittent eruptions and periods of slow boil, the sex debates in Western feminism, and in Canadian feminism specifically have yielded no consensus.[20] In some cases, it feels to me that the 'pro legal reform/anti-porn' and the 'anti censorship/pro-porn' tendencies have hardened into cemented polarities. Clearly, on issues of power, morality, pleasure, danger, and the law there is little agreement.

Deep splits endure among feminists about what pornography is, what it represents, and how to deal with it; the *Bad Attitude* case did not succeed in galvanizing the factions. In Canada, diverse constituencies of feminists including the Women's Legal Education and Action Fund (LEAF) identify pornography as a key site of women's subordination (see Gotell 1997). In their *Butler* factum prepared for the Supreme Court of Canada in 1992, LEAF submits that 'pornography is a form of hate propaganda against women', and as such it 'undermines the equality of women' (LEAF 1991*a*: 16, 19). LEAF lawyers Kathleen Mahoney and Linda Taylor conclude that 'The pervasive presence of pornography thus deters women's equal access to participation in community life' (ibid: 19).

Queer theorist Julia Creet astutely observes: 'A [feminist] movement built on the repudiation of sexual objectification has had a very difficult time embracing sex and its inherent complexity without questioning the tenets of the movement itself' (Creet 1991*a*: 139). Feminists politicized through anti-violence and anti-rape activism, and through their own and others' personal experiences of sexual danger (for instance, incest, rape, harassment), regularly point to commercial heterosexual pornography as a cause of women's suffering. Because pornography is viewed by many as a graphic embodiment of women's inequality, it has long been the focus of women's anger and outrage. Catharine MacKinnon writes that showing porn to men is 'like saying "kill" to a trained guard dog' (MacKinnon 1993: 12) However long-time gay activist Chris Bearchell warns: 'Porn is an easy target—it's visible, officially disapproved of and relatively controllable. The abusive situations faced by many women and young people, on the other hand, have tended to be invisible, condoned and very difficult to change' (Bearchell 1993: 40). In others words, erasing porn will not eradicate gendered (as well as racialized and classed) power relations.

There is a long history of feminist criticism of pornography, and a small but significant body of literature that isolates sadomasochism as especially anti-woman hate literature. The feminist anthology *Against Sadomasochism* (1982) contains contributions from Judith Butler and the late Audre Lorde. And there has been a recent revival of feminist commentary on the evils of lesbian s/m in the work of Didi Herman (1994), Janice Raymond (1992), Reina Lewis and Karen Adler (1994), Ann Scales (1994), Sheila Jeffreys (1994), and Karen Busby (1994), among others. Unfortunately, the pinpointing of lesbian s/m fantasy plays directly into the hands of Christian coalitions, right-wing politicians, and other moral conservatives who view pornography, s/m porn especially, as a foul assault on (white, middle-class) family values.

Unable to stamp out actual, practised lesbian s/m, critics must content themselves with controlling a proxy: the images of sexual behaviour (see Vance 1989: 43).

Lesbian feminist legal theorist and activist Didi Herman, in an attempt to theorize the *Butler* decision in relation to s/m porn and practice, makes a surprisingly conservative, sex-negative assertion that 'the law has an *inevitable and legitimate role* to play in regulating desire' (her emphasis) (Herman 1994: 6).[21] In a paper delivered to the Canadian Sociology and Anthropology Association in 1994, Herman maintains that s/m porn and practice (both gay and straight) 'violate the core values that anchor our condemnation of genocide and other simi lar practices—core values such as respect, empathy and substantive equality' (ibid. 12). She concludes that '[s/m porn and practice] are morally reprehensible' (ibid. 13). Given my concerns in this chapter, Herman's invalidation of lesbian s/m imagery on moralistic rather than empirical grounds affirms Judge Paris's ruling in *R.* v. *Scythes* that such imagery imperils women's equality. Her notion of 'core' values smacks of universalism and has its roots in an ahistorical notion of culture as unchanging and uncontested. She implies that makers, users, and supporters of lesbian s/m imagery are not only disrespectful; they are unconcerned about actual lived violence and despair in women's lives. Moreover, Herman seems to suggest that the eradication of s/m imagery will hasten women's actual, lived equality. In opposition, feminist sociologist Thelma McCormack asserts that censorship of so-called harmful porn overprotects women, infantilizes women, and contributes to the dependency of women; it does not help in achieving women's equality (McCormack 1993*b*: 30). Herman supports state censorship of what she views as condemnable s/m porn. By contrast, McCormack warns that 'Censorship is the fastest and cheapest way of seeming to deal with the psychological uncertainty we feel about our social lives, our pervasive sense of being manipulated' (ibid. 33).

Herman's emotional equation of s/m porn and practice with genocide and moral corruption neither elucidates the porn's allegedly objectionable properties nor makes room for candid discussion of why s/m imagery pushes her buttons one way, and pushes mine (and others') another, and what, if anything, is to be done about it. In addition, her conflation of s/m porn and genocide trivializes actual instances of genocide and enables, if not fuels, anti-queer backlash. It enjoins right-wing moralizing discourse that calls for policing sexualities rather than encourage democratic discussion of alternative sexualities and pleasures.[22] Herman's endorsement of obscenity law postpones engagement with issues of power that have vexed feminists for over a century and invites further state suppression of lesbian sexual texts that may possess no other raison d'etre than readership arousal: dirt for dirt's sake. In effect, arguments such as Herman's, much like obscenity law, act to circumscribe the imaginability of homosexuality itself.

By avoiding analysis of the structure of pornographic fantasy and its place within the field of social power, Herman forecloses talk of contradictions and complexities lived by women (and men) of all sexual persuasions in favour of renewing binaries of us/them, good homo/bad homo, and madonna/whore. Perhaps most significantly, Herman's conception of representation as *debasing and discriminatory action* situates fantasy as the causal link, as if, Judith Butler argues, 'fantasy could suddenly transmute into action' (Butler 1990: 113–14) It is this very 'truth' that is enshrined in the Supreme Court's *Butler* decision, and it is this 'truth' that Judge Paris deployed in his ruling against the lesbian sex magazine *Bad Attitude.* Rather, no pornographic text (s/m or other) operates as a site of singular, univocal meaning: textualized fantasy does not supply a single point of identification for viewers (ibid.). As such, women (lesbian and non lesbian) are and can be agents of pornographic fantasy. Whoever she is, the woman pictured in erotic texts is not *fixed in meaning* as an injured, assaulted object; her subject position as unilaterally oppressed victim is not stable. Once we accept this, we then recognize that there can be no definitive acts of harm that flow from exposure to sexual images, s/m or not.

Other feminists have been equally adamant in their critique of lesbian s/m porn and practice. In *Women's Studies International Forum*, British writers Reina Lewis and Karen Adler argue that 'Sm's presentation of itself as a hip new lifestyle inhabited by tops and bottoms rather than sadists and masochists, belies the actual violence inherent in sm discourse and practice' (Lewis and Adler 1994: 435). Without detailing how, empirically, they arrived at their conclusions, they elaborate their standpoint: '[S/m's] separation of the sexual from the emotional, social and political aspects of lesbian lives, coupled, moreover, with a liberationist vision of the sexual experience itself, negates any regard for the future of commitment beyond the single sexual encounter . . . the long-term relationship is excluded from the realm of fantasy' (ibid.). Here we see the inference of causation: (violent) s/m porn flagrantly promotes the casual, recreational, snappy, and guiltless fuck and as such jeopardizes the lesbian reader's ability to differentiate good from evil. By combining the super-valuation of long-term lesbian unions with essentialist notions of lesbians' inherent nurturing, egalitarian, and monogamous 'nature', Lewis and Adler not only reinforce highly conservative notions of proper sexual conduct; they scapegoat s/m porn as a 'creeping colonization' in the absence of any data that confirm their fear of a lesbian s/m epidemic. (Certainly in Canada, with lesbian pornography routinely snatched at borders and from bookstores, alarmist dread of colonization seems laughably misplaced.)

American Ann Scales is a self-avowed radical feminist who recently analysed obscenity legislation in Canada: 'Butler is the law. It is still the best that any nation on earth has done so far to protect women from the harms of pornography—that specific propaganda that constructs women as *expendable* (Scales 1994: 363–4) (her emphasis).[23] Having enjoined 'all gay men and lesbians to withdraw from the war on *Butler*', having announced her support for Judge Paris's decision in *R.* v. *Scythes*, Scales goes to great lengths in the *Canadian Journal of Women and the Law* to meditate on her disgust for lesbian s/m porn (ibid. 350). She refers to Trish Thomas's 'Wunna My Fantasies' as a 'positive-outcome rape story' and suggests that it is as 'violent' and 'dehumanizing as what is common in mainstream pornography' (ibid. 375). In one of a series of bald generalizations *à la* Malamuth in *R.* v. *Scythes*, Scales states: 'Though the genders may be rearranged in gay and lesbian pornography, if the turn-on requires domination and subordination, then those materials affirm the social hatred of women . . . The value enacted, therefore, even in some gay and lesbian materials, is that it is socially acceptable, indeed, desirable, to turn women (or their surrogates) into things, to deprive us of our selves, and to screw us to death' (ibid. 365). Scales maintains a paternalistic position in speaking for the 'victimized' bottom instead of letting the bottom speak for herself.

Of the multiple, unpacked assumptions at work in Scales's piece, one is that s/m lesbians are falsely conscious dupes who stupidly, selfishly, and violently poison the sexual climate and put (non-s/m) women at risk of annihilation. Another assumption, and one shared by Herman, Lewis, Adler, and others, is the claim that the image itself does the screwing: a literalist reading of pornography as a practice innately harmful to women. Winding down, Scales concludes: 'Lesbians have a powerful argument about our need to build and expand our interpretive communities . . . But does the building of the interpretive, supportive community require trafficking in what would otherwise be pornography? Put in a less loaded way, can't we have sex without tolerating abusive sex, or what we want to call "depictions" thereof?' (Scales 1994: 381). First, I interpret Scales to be saying that the one and only by-product of reading pornography is real, live, hurtful sex. Second, she seems to yearn for an uncontaminated space populated by female bodies that manifest extra-discursive innocence free from the taint of sexually explicit texts, and free from all base desire to communicate (and fantasize) about sex, turn-ons *and* turn-offs. Like her anti-porn colleagues, Scales appears unable or unwilling to imagine women (and lesbians) as other than victims of textually mediated male oppression, hate, and torture.

In October 1993, on a panel organized in Toronto by Media Watch—the Canada-wide feminist advertising watchdog—well-known lesbian anti-porn advocate Susan Cole reinscribed the judgmental dichotomy of good girl/bad girl (and her own identification with goodness) by confessing that she did not protest the police seizure of *Bad Attitude* in the spring of 1992 because she could not, 'in good faith', endorse the 'torture and pain inflicted by one woman on another.' I argue that the reading 'It's two women hurting each other' smacks of simplistic, moral indignation and a rigid refusal to *learn about* the actual particulars of s/m sex and fantasy.[24] Moreover, it closes off insight into how one's own sexual fantasies may contain elements of the same power that is honestly and formally played with in s/m imagery. Several months later in Toronto, New York art critic Liz Kotz argued that a 'tactically motivated disavowal of the dark, troubling registers of sexuality, including aggressive s/m', will only result in constricted notions of pleasure, sex, and the body (Kotz 1994). I agree. Habitual genuflection to the negative frame of s/m, snuff, and kiddie porn, such as that exercised by the anti-porn feminists above, prohibits self-reflexive dialogue about the murky, scary, contradictory zone of sexual desire between the ears where force, raw aggression, surrender, and control often pervail.

I have no quarrel with the right of anti-porn feminists to publicize their positions. What I object to is the use of established and influential scholarly journals and conferences—authority-ascribing fora—to broadcast views that grant validity and credibility to moral claims *under the guise of social science.* In feminist anti-s/m tracts, a roaring silence surrounds how 'harm' or 'actual violence' is defined, calculated, and measured; instead, we find s/m porn advanced as a fully transparent and seamless category—the receptacle of all that is distastefully vile and injurious. The minds and bodies of queer (and straight) writers and readers of lesbian s/m porn are never present in feminist critiques of the sub-genre. In a recent issue of the *Canadian Journal of Law and Society*, legal scholar (and LEAF member) Karen Busby avowed: 'LEAF is committed to affirming the social and sexual identities of lesbians through law' (Busby *et al.* 1994: 184). And yet I deduce from LEAF's implicit anti-s/m stance that the social and sexual identities of lesbians are not all equal and, as such, are not equally defensible in court (or anywhere else). In my view, common to all feminist denouncers of lesbian s/m porn and practice is the standpoint of *not knowing*. In the place of knowledge, we find conjecture about what lesbian s/m fantasy is, how it works, and whom it 'harms'. But on what grounds might 'harmful materials' be distinguished from 'non-harmful materials'? Who decides? And how do these very questions reveal capitulation to the power of law, that is, *Butler*, to set the terms of debate and the parameters of 'truth'? Foucauldian theorist David Halperin reminds us that, '["truth"] licenses "experts" to describe and objectify people's lives, especially the lives of those who, for whatever reason, happen to find themselves most fully exposed to the operations of disciplinary power' (Halperin 1993: 88). Crown attorneys and judges seeking to criminalize lesbian (and gay) pornographers need look no further than this recent wave of feminist academic 'truth' about s/m for arguments that perfectly buttress the letter of Canadian obscenity law. In what follows, I show how some queerly located sexperts are leading us in radically other directions.

Cracking the Whip

Just over ten years ago, in the pathbreaking Canadian anthology *Women Against Censorship*, Lorna Weir and Mariana Valverde advised: 'Our strategies for creating lesbian culture cannot be achieved through the law, police and courts. We do not need a legal defence as much as a cultural offense' (Valverde and Weir 1985: 105) In the same volume, critic Varda Burstyn called for 'pluralistic work that reflects the variety of sexual lifeways that exist in our society' (Burstyn 1985*a*: 156). In 1997, lesbians, gays, bisexuals, transsexuals, and transgenders continue to struggle to combat the internalized shame, fear, and self-hatred we are taught in a heterosexist, gender-bound, and homophobic culture. Part of this struggle necessitates access to a vast range of images that name lesbian sexual difference and celebrate the diversity and complexity of our sexual, emotional, intellectual and spiritual selves.

Simply stated, the production of sexually explicit images highlights what is specific and unique to lesbian and gay communities: our same-sex desire. Erotic images validate our sexuality as one healthy, meaningful, and empowering part of our lives as lesbians (and gay men). Sexually explicit images produced by and for lesbians challenge the barrier of sexual fear, inhibition, ignorance, and shame by unapologetically foregrounding lesbian desire, and thus expanding the realm of knowable human sexual expression. Lesbian writer Pat Califia describes why she wrote *The Lesbian S/M Safety Manual* (1988): 'The purpose was to educate women who do s/m with other women about ways to fulfil fantasies about dominance and submission in ways that are emotionally and physically safe, provided that both partners are consenting adults and both of them find these types of fantasies mutually pleasurable' (cited in Fuller and Blackley 1995: 58). Mistress Patricia Marsh, a professional dominatrix in New York, remarks on the therapeutic value of s/m: 'Some people who are into s/m either as dominants or submissives are people who were abused and it is their way of healing. It is their way of owning it again; it is healing for them to get over the powerlessness they had in the abuse situation. It is a way of becoming powerful and saying I want this experience and I am turning it into pleasure' (cited in Bell 1995: 125).

Still, depictions of lesbian sexuality remain hard to find. Philosopher Marilyn Frye wryly observes the enduringly 'inarticulate' character of lesbian sex (Frye 1988), and theorist Judith Roof remarks on the 'inconceivability of lesbian sexuality' (Roof 1991: 245). In Canada, the challenge to make lesbian sexual desire visible and speakable is being led by intrepid video and filmmakers Midi Onodera, Lorna Boschman, Kika Thorne, Candi Pauker, Shani Mootoo, Joyan Saunders, Margaret Moores, Lynne Fernie, Aerlyn Weissman, Almerinda Travassos, and Kathy Daymond (see Bell 1997); photographers Li Yuen, Cyndra MacDowall, Ellen Flanders, Heather Cameron, Jennifer Gilmor, and the duo Average Good Looks; poets Dionne Brand, Brenda Brooks, Chrystos, Daphne Marlatt, Betsy Warland, and Carolyn Gammon; visual artists G. B. Jones, Shonagh Adelman, Buseje Bailey, the Kiss & Tell collective, Cynthia Lo, and Stephanie Martin; writers Donna Barker, Marusia Bociurkiw, Sarah Sheard, Mona Oikawa, Tamai Kobayashi, Ingrid MacDonald; and performance artists Gwendolyn, karen augustine, Elaine Carol, Lisa Lowe, Lorri Millan, and Shawna Dempsey, among many others.[25]

Willing to push the limits of their own sexual imaginations, many of these artists explore sexual turf that is uncomfortable and unfamiliar: dykes with dicks, inter-racial lesbian sex, the anatomy of orgasm, dykes who do boys, group sex, anonymous and casual sex, leather, bondage, and s/m. In part, this new wave of work signifies the moxie of generation of young lesbians and bisexuals determined to rebel against their symbolic 'mothers' and the positive-image school of lesbian and feminist image-making (Creet 1991*a*). In her introduction to *Macho Sluts*, Pat Califia notes:

> 'Feminist erotica' that presents a simplistic view of lesbian sex and two women in love in a bed who embody all the good things that patriarchy is trying to destroy isn't very sexy. This stuff reads as if it were written by dutiful daughters who are trying to persuade Mom that lesbian sex isn't dirty, and we really are good girls after all. It isn't challenging or stirring enough. The auto-erotically inclined lesbian reader deserves more bang for her buck. And Mom is never going to believe that nice girls put their hands in other girls' panties, anyway . . . lesbian writers have got to loosen up, drop our drawers, spread our cheeks, stick out our tongues, get nasty. (Califia 1988: 13)

Those who have actually seen lesbian s/m imagery (not an easy task) do not all describe it in glowing terms. In a culture still searching for images that reinforce individual and community pride and strength, efforts made to explore power, domination/submission, role-playing, costuming, and so on are often viewed as counter-productive, if not damaging. Some feel that exposing 'dirty laundry' needs to be avoided for fear of ceding ground to the fundamentalist and political right wing and their anti-woman, anti-homosexual, and racist ideologies. Others are afraid that the images may serve to reinvigorate age-old sexological descriptions of female homosexuals as sexually insatiable, promiscuous, aggressive, jealous, rough, self-loathing perverts. In 1954, popular American psychoanalyst Frank Caprio named lesbians as unhappy, sexually maladjusted and prone to extreme jealousy, sexual immaturity, and sadomasochistic tendencies. He concluded that '[lesbians] can be restored to normal sex outlook by sympathetic and expert treatment, usually at the hands of a psychiatrist or psychoanalyst who believes in cure' (Caprio 1954: 171, 294).

Vancouver's Kiss & Tell visual art collective comment: 'We love making representations of our own sexuality. What we don't love is how state censorship denies our rights and threatens our queer culture. Making lesbian sex art isn't safe. It's not invisible and it's not always nice' (Kiss & Tell 1994: 1, 12). They talk about how their collaborative show, 'True Inversions', was used to spread homophobic hatred and to threaten arts-council funding in 1992 in the province of Alberta (ibid. 59–74). And yet even in the current climate of severe 'obscenity chill', the drive to render lesbian eroticism a movable threat stubbornly pushes ahead (Barclay and Carol 1992–3: 18–28).

Within the past five years irreverent risk takers have launched sex magazines *Lezzie Smut* (Vancouver), *Lickerish: polymorphous queer candy* (Toronto), and *Frighten the Horses* (San Fransisco) and the fanzines *SMACKS, BIMBOX*, and *Pussy Grazer*. The editors of Vancouver's *Lezzie Smut* lay out their publishing objective in their first editorial in September 1993:

> This is a magazine about sex. About dyke sex. About what we do in bed (on the floor, in the elevator, when no one's looking on the bus. When they are looking). What we do, what we would like to do, what we are afraid of doing. We made it for you, to get you off, to get you thinking, to get you to write, take pictures, take chances. We made it for us too, because we wanted smut. We wanted flesh skin lips sex. And shucks, gals, as we all know porn for women by women is hard to come by on this side of the border. We made it because it's the best way to fuck over Canada customs, to refuse to let them limit our desires. We made it because we are exhibitionists. We made it because this city needs a space for dykes to see themselves. A sex rag. Something to whack off to. (*Lezzie Smut* 1993: 5–6)

When I interviewed her in early 1994, then co-editor/publisher of *Lickerish: polymorphous queer candy* Jennifer Gillmor cited the 1993 obscenity ruling against *Bad Attitude* (which continues to publish her photographs) as instrumental in her decision to launch her own queer sex magazine (Gillmor 1994). 'Lickerish' was chosen as the title because it means 'eager to taste or enjoy, greedy, desirous, tempting the appetite, having or suggesting lustful desires'. In the editorial in the first issue, Gillmor and co-editor Janet Lee Spagnol state: 'some publications have been banned in Canada. [We were] frustrated as consumers knowing that virtually all of our pornography is imported and therefore, not specifically culturally relevant to us. *Lickerish* is our statement against the criminalization of art and desire. The recognition of the frustration was our catalyst in deciding that we need our own forum in Canada for explicit work by women and men from varying sexual deviations . . . We sexual beings often seem most brimming with creativity when flooded with feelings of lust and passion' (Gillmor and Spagnol 1994: 1).

Lesbian s/m porn mounts a potent counterclaim *because* it performs excessive female sexuality and iconography in defiance of residual, Victorian definitions of (white, bourgeois) femininity. Images like those in *Bad Attitude* may disturb, dismay, or disgust viewers. I am not always comfortable with descriptions of sexual acts in lesbian-made porn, and recognize that sexually explicit words and pictures are not uniformly liberatory. It is important and necessary to challenge sexist and racist portrayals of women in all pornographic disourse. At the same time, I predict that unless collective, loud-mouthed support is secured for alternative sexual discourses such as lesbian s/m fantasy, 'we-deviants' can anticipate successive rulings whereby legislators decide for us what is 'degrading', 'dehumanizing', and 'obscene'. The libidinal scope of Canadian lesbian cultural workers sketched above is proof of their high-amped assault on the moral certitudes of the status quo. This work alone will never hobble obscenity law, but it does help to seed a context from which to better explain and critically defend radical sexual pluralism in the future (Weeks 1991).

In 1997, as in the late nineteenth century, sexuality remains a site of contested meanings. Today, more and more feminists want space and language to describe sexual techniques, etiquette, fantasy, and vocabulary from the pivotal standpoint of female sexual subjectivity. It is possible that these new spaces may afford women different ways of configuring their own sexual identities and practices (see Smith 1995: 202). As such, repressive legal discourse that squeezes off conversations and blots out depictions seems patently premature (Tisdale 1994; Strossen 1995). The foregrounding of sexual and moral peril in an already erotophobic climate serves to reinforce, even heighten, feelings of sex-related pessimism and shame. Cindy Patton defines erotophobia as: 'The terrifying, irrational reaction to the erotic which makes individuals in society vulnerable to the psychological control of cultures where pleasure is strictly categorized and regulated' (Patton 1986: 103). My view is that rather than classify s/m fantasy and other non-conformist sexual tastes morally bad and dirty, hence punishable by law, we need to decriminalize depictions of consensual sex across a range of desires and discourses.

Knowledge of lesbian s/m image-making expands and positively deepens the range of female sexual possibilities across the spectrum of sexual preferences. At the same time, African American theorist Jackie Goldsby has pointed out that white narratives, icons, and ideologies have prevailed in the field of lesbian and gay sexual representation (Goldsby 1990: 15). However, increasing numbers of lesbians and gay men of colour, including Isaac Julien, Kobena Mercer, Donna Barker, karen augustine, Laverne Monette, and Dionne Brand are entering the scene as producers and critics of s/m imagery, and of sexually explicit materials in general.[26] Many have located their criticisms of s/m imagery (especially bondage, whipping, body marking) in specific histories of African American, Caribbean Canadian, black British, and Jewish persecution. Still, as the writings of Tina Portillo (1991), Donna Barker (1988), and Kobena Mercer (1991, 1992), and the films of Isaac Julien and Richard Fung attest, there is no agreement about what s/m means, how the signs might be used, and whether or not they are recoverable from racist and sexist trappings. Nor is there uniform support among producers and critics of colour for state sexual censorship as a solution.

CONCLUDING THOUGHTS

Religious and medical prohibitions against homosexuality combined with state criminalization of homosexual practices (including consensual activities) in Canada until 1969 have made it difficult for gay men, lesbians, and bisexuals to openly experiment with, and to celebrate their sexual differences.[27] Today, the age-old equation of homosexuality with sin, sickness, and/or criminality continues to drive many queers to secrecy and shame. Morally conservative discourse on obscenity in Canada continues to be vengefully formulated through coalitions of anti-porn feminists and neo-conservatives: the Coalition for Family Values, members of the Reform Party, Canadians for Decency, Citizens United for Responsible Education (CURE), REAL women, and the Conference of Catholic Bishops, among others.[28] Over fifty years ago, during the Third Reich in Germany, lesbians, single mothers, and prostitutes were gassed as 'anti-social women' alongside Jewish peoples in Nazi death chambers. Decades later, in the 1990s, lesbian makers and readers of s/m fantasy have been reclassified in law as criminals *predisposed to anti-social behaviour*. To communities of lesbians shaped by the historical legacy of persecution and invisibility, the remaking of the 'lesbian pervert' in obscenity rulings is an all-too-familiar twist of the knife.

In order to fight repressive state, medical, and religious discourses and practices, lesbians, gays, bisexuals, and friends need to pursue alliances with all communities who have experienced histories of intimidation – for example, coalitions amongst Black, Asian, and First

Nation communities and communities of sex-trade workers, the disabled, and AIDS activists. Ambitiously, we need to persuade queers and queer positive supporters that state sexual regulation has an impact on all of our sexualities, not just on those of perverts. Scapegoating the 'deviants', turning around to leave them holding the sexuality bag, marks a selfish, short-sighted betrayal. Moreover, I believe that we stand to benefit collectively from combining protests against state sexual censorship with organized action against the dismantlement of the Canadian welfare state, racist immigration policies, intensified regulation of sex-trade workers, and the coordinated reassertion of 'family values'.

Even though most s/m porn represents heterosexual women dominating and disciplining men (McClintock 1993: 211), disciplinary modes of state control such as sexual censorship laws instruct the systematic harassment of producers and consumers of queer images; hundreds of thousands of taxpayers' dollars are dedicated to processes of containment and normalization. In her 1993 case study of three lesbian and gay bookstores in Canada—L'androgyne in Montreal, Glad Day Bookshop in Toronto, and Little Sister's in Vancouver—Catherine Jones concluded that the personal costs of being subjected to, and demoralized by, death threats, fire bombs, and the scrutiny of police and customs officials are immeasurable.[29] In January 1996, Justice Kenneth Smith of the BC Supreme Court ruled that Canada Customs officials contravened the Charter of Rights and Freedoms in their regulation of lesbian and gay materials, but he did not declare sections of the Customs Act unconstitutional, which may mean business/censorship as usual.[30] Bookstore workers and anti-censorship activists suspect that Project P (the joint Metro Toronto Police and Ontario Provincial Police anti-porn squad) is primed to raid Glad Day Bookshop in Toronto again, this time for trafficking material that openly condones cross-generational sex—the newsletter of the North American Man/Boy Love Association NAMBLA. Admittedly, perceptions of NAMBLA among lesbians and gay men are extremely mixed. For example, the NAMBLA organization was banned from the 1994 Stonewall Anniversary parade in New York City, and welcomed in the counter-parade of sex radicals and AIDS activists. Whether Project P raids Glad Day for stocking the NAMBLA bulletin or not, full-fledged moral panics over youth sexuality have raged over the past two years.

In general terms, I feel strongly about increased access to materials that foreground the plurality of perverted and inverted desires. I want pornographies or eroticas that figure multi-sexual, multi-abled, multi-racial, and generationally mixed bodies, all wet and sticky. Perhaps more than anything, I would like to hear a lot more talk about what people like sexually and what they/we might want to find on fields of representation. In particular, I look forward to stepped-up sexual commentary from lesbians, gays, and bisexuals of colour. It behoves lesbian and feminist academics such as Didi Herman who have made public their concern about devoting so much time to 'this tired [sex] debate' when 'there are far more important things to worry about in the world', to reconsider their own investments in the legal sanctioning of hetero-normativity (Herman 1994: 25). I argue that as long as the state/moral regulation of lesbian sexual materials persists, there will be a need for action on multiple fronts, including the fight for expanded access to the production and dissemination of alternative sexual discourses. In this case, I hardly consider battles for access to resources a luxury, indulgent pastime, or 'fetishism' (ibid. 24).

More than eighty years after Dr Howard Kelly's equation of 'good women' with sexual ignorance, we have only had a peek at what a lesbian, bisexual, or straight feminist sexual imagination might hold, or in what terms it might be conveyed. Today it perturbs me to think that sex-positive sparks such as *Bad Attitude* magazine may be extinguished before their chance to ignite into flame. In this chapter I have shown how and why the defence team headed up by lawyer Clare Barclay failed to save *Bad Attitude* from the trap of feminist-informed obscenity law designed to 'protect women from harm' and legislate 'women's equality'. In the Ontario Court, *Butler* was deployed by the Crown, and by Judge Paris, to adjudicate contesting epistemologies: a troublingly conservative, moralistic, and sex-negative feminism won the day in February 1993. In *R.* v. *Scythes*, lesbians who fantasize and practise s/m are scapegoated as the monsters from whom (all) women need and deserve protection. Indeed, we may conclude that these 'bad' lesbians—like the 'congenital inverts', 'sex variants', and 'bulldaggers' who preceeded them—are not women, and as such, their equality before the law need not be promoted or protected. *R. v. Scythes* confirms that s/m lesbians have become super-markers of female deviance and pathology, split off from 'good' women (and even 'good' lesbians) who uphold the sanctity of long-term, monogamous, loving relationships and nuclear families. Upon extending the logic of this binary stance, we find that those of us who defend *Bad Attitude* and publications like it can only appear as unintelligible, anti-feminist heretics. Moreover, under this regime, our challenges to the defective social-science data that structure Canadian obscenity law amount to nothing more than non-scientific prattle.

In the end, to the extent that lesbian s/m discourse impinges uncomfortably on what the unqueer centre postulates as 'normal' and 'natural', it will continue to be prohibited as surely as its prohibition is eroticized in the service of (illicit) fantasy. Ironically, it is the very limits of bourgeois morality and gendered propriety that fantasy, lesbian s/m fantasy in particular, loves to manipulate and disrupt. I submit that the scope of the feminine sexual imaginary is all the more rich because of it.

Notwithstanding Diana Fuss's homo rereading of mainstream women's magazines, I for one refuse to be content with sucking 'lesbian content' out of *Elle, Vogue, Cosmopolitan,* and *Mirabella* or, for that matter, *Hustler, Penthouse,* and *Forum* (Fuss 1992: 713–37). I don't want to squirrel away my illegal desires until it is safe to do otherwise. Instead, I intend to continue pushing for lesbian criminality in all of its glorious manifestations, both real and imagined.

Notes

1. Patricia McVicar, in Ontario Provincial Police report of the charges under the Canadian Criminal Code (R.S.C. 1985) for possession (s.163(2a)) and sale (s. 163(2a)) of obscene material, in *R.* v. *Scythes* (16 February 1993), Toronto (Ont. Ct. Prov. Div.) [unreported], 5–6. McVicar was not responding to a complaint about either the bookstore or *Bad Attitude*.
2. On campaigns against venereal disease, see Cassel 1988. On the homo-purges of the 1950s, see Kinsman 1995 and Kimmel and Robinson 1994. On crime comics and romance literature in the 1950s, see Adams 1994.
3. In his final 'Summation', Crown Attorney, Charles Granek said this about my testimony: 'I think it's important to recognize the bias that [Dr Ross] has in terms of these issues and I merely cite to Your Honour in my cross-examination the comments that she was making about her views of censorship, how there ought to be a rather liberal opening up to some pretty serious types of articles that I was questioning her about' (Granek 1992*b*: 43)
4. Carole Vance is cited as identifying s/m as the epicentre of harm in feminist anti-porn politics in Fuller and Blackley 1995: 58.
5. Here I'm adapting the provocative insights of Judith Butler, worked up in her essay 'Critically Queer' (1993. 20–2)
6. I am not suggesting here that lesbian s/m is only a set of campy, theatrical tastes or aesthetics. It clearly involves much more than stylish codes, though the codes themselves are integral to the shaping of s/m identities and practices.
7. In her article 'Here, Clitty, Clitty' (1995), Marie Caloz tackles the trend in lesbian consumption of gay-male video pornography. She writes: 'It might

seem a trifle odd that the pussy-down set would go hard for nine-inch males dicking it out. But it makes sense. Off-the-rack lezzie smut comes in two varieties—and little of it has to do with the real thing. Either you get islands of silicon implant bobbing in a sea of coiffed peroxide blonds, spreading it for the straight guy who can hardly believe his luck, or it's the kind of porn dykes tend to put out for themselves: an epic lifetime of foreplay riding on a tide of meaningful Bergmanesque glances and Hallmark card sentiment. When you finally get to the main event, the credits roll. The wet factor rating is definitely sub-Saharan' (p.49).

8. For a provocative recasting of femme sexuality through analysis of what it means to 'get fucked', see Cvetkovich 1995.
9. Pat Califia has recently drawn attention to the fact that tops need to be more aggressive about asking for what they want and stop acting like a 'bunch of codependents held hostage by rapacious bottoms'. See Califia 1992. Also on the dynamics of s/m, see contributions to John Preston's edited collection, *Leatherfolk* 1991). I want to thank Tim Timberg for pointing out that in much feminist and legal discourse, the bottom in s/m porn is seen as equivalent to the essentialized woman/victim in heterosexual porn. However, if bottoms/women are empowered and consent to sexual play, there is no degradation and humiliation—a very frightening concept for institutionalized heterosexism.
10. For an early discussion of this topic, see Valverde and Weir 1985.
11. Only after I wrote this section did I discover that 'Jessie' was Califia's first published piece of pornographic fiction. In *Restricted Entry: Censorship on Trial* (1995), this is how she talks about it: 'That story was a breakthrough for me as a writer. I was able to complete it. I was eventually able to share it with others and it became more than a work of fiction. It became an organizing tool. It became a way to signal to other women who might be interested in the sexual practices that there was someone else . . . who was available to discuss those things with them. And it gave other women permission, whether they were writers or not, to start to think about and make that sexuality more public' (p.59).
12. Several months before the trial, my partner and I had a little spat about why I had 'wasted my money' purchasing Madonna's *Sex*. Little did I know that I'd later be using it as sure-fire evidence of changing community standards about pornography in an Ontario court.
13. In the appendix to their volume, *Restricted Entry: Censorship on Trial*, Janine Fuller and Stuart Blackley include a detailed description of Memorandum D9–1–1.
14. In her MA thesis, Kirstie Lang analyses the debates surrounding the controversy generated by the exhibition of Robert Mapplethorpe's retrospective, 'The Perfect Moment' in the United States in 1989–90. See Lang 1995.
15. For analysis of the obsessive figuring of lesbian bodies in sexological photography in the 1930s, see O'Brien 1994.
16. For more detailed discussion of the dynamics of heterosexual s/m, in particular, the role of women as dominatrices in commercial s/m, see McClintock 1993: 211
17. In a disturbing, MacKinnon-esque research paper on gay male pornography, Canadian Christoper Kendall makes the argument that 'harms-based

research' on the 'effects of heterosexual pornography . . . [offers] findings that are equally applicable within the context of gay male pornography' (Kendall 1993: 38). Kendall references Malamuth's testimony in *R.* v. *Scythes* as away of buttressing his own conclusions that gay male porn promotes 'shared degradation', 'contributes to the real abuse of real people', and 'normalizes male sexual aggression' (p. 58) .

18. It is important to note that *R.* v. *Butler* states that the audience to which sexually explict material is addressed is not relevant to the determination of community standards (1992: 477–8).
19. By contrast, the courtroom at the British Columbia Provincial Court (Vancouver) during the Little Sister's bookstore's month-long challenge to Canada Customs censorship was routinely packed. This reflects the bookstore's almost ten-year battle to defend lesbian and gay literature from 'prior restraint' and destruction at the Canada/U.S. border; it reflects the case's high profile in national and international media; it reflects the 'celebrity roster' of literary stars who testified for the bookstore (such as Jane Rule, Pat Califia, Nino Ricci, Pierre Berton); and it reflects the high level of queer and queer-positive community involvement—emotional, political, and financial—in the case itself.
20. For some of the key, recently published texts that address questions of sex, pornography, and censorship, see Gibson and Gibson 1993; Smith 1993; Assiter and Avedon 1993; Kiss & Tell 1994; Goldsby 1993; augustine 1994; Segal and McIntosh 1992; Gwendolyn et al. 1994; L. Williams 1990; McCormack 1993*b*; Butler 1990; B. Brown 1993; Lacombe 1994; and Adelman 1994.

    Very little critical writing has been published on lesbian sexual images and texts, particularly s/m. Exceptions include Creet 1991*a* and Henderson 1992.
21. Here, I use the terms surprising and sex-negative because Herman's stance on s/m porn and practice seems internally inconsistent with her on-going, trenchant exploration of lesbian and gay identities, communities, and legal battles for freedom from discrimination. There is clearly something about s/m and the way it touches hot buttons that warrants further inquiry. See Herman's thoughtful analysis of the Christian Right's anti-homosexual discourse: '"Then I Saw a New Heaven and a New Earth": Thoughts on the Christian Right and the Problem of "Backlash"', forthcoming in Leslie Roman and Linda Eyre, eds, *Dangerous Testimonies: Struggles for Equality and Difference in Education* (New York: Routledge).
22. My thanks to Leslie Roman for helping me think through the implications of treating s/m porn as equivalent to lived genocide.
23. On the surface, it seems surprising that Ann Scales testifted on behalf of Little Sister's bookstore in their case against Canada Customs in October 1994. Joe Arvay, counsel for the bookstore, felt that Scales would be a useful witness, given her well-known heralding of *R.* v. *Butler* as a feminist victory. Indeed, in part because Scales was conveniently disqualified on the stand from commenting on the links between pornography and harm to women, Arvay was successful in artfully managing her articulation of pro-lesbian/gay, anti-censorship statements.
24. Susan Cole told me after the panel at Harbourfront that she now considered herself to be anti-censorship given her recent foray into writing and staging

play, 'Fertile Imagination'. That she made this comment in private and retained her public, pro-censorship stance is both perplexing and unsettling.

25. On recent trends in lesbian and feminist sex-related art practice, including the work of Canadians G. B. Jones and Kiss & Tell, see Adelman 1995.
26. On issues of race, racism, and pornography, see Goldsby 1993; Mercer 1992 and 1991; augustine 1994; Fung 1991 and 1993; Barker 1988; and Portillo 1991. Ever-irreverent, British black gay filmmaker Isaac Julien has made a short film, *The Attendant* (1993), that deliberately complicates debates about race/racism and s/m representation. He has also written about his film in 'Confessions of a Snow Queen' (1993).
27. For a more detailed examination of state and religious discourses on homosexuality, see Kinsman 1995.
28. On CURE's Sue Careless's trip to Ottawa to drum up support for their anti-homosexual campaign, see Oldham 1993. For more on CURE, see Pegis 1993. In part, CURE has focused energy on protesting the Toronto Board of Education's new set of curriculum guidelines, a resource manual designed to combat homophobia and heterosexism. For one teacher's positive response to the Board's resource guide, see Ricker-Wilson 1993. The Toronto Board's curriculum guide is in direct contrast to Saskatchewan's Teen-Aid program designed by the province's Pro-Life Association and taught yearly to more than 20,000 students in 203 primary and secondary schools. The program extols chastity/abstinence, the sanctity of marriage, and negative views on homosexuality. See Mitchell 1993.
29. See Jones 1993. Also, see E. Brown 1993*a*, and Hough 1994. And for more on Canada Customs, see Johnston 1993 and O. Gillmor 1993. On the Little Sister's court challenge to Canada Customs, see Leiren-Young 1994; Dafoe 1994; and Fuller and Blackley 1995.
    On the ruling in the Little Sister's bookstore challenge to practices of prior restraint by Canada Customs officials, see Cernetig 1996 and Rupp 1996.

References

Adams, Mary Louise. 1993. 'Precedent-Setting Pulp: Women's Barracks Was Deemed "Exceedingly Frank."' *X-tra!*, 3 September, 21.

——1994. 'The Trouble With Normal: The Social Construction of the Teenager in Post-War Ontario.' Ph.D. dissertation, OISE, University of Toronto.

Adelman, Shonagh. 1994. *Skin Deep*. Toronto: A Space Gallery.

——1995. 'Girrly Pictures.' *Border/Lines* no.37: 28–35.

Allen, Carol, and Rosamund Elwin. 1993. *Getting Wet: Tales of Lesbian Seduction*. Toronto: Women's Press.

Assiter, Alison, and Carol Avedon, eds. 1993. *Bad Girls and Dirty Pictures: The Challenge to Reclaim Feminism*. London: Pluto Press.

augustine, karen/miranda. 1994. 'Bizarre Women, Exotic Bodies and Outrageous Sex: Or if Annie Sprinkle Was a Black Ho She Wouldn't Be All That.' *Border/Lines* 32 (Spring): 22–4.

Backhouse, Constance. 1991. *Petticoats and Prejudice: Women and Law in Nineteenth Century Canada*. Toronto: Women's Press.

Bad Attitude: Lesbian Erotic Fiction. 1991*a*. Vol. 7, no. 4.

——1991*b*. 'Editorial: Gay Bashing.' Vol. 7, no. 4: 2.

Barber, Karen, ed. 1991. *Bushfire*. Boston: Alyson Publications.

Barclay, Clare. 1992. 'Summation.' *R*. v. *Scythes* (16 January 1993), Toronto (Ont. Ct. Prov. Div.) [unreported] 6–24.

Barker, Donna. 1988. 'S & M Is an Adventure.' *Fireweed* no.28: 115–21.

Bearchell, Chris. 1983. 'Art, Trash and Titillation: A Consumer's Guide to Lezzy Smut.' *The Body Politic*, May, 29–33.

Bell, Shannon. 1995. *Whore Carnival*. Brooklyn: Autonomedia.

——1997. 'On ne peut pas voir l'image [The image cannot be seen]'. 'Shaping *Butler*: The New Politics of Anti-Pornography.' In *Bad Attitude/s on Trial: Pornography, Feminism, and the 'Butler' Decision*, ed. Brenda Cossman, Shannon Bell, Lise Gotell, and Becki L. Ross, 199–242, Toronto: University of Toronto Press.

Bergman, David. 1993. 'Introduction.' In *Camp Grounds: Style and Homosexuality*, ed. David Bergman, 3–18. Amherst: University of Massachusetts Press.

Bright, Susie. 1990. *Susie Sexpert's Lesbian Sex World*. San Francisco: Cleis Press.

—— 1992. *Susie Bright's Sexual Reality: A Virtual Sex World Reader*. San Francisco: Cleis Press.

Brown, Beverly. 1993. 'Troubled Vision: Legal Understandings of Obscenity.' *Perversity: a journal of culture/theory/politics* 19 (Spring): 29–44.

Brown, Eleanor. 1993*a*. 'Customs Targets Gay Book Distributor.' *X-tra!*, 28 May, 13.

—— 1993*b*. 'Harrassment Escalates'. *X-tra!*, 24 December, 1.

Burstyn, Varda. 1985*a*. 'Beyond Despair: Positive Strategies.' Chapter in *Women Against Censorship*. Vancouver: Douglas and McIntyre.

—— 1985*b*. *Women Against Censorship*. Vancouver: Douglas and McIntyre.

Busby, Karen. 1994. 'LEAF and Pornography: Litigating on Equality and Sexual Representations.' *Canadian Journal of Law and Society* 9, no. 1 (Spring): 165–92.

Butler, Judith. 1990. 'The Force of Fantasy: Feminism, Mapplethorpe, and Discursive Excess.' *differences: a journal of feminist cultural studies* 2 (Summer): 105–25.

—— 1993. 'Critically Queer.' *GLQ: A Journal of Lesbian and Gay Studies* 1, no. 1: 20–33.

Califia, Pat. 1981. 'Feminism and Sadomasochism.' *Heresies, The Sex Issue* 12, reprinted in Pat Califia, *Public Sex: The Culture of Radical Sex*, 165–74. San Francisco: Cleis Press 1994 (cited to first printing).

—— 1988. *Macho Sluts*. Boston: Alyson Publications.

—— 1992. 'The Limits of the S/M Relationship, or Mr. Benson Doesn't Live Here Anymore.' *Out/Look* (Winter): 15–21.

—— 1993. '*Sex* and Madonna, Or, What Do You Expect From a Straight Girl Who Doesn't Put Out on the First Five Dates?' In *Madonnarama: Essays on*

Sex and Popular Culture, ed. Lisa Frank and Paul Smith, 169–84. San Francisco: Cleis Press.

Caloz, Marie. 1995. 'Here, Clitty, Clitty: Fag Porn Is Fast Becoming the Choix du Jour for Lesbians.' *X-Tra!*, 24 November, 49.

Caprio, Frank. 1954. *Female Homosexuality: A Psychodynamic Study of Lesbianism*. New York: The Citadel Press.

Cassel, Jay. 1988. *The Secret Plague*. Toronto: University of Toronto Press.

Cernetig, Miro. 1996. 'Censorship Discriminates against Gays, Court Says.' *Globe and Mail*, 20 January, A1.

Congress of Canadian Women. 1952. 'Proceedings of the Special Committee on Salacious and Indecent Literature.' Submission to the Senate, 25 June.

Cossman Brenda. 1997. 'Feminist Fashion or Morality in Drag? The Sexual Subtext of the *Butler* Decision'. 'Shaping *Butler*: The New Politics of Anti-Pornography.' In *Bad Attitude/s on Trial: Pornography, Feminism, and the 'Butler' Decision*, ed. Brenda Cossman, Shannon Bell, Lise Gotell, and Becki L. Ross, 107–51, Toronto: University of Toronto Press.

Creet, Julia. 1991*a*. 'Daughter of the Movement: The Psychodynamics of Lesbian S/M Fantasy.' *differences: a journal of feminist cultural studies* 3, no. 2 (Summer): 135–59.

——1991*b*. 'Lesbian Sex/Gay Sex: What's the Difference?' *Out/Look* no. 11: 29–34.

Crimp, Douglas, and Michael Warner. 1993. 'No Sex in *Sex*.' In *Madonnarama: Essays on Sex and Popular Culture*, ed. Lisa Frank and Paul Smith, 93–110. San Francisco: Cleis Press

Cvetkovich, Ann. 1995. 'Recasting Receptivity: Femme Sexualities.' In *Lesbian Erotics*, ed. Karla Jay, 125–46. New York: New York University Press.

Dafoe, Chris. 1994. 'Little Sister v Big Brother'. *Globe and Mail*, 8 October, C1, C2.

Fish, Stanley. 1989. Doing *What Comes Naturally: Change, Rhetoric and the Practice of Theory in Literary and Legal Studies*. Chapel Hill, NC: Duke University Press.

Flanders, Ellen. 1993. 'Feminism and Censorship.' *Ideas*, CBC Radio Works, Toronto, October, 9.

Foucault, Michel. 1980. *The History of Sexuality*, trans. Robert Hurley. New York: Vintage Books.

Freedman, Jonathon. 1992. 'Testimony.' Transcripts from *R.* v. *Scythes* (16 January 1993), Toronto (Ont. Ct. Prov. Div.).

Frye, Marilyn. 1988. 'Lesbian Sex.' *Sinister Wisdom* (Summer/Fall).

Fuller, Janine, and Stuart Blackley. 1995. *Restricted Entry: Censorship on Trial*. Vancouver: Press Gang Publishers.

Fung, Richard. 1991. 'Looking for My Penis: The Eroticized Asian in Gay Video Porn.' In *How Do I Look? Queer Film and Video*, ed. Bad Object Choices, 145–68. Seattle: Bay Press.

—— 1993. 'Shortcomings: Questions about Pornography as Pedagogy.' In

Queer Looks: Perspectives on Lesbian and Gay Film and Video, ed. Martha Gever, John Greyson, and Pratibha Parmar, 355–67. Toronto: Between the Lines.

Fuss, Diana. 1989. *Essentially Speaking: Feminism, Nature and Difference*. New York and London: Routledge.

——1992. 'Fashion and the Homo-Spectatorial Look.' *Critical Inquiry* 18 (Summer): 713–37.

Gammon, Carolyn. 1992. *Lesbians Ignite*. Charlottetown, PEI: Gynergy Press.

Gibson, Pamela C., and Roma Gibson, ed. 1993. *Dirty Looks: Women, Pornography, Power*. London: British Film Institute Publishing.

Gillmor, Don. 1993. 'Strange Customs.' *Saturday Night* (March): 31–3, 66–7.

Gillmor, Jennifer. 1992. 'In-Chief and Cross-Examination.' Transcripts from *R.* v. *Scythes* (16 January 1993), Toronto (Ont. Ct. Prov. Div.), 16–22.

——1994. Interview with Becki Ross.

Gillmor, Jennifer, and Janet Lee Spagnol. 1994. 'Editorial.' *Lickerish: polymorphous queer candy* 1, no. 1 (Winter): 1.

Goldsby, Jackie. 1990. 'What It Means to Be Colored Me.' *Out/Look* 9 (Summer): 8–17

—— 1993. 'Queen for 307 Days: Looking B(l)ack at Vanessa Williams and the Sex Wars.' In *Sisters, Sexperts and Queers: Beyond the Lesbian Nation*, ed. Arlene Stein, 110–28. New York: Plume.

Gomez, Jewelle. 1987. 'Come When You Need Me.' In *The Leading Edge*, ed. Lady Winston, 161–71. Denver: Lace Publications.

Gotell, Lise. 1997. 'Shaping *Butler*: The New Politics of Anti-Pornography.' In *Bad Attitude/s on Trial: Pornography, Feminism, and the 'Butler' Decision*, ed. Brenda Cossman, Shannon Bell, Lise Gotell, and Becki L. Ross, 48–106, Toronto: University of Toronto Press.

Granek, Charles. 1992*a*. 'Cross Examination of Jennifer Gillmor.' Transcripts from *R* v. *Scythes*, 14 December.

——1992*b*. 'Cross-examination of Becki Ross.' Transcripts from *R. V. Scythes*, 14 December.

——1992*c*. 'Summation'. Transcripts from *R.* v. *Scythes*, 18 December.

Gwendolyn, Karen/miranda augustine, Susan Cole, Becki Ross, Midi Onodera, and Karen Busby. 1994. 'Politics of Desire: Pornography, Erotica, Freedom of Expression: Proceedings of MediaWatch Panel, October 1993.' *Fireweed: A Feminist Quarterly* 42 (Winter): 22–40.

Halperin, David. 1993. 'Bringing Out Michel Foucault.' *Salmagund* no. 97 (Winter): 69-89.

Henderson, Lisa. 1992. 'Lesbian Pornography: Cultural Transgression and Sexual Demystification.' In *New Lesbian Criticism*, ed. Sally Munt, 173–92. New York: Columbia University Press.

Herman, Didi. 1994. 'Law and Morality Re-Visited: The Politics of Regulating Sado-Masochistic Porn and Practice.' Paper delivered at the Canadian and American Law Society Association conferences, Calgary and Phoenix, June.

Hough, Robert. 1994. 'Degrading Customs.' *Globe and Mail*, 12 February, D1, D5.

Hustler. 1990. 'Stream of Cuntiousness.' March: 36–41.

——1993. 'Nicki and Bronson: Aquavelvet.' Photographed by Matti Klatt. March: 96–104.

Jarvie, Suzanne. 1992. 'In-Chief and Cross-Examination'. Transcripts from *R.* v. *Scythes*, 14 December, 23–7.

Jeffreys, Sheila. 1994. *The Lesbian Heresy: a feminist perspective on the lesbian sexual revolution*. London: Women's Press.

Johnston, Lucinda. 1993. 'Saving Canada from "Betty Page."' *Canadian Bookseller*, February: 30–3.

Jones, Catherine. 1993. 'Patrolling the Borders: Censorship and Gay and Lesbian Bookstores, 1982–1992.' MA thesis, Dept. of Canadian Studies, Carleton University, Ottawa.

Kendall, Christopher N.. 1993. '"Real Dominant, Real Fun!": Gay Male Pornography and the Pursuit of Masculinity.' *Saskatchewan Law Review* 57: 21–57.

Kessler-Harris, Alice. 1987. 'Equal Employment Opportunity Commission v. Sears, Roebuck and Company: A Personal Account.' *Feminist Review* 25: 46–69.

Kimmel, David, and Daniel Robinson. 1994. '"Certain Sensitive Position": Anti-Gay Security Regulations and the Canadian Civil Service, 1955–1970'. Unpublished manuscript, Toronto.

Kinsman, Gary. 1995. '"Character Weaknesses" and "Fruit Machines": Towards an Analysis of the Social Organization of the Anti-Homosexual Purge Campaign in the Canadian Federal Civil Service, 1959–1964.' *Labour/Le Travail* 35 (Spring): 133–61.

Kiss & Tell, eds. 1994. *Her Tongue on My Theory: Images, Essays and Fantasies*. Vancouver: Press Gang Publishers.

Kotz, Liz. 1994. 'Keeping Secrets and Other Stories: On Lesbian Representation.' Panel presentation, A Space Gallery, Toronto.

Lacombe, Dany. 1994. *Blue Politics: Pornography and the Law in the Age of Feminism*. Toronto:University of Toronto Press.

Lang, Kirstie. 1995. 'Freezing the "Perfect Moment."' Unpublished MA thesis, Department of Curriculum Studies, University of British Columbia.

LEAF. 1991*a*. 'Factum of the Intervenor, Women's Legal, Education and Action Fund.' *Butler* v. *R.*, [1992] 1 S.C.R. 452, [1992] 8 C.R.R. (2d) 1.

——1991*b*. 'Keegstra, Andrews, Smith and Taylor: Supreme Court Upholds Prohibitions on Hate Literature.' *LEAFLines* 4, no. 2 (March).

Leiren-Young, Mark. 1994. 'Breaking the Ties That Bind: Can a Small Bookstore Take on the Feds and Win?' *Georgia Straight* 25 (7–14 October): 11, 13, 15, 17.

Lewis, Reina, and Karen Adler. 1994. 'Come to Me Baby or What's Wrong with Lesbian S/M.' *Women's Studies International Forum* 17, no. 4: 433–41.

Lezzie Smut. 1993. 'Editorial: Show Us Yours.' Vol .1, no. 1 (September): 5–6.

Linden, Robin Ruth, et al., eds. 1982. *Against Sadomasochism: A Radical Feminist Analysis*. East Palo Alto, Calif.: Frog in the Well Press.

McClintock, Anne. 1993. 'Maid to Order: Commercial Fetishism and Gender Power.' *In Dirty Looks: Women, Pornography, Power*, ed. Pamela C. Gibson and Roma Gibson, 207–32. London: British Film Institute Publishing.

McCormack, Thelma. 1993*a*. 'If Pornography Is the Theory, Is Inequality the Practice?' *Philosophy of the Social Sciences* 23, no.3 (September).

—— 1993*b*. 'Keeping Our Sex "Safe": Anti-Censorship Strategies vs. The Politics of Protection.' *Fireweed: A Feminist Quarterly* 37 (Winter): 25–34.

MacKinnon, Catharine 1993. *Only Words*. Cambridge: Harvard University Press.

Madonna. 1992. *Sex*. New York: Time Warner Books.

Malamuth, Neil. 1992. 'In-Chief and Cross-Examination.' Transcripts from *R.* v. *Scythes*, 14 December, 3–78.

Mercer, Kobena. 1991. 'Skin Head Sex Thing: Racial Difference and the Homoerotic Imaginary.' In *How Do I Look? Queer Film and Video*, ed. Bad Object Choices, 169–210. Seattle: Bay Press.

——1992. 'Just Looking for Trouble: Robert Mapplethorpe and Fantasies of Race.' In *Sex Exposed: Sexuality and the Pornography Debate*, ed. Lynne Segal and Mary McIntosh, 92–110. London: Virago.

Mitchell, Alanna. 1993. 'Faith, Hope and Chastity.' *Globe and Mail*, 18 February, A1.

Mitchinson, Wendy. 1991. *The Nature of Their Bodies: Women and Their Doctors in Victorian Canada*. Toronto: University of Toronto Press.

Nazarieff, Serge. 1988. *Jeux de Dames Cruelles, 1850–1960*. Berlin: Taco.

Nestle, Joan. 1987. *A Restricted Country*. Ithaca, NY: Firebrand Books.

Newton, Esther. 1993. 'Role Models.' In *Camp Ground: Style and Homosexuality*, ed. David Bergman, 39–53. Amherst. University of Massachusetts Press.

O'Brien, Kelly. 1994. 'Turning Deviant Bodies into Visible Objects of Knowledge: A Look at the Way *Sex Variants* Sees Lesbians.' Unpublished manuscript, Toronto.

Oldham, Jim. 1993. 'Spreading the Word: CURE Founder Travels to Ottawa to Sow New Seeds.' *X-tra!*, 30 April, 11.

Pally, Marcia. 1994. *Sex and Sensibility: Reflections on Forbidden Mirrors and the Will to Censor*. Hopewell, NJ: Ecco Press.

Patton, Cindy. 1986. *Sex and Germs: The Politics of AIDS*. Montral: Black Rose Books.

Pegis, Jessica. 1993. 'A Sick Body of Evidence: CURE Scrapes Bottom to Find "Scientific" Support for Its Homophobic Agenda.' *Xtra*, 3 September, 17.

Portillo, Tina. 1991. 'I Get Real: Celebrating My Sadomasochistic Soul.' In *Leather-Folk: Radical Sex, People, Politics and Practice*, ed. Mark Thompson, 49–55.

Preston, John, ed. 1991. *Leatherfolk*. Boston: Alyson Publications.

Raymond, Janice. 1992. 'Pornography and the Politics of Lesbianis.' In *Pornography: Women, Violence and Civil Liberties*, ed. Catherine Itzin, 166–78. London: Oxford University Press.

Richardson, Bill. 1995. 'Of Fabulous Thighs and Delicate Eyes.' *Georgia Strait* 29, no. 1460: 17.

Ricker-Wilson, Carol. 1993. 'Tolerance in Our Schools Cannot Be One Dimensional.' *Toronto Star*, 13 April, A17.

Roof, Judith. 1991. *A Lure of Knowledge: Lesbian Sexuality and Theory*. New York: Columbia University Press.

Ross, Becki. 1992. 'In-Chief and Cross Examination.' Transcripts from *R.* v. *Scythes*, 3–109.

—— 1993. 'Trish Thomas: Reborn in Porn.' *X-tra!*, 11 June, 27.

Rupp, Shannon. 1996. 'B.C. Court's Ruling Falls Short, Bookstores Say.' *Globe and Mail*, 23 January, A9, A10.

Scales, Ann. 1994. 'Avoiding Constitutional Depression: Bad Atttitudes and the Fate of Butler.' *Canadian Journal of Women and the Law* 7: 349–92.

Sedgwick, Eve. 1990. *Epistemology of the Closet*. Berkeley: University of California Press.

Segal, Lynne. 1993. 'Does Pornography Cause Violence? The Search for Evidence.' In *Dirty Looks: Women, Pornography, Power*, ed. Pamela C. Gibson and Roma Gibson, 5–21. London: British Film Institute Publishing.

Segal, Lynne, and Mary McIntosh. 1992. *Sex Exposed: Sexuality and the Pornography Debate*. London: Virago.

Smart, Carol. 1989. *Feminism and the Power of Law*. London: Routledge.

Smith, Anna Marie. 1993. '"What Is Pornography?": An Analysis of the Policy Statement of the Campaign Against Pornography and Censorship.' *Feminist Review* 43 (Spring): 71–87.

—— 1995. '"By Women, For Women and About Women" Rules OK?: The Impossibility of Visual Soliloquy.' In *A Queer Romance: Lesbians, Gay Men and Popular Culture*, ed. Paul Burston and Colin Richardson, 199–215. London and New York: Routledge.

L. 1993. 'A Feminist Critique of "The" Feminist Critique of Pornography' *Virginia Law Review* 79: 1099.

Strossen, Nadine. 1995. *Defending pornography: Free Speech, Sex and the Fight for Women's Rights*. New York: Scribner

Thomas, Trish. 1991 'Wunna My Fantasies.' *Bad Attitude* 7 no. 4: 25–9.

Tisdale, Sallie. 1994. *Talk Dirty to Me: An Intimate Philosophy of Sex*. New York: Doubleday.

Toobin, Jeffrey. 1994. 'X-Rated' *The New Yorker*, 3 October, 70–8.

Valverde, Mariana. 1991. *The Age of Light, Soap, and Water: Moral Reform in English Canada 1885–1925*. Toronto: McClelland and Stewart.

——1996. 'Social Facticity and the Law: A Social Expert's Eyewitness Account of Law.' *Social and Legal Studies* 5, no.2 (June): 201–17.

Valverde, Mariana, and Lorna Weir. 1985. 'Thrills, Chills and the "Lesbian Threat" or, The Media, the State and Women's Sexuality.' In *Women Against Censorship*, ed. Varda Burstyn, 99–106. Vancouver: Douglas and McIntyre.

Vance, Carol. 1989. 'The War on Culture.' *Art in America* 77, no. 9: 39–45.

Weeks, Jeffrey. 1991. *Against Nature.* London: River Oram Press.

Williams, Linda. 1990. *Hard Core: Power, Pleasure and the Frenzy of the Visible.* London: Pandora.

Winston, Lady, ed. 1987. *The Leading Edge.* Denver: Lace Publications.

List of Cases

R. v. *Butler*, [1992] 1 S.C.R. 452.

R. v. *Scythes* (16th January 1993), Toronto (Ont.Ct.Prov.Div.) [unreported].

15

Avoiding Constitutional Depression

Bad Attitudes and the Fate of Butler

Ann Scales

This article explores the controversy about the application of R. v. Butler, *Canada's new interpretation of 'obscenity', to sexually explicit gay and lesbian materials. It is argued that the attack perceived by gay and lesbian communities is not the fault of the* Butler *decision. There are surely problematic legal doctrines, but those were retained from the pre-*Butler *regime. More important is how* Butler *is being distorted, not only as a weapon against gay men and lesbians, but also to preclude realization of the decision's promise as a means to protect victims of mainstream pornography. The article discusses some possible distinctions between sexually explicit lesbian materials and mainstream pornography, which should be considered by judges obliged to enforce the* Butler *decision. The author concludes, however, that at least so long as those distinctions are unproven, gay men and lesbians need to withdraw from the war on* Butler. *Rather, those communities need to join in solidarity with other disadvantaged groups to educate about Butler's real meaning and promise, and to strive for its uniform, non-discriminatory enforcement. The article considers, finally, how 'postmodernist' arguments might be approriated by pornographers to defeat the purpose of Butler.*

During the spring term of 1993, I was honoured to be the Walter S. Owen Visiting Professor at the University of British Columbia Faculty of Law. This paper is a revised version of the 'Owen Lecture', at UBC on 16 March 1993. That lecture transpired in the middle of a political firestorm about gay and lesbian sexual expressions, my involvement in which unfolded as follows.

Ann Scales, from 'Avoiding Constitutional Depression: Bad Attitudes and the Fate of Butler', Ann Scales, edited extract from *Canadian Women's Law Journal*, vol VIII, 1994, 250–72, reprinted by permission of the author.

INTRODUCTION

A decade before my visiting stint at UBC, I had enjoyed a collegial exchange of letters with Professor J. C. Smith of the UBC Law Faculty. We met face to face in February of 1986, when I was invited to come to UBC to debate pornography regulation.

That event is memorable for any number of reasons: (1) The student at UBC who arranged the logistics actually said, 'we couldn't get MacKinnon, so we invited you.' No amount of sodium pentothal could make me remember the identity of the speaker. I was, however, utterly charmed by that person's honesty, and felt fully appraised of the situation; (2) The day of the event witnessed one of the biggest blizzards in Vancouver history. My cab got into a wreck on the way from the downtown hotel, which made me late for the event. I didn't think it mattered, because the snowstorm was so intense that I was sure no one would show up. Yet, when I arrived at UBC, the lecture hall was packed to the gills; (3) My happiness about the turnout was fully justified by the discussion. By 1986, feminist debates about pornography in the US had become hotly polarized. That situation was painful, among other reasons, because it was and remains so obstinately abstract. Though US activists Catharine MacKinnon and Andrea Dworkin had articulated a coherent feminist approach to pornography,[1] no US jurisdiction has yet put such a law into effect.[2] In the US, the argument always gets stuck on how the foundations of the republic would crumble should we even try. On the other hand, at this snowbound event at UBC, a huge crowd had shown up, and was giving serious consideration to what could and/or should be done.

There is an additional anecdote from the 1986 event which I must report, because this paper is dedicated to J. C. Smith, who was the otherwise very quiet 'moderator' of the debate. In the period following the debate, someone asked me the inevitable 'strange-bedfellows' question: 'aren't you and Catharine MacKinnon and Andrea Dworkin in bed with right-wing women?' Before I could respond to the argument that radical feminists are the pawns of the far right, Professor Smith leapt to his feet and said, 'if right-wing women would spend more time in bed with Scales, MacKinnon, and Dworkin, and less time in bed with their right-wing husbands, the world would be a better place.'[3] The sexualized nature of the 'bedfellows' question and J. C.'s answer notwithstanding, I was amazed by the frankness of his comment, which, in the US in 1986, might have caused a riot.

Thus was I introduced to Canadian law students as a radical feminist, and thus did I acquire my first sense that Canadian and US constitutional legal interpretations might operate in different realities. This paper is about how that sense of difference was borne out, and about the courage it has taken and will take for Canadian constitutional interpretations to maintain that difference.

I do not intend to reinvent the debates among Charter-watchers. As I am not a Canadian lawyer, I cannot speak with authority even to specific Charter sections or adjudicative doctrines. My concern is rather with the political matrix surrounding specific litigation, namely the case brought by Little Sisters Book and Art Emporium, Vancover's gay and lesbian bookstore, against Canadian Customs challenging seizures of gay and lesbian materials.[4] That case, I believe, presents the risk of constitutional depression, which debilitating condition can and must be avoided.

I use the term 'depression' in the practical way that it can be distinguished from despair.[5] Despair means the loss of hope or confidence, on a temporary basis. Depression refers to an on-going sense that despair will never, and can never, go away. In the constitutional realm, depression is produced by multiple layers of denial, abstraction, obfuscation, and a pervasive 'not-the-point-ness' in adjudication. I believe that the constitutional situation in the United States has gone beyond a state of despair, to widespread depression.[6]

In reporting my own malady, I should note that the trajectory of my legal career tracks a dreadful period for progressive US constitutionalism, particularly on gender issues. For example, I was accepted into law school in the year that the US Supreme Court decided that discrimination on the basis of pregnancy was not sex discrimination.[7] That was once the law in Canada, but has since been reversed.[8] In the US, however, that view has not only *not* been reversed, but was reiterated recently in *Bray* v. *Alexandria Women's Health Clinic*,[9] which held that the harassment by 'Operation Rescue' of women seeking abortions was not sex discrimination.[10]

US Supreme Court Justice Antonin Scalia, writing for the majority, put it this way:

> Whatever one thinks of abortion, it cannot be denied that there are common and respectable reasons for opposing it, other than hatred of or condescension toward (or indeed any view at all concerning) women as a class—as is evident from the fact that men and women are on both sides of the issue . . .[11]

There are three things in this short quote that exemplify

constitutionally depressing patriarchal power. First, for Scalia to assert that it is possible to be against abortion without having *any* view of women, he reinforces a deeply socially-constructed and usually invisible view of women's natural place, attributes, and just desserts. We are essentially breeding instruments, and there can be no harm to us as a class by treating us, however brutally, as such.[12]

Second, Scalia demonstrates how, if male power can get some women to be against women, that always proves that *no women are ever being hurt* by whatever male power does. This was at work in the confirmation hearings for US Supreme Court Justice Clarence Thomas, after he had been accused of sexually harassing Professor Anita Hill. Thomas brought in other of his former female co-workers to testify that he never harassed them: he therefore could not have harassed Anita Hill.[13] That it why some allegedly highly-paid female sex models[14] are so salient in discussions of pornography: if they are consenting and reaping economic rewards, then all women must really consent to all the ways pornography is produced and used.

Third is Scalia's game-winning evocation of point-of-viewlessness, also a fundamental patriarchal format: since I, Scalia, have the power to deny any hatred of women, I can grant point-of-viewlessness on 'the woman question' to Operation Rescue, which can then grant it to its showpieces, its complicit female members.

This is the ideal of US constitutional decision-making, a valorization of positionlessness. The existence of hatred need not be acknowledged, complicity in hateful practices remains concealed, and power is as comfy as ever. One is reminded of Patricia Williams' wonderful description of impersonal writing styles:

> It it not only a ruse, but a warm protective hole to crawl in, as if you were to throw your shoe out the front door while insisting that no one's home.[15]

Scalia's shoe-throwing exercise must have thrilled Operation Rescue. He validated their favorite fetish: the 'ego in utero', that privileged being that simply has and is simply automatically entitled to have convictions, which convictions are not determined, unduly influenced, or even necessarily connected to anything else going on in the world.[16]

This ego informs all of US constitutionalism. We are miles from relinquishing or even acknowledging the ideal of the John-Wayne-rugged-individualist who can make up his own mind, damn it, whose entitlement to his opinion is always more important than the blood in the streets. The conspicuously entitled subject is the sole measure of justice. John Wayne would supply the US meaning to the Latin inscription over the main entrance to the UBC Faculty of Law: 'Let Justice be done, though the heavens may fall.'

In the *Little Sisters* litigation, there it a sense that the heavens will fall. At stake is not only the well-being of gay and lesbian Canadians, but also the meaning of *R.* v. *Butler*,[17] Canada's revolutionary new definition of obscenity as that which presents a risk of harm to women. While I was teaching in Canada, and again when I returned to testify, I had the sense that, in the public imagination, there were only two polar alternatives in the *Little Sisters* case: either seriously dilute *Butler*, or enforce it in a fundamentally contextless way. That is, there were two competing political alliances: one could decide that it would be acceptable if *Butler* were *never* enforced (required in order to preserve gay/lesbian Canadian communities), or one could decide that the enforcement of *Butler* was more important than the survival of those gay/lesbian communities. The choices seemed to be, whose blood will flow? Whose lives matter less? The women who are victims of mainstream pornography, or their lesbian sisters whom they have probably never met?

That of course is a false choice. Victims of mainstream pornography are often lesbians, and we are all diminished by the harms of pornography. Crucially, what *wasn't* said in the popular conversation was that lesbians were being asked to ignore those facts: 'oh, it's just them, it isn't us.' What *wasn't* said was that this was a ransom offer, a trade of consumable women for the marginal acceptability of gay/lesbian Canadians. What *wasn't* said was that the gay/lesbian communities were being used to de-legitimate *Butler*. And it followed that the *Butler* decision itself would not be read; it became, instead, a symbolic object of hatred and division.

In this paper, I will first present my account of what has happened so far, that is the 'divide and conquer' strategy at its best, which, when unnamed, is a leading cause of constitutional depression. The rest of this paper tracks the course of my thinking about Canadian obscenity law and about the sexually explicit materials at issue in the *Little Sisters* litigation. Thus, after noting some pitfalls in Canadian obscenity law, I will present the best arguments for constitutional protection of the lesbian materials at issue in the *Little Sisters* case,[18] (including some of the so-called 'sado-masochistic' materials).

In doing so, however, I am not saying that all of those materials should be protected. Indeed, I have come to the firm conclusion that insofar as any of the lesbian materials present a risk of harm to women, they are obscene, and prohibited under Canadian criminal law. Any apparent equivocation in what follows is because of my concern that the risks of harms from the lesbian materials could be different, and because, given rampant homophobia, even the same harms would be identified and evaluated differently.

Canadian customs, police, and judges thus far have not shown much sensitivity to the persecution and present needs of gay/lesbian communities. Charter jurisprudence, however, requires all of them to develop that sensitivity. Unlike constitutional adjudication in the United States, Charter interpretation is committed to putting rules, interpretive competitions, and people *in context:*

> The contextual approach attempts to bring into sharp relief the aspect of the right or freedom which is truly at stake in the case as well as the relevant aspects of any values in competition with it. It seems to be more sensitive to the reality of the dilemma posed by the particular facts and therefore more conducive to finding a fair and just compromise between the two competing values under s. 1.[19]

The relevant context in any Canadian obscenity case is the oppression of women, in all the monstrous ways that it is maintained, and whatever painful investigation that might require. The context of the *Little Sisters* case also involves atrocities perpetrated against gay and lesbian people, children, and people of colour. All of these categories overlap in ways that put extraordinary demands upon the commitment to contextualization.

Lesbians, their political allies and co-affected communities, must participate in the tasks of education, of contextualization. That requires that we continue having very difficult conversations among ourselves, and with others. This paper is intended to contribute to that discussion. Whatever the outcome in the *Little Sisters* matter, at least let the materials at issue be understood—whether they be exonerated or condemned—in context.

BUTLER HAPPENED: DEPRESSION LIFTS, THEN THREATENS AGAIN

The political situation is deep, because the gay and lesbian materials are being judged by Canada's new obscenity standard. In February of 1992, in *R.* v. *Butler,*[20] the Supreme Court of Canada reinterpreted the term 'obscenity', as it is used in the federal *Criminal Code.*[21] Obscenity had previously been understood in terms of prevailing standards of decency. Since 1992, obscenity is no longer about that.[22] While there is still a dimension of morality,[23] obscenity in Canada is now measured by the harm it inflicts, particularly harm to women.[24] Obscenity in Canada is now about gender equality.[25] Crucially, the Supreme Court identified non-violent materials which are 'degrading or dehumanizing' as a regulable category.[26] In shifting the emphasis in obscenity law from morality to gender-based harm—specifically the degradation and dehumanization of women—the Supreme Court took an historic step toward whatever justice might turn out to be.

I will never forget the moment—I was standing outside one of the few women's rest rooms at the University of New Mexico School of Law—when I heard about the *Butler* decision in February 1992. I was thrilled, because, in the US, I have long allied myself with the so-called 'anti-pornography radical feminists'. That is, I have supported the MacKinnon/Dworkin pornography ordinance, which provides a civil action for sex discrimination to victims of pornography.[27] Very soon after *Butler*, however, my First-Amendment-absolutist friends called to gloat, having read US press reports that the first prosecutions under the *Butler* standard were against gay and lesbian bookstores. That of course is only partly true.[28]

In the US, whenever any restriction on speech is used against the expression of the relatively powerless, *that is the end of the argument.*[29] Once any instance of that entirely predictable phenomenon comes to pass, US lawyers lie down and roll over. But please consider, even when most exercised in the US debates over the civil pornography ordinance, I would not have asserted that it would unproblematically *work.* Effectiveness is a long-term question. If such ordinances were in effect long enough in enough places, then one could assess whether the pornography industry would be forced to change, or whether women would be differently empowered in the ongoing struggle for other than pornographically defined selves. Of more immediate importance, had such ordinances gone into effect, a long *interpretive competition* would have ensued. An inevitable part of that competition would have been the attempted co-optation of the ordinance by a conspiracy of pornographers and their apologists.

In the first stage of this competition in Canada, the Supreme Court has made a courageous move toward a new paradigm of pornography. The engine of *Butler* was gender equality, which when understood in other than a formal, empty, liberal way,[30] is about the redistribution of power. Given that, did anyone expect those who stood to lose power to give it up gleefully? How could anyone be shocked that this newly configured power would immediately be twisted into a weapon for the enforcement of sexual orthodoxy? From a gay and lesbian perspective, this particular move was inevitable: in a society that hates us so much, any shift in cultural situation will be an occasion to escalate our demise. In a society that really wants us dead, *Butler* would be taken as yet another occasion to eliminate any trace of us.

Butler itself said nothing about gay and lesbian people. State officials made the decisions to take *Butler* to the throats of fragile communities (such as gay men and lesbians), and the press jumped on that as if the heavens had indeed fallen.[31] We should not be surprised when the conversation in the lesbian and gay communities takes the form: '*Butler*—UGH.'[32] Nor should we be surprised if women who supported *Butler* feel attacked and defensive.[33] Did anyone think that power was as dumb as it sometimes looks? If the divide-and-conquer strategy weren't stunningly, reliably effective, it would have been abandoned long ago.

WHAT NOW?

But here we are. It is important to describe what the *Little Sisters* case involves. The case (again, brought *prior* to *Butler*) is in large part a challenge to Canadian Customs' arbitrariness. Customs is a relatively unaccountable agency, and its long-standing arbitrariness is the subject of much dispute, regarding a wide range of publications and goods.[34] The *Little Sisters* case is thus, in part, about making Customs conform to Parliament's superior law—whatever that law was, is, and will be—and forcing Customs to administer the law in a consistent way.

But *Little Sisters* is also an equality case. Customs' seizures of materials headed for the bookstore have been monumentally and stupidly overbroad. The materials alleged by Customs to be obscene are hundreds of books and magazines, including lesbian romance novels that contain no violence and almost no sex, as well as academic books about homosexuality, as well as academic books about pornography. So far as I can determine, most of the titles at issue in the case do not meet the harm-based standard of *Butler*. Thus, *Little Sisters* is an easy case with respect to the overbreadth of Customs' power, and eventually, Canadian courts will condemn it. In the meantime, of course,

Little Sisters Bookstore and the communities it serves suffer, and I do not underestimate that economic and social deprivation.

There are three ways that equality considerations come into play: (1) If the overbreadth of Customs practices is exercised disproportionately with regard to gay/lesbian materials, as opposed to mainstream pornography materials (which I believe to be true);[35] (2) If gay/lesbian materials that *meet* the harm-based standard of *Butler* are seized disproportionately as compared to mainstream 'male on female' materials (which I believe also to be true, not only as a matter of discriminatory administrative discretion, but also because it is only in the gay/lesbian contexts that the authorities can understand the meaning of 'degradation and dehumanization'); and (3) If the equality-driven, harm-based standard of *Butler* is being ignored (which is manifestly true, particularly in the practices of Customs).

Butler is not perfect, is very threatening to pornographers, and requires extreme measures to undermine it. Pornographers needed to pick a good battleground, and that is where the gay and lesbian communities came in. Battlegrounds get trampled upon; it was convenient that this turf was already beaten down.

There are at least three aspects of the *Butler* decision itself that make this bloody scenario possible. First, *Butler* interprets a section of the *Criminal Code*, in contrast to the MacKinnon/Dworkin ordinance, which, in creating a civil action for sex discrimination, places the first interpretive moves in the hands of victims of pornography, to identify what is pornographic, and to demonstrate the harms therefrom.[36] In criminal prosecutions or customs seizures, the first interpretive moves are in the hands of public officials: that is, those invested by the *status quo* wish a uniquely legitimated authority to use physical force, which force is usually deployed to protect the *status quo*, to wit, the persecution of women in pornography.

I am aware that some anti-pornography feminist lawyers believe the civil action is the wrong way to go, because it 'privatizes' the harms, that is, makes the harms of pornography into a set of personal problems, privately realized and privately pursued. I disagree with that assessment, first because of the difference between civil rights actions and torts: civil rights claims, though brought by private persons, represent a public commitment to equality, as opposed to mere compensation. In addition, the present situation in Canada, I hope, is a stepping stone toward the civil rights approach.[37] *Butler* is the beginning, rather than the end, of this historic tale. In the meantime, though public officials are having a hard time getting it, or though they may be resisting it, *Butler* is *the law*. It is still the best that any nation on earth has done so far to protect women from the harms of pornography.

The other two immediate problems with *Butler* are the ways that it adheres to traditional obscenity law, as opposed to more progressive concepts of pornography regulation. The concept of obscenity lives in a moralistic, paternalistic universe.[38] The value of *Butler* will be in whether it can bridge the gap between obscenity and pornography regulations.

Butler interpreted the section of the *Criminal Code* that defines 'obscenity', so that is still the technically relevant term in Canada. 'Obscenity' is a moral issue; the term literally means 'filth',[39] its regulation is about protecting mainstream sensibilities against offense.

The term 'pornography' literally means, 'descriptions of prostitutes or of prostitution.'[40] In the radical feminist lexicon, 'pornography' identifies that specific propaganda that constructs women as *expendable*. This feature of pornography is illustrated by the statistic that, in Canada, prostitutes suffer a homicide rate *40 times* the national average.[41] And you don't hear much about that.[42]

The critical conjure in the construction of pornography is in the *eroticization* of the consumption of women. In pornography, inequality is sexy. The hatred, defilement, and annihilation of women portrayed in pornography is sexy. Cruelest of all, pornography constructs women as loving their own annihilation. Oppression becomes mutuality, hate becomes love, and torture becomes consent.[43]

'Pornography' is an extraordinarily profitable and wholly-owned subsidiary of male dominance. When women as a class can be successfully portrayed as whores (when whores exemplify the expendability of women),[44] then women become expendable as a group, within which group each individual woman is a potential 'disappeared one'. Each individual woman can't help but confront her disappearability *as a woman* at some level. And thus (Justice Scalia, wherever you are), lots of women have life-or-death incentive to discover why male superiority is such a swell idea.

Within this radical feminist analysis, the fact that sexually explicit materials are gay and lesbian does not automatically exempt them from regulation under *Butler*. Pornography exists only in the context of a gendered society, which equates maleness with domination and femaleness with subordination, maleness with objectification and femaleness with the-objectified. Though the genders may be rearranged in gay and lesbian pornography, if the turn-on requires domination and subordination, then those materials affirm the social hatred of women. An MacKinnon put it:

> [E]xactly what is defined as degrading to a human being, however that is socially defined, is exactly what is sexually arousing to the male point of view in the pornography, just as the one to whom it is done is the girl regardless of sex.[45]

The value enacted, therefore, even in some gay and lesbian materials, is that it is socially acceptable, indeed, desirable, to turn women (or their surrogates) into things, to deprive us of our selves, and to screw us to death.

The *Butler* decision, though historic in its recognition of the harms from pornography, hangs in a purgatory between obscenity and pornography. In residual adherence to the obscenity regime, the *Butler* court allowed its test of degradation or dehumanization to depend upon community standards of tolerance.[46] That portion of the test is a set-up for misunderstanding. Consider the much-maligned case of *Glad Day Bookshop, Inc.* v. *Canada* (*Deputy Minister of National Revenue*).[47] This case, brought by Toronto's Glad Day bookstore before *Butler*,[48] challenged Customs' seizure of various sexually explicit gay male materials, from magazines to comic books.

After *Butler* and claiming to enforce it, Judge Hays deployed a strictly morality-based, pre-*Butler* standard to find all of the materials at issue obscene. Though presented with evidence that the nine publications at issue were not harmful,[49] Judge Hays didn't rely on consideration of harm at all, much less focusing on harms to women.[50] Instead, he condemned all the materials as degrading or dehumanizing, on the grounds that they did 'not contain any real human relationship', were 'encounters without any real meaningful human relationship', did not 'arise from any ongoing human relationships', had 'no human dimension', were casual encounters among strangers, and were otherwise 'subhuman'.[51]

Judge Hays was clearly predisposed to seeing male homosexuality as degrading.[52] Stuck in the moral universe of traditional obscenity law, Judge Hays unfortunately did not provide any guidance on the aspects of the materials before him which might have violated *Butler*, and there were many.[53]

Given *Butler's* adherence to a community tolerance test, however, I can imagine how this happened. For example, having just stated that 'dehumanizing or degrading' material is obscene, 'not because it offends against morals but because it is perceived by public opinion to be harmful to society, particularly to women',[54] the *Butler* Court goes on to quote Justice Bertha Wilson from an earlier case:

> The most that can be said, I think, is that the public has concluded that exposure to material which degrades the human dimensions of life to a *sub-human* or *merely physical dimension* and thereby contributes to a process of *moral* desensitization must be harmful in some way.[55] [Emphasis added]

This quote is the only reference in *Butler* to subhumanity, mere physicality, and specifically moral diminishment. I am not sure why it is in the opinion, but I can see why lower court judges might see an opening still to impose their own moralities. I am confident that later decisions will avoid that temptation.[56]

The most infamous post-*Butler* case may or may not have grasped the distinction between the new harm-based law and the regime of morality. *R* v. *Scythes*[57] involved the seizure by Toronto police 'before the ink was dry on the *Butler* decision',[58] and subsequent criminal prosecution, of an issue of the US lesbian magazine *Bad Attitude.* Though the Crown relied on several features of this particular issue, Judge Paris stated that 'the prosecution must stand or fall on the basis of one article entitled "Wunna My Fantasies".'[59]

In that piece, one woman follows another to a school shower, surreptitiously cuffs and blindfolds her, pulls her to the floor and has rough and painful sex with her. Then, as Judge Paris put it, 'The woman is immediately aroused by the acts of the writer, becomes an eager participant and eventually has an orgasm.'[60]

Compared to the conventional morality at work in the *Glad Day* case,[61] at least Judge Paris tried to employ the harm standard of *Butler.* He also gave some direct consideration to the lesbian context of the expression, in these two critical passages:

> I have detected during this trial a concern that the Court will find relevant the sexual orientation of Bad Attitude. In recent years, many courts and tribunals have struck down laws and practices held to discriminate against gays. This is an indication that our society has moved beyond tolerance to the actual recognition that homosexuals form an essential part of our community. It follows then that as members of a sexual minority they have the right to communicate publicly on the subject that binds them together. That right however, will on occasion be curtailed in the public interest. *The community tolerance test is blind to sexual orientation or practices.* Any consideration given to the sexual orientation of the material would constitute an unwarranted application of the test . . .
>
> This material flashes every light and blows every whistle of obscenity.

Enjoyable sex after subordination by bondage and physical abuse at the hands of a total stranger. *If I replaced the aggressor in this article with a man there would be very few people in the community who would not recognize the potential for harm.* The fact that the aggressor is a female is irrelevant because the potential for harm remains.[62] [Emphasis added]

I agree with the outcome in this case, but not completely with the analysis. Sexual orientation, I believe, *did* matter.[63] In addition, Judge Paris employed an abstract, almost algebraic notion of equality: that is, whenever 'x' can plausibly be substituted for 'y', the answer is obvious, as if the social contexts for groups 'x' and 'y' were the same. If this notion were truly in the hearts and minds of Canadian police and customs, there would have been massive busts and seizures of mainstream pornographic materials since *Butler*.[64] I am inclined to believe that had the 'Bad Attitude' perpetrator been a man instead of a woman, the harm would have been legally *invisible*. I defy anyone to show me that the thousands of 'positive-outcome' rape scenes in mainstream pornography (most of which is available in Canada) hold much prosecutorial interest for any of the powers-that-be.

The third, and most troubling aspect of the *Butler* decision is in its retention of the 'internal necessities test' or 'artistic defence'. That is, '[e]ven material which by itself offends community standards will not be considered [an] undue [exploitation of sex] if it is required for the serious treatment of a theme.'[65]

Here we have, live and in person, the proverbial exception that swallows the rule. Every piece of pornography seriously expresses the most serious of political themes: consuming women sustains male superiority. The better pornography does its job, the protected it is.[66] The artistic defence is thus incompatible with the harm-based approach to pornography. Even the US Supreme Court, unrenowned for its fluency in articulating harms, has recognized that fact. In holding that the definition of child-pornogaphy need not include a consideration of other merit of the materials at issue, the US Supreme Court stated: 'It is irrelevant to the child [who has been abused] whether or not the material . . . has a literary, artistic, political, or social value.'[67]

There is still this conundrum in the US: if we recognize that *children* are harmed in the production and distribution of pornography, why can't we recognize that similar harms befall *women*? But the Canadian Supreme Court has gone beyond that. If the Court really believes that pornography harms women, why is it relevant to the abused individual or group that the material has some other value? This trap fell shut on me when testifying on behalf of the Little Sisters bookstore. One of the books I was asked to read for the trial was Pat Califia's novel, *Doc and Fluff*.[68] On one hand, the novel contains gratuitous and sometimes glorified sado-masochistic sex, most savagely in an encounter between men.[69] On another hand, it is a story of brutal female vengeance for a brutal rape of a sister,[70] which is indeed a serious political theme. The questions from counsel for Little Sisters focused solely on the latter.[71] I suppose he was just doing his job, and unfortunately, I was just doing mine. It was easy to identify the artistic defence. It was easy to articulate the political content of this violent novel.[72]

There are, therefore, major ambiguities and opportunities for backsliding in the *Butler* decision. These problems were not created by *Butler*, but merely retained from an earlier regime. I believe the problems will be worked out with reference to the harm-based analysis. In the meantime, gay and lesbian Canadians are better off, because *Butler* replaces 'decency' with 'harm' as the normative standard for defining obscenity. *We could not have won the decency arguments.*[73] But from within the harm/equality paradigm, we have lots to say about how various sexually explicit materials either enrich or further diminish us as historically disadvantaged groups.[74]

THE CONTEXT OF LESBIAN S/M MATERIALS

The great news for gay and lesbian Canadians is that, after *Butler*, sexually explicit gay and lesbian materials will not be deemed 'degrading or dehumanizing' simply because they *are* gay and lesbian. The bad news is that in the gay and lesbian communities, and perhaps in the *Little Sisters* courtroom, the meaning of *Butler* for gays and lesbians is coming down to particular sub-classes of sexually explicit materials, that is so-called 'sado-masochistic', 'bondage and discipline', and other materials that portray violence or threats of violence.

As has been true since I can remember, almost everyone seems to want to draw a distinction between pornography and erotica. Almost everyone seems to believe that—somewhere out there—we can find reliably different definitions. This tired enterprise is legally irrelevant. The law has no business defining 'erotica'. The law can only decide *what is pornography.* There is pornography, and there is everything else. If something from the category of 'everything else' turns you on, so be it. Therefore, in order for gay and lesbian Canadians to protect their expressions, they must demonstrate, not that the materials are a turn-on, but that they are not pornography. The question is whether or not *Butler* prohibits them.

Prior to the Owen Lecture, I discussed with various groups the possibility that *Butler* could be vigorously reaffirmed *and* that all the lesbian materials at issue in the *Little Sisters* case *could* be found not obscene, including, perhaps, those materials that are 'sado-masochistic'. In having those discussions, there was a logically prior, definitional problem with 'sado-masochistic' materials. It is also illustrative of why *Butler* is a good thing for lesbians.

Though there are 'line-drawing' disputes among S/M adherents,[75] I don't think there is disagreement within that community that those very practices debated are indeed sado-masochistic. The problem resides in the lack of clarity of that concept to non-S/M lesbians, and particularly to straight people. For a lesbian to wear a leather jacket, sport a tattoo, or have very short hair would be, for many people, sure signs of degradation and dehumanization. A major theme in anti-lesbian propaganda is that we trick 'normal' women into lesbian sex.[76] By our very existence, we disturb (and some would say, do violence to) conventional gender roles. There is a common point of view that all lesbian sex is degraded sex, such that all descriptions of it are obscene.

It is only after *Butler* that we have an opportunity to expose the bare, irrelevant morality in those suppositions. We have an opportunity to explain how *being* lesbian is such an outsider status that we have often found our identity in non-conformity, subversion, and daring. However, we therefore also have an obligation to distinguish among expressions of our sexual practices that are potentially harmful to women and those that are not.

Notes

1. The MacKinnon/Dworkin ordinance creates a civil rights cause of action for *sex discrimination* for victims of pornography. The model ordinance defines 'pornography' as follows:

   1. Pornography is the graphic sexually explicit subordination of women, whether in pictures and/or in words that also includes one or more of the following:

      (i) women are presented dehumanized as sexual objects, things, or commodities; or

(ii) women are presented as sexual objects who enjoy pain or humiliation; or
(iii) women are presented as sexual objects who experience sexual pleasure in being raped; or
(iv) women are presented as sexual objects tied up or cut up or mutilated or bruised or physically hurt; or
(v) women are presented in postures of sexual submission, servility or display; or
(vi) women's body parts – including but not limited to vaginas, breasts, or buttocks – are exhibited such that women are reduced to those parts; or
(vii) women are presented as whores by nature; or
(viii) women are presented being penetrated by objects or animals; or
(ix) women are presented in scenarios of degradation, injury, torture, shown as filthy or inferior, bleeding, bruised, or hurt in a context that makes these conditions sexual.

2. The use of men, children, or transsexuals in the place of women in (1) above is pornography for purposes of this law. The model ordinance lists four sex discriminatory practices: 1. Coercion into pornography; 2. Trafficking in pornography; 3. Forcing pornography on a person; and 4. Assault or physical attack due to pornography. A violation of any of these gives rise to no criminal penalty, but may include civil damages, injunctions, and attorneys' fees. 'Model Anti-Pornography Law', in Andrea Dworkin, "Against the Male Flood: Censorship, Pornography, and Equality', (1985) 8 Harvard Women's Law Journal I at 24.

2. Three US municipalities (Minneapolis, Minnesota; Indianapolis, Indiana; and Bellingham, Washington) adopted the MacKinnon/Dworkin pornography ordinance, but it never became effective, so the argument that such regulation will backfire is speculative in the extreme. The legal history of those three municipal legal results is as follows. Amendment to the Minneapolis, Minn., Code of Ordinances, tit. 7, c. 139 (Dec. 30, 1983) (vetoed by the mayor January 5, 1984; reenacted in amended form on July 13, 1984; vetoed by the mayor on the same day); Indianapolis, Ind., City-County General Ordinance No. 24, c. 16 (May 1, 1984) (held violative of the First Amendment in action for declaratory judgment, *American Booksellers Ass'n* v. *Hudnut*, 598 F.Supp. 1316 (S.D. ind. 1984), *aff'd per curiam*, 771 F.2d 323 (7th Cir. 1985) *aff'd mem.* 475 U.S. 1001 (1986), *rehearing denied.* 475 U.S. 1132 (1986); Bellingham, Wash, Initiative 1C (November 8, 1988) (passed by 62 per cent of the voters) (held violative of the First Amendment in action for declaratory judgment in *Village Books* v. *City of Bellingham*, No. 88-1470) (W.D. Wash. Feburary 9, 1989)).
3. This is surely paraphrased to some extent, due to my astonishment at Professor Smith's outburst. For my later analysis of the 'strange bedfellows' argument, see Ann Scales, 'Feminist Legal Method: Not So Scary', (1992) 2 U.C.L.A. Womens's Law Journal 1 at 5–10.
4. *Little Sisters Book and Art Emporium* v. *Canada* (*Minister of Justice*), Vancouver Registry No. A901450 (B.C.S.C.) filed June 1990 [hereinafter *Little Sisters*]. See

also *R* v. *Butler*, [1992] 1 S.C.R. 452 [hereinafter *Butler*]. I am aware that there was a pre-*Butler* challenge to Customs regarding seizure of gay male materials, wherein the court purported to use the *Butler* standard to hold all the materials obscene: *Glad Day Bookshop Inc.* v. *M.N.R.* (14 July 1992), O.J. No. 1466 Ont. H.C. (Gen. Div. (on appeal) [hereinafter *Glad Days*]. See *infra* notes 47–53. I know as well that there was a very high-profile criminal seizure of the lesbian magazine *Bad Attitude* against the same bookstore: *R* v. *Scythes* (16 January 1993), O.J. No. 537 Ont. Prov. Ct. [hereinafter *Scythes*]. See *infra* notes 57–63. I am focusing on the *Little Sisters* civil action only, in part because I was a witness in the case (on 21 October 1994). More importantly, like *Glad Day*, the *Little Sisters* matter was instituted well before the *Butler* decision, so it, too, underscores how *Butler* is being *used*, rather than enforced. Also, the *Little Sisters* case involves a range of materials far greater than that at issue in the criminal prosecution of Glad Day (one magazine) or in its civil action against customs (nine different items). At last count, there were 370 titles at issue in the *Little Sisters* litigation. Telephone conversation with Irene Faulkner, articling at Arvay & Finlay, solicitors for Little Sisters (30 September 1994). Therefore, the scope of *Butler* is being tested to a far greater extent.

5 My talented psychiatrist drew this distinction for me many years ago.

6. In fairness, I should say that since I gave the Owen Lecture, things are looking up a bit in US constitutional law, at least with regard to President Clinton's appointments to our Supreme Court. Ruth Bader Ginsburg, a hero and mentor to many progressive lawyers, has taken her rightful place there. Stephen Breyer has potential. It remains to be seen what they can do to resolve our constitutional depression.

7. *Geduldig* v. *Aiello*, 411 U.S. 484, 496 n.20 (1974) (no violation of constitutional equality guarantee in excluding pregnancy related services from disability insurance system for California state employees; in essence, no sex discrimination so long as pregnant women and pregnant men are treated the same).

8. See *Bliss* v. *Canada (AG.)*, [1979] 1 S.C.R. 183, overruled (in large part due to UBC Dean Lynn Smith) in *Brooks* v. *Canada Safeway*, [1989] 1 S.C.R. 1219. As Chief Justice Dickson said in the latter case: 'It is difficult to conceive that distinctions or discriminations based upon pregnancy could ever be regarded as other than discrimination based upon sex, or that restrictive statutory conditions applicable only to pregnant women did not discriminate against them as women'. (*Ibid.* at 1243–44).

9. __ U.S. __, 113 S.Ct. 753(1993) [hereinafter *Bray*].

10. *Ibid.* The technical legal question was whether Operation Rescue's blockades of abortion clinics—and harassment of women and personnel entering those clinics—violated the federal *Ku Klux Klan Act of 1871*, 42 U.S C. sec 1985(3). That statute criminalizes conspiracies to deprive persons of their equality rights. According to US Supreme Court interpretations of this law, the women's clinic would have to show that Operation Rescue was motivated by 'invidious discriminatory animus' toward women as women. The Court accepted Operation Rescue's contention that they were motivated not by animus toward women, but by their commitment to protect the unborn through this physical intervention. Since the decision in *Bray*, the US Congress has passed the *Freedom of Access to Clinic Entrances Act of 1994*, 18

U.S.C.A. s. 248, which provides federal penalties for using force, threats of force, or intimidation to interfere with persons entering clinics or with clinical facilities. That new stature is now being challenged as a violation of (you guessed it!) freedom of speech. In all cases brought to date, the courts have sustained the constitutionality of the Act. See *U.S.* v. *Brock*, ___ F.Supp. ___ (slip. op. E.D. Wisc., September 23, 1994); *Reily* v. *Reno*, ___ F. Supp. ___, 1994 WL 442826 (D. Ariz. 1994); *Cook* v.*Reno*, ___ F. Supp. ___, 1994 WL 422316 (W.D. La. 1994) (appeal filed #94-2676, 11th Cir.); *Council for Life Coalition* v. *Reno*, ___ F. Supp. ___, 1994 WL 363132 (S.D. Cal. 1994); *American Life League* v. *Reno*, 855 F. Supp. 137 (E.D. Va. 1994) (appeal filed, #94-1869, 4th Cir).

11. ___ U.S. at ___, 113 S. Ct. at 760.
12. Though the constitutional right to abortion was 'secured' in the US over twenty years ago, *Roe* v. *Wade*, 410 U.S. 113 (1973), that decision was based on the right to privacy rather than on women's equality concerns. Therefore, the conversation about abortion in the US has little to do with women, and lots to do with the abstract concept of personal autonomy. Abortion will remain an intractable issue until we achieve full and genuine equality for women. See *e.g.* Catharine A. MacKinnon, 'Reflections on Sex Equality Under Law', (1991) 100 Yale Law Review 1281. The abstract lie that Operation Rescue has no position on women is matched by the lie implicit in the rallying cry of 'no abortion on demand', as if abortion were something women do just for fun, as if there were no anguish, medical need, or dire necessity attached to the decision to terminate a pregnancy.
13. There was also a rather loose evidentiary standard at work. As Professor MacKinnon pointed out, it was as if an accused bank robber brought in the testimony of officers of all the banks he *didn't* rob. Catharine MacKinnon, 'Truth to Power' (Lecture at the University of New Mexico, 31 January 1992).
14. I use the qualifier 'allegedly', because I have seen no evidence that any sex workers are truly 'highly-paid'. The sex industry in all of its incarnations has a unique economic structure: undoubtedly a lot of money changes hands, but almost all of it goes into the hands of pimps, in all of *their* incarnations.
15. Patricia J. Williams, *The Alchemy of Race and Rights* (Cambridge, Mass. Harvard Univ. Press, 1991) at 93.
16. This fictional character was central in deciding the unconstitutionality of the MacKinnon/Dworkin pornography ordinance in Indianapolis, Indiana. Having accepted 'the premises of the legislation' (i.e. that pornography causes harm to women), Judge Easterbrook went on to say that '[a]ll of these unhappy effects depend on mental intermediation', so that the regulation of pornography would be 'thought control'. *American Booksellers Ass'n, Inc.* v. *Hudnut.* 771 F. 2d 323, 329 (7th Cir. 1985), *aff'd mem.* 475 U.S. 1001 (1986). In the US, constitutional reality is determined by what powerful heads believe they can mediate. Whatever happens, happens *only*, in Andrea Dworkin's immortal phrase, 'in the head, a vast cavern somewhere north of the eyes'. Dworkin, *supra* note 1 at 3.
17. *Butler, supra* note 4. For a fuller description of the *Butler* decision, see notes 20–26, and accompanying text, *infra*.
18. Though both lesbian and gay materials are at issue in the *Little Sisters* case, I will write almost exclusively about the lesbian stuff, partly because of the

political conundrum about the relationship between gay males and lesbians, but mostly because I know more about the lesbian materials.

19. *Edmonton Journal* v. *Alberta* (*Attorney General*), [1989] 2 S.C.R. 1326 at 1355–56 (opinion of Madam Justice Wilson). The contextual approach has required an expressly non-formalistic approach in equality cases under the Charter. As Madam Justice Wilson stated in *Andrews* v. *Law Society of British Columbia*, [1981] 1 S.C.R. 143 at 164 [hereinafter *Andrews*]:

    > [Equality] is a comparative concept, the condition of which may only be attained or discerned by comparison with the condition of others in the social and political setting in which the question arises . . .

    Mr Justice McIntyre emphasized, *ibid.* at 168:

    > Consideration must be given to the content of the law, to its purpose, and its impact upon those to whom it applies, and also upon those whom it excludes from its application. The issues which will arise from case to case are such that it would be wrong to attempt to confine these considerations within such a fixed and limited formula.

20. *Butler, supra* note 4.
21. In the relevant section, obscenity is defined as: 'any publication a dominant characteristic of which is the undue exploitation of sex, or of sex and any one or more of the following subjects, namely crime, horror, cruelty and violence . . .' *Criminal Code of Canada*, R.S.C. 1985, c. C-46, s. 163(8).
22. *Butler, supra* note 4 at 479: degrading or dehumanizing material fails community standards test 'not because it offends against morals but because it is perceived by public opinion to be harmful to society, particularly to women'; at 491–92: objective of maintenance of 'decent society' is no longer defensible in view of the *Charter, infra* note 24.
23. The *Butler* court noted that the notions of moral corruption and harm to society are 'inextricably linked. It is moral corruption of a certain kind which leads to the detrimental effect on society.' *Supra* note 4 at 495. Indeed, there is a widespread conviction that harm to women—especially rape and battering—are social 'goods'.
24. Discrimination against women is twice prohibited by the *Canadian Charter of Rights and Freedoms*, Part I of the Constitution Act, 1982, being schedule B to the *Canada Act 1982* (U.K.), 1982, c. 11 [hereinafter the *Charter*], ss. 15 & 28. Section 15 provides: '[E]very individual is equal before and under the law and has the right to the equal protection and equal benefit of the law without discrimination, and in particular, without discrimination based on race, national or ethnic origin, colour, religion, sex, age or mental or physical disability.'

    Section 28 provides: 'Notwithstanding anything in this Charter, the rights and freedoms referred to in it are guaranteed equally to male and female persons.'
25. I recognize that nowhere does the *Butler* court cite the gender equality provisions of the *Charter*. Nonetheless, in its repeated references to gender equality, the court clearly means to rely on the *constitutional* version of the idea. That had to have been true because the Court, in its balancing under the *Charter*, s. 1, found gender equality to outweigh the constitutional guarantee of freedom of expression under the *Charter*, s. 2(b). The *Butler* opinion relies explicitly on

harms to women (and/or children) from pornography in at least seven instances. See *supra* note 4 at 479: focus on harm, 'particularly to women'; at 493: noting how pornography reinforces harmful male-female stereotypes (quoting *Report on Pornography by the Standing Committee on Justice and Legal Affairs* (MacGuigan Report) (1978), at 18:4); at 485: describing harm as 'physical or mental mistreatment of women by men, or, what is perhaps debatable, the reverse'; at 497: noting goal of achieving 'true equality between male and female persons'; at 500 describing how in pornography, '[women], particularly, are deprived of unique human character or identity and are depicted as sexual playthings . . .' (quoting *R.* v *Wagner* (1985), 43 C.R. (3d) 318 at 331); and at 501: noting analogy of obscenity to hate propaganda against 'a significant portion of the population'. In the most colourful passage, the *Butler* court, at 479, quotes Ferg, J., from *R.* v. *Ramsingh* (1984), 14. C.C.C. (3d) 230 at 239 [hereinafter *Ramsingh*], on the type of material that qualifies for the label 'degrading or dehumanizing':

> [Women] are exploited, portrayed as desiring pleasure from pain, by being humiliated and treated only as an object of male domination sexually, or in cruel or violent bondage. Women are portrayed in these films as pining away their lives waiting for a huge male penis to come along, on the person of a so-called sex therapist, or window washer, supposedly to transport them into complete sexual ecstasy. Or even more false and degrading one is led to believe their raison d'être is to savour semen as a life elixir, or that they secretly desire to be forcefully taken by a man.

26. Pornography can be usefully divided into three categories: 1. Explicit sex with violence; 2. Explicit sex without violence but which subjects people to treatment that is degrading or dehumanizing; and 3. Explicit sex without violence that is neither degrading nor dehumanizing. . . . [T]he portrayal of sex coupled with violence will almost always constitute the undue exploitation of sex. Explicit sex which is degrading or dehumanizing may be undue if the risk of harm is substantial. Finally, explicit sex that it not violent and neither degrading nor dehumanizing is generally tolerated in our society and will not qualify as the undue exploitation of sex unless it employs children in its production.
    Butler, supra note 4 at 484–85.
27. See *supra note* 1.
28. It is true with respect only to the highest-profile case, *R.* v. *Scythes, supra* note 4, which was the criminal seizure of a particular issue of *Bad Attitude* from Glad Day Books a very short time after *Butler* was announced. See *infra* notes 57–63, and accompanying text. Both *Little Sisters* and *Glad Day*, which were civil actions against Customs, were begun well before *Butler*. In the only one of those two cases decided to date, *Glad Day*, sexually explicit gay male materials were found to be obscene. See *infra* notes 47–53, and accompanying text. Regarding treatment of 'mainstream', male-on-female materials, I cannot believe that the *Butler* harm-based standard (particularly on its 'dehumanization or degradation' prong) is being applied in the same way by either Customs or the police. There are unfortunately few reported cases (which by itself tells us something), and no official comparative data available. Suffice it to say, however, that since *Butler*, the mainstream industry has

thrived. For example, since *Butler*, Canadian pornography king Randy Jorgensen has expanded the number of his stores from 60 to 86. Jeffrey Toobin 'X-Rated', *The New Yorker* (3 October 1994) 70 at 75 (hereinafter 'The New Yorker').

29. A telling example comes from a recent interview with civil libertarian columnist Nat Hentoff:

> DEF ['The Defender', interviewing magazine] . . . this is one of the things that the Left has set out to obliterate, the concept of the individual. The attack for example, on white males in the university, which I find particularly horrendous because however powerful you regard white males in this society at large, when they're students, they're at the bottom of the totem pole. When Catharine MacKinnon [sic] bullies a male student because he's male, as I have seen her do, it's against everything that education is supposed to stand for.
> HENT [Hentoff]: I'll give you a quick story on Catharine McKinnon [sic]. Her main thrust for years, you know, has been to obliterate, to make illegal, all kinds of pornography which she defines so broadly that the censors can include the Old Testament. They wanted to do the same thing in Canada, and they succeeded in the Canadian Supreme Court, largely because of her and the brief she filed. What do you think was the first publication that was taken off the stands by the police in Toronto? It was a lesbian magazine.
> DEF: Perfect. What did she expect? . . .

'Interview with Nat Hentoff', *The Defender* (May 1994), 8–9 (hereinafter 'The Defender'). There is too much to comment on here: the difference between a civil action and censorship, whose totem pole is being described, why Hentoff would leave out the New Testament, etc. I would advise Canadian readers that, in the US, in order to fully demonize Professor MacKinnon, it has been necessary to disappear LEAF and blame *Butler* entirely on her. Two items are more to my textual concerns: 1. MacKinnon might well have expected and *applauded* the bust at that particular lesbian magazine, see *infra* note 45, and accompanying text; and 2. The 'quick story' is all that is offered to discredit MacKinnon, pornography victim advocacy, and Canadian constitutionalism.

30. The Canadian Supreme Court had already abandoned the formal, empty, liberal definition of equality. In *Andrews, supra* note 19, the court—in stupendous multiple distinctions to US law—had defined the command of s. 15 equality in the *Charter* to require in its interpretation: 1. A generous, purposive approach to the goal of equality; 2. An effects-based (rather than intention-driven) assessment; 3. An abandonment at the requirement of proof of 'similar situation', 4. A finding of inequality based on proof of harm, prejudice, or disadvantage; and 5. An allowance that groups other than those enumerated in s. 15 would, by analogy, be entitled to s. 15 scrutiny. The principles of *Andrews* made all subsequent equality cases, including *Butler*, possible and necessary. For a concise description of the relevance of *Andrews* to Canadian equality jurisprudence generally, see Kathleen A. Mahoney, 'The Constitutional Law of Equality in Canada', (1992) 44 Maine Law Review 229.

31. See 'The Defender', *supra* note 29; also see *e.g.* John Leo, 'Censors on the Left', *U.S. News and World Report* (4 October 1993); Tim Kingston, 'Canada's New Porn Wars;', *San Francisco Bay Times* (4 November 1993); Leanne Katz,

'Censors' Helpers', *The New York Times* (3 December 1993) 15; Ted C Fishman, 'Northern Underexposure', *Playboy* (June 1994); Thelma McCormack 'Keeping Our Sex "Safe": Anti-Censorship Strategies vs. the Politics of Protection', *Fireweed (Winter 1993), 25.*

32. See *e.g.* Michael Rowe, 'Oh Canada: Another Obscenity at the Frontier', *Harvard Gay and Lesbian Review* (Fall 1994), 17; Lucinda Johnson 'Censorship and Receiving', *Fuse Magazine* (May/June 1993) 10; Catherine Creede 'Censorship and Mainstream Media', *Fuse Magazine* (Winter 1992/93), 13; Christopher Eamon, 'The Rhetoric of Degradation: How the Anti-Porn Lobby Sold Us Out', *ibid.* 16; Clare Barclay and Elaine Carol, 'Obscenity Chill: Artists in a Post-Butler Era', *ibid*, 18.
33. These sentiments were clear to me at the workshop entitled 'Women's Right to Speak: Section 2 as Both Sword and Shield' (National Association of Women and the Law Conference, Vancouver, 20 February 1993). On why anti-pornography feminists, and members of LEAF in particular, do not deserve to be put in a defensive position, see the excellent article by Karen Busby, 'LEAF and Pornography: Litigating on Equality and Sexual Representations' (1994) 9 Canadian Journal of Law and Society 165.
34. See Jamie Lamb, 'Border Blues: Customs Mysterious Ways Impossible to Compute', *Vancouver Sun* (7 December 1994), A3 (describing arbitrary seizure, detention, and/or taxation of all manner of imports). Customs did not change its own regulations after *Butler*: the schedule at seizable goods published on 12 June 1991, remained in effect, unchanged until 29 September 1994. On that date, at the pre-trial hearing in the *Little Sisters* matter, Customs eliminated descriptions of 'anal penetration' from its grounds for detention or seizure. Telephone conversations with Irene Faulkner (30 September 1994). Compare *Revenue Canada Customs and Excise, Memorandum D9-1-1*, s. 6(a)(8)(1991), prohibiting importation of 'goods which depict or describe sexual acts that appear to degrade or dehumanize any of the participants, including . . . depictions or descriptions of anal penetration, including depictions or descriptions involving implements of all kinds . . .' with *Revenue Canada Customs and Excise, Memorandum D0-1-1* (29 September 1994).
35. Customs' discrimination among seizures is difficult to prove directly, as Customs is not obliged to publish data about its relevant activities. See Busby, *supra* note 33 at 186–87, noting how discrimination by Customs might be inferred. Customs' deletion of depictions of anal penetration as a criterion for seizure, on the eve of trial in *Little Sisters*, suggests that agency's awareness of its past discriminatory practices toward at least gay men. See *supra* note 34.
36. See *supra* note 1.
37. In establishing pornography as an equality concern, *Butler* provides the constitutional basis for any subsequent anti-pornography legislation to be enacted at any level in Canada. In the US, by contrast, pornography has not been understood as an equality concern, and its regulation does not fit into established exceptions to the First Amendment guarantee of freedom of expression. See *American Booksellers Ass'n. v. Hudnut*, 771 F. 2d 323 (7th Cir. 1985), *aff'd mem.* 475 U.S. 1001 (1986), *rehearing denied*, 475 U.S. 1132 (1986). Therefore, civil rights actions for harms inflicted by pornography are, constitutionally speaking, out of the question, at least until a courageous judge with a very different point of view takes another crack at that concept.

38. When consulted about LEAF's intervention in *Butler*, co-author of the Pornography Ordinance *supra* note 1, Andrea Dworkin advised that women should not support obscenity laws, even if redefined:

    'Obscenity law is a total dead-end in dealing with the pornography industry. The whole idea of obscenity law is based on the idea that women's bodies are filthy and shouldn't be displayed, and that homosexuality is disgusting and shouldn't be seen. I think obscenity laws are real censorship laws, easy to use against literature that should be protected, and hard to use against what really harms women'. The seizure of her own books by Canada Customs, she said, was a typical abuse of police power.

    'The New Yorker', *supra* note 28 at 78 (quoting Andrea Dworkin).
39. The Oxford English Dictionary acknowledges the 'doubtful etymology' of the term 'obscene', but defines it as: 'offensive to the senses, or to taste or refinement; disgusting, repulsive, filthy, foul, abominable, loathsome . . .; offensive to modesty or decency; expressing or suggesting unchaste or lustful ideas; impure, indecent, lewd . . .' *The Compact Oxford English Dictionary* 2d ed. (Oxford: Clarendon Press, 1991), at 1195.
40. *Ibid.* at 1391.
41. *Report of the Special Committee on Pornography and Prostitution, Pornography and Prostitution in Canada* (Ottawa: Supply and Services) (1985), at 50.
42. What one does see about the murder of prostitutes is usually in the context of a liberal argument that prostitution should be de-criminalized. See *e.g.* Daniel Wood, 'Streets of Broken Dreams', *Vancouver Step* (March/April 1993), 59. But that argument misses the crucial question of how prostitutes are so gone from the social landscape as to make their slaughter almost invisible. In her famous article, 'Split at the Root: Prostitution and Feminist Discourses of Law Reform', (1992) 5 Yale Journal of Law & Feminism 47, Professor Margaret Baldwin demonstrates how various feminist analyses of prostitution tend to enhance rather than to undermine the dichotomy between 'prostitutes' and 'other women.' *Ibid.* at 48. In other feminist crusades, such as those against sexual harassment, domestic battering, and pornography, an underlying appeal is that the victims are *not* selling their sex, but are having it taken from them. *Ibid.* at 67. Thus, feminism is sometimes

    driven by a tacit recognition that legal regulation of sexual violence and sex discrimination at bottom always functions as some form of judicial review of a man's conclusion that a complaining woman was, in fact, a whore, and therefore a permissible target of misogynist rage, contempt, and sexual use. The fate of a woman's claims on justice, we all seem to know somewhere, crucially depends on her success in proving that she is not, and never has been, a prostitute.

    Ibid. at 81. The 'virgin/whore' dichotomy is a serious trap for all women, see *infra* note 100 and accompanying text, and its psychological power retards feminist efforts to respond to the needs of our sisters embroiled in prostitution.
43. The *Butler* court seemed to grasp the centrality of these reversals: 'In the appreciation of whether material is degrading or dehumanizing, the appearance of consent is not necessarily determinative. Consent cannot save

materials that otherwise contain degrading or dehumanizing scenes. Sometimes the very appearance of consent makes the depicted acts even more degrading or dehumanizing.' *Supra* note 4 at 479.

44. Baldwin, *supra* note 42.
45. Catharine A. MacKinnon, *Toward a feminist Theory of the State* (Cambridge, Mass.: Harvard Univ. Press, 1989) at 211.
46. > [T]here is a range of opinion as to what is degrading or dehumanizing . . . Because this is not a matter that is susceptible of proof in the traditional way and because we do not wish to leave it to the individual tastes of judges, we must have a norm that will serve as an arbiter is determining what amounts to an undue exploitation of sex. That arbiter is the community as a whole.

    Butler, supra note 4 at 484.
47. *Supra* note 4.
48. The case was brought in 1990, but, according to Karen Busby, the trial was delayed pending a decision in *Butler*. Busby, *supra* note 33 at 185. The *Glad Day* matter is now on appeal.
49. *Glad Day, supra* note 4 (O.J.) at 27.
50. There is some question whether *Butler*, its focus being on inequality of women, should apply to sexually explicit gay male materials at all. As the *Butler* court noted:

    > Harm in this context means that it predisposes persons to act in an anti-social manner as, for example, the physical or mental mistreatment of women by men, or, perhaps debatable, the reverse.

    Butler, supra note 4 at 485.
51. *Glad Day, supra* note 4 (O.J.) as 38. In a post-*Glad Day* ruling, the same Province countered Judge Hays' interpretation of *Butler*. The Ontario Court of Appeal held that heterosexual adult videos' failure to portray meaningful relationships, or anything except physicality, did not make them obscene within the meaning of *Butler: R.* v. *Ronish* (1993), 26 C.R. (4th) 75 at 82, 89–92, 95–96 (Ont C.A.) (ordering new trial concerning distribution of 'Oriental Taboo', 'D-Cup Delights', 'La Bimbo', 'The Honeymooners', 'Lawyers in Heat', 'Kinky Sluts', 'Secret Action Man', and 'Suzy Superstar Three') [hereinafter *Ronish*].
52. Thus, Judge Hays stated with respect to a video entitled 'Hard Choices': 'It does not involve violence but in a part which was not shown to the Court, Counsel for the Appellant advises that these are scenes of anal intercourse involving three males. This, of course, is not permissible activity under the provisions of the *Criminal Code*.' *Glad Day, supra* note 4 (O.J.) as 36. This aspect of Judge Hays' ruling is now clearly wrong, given Customs' deletion of materials describing anal penetration from its schedule of seizable goods. See *supra* note 34.
53. In the materials at issue in that case (videos, magazines, and comics), Judge Hays notes (just in passing) that three of the nine publications involved bondage; five involved urination and/or defecation. Another of the items, 'Movie Star Confidential', describes a scenario that closely corresponds to the worst messages sent by mainstream pornography, as identified by Judge Ferg in *Ramsingh,. supra* note 25 at 239. As Judge Hays described it '[Movie Star Confidential] is supposedly a comic strip concerning an aging movie actress. It

depicts sexually explicit activity. It also depicts a messenger of the actress paying men to attend at her home and ejaculate on her in her bath tub so she could satisfy her desire to bath [sic] in semen:' *Glad Day, supra* note 4 (O.J.) at 38.

54. *Butler, supra* note 4 at 479.
55. *Ibid.* at 480, quoting *Towne Cinema Theatres Ltd.* v *R.*, [1985] 1 S.C.R. 494 at 584, Wilson J.. *Towne Cinema* was the case that gave a modem imprimatur to the 'community standards of tolerance' test, and described its contours.
56. As the Ontario Court of Appeal subsequently did in another case. See *R.* v. *Ronish, supra* note 51.
57. *Supra* note 4.
58. Bushy, *supra* note 33 at 185.
59. *Scythes, supra* note 4 (O.J.) at 3; Trish Thomas, 'Wunna My Fantasies', (1991) VII: IV *Bad Attitude* 25.
60. *Scythes, ibid.*
61. See *supra* notes 47–53 and accompanying text.
62. *Scythes, supra* note 4 (O.J.) at 5,7.
63. This belief is based on the last paragraph of the opinion:

> Madonna's book called *Sex* was offered to show the public tolerance to this type of material. One photograph of particular relevance shows a so-called playful rape scene in a school gymnasium. I received very little information on the distribution of this book. I am told however that few were available and were sold immediately. I find the sample too small to be a reliable indication of the public's reaction to its distribution.

Ibid. at 7. Madonna's book was widely available and became a best-seller in Canada. See 'The New Yorker', *supra* note 28 at 75. (Madonna's book avoided much scrutiny because its publisher sought and obtained 'pre-clearance' from Customs. *ibid* at 76). Even so, why was the scope of distribution even relevant? According to the publisher of *Bad Attitude*, her short-lived distribution in Canada was 'only ever about 50 copies'. Telephone conversation with Jasmine Sterling (15 September 1994). So there are two relevant differences: money talks, and the scene described from Madonna's book was a *heterosexual* 'playful rape'.

64. I can find no data on the frequency of post-*Butler* prosecutions of 'main-stream' male-on-female materials as opposed to prosecutions of lesbian/gay materials, though the latter surely get more press. But see *supra* note 35. In the major post-*Butler* decision involving prosecution of mainstream pornographic materials, the Ontario Court of Appeal found six out of 31 representations to be obscene, while remanding others for new trial. *R.* v. *Ronish, supra* note 51 (reviewing five consolidated appeals). Among the materials found obscene were three videos: 'Bung Ho Babes' (depicting male prison warden ordering female prisoners to undress, and one of them to spank another), *ibid.* at 85; 'Made in Hollywood' (depicting male battering of a woman during intercourse), *ibid.* at 86; and 'Dr. Butts' (depicting pain inflicted on woman during anal rape). *Ibid.* Other materials found obscene were undifferentiated videos taken from a satellite dish and shown in a bar. Included scenes were of necrophilic sex with a woman in a coffin and a male biting a woman's vagina. *Ibid.* at 86–97. In the same opinion, a portrayal of a man spanking a woman

was affirmed to be 'minor or minimal', hence, not obscene. *Ibid.* at 84, 90–93. It wasn't Madonna, was it?

65. *Butler, supra* note at 482. Compare in this regard, the US test for obscenity:

> (a) whether 'the average person, applying contemporary community standards' would find that the work, taken as a whole, appeals to the prurient interest . . . (b) whether the work depicts or describes, in a patently offensive way, sexual conduct specifically defined by the applicable state law and (c) whether the work, taken as a whole, *lacks serious literary, artistic, political, or scientific value.*

 Millers v. *California*, 413 U.S. 15, 24 (1973) (emphasis added). Even if the US standard was not largely situated in a moral regime ('prurient interest', 'patently offensive way'), the third prong at the *Miller* test, almost always absolves materials alleged to be obscene.

66. In the decision invalidating the MacKinnon/Dworkin ordinance as enacted in Indianapolis, Indiana, the United States Court of Appeals expressly recognized the political value of pornography. Having 'accepted the premises of the legislation' (i.e. that pornography causes harm to women), Judge Easterbrook went on to say that, 'this simply demonstrates the power of pornography as speech.' *American Booksellers Ass'n* v. *Hudnut*, 771 F. 2d 323, 329 (7th Cir. 1985), *aff'd mem.* 475 U.S. 1001(1986).
67. *New York* v. *Ferber*, 458 U.S. 747, 761 (1982), quoting Memorandum of Assemblyman Lasher in Support of [the New York state child pornography statute]. The holding of *Ferber* was that, for purposes of criminalizing the production and distribution of *child* pornography, the states may define what constitutes child pornography without being limited to the test for (adult) obscenity required by *Miller* v. *California*, *supra* note 65. *Ferber* at 756.
68. Pat Califia, *Doc and Fluff: A Dystopian Tale of a Girl and her Biker* (Boston: Alyson Publications, 1990).
69. *Ibid.* at 45–52.
70. *Ibid.* at 91–94.
71. In cross-examination, Counsel for the Crown also focused largely on the rape scene in *Doc and Fluff*, which really was necessary to the treatment of Califia's theme (not unlike the gang-rape scene in the 1991 movie 'The Accused'), rather than focusing on the other violent, S/M scenes which were largely gratuitous.
72. My testimony otherwise focused largely on the arbitrariness of Customs' practice. *Doc and Fluff* had been prohibited by Customs from entering Canada (at least initially; I do not know whether it is now available). I compared it to another book which was (at least initially) prohibited: Karen Barber (ed.), *Bushfire: Stories of Lesbian Desire* (Boston: Lace Publications, 1991). This collection of 16 short stories, though occasionally sexually explicit, is highly romanticized and non-controversial. I surmise it was prohibited because of one paragraph in a short story by Molly Martin entitled 'The Helper', wherein the narrator's sexual partner inserts a finger into the narrator's anus. The narrator states that she is 'shocked', as she had 'never had a lover put a finger in my ass'. *Ibid.* at 59. After some Customs official spent a lot of time finding this passage, it would have technically fallen within that provision of the

Customs Memorandum (since rescinded) which prohibited importation of depictions of anal penetration. See *supra* note 34.

73. Thanks to Sheila McIntyre for this formulation.

74. Through the Supreme Court has not found gays and lesbians to enjoy protection under s.15 of the *Charter*, at least four lower courts have done so. *Douglas* v. *Canada* (1992), 98 DLR (4th) 129 (F.C.A.) (invalidating Armed Forces' release of serviceperson for homosexuality); *Knodel* v. *British Columbia* (*Medical Services Commission*) (1991), 66 D.L.R. (4th) 444 (B.C.S.C) (including same-sex partner within Medical Services Act (B.C.) definition of 'spouse'); *Brown* v. *British Columbia* (*Minister of Health*) (1990), 66 D.L.R. (4th) 444 (though s.15 precludes discrimination on basis of sexual orientation, it does not require the province to fund AZT treatments); *Veysey* v. *Canada* (*Commissioner of the Correctional Services*), (1989), 39 Admin L.R. 161, varied (1990), 43 Admin L.R. 316 (prison officials must consider allowing same-sex partner to participate in family visiting programme), aff'd on other grounds (31 May 1990), Court file A-557–89 (F.C.A.).

75. See, for example, the letters to the editor in (1991) VII: IV *Bad Attitude* 3, discussing 'ongoing controversy within the Leather-S/M-Fetish community about what activities are okay, acceptable S/M activities and what are not acceptable'.

76. This perception is powerfully reinforced by the thousands of 'fake' representations of lesbians in mainstream pornography, literature, and popular media:

> The fantasy which probably characterizes male thoughts on the lesbian question is the one which sees lesbians as super-whores, sex fiends who need to molest, humiliate or even torture a defenceless sexual object, namely another woman. The sexual object is invariably imagined as 'not a real lesbian . . .' When the [aggressive lesbians] get their just desserts by committing suicide or . . . being killed . . . the public is expected to be relieved that the sweet young female in question can now become the property of a man.

Mariana Valverde, *Sex, Power and Pleasure* (Philadelphia: New Society Publishers, 1987), at 89,95.

16 On Prostitution

Two Broadsheets and a Statement

Movimento Femminista Romano

The following is the text of the leaflet that Turin's Feminist Alternative group has tried to distribute outside the daily La Stampa *where, in recent days, the newspaper has been trying to collect 50,000 signatures for the proposal by popular initiative to reform the Merlin law, alongside the similar proposed bill put forward by 29 Christian Democratic deputies.*

Prostitution exists.

It's not a matter of hiding the prostitutes.

It's a matter of eliminating prostitution.

As women, we are against a society where any man can buy a woman. As women we have never been disturbed by prostitutes. Instead it is their clients who, in public places, accost us 'intentionally', 'continually' and 'unequivocally', offering us their sexual services and preventing us from walking through the streets in peace. Will 50,000 signatures really be enough to ensure that women are no longer bothered when they go out at night? Is it not perhaps the first step towards reopening brothels? Let us not forget that in Turin prostitution brings in 150 billion lire a year. Will you sign? Then you agree that prostitution should continue to exist but behind closed doors. Your signature would be better used supporting a campaign for courses of sex education in all schools, for the establishment of family planning clinics in all quarters of the city, for making abortion available and free to all women.

The Roman Feminist Movement shares the Feminist Alternative group's initiative and invites women to meet at 9 p.m. on Wednesday

Movimento Femminista Romano, 'On Prostitution: Two Broadsheets and a Statement, from *Italian Feminist Thought*, ed. Paola Bono and Sandra Kemp (Blackwell, 1991), 64–9. Every attempt has been made to obtain permission to reproduce this article. Please contact Oxford University Press with queries.

3rd January 1973 at the movement's base in Via Pompeo Magno no. 94 (Prati), tel. 386503, in order to discuss the possibility of opposing the proposals for the reform of the Merlin law.

(Only women are invited to attend)

Let's save morality. Let's preserve children from scandal. Let's protect public health and women's dignity. Under these banners Christian Democratic deputies, supported by a campaign led by the Turin newspaper *La Stampa* to collect 50,000 signatures for an analogous bill by popular initiative, have presented a bill to the chamber. This bill, with the pretext of attacking prostitution, actually leads to the limitation of personal freedom and freedom of movement for all us women. In fact every woman who finds herself on the street, especially at night, will be subjected to a personal evaluation by those (that is, the police) in charge of enforcing its norms. They will be able to decide at their own discretion whether or not they are dealing with a prostitute. And this suspicion, with a police warrant, could lead to an arrest of up to ninety-six hours with no means of defence.

As regards prostitution itself, it is significant the way yet again an attempt is being made to lay all the weight and moral blame on the woman rather than on the clients who allow themselves to pay a human being to gratify their own sexual pleasures.

Prostitution is a product of the patriarchal society, which invented the double standard, and in particular of the patriarchal-capitalist society that excludes women from the work market, pushes them into consumerism and forces them to various forms of prostitution in order to survive.

Prostitution is a male problem. If the 'sad spectacle of accosting', the invitation to 'sexual intercourse, and to illicit trading of the body'. exists, then it is offered by men who attempt to accost, invite and offend any woman who happens to be passing by in the street. And for the umpteenth time we women are forced to hide in the ghettos of our houses.

Do they wish to apply repressive laws? In that case let them start by stopping men who molest and hassle women. They want sanitary control on venereal diseases? Every car that slows down near a woman is a threat. Enough false moralism!

This letter has been sent to various newspapers; if they choose to publish it, they should do so in its entirety.

What follows was read out on 25.2.73 during the meeting convened by the Roman Feminist Movement in the Sala Belloch on 'feminine prostitution in Italy'.

The Roman Feminist Movement, following the presentation:

1 of the proposal of law for the revision of the present Merlin law by 29 Christian Democrat deputies
2 of the proposal of law by popular initiative promoted by the Turin daily *La Stampa*

believes it is important to attempt to bring together all the women's groups interested in the problem in order to discuss not only the negative implications of the eventual approval of the above laws, but the problems of prostitution in general. As feminists we believe the Merlin law is positive in as much as it does not regulate and therefore does not punish prostitution, but tends to eliminate the exploitation of those who actually practise prostitution. It is because of this law that since 1958 prostitution has no longer been an offence in Italy even if, as we will see, prostitutes do not enjoy the same rights as other citizens.

The Merlin law, therefore, does not regulate prostitution but sanctions the abolition of brothels, punishes the instigation of or profit from prostitution, and prohibits the compilation of lists either by the police or by the health authorities.

The only offence that can at present be committed by anyone practising prostitution, according to the Merlin law, is the offence of 'inviting anyone to libertinism in a scandalous or molesting manner'. For this offence not only can the woman be punished but also whoever follows her in a car in a troublesome way, whoever importunes another person and offers sexual services in a molesting manner: in other words a large part of the male population could be punished.

We believe that it is important that a law should exist which, in principle, serves to catch indiscriminately whoever, man or woman, invites anyone to libertinism with harassment, and that it should not place the responsibility solely on whoever practises prostitution. For this offence the present law provides, however, not for preventative arrest but for denouncement to a judge who can inflict detention or enforce a fine. It is precisely the 'liberality' of this article that has drawn the fury of the counter-reforming crusaders of the Christian Democrats and the daily *La Stampa*.

In both proposals of law the penalties are made harder and can be applied only to whoever practises prostitution, even if not in a scandalous or troublesome manner.

In the projected laws neither the accoster nor the client can be punished, because they say the act of accosting must be continuous and unequivocal. In order to be able to talk of a continuous offence it is obvious that the persons in question should be under control; in other words, the existence of lists drawn up by the police, which we believe were never destroyed, would be legalized.

The repression of prostitution on the streets is not, however, to be considered an aim in itself, the idea of only a few puritans: it is part of a much wider plan for the control of the whole population, even if as usual women will be the first to suffer.

With the ominous provision of the establishment of a police warrant that would enable any policeman to arrest for up to ninety-six hours any person he suspected of intending to commit an offence (and in our case of intending to accost) one can say without exaggerating that it would become dangerous for any one of us women to go out at night without a man.

In contrast to the Merlin law, which provides for detention only in cases of the re-establishment of brothels and not in cases of prostitution by one person in their own house, the new proposals for law would lead, because of the possibility of denouncement by others within the building, to the creation of ghetto areas reserved for prostitution, such as already exist in other countries.

Both proposals would furthermore re-enforce the sanitary listing of persons practising prostitution: this would be justified by the alarming increase in venereal diseases. We believe that the spread of venereal diseases in Italy is favoured not by prostitution but by the aura of shame and ignorance that has always accompanied such diseases: a situation aggravated by article 554 of the fascist penal code to defend the health of the Italian race. This article, which no parliament, in 27 years of 'democracy', has proposed annulling, allows for penalties of imprisonment for up to three years for anyone who, aware of being a carrier, spreads a venereal disease. The fear of such a penalty inflicts on anyone, but especially the young, psychological conditions that lead to hiding a disease that the law believes is an offence, thereby making medical intervention more difficult. It is discriminating to impose only on women prostitutes certain health passes when this disease is contracted by men as well as by women. It is clear that in Italy it is the clients of prostitution, that is to say a majority of the male population, who spread venereal disease.

It is otherwise impossible to understand how women in brothels could be infected, if not by those visiting from outside, considering that the women were found to be healthy on entering the houses.

Therefore if a health pass is to be issued let it be issued for the whole population. But this will certainly never be proposed!

For these reasons we consider as positive the Merlin law, which in 1958 represented an attempt to overcome the patriarchal law which deprives women of the possibility of managing their own bodies. We do, however, denounce the lack of correct application of the law, because it is never interpreted in the spirit with which Senator Merlin proposed it; that is, trying to make it easier for anyone who wanted to abandon prostitution to do so.

From the little evidence collected, it seems that this very law is used to perpetuate prostitution as it serves this society. The cases brought against keepers of brothels and profiteers are very few. Even when a woman denounces an exploiter the case is bogged down or proceeds very slowly. Every time a brothel is discovered the press carries only the names and surnames of the women involved, but never those of the clients caught in the act. Most women prostitutes tell us they cannot obtain a driving licence because they do not have a certificate of 'good conduct'. They cannot set up any business venture for five years after giving up prostitution. This necessitates accumulating millions of lire on which they must live for five years, which is almost impossible, as the violence these women suffer from their clients imposes on many the necessity of having a protector, who then appropriates a large part of their takings.

These women are, however, 'known' by the police, and their reinstatement into business is extremely difficult if not impossible in a society which virtually precludes these women from external work and which needs prostitution as a release valve for violence.

Anna, Matilde, Giuseppina, Paola

MALE SEXUALITY—PERVERSION *MOVIMENTO FEMMINISTA ROMANO*, 1976

Patriarchal society is based on authoritarian-exploitative relationships, and its sexuality is sadomasochistic. The values of power, of the domination of man over the other, are reflected in sexuality, where historically woman is given to man for his use. Sexual language also incorporated this concept: it is not by chance that one says that man 'takes' woman and that she 'gives herself' to him, or that man 'possesses' woman.

The idea of woman as man's property is fundamental to her oppression and she is often the only possession that dominant men allow exploited men to keep.

The very expression 'proletarian class' means 'he who possesses issue', and it goes without saying that it also means 'he who possesses the means, namely the woman, to produce issue'.

In other words woman is given to the (exploited) man as compensation for his lack of possessions.

Furthermore, man's frustrations as subordinate in a power-relationship is eased by the possibility of turning himself from oppressed into oppressor.

The transformation of sexuality into a sadomasochistic model of power and submission means that effectively what in the male world is defined as sexuality is none other than perversion.

Male frigidity, that is to say the impossibility of expressing true sexuality, is fundamental to this perversion. Man tries to conceal this frigidity behind a behaviour that is defined as 'virile' and 'active' and which in reality is an ideological concept for mystifying violence.

In patriarchal society virility is the same as violence.

The symbol of virility, *the erect phallus*, is therefore the symbol of violence.

But to the extent that virility equals violence it is not a vital force but only a cover for the real frigidity. The erection of the penis is not a sign of sexual vitality, but only a conditional reflex.

Man, while he seeks to hide his own frigidity, tries to force onto the woman an open and accepted frigidity. Woman must be the inert and passive object that, when moulded and manipulated by violence, will give the frigid man an illusion of vigour

This leads to the total oppression of woman's sexuality and of her own identity.

Overwhelming woman's sexuality means crushing her vitality, her creativity, creating in her a masochism that makes her an object to be exploited more easily.

True sexuality is the spontaneous reaction to stimuli, whether psychological or physiological, that come together to obtain sexual pleasure, and it is also the awareness of the whole body as a source of sexual creativity. Spontaneity and the ability to control pleasure, which are indispensable for this creativity, cannot exist in patriarchal society, where they are repressed so that the sexual urge can be channelled into a perversion based on violence, fear and frigidity.

We denounce as the latest form of woman's oppression the idea of a 'sexual revolution' where woman is forced to go from being one man's object to being everybody's object, and where sadomasochistic pornography in films, in magazines, in all the forms of mass media that brutalize and violate woman, is bandied about as a triumph of sexual liberty.

This is freedom for the woman in the same way as the Nazis interpreted freedom when they wrote on the doors of Auschwitz 'work is freedom'.

The discovery that sexual oppression is the mainstay of male power, thus one which renders women different from any other oppressed group, was only possible when we began to free ourselves from all present structures and ideologies.

Part III. An Historical and Cultural Analysis of Sexuality, Imperialism, and Modernity

17 Obscenity and the Origins of Modernity, 1500–1800

Lynn Hunt

PORNOGRAPHY HAS A HISTORY

Pornography still provokes intense debate, but in Western countries it is now generally available to adult consumers and scholars alike. When you make your way to the Reserve Room of the Bibliothèque Nationale in Paris, for instance, there are only a few reminders of the secrecy formerly shrouding the famous Collection de l'Enfer. As late as 1992 you still had to fill out a form explaining your 'precise reason for request'. The asterisk on the front of the form referred you to the back where it said, 'general or vague terms ("scientific research," "documentation," "personal research") will not be accepted.' When you read those words of warning it is hard not to think of prim, worried librarians trying to keep dirty books out of the hands of the wrong people; most likely aging men in fraying suit jackets who would occupy their seats in search of something other than scholarship. It is a measure of the changing times that no one ever questions your responses any more.

The very existence of the Collection de l'Enfer or its English counterpart, the Private Case of the British Library, gives a sense of definition and clarity to pornography that it has not always had. Pornography did not constitute a wholly separate and distinct category of written or visual representation before the early nineteenth century. If we take pornography to be the explicit depiction of sexual organs and sexual practices with the aim of arousing sexual feelings, then

Lynn Hunt, from 'Obscenity and the Origins of Modernity, 1550–1800', edited extract from *The Invention of Pornography*, ed. Lynn Hunt (Zone Books, 1993), 9-18, 24–5, reprinted by permission of the author and the publisher.

pornography was almost always an adjunct to something else until the middle or end of the eighteenth century. In early modern Europe, that is, between 1500 and 1800, pornography was most often a vehicle for using the shock of sex to criticize religious and political authorities. Pornography nevertheless slowly emerged as a distinct category in the centuries between the Renaissance and the French Revolution thanks, in part, to the spread of print culture itself. Pornography developed out of the messy, two-way, push and pull between the intention of authors, artists and engravers to test the boundaries of the 'decent' and the aim of the ecclesiastical and secular police to regulate it.

Although desire, sensuality, eroticism and even the explicit depiction of sexual organs can be found in many, if not all, times and places, pornography as a legal and artistic category seems to be an especially Western idea with a specific chronology and geography. As a term in the modern sense, pornography came into widespread use only in the nineteenth century. For some commentators, consequently, the late eighteenth and early nineteenth centuries were critical in the development of a modern notion of pornography. But the main lines of the modern pornographic tradition and its censorship can be traced back to sixteenth-century Italy and seventeenth- and eighteenth-century France and England (albeit with important antecedents in ancient Greece and Rome). Thus, the essays that follow shall focus on this time period and these places.

Pornography came into existence, both as a literary and visual practice and as a category of understanding, at the same time as—and concomitantly with—the long-term emergence of Western modernity. It has links to most of the major moments in that emergence: the Renaissance, the Scientific Revolution, the Enlightenment and the French Revolution. Writers and engravers of pornography came out of the demimonde of heretics, freethinkers and libertines who made up the underside of those formative Western developments. For this reason, a historical perspective is crucial to understanding the place and function of pornography in modern culture. Pornography was not a given; it was defined over time and by the conflicts between writers, artists and engravers on the one side and spies, policemen, clergymen and state officials on the other. Its political and cultural meanings cannot be separated from its emergence as a category of thinking, representation and regulation.[1]

Early modern pornography reveals some of the most important nascent characteristics of modern culture. It was linked to freethinking and heresy, to science and natural philosophy, and to attacks on absolutist political authority. It was especially revealing about the gender differentiations being developed within the culture of modernity. Although no judgment is offered here on the value of modern pornography, understanding its history is an essential element in understanding the current debates.

The need for a historical perspective was recognized in the 1986 Meese Commission report on pornography, which complained that 'the history of pornography still remains to be written.'[2] The 1,960-page final report included only sixteen pages on the history of pornography in all times and all places (that is, less than one percent of the total report) and another forty-nine pages on the history of the regulation of pornography. This disproportion between the history of the practice and the history of its regulation is significant, since pornography has always been defined in part by the efforts undertaken to regulate it.

The Commission's brief historical overview was, however, surprisingly good. It argued that the control of written and printed works in Europe from medieval times through the seventeenth century was undertaken primarily in the name of religion and politics, rather than in the name of decency, and it showed that modern obscenity laws only took shape in the early nineteenth century. The first conviction in the United States for the common law crime of obscene libel, for instance, took place in 1815 in Pennsylvania, in the case of *Commonwealth* v. *Sharpless.* As the Meese Commission report shows, while regulation of pornography was not invented in modern times, regulation in the early nineteenth century marked a clear departure from earlier concerns.[3]

In *The Secret Museum*, Walter Kendrick traced the origins of modern attitudes toward pornography with more precision. Kendrick attributed the invention of pornography to the conjunction of two very different events at the end of the eighteenth and during the early decades of the nineteenth century: the creation of 'secret museums' for objects classified as pornographic and the growing volume of writing about prostitution. Kendrick situated the secret museum (whether in the form of locked rooms or uncataloged holdings) in the long-term context of the careful regulation of the consumption of the obscene so as to exclude the lower classes and women. With the rise of literacy and the spread of education, expurgation of the classics was required; this practice, insofar as English-language books are concerned, began in the early eighteenth century, flourished throughout the nineteenth, and came to an abrupt though incomplete end at the time of World War I. Thus, the prospect of the promiscuity of representations of the obscene—'when it began to seem possible that anything at all might be shown to anybody'[4]—engendered the desire for barriers, for catalogs, for new classifications and hygienic censoring.

In other words, pornography as a regulatory category was invented in response to the perceived menace of the democratization of culture. As the Meese Commission itself noted, albeit with a somewhat loose sense of chronology and a penchant for under statement, 'until the last several hundred years, almost all written, drawn, or printed material was restricted largely to a small segment of the population that undoubtedly constituted the social elite'.[5] It was only when print culture opened the possibility of the masses gaining access to writing and pictures that pornography began to emerge as a separate genre of representation.

As Kendrick argued, the concept of pornography was historically shaped, and its development as a category was always one of conflict and change. Pornography was the name for a cultural battle zone: '"pornography" names an argument, not a thing.' Obscenity has existed just as long as the distinction between private and public behavior, yet around the middle of the nineteenth century, according to Kendrick, something changed in the balance between obscenity and decency, private and public, and pornography emerged as a distinct governmental concern.[6]

The middle of the nineteenth century was certainly crucial in linguistic terms. The word *pornography* appeared for the first time in the *Oxford English Dictionary* in 1857, and most of the English variations on the word (*pornographer* and *pornographic*) date from the middle or the end of the nineteenth century. The words emerged in French a little sooner. According to the *Trésor de la langue française*, *pornographe* surfaced first in Restif de la Bretonne's treatise of 1769 titled *Le Pornographe* to refer to writing about prostitution, and *pornographique, pornographe* and *pornographie* in the sense of obscene writing or images dated from the 1830s and 1840s.[7] The Collection de l'Enfer of the Bibliothèque Nationale was apparently set up in 1836, though the idea had been in the air since the Napoleonic regime and perhaps even earlier.[8] Thus, in the decades just before and just after the French Revolution, the term begins to gain consistency, a fact that is far from accidental.

The earliest modern usage of the term *pornography* that I have been able to find is in Etienne-Gabriel Peignot's *Dictionnaire critique, littéraire et bibliographique des principaux livres condamnés au feu, supprimés ou censurés*, published in Paris in 1806. Peignot was interested in cataloging not only the books but the reasons for censoring them. In his preface, he established three classes of reasons: religious, political and moral. Included in the moral class were those books that disturbed the social order and contravened good morals. This class of suppressed books was further subdivided: books that, though not obscene, were filled with 'bizarre and dangerous opinions', such as Rousseau's *Emile* and the works of Helvétius; immoral books written in prose which 'one calls *sotadique* or pornographic'; and works of the same kind written in verse. Pornography is here clearly associated with immorality and with the need to protect society.[9]

Peignot was trained as a lawyer and worked as a librarian and school inspector. As a consequence, he was no doubt especially alert to the concerns characteristic of modern discussions of pornography: legal regulation, library classification and consideration of the effect on morals. Peignot began his dictionary in ways reminiscent of all the early catalogers of pornography and of much current commentary, that is, with assurances that he recognized the 'delicacy' of his subject: 'I did my best to treat it decorously, that is, in a fashion designed not to shock any opinion but to inspire horror for these debaucheries of the spirit which have justly provoked the severity of the laws.' Yet, again like his successors, he insisted on the need to pursue such investigations rigorously and evenhandedly. Some books have been unjustly censored, he argued, and many writers and booksellers were punished too severely when all that was required was the simple suppression of publication. Peignot was grappling with the problem of print in a supposedly modern society; books should not be suppressed just because religious and political authorities do not like them but rather because they offend some basic shared sense of the social order.[10]

Peignot recognized the contradiction implicit in openly discussing pornographic literature: If you write about the loathsome, don't you give it the very publicity that a good moral order would try to suppress? To get around this problem, Peignot announced that he had cited very few pornographic works even though they were 'unfortunately all too numerous'. He gave two reasons for his reticence: it would be dangerous to make the books known, and few of them had been publicly condemned. The police, he claimed, ordinarily took these books away in secret. He then gave a representative list of the most abhorrent and included several, though not all, of them in his dictionary. Peignot thus placed himself exactly on the crucial battleground identified by Kendrick: on the border between the zones of darkness and light, the secret and the revealed, the hidden and the accessible. Peignot was extending the zone of light by compiling his dictionary even while supposedly condemning certain books to darkness.[11]

From the way Peignot tossed off his list of the most repugnant, immoral books, it is clear that a kind of galaxy of the most explicit pornographic writing was already in place in the minds of connoisseurs at the beginning of the nineteenth century. At the top of Peignot's list of prose works was the *P—des Ch—; Th—ph—*, and the *A—des d—*. Since the author of the first was listed as well as the 'translator' of the last, it is clear that Peignot expected to fool no one by failing to list the full titles: *Histoire de Dom Bougre, portier des Chartreux* (1741), *Thérèse philosophe* (1748) and *L'Académie des dames* (1660). He included in the same category the libertine works of both Fromaget (author of *Le Cousin de Mahomet,* 1742) and Crébillon fils; *Les Bijoux indiscrets, Jacques le fataliste* and *La Religieuse* of Diderot; *Les Liaisons dangereuses* of Laclos; *Le Poëte* (Pierre-Jean-Baptiste Desforges, 1798); and the *Veillées conjugales* and the *Galerie des six femmes* of Desf—(presumably *Galerie des femmes* by Victor-Joseph-Etienne de Jouy, 1799). He listed several works in verse as examples of that genre, including the *Pucelle d'Orléans* of Voltaire (1755), *Chandelle d'Arras* of Dulaurent (1765), the *Ode à Priape* of Piron (1710) and the *Epigrammes* of Jean-Baptiste Rousseau, in circulation since the early eighteenth century (Figure 1).[12]

Peignot reserved his only extensive commentary in the preface for the one work—seized by the police—that 'includes all that the most depraved, cruelest, and most abominable imagination can offer in the way of horror and infamy': *Justine.* His reference to the two editions, to the engravings, and to the initials of the author (M.D.S—) again make clear that Peignot expected many if not most of his readers to be familiar with this work of Sade's. However, Sade does not appear in the dictionary itself, for, as Peignot insists, we should 'penetrate no further into the sewers of literature'.[13]

Thus, by 1806 at the very latest, a French pornographic tradition had been identified. In the main body of his dictionary, however, Peignot listed suppressed books only in alphabetical order, with no distinction made between pornography, heresy, political subversion and philosophic radicalism. Aretino's sonnets (1527) and *L'Ecole des filles* (1655) are listed along with La Mettrie's materialist tract *L'Homme machine* (1748) without much discussion of their differences. If, as Peter Wagner has argued, pornography 'becomes an aim in itself'

FIGURE 1 The Pornographic Author. Frontispiece to *Histoire de Dom B—, portier des Chartreux* (Frankfurt edition, 1748).

sometime after the middle of the eighteenth century, rather than merely an adjunct to other forms of criticism of church and state, the distinction was still not widely understood.[14] Robert Darnton has demonstrated that the French government of the ancien régime prohibited all books that threatened religion, the state or good morals, and all these were indiscriminately labeled 'philosophical books', whether they were politically motivated scandal sheets, metaphysical treatises, anticlerical satires or pornographic stories.[15] By the time of Napoleon's empire, critics such as Peignot were beginning to think of pornography as a separate category of bad books, but the separation was still far from complete.

. . .

Although French works formed the core of the pornographic tradition in the seventeenth and the eighteenth century, the first modern source cited by every expert on pornography—and by many of his would-be successors—is the sixteenth-century Italian writer, Pietro Aretino. Aretino made two contributions to the tradition, one in prose and the other in sonnet form. His *Ragionamenti* (1534–1536) became the prototype of seventeenth-century pornographic prose. In the *Ragionamenti,* Aretino developed the device of realistic and satirical dialogues between an older, experienced woman and a younger, innocent one. This dialogue form had a long life; it completely dominated seventeenth-century pornography in every language, and it still appears, for example, in Sade's *La Philosophie dans le boudoir* (1795), 250 years later. The most influential section of the *Ragionamenti* was the dialogue in the first part, which deals with the lives of whores. Soon, this section alone was widely circulated in Spanish, Latin, German, Dutch, French and English.[16]

Aretino also composed a series of sonnets, known as the *Sonnetti lussuriosi* (listed in Peignot's *Dictionnaire*), to accompany a series of erotic engravings in which the various positions for lovemaking were graphically depicted. The engravings had been published without text in 1524 and suppressed by order of the pope. Aretino's name was quickly associated with the illustrations as well, even though they did not come from his hand, and 'Aretino's postures' became the name commonly given to the entire collection of imitations and variations supposedly drawn from the sixteenth-century original. References to Aretino's postures abound in seventeenth-century English drama, for instance, and especially in works of pornography.[17] When an English translation of *L'Ecole des filles* was advertised in a London newpaper in 1744, the advertisement described the book as adorned with twenty-four curious prints, 'after the Manner of Aratine *[sic]*'.[18]

In the minds of his successors, Aretino stood for the basic pornographic intention. The name *Aretino* represented what Peter Wagner has defined as pornography: 'the written or visual presentation in a realistic form of any genital or sexual behavior with a deliberate violation of existing and widely accepted moral and social taboos.'[19] Aretino seemed to take this role on himself. In a letter of dedication he defended his action as countering hypocrisy and celebrating bodily pleasures:

> I renounce the bad judgment and dirty habit which forbid the eyes to see what pleases them most. . . . It seems to me that the you-know-what given us by nature for the preservation of the species should be worn as a pendant round our necks or as a badge in our caps, since it is the spring that pours out the flood of humanity.[20]

Aretino brought together several crucial elements to form the basis of the pornographic tradition: the explicit representation of sexual activity, the form of the dialogue between women, the discussion of the behavior of prostitutes and the challenge to moral conventions of the day.

In this book's opening essay, Paula Findlen sets Aretino in the context of sixteenth-century Renaissance culture and the creation of a new marketplace for the obscene. Aretino was only one of many authors and engravers who produced forbidden works on the fringes of the new print culture. Images of amorous encounters, which had been previously confined to humanist circles and were often in the form of high art, now circulated in cheap reproductions designed for a more popular audience. Sixteenth-century pornography relied heavily on classical models, including the revival of Roman poems to the god Priapus, which circulated in manuscript form during the fifteenth century. In its reliance on classical themes, pornography in the sixteenth century was not especially innovative. Rather, it was the diffusion through print culture that marked a significant new departure.

Sixteenth-century humanists also wrote a kind of 'academy pornography', designed for limited distribution to an educated elite, in which local politics were dissected in sexual terms. Findlen analyzes one of them, Vignali's *La Cazzaria* (1525–1526), which depicts Sienese factional struggles in terms of competition between Pricks, Cunts, Balls and Asses. Such works provided the prototypes for seventeenth- and eighteenth-century political pornography. In the sixteenth-century versions of pornography, sodomites and prostitutes were already depicted as privileged observers and critics of the established order, thanks to their membership in the 'third sex'. Aretino and his peers, when compared to those who wrote in the pre-sixteenth-century literary forms, can be seen to have inaugurated a literary tradition which was new in two respects: it appealed to a broader audience thanks to the use of printing, and it employed political satire, which would play an increasingly important role in the next two centuries.

Works inspired by Aretino appeared immediately, beginning with the pseudo-Aretine *La Puttana errante* (1531). The next major moment in the establishment of a pornographic tradition came a century later in France, in the late 1650s, with the publication of *L'Ecole des filles* and *L'Académie des dames* (published originally in Latin as *Aloisiae Sigaeae Toletanae Satyra Sotadica de arcanis Amoris et Veneris* ... in 1659 or 1660, Figure 2). The last professed to be a translation, by a Dutch philologist, from a work originally composed in Spanish by a woman, Luisa Sigea. It was, in fact, written by a French lawyer, Nicolas Chorier. This convoluted story shows how the pornographic tradition was almost immediately imagined, both by authors and readers, to be European rather than narrowly national.

The publication of *Lacadémie des dames* in Latin was probably designed to evade prosecution rather than to ensure an international audience, but the internationalization of the tradition can be seen in the diversity of places of publication for such books (Figure 3). Experts disagree, for example, about whether *L'Académie des dames* was first published in Lyon, Grenoble, or the Dutch Republic, the final being a well-established haven for publishers of forbidden books. These books were immediately available in England. Pepys bought his copy of *L'Ecole des filles* in 1668, and another English diarist records knowledge of the Latin edition of *L'Académie des dames* in 1676 (the French edition appeared in 1680). An English translation of *L'Académie des dame* appeared in 1684.[21] Likewise, in the eighteenth century English pornography was quickly translated into French; the French translation of Cleland's book appeared only two years after its English publication.

David Foxon has claimed that 'pornography seems to have been born and grown to maturity in a brief period in the middle of the seventeenth century'.[22] At that time sex became intellectualized, particularly in the two books just cited. One sign of this new experience of sex was the use of what are now called *sex aids*, with the reading of

JOANNIS MEURSII

ELEGANTIÆ

LATINI SERMONIS

SEU

ALOISIA

SIGÆA TOLETANA

De arcanis Amoris & Veneris

Adjunctis Fragmentis quibusdam Eroticis.

PARS PRIMA.

LUGD. BATAVORUM,

EX TYPIS ELZEVIRIANIS.

CIƆ IƆCC LVII.

FIGURE 2 Title page to one of the Latin versions of *L'Académie des dames* (1678).

FIGURE 3 Title page to a nineteenth-century French reprint edition of *L'Académie des dames* (despite its claims to being published in Grenoble, 1680). This engraving may have been added in the nineteenth century.

pornography being a prime example. In the 1660s, imported Italian dildos, as well as condoms, first became available in London.[23] Almost all the themes of later prose pornography were present by 1660: the self-conscious aim of arousing sexual desire in the reader, the juxtaposition of the material truth of sex against the hypocritical conventions of society and the rulings of the church, and, new in the seventeenth century, the cataloging of 'perversions' as so many variations on a self-justified, amoral gratification of the senses (even when some of these perversions were supposedly condemned). These aspects, as well as the emergence of libertinism as a mode of thought and action, were related to the new emphasis on the value of nature and the senses as sources of authority.[24] From the beginning, pornography had close ties to the new science as well as to political criticism.

Because pornography first emerged in the sixteenth century, and developed concomitantly with print culture, it is hardly surprising that its next big step forward in the seventeenth century was closely related to the development of the novel, which was the most important new genre of that culture. The publication of *L'Ecole des filles* and *L'Académie des dames* signaled the displacement of the center of pornographic writing from Italy to France, and this shift occurred just when French novels were increasingly being differentiated from the romance as a genre. Marie-Madeleine Pioche de Lavergne, countess de Lafayette, for example, published her influential novels between 1662 and 1678.

Just how the development of the novel and pornography were related in the seventeenth century is far from clear, however, and it is a topic that bears further investigation. As Joan DeJean shows in her essay, the pornographic originality of *L'Ecole des filles* was exaggerated by contemporaries and later literary historians because it was included in the repression of texts linked to the Fronde (1648–1653), the internal civil war of nobles and magistrates against the crown and its ministers. *L'Ecole des filles* was linked to the novelist Paul Scarron and his wife, Françoise d'Aubigné, the future Madame de Maintenon and mistress of Louis XIV, and to Louis's disgraced minister of finances, Nicolas Fouquet, who had in his possession one of the few surviving copies. DeJean speculates that the authors of *L'Ecole des filles,* whomever they were, were experimenting with various forms of prose fiction at a moment when the novel as a genre was far from fixed or settled. Both *L'Ecole des filles* and *L'Académie des dames* show traces of the effort to combine Aretino's dialogue between women with many of the elements of the emerging novel.

Between the publication of these two works in the middle of the seventeenth century and the next major recasting of pornographic writing in the 1740s, pornography stagnated as a genre.[25] Pornography, however, continued to be published in this period, and much of it was explicitly related to political issues, as is shown in the essay by Rachel Weil on English Restoration political pornography. During the Fronde in France, pornographic pamphlets had attacked the Regent, Queen Mother Anne of Austria, and her presumed lover and adviser, Cardinal Mazarin. Libertine and libelous pamphlets were also published against Queen Christina of Sweden after her conversion to Catholicism in 1654.[26] Despite the continuing flow of pornographic pamphlets, no new major works emerged to join the classics of the tradition.

Then, in the 1740s, pornographic writing took off with the rapid-fire publication of a series of new and influential works: *Histoire de Dom Bougre, portier des Chartreux* (1741); *Le Sopha* by Crébillon fils (published 1742, written 1737); *Les Bijoux indiscrets* by Diderot (1748); *Thérèse philosophe* (1748); and Cleland's *Fanny Hill* (1748–1749), to name only the best-known works. These classics of the genre appeared in a very short period of time, all of them now utilizing the extended novel form rather than the previous Aretinian model of a dialogue between two women. Did pornographers, as some have suggested, have to await the development of the novel in its eighteenth-century form—Richardson's *Pamela* was published in 1740—before they could advance their own prose efforts? And if so, how was the new novelistic form of writing so quickly assimilated into the pornographic tradition?

The link between pornography and the novel in the eighteenth and nineteenth centuries has been commented on by many. Steven Marcus has argued, for example, that 'the growth of pornography is inseparable from and dependent upon the growth of the novel'. Yet his analysis is very general and, therefore, vague. He attributes both pornography and the novel to the 'vast social processes which brought about the modern world': the growth of cities and with them of an audience of literate readers; the development of new kinds of experience, especially privatization; and the splitting off of sexuality from the rest of life in an urban, capitalist, industrial and middle-class world. Pornography, for Marcus, is 'a mad parody' of the new, private experience set up by these social changes.[27]

Such a broad analysis, though not without merit, fails to explain the timing of the major bursts in pornography and especially the differences among countries. If pornography reflects (and reflects upon) the growth of cities, literacy and privatization, then why don't the writers of the Dutch Republic—arguably the most urban, middle-class, literate and privatized country—specialize in the genre? Much early modern pornography was published in the Dutch Republic, but little was written originally in Dutch, as Wijnand W. Mijnhardt's essay on politics and pornography demonstrates. Although Dutch writers produced a few home grown pornographic novels in the last decades of the seventeenth century, sometimes as direct imitations of Aretino, the increased pornographic output the French and English experienced in the 1740s passed by the Dutch almost unnoticed. Instead, as Mijnhardt argues, the Dutch turned away from their previous openness about the public discussion of sexuality, which was so evident in the numerous sexual and erotic manuals published in the late seventeenth century, and removed all sexual references from the public sphere, whether in brothels, paintings or pornographic books.

It hardly seems coincidental that the rise in pornographic publications in the 1740s also marked the beginning of the high period of the Enlightenment as well as a period of general crisis in European society and politics. The year 1748, so rich in pornographic publications, was also the year of publication of Montesquieu's *L'Esprit des lois* and La Mettrie's *L'Homme machine.* Darnton has shown that pornography was often enlisted in the attack on the ancien régime, but he describes such politically motivated pornographic writing as the underside or lowlife of Enlightenment literature.[28]

Others have postulated a closer relationship between pornography and the Enlightenment's stinging criticism of clerical rigidity, police censorship and the narrowness and prejudices of conventional mores. Aram Vartanian argues that eroticism in general played an important, if neglected, role in providing creative energy to the Enlightenment as a movement. His exemplary philosopher, Diderot, wrote pornography (and was imprisoned for it in 1749), and, according to Vartanian, the Enlightenment provided a climate favorable to the progress of 'literary sexology', which began with pornography. He attributes the resurgence of the erotic in literature and painting in the eighteenth century to the Enlightenment's understanding of nature: sexual appetite was natural; repression of sexual appetite was artificial and pointless; and the passions might have a beneficial influence in making humans happy in this world. Sexual enlightenment was consequently a part of the Enlightenment itself.[29]

Margaret C. Jacob's essay on the philosophical and social content of pornography in the seventeenth and eighteenth centuries traces this radical side of the Enlightenment. She shows that pornography was first naturalist and then profoundly materialist in inspiration. Eighteenth-century pornography was Lockeian and La Mettrian in philosophy, and a large part of its shock value rested on its materialist underpinnings. Materialist thinkers such as La Mettrie seemed to be drawn inexorably from their writings on the soul's subordination by physical influences toward efforts to theorize pleasure, as with La Mettrie's own *L'Art de jouir*. Diderot, also a materialist, wrote pornographic novels along with his more conventional, philosophical, yet nonetheless threatening, works. As Diderot remarked in one of his letters, 'There is a bit of testicle at the bottom of our most sublime feelings and our purest tenderness.'[30]

The burst of publication in the 1740s may have been related, in addition, as Jacob suggests, to a more general crisis in the French state caused by the unsuccessful prosecution of the War of Austrian Succession. The war ended in 1748 in a stalemate that carried with it the prospect of continuing decline in influence for the French. Materialist philosophy and pornography were both ways of criticizing the status quo at a time when the status quo was weakening.

By the end of the 1740s, the pornographic tradition was becoming well established and was clearly linked to the novel in form. By then, French publications predominated in the genre, despite the remarkable international influence of *Fanny Hill*. Between the 1740s and the 1790s French pornography turned increasingly political. As criticism of the monarchy grew more strident, pornographic pamphlets attacked the clergy, the court, and, in the case of Louis XV, the king himself.

In the 1790s, the French Revolution let loose another cascade of pornographic pamphlets directly linked to political conflicts and, at the same time, the early modern pornographic tradition culminated in the writings of the Marquis de Sade. Virtually all of the themes of modern pornography were rehearsed by Sade; indeed, he specialized in the cataloging of pornographic effects. Rape, incest, parricide, sacrilege, sodomy and tribadism, pedophilia and all the most horrible forms of torture and murder were associated with sexual arousal in the writings of Sade. No one has ever been able to top Sade because he had, in effect, explored the ultimate logical possibility of pornography: the annihiliation of the body, the very seat of pleasure, in the name of desire. This ultimate reductio ad absurdum of pornography would not have been possible without the prior establishment of a pornographic tradition. By the early nineteenth century, when efforts at regulation for moral purposes expanded dramatically, the police, the writers, the printers and the readers all knew what the models were.

PORNOGRAPHY AS POLITICS AND SOCIAL COMMENTARY

From the days of Aretino in the sixteenth century, pornography was closely linked with political and religious subversion. Aretino decided to write sonnets to accompany obscene engravings when he heard of the arrest of the engraver of the original sixteen postures. The identification between pornography and political subversion could also work in reverse: *L'Ecole des filles* was assumed to be wildly pornographic because it was the subject of a determined political repression. As Rachel Weil argues, however, political pornography was continuous with other forms of political commentary and not always easily separated out as a genre. Charles II's potential tyranny was often represented in sexual terms, but the argument that despotic kings resembled Eastern tyrants could be found in more formal political works as well. The link between debauchery and tyranny or despotism could be found throughout the seventeenth and eighteenth centuries. It culminates in the flood of pamphlets attacking Marie Antoinette and other leading figures of the French court after 1789, which I discuss in my essay on pornography during the French Revolution.

Pornography's relationship to the novel as a form of narration heightened its reputation as an oppositional genre, because the novel itself was under severe attack through the eighteenth century. Jean Marie Goulemot has shown that pornography engaged the same paradoxes of imagination and reality as the novel, and novels were also regularly condemned for their capacity to incite desire. Some pornography, then, is simply a specialized version of the novel; it plays upon the imagination of the reader to create the effect of real sexual activity, all the while, of course, being purely imaginary. But there seems to be an important gender differentiation that Goulemot misses in his analysis: women were thought especially susceptible to the imaginative effects of the novel, while men were usually assumed—rightly or wrongly—to be the primary audience for pornographic writing, at least until the end of the eighteenth century.[31] If pornography is just a subset of the novel, why is it imagined to be so different in its gender audience and effects?

Pornography, like the novel, was often associated with libertinism.[32] Libertinism followed the same trajectory as pornography; under the influence, in part, of the new science, it took shape in the seventeenth century as an upper-class male revolt against conventional morality and religious orthodoxy, and then spread more broadly in the eighteenth century into the artisanal and lower middle-class circles of many Western countries especially England and France. Libertines were imagined to be free thinkers who were open to sexual, and literary, experimentation. By the definition of their adversaries in church and state, libertines were the propagators of and audience for pornography.

Pornographic novelists explored realist techniques of writing which became increasingly important in the eighteenth century. In *La Philosophie dans le boudoir,* for example, Sade parodied the interminable scenes of seduction found in novels such as Richardson's *Pamela.* This truth-telling trope of pornography went back to Aretino. 'Speak plainly,' the prostitute Antonia insists in the *Ragionamenti,* 'and say "fuck," "prick," "cunt" and "ass". . . .' Similarly, in *Histoire de Dom Bougre* a libertine nun explains the true meaning of the expression 'to be in love': 'When one says, the Gentleman . . . is in love with the Lady . . . it is the same thing as saying, the Gentleman . . . saw the Lady . . . the sight of her excited his desire, and he is dying to put his Prick into her Cunt. That's truly what it means.'[33]

In her essay on the obscene word, Lucienne Frappier-Mazur explores the significance of the language of transgression. The obscene word played on the contrast between different social registers of language—crude and elegant, lower and upper class, masculine and feminine—in order to achieve its effect. To enact social transgression and a kind of hyperrealism, obscene language fetishizes certain words related to sex; the obscene word substitutes for the body part in question but, in the process, acquires the status of a fetish. As a consequence, the realism paradoxically devolves into a form of the grotesque, where penises are always huge, vaginas multiply in number and sexual coupling takes place in a kind of frenzy that is hardly 'realistic'. This results in pornography that is imaginary and at times fantastic even though its effects on its readers are very real.

One of the most striking characteristics of early modern pornography is the preponderance of female narrators. Frappier-Mazur emphasizes the structures of voyeurism and eavesdropping that are established by female narrators, which turn the male readers of such works into complicit third parties. Both Margaret C. Jacob and

Kathryn Norberg address the issue of the female narrator, but with a different focus. They emphasize the potential for social and philosophical subversion in female narration. Materialist philosophy, for example, required that women be materially or sexually equivalent to men; otherwise, all bodies in nature would not be equally mechanical. Randolph Trumbach argues in his essay on eighteenth-century England that male sexuality was codified before female sexuality to eliminate the legitimacy of male homosexual relationships, with the result that men were less likely than women to be represented as sexually polymorphous. (Sade's male characters are the exception in this respect rather than the rule.) Thus the issue of the female narrator and her transgression of expected female roles goes to the heart of questions of sexual difference.

In her essay on the pornographic whore, Norberg focuses on the privileged figure of early modern pornographic literature, the prostitute. From Aretino's dialogues onward, the female narrator is often a prostitute by occupation. The pornographic whore, such as Margot (the stocking mender who is the main character of *Margot la ravaudeuse*, 1750), is most often portrayed as independent, determined, financially successful and scornful of the new ideals of female virtue and domesticity. Such texts, written by men, consequently elide the very sexual difference that was increasingly coming into vogue in medical tracts and domestic manuals.

Margot and the other prostitute narrators in the pornographic novel were always astute social observers, and they saw much of the social world because of their unique position. They resemble in many respects the foundlings and bastards who are the staple of the early realist novel. Both the pornographic and the realist novel endeavored to reimagine and represent the social world during the eighteenth century. The pornographic novel in the eighteenth century was a kind of reductio ad absurdum of the realist novel, and, as such, it is immensely revealing of the social concerns of the time. Margot and characters like her are usually born poor and see much of the underside of life, but they also make their way to the opera, to the world of the salons and to the highest levels of church and government, thanks to their profession.

This is not to say, however, that the pornographic novel transparently represented the social. As Stephen Marcus has asserted, the 'governing tendency' of pornography 'is toward the elimination of external or social reality'. In *pornotopia*, Marcus's term for the utopian fantasy implicit in pornography, space and time only measure the repetition of sexual encounters, and bodies are reduced to sexual parts and to the endless possibilities of their variation and combination (a materialist vision if there ever was one). As a result, pornography 'regularly moves toward independence of time, space, history, and even language itself'.[34] In a similar vein, Angela Carter argues that pornography reinforces by its very nature the tendency to think in universals:

> So pornography reinforces the false universals of sexual archetypes because it denies, or doesn't have time for, or can't find room for, or, because its underlying ideology ignores, the social context in which sexual activity takes place . . . Therefore pornography must always have the false simplicity of fable.[35]

The ultimate in this tendency toward erasure of the standard coordinates of time, space and social reality can be found in Sade's underground caverns, forest lairs and solitary castles, all of which are so many versions of the ideal brothel.

Yet pornography also invariably engaged the social, whether in its efforts to give realistic descriptions of characters or in more abstractly coded ways. Carter insists that 'sexual relations between men and women always render explicit the nature of social relations in the society in which they take place and, if described explicitly, will form a critique of those relations, even if that is not and never has been the intention of the pornographer'.[36] In the early modern period, it often was the intention of the pornographer to criticize existing social and sexual relations. Accounts of conversations about whores or between them were perhaps the favorite devices of early modern pornography, and they were frequently used to reveal the hypocrisy of conventional morals. Descriptions of brothels were used to attack leading aristocrats, clergymen, and, in France, even Marie Antoinette. The pornographic pamphlet *Les Bordels de Paris, avec les noms, demeures et prix* . . . (1790), for instance, was devoted to denouncing the queen's own brothel and was filled with detailed descriptions of her orgies with various aristocrats and clergymen. The prostitute, moreover, was the public woman par excellence and hence an essential figure for discussing the roles of women, the supposedly excessive powers of some politically active women and the general commercialization of social relationships.

As Trumbach demonstrates, the social context for the consumption of pornography was most often a masculine one. It was men who sang obscene songs in the street, cited gross verses at male gatherings and socialized at brothels, even though pornographic prints seemed to have been aimed at women and men alike. Male sexuality, paradoxically, is one of the obscure areas in much pornography. Although early modern pornography was written by men for a presumably male audience, it focused almost single-mindedly on the depiction of female sexuality, as if male sexuality were too threatening to contemplate. Implicit in much early modern pornography is the question of sodomy: Were men (except for the Catholic clergy, who were depicted as capable of anything) to be imagined as sexually ambidextrous and polymorphous, that is, like women, or not?

Trumbach explores this question by focusing on the sexual ideology of John Cleland, author of *Fanny Hill*, and his presumed readers. Cleland and others like him were attracted to the religions and sexual representations of ancient Greece, Rome and India. They may have dreamed of inaugurating a new deistic, libertine religion of their own that included homoerotic rituals. A fraternity of this sort was established by Sir Francis Dashwood at Medmenham Abbey in the 1750s, although those who participated, including the notorious John Wilkes, insisted on its heterosexuality. Similar notions were taken up later in the century by Richard Payne Knight, who wrote extensively about the cult of Priapus as an alternative stamped out by the arrival of Christianity. Sodomy seems to be linked in various ways with these cults, and Trumbach suggests that Cleland and Payne Knight might well have been sodomites themselves. From the time of Aretino forward, pornography and sodomy were intertwined in various ways, not least in the minds of the police. Sade's exaltation of sodomy in his works in the 1790s grew out of and reinforced this connection.

A major turning point in the social and political functions of pornography seems to have been reached sometime between the 1790s and the 1830s, depending on the country (earlier in France, later in Britain). Until the end of the 1790s, explicit sexual description almost always had explicitly subversive qualities. At the end of the 1790s, pornography began to lose its political connotations and became instead a commercial, 'hard-core' business. At this point, which Wagner attributes too narrowly to the novels of Restif de la Bretonne and Andrea de Nerciat, 'nothing remains to be said on the ideological level . . . sexual pleasure is the only aim left'.[37]

Obscenity continued to serve political purposes in England until the early 1800s. Iain McCalman has shown, for instance, how 'obscene populism' animated radical printers during the Queen Caroline Affair in the early 1820s, but by the 1830s, he claims, the purpose of sexual arousal had replaced radical populist and libertine elements in underworld publishing. As a consequence, the social character of the audience for pornography was also transformed, or perhaps merely reverted to an older configuration. After the 1820s, pornography for sexual arousal was bought by male aristocrats, professionals and clerks but not by the working classes. Printers of the new pornography left or were chased from radical political circles.[38]

There is less known about parallel developments in France, although their turning point seems to have come earlier, during the revolution of 1789. During the decade of revolution, as I argue in my essay, pornography reached a wider audience in France, both in social terms and in numbers, than it had ever touched under the ancien régime. Kathryn Norberg demonstrates the similar ways in which the image of the whore changed in the 1790s. The whore comes down off her social pedestal and is available to all men; even the pornographic prostitute is democratized. By 1795, perhaps as an ironic result of this democratization, explicitly political pornography began to die a slow death in the country of revolution. Despite some revivals of political pornography at the end of the 1790s, most pornographic works thereafter were, as Wagner argues, entirely devoted to sexual arousal. The police still found these works dangerous, as the determined harassment of Sade shows, but the danger was perceived as moral and social rather than political. The shock of the French Revolution helped galvanize the policing of pornography everywhere in Europe. As a consequence, censorship for exclusively moral reasons got under way just when pornography stopped being social and political criticism.

Thus, pornography has a peculiar, even paradoxical relationship to democracy. In the sixteenth and seventeenth centuries, pornography was written for an elite male audience that was largely urban, aristocratic and libertine in nature. In the eighteenth century, the audience broadened as pornographic themes entered populist discourses, a development given even greater impetus by the French Revolution. But the democratization of pornography was not a straight, one-way street. David Underdown has shown how, during the English Civil War, a royalist newspaper could use sexual slander to attack the revolutionary government, accusing it of being composed of cuckolds and fornicators who allegedly used words like ‘freedom’ and ‘liberty’ as passwords for entering brothels.[39] Similarly, in the first years of the French Revolution of 1789, royalist papers and pamphlets used scatological and sexual insults to attack the new constitutional monarchy and, in particular, its more democratic supporters. Pornography was not a left-wing preserve. Moreover, pornography had much less appeal, it appears, in the Dutch Republic, where there were no kings, no effective courts, no entrenched privileged nobility and no established church. Pornography seems not to have been just a tactic of democratic propaganda, but a variable arm of criticism whose use was shaped by local circumstances.

Pornography developed democratic implications because of its association with print culture, with the new materialist philosophies of science and nature and with political attacks on the powers of the established regimes. If all bodies were interchangeable—a dominant trope in pornographic writing—then social and gender (and perhaps even racial) differences would effectively lose their meaning. Early modern pornographers were not intentionally feminists *avant la lettre*, but their portrayal of women, at least until the 1790s, often valorized female sexual activity and determination much more than did the prevailing medical texts. *Thérèse philosophe*, *Margot la ravaudeuse* and *Julie philosophe* had much more control over their destinies than was apparent in other representations of women during that time.

Yet there was another side to this picture, which became more apparent toward the end of the eighteenth century. In the novels of Sade, determined, libertine women were the minority among the legions of female victims. Women's bodies might be imagined as equally accessible to all men, whether in Restif de la Bretonne's tract, *Le Pornographe*, which advocated the establishment of giant houses of prostitution, or in Sade's proposal of mammoth Temples of Venus in *La Philosophie dans le boudoir*. The point of such establishments was not the liberation of women but the community of women to service men. In this period, ranging from the sixteenth to the eighteenth century, pornography as a structure of literary and visual representation most often offered women's bodies as a focus of male bonding. Men wrote about sex for other male readers. For their own sexual arousal, men read about women having sex with other women or with multiple partners. The new fraternity created by these complex intersections of voyeurism and objectification may have been democratic in the sense of social leveling, but in the end it was almost always a leveling for men.

The male-bonding effect of most pornography no doubt accounted for its total incompatibility with the new ideals of domesticity that were developing in the eighteenth and nineteenth centuries.[40] The ideology of a separate, private sphere for women depended on a reassertion of fundamental male and female sexual (and, therefore, social and political) difference. Pornography, in contrast, always intentionally transgressed the boundaries establishing difference. As Mijnhardt demonstrates in his essay on the Dutch Republic, the Dutch were among the first in Europe to actively celebrate the private and domestic spheres of life, and this may account, in part, for the Dutch rejection of pornography in the eighteenth century. As new biological and moral standards for sexual difference evolved, pornography seemed to become even more exotic and dangerous. It had to be stamped out. Much—though certainly not all—of our modern concern with pornography follows from that conviction.

Notes

1. My understanding of pornography has been inspired in part by Michel Foucault's many works on the historical emergence of the discourses of modern life: as with medicine, madness, the prison and sexuality, pornography should be understood as the product of new forms of regulation and new desires for knowledge. Although Foucault's interest in pornography and especially the Marquis de Sade is apparent in many of his works, he did not devote any sustained attention to this subject. On Sade, see Michel Foucault. *The History of Sexuality:* vol. 1: *An introduction*, trans. Robert Hurley (New York: Random House, 1980), pp. 148–49.
2. U.S. Department of Justice, *Attorney General's; Commission on Pornography, Final Report*, 2 vols. (Washington, DC: 1986), p. 233.
3. The conclusion of the historical section of the Meese Commission report is, nonetheless, disappointingly vague: 'To conclude that inhibition, in some form or another, of public discussion and representations of sexual practices is a totally modern phenomenon is to overstate the case and to misinterpret the evidence from earlier times. But to assume that public discussions and descriptions of sexuality were, prior to 1850, always as inhibited as they were in English speaking countries from 1850 to 1950 is equally mistaken' (Department of Justice, *Attorney General's Commission*, p. 236).
4. Walter Kendrick, *The Secret Museom: Pornography in Modern Culture* (New York: Penguin, 1987), p. 57.
5. Department of Justice, *Attorney General's Commission*, p. 235.
6. Kendrick, *The Secret Museum*, p. 31.
7. *Trésor de la langue française* (Paris: Centre Nationale de la Recherche Scientifique, 1988), vol. 13, pp. 786–87.
8. For a discussion of the relevant literature, see Annie Stora-Lamarre, *L'Enfer de la IIIe République: Censeurs et pornographes*, (*1881–1914*) (Paris: Imago, 1990), pp. 14–15.
9. Etienne-Gabriel Peignot, *Dictionnaire critique, littéraire et bibliographique des principaux livres condamnés au feu, supprimés ou censurés*, 2 vols. (Paris, 1806), vol. 1, p. xij. All translations from the French are mine unless otherwise noted. Peignot used the terms *pornographique* and *sotadique* as synonyms. *Sotodique* comes from the Latin *sotadicus*, which is based on the Greek name of an

obscene poet, Sotades. I am grateful to my colleague Ruth Mazo Karras for help in tracing the meaning of *sotadique*.

10. Ibid., p. vij.
11. Ibid., pp. viij–xij.
12. Full titles (Peignot gave abbreviated titles) and publication information come from *Dictionnaire des oeuvres érotiques: Domaine français* (Paris: Mercure de France, 1971).
13. Peignot, *Dictionnaire*, pp. xxiv–xxv.
14. Peter Wagner, *Eros Revived: Erotica of the Enlightenment in England and America* (London: Secker & Warburg, 1988), p. 6.
15. Robert Darnton, *Edition et sédition: L'Univers de la littérature clandestine au XVIIIe siècle* (Paris: Gallimard, 1991), especially pp. v, 13–16.
16. The essential bibliographic work was undertaken by David Foxon, *Libertine Literature in England, 1660–1745* (New Hyde Park, NY: University Books, 1965), pp. 25–27.
17. My account is taken from Kearney, *A History*, pp. 24–29.
18. Foxon, *Libertine Literature*, p. 3.
19. Wagner, *Eros Revived*, p. 7.
20. Quoted in Foxon, *Libertine Literature*, pp. 19–20. Paula Findlen gives a slightly different translation in her essay, 'Humanism, Politics, and Pornography in Renaissance Italy', in Lynn Hunt (ed.), *The Invention of Pornography* (New York: Zone Books, 1993), pp. 49–108.
21. Kearney, *A History*, pp. 29–52.
22. Foxon, *Libertine Literature*, p. ix. Foxon is an indispensable source for seventeenth-century development.
23. Lawrence Stone, *The Family, Sex, and Marriage in England, 1500–1800*, abridged ed. (New York: Harper & Row, 1977). pp. 333–34.
24. Foxon, *Libertine Literature*, pp. 48–49.
25. Kearney, *A History*, p. 53. No adequate explanation of this stagnation has been offered.
26. Susanna Åkerman, *Queen Christina of Sweden and Her Circle: The Transformation of a Seventeenth-Century Philosophical Libertine* (Leiden: E. J. Brill, 1991), especially appendix 2, 'The Libertine Pamphlets,' pp. 310–15. It is unclear from Åkerman's analysis just how explicit these pamphlets were. My thanks to Paula Findlen for this reference.
27. Steven Marcus, *The Other Victorians: A Study of Sexuality and Pornography in Mid-Nineteenth-Century England* (New York: Basic Books, 1974), p. 282.
28. Robert Darnton, *The Literary Underground of the Old Regime* (Cambridge, Mass.: Harvard University Press, 1982).
29. Aram Vartanian, 'La Mettrie, Diderot, and Sexology in the Enlightenment', in Jean Macary (ed.), *Essays on the Age of Enlightenment in Honor of Ira O. Wade* (Geneva: Librarie Droz, 1977), pp. 347–67.
30. As quoted in R. F. Brissenden, '*La Philosophie dans le boudoir*; or, A Young Lady's Entrance into the World', *Studies in Eighteenth Century Culture* 2 (1972), pp. 113–41, quote p. 124.
31. Jean Marie Goulemot, *Ces Livres qu'on ne lit que d'une main: Lecture et lecteurs de livres pornographiques au XVIIIe siècle* (Aix-en-Provence: Alinéa, 1991). In fact, the gendering of pornography is still up for debate.

32. On libertinism in general, see Péter Nagy, *Libertinage et révolution*, trans. Christiane Grémillon (Paris: Gallimard, 1975), p. 29.
33. As quoted in Robert J. Ellrich, 'Modes of Discourse and the Language of Sexual Reference in Eighteenth-Century French Fiction', in Robert P. Maccubin (ed.), *Unauthorized Sexual Behavior during the Enlightenment*, a special issue of *Eighteenth-Century Life* 9 (May 1985), p. 222.
34. Marcus, *The Other Victorians*, pp. 44–45, 268–71.
35. Angela Carter, *The Sadeian Woman: An Exercise in Cultural History* (New York: Pantheon, 1978), p. 16.
36. Ibid., p. 20.
37. Wagner, *Eros Revived*, p. 214.
38. Iain McCalman, *Radical Underworld: Prophets, Revolutionaries and Pornographers in London, 1795–1840* (Cambridge, UK: Cambridge University Press, 1988), especially pp. 204–321.
39. David Underdown, '*The Man in the Moon*: The Upside Down World in Popular Journalism, 1649–1650', a draft paper kindly lent to me by the author.
40. Lynn Hunt, "The Unstable Boundaries of the French Revolution', and Catherine Hall, 'The Sweet Delights of Home', in Michelle Perrot (ed.). *A History of Private Life:* Vol. 4. *From the Fires of the Revolution to the Great War*, trans. Arthur Goldhammer (Cambridge, Mass.: Harvard University Press, 1990), pp. 13–94.

18 The Colonial Harem

Images of a Suberoticism

Malek Alloula

> (Photography) leads me to distinguish the 'heavy' desire of pornography from the 'light' (good) desire of eroticism.
>
> Roland Barthes, *Camera Lucida*

The figures of the harem are not infinite, whereas the quest for the harem is: it belongs to obsession.

Never has this feature, the obsessive in and of the postcard, been expressed as vehemently and as abundantly—bared so to speak—as in the present series, dedicated to the exhibition of breasts.

We have here the equivalent of an anthology of breasts. And an anthology aims at exhaustive coverage, so the viewer gets to know a large variety of bosoms: first the Beduin, then the Kabyl, then the 'Uled-Nayl, and so on. There emerges from this anthology a sort of half-aesthetic concept: the Moorish bosom, the exclusive property of the exotic postcard, which sets down its canon.

Generally topped off with a smiling or dreamy face, this Moorish bosom, which expresses an obvious invitation, will travel from hand to hand to reach its destination. All along the trajectory, from sender to addressee, it will be offered to view, without any envelope to ensure the intimacy of a private correspondence.[1] Even after its arrival, it will be solicited whenever the *colony and its indiscreet charms* are evoked.

The use of this type of postcard cannot be entirely foreseen: it goes from jocular smuttiness between correspondants ('The lucky bastard! He sure doesn't get bored over there!') to lover's stratagem (the soldier who wants his girlfriend to believe that temptations are numerous) and includes the constitution of comparative 'knowledge' (the

Malek Alloula, 'The Colonial Harem: Images of a Suberoticism', from *The Colonial Harem*, trans. Myrna Godzich and Wlad Godzich (University of Minnesota Press, 1986), reprinted by permission of the author and the publisher.

Moorish bosom compared with the Asian). To these various uses, one must add the periodic report on one's physical and mental health sent to sundry relatives: 'I send you these few lines in order to bring you up on what has been happening to me.'

Given the range of possible uses, and to satisfy somewhat all the tastes of his faithful and extensive clientele, the photographer will operate in all registers: the exhibition of breasts will be carefully considered.

Three variants order this ensemble. First, the 'artistic' variant: it requires that between the breasts and the eyes there be interposed some gossamer fabric that leaves visible the curves of the bosom. Here the photo maintains an ambiguity between modest reserve and whispered beckoning. Flimsily covered by gauze or tulle, and posing in backlight (to ensure the graphism of her form), the model will be shown wearing her jewels to better suggest intimacy, the very intimacy in which the entire 'scene' is bathed and to which the viewer is invited.

The second variant could be characterized as that of *roguish distraction*. Troublesome and shameless, one of the breasts, sometimes both for good measure, takes advantage of an opening in the clothing to peek out and parade its nipple under the nose of the spectator. Still in this variant, it may happen that the weight of the breasts is sufficient to open the bodice and thus to permit a view from above upon a well-endowed bosom. What was only half-suggested in the first variant becomes half-explicit here. The garments and the jewels are still present but only as accessories to the operation of showing off: they are the setting in which the breast is displayed. Incidentally, this variant insists on the *practical* side of the clothing of these ladies. Pieces of cloth held with clasps, bolero jackets unencumbered by buttons, transparent and low-cut bodices—these are the elements of an attire of *permissiveness*, which avoids the brassiere, the high-necked blouse, and other constraining trifles. This suggestive and unstable looseness of appearance becomes a component of pornography, but it matters little to the photographer.

The third variant could be familiarly called that of the *display*. The bust, at last freed from the garments designed only to be removed, offers itself either with arrogance or with submissive humility. Accessories are reduced to the absolute minimum: sometimes a few jewels hang from the neck to the breasts. Most often, the breasts are the only ornament of the model. This variant does have the merit of putting an end to any 'artistic' reverie on the part of the spectator: the evidence speaks for itself. It also brings commentary to a halt.

Scenes and types. Young Moorish woman.

Scenes and types. Moorish woman.

Beduin woman.

Woman from the Far South of the Oran District.

Some features are nonetheless shared by all three variants. To begin with, they are all captioned as if they are innocent family portraits. The word *bust*, so often reiterated, is itself connoted to such an extent by its pictorial referent that it ceases to be, through a sort of prophylaxis, the synonym of *bosom* or of *breasts*. The photographer operates in the vast category of the 'nude', no longer the preserve only of painters and sculptors. From the technical point of view, all the photographs are taken in medium shot. There is only one full-length portrait (p. 385); this exception confirms the rule that the focus be set on the breasts and nowhere else.

Three captions deserve comment by the heavy and licentious complicity they establish, which duplicates soliciting by an invitation of the kind: 'Want to party, honey?' The first of these captions (p. 391) is 'Contemplating'. The card represents a young woman contemplating her breasts as if to orient the viewer's gaze toward what she herself already admires in an almost amorous fashion.[2]

The second caption reads 'The Cracked Jug': (p. 392). The model does hold a jug balanced on her right hand, but the jug is quite undamaged! The pictorial reminiscence meant to be recalled by the card is a wink of collusion for barracks denizens.

As for the third card, which represents a woman, somewhat more mature than the others, her hands clasped behind her head in a gesture designed to uplift her breasts, it is captioned with the same disarming humor: 'Oh! Is it ever hot!' (p. 393).

This series, whose aims and concerns are so obvious, uses particularly attractive models. The great beauty of some of them could lead one to feelings of nostalgia accompanied by a posthumous tribute to the art of the photographer. In fact, such an 'aestheticizing' temptation has not failed to give rise, here and there, to some such undertakings, attempting to capitalize on a few very rare exceptions. The extraordinary portrait on p. 398 or the fantastic surrealism of the postcard on p. 402 might be the figures of such a temptation if we could but forget their end.

It is on 'accomplishments' of this sort that a lucrative business of speculative card collecting has been built and continues to thrive. It is also by means of this type of 'accomplishment' that the occultation of meaning is effected, the meaning of the postcard that is of interest to us here.

Summarily, and in its customarily brutal idiom, the colonial postcard says this: these women, who were reputedly invisible or hidden, and, until now, beyond sight, are henceforth public; for a few pennies,

Moorish woman from Constantine.

Algiers. Moorish woman in housedress.

Algiers. Moorish woman.

Contemplating.

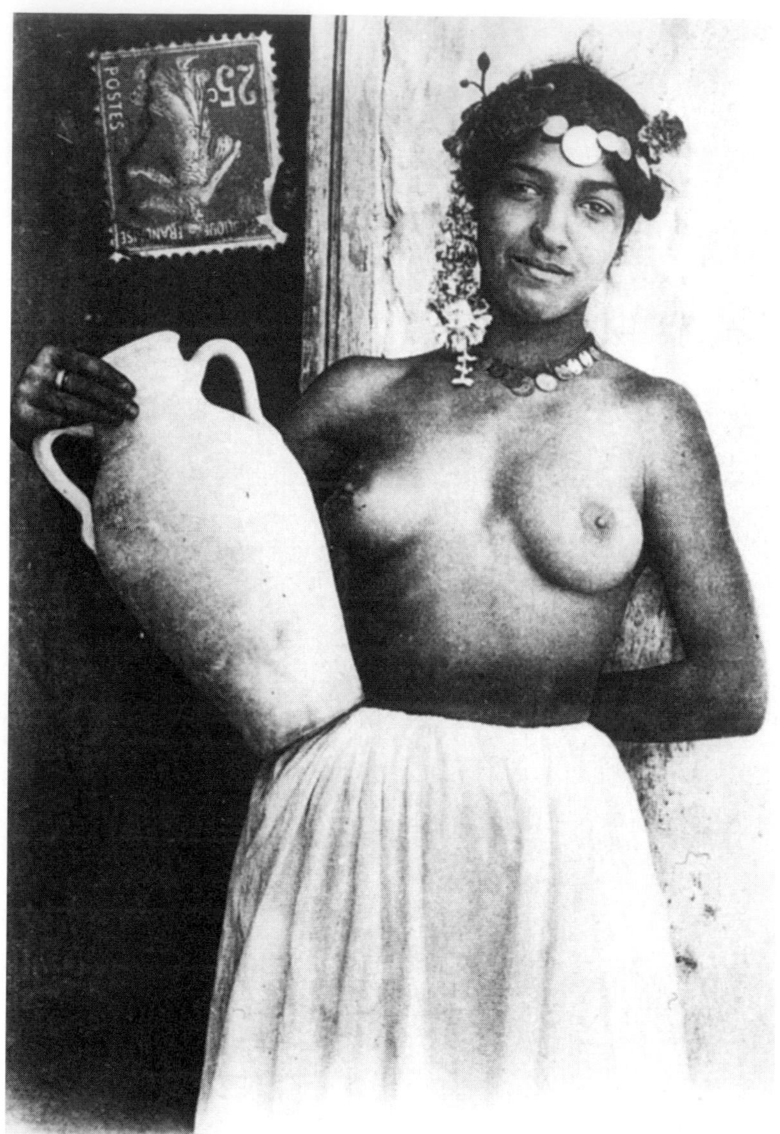

Scenes and types. The Cracked Jug.

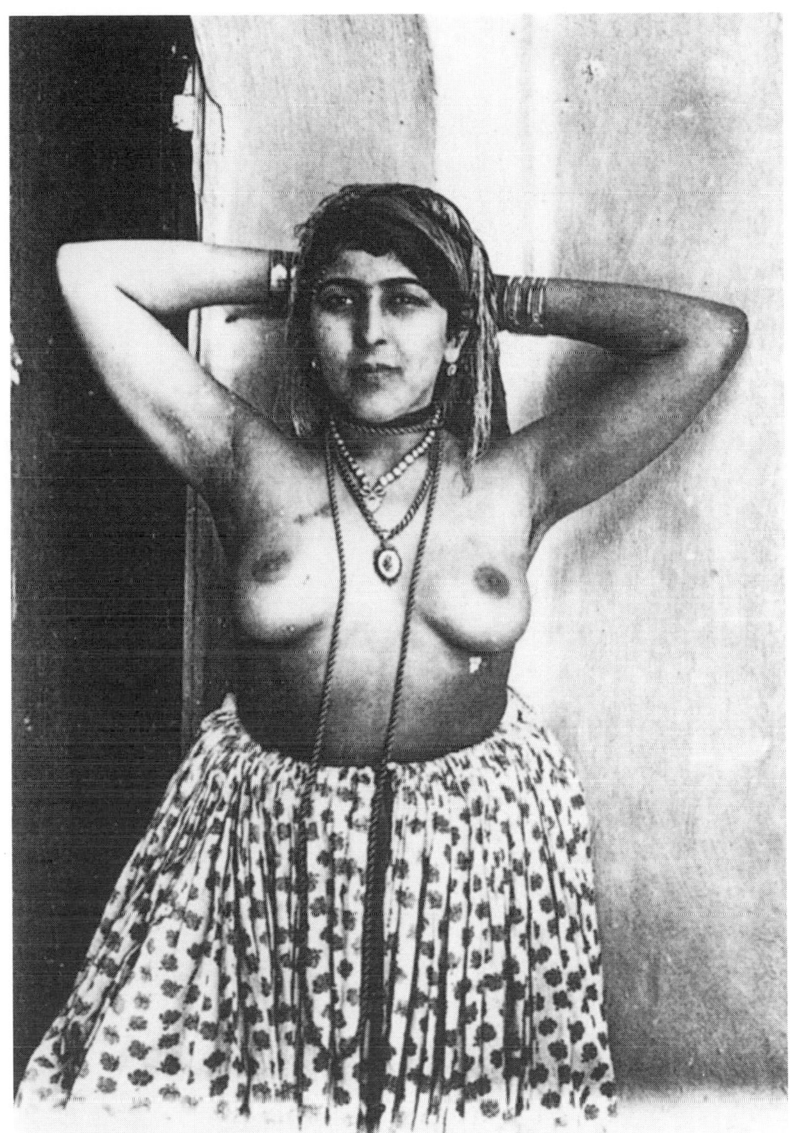

Scenes and types. Oh! Is it ever hot!

Scenes and types. 'Uled-Nayl.

Scenes and types. Moorish woman.

Scenes and types. Young woman from the Algerian South.

and at any time, their intimacy can be broken into and violated. They have nothing to hide anymore, and what they show of their anatomy—'eroticized' by the 'art' of the photographer—is offered in direct invitation. *They offer their body to view as a body-to-be-possessed*, to be assailed with the 'heavy desire' characteristic of pornography.

It is not enough for the colonial postcard to be the rowdy form of this soliciting in public places; it must also be the deceitful expression of symbolic dispossession. The model, in selling the image of her body (dispossession through remuneration), sells at the same time, by virtue of her exemplariness, the image of the body of Algerian women as a whole (extended dispossession).

But the postcard is also one of the illustrated forms of colonialist discourse, its chatty and self-satisfied imagery. In and of itself, it does not speak (it is a photograph of unrelieved flatness, completely summed up by, and in, its surface): *it is spoken*. Its meaning resides elsewhere; it comes from outside itself. It preexists the postcard, but the card gives it a form (the elementary image) that extends it. What it says in its idiom (that of the icon) has already been said by other means, much more brutal and more concrete: the means of operative colonialism.

A ventriloquial art, the postcard, even—and especially—when it pretends to mirror the exotic, is nothing but one of the forms of the aesthetic justification of colonial violence. Such a status of infeudation is constitutive of the postcard.

A form of degraded art, since it is never present in what it represents and, as a result, is without specific finality, the postcard derives from colonial discourse its only, rather shabby, justification. Its constitutive illegitimacy turns it into a hollow and malleable form filled with a discourse that it proceeds to amplify by disseminating it widely but in front of which it effaces itself. Hence its duplicity.

Another version of this duplicity, the discourse that underlies it and forms its armature, is presented as a fragmented discourse through the partial and isolated illustrations that it provides of it. It scrambles its meaning through repetitions and reiterations; it misleads attempts at deciphering it through aesthetic 'accomplishments'. But though it be an atomized rerun of this discourse, it is, in each instance, its total and accomplished expression, its ever renewed reiteration.

When, as here, it exhibits the body of the *algérienne* laid bare, the postcard obeys another injunction of the same colonial discourse: the injunction of the repressed. The postcard authorizes and ensures *the return of this repressed*; it is its ideal mediation since it does not

Scenes and types. Moorish woman.

surround it with any clandestinity; on the contrary, it displays it everywhere and draws all eyes to it.

The postcard is an immense *compensatory undertaking*, an imaginary revenge upon what had been inaccessible until then: the world of Algerian women. Imprinted on the cards, they are the figures of a Parousia: they are reborn, but this time they are available and consenting, welcoming and exciting, submissive and possessed. The postcard can represent them in this way, runs the rationalization, because that which established and maintained the prohibition around them, namely male society, no longer exists. The imaginary abolition of prohibition is only the expression of the absence of this male society, that is, the expression of its defeat, its irremediable rout.

Offered up, body and soul, these *algériennes* are the metaphorical equivalent of trophies, of war booty. *The raiding of women has always been the dream and the obsession of the total victor. These raided bodies are the spoils of victory, the warrior's reward. In this case, the postcard is an enterprise in seduction directed to the troops, the leering wink in the encampments.*

Better yet, displaying, as it does, the traces of this imaginary achievement in the very midst of the society it is 'photographing' (the vanquished society), the postcard is the blustering proclamation of the victory bulletin, the final trumpet flourish.

Raided, possessed but always offered with the bonus of a smile and elegance, these women are phantasmically freed by the postcard from their prison, the harem.[3] The postcard lifts the veil from them and grants them a space (that of the postcard) in which they can romp and frolic to their hearts' desire.

But this space, transparent now, where bodies are taken without any possibility of refusal, where they abandon themselves even more if that is possible, is the *very space of orgy*: the one that the soldier and the colonizer obsessively dream of establishing on the territory of the colony, transformed for the occasion into a bordello where the hetaeras are the women of the conquered, these *algériennes* whom the postcard in its guise as a good and wise madam offers for *selection*.

The harem has become a brothel: it is the last avatar but also the *historical truth* of an Orientalism the presuppositions of which are no longer masked by the postcard. Moreover, it displays them and sends them touring. It underscores their meretricious tendencies. Colonialism is indeed the final morality of Orientalism and exoticism. But it is the morality of a procurer and a bawd.

Scenes and types. Moorish bust.

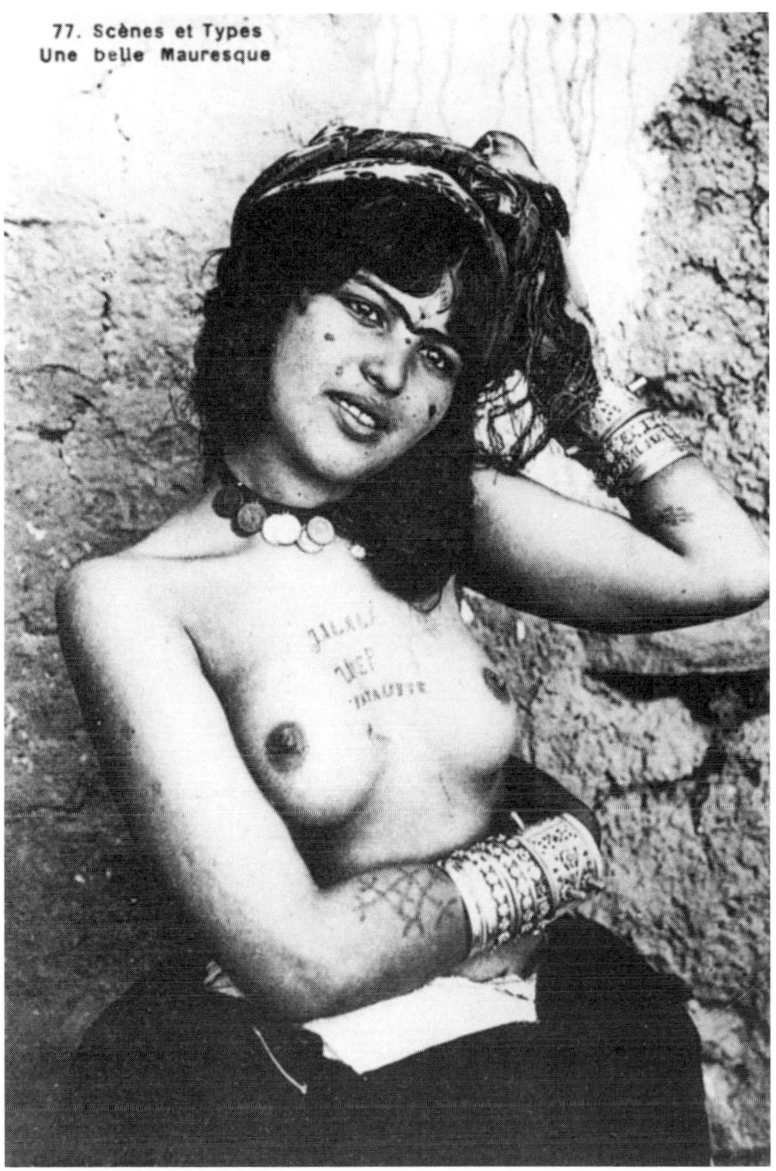

Scenes and types. A beautiful Moorish woman.

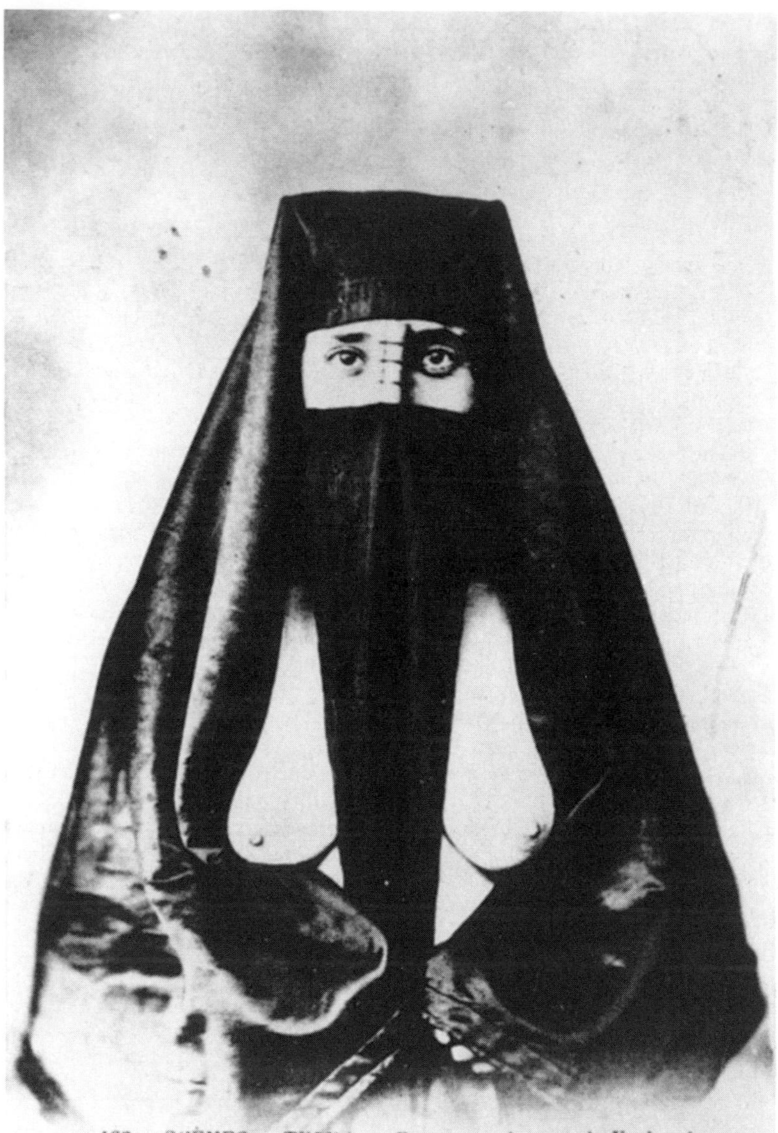

Scenes and types. Arabian woman with the Yachmak.

Voyeurism turns into an obsessive neurosis. The great erotic dream, ebbing from the sad faces of the wage earners in the poses, lets appear, in the flotsam perpetuated by the postcard, another figure: that of *impotence.*

Notes

1. 'The age of Photography corresponds precisely to the explosion of the private into the public, or rather into the creation of a new social value, which is the publicity of the private: the private is consumed as such, publicly.' Roland Barthes, *Camera Lucida,* p. 98. The colonial postcard is the seeing and accomplished form of the 'publicity of the private'. *Only it forgets that it gained access by breaking and entering and perpetrating violence.* The postcard erases the traces of its crime.

   The postcard is also the negation of intimacy. Much could be said here about its exhibitionism as well as about that of its clientele.

   Viewed and visible, the postcard is also seeing. Its two faces complete each other. Its reflecting face (recto) and its blind face (verso) are both spaces of saturation: here the chit-chat, there the redundant signs of representation.

   No envelope can contain a postcard. Hidden, it immediately ceases to be.
2. This redoubling of the gaze is rather surprising in such a mediocre series. Superimposing upon the same surface the narcissism of the model with the voyeurism of the spectator makes them complementary.

   It is strange that in this way an articulation that has nothing obvious about it is apprehended. Such a happenstance of theoretical chance in no way absolves the pornographic aim.
3. A resurgence of this phantasm of liberation occurred on a fine 13 May 1958 when a blunt *géné ralesse* proposed to Algerian women that they seek their liberation *within* France by dropping the veil. She was, of course, surrounded by troopers. She had forgotten, however, that her veil trick had been understood for over half a century, not an altogether negligible period. But colonialism knows no history.

Erotic Autonomy as a Politics of Decolonization

An Anatomy of Feminist and State Practice in the Bahamas Tourist Economy

M. Jacqui Alexander

And the Trees Still Stand

We are here
because you beat back the bush
because you raked rocks and stones
because you pitched scalding tar
to make that road
You uprooted lignum vitae trees
to turn that unchartered road
into a journey with landmarks
And because you replanted
those trees of life
we are here[1]

Marion Bethel wrote this tribute to the women of DAWN[2] and in memory of the women of the suffrage movement who severed the colonial connection between property ownership, respectability, and citizenship. She uses this poem to establish a deliberate link with a particular history of women's political struggle in the Bahamas. Foregrounded in Bethel's incantation is a conscious political move on the part of women in the contemporary women's movement in the Bahamas to choose from particular feminist genealogies, particular histories of struggle especially at a moment when the legacy of British gentility and respectability continues to assert itself and threatens to mold and usurp understandings of the self. According to Bethel, the

M. Jacqui Alexander, from 'Erotic Autonomy as a Politics of Decolonization: An Anatomy of Feminist and State Practice in the Bahamas Tourist Economy', edited extract from *Feminist Genealogies, Colonial Legacies, Democratic Futures*, ed. M. Jacqui Alexander and Chandra Talpade Mohanty (New York: Routledge 1996), reprinted by permission of the author and Taylor and Francis/Routledge Inc.

choice of a legacy is fraught with bush, entangled, and unchartered road; a tumultuous journey out of which a path must be cleared. But she also suggests that the political strategic work of movement-building involves danger, pitching scalding tar, simultaneously deploying tools that might entrap, ensnare, or liberate. These symbols of contradiction and liberation deliberately evoke the ideological dialectic in which the women's movement is now positioned.

These symbols of contradiction are nowhere more transparent than in the Sexual Offences and Domestic Violence Act of 1991. It is a moment of crisis where the state moved on the one hand to criminalize lesbian sex (a move intended to foreclose desire between women) and, on the other, to re-establish primogeniture under the guise of protecting 'other' women against domestic violence. But why was it necessary for the state to shore up its inherited power? Why this reinvention of hetropatriarchy? What, to use Lynda Hart's terms, are the productive breaks in the 'heteropatriarchal symbolic order' that require the state to clothe itself, as it were?[3] I want to argue here that there are certain functions of heteropatriarachy which supercede the sexual or the marking of sexual difference. At this historical moment, for instance, heteropatriarachy is useful in continuing to perpetuate a colonial inheritance (which is why I use the term neocolonial) and in enabling the political and economic processes of recolonization.

By 'recolonization', I mean the attempts by the state, and the global economic interests it represents, to achieve a psychic, sexual, and material usurpation of the self-determination of the Bahamian people. In this regard, heteropatriarchal recolonization operates on at least three levels simultaneously. At the discursive level, it operates through law, which is indispensable in the symbolic and material reproduction and consolidation of heteropatriarchy and in the elaboration of a cathectic structure based primarily in sexual difference. Indeed, law forges a continuity between white imperial heteropatriarchy—the white European heterosexual inheritance—and Black heteropatriarchy.

In the accounts of domestic violence, state managers recodified the texts in terms of class-based symbols of the matrimonial home in order to continue the somewhat orderly patrilineal transfer of private property under the most disorderly and injurious circumstances of wife-beating, rape, sexual abuse, and incest. This literal resituation of the law of the father and the privileges of primogeniture through state domestication of violence not only distanced parliamentary partriarchy from domestic patriarchy but also narrowed the definitions of violence which feminists had linked to the organizing episteme of heteropatriarachy itself.[4] From the official story, we know almost nothing about women's experiences of violence in the home. These were ideologically fragmented in the legal text. Women were made culpable for not reporting these acts (perpetrated against themselves and their daughters) and the burden of criminality was shifted onto them, drawing them more tightly into the state mechanisms of surveillance, positioning them simultaneously as victim and policer, all under the ideological gaze of the heteropatriarchal state as protector.

Psychic recolonization occurs not only through the state's attempts to produce a servile population in tourism but also through it's attempts to repress, or at least to co-opt, a mass-based movement led by feminists. In other words, it seems the law (positioned as order) functions both to veil ruptures within heteropatriarchy and to co-opt mobilization of another kind, that is, the sort of popular feminist political mobilization that made the break visible in the first place. It would be necessary for the state to work, and work hard, to recast the official story, to displace popular memory of the people's struggle with the state's own achievements (in this instance, The Sexual Offences and Domestic Violence Act of 1989). But the fact is that Bahamian feminism, however ambiguously or contradictorily positioned, helped to provoke the political rupture by refusing the state conflation of heterosexuality and citizenship and by implicating the state in a range of violences. In this regard, then, and as a prelude, I would like to locate myself within this narrative.

I write as outsider, neither Bahamian national nor citizen, outside the repressive reach of the Bahamian state, recognizing that the consequences of being disloyal to heterosexuality and, therefore, to the Bahamian state fall differently on my body than on the bodies of those criminalized lesbians in the Bahamas for whom the state has foreclosed (if only temporarily) any public expression of community. Against the state's recent moves at reconsolidating heterosexuality, I write as outlaw in my own country of birth; both states confound lesbian identity with criminality. I write, then, against the 'myth of lesbian impunity'.[5] However, I am not an outsider to the region, for feminist solidarity crosses state-imposed boundaries. And, unlike the Bahamian state, which almost entirely aligns itself with the United States and foreign multinational-capitalist interests, a regional feminist movement, of which Bahamian women are a part, consciously chooses links with the wider Caribbean region and with diasporic women living elsewhere.

I live in the United States of North America as a noncitizen, an alien, as 'immigrant' and 'foreigner', and perennial suspect, at a time when the American state is still engaged in reinventing and redrawing its own borders.[6] As a 'legal' alien, I am subject to being convicted of crimes variously defined as 'lewd, unnatural, lascivious conduct; deviate sexual intercourse; gross indecency; buggery or crimes against nature'.[7] I am simultaneously writing against hegemonic discourses produced within metropolitan countries, and even within oppositional lesbian, gay, and bisexual communities that position the Third World as barbaric (in contrast to American civilized democracy), even in the midst of the daily escalation of racist and homophobic violences (which the state itself legitimates), the sexualization of citizenship from both secular and religious fundamentalisms, and the consolidation of heterosexism and white supremacy through new population control policies which link the terms of 'foreign aid' (read 'imperialism') to the presence of nuclear families.[8] I write out of a desire to contradict prevalent metropolitan impulses that explain the absence of visible lesbian and gay movements (in this instance in the Caribbean) as a defect in political consciousness and maturity, using evidence of publicly organized lesbian and gay movements in the U.S. (as opposed to elsewhere) as evidence of their originary status (in the West) and superior political maturity. These imperial tendencies within oppositional movements (witness the imperialist practices within white gay tourism) have occasioned a marked undertheorization of the imbrication of the imperial and the national, of the colonial within the postmodern.[9] Such theorization might enable a more relational and nuanced understanding of the operation of state processes between neocolonial and advanced-capitalist states around their systematic practices of heterosexualization, for, clearly, both states, although differently positioned, are constantly involved in the reconsolidation of borders and in the repressive deployment of heteropatriarchy in domains other than the sexual.[10]

In what follows, I analyze the state mobilization and reinvention of heteropatriarchy within the Sexual Offences and Domestic Violence Act of 1991. I argue that the state's interest in domestic violence is tangential to a deeper interest: the literal resituation of the law of the father and of primogeniture which preserves in tact the transfer of property even in the event of disruptive violence within heterosexual marriage. Clearly questions arise about whether women's interests can even be fully consonant with those of the state; or even when they ostensibly coincide, as is the case with domestic violence, do women's interests supercede state interests.

DOMESTICATING VIOLENCE OR FEMINISTS PUBLICIZE THE 'PRIVATE'

For many women in the Bahamas, the popular feminist mobilization of the mid-1980s recalled the time three decades earlier when the Women's Suffrage Movement agitated for—and won—the right for all adults to vote. Then, the colonial state had made ownership of property, wealth, whiteness, and masculinity the primary condition of citizenship. In fact, owners of real property could vote more than once if they owned land in more than one constituency.[11] However, universal adult suffrage severed the colonial link between ownership of property, colonial respectability, manliness, and rights of political representation, and conceded the right to vote to the majority of Black Bahamians (both men and women), the bulk of whom were working class. Not only did the contemporary feminist movement reach back and draw upon strategies of political education and mobilization such as public meetings, marches and rallies, petitions and demands for legal protection, but, like its progenitor, it also refused the narrow designation of 'the woman question' and formulated its political vision in terms of mass-based struggle for popular justice. In general, both the movement for universal suffrage of the 1950s and the political platform of violence against women of the 1980s and 1990s were formulated in terms that implicated sexual politics in the very organization of social relations rather than as a peripheral category of significance pertaining only to women.

The recent mobilization based on violence against women functioned as a point of convergence for very many different women's organizations. Among them were: the Women's Desk, contradictorily positioned between the state machinery (as evidence of its international obligations to 'women's rights') and the women's movement; Lodges with an active membership anchored within an African-based spiritual cosmology; The Women's Crisis Center; professional women's organizations, such as ZONTA; church-affiliated women's groups; autonomous feminist groups; and individual women parliamentarians. All of these groups had different, often conflicting theories about the origins of violence and the most effective strategies to combat it.[12] Nonetheless, for the majority of them, violence was defined not so much in terms of a social history of violence but as the cumulative coagulation of sexual 'offences' (such as rape, incest, woman, or wife battery), and sexual harassment perpetrated by men against women. The combined work of these organizations—particularly the Women's Desk, which, through a series of workshops and seminars, had identified 'violent crimes against women' as a major organizational focus—gave collective force to a political agenda that would shape the public conscience for more than a decade.[13]

Prior to 1981, when the Women's Desk was created, the Women's Crisis Center had begun to document an increased incidence of rape and incest. After a major mobilization against rape, it turned its attention to the violence of incestuous familial relations. Most acts of incest were committed against girls under ten years old.[14] Female victims of incest outnumbered male victims by a ratio of almost ten to one. Three- and five-year-old girls were being brought to hospitals where they were diagnosed with spontaneous orgasms and sexually transmitted diseases.[15] Combined cases of physical and sexual abuse were being reported to social services at a rate of three to five daily. All together, these data shattered the myth of the sanctity, safety, and comfort of the matrimonial home. Two 'Take Back the Night' marches had underscored the violence of the streets, where 'strangers' presumably committed at least 25 per cent of all physical and sexual abuse. In addition, a series of radio and television broadcasts sponsored by the Women's Crisis Center challenged the media's self-imposed silence around physical and sexual violence perpetrated against women. When the media did report such cases, they gave the impression that the abuses were idiosyncratically imagined and enforced or simply irrational and, therefore, extreme.[16]

In addition to insisting that incest be removed from the colonial penal code as 'unlawful carnal knowledge' and be treated instead as a separate crime, the first petition against incest, which the Center drafted in March 1988, demanded the following: that the proceedings against such crimes occur in chambers; that the names of survivors not be published; that some safe refuge be provided for girls taken out of homes; that reporting to the police of sexual abuse from *professionals* be mandatory; and that court-mandated psychological evaluation and treatment be provided for the offenders. Besides organizational endorsement from the Church (which sidestepped the question of violence against women to define incest as an infraction against the Divine) and some members of the medical profession (who worried that if incest continued at the current rate, family groups would be extinct by the year 2000), civic groups, lawyers, and 10,000 Bahamians who were not organizationally affiliated agreed that evidence needed to be presented to the state about pervasive sexualized violence; that the state ought to do something that neither private organizations nor individual citizens felt empowered to do. Indeed, the mobilization pointed to something far deeper and far more profoundly disturbing than individual criminality or individual concupiscence would suggest, and gave some official recognition to what Bahamians all knew or suspected to be true: that the normalization of violent sex inside and outside of the family had produced a real existential dilemma. Something had gone terribly amiss in the human organization of things. And in 'a small place', like the Bahamas, such a public, mass-based move at denaturalizing violence could not help but infuse the fabric of daily life with a new, albeit contentious vocabulary on sexual politics. It would challenge inherited definitions of manliness, which had historically been based on ownership—sometimes as owner of property—but more often as owner and guardian of womanhood.[17]

Not all segments of the movement understood violence solely in terms of the combined expression of physical and sexual abuse. Denaturalizing violence meant that it could also be linked to the imperatives of the political economy and exposed in its imbrication with the organizing logic of heteropatriarchy itself. This is what other segments of the movement effected: in particular, DAWN, an autonomous women's organization (not linked to church, party, or state), refused the inherited legal conflation of wife and mother. The members of DAWN argued that the existing legal mandate requiring wives to cohabit with their husbands and, implicitly, to bear offspring did not necessarily compel motherhood.[18] Women, those with 'husbands' and those without, were free to engage in heterosexual sex for pleasure alone, without having to satisfy the patriarchal state's desire for biological paternity or reproduction.[19]

Within the broad framework of reproductive freedom, DAWN politicized the state's recirculation of the modernization discourses of the 1950s, which had marked women's bodies with a recalcitrant, unruly sexuality—as reproducing too much, threatening the 'body politic', and threatening 'development' and progress. In its public mobilizations against the introduction of Norplant and other pharmaceuticals into the Bahamas, DAWN implicated Black masculinity (in this instance, the state, organized medicine, and Planned Parenthood) in the white, imperial forfeiture of women's agency. The state had acquiesced to the unexamined introduction and diffusion of Norplant, an invasive birth-control procedure, without the knowledge or consent of women, enabling and reinforcing the metropolitan ideology of backward Third World women as silent, yet willing receptacles of the technologies of development and modernity.[20] Generally then, DAWN challenged state enforcement of compulsory motherhood and, with it, the overall colonization of citizenship and subjectivity within normative heterosexuality. It expanded the definition of violence against women to include ongoing state economic violence and the 'silent' destruction of 'citizens' and 'noncitizens' alike. In this sense, DAWN aligned itself with the regional feminist movement of the Caribbean, which resisted state attempts to domesticate violence and saw violence against women along a continuum of patriarchal violences expressed in different sites and within different domains. Violence within the domestic sphere, then, did not originate there, but drew strength from, and at times was legitimated by, larger organized state and economic violence, which was itself responsible for the increase in sexual violence within the home.[21]

It was this larger feminist vision of the historicized violences of heteropatriarchy, only partially understood as 'sexual offences', that the state co-opted, narrowed, and brought within its juridicial confines as the Sexual Offences and Domestic Violence Act of 1991.[22] The passage of this legislation became a major symbol of victory for women and for feminists. Incest, sexual harassment, and sexual assault of a spouse (*almost* defined as rape) were introduced as new crimes. Incest of an adult on a minor or dependent carried, upon conviction, the possibility of life imprisonment and a minimum sentence of seven years. However, only the attorney general, not the women who were incested, sexually harassed, or assaulted, could be relied upon to present true testimony to the court. Moreover, these sexual offences were spatially separated in the legal text from domestic violence, contradicting what women had demonstrated: that almost all instances of violent sex were accompanied by violent physical coercion. The popular demand for professionals to report on incest and sexual abuse of minors and dependents was transformed in the legislation to the following:

Any person who a) is the parent or guardian of a minor; b) has the actual custody, charge or control of a minor; c) has the temporary custody, care, charge or control of a minor for a special purpose, as his attendant, employer or teacher, or in any other capacity; or d) is a medical practitioner, or a person registered under the Nurses and Midwives Act, and has performed a medical examination in respect of a minor, and who has reasonable grounds for believing that a sexual offence has been committed in respect of that minor, shall report the grounds for *his* belief to a police officer as soon as reasonably practicable. (emphasis mine)

The penalty for failure to report is a fine of $5,000 or imprisonment for two years, the same penalty for an employer who has sexually harassed his employee.

But precisely because there are these significant disjunctures between what women demanded and what was conceded, precisely because women (and not just *any* person) are drawn into the state's mechanisms of surveillance in ways they had not anticipated, it becomes clear that, in this instance, the state folded its own interests into a disciplinary narrative that it could later claim, (by virtue of its name at least), as evidence of *its* benevolent paternalism. History was being constantly renarrativized in these terms: Women's Crisis Week was 'proclaimed by the (then) Prime Minister Linden Pindling [to be] aimed at increasing public awareness of family violence';[23] 'Only the Bahamas has enacted legislation pertaining to sexual harassment';[24] 'MPs Passed the Sexual Offences Bill to provide greater protection for women on the job. . . . The bill was an important piece of social legislation, particularly sections outlawing sexual harassment on the job and domestic violence.'[25] Parliamentarians invoked a Bahamas residing at the pinnacle of constitutional evolution: 'We happen to have, unlike the British, a written constitution which has embodied in it . . . certain principles with regard to freedom of conscience which protects your rights of privacy.'[26] Clearly, the state's desire to usurp the popular narrative of struggle and convert it into a hegemonic narrative of deliverance, seen *only* as initiated by itself as benign patriarch is paramount. It is crucial that we understand, therefore, the uses to which 'sexual offences' and 'domestic violence' were put and these social and material practices were converted into categories that were deployed by the state to do its own work.

ENSURING THE LAW OF THE FATHER: DOMESTIC VIOLENCE AS PROXY

There was never an organized demand to criminalize lesbianism during the political mobilization for the passage of the Sexual Offences and Domestic Violence Act. The organized feminist demand coalesced around the restraining of violent domestic patriarchy. Behind closed doors, however, state managers sought to keep the erotic within the boundaries of the domestic heterosexual home, disrupted as it was by wife beating, rape, and incest. If husbands now had to rely upon the consent of their wives for sex, if they could no longer resort to physical and psychic violence or coercion in the 'matrimonial' home, if, in other words, domestic patriarchy were in perennial need of restraint, then heterosexuality itself was at risk, and therefore needed to be defended. On no account could it be forfeited. In other words, from the state's vantage point erotic autonomy for women could only be negotiated within the narrow confines of a disrupted heterosexual. Autonomous eroticism could only go so far—it could not leave the confines of the matrimonial bed to inhabit a space that could be entirely oppositional to it, entirely unaccountable to it, or even partially imagined outside of it. Much like colonial master narratives in which masters could not imagine or anticipate their absence (for power cannot predict its own destruction), so, too, heterosexuality remains unable to imagine *its* own absence. The state as surrogate patriarch can distance itself from violent domestic patriarchy only temporarily, in order to appear more progressive than it, for ultimately it comes to the defense of the domestic patriarch in legally recouping the matrimonial bed. And while women and feminist groups may make demands on the state, indoing this historical, homosocial, ultimately homophobic bonding is a formidable task indeed.

One the one hand, women and women's groups, in spite of differences in their ideological and material class base, appear to have derivative access, if not direct access, to the state. In this sense, then, the political economic serviceability of working-class women in tourism is matched by women's serviceability in another domain, for the state can draw upon women's political mobilizations as evidence of its own legitimate and advanced political governance, as evidence of its constitutional, even politically mature evolution, as evidence that democracy is working. Establishment of a woman's desk, a place behind which women can only presumably sit, provides international legitimacy for the state which is seen as adhering to civilized international conventions. The links that these groups have established make it possible for the state to allow only certain women in as symbolic representatives of women's struggles, while simultaneously continuing to diffuse certain narrow definitions of femininity. How can feminists rely on a patriarchal state that draws epistemic fodder from sexualized, imperial, regressive symbols, while making emancipatory demands upon it? How can feminists continue to lay claim on a thoroughly corrupt state? What are the responsibilities of feminists within the state apparatus to those on the outside? Even as feminist mobilizations help to provoke ruptures in heteropatriarchy and compel the state to work harder to reconstitute itself, they have not been able to interrupt sexualized practices within tourism, which occupy a sacred place in the Bahamas.

It would seem that in this moment of the historical evolution of the Bahamian state, emancipatory feminist projects are hard pressed to continue to draw legitimacy from the state. It seems crucial for the feminist movement to reformulate a new vocabilary for an understanding of domestic violence, for instance, in terms that are not located within the state's mechanisms of surveillance. Instead of being premised within the state's misrepresentation of domestic violence and its deployment of the law of the father, feminists would need an emancipatory praxis that would dissolve the carefully programmed dimensions of the survivors' internal psychic landscape that has taught her: 'if mih man don't beat me, he don't love me;' 'is so man stop;' or that her daughter is 'too womanish for she own good and it can't have two woman living in one house;' or that more generalized, internalized shame that begets silence and the conviction that women are women's worst enemies and only men are women's best friends. One would urgently need an emancipatory praxis that deconstructs the power of heterosexual lore that positions women as their own worst erotic enemies and rivals, that might explode mothers' inherited discomfort with the emerging, restless sexuality of their own daughters, a sexuality that is often viewed as threatening and anxious to usurp. We might have to speak the unspeakable and name the competitive heterosexuality, an unnamed homosexual desire between mother and daughter, its complicated, as yet unspecified origins, and its contradictory societal sanctions and approbations. It would be an emancipatory praxis anchored within a desire for decolonization, imagined simultaneously as political, economic, psychic, discursive, *and* sexual.

A major challenge lies, therefore, in crafting interstitial spaces beyond the hegemonic where feminism and popular mobilization can reside. It would mean developing a feminist emancipatory project in which women can love themselves, love women, and transform the nation simultaneously. This would mean building, within these interstices, new landmarks for the transformative power of the erotic, a meetingplace where our deepest yearnings for different kinds of freedom can take shape and find rest.

Notes

This essay would not have been possible had it not been for the women and men in the Bahamas who have been an integral part of movements for social justice. I am profoundly indebted to them and to DAWN for their willingness to be candid under conditions of state repression. I am also grateful to Linda Carty, with whom I did the field work for this essay and with whom there were many late-night conversations to sort through the inevitable residues of research insights. Two in the field are infinitely better than one. I also benefited enormously from the meticulous readings of Marion Bethel, Linda Carty, Jinny Chalmers, Cynthia Enloe, Barbara Herbert, Jerma Jackson, Gary Lemons, Chandra Talpade Mohanty, and Mun Wong, I trust that I have used them wisely. Thanks also to Ana Christie for being a resourceful and patient research spirit, and to Jessica Badonsky for assisting in the job of assembling notes. Mo dúpẹ̀.

1. Marion Bethel, 'And the Trees Still Stand', in Marion Bethel (1994) *Guanahani, Mi Amor Y Otras Poemas* (Cuba: Casa de las Americas), p. 44.
2. The acronym DAWN stands for Developing Alternatives for Women Now. The group was formed in 1986 and from the outset operated as an autonomous women's organization. Beginning with a multifaceted feminist ideology, one of its first tasks was to challenge the state and organized medicine in 1989 on the introduction of Norplant. It has simultaneously politicized questions of women's history, cultural and artistic production, domestic violence and violence against women, and has also held annual women's fairs.
3. Repression of other kinds also exist. For example, there is a section in the general orders that curtails political activity of public servants. See general orders, 'Utterance on Political and Administrative Matters, Statement #932' (1982) Nassau, Bahamas. The injunction reads as follows: 'A public officer must in no circumstances become publicly involved in any political controversy, unless he becomes so involved through no fault of his own, for example, in the proper performance of his official duties; and he must have it in mind that publication either orally or in writing of any material, whether of direct political interest or relating to the administration of the Government or of a Department of Government or any matter relating to his official duties or other matters do not affect the public service.' See also 'An Act to Amend the Law Relating to Sexual Offences and to Make Provisions in respect of Related Circumstances Involving Parties to a Marriage'

(Date of Assent 29 July1991) (Nassau: Bahamas, Government Printing Office 1991).

4. The recodification of primogeniture here is somewhat paradoxical since from 1982, women's groups have influenced the state to erase primogeniture. A bill, brought before Parliament since that time, now sits on the back burner.
5. *Op. cit* Lynda Hart (1994) Fatal Women: Lesbian Sexuality and the Mark of Aggression (Princeton: Princeton University Press), p. 5.
6. This is one area that has been remarkably undertheorized in the understanding of the American state—the extent to which an advanced capitalist state can be simultaneously nationalist, or even hypernationalist, intervening abroad, while vigorously engaged in the redrawing of its own borders at home. Unfortunately, nationalism has come to be more easily associated with Third World and not advanced capitalist states.

   The specific reference here is to the Californian mobilization in 1995, Proposition 187, against undocumented workers, whom the US North American state defines as 'illegal aliens'. The effect of this Right-wing mobilization would be to deny schooling, health care and a range of social services to both these undocumented workers and their children. Variations of Proposition 187 are being undertaken in different states.
7. Ruthann Robson (1992) *Lesbian (Out)Law: Survival under the Rule of Law*, (Ithaca, NY: Firebrand Press), p. 58.
8. The most significant gesture here is the convergence of Right-wing mobilization inside the American state surrounding family values and the deployment of foreign 'aid' in its service. The United States Foreign Relations Committee has, for instance, formulated a policy that links the terms of foreign aid to the outlawing of abortions and increasing sterilization programs, in other words, the further institutionalization of population control at the expense of birth control.
9. Inderpal Grewal and Caren Kaplan (eds.) (1994) *Scattered Hegemonies: Postmodernity and Transnational Feminist Practices* (Minneapolis: University of Minnesota Press). For a more extended analysis of the deployment of these gestures within white gay metropolitan tourism, see M. Jacqui Alexander, 'Imperial Desire/Sexual Utopias: White Gay Capital and Transnational Tourism,' in Ella Shohat (ed.) (1998) *Talking Visions: Multicultural Feminism in a Transnational Age* (Boston: MIT Press).
10. Janet Halley, 'The Construction of Heterosexuality', in Warner, *ibid.*, pp. 82–104; see also Kendall Thomas, 'Bowers vs Hardwick: Beyond the Pleasure Principle', in Dan Danielsen and Karen Engle (eds.) (1995) *After Identity: A Reader in Law and Culture* (New York: Routledge).
11. Edda Dumont, 'Franchise has not Solved All Women's Problems', (Interview with Lady Butler) *Nassau Guardian* 19 November 1987, p. 2
12. There is both a range and plethora of women's organizations ranging from girl guides and trade union gropings to Business and Professional Women's organizations and feminist groups. A listing compiled by the Women's Desk reveals that there are approximately 67 women's organizations. Women's Affairs Unit, *Directory of Women's Groups* (Nassau, Bahamas: Government Printing Office, 1991).
13. The Women's Desk, established in 1981, was upgraded in 1987 to a Women's Affairs Unit but is still located within the Ministry of Youth, Sports, and

Community Development. It has been consistently plagued by a lack of funds. Constraints it faced in 1993 included the following: (1) inadequate funds for execution of program activities; (2) lack of trained staff in unit; (3) unit unable to meet the demands of the public; (4) no approved national policy (on women) and (5) unclear status. Women's Desk internal memorandum, 1989. See also Audrey Roberts, 'The Changing Role of Women's Bureaux in the Process of Social Change in the Caribbean', Keynote presentation for the tenth Anniversary Celebration of the Women's Affairs Unit, 17 June 1991.

14. Interviews with Sandra Dean Patterson, Director of the Women's Crisis Center and Sharon Claire and Camille Barnett, College of the Bahamas, June 1993.
15. *Ibid.* Interviews with Sexual Offences Unit at the Criminal Investigation Division, CID, Bahamas, June 1993.
16. The following provide an indication of the kind of sensationalism generated in the media: 'Sixteen-Year-Old School Girl Mother—Teenage mothering is no fun', 22 March 1986, *The Tribune*; 'Thirteen year-old Girls Sexually Molested by a Knife-Wielding Man', July 26, *The Tribune*; 'False Cry of Rape Puts Lady Accountant in Jail' (convicted of endeavor to deceive) 18 September 1986 *The Tribune*; 'Visitor is Raped at Gunpoint at Paradise Beach', 8 October 1986, *The Tribune.* Also interviews with Alfred Sears and Marion Bethel, Nassau, June 1993.
17. Interviews with Alfred Sears and Marion Bethel, Nassau, June 1993.
18. See here, General Laws, 'Personal Rights Arising from Marriage and Property Rights during Marriage' Part 3, subsection 2 relating to the rights of consortium and the duty of the wife to cohabit with her husband. It states: 'it is the duty of the wife to reside and cohabit with her husband.' There is no such requirement specified for a husband.
19. 'DAWN Galvanizes Resources to Address Issues Arising from Sex Violence Bill', *Nassau Guardian*, 25 November 1989
20. Interview with Therese Huggins, Member of DAWN, Bahamas, June 1993.
21. The link between domestic sexual violence and state economic violence has been made by CAFRA, the Caribbean Association for Feminist Research and Action and by SISTREN, a women's collaborative theatre group. See, for example, *CAFRA News.* Newsletter of the Caribbean Association for Feminist Research and Action, 'Women and Sexuality, Vol. 8, No. 1, 2, January–June 1994. See also Honor Ford Smith (1986) *Lionheart Gal: Lifestories of Jamaican Women* (London: The Women's Press).
22. *Ibid.* (Sexual Offences Act).
23. 'Women's Crisis Week', *Nassau Guardian*, 29 September 1989.
24. 'MPs Passed the Sexual Offences Bill to Provide Greater Protection for Women on the Job', *The Tribune*, 17 May 1991; 'Magistrate Supports Move to Educate Public about Incest', 23 June 1986, *Nassau Guardian.*
25. Alicia Mondesire, Leith Dunn, (1994) 'Towards Equity in Development: A Report on the Status of Women in 16 Commonwealth Caribbean Countries', prepared for the Fourth World Congress on Women (Georgetown: Guyana), p. 50.
26. *Ibid.*

20 The Sexual Exploitation of Women and Girls

A Violation of Human Rights

Dorchen A. Leidholdt, Esq.

Like many activists in the struggle to name and claim women's human rights, I wear more than one hat. In addition to serving as Coexecutive Director of the Coalition Against Trafficking in Women, I am the Director of the Center for Battered Women's Legal Services in New York City. The Center provides representation to domestic violence victims in a wide array of legal proceedings. It will come as no surprise to many in this audience of human rights activists, who know only too well that practices of violence and exploitation are interconnected, that several of my clients in addition to having been battered by their partners have been subjected to horrifying sexual exploitation.

There is Raya, who as an 18 year old in Sri Lanka, was approached by an American man who offered her work as a caregiver to his elderly mother. Instead of taking her to the United States, he took her to Abu Dabi, where he kept her in a house with other women he had similarly lured from Sri Lanka and other poor countries. There she became his slave, serving him sexually and eventually bearing him children.

There is Sasha, advertised in a catalogue to Western men, interested in acquiring subservient Eastern European brides. When Sasha turned out to be a human being instead of a compliant blow-up doll, her new husband beat her and threatened her with a loaded gun.

And there is Andrea. A fashion model in Brazil, Andrea moved to

Dorchen A. Leidholdt, Esq., 'The Sexual Exploitation of Women and Girls: A Violation of Human Rights', from a paper presented to the Working Group on Contemporary Forms of Slavery, subgroup of the Human Rights Commission of the UN, June 1998, Geneva, Switzerland. It was subsequently published in *Making the Harm Visible*, Donna Hughes *et al.* (ed), (Coalition Against Trafficking in Women, 1999). Every attempt has been made to obtain permission to reproduce this article. Please contact Oxford University Press with queries.

the United States to further her career. When her visa expired, she could no longer find work. A friend told her about an easy way to make good money—as a call girl for an escort service. The money was good, but the only way Andrea could do what she had to to make it was by using drugs, supplied by the driver for the escort service. He became her pimp and abuser, as she spiralled downward into a cycle of sexual exploitation, drug addiction, and destitution.

I mention these examples to bring actual experiences of sexual exploitation to what is too often an abstract discussion. I also mention these examples to highlight a problem with recent formulations by policymakers, who claim to be interested in developing strategies to address the human rights crisis of trafficking in women. Some recent definitions of trafficking are so narrow and legalistic that they fail to address the situations of Raya, Sasha, and Andrea, and millions of other women victimized by pimps, traffickers, and other sexual exploiters. Too often, trafficking in women is addressed in isolation from other related practices of sexual exploitation, like sex tourism and prostitution. Distinctions are made, often in the name of the victims, that in fact serve only to protect the industry and its customers at the expense of women and children they exploit.

The first distinction that is made is that between sex trafficking and organized prostitution. The fact is that sex trafficking and organized prostitution are inextricably connected and share fundamental characteristics and dynamics. The victims who are targeted are the same—poor, minority, or so-called Third World women and children, frequently with histories of physical and sexual abuse. The customers are the same—men with disposable incomes who achieve sexual gratification by purchasing and invading the body of a woman or a child. The dynamics of power and control employed by the profiteers are the same, whether they take the form of violence and threats of violence, debt bondage, torture, imprisonment, and/or brainwashing. The harm to the victims is the same—trauma, sexually transmitted diseases, drug and alcohol addiction, the physical toll of beatings by customers and pimps, the psychological toll of repeated and unwanted sex, and the destruction of a sense of self, identity, and sexuality. The harm to society is the same—the fortification of gender-, race-, and socioeconomic-based hierarchies.

The reality is that organized prostitution constitutes the economic and structural foundation of sex trafficking. Many of the women and girls who are trafficked start out being prostituted to local men by local pimps and brothel owners. Often, when they are deported back to their countries of origin, they are prostituted again, locally. Sex tourism, frequently the launching pad for sex trafficking, involves the sexual exploitation of women in their countries of origin. The countries that are the largest importers and exporters of trafficked women are those countries with the largest and most entrenched and lucrative local prostitution networks.

The second distinction that is frequently made is between the sexual exploitation of children and adults. The problem with this is that by failing to criticize the sexual exploitation of adults, especially adult women, this distinction inadvertently legitimizes it. To decry the sexual exploitation of a 15-year-old girl but to fail to speak out against the sexual exploitation of her 18-year-old sister is to tacitly sanction the exploitation of the older girl.

The sexual exploitation of children is inextricably connected to that of adults. Studies show that in the West, at least 70 per cent of adults in prostitution were sexually abused as children. Studies also show that the average age of entry into prostitution is 16 or younger. It is clear that the sexually exploited children of today are the prostituted adults of tomorrow. As the French abolitionist organization, Le Nid declares, 'In every "whore," there is a little girl murdered.' Although some sex industry consumers prey only on children, many sexually exploit girls and women interchangeably. We will not be able to end the sexual exploitation of children until we take a stand and develop strategies against the sexual exploitation of all human beings.

The third and most problematic distinction that has recently emerged is that between so-called forced and so-called voluntary prostitution. By limiting the pool of people who can claim the status of victims while at the same time protecting large segments of the sex industry, this is the best gift that the pimps and traffickers could have received. This distinction is predicated on an illusion of sexual exploitation that is freely chosen; an illusion that can be maintained only by ignoring all of the social conditions that force women and girls into conditions of sexual exploitation. The proponents of this distinction are sending this message: 'Ignore the poverty, the familial pressure, the incest, the domestic violence, the lack of employment options. Just ask if someone pointed a gun at her head or defrauded her. No gun. No fraud. No problem. Not only is she voluntarily in the sex industry; she is a "sex worker"' In this analysis, the pimp who recruited her into prostitution and the brothel owner who reaps profits from prostituting her are rehabilitated as so-called 'third-party managers'.

What are the consequences of conceptualizing prostitution as free or forced, and the legitimization of prostitution as 'sex work' that inevitably follows? There are many. First, governments, especially those of poor countries, realize that they can reduce their unemployment rates and increase their gross national products by moving unemployed women and girls into organized prostitution. This is most likely to happen in countries with strong internal sex industries fuelled by the profits of sex tourists. One such country has gone so far as to tout prostitution as acceptable work for poor women. It did so in its 1996 report to CEDAW, stating, 'Recognized prostitution in Belize is a gender-specific form of migrant labor that serves the same economic function for women as agricultural work offers to men and often for better pay.' I should note that Belize's position is supported by a recent report distributed by the ILO that urges countries to factor sex industry profits into their national financial accounting.

When prostitution is accepted as sex work, it becomes even more difficult for poor women and girls, often socialized into an ethos of female self-sacrifice, to resist economic and familial pressure to enter prostitution. As the numbers of prostituted women and girls increase, growing numbers become infected with HIV and die of AIDS, while a smaller but still significant percentage are murdered by pimps or customers. Those women fortunate enough to survive sexual exploitation are left, like Andrea, with no job skills, traumatized from years of enduring unwanted sex and violence, and physically debilitated from sexually transmitted diseases and the substance abuse necessary to endure the sex of prostitution. What is available to these women? Destitution or a job as a madam or mama san, helping the pimps control the younger women who are still marketable commodities.

When prostitution is recognized as 'sex work', legalization follows. Pimps, sex industry cartels, and sex businesses openly flourish, regulated only by the demands of the market. Men and boys are sent the message that purchasing the body of a woman or girl for sex is no different from buying a pack of cigarettes. With no social stigma attached to buying the bodies of women and girls, the demand escalates. At the same time, women and girls increasingly internalize the message that the female body is a marketable commodity. Girls begin to see prostitution as a career option, unaware that 'sex work' is a trap that will deprive them of control over their lives. When prostitution is legitimized as sex work, its values and dynamics spill over into other areas of society, influencing the valuation and treatment of women and girls and lowering their status.

Some have argued that since criminal sanctions have not slowed the growth of the sex industry or lessened the exploitation of victims, the only recourse is to recognize prostitution as sex work and legalize the sex industry. Criminal sanctions have not worked, it is true, but that is because in most instances they have been directed against the victims. Few governments invest law enforcement resources in the investigation and prosecution of sex industry profiteers and fewer still direct criminal sanctions against the customers, who fuel the demand side of the industry. And while some countries have conducted effective and well-funded campaigns against domestic violence and rape, with shelters, counselling, and legal services for victims, women and girls in conditions of sexual exploitation have been denied the support and advocacy given other victims of male violence.

How can we begin to address the exploitation and enslavement of women and girls by local and global sex industries? How can we end sex trafficking? To begin, we must take the following steps:

1. Recognize that sex trafficking, sex tourism, prostitution, and other forms of sexual exploitation are interrelated practices of gender-based domination and control; that every woman and girl has a right to be free from sexual exploitation.

2. Educate legislators and policy-makers, NGOs, and the public that all forms of sexual exploitation—whether the result of force and deception or poverty and social inequality—are practices of discrimination and human rights violations.

3. Advocate for local, national, regional, and international law enforcement strategies that penalize sex industry profiteers and consumers while decriminalizing their victims.

4. And, finally, urge governments and social service agencies to develop and/or expand shelters and counselling services, medical care providers, and legal services for all victims of male violence against women, including sex industry victims and survivors.

Looking for Women's Rights in the Rainbow

Pornography, Censorship, and the 'New' South Africa

Lliane Loots

INTRODUCTION

After the first democratic election ever held in South Africa on the 27th of April 1994, South Africa ostensibly shed the shackles of apartheid legislation and became what Archbishop Desmond Tutu had so often called South Africa: a 'Rainbow Nation'. With the thrill of 'one person, one vote' keeping South Africans euphoric for some time, it was only awhile later that the golden haze of this 'rainbow' started to cloud over. The depth of the legacy of apartheid law started to manifest itself in how difficult it was for our 'new' South Africa to begin shifting and changing legal practices. South Africa's National Party government had hegemonically constructed and used a legal system to justify racist apartheid state power. While this legal system operated in many seemingly non-race related areas, such as the censorship of sexually explicit material, these legal practices functioned not to investigate gender-related oppressions but acted either to mask a racist agenda, or to re-inform, in this instance, the censorship of political material. One of the great legacies of apartheid law was the conflation of censorship of political material with the censorship of sexually explicit material such that censorship became a state apparatus for justifying political power—issues around gender and the lack of equality afforded women (both black and white) in South African society was almost never part of a social and political agenda.

With the end of apartheid and the beginning of a new emerging democracy, these past intricate legal operations were not easily shed, with new legal practices around sexually explicit material often playing off the fear of returning to a system of censorship such that the potential availability of this material was somehow linked to 'free speech'. What has been, and is, clear in the shifting legal practices around the censorship and/or availability of sexually explicit material in South Africa, is that a gendered critique has not been considered nor has a concern for women's rights been expressed. One is left wondering just how strongly women are represented in this 'rainbow' which, as an analogy, uses the joy of multi-culturalism and race and colour as *the* defining factor of our new nation.

Apartheid has often been 'reduced' to being seen entirely as a race related issue and this has, mistakenly, led to a type of reductionist thinking that believed that getting rid of an apartheid government in South Africa would automatically result in a democratic and fair society. Apartheid has always been a type of meta-narrative for South Africa but, like all grand narratives, contains within it many interconnected levels of oppressions. Issues such as, though not exclusively, of gender and class oppression were upheld and indeed informed by apartheid. One of the great myths of anti-apartheid activism has been the need to contain opposition against the National Party government to a fight against racism; this was done such that often women's issues (as one example) were relegated to secondary concerns in a greater fight for political and social freedom in South Africa. One clear example of this was, just prior to the first democratic elections in South Africa in 1994, the African National Congress Women's League (ANCWL) began a mass campaign against the proposed South African launch of the sexually explicit magazine *Penthouse*. Given that the ANC was gearing itself up to win the upcoming elections, the highest level of the ANC electorate informed the ANCWL that their campaigning around *Penthouse* was a potentially divisive strategy that was diverting the *real* struggle. The ANCWL was forced to drop the campaign and made to focus on what the primarily all-male ANC electorate felt were the 'real' issues. This speaks of a potentially naive attitude to the understanding of how categories of power (such as race, class, and gender) interconnect in the governance of citizens lives—whether this be social or political.

This way of thinking has left South Africa with a strange type of legacy in which we still articulate gender concerns, for example, as secondary to a national endeavour of creating a free and equal society. The lack of interrogation of seeing how apartheid has left South Africa with multi-layered wounds and interrelated levels of oppression (such as race, class, and gender) has profound impact on the way our new legal system is beginning to redefine and re-regulate social and political practices. This is perhaps best demonstrated by the way in which both apartheid and post-apartheid governance has chosen to deal with censorship of pornography. The issues are complex and layered given that, unlike most First World countries, South Africa has newly emerged as a developing nation having rid itself of the shackles of one of the legally most oppressive governance systems in the world. This historic moment of going into a democratic system of government offers an interesting point from which to rethink a discussion around sexually explicit material and the availability of pornography.

In this light, this article will deal first with problems inherent in defining what constitutes pornography and will thus draw on some of the North American feminist debates around this issue. In order to make legislation concerning sexually explicit material, the law requires a workable definition; this is offered up as the first potential problem area for women's voices to be heard. Secondly, this article will deal with the censorship and legal ramifications of sexually explicit material under apartheid law. Thirdly, the legal shifts in post-apartheid law around sexually explicit material will be investigated in the light of South Africa's new constitution—arguably one of the most progressive in the world with our Bill of Rights forming Chapter 2 of the main body of the Constitution. This is unlike the U.S. Bill of Rights which is an appendix to the U.S. Constitution. Finally, this article will reflect on how women's concerns have (or have not) been addressed in the legal, political, and social dealings of sexually explicit material and will investigate what this might further mean for wider gender concerns in South Africa's emerging democracy.

DEFINING PORNOGRAPHY

Defining pornography is a difficult and problematic issue primarily because there is very little consensus amongst the legal fraternity and feminists alike on exactly what constitutes pornography. Every person writing about pornography appears to conceptualize and therefore define it differently. Furthermore, however one may choose to define pornography, the choice often depends on the purpose for which it is formulated. If the purpose, for example, is to draft legislation to regulate or censor pornography, then the definition will focus on certain legal issues and thus influence how people think about the legal availability of sexually explicit material. In this context, who formulates the definition is also important, because whoever controls the definition will decide the framework within which the laws are formulated, as well as the views and images that the law will seek to suppress (McElroy 1995: 41).

Issues around sexually explicit material (unlike any other within feminist discourse) seem to have split the feminist movement into two schools of thought, labelled as anti-pornography and anti-censorship. These are loosely categorized as representing radical and liberal feminism, respectively. This categorization, which casts the feminist response to sexually explicit material as binary opposites, is deceptive as it 'blurs the dialogue and the debates in the grey areas between these two polar extremes where there could be and is an overlap or consensus on certain issues' (Badat 1998: 86). Primarily what the North American feminist debates on pornography bring to the discussion is an articulated need to address sexually explicit material not simply as a legal issue around regulation or censorship, but a profound need to address the politics of gendered media representation. While the conclusions reached for action vary between schools of feminist thought, both groups have placed the discussions around sexually explicit material firmly on a gendered political agenda—an area where South African debates on sexually explicit material need to move.

The radical feminist position is best exemplified by Andrea Dworkin (1981) who, through her book, *Pornography: Men Possessing Women*, spearheaded the feminist campaign against sexually explicit material in the early 1980s in North America. Dworkin analyses sexually explicit material as a specific genre which celebrates and justifies male power. She sees all sexually explicit material as harmful because its very existence discriminates against women by representing and encoding women as sexual objects always available to men. Dworkin sees sexually explicit material as central to women's oppression, as she states: 'We will know that we are free when pornography no longer exists. As long as it does exist, we must understand that we are the women in it: used by the same power, subject to the same valuation' (1981: 224). This understanding of sexually explicit material as *the* reason for women's global oppression led Dworkin towards the legal call for censorship of all sexually explicit material[1]:

> In the system of male sexual domination explicit in pornography, there is no way out, no redemption: not through desire, not through reproduction. The

woman's sex is appropriated, her body is possessed, she is used and she is despised: the pornography does it and the pornography proves it. (1981: 223)

Opposing this belief in the 'all-pervasive power of pornography in the oppression of women' comes the liberal feminist position best exemplified by the North American group called Feminists Against Censorship (FAC), which formed in 1989. This group of women came together, in part, to oppose radical feminist ideas around the call for censorship of sexually explicit material: 'Our aim is to make certain that the pro-censorship position is not seen as the only feminist perspective on pornography' (Ellis 1990: 22). FAC expressed the concern that if all sexually explicit material is to be censored then the very real need for women to experiment, through text and media, with definitions of their own sexuality (whether heterosexual or homosexual) has the potential to be contained and silenced. Thus, liberal feminists place the onus of censorship on the individual within society to view and respond to material as she sees fit. For liberal feminism, censorship in one area cannot be separated from censorship in another. Censorship works against a desire to create a democratic society in which diversity of views and behaviour is tolerated. Liberal feminists question the radical feminist assumption that pornography is the central issue in feminist politics, arguing that need to address issues around the gendered nature of education (for example) are just as important for feminists in the fight for equality. They reject censorship of sexually explicit material as, in their view, it prevents members of society from choosing for themselves what they do and do not want to read and watch. For liberal feminists, censorship of sexually explicit material is another form of patriarchal power—for those who wield power can easily fall into the belief that they know what is best for others. As FAC states:

Suddenly the feminist movement that once fought for freedom and sexual self-determination is advocating giving power over our lives to the judges and police: suddenly what is said about our freedom and sexual desires sounds like the ravings of the right. Suddenly feminism is about censorship rather than opening up possibilities. (Ellis 1990: 27)

Both these feminist positions around sexually explicit material have merit; however, both fall into theoretical traps.

Radical feminism makes the error of globalizing women's oppression which renders categories of difference invisible. Questions of the interconnection of race and class (for example) with women's oppression is ignored, such that issues of class exploitation and racism in pornography are disregarded over the all-consuming desire to define women as a monolithic 'community'. Furthermore, by defining pornography as a central patriarchal tool in oppressing women, the possibility for sexually explicit material about women's desires and women's sexuality is denied. The radical feminist call for censorship is also problematic as it offers a potentially difficult alliance with right-wing politics; a politics that would call for the censorship of sexually explicit material on the grounds that it is (amongst other things) anti-family—a constructed institution which has been severely criticized by radical feminism.

Liberal feminism's easy distinction between what constitutes pornography and what constitutes erotica is perhaps also made too easily. Implicit in their distinction is the understanding that there is such a thing as 'good' sexuality and 'good' representations of sexuality (erotica) and opposite it, 'bad' sexual representations (pornography). To assume that because, for example, women make sexually explicit material that it will not be an objectification of the female body, is an assumption which is potentially dangerous and which, ironically, like radical feminism, assumes that if women do something it has to be 'good'.

Thus, while both the liberal and radical (North American) feminist positions offer insights into the debates around sexually explicit material, attention has to be turned to investigate these debates (and how they inform) the South African context to assess how the specific South African historic process has informed a unique understanding of censorship.

In the context of South Africa we also have the thorny issue of cultural practice looming over what we define as sexually explicit. For example, do women photographed bare-breasted wearing traditional dress come under review as pornography, or indeed as sexually explicit representation? The answer is a much contested one and one which highlights the crux of the debates around censorship of sexually explicit material. Naked bodies and bare breasts are not in and of themselves pornographic. It is, rather, the way in which they are represented (or photographed) and in which arena they are viewed that constructs material as sexually explicit. As feminists, the issue that needs to be addressed most profoundly is that (primarily) it is women's bodies which carry the burden of sexually constructed representations and the issue of legislating or censoring sexually explicit material, does not, of necessity, address the lived reality of how the media does and can be allowed to represent women's bodies and sexuality.

SEXUALLY EXPLICIT MATERIAL AND APARTHEID LEGISLATION

Censorship of sexually explicit material in South Africa under apartheid legislation has been the historical domain of a secretive (generally white male) censorship board working with section 47.2(a) of the South African Publications Act of 1974. The Act states:

> For the purposes of this act any publication, object, film, public entertainment or intended public entertainment shall be deemed to be undesirable if any part of it:
>
> (a) is indecent or obscene or is offensive or harmful to public morals.

What becomes apparent in investigating the past workings of this law under apartheid legislature and the possible implications of it, is the difficulty of defining what is in fact 'indecent', 'obscene', or 'offensive'. Given that South Africa is a multi-cultural society with a host of religious practices and political viewpoints, it becomes impossible to have a single definition of any of the above terms. Implementing obscenity legislation around sexually explicit material thus became a highly controversial political and personal act of informing dominant apartheid-informed ideologies.

Section 47.2(a) of the Publications Act of 1974 also implied a South African 'community' with a common understanding of what constitutes a moral practice. The South African censorship board in the apartheid era, was made up of non-elected, primarily white men who clearly served National Party policy. The 'moral' prerogative set up by obscenity legislation served not only a narrowly defined community, but also served obvious National Party political ends. With this difficulty in creating a definitive understanding of 'obscene' and what, singularly, is found to be 'harmful to public morals', comes the added (and more controversial) task of creating consensus around what defines pornography and pornographic material. As indicated by previous discussion, this is not simply a semantic problem, as an inability to offer a definition precludes clear legal practices around issues pertaining to sexually explicit material.

South Africa, under apartheid was, for many years, subject to restrictive and oppressive censorship legislation. Past research efforts into pornography and censorship in South Africa have been limited, to say the least, with the predominant view being that some control is justified, since pornography and portrayals of certain types of violence give rise to anti-social behaviour and crime (Sonderling 1990). Sonderling finds this argument to be 'a paradoxical contradiction' (1990: 41), since at the time when these views were expressed, pornography was not legally available or even accessible to most South Africans due to particularly stringent censorship legislation. Sonderling (1990) contends that the inclusion of pornography in the debates around censorship was an effective tactic used consciously or unconsciously, to divert attention away from the real aim of censorship, which was National Party political control. The assumption that in South Africa publication control was aimed primarily at combating pornography was in fact a smoke screen for insidious political censorship. Pornography, under the apartheid regime, was not of such overwhelming importance to justify the existence of strict censorship laws. The laws, however, did impact on the publication, distribution and even possession of 'indecent' and 'obscene' material. Obscenity legislation in South Africa was also advanced to uphold strict conservative and moral ethics, as is evident from the preamble to section 47.2 of the 1974 Publication Act, which pledged to uphold a Christian view of life—the apartheid National Party upholding itself as a Christian national government. Censorship of sexually explicit material in South Africa thus cannot be considered in isolation from other legislation which promoted and entrenched racial discrimination.

Interestingly enough, Itzin (1992), commenting on obscenity legislation in Britain, also notes—similarly to the points made around the South African context of obscenity legislation—that the deliberate vagueness of the definitions of 'obscenity' and 'indecency' leaves the legislation open to abuse. Consequently, these obscenity laws have been used as instruments to justify the censoring of art and literature, to oppress gays and lesbians, and to control women's fertility. Morality has been used as a smoke screen for political suppression, since the original target of any state censorship was not sex but politically subversive material/literature.

Within the South African context, the debates around sexually explicit material started gaining momentum and prominence around the time of the unbanning of the African National Congress (ANC) in 1990 and towards the time of the first democratic elections (27 April 1994). This came as a result of an overriding concern with the hitherto denied democratic right of freedom of speech and expression. This concern arose as a direct result of the political and press censorship that had occurred under National Party rule in South Africa. It is significant to reflect on how producers of pornography have used (and are using) this political climate as the bandwagon on which issues of sexually explicit material must climb. Joe Theron, the South African editor of *Hustler*, for example, has said:

> History has proved that the best societies are those in which freedom of speech and expression exist. . . . We at *Hustler* defend the rights of individuals and organisations—be they religious, political, or 'pornographic'—to have their say in a free and democratic society. (*Daily News*, 21 November 1994)

Clearly, Theron is fusing the notion of political censorship with the censorship of sexually explicit material. His assumption is that censoring the writing of Karl Marx (as was done under apartheid), for example, is the same as not allowing adults to read/view *Hustler* magazine. What is rendered invisible by this argument is that Marx's writing was banned because of its potentially subversive power to challenge the status quo of a racist, capitalistic minority rule. *Hustler* magazine, as one of many examples of sexually explicit materials, does not challenge racist, capitalistic and patriarchal assumptions around women. Rather it reinforms the status quo on how to continue viewing the female body as a sexual object. While it becomes easy to slip into a radical feminist position at this point, the need arises to separate issues of the censorship of sexually explicit material from political censorship—especially to address the praxis of a new South African post-apartheid legal system.

With the end of apartheid, one of the highest democratic ideals that we are striving for is the need for freedom of speech and expression. This democratic right should not, however, render invisible the need to analyse sexually explicit material from the past position of censorship, and also, more importantly, with an understanding that it is primarily the naked representations of women's bodies that are displayed and objectified. The very real need to address what it means to women (and men) to have their bodies open and displayed has not, as yet, entered, in any meaningful way, the debates. The primacy given to the right of Freedom of Speech and Expression (clause 16 of the South African Bill of Rights) has eclipsed the fact that the South African Bill of Rights has three other clauses which carry immediate relevance to the debates around the potential censoring of sexually explicit material. The first is clause 14, which states that:

> Everyone has the right to privacy, which includes the right not to have—
> a. their person or home searched;
> b. their property searched;

c. their possessions seized; or
d. the privacy of communication infringed.

It is conceivable that producers of sexually explicit material could use clause 14 to justify the individual right to own/view/read sexually explicit material as it is a private act and thus protected by our Bill of Rights. Thus, the owning and viewing (or reading) of sexually explicit material, when done in the privacy of the individuals' home (i.e. within the private arena), cannot justify state intervention nor the state seizing this material.

Further adding to the complexity of formulating a coherent policy and practice around sexually explicit material are the following two clauses of the South African Bill of Rights which argue against the creation or existence of pornography. Clause 9, the Equality Clauses, which secures citizens of South Africa the right to equality before the law, states in subsection 9.3:

> The state may not unfairly discriminate directly or indirectly against anyone on one or more of the following grounds, including; race, gender, sex, pregnancy, marital status, ethnic or social origin, colour, sexual orientation, age, disability, religion, conscience, belief, culture, language, and birth.

Following from this clause, it could be argued that (some) sexually explicit material is not about equality. Women are represented as objects for male sexual gratification and male ownership; a status which unfairly discriminates against the individual on the grounds of her gender. Thus, the existence of (some) sexually explicit material undermines the equality of women before the law.

Alongside this could be placed clause 10, which enshrines all South Africans' fundamental right to Human Dignity. It states:

> Everyone has inherent dignity and the right to have their dignity respected and protected.

Some sexually explicit material, it could be argued, does not respect the (bodily) dignity of women (and men) and thus infringes on women's rights to be full and equal citizens—both legally and politically.

It thus becomes clear that even within South Africa's progressive constitutions in the world lie a great many potential contradictions around constitutional practice surrounding the availability of sexually explicit material. What does need to be addressed is the way in which a post-apartheid climate has given South Africans a deep (and understandable) fear of any form of censorship thus privileging clause 16 of the Bill of Rights. While one needs to fight for the right to enshrine a culture of free speech and expression, it becomes equally important that this 'free speech' is not, once again, male voices that, through patriarchal (and capitalist) structures, deny women the chance to speak out. Privileging clause 16 of South Africa's Bill of Rights has had the hegemonic effect of silencing women's opposition to (some) sexually explicit material not on the grounds of censorship and free speech, but on the grounds of discriminatory and sexist representation—issues that have not entered the South African debate around pornography.

SEXUALLY EXPLICIT MATERIAL AND POST-APARTHEID LEGISLATION

The introduction of a Bill of Rights into the Constitution of South Africa (adopted 8 May 1996) thus presents a whole new set of factors for consideration. As discussed, the protection of rights to privacy, dignity, equality, and in particular, freedom of speech and expression, places the validity of censorship legislation in question. The protection of, for example, freedom of speech and expression, entails 'complex problems of balancing competing interests' (Badat 1998: 88). According to Cachalia *et al.* (1994), the outcome of disputes regarding the guarantee of freedom of speech and expression will depend on the value that the Constitutional Court is prepared to place on this right, and the extent to which it will be inclined to subordinate other interests. Cachalia *et al.* authoritatively also go on to state, importantly, that in no country is freedom of speech and expression absolute.

Having, however, disbanded the censors board as unconstitutional as a result of the *Hustler* case, the new South African government renegotiated the need for some form of control over production, distribution, and availability of sexually explicit material. In 1996 the Films and Publications Act 65 was set up which, as a result of over 5,000 oral and written submissions to parliament, ostensibly shifts the focus around sexually explicit material from censorship and control to classification.

Desmond Lockley, the chairperson of this particular portfolio committee, has said that the new Bill is not about pornography, but rather is about films and publications and how we (as a democratic country) can regulate the distribution of material. Interestingly enough this has given rise to two new boards—the Film and Publication Board and the Review Board. Neither are labelled as a censors board, they now define their tasks as regulation and classification of material. It becomes important in terms of gender and race representation that the offices born by both boards are democratically elected and that all proceedings are now publicly available for scrutiny. This, in the first instance, distinguishes these publication 'control' boards from the Censorship Board that operated under the old apartheid dispensation. Once again, however, this newly discovered transparency does not, in and of itself, solve the legal ramifications of defining what constitutes pornography, so that even a Review Board will have to have some form of consensus over a working definition. It must be noted, however, that given the transparency of the election of committee office bearers (for both the Review Board and the Classifications Committee), the move is a welcome one for democratic South Africans.

The true effect of this legislation on the production and distribution of sexually explicit material is yet to be ascertained. It has, however, been described as reflecting 'the unresolved status of the pornography debate' (Smith 1997: 293). On examining the new Film and Publications Act 65 of 1996, it is clear that, once again, the use of incomprehensible terms and definitions create an uneasy situation where interpretation and the acting out of the law may prove problematic. The object of this new Act is to regulate the distribution of certain publications and to regulate the exhibition and distribution of certain films, by means of classification, i.e. the imposition of age restrictions and the giving of consumer advice; with obvious due regard to individual rights enshrined by the constitution. It appears, however, that the Act does more than its proposed objectives. While the Film and Publication Act does not use words like 'ban' or 'censor', it does in fact place restrictions on certain publications and films, and even prohibits the distribution and possession of certain material— which ironically, amounts to nothing short of censorship and control. As stated previously by Cachalia *et al.* (1994), the right to freedom of speech and expression is never, even within a democracy, an unquestioned and unregulated right, thus bringing into profound question the way in which the right to freedom of speech and expression has been manipulated to serve, once again, some form of social and political end.

'NEW' PROBLEMS FOR WOMEN

Before the Film and Publication Act was passed in South Africa, the Freedom of Expression Institute (FXI) issued a response to the proposed Act 65 (to serve before the Parliamentary Select Committee) in which it recorded its opposition to all forms of banning of films and publications. In its response against censorship, the FXI confronted the argument that pornography is harmful to women and therefore should be restricted. The FXI counter-argument (FXI 1995) was based on three grounds, reminiscent of anti-censorship arguments canvasses by North American liberal feminists; these state (as quoted in Badat 1998: 91–2):

1. The focus on censoring pornography diverts attention from the root cause of discrimination and violence against women, of which violent, misogynist pornography is merely one symptom. In addition, those in favour of censorship dilute the accountability of men who commit violence against women by displacing their responsibility onto the makers of the pornography instead of themselves.
2. By undermining free speech, censorship would deprive society of a powerful tool for advancing women's equality. The FXI claims that free speech is a powerful tool to fight against discrimination and misogyny, as well as to seek social change.
3. Censorship schemes are usually enforced in a way that discriminates against marginalised groups, including women.

While it must be acknowledged that the new South African Films and Publications Act does to some extent relax the previous legal positions, especially with regard to possession of sexually explicit material, it by no means offers a significant departure from the restrictive legislation of the past. The few references to 'gender' in the Act are the only slight evidence of concessions granted to the implication of women in the pornography and censorship debate.

CONCLUSION

The legal ramifications around sexually explicit material and its censorship/control/regulation in the post-apartheid South African context have not, as yet, been pushed to the limit. It remains the domain of lobbyists and the workings of a very young South African Constitutional Court to see what policies and practices will be further formulated. This, however, remains an important debate for women, as the outcome will have personal implications for our lives. As women we need to remain vigilant and watch how our South African Constitution is put into practice. South African women need to enter the debate around pornography to ensure, first, that specifically women's concerns around the gendered nature of the discrimination potentially implicit in pornography, is not rendered secondary to a politically constructed privileging of freedom of speech and expression that, ironically, has the potential to silence women's voices. Secondly, it would seem that it is primarily up to South African women to make sure that issues around sexually explicit material are addressed as multi-layered problems that are not only about gender but that are profoundly affected by issues such as race and class as well. In theory at least, all clauses within the South African Bill of Rights carry equal weight. Once again, attention needs to be drawn to the privileging of clause 16 (Freedom of Speech and Expression) by the producers of sexually explicit material, as this is a political (and economic) manœuvre that carries profound gendered consequences. It needs to also be remembered, in a profoundly gendered way, in South Africa's present climate of democracy and freedom of speech, that clause 16 of the Bill of Rights, carries the following subsection—16.2(c):

> The rights (of Freedom of Speech and Expression) do not extend to—
> c.advocacy of hatred that is based on race, ethnicity, gender or religion, and that constitutes incitement to cause harm,[2]

Notes

1. It is important to note that Dworkin does not make any distinction between pornography and erotica. She states:

   > In the male sexual lexicon, which is the vocabulary of power, erotica is simply high-class pornography: better produced, better packaged, designed for a better class consumer. . . . In the male system erotica is a sub-category of pornography (1981: preface).

2. The author wishes to acknowledge two important research sources towards this article:

   (1) A short article written previous by the author for the South African journal *AGENDA*: Loots, L. (1996), 'Pornography and the Body Politic', *AGENDA*, 31.

   (2) The scholarship and advice offered by Jamila Badat as a graduate student in the Centre for Gender Studies (UND) and as a lecturer in Private Law

in the Law Department at the University of Durban/Westville—South Africa.

References

Badat, J. (1998), 'Marked XX—Censorship and Pornography', *AGENDA*, 38.

Cachalia, A., Cheadle, H., Davis, D., Haysom, N., Maduna, P., and Marcus, G. (1994), *Fundamental Rights in the New Constitution* (Kenwyn: Juta).

Dworkin, A. (1981), *Pornography: Men Possessing Women* (London: The Women's Press).

Ellis, K. (1990), 'Feminism and Pornography', *Feminist Review*, 36.

FAC (1990). 'Leaflet', *Feminist Review*, 36.

Freedom of Expression Institute (1995), 'First Draft of FXI Response to the Film and Publications Bill as Amended', unpublished discussion document.

Itzen, C. (Ed.) (1992), *Pornography: Women, Violence, and Civil Liberties* (Oxford: Oxford University Press).

Loots, L. (1996), 'Pornography and the Body Politic', *AGENDA*, 31.

McElroy, W. (1995), *XXX: A Women's Right to Pornography* (New York: St Martin's Press).

Smith, N. (1997), 'Policing Pornography', *South African Journal on Human Rights*, 13(2).

Sonderling, S. (1990), 'New and Old Voices from the Ship of Fools: The South African Pornography Debate', *Communicato*, 16(2).

22 Tambien Somos Mujeres

We Are Women, Too—Cuban Prostitutes after the Revolution

Victoria Ortiz

When 1959 dawned in Cuba, the brand-new revolution faced an almost overwhelming array of social, economic, and political problems, both internal and external. Emerging from a long history as a colony first of Spain and then—virtually—of the United States, Cuba appeared ill-equipped to resolve the difficulties involved in rising out of the oppression and exploitation of centuries. In fact, a multi-pronged approach to tackling the curing of ingrained and seemingly immutable social ills led the small island nation to achieve a degree of broad communal change that has been internationally hailed and often cited by the United Nations and non-governmental organizations as a model for planned social reform.

One of the most oppressed groups in Cuban society was its women, battered over the years by an economy that excluded and exploited them, by a society that reviled and abused them, by a culture that disempowered and objectified them, and by an ideology that forced them into roles impossible to fulfil in the context of the multiple subjugations by which they were dominated. In 1959, less than 10 per cent of Cuban women worked outside the home, and those who were employed were, overwhelmingly, domestic workers. The demographic pool from which the majority of Cuban domestic workers were drawn was the increasingly impoverished rural population that suffered the traditional scourges of Third World peasants: seasonal unemployment for most non-land-owning peasants; very large families and very few resources to care for them; lack of education and other social programmes; impossibility of landownership because of increased capitalization of land holdings; and backbreaking and unrewarding labour that was remunerated at barely subsistence levels. Young women (and young men) left their homes and families in the rural areas and fled to the towns and cities, hoping for well-paying work. Because they were largely illiterate, or at least barely educated, and had received no job training of any kind that would make them employable in urban jobs (service industry, factories, offices), these women most often found jobs as maids in the homes of middle- and upper-class families.

But the vicissitudes of both the economy and the moods and attitudes of employers steered or forced many thousands of women into prostitution as the only economically viable alternative to starvation. Most prostitutes had spent time as washerwomen or servants, or in some cases bar waitresses or hostesses, before realizing that while the degree of mistreatment and exploitation might not change that much from 'legitimate' employment to working in 'The Life', the income difference was significant.

At the triumph of the Cuban Revolution, the leadership was well aware that the new society's longevity would only be assured if the entire population became participants in the construction of an economically and socially different order from that which had been replaced. The full integration into daily political, economic, and social life of all Cubans became an early priority for the revolutionary leaders. Programmes were developed early on to educate or re-educate, to train or re-train, Cuban workers, peasants, young people, and—remarkably—women. The Federation of Cuban Women ('FMC'—Federación de Mujeres Cubanas) assumed command of those programmes that were specifically aimed at preparing for full citizenship three clearly identified groups: peasant women, domestic workers, and prostitutes, the three groups of women most oppressed by colonialism, imperialism, and underdevelopment. The programmes tailored to the needs and realities of each of the three groups were all based on the view that the participants would need to learn new aptitudes as well as new attitudes in order to develop and grow: this meant the teaching of basic literacy, basic elementary-school subject matter, economically viable skills such as dressmaking, hairdressing, and secretarial skills, as well as history and citizenship in the context of a socialist revolution.

Of all these women, those for whom the changes brought by these revolutionary programmes were the most dramatic were undoubtedly the prostitutes. The schools for prostitutes were initially established throughout the country, mostly in rural areas, and were staffed by young women often with little or no prior experience as teachers or 'rehabilitators'. Because the FMC was not limited to a middle-class membership, but rather functioned throughout the society and incorporated working-class and peasant women, students, professionals, factory and farm workers, office workers, and housewives, those who planned and implemented the schools for former prostitutes understood their target population well.

The schools were generally in semi-rural areas, not too far from the towns or cities where the students had worked as prostitutes. In the early days many of the women continued as prostitutes because they needed the income to help support their families, but gradually they learned new trades or professions and entered the mainstream workforce. The schools generally were organized as farms, and the students and staff collaborated in the production of as many crops or farm products as possible in order to meet the community's need for meat, dairy goods, and vegetables as much as possible. The schools provided nurseries and daycare facilities for those women with infants or young children; there was medical and psychological counseling for the women who were fighting drug or other substance abuse, as well as psycho-social problems stemming from a lifetime of low self-esteem and social condemnation; there was legal help for women who were in trouble with the justice system; and there was serious job retraining, making it possible for the former prostitutes ultimately to join the workforce with new skills and interests. The graduates of these schools went on to hold jobs as bank tellers, factory workers, government office workers, seamstresses, daycare workers, and the like. Many of them, following the overwhelming social trend in the 'new Cuba', chose also to pursue advanced education and went on to receive high school diplomas and eventually college degrees.

The Cuban experience with re-educating and re-training prostitutes was remarkable on many fronts. It should not be forgotten that the FMC implemented its programmes in the context of a society that had historically both objectified and reviled women, a society where prostitution of many kinds had been a mainstay of an economy based on tourism, gambling, and the illicit drug trade. It is a tribute both to the stubbornness of the FMC's founders and to the farsightedness of the Cuban revolution's male and female leaders that the schools for prostitutes (as well as those for peasant women and housewives) truly succeeded in salvaging for society and for themselves thousands of women who otherwise would have continued being exploited and abused in their lives as sexual servants. Prostitution in pre-revolutionary Cuba was recognized as an economic component of a decaying society: the revolutionary leadership did not moralize about the sins of prostitutes but rather saw the many forms taken by the economic exploitation of women and determined to attack them on all fronts. The goal and the actual outcome of the revolution's programmes for women were the incorporation of *all* Cuban women into the nation's social, economic, and political life.

Further information about prostitutes in Cuba and about Cuban women generally may be found in: Elizabeth Stone (ed.), *Women and the Cuban Revolution: Speeches and Documents by Fidel Castro, Vilma Espín and Others* (New York: Pathfinder Press, 1981); Margaret Randall, *Cuban Women Today: Interviews with Cuban Women* (Toronto: The Women's Press, 1974); Margaret Randall, *Women in Cuba: Twenty Years Later* (New York: Smyrna Press, 1981); Maxine Molyneux, *State, Gender and Institutional Change in Cuba's 'Special Period': The Federación de Mujeres Cubanas* (London: Institute of Latin American Studies, 1996); Vilma Espín de Castro, *La mujer en Cuba* (La Habana: Editora Politica, 1990); Isabel Larguía, *Hacia una concepción de la mujer* (La Habana: Editorial de Ciencias Sociales, 1983); Oscar Lewis, *Four Women: Living the Revolution: An Oral History of Contemporary Cuba* (Urbana: University of Illinois Press, 1977).

Part IV. Breaking Open the Ground of Sex and Gender

Seducing Women into 'a Lifestyle of Vaginal Fisting'

Lesbian Sex Gets Virtually *Dangerous*

Amber Hollibaugh

Reverend Louis Sheldon, Director, Family Values Coalition, on 28 March 1994, discussing the *Safer Sex Handbook for Lesbians*, produced by the Lesbian AIDS Project of Gay Men's Health Crisis and available at a youth peer educators' conference held in New York City:

This is it. I'm sorry, I thought you'd seen it. Is this your first time for—it's wild. I mean it's absolutely, it's so grotesque, it's so vulgar, it is so obscene that when I first saw it, I had to put it down. I couldn't look at it because it's pornography.

Duffy. (radio show host of 'Live in L.A.'). This is, this is filth.

Sheldon. This is filth, this is pornography.

Duffy. Hold on Lou, for just a second. I want to tell you what Lou has just handed me. This is a book that's about three inches by five inches, just about the size of one of those photographs you would get when you send in your film. What you can see is a nude woman. I'm assuming this is a woman—

Sheldon. Yes, it is.

Duffy. Yes, 'cause it's a safe sex handbook for lesbians. This person has gloves on—

Sheldon. Latex gloves.

Duffy. Latex gloves. There's no polite way to say this, friends, on her left breast there is a ring that has been pierced through the nipple. There is in her belly button a pierced ring that goes through her belly button. She's holding her right breast with a gloved hand and you can see all this and, I hate to say this, Lou, but her center finger which is down covering most of her pubic hairs, has disappeared.

Sheldon. That is correct.

Amber Hollibaugh, 'Seducing Women into 'A Lifestyle of Vaginal Fisting': Lesbian Sex gets *Virtually* Dangerous', from *Policing Public Sex: Queer Politics and the Future of AIDS Activism*, Amber Hollibaugh (South End Press, 1996), 321–36, reprinted by permission of the author and the publisher.

Duffy. To see that this is being passed out and then you open it up, I mean, it is inside. Here's—as you open it up, kissing, here's two women kissing and I mean, it just goes on and on. They're distributing this and here—it's awful.

Sheldon. See, the bottom line to this, uh, Duffy, is that they're telling these young children how they can counsel lesbians not to get the HIV virus infection. And what they're saying is because lesbians, this particular brochure produced by the homosexual community, remember that it is not us who is saying this about them, they say this about themselves: that lesbians are now into vaginal fisting. I've heard of homosexuals, gays, into rectal fisting, but this is vaginal fisting. And I want to tell you that a woman can die—the vaginal, the vagina is not made to have a fist placed in it for such purposes as this booklet is trying to say. And what their purpose in this booklet is to say to young children, you must wear a latex glove. As you do vaginal fisting, wear a latex glove. Then it goes on to tell you what to put on the latex glove, then it goes on to tell you all these other things.

And as we showed this on the floor of the Congress, as men were com— as men and women were coming into the floor of the Congress, we went there with fear and timidity and I tell you we prayed before we went, 'cause I've never given out pornography. I don't participate in any kind of pornography. But when these were sent to me by dear Mary Cummings, a 74-year-old grandmother, president of School District 24 in Queens, New York, she said, 'Lou, you've got to tell the Congressman.' I gave it to Congressman Mel Hancock; Mel Hancock said, 'I will instruct the sergeant-at-arms not to touch you. You may give this out on the street, at the foot of the steps of the House side of the U.S. Capitol as they come in to vote.' And we did that. And I want to tell you all you-know-what broke loose. I mean, I'm actually giving this out . . .

Duffy. Friends, I can't tell you where this has hit me. To think that the Bible is excluded from our curriculum and this kind of filth is included. I mean, doesn't that strike you the same way it strikes me? Doesn't that just make you ill? Doesn't it just make your tastebuds reverberate with bad taste? We've got to do something, Lou. What can we do? The brochure? . . .

Sheldon. You know, it's produced in New York City. If anyone wants a copy of this, we'll send it to them, to show them what New York City tax dollars are going for. But what we need to do is to just impact upon our Senators and say to them, 'Look, we're not homophobic. We have compassion. We're concerned about those that have gender identity conflict, but we don't want to affirm a lifestyle of vaginal fisting.' And this is exactly the simple and short of it.

Duffy. Well, folks, there it is. There's the problem that confronts us . . .

THE LESBIAN PROBLEM THAT CONFRONTS US

> RADICAL GAYS USE THE PUBLIC SCHOOLS TO RECRUIT OUR KIDS
>
> (Ray Kerrison, *New York Post*, 16 February 1994)
>
> DISGUSTING WAY GAYS BRAINWASH OUR SCHOOLKIDS; Mixing Porn With Suicidal Sex Advice
>
> (Ray Kerrison, *New York Post*, 9 March 1994)
>
> 12 YEAR OLDS ARE TAUGHT THE RAWEST GAY SEX TECHNIQUE—With the Board of Education's Blessing
>
> (Mona Charen, *New York Post*, 14 March 1994)

Lesbian sex, queer girls with disappearing fingers, lesbians with fists up each other's vaginas, sucking and fucking, vulgar women-to-women porn, dyke HIV, public debates on lesbians' right to unrestricted erotic terrain? Lezzies? He/Shes? Girl-to-girl HIV sexual transmission? How in the hell did lesbians get in this picture?

In late 1994, in the above radio talk show exchange, in these newspaper headlines, and on CNN, the first barrage of attacks against the Lesbian AIDS Project's *Safer Sex Handbook for Lesbians* appeared in an unprecedented debate. Discussions suddenly emerged about lesbian sexuality, HIV education, public morality, and lesbian sexual safety. This cause celèbre was kicked off when a youth peer-educators' conference was held in New York City to update young HIV counselors with the most recent information they might need to teach other young people about AIDS—what it is, how the virus is transmitted, and how to protect themselves against it. Some local new right organizations heard about the conference and sent their own kids in as spies, asking them to collect all the literature they could find and to attend the workshops being offered.

In the hallways, a multitude of AIDS organizations who were asked to attend displayed their own literature. The *Safer Sex Handbook for Lesbians* was on GMHC's literature table along with 15 or 20 of its other brochures, covering all aspects of HIV/AIDS. Many organizations had set up tables, but for the new right, only two brochures seemed to fascinate them: the *Safer Sex Handbook for Lesbians* and another GMHC brochure called *Listen Up*, targeting young gay men of color.

This completely new attack against lesbian sexuality by the new right caught everyone off guard, including AIDS organizations, feminists, lesbian/gay/bi/trans rights groups, and civil rights groups like People for the American Way. Because lesbian sexuality had never been the focus of the new right (in fact we are hardly evident as independent agents in most of its literature and public speaking), most of us were unprepared for this ferocious onslaught. In doing AIDS work, many of us had come to expect the routinely manufactured sexual outrage the new right fashions whenever it needs a convenient crisis or a reason to cut the budget, but their fabricated fury had never before been generated by images of lesbian sexuality and safer sex information.

Lesbians have never been part of the debates that have continuously swirled and receded around HIV and safer sex information these last 15 years of the epidemic. Homosexuals, gays, and gayness were male, and gay was guy. In fact, within and outside the gay community, we have been the great 'disappeared' when issues of sexuality or HIV are defined. Even within the little-considered world of women's sexuality, risk, and HIV, for lesbians, our sexuality and HIV sexual danger have been almost totally absent from the public debates that have been such cultural markers throughout the life of the pandemic. Only in the feminist porn wars of the 1980s was lesbian sexuality central, visible and pivotal in characterizing the issues at stake in the larger political debates of that struggle and that movement.

This sudden recognition of lesbian sexuality by the new right marks our entry into a new era. It is not merely a superficial trend like the straight media talking about lesbian chic; it is a time when our sexuality, in all its extraordinary variation, is finally being revealed, even to us. We are debating it, writing about it, disagreeing about it, teaching each other about new sexual options. All of this is exploding inside our communities at the same time as we have become more visible. We have only just begun the job of opening the windows around our own sexualities.

Women, though, have been attacked and sexually caricatured throughout the epidemic. When those attacks have occurred against women who are HIV+ or suspected of 'carrying AIDS', these women have generally been represented as a problem stemming from our lack of sexual morals. This is also underscored by the inherent racism of the new right against women of color, its assumptions about 'promiscuous' sexual partnering, and its suggestion that we are a sexual threat because our bodies are vectors of infection for 'innocent' men or children. Women who have AIDS (or are at risk for HIV) are always represented as whores, users, or unknowing victims: the three bitter female categories of blame used to explain women's internal liability and fault in the epidemic. In all the new right's different constructions of moral accountability, HIV was either queer and male or straight and female. Straight men were represented as victims of female immorality or dangerous faggots, but never as the transmitters of HIV. And lesbians? We didn't even exist—that is, not until the *Safer Sex Handbook for Lesbians* entered the picture.

CONTROL OF WHOSE BODIES? THE STATE, LESBIAN HISTORY, AND GAY MALE SEXUAL DESIRES

The current battle over the *Safer Sex Handbook for Lesbians*, as well as the issues raised around the current public sex debates, were preceded by the feminist porn wars of the early 1980s, often called the 'sex wars'. The vicious battles of the sex wars have left fields still strewn with corpses, and they continue to haunt us in current AIDS clashes, especially as the new right has grown in strength. The struggle around public sex has forced us to discover once again that our movements—Women's Liberation, Lesbian-Feminist Liberation, or Gay Liberation—do not guarantee agreement on issues as volatile as desire, sexual practices, and control of our own bodies. As we saw in the 1980s porn wars among feminists, and in the early fights among gay men about what exactly constituted safe sex in the late 1970s, and now in the public sex debates currently raging, we are faced again with the painful lessons that our communities are perfectly capable of betraying each other's erotic desires to the State in the name of 'safety', or to shore up a questionable victim defense to create a hierarchy of risk and innocence. As a group, we are more than capable of blaming each other for the literal genocide caused by the State's inaction and its criminal unwillingness to protect our lives in the face of this epidemic. Somehow, it is easier to blame each other for society's sexual hatred of lesbians and gay men, which sustains these policies against us, as well as against women and people of color, rather than name the real problems we confront in the fight for sexual and social freedom and justice.

For lesbians, we were made more vulnerable as a legacy of that earlier feminist battle over sexuality and because we have few places in which to learn about our own desires and no safe places in which to gain sexual self-knowledge. Straight white men don't lose their 'reputations' or their lives for being sexual (although they can for being faggots), and no men end up pregnant or on an abortionist's table as the end play of sexual experimentation.

One of the things I most envied and admired about gay men after Stonewall was that they could go to clubs and baths and parks and parties, watching, exploring, and learning the range of what was sexually possible for men to do with each other. Regardless of their individual decisions about monogamy, friendship, and desire, they had avenues to sexual exploration and sexual knowledge that were closed to me as a lesbian.

The history of lesbian struggles has not been the same as that of gay men, often leaving gay men with a sense that the issues debated by lesbians have no meaning for or impact on their own political issues. While the feminist 'sex wars' are the vital link and the political precursor to this current division about public sexuality, most gay men don't know much about them, and usually have not been able to make the connections between the pornography battles that occurred among feminists and the public sex debates that have been so crucial to gay men in the 1980s and now again in the 1990s. Once boiled down, the parallels are strikingly similar in all these arguments, and expose how they rest on many of the same fundamental questions: the role of the State in regulating sexual behaviour, the meaning of desire, and the need for danger in our erotic lives. Perhaps the most important parallel involves the demand to control our own bodies, a fundamental feminist tenet that usually erupts around abortion struggles, but which is also the basis for how each of us frames responsibility and safety when discussing safer sex, partnering, control, desire, and personal responsibility.

QUEER GIRLS IN DANGER

The fight to limit sexual awareness and HIV information for marginal communities has had tragic results, many of which we are now seeing first hand. The number of young gay men who are now not practising safer sex, and not even thinking it is relevant to them, as well as the exploding HIV infection rates for gay men of color, are cataclysmic examples of homophobia, sexual silence, racism, and a too-perfect example of how all of these issues often combine toward one devastating end. This is true for various lesbian communities too, where the legacies of earlier feminist struggles about sexuality (together with many other factors) generated the current and tragic lack of HIV awareness in most lesbian communities and the communities where lesbians build their lives. By shutting down discussion within lesbian communities about desire, sexual activities, class and race experiences, and our many erotic differences, we have remained outside the vital exploration about AIDS and our own risks within our communities for too long, sending to the hinterlands of shamed hetero- or bisexuality any woman who has ever fucked a man, as well as any women who ever used drugs.

Yet lesbian communities are as diverse in our sexual practices as we are in our class, color, sexual histories, or drug use. Popular renditions of lesbianism rarely capture the experience of the majority of women who love or have sex with other women. The bulk of women who love other women are not involved in the political or cultural movements of the Lesbian Nation. They remain working-class and poor women, women of color and white women, who do not fit easily into the new 'lesbian chic' or the political lesbian culture of the 1990s any better than many of us fit into the lesbian-feminism of the 1980s, for the same reasons—*wrong color, wrong class, wrong background, wrong desires, wrong sexual histories.*

The majority of lesbians live in a world altered by the gay liberation movement and the feminist, civil rights, and AIDS movements, but they are not a central component of it. Yet these debates about our sexuality and public morality deeply affect the day-to-day desires of vast numbers of lesbians and gay men. They also impact upon the ability to fight for our own erotic rights within the various communities of birth or language we call our homes, or to know what is important to understand about sexual dangers so that we can protect each others' erotic lives.

Few lesbians openly discuss their sexual habits with anyone but their lovers, and often not even with them. We have inherited the dreadful legacy of social constraints on women, which require sexual modesty and erotic ignorance. No one gets good information in this culture, but men are at least expected to be sexual and are therefore assumed to have the right to be interested in and to act upon their own desires and pleasures. Boys are not punished for showing sexual curiosity or, since they're supposed to run the fuck, for learning how to 'do it'. For women, the field is rigidly limited—and for lesbians, the field seems empty. The price for showing sexual interest in another woman is almost too high.

When HIV hit, it made us sitting ducks for misinformation about different sexual and social practices and the particular dangers that could put a lesbian at risk. We did not want to recognize or discuss our underground sex with men, and we didn't want to see the drug use which tears our communities apart. Instead, the only topic we would discuss was sexual transmission between women partners. We refused to ask the central question—how do lesbians get AIDS? Since there was no good data out there about women's sexual risks except through unprotected sex with a man, and since lesbian sexuality is always collapsed into oral sex, we rationalized, 'it isn't our issue'. As a result, lesbians continued to get infected in the ways that all women are vulnerable, especially through drug use and unprotected sex with men. Additionally, we continued to put each other at risk sexually because we refused to recognize our culpability vis-à-vis any sexually transmitted disease between female partners, including HIV. It's as though we couldn't even think about it, couldn't bear to imagine ourselves any deeper inside this epidemic than we already were as lesbians in a devastated gay community. It was already too much, too painful, too terrifying.

All communities are in denial about HIV, including parts of the gay male community. There, HIV is about 'older' men or promiscuous men or unsafe men, any kind of man that isn't like the one in the mirror. For lesbians too, the distancing continues, but for us the excuses are really about color and class and sexual desires we refuse to acknowledge that we have. 'Oh, I'm not like her, I'm not poor—or Black—or Latina—or a junkie—or a bar dyke—or sleeping with men—or having 'rough' sex—I'm a real lesbian.' Realness. But there are some other reasons we couldn't see what was happening within our communities. We didn't know how to acknowledge women unlike ourselves or from communities, sexualities, or cultures we had no built-in connection to. And since we rarely discuss our sexual activities (except as an accusation of failure during a breakup), we also couldn't recognize the myriad activities and circumstances which could put us at risk sexually. Dildos, multiple and unprotected sexual partners, sex toys, sex during menstruation, female ejaculation, STDs as a co-factor if one partner is infected—none of these things were acknowledged and discussed as risks, leaving HIV+ lesbians isolated from both information and community, and leaving everyone else saying lesbians needn't worry.

The irony in the current eruption over the *Safer Sex Handbook for Lesbians* is that, until now, lesbian sexuality has never had the public space or enough political power to engender any debate at all. Few people aside from lesbians ourselves have any idea about (or interest in) the variety of desires, identities, and sexual practices possible between women. Gay male sexuality has been discussed, first because of its publicly explicit sexual liberation ideology and practices in the 1960s and 1970s, and later, tragically, because of the onset of the AIDS epidemic. But for lesbians, this attack by the new right against the *Safer Sex Handbook for Lesbians* is the first to publicly engage with our desires within the debate about the public and common sexual landscape of the US and the lesbian erotic. It brings us full circle to those earlier feminist battles about desire and danger. Then, as now, the underlying question remained—whose sexuality would be the axis at our communities' erotic center?

SEX WARS, ROUND 2: WE BECOME 'THE PROBLEM ITSELF'

It was in those earlier skirmishes that some of us who are now AIDS activists first fought over issues of sexuality and state power, over who was a 'victim' and who a perpetrator, over definitions of sexual responsibility and community values, over our right to explicit public expressions of sexuality. Some of us were deemed too deviant, *too sexually ruined*, for the feminist movement—finally, much too queer, too butch or femme or S/M, too into the union of power and sexual desire, too untrustworthy in our hungers. It was after that set of battles that some of us limped away from the feminist and lesbian-feminist movements. It was precisely over these issues (and all that they disclosed about the emerging divisions between women who had once thought of each other as 'sisters') and our common fight that some of us began to see how these differences of experience for women of different classes, colors, sexual histories, and erotic needs could not be subsumed inside 'the sisterhood'. It was there that many of us learned again about the abstract-sounding issues of experience, background, class, and race as we saw ourselves become expendable, or worse, were told that if we didn't shut up or change our radical sex politic, we would be defined as the problem itself.

That earlier battleground was the foundation for the current battles and the emerging shock waves appearing on the geography of gay male sexuality. Again, like a crazy song that repeats itself, we have come down to *whose sexualities, whose desires, whose bodies* will be at the center of the current AIDS movement, and whose will be left outside; whose erotic lives will be made to appear perilous, dangerous, abnormal, genocidal, or invisible. It is not an accident that this is happening at the same time as the growing 'homosexual' equal rights movement is attempting to move us from the cultural margins of our supposed sexual 'deviance' into the social and economic mainstream, as books like Bruce Bawer's *A Place at the Table* make evident. HIV and the debates it engenders create a tempting, vulnerable, and logical place to fight out these political differences—over whose movement this is, where it's going, and who exactly is driving the car—these are the crucial issues when we're talking about radical change or 'gay' assimilation. Because the safer sex debate immediately generates so much passion, it is easy to shut down dialogue and difference with a mere suggestion that any oppositional position on public sex or multiple partnering, anonymous fucking, girls (or guys) with dangerous cocks, or our explicit queer desires will result in our HIV infection, our self-generated murder, or at least that we will profoundly contribute to our communities' sexual genocide.

The new right has proved itself a master at manipulating our society's cultural fears about sexuality and homosexuality. Like its ideology of racism, which created 'the welfare cheat', or its myth of the unmarried women eating bonbons while having kids by the pound—a problem blamed on women's liberation or on the black community and lesbian women for undoing the family—its propaganda about the dangers of allowing the creation of gay family, and its ideologies of bootstrap, survival-of-the-fittest economics mask class structures and class issues in this country, while targeting those too vulnerable or powerless to resist. And at least parts of our communities are falling for it.

The tragedy of this fight among us over sexual desire and HIV is that it helps mask the larger enemy around us, one who would like to see us disappear altogether, even if it literally means letting us die. It also helps cloak the spinelessness of many liberals in this culture who refuse to stand up and fight for lesbian and gay rights. They are too frightened to lift their heads above their own heterosexually protected sheets and engage in the real contest to help create a general climate of explicit, sex-positive education and a movement for sexual power which can fully incorporate lesbians, gay men, bisexuals, and transgender people.

In this larger fight, we all need to rethink many issues, not just lesbian or gay civil and sexual rights. The deeper agenda of confronting sexual shame and ignorance, sexual oppressions, and power imbalances of all kinds rests upon and is linked to the larger social issue of how to build a democratic and compassionate society as opposed to what we have right now: a culture that is daily growing more terrified of its own citizens and all their passions. It would mean addressing the underlying issues of who has and who has not, and it would mean, for those of us fighting for genuine sexual empowerment, that our struggle must by necessity be linked and integrated with issues of gender, class, and race differences. Gay and lesbian liberation is not an isolationist issue; it comes from somewhere and rests on many compounded things. If gender differences support the structures of social oppression for women, if race and class make some members of the queer community less valuable than others in this country, these issues must be recognized for their concrete interdependence. Fighting to eradicate racism is as much our fight as the fight for sexual liberation. We can't afford to forget the connections between race, class, and gender when we are building and defending a movement for sexual freedom. Whose desires, whose imaginations, whose behaviors will each of us be ready to defend, and whom will we each be willing to leave behind?

THE NEW RIGHT AND US: THE DANGER AND THE CHALLENGE

Part of what makes this firestorm about lesbian sexuality so interesting is what it reveals about the unstated assumptions of the new right about lesbian sexuality, what they had thought constitutes queer girl sexual desires and practices, or more to the point, what it couldn't possibly incorporate—namely, *penetration.* In reading right-wing documents, it quickly becomes obvious that the social meanings constructed for our deviance had to do with a kind of blind heterosexism—an inability to imagine 'what we really do in bed'. Their ideas were never based on the possibility of genuine sexual attraction to another woman, but instead upon the assumption of a defect within lesbians which made it impossible for us to attract or hold a man—that we are too ugly to get a 'real' man, or that we have been raped or somehow deeply betrayed by men and therefore seek a sort of pathetic refuge with other women, that we are spinsters—never desired by a man, etc. Lesbianism is always assembled in their arguments as a *vacancy at the center*, a sad, unfulfilling, and counterfeit erotic system that cannot stand on its own. Yet, as the *Safer Sex Handbook for Lesbians* makes clear, we aren't actually lacking in any sexual pleasures; the range of our sexual practices shows that everything is possible and easily taught, built, or bought outside the current boundaries of our existing sexual/gender system.

This is occurring at the same time that new right media figures are attacking us for those very desires, while they pore over newly created and explicit sexual information about lesbian erotic practice. And fascinated with lesbianism they are! Over and over, they can't resist quoting long and detailed paragraphs from the *Safer Sex Handbook for Lesbians*, while offering shocked disclaimers to their listeners and readers as they continue to scan the page. Like peep-show voyeurs, they want to read erotic materials and repudiate any interest in them at the same time. These are people who have always wanted to know about sex but were terrified to ask, especially, as straight men, about lesbian sex. This becomes particularly clear when, in article after article, they repeatedly return to the issue of lesbian vaginal fisting, one of the activities discussed in the safer sex brochure. They're mesmerized by it, can't stop talking about it, keep habitually returning to it. Their fascination is a dead give-away. After all, the idea that they can be replaced sexually, that their cocks aren't the only way to give pleasure and penetration to a woman, must be shocking to them, a continuation of the fear and titillation that lesbianism has always contained for heterosexual men.

They do something else. They pretend that the brochure is advocating fisting for 12-year-old girls and then go on to claim that 'fisting often leads to death', especially in the pages of the new right monthly *The Lambda Report*, a journal whose only purpose is to 'monitor the homosexual agenda in American culture and politics'. The claim that 'fisting often leads to death' is drawn from an article in a respected professional forensic journal that details the death of a woman from internal vaginal and rectal injuries due to penetration. When I looked up the article, what I found shocked me. This was not the story of a woman injured while making love with her female partner; it was the documented case of a woman who was sexually attacked, assaulted by a *male* perpetrator who had rammed his fist and arm up her vagina and rectum until she died. This is what they quoted to prove that *lesbian* sex is dangerous. This is how far they are willing to take their vicious misrepresentations of our sexuality. This also may be what they need to believe when faced with a group of women for whom they are sexually unnecessary.

Fisting is a pleasure that is not defined by gender. It is often recommended to women and their partners in preparation for childbirth, but is demonized after the child is born. But all these arguments are made by men who have historically refused to care about the lives of the women who were giving birth and often dying in the process—men who have left in droves when the kids were more than they anticipated. The list of deadbeat dads could paper the world. Women's lives, both reproductive and sexual, have never been much more than the canvas for the male brush—our deaths, like our pleasures, have mattered just as little.

When I first saw the new right's claims about fisting, I thought they were merely ludicrous and foolish, but as I saw this assertion reappear incessantly, I realized its reason and its danger. Lesbians have few resources for decent, non-judgmental sexual information. We are bombarded with messages not to come out and are discouraged from experimenting sexually once we have come out, through distorted representations of our erotic female-to-female desires as dangerous, sick, or injurious. Powerful safer sex information for lesbians, like the material in the handbook, is also dynamic, sexually positive sex information, period, and we are starved for it. It counteracts the messages that surround women suggesting that lesbianism and lesbian sexual desires are ridiculous, unhealthy, and without erotic heat. What is it again that we do in bed?

THE QUESTION THAT REMAINS FOR ALL OF US: WILL WE ABANDON EACH OTHERS' DANGEROUS DESIRES?

When the new right mounted its attack against the *Safer Sex Handbook for Lesbians*, our own lesbian communities were still torn apart by debates about lesbians and HIV risk. The only other place we could have looked for help was from gay men. But most gay men, regardless of how committed they are to lesbian and bisexual women's rights, have never before had to defend lesbian sexuality or women's bodies, and were totally confused about how to handle this new onslaught. This left the Lesbian AIDS Project's handbook defenseless. We watched as a conservative justification was marshaled, while gay, AIDS, and civil rights organizations rushed in to say that the materials were never meant for minors—without defending their content—trying to create some safety for AIDS organizations which were already fiercely under attack from the likes of Jesse Helms.

The problem, of course, with a conservative defense is that you can't argue for the beauty or power or right of your own or others' sexuality when you are also arguing for sexual privacy—the don't-ask-don't-tell argument. When we say that children or youth are inappropriate members of our communities as targets of sexual education, we desert them to the same forces that shaped and mis-shaped us. And we leave ourselves vulnerable to the next attack because of a defense that we ourselves have made unspeakable.

For lesbians, what the lack of a sexual defense meant was that lesbian desire and our right to know about our sexuality, both for our protection against HIV and for our need for erotic knowledge, got abandoned. And men who were potential allies, including gay men, showed a deep discomfort with talking about women's bodies, lesbian desires, and sexual practices, with saying 'vagina' or 'clitoris', and with knowing enough about our erotic lives to marshal an argument which was intelligently informed about lesbian sexuality and practices. They were up against the wall this time; in the midst of a battle about female desires and lesbian lusts, they would have had to defend the right for lesbians to control our own bodies and the terms of our own sexual debates and cravings. That is what it would have taken to actually defend the handbook. It is also what it will take to defend gay men's right to public sex, a sexual practice which is risky, difficult, and even potentially life threatening. Who, then, will have the power to decide?

This question has also been at the core of all the battles surrounding HIV since the beginning of the epidemic. It is the issue that frames the question of testing (mandatory or voluntary), and that stands right at the edge of the table when we're talking about safer sex. Will we allow sexuality, for the greater good (for the State or humanity, for procreation or God), to be regulated if our survival or death are at issue? Will an individual be allowed to take life-threatening chances with his or her own life, or another's life, for desire? Is any sexuality, any form of desire, worth that much?

I think that we, more than most people, know the answer to that question, because it is a question that each of us has faced before, with similar terror of the answer. We have all had to come out. In a culture where heterosexuality is the only justified system and homosexuality is presented as the death of all hope or future, when queerness itself seems to represent extinction, each of us has dared to step over that line to find our own answers. I do not think HIV, or our deepest erotic desires, are somehow different from the experience of coming out. What is worth living to experience is worth risking everything for. It is also worth fighting within our communities for safety and the courage to love and protect each other. But the ability to make a choice is everything in the doing of it. The State could not finally make me straight, nor can it decide that my loving of women must be regulated by its morality, even if it argues that regulation is necessary to save my life. In this culture at least, only we have loved each other enough to try and keep each other alive. It has been gay people who have taken on the battle to educate, inform, care for, and bury our own, not the State. And it is also the gay community, at its best, that has fought for the value and honoring of other lives and communities also radically affected by this pandemic. It is our own particular terrible legacy, and a tribute to ourselves and our furious refusal to give up on our own lives or any other community's survival.

Just Looking for Trouble

Robert Mapplethorpe and Fantasies of Race

Kobena Mercer

How does 'race' feature in the politics of anti-pornography? Well, it does and it doesn't. 'Race' is present as an emotive figure of speech in the rhetoric of certain feminist anti-pornography arguments; yet 'race' is also markedly absent, since there appears to be no distinctly black perspective on the contentious issues of sexuality, censorship and representation that underpin the volatile nature of the anti-porn debate. Although Audre Lorde and Alice Walker made important contributions early on in the debate in the United States over a decade ago, the question of pornography has hardly been a top priority on the agenda of black feminist politics in Britain in the 1980s and early 1990s.[1] If it is indeed the case that white and black women have not been equally involved in the anti-porn movement, or have not made it a shared political priority, then we have to ask: What role does 'race' play in the discourse of anti-pornography which has come mainly from white women?

'RACE' AS AN ISSUE IN ANTI-PORNOGRAPHY FEMINISM

When 'race' is invoked to mobilize moral support for anti-pornography positions, it tends to function as a rhetorical trope enabling a race and gender analogy between violence against women and incitement to racial hatred. In their recent campaigns, Labour MPs Clare Short and Dawn Primarolo have frequently used this analogy to argue that

Kobena Mercer, 'Just Looking for Trouble: Robert Mapplethorpe and Fantasies of Race', from *Sex Exposed: Sexuality and the Pornography Debate*, eds. Lynne Segal and Mary McIntosh (Virago Press/Rutgers University Press, 1993), 92–110, reprinted by permission of the author and publisher.

just as black people are degraded by racist speech and hurt by racial violence, so women are harmed and victimized by sexist and misogynist representations which portray, and thus promote, the hatred and fear of women that erupt in all acts of male violence. It follows, so the argument goes, that just as the law is supposedly empowered to prohibit and punish incitement to racial hatred, new regulative legislation is needed to 'protect' women from the harm and danger of male violence that pornography represents. Yet the 1965 Race Relations Act, which sought to prohibit racist speech, has never been particularly beneficial to black people—more often than not it has been used against black people to curtail our civil rights to representation, and was proved to be notoriously useless and ineffective by the rise of new racist and fascist movements in the 1970s. Just as most black people know not to entrust our survival and protection to the state, one ought to question any argument, feminist or otherwise, that seeks to extend the intervention of the state in the form of prohibitionary legislation.

Indeed from a black perspective, the problem lies with the very analogy between racial hatred and male violence because it is based on a prior equation between those sexually explicit words and images labelled 'pornographic' and those acts of violence, brutality and homicide that do indeed take place against women in 'real life'. This equation—that 'pornography is the theory, rape is the practice'—is central to the radical feminist anti-pornography argument that gained considerable influence in the USA during the 1980s and is gaining ground in Britain now. One of the most worrying aspects of these developments is the strange alliance that has evolved between radical feminists demanding censorship in the name of women's freedom, and the anti-obscenity lobby of the New Right whose demands for the prohibition of sexual representations have always been part of the moral agenda of mainstream conservatism. For entirely different reasons, these two groups seek further state regulation of pornography, yet their convergence on this objective has created a wider constituency of support for a policy of cultural censorship. Where do black people stand in relation to this unhappy alliance?

While anti-porn feminists are more likely than their neo-conservative counterparts to observe that pornography itself is violently racist, one has to question the highly emotive way in which 'race' is used only to simplify complex issues and polarize opinion, as if everything were a matter of black and white, as if everything depended on whether you are simply for or against pornography and, by implication, male violence. In a theoretical defence of the radical feminist view that pornography does not merely reflect male violence but is itself a form of violence even as representation, Susanne Kappeler uses 'race' precisely in this way—not only to justify the unproven equation between images of sexual violence and actual violence experienced by women, but to elicit a moral response of horror and outrage that lends further credence to the anti-porn argument. At the beginning of her book *The Pornography of Representation*, by means of a graphic description of photographs depicting a black African man—one Thomas Kasire of Namibia —shown mutilated, tortured, and obliterated for the gratification of his white male European captors, Kappeler hopes to persuade us that, essentially, all pornography entails that women experience the same kind of actual violence as the brutal, sadistic and murderous violence of the colonial racism that resulted in the death of this black man.[2] Not only does this analogy reduce 'race' to rhetoric—whereby the black/white polarity serves to symbolize an absolute morality based on an either/or choice between good and evil—but it offers no analysis of racial representation in pornography, nor of black people's experiences of it, as Kappeler nowhere acknowledges the relative absence of black women in defining the feminist anti-porn agenda, or the fact that black feminism, in all its varieties, has certainly not prioritized the issue as a touchstone of revolutionary morality.

Each of these issues concerning race, representation and sexual politics has arisen in the very different context of Robert Mapplethorpe's avowedly homoerotic photography, which was at the centre of a major controversy in the United States during 1989 and 1990. Paradoxically, as a result of the campaign led by Senator Jesse Helms to prevent the National Endowment for the Arts from funding exhibitions of so-called 'indecent and obscene materials', Mapplethorpe's photographs have come to the attention of a far wider audience than at any point in his career before his death, from AIDS, in 1989. Although Helms's proposed amendment to NEA funding criteria was eventually defeated, the virulent homophobia that characterized his campaign against Mapplethorpe's 'immoral trash' has helped to create a climate of popular opinion favourable to cultural repression. Just as self-censorship has become routine among art-world decision-makers, so the policing and prosecution of cultural practitioners—from feminist performance artist Karen Finley to the black rap group 2 Live Crew—has also become commonplace. What is truly disturbing about these trends is both the way in which the New Right has successfully hijacked and appropriated elements of the feminist anti-pornography argument, and the way in which some feminists have themselves joined ranks with the law-and-order state. An instance of this occurred in Cincinnati in 1990 when feminist campaigners aligned themselves with the city police department to close down the touring Mapplethorpe retrospective and prosecute the museum director responsible for the exhibition, Dennis Barrie, for the violation of 'community standards'.

MAPPLETHORPE'S BLACK MALE NUDES

In this context, I would like to offer a contribution to the debate on pornography that is based on my reading of Mapplethorpe's troublesome images of nude black men. Although the attack on Mapplethorpe focused mainly on his depictions of gay male sadomasochism and portraits of naked children, his black male nudes are equally, if not more, problematic—not only because they explicitly resemble aspects of pornography, but because his highly erotic treatment of the black male body seems to be supported by a whole range of racist myths about black sexuality.

To shock was always the key verb in the modernist vocabulary. Like other audiences and spectators confronted by the potent eroticism of Mapplethorpe's most shocking images, black audiences are not somehow exempt from the shock effect that Mapplethorpe's images so clearly intend to provoke. Indeed, it was this sense of outrage—not at the homoeroticism, but at the potential racism—that motivated my initial critique of the work, from a black gay male perspective. I was shocked by what I saw: the profile of a black man whose head was cropped—or 'decapitated', so to speak—holding his semi-tumescent penis through the Y-fronts of his underpants, which is the first image that confronts you in Mapplethorpe's 1982 publication *Black Males*. Given the relative silence of black voices at the time of Mapplethorpe's 1983 retrospective at the Institute of Contemporary Arts in London, when the art world celebrated his 'transgressive' reputation, it was important to draw critical attention to the almost pornographic flamboyance with which Mapplethorpe, whose trademark is cool irony, seemed to perpetuate the racist stereotype that, essentially, the black man is nothing more than his penis.

Yet, as the context for the reception and interpretation of Mapplethorpe's work has changed, I have almost changed my mind about these photographs, primarily because I am much more aware of the danger of simply hurling the accusation of 'racism' about. It leads only to the closure of debate. Precisely because of the hitherto unthinkable alliance between the New Right and radical feminism on the issue of pornography, there is now every possibility that a critique which stops only with this kind of moralistic closure inevitably plays into an anti-democratic politics of censorship and cultural closure sought by the ascendant forces of the New Right. In what follows, I explain how and why I changed my mind.[3]

Picture this: two reasonably intelligent black gay men pore over Mapplethorpe's 1986 publication *The Black Book*. When a friend lent me his copy, this was exactly how it circulated between us: as an illicit and highly troublesome object of desire. We were fascinated by the beautiful bodies and seduced by the pleasure in looking as we perused the repertoire of images. We wanted to look, but we didn't always find what we wanted to see. This was because we were immediately disturbed by the racial dimension of the imagery and, above all, angered by the aesthetic objectification that reduced these individual black men to purely abstract visual 'things', silenced in their own right as subjects and serving mainly as aesthetic trophies to enhance Mapplethorpe's privileged position as a white gay male artist in the New York avant-garde. In short, we were stuck in a deeply ambivalent structure of feeling. In an attempt to make sense of this experience, I drew on elements of feminist cultural theory.

The first thing to notice about Mapplethorpe's black males—so obvious that it goes without saying—is that all the men are nude. Framed within the generic conventions of the fine-art nude, their bodies are aestheticized and eroticized as 'objects' to be looked at. As such, they offer an erotic source of pleasure in the act of looking. But whose pleasure is being served? Regarding the depiction of women in dominant forms of visual representation, from painting to advertising or pornography, feminist cultural theory has shown that the female image functions predominantly as a mirror-image of what men want to see. As a figment of heterosexual wish-fulfilment, the female nude serves primarily to guarantee the stability of a phallocentric fantasy in which the omnipotent male gaze sees but is never itself seen. The binary opposition of seeing/being seen which informs visual representations of the female nude reveals that looking is never an innocent or neutral activity, but is always powerfully loaded by the gendered character of the subject/object dichotomy in which, to put it crudely, men look and women are there to be looked at.

In Mapplethorpe's case, however, the fact that both artist and model are male sets up a tension of sameness which thereby transfers the *frisson* of 'difference' from gender to racial polarity. In terms of the conventional dichotomy between masculinity as the active control of the gaze, and femininity as its passive visual object, what we see in Mapplethorpe's case is the way in which the black/white duality of 'race' overdetermines the power relations implicit in the gendered dichotomy between subject and object of representation.

In this sense, what is represented in Mapplethorpe's photographs is a 'look', or a certain 'way of looking', in which the pictures reveal more about the absent and invisible white male photographer who actively controls the gaze than they do about the black men whose beautiful bodies we see depicted in his photographs. In so far as the pictorial space excludes any reference to a social, historical, cultural or political context that might tell us something about the lives of the black models who posed for the camera, Mapplethorpe facilitates the projection of certain racial and sexual fantasies about the 'difference' that black masculinity is assumed to embody. In this way, the photographs are very much about sexual investment in looking, because they disclose the tracing of desire on the part of the I/eye placed at the centre of representation by the male gaze.

Through a combination of formal codes and conventions—the posing and posture of the body in the studio enclosure; the use of strong chiaroscuro lighting; the cropping, framing and fragmentation of the whole body into parts—the 'look' constructed not only structures the viewer's affective disposition towards the image but reveals something of the *mise en scène* of power, as well as desire, in the racial and sexual fantasies that inform Mapplethorpe's representation of black masculinity. Whereas the white gay male sadomasochist pictures portray a subcultural sexuality that consists of 'doing' something, the black men are defined and confined to 'being' purely sexual and nothing but sexual—hence hypersexual. We look through a sequence of individually named African-American men, but we see only sexuality as the sum-total meaning of their black male identity. In pictures like 'Man in a Polyester Suit' (1980), apart from the model's hands, it is the penis, and the penis alone, that identifies him as a black man.

Mapplethorpe's obsessive focus on this one little thing, the black man's genitals, and the way in which the glossy allure of the quality monochrome print becomes almost consubstantial with the shiny, sexy texture of black skin, led me to argue that a certain racial fetishism is an important element in the pleasures (and displeasures) which the photographs bring into play. Such racial fetishism not only eroticizes the most visible aspect of racial difference—skin colour—but also lubricates the ideological reproduction of 'colonial fantasy', in which the white male subject is positioned at the centre of representation by a desire for mastery, power and control over the racialized and inferiorized black Other. Hence, alongside the codes of the fine-art nude, Mapplethorpe seems to make use of the regulative function of the commonplace racist stereotype—the black man as athlete, mugger savage—in order to stabilize the invisible and all-seeing white subject at the centre of the gaze, and thereby 'fix' the black subject in its place not simply as the Other, but as the object in the field of vision that holds a mirror to the fears and fantasies of the supposedly omnipotent white male subject.

According to literary critic Homi Bhabha, 'an important feature of colonial discourse is its dependence on the concept of "fixity" in the ideological construction of otherness'.[4] Just as Mapplethorpe's photographs of female body-builder Lady Lisa Lyon seem obsessively to pin her down by processing the image of her body through a thousand cultural stereotypes of femininity, so the obsessive undercurrent in his black male nudes would appear to confirm this emphasis on fixity as a sign that betrays anxiety as well as pleasure in the desire for mastery. Mapplethorpe's scopic fixation on the luxurious beauty of black skin thus implies a kind of 'negrophilia', an aesthetic idealization of racial difference that merely inverts and reverses the binary axis of colonial discourse, in which all things black are equated with darkness, dirt and danger, as manifest in the psychic representations of 'negrophobia'. Both positions, whether they overvalue or devalue the visible signs of racial difference, inhabit the shared space of colonial fantasy. These elements for a psychoanalytic reading of fetishism, as it is enacted in the theatre of Mapplethorpe's sex–race fantasy, are forcefully brought together in a photograph such as 'Man in a Polyester Suit'.

The use of framing and scale emphasizes the sheer size of the big black penis revealed through the unzipped trouser fly. As Fanon said, when diagnosing the terrifying figure of 'the Negro' in the fantasies of his white psychiatric patients, 'One is no longer aware of the Negro, but only of a penis: the Negro is eclipsed. He is turned into a penis. He *is* a penis.'[5] By virtue of the purely formal device of scale, Mapplethorpe summons up one of the deepest mythological fears in the supremacist imagination: namely, the belief that all black men have monstrously large willies. In the phantasmic space of the white male imaginary, the big black phallus is perceived as a threat not only to hegemonic white masculinity but to Western civilization itself, since the 'bad object' represents a danger to white womanhood and therefore the threat of miscegenation, eugenic pollution and racial degeneration. Historically, in nineteenth-century societies structured by race, white males eliminated the anxiety that their own fantastic images of black male sexuality excited through rituals of aggression in which the lynching of black men routinely involved the literal castration of the Other's strange fruit.

The historical myth of penis size amounts to a 'primal fantasy' in Western culture in that it is shared and collective in nature—and, moreover, a myth that is so pervasive and firmly held as a folk belief that modern sexology repeatedly embarked on the empirical task of actually measuring pricks to demonstrate its untruth. Now that the consensual management of liberal race relations no longer provides available legitimation for this popular belief, it is as if Mapplethorpe's picture performs a disavowal of the wish-fulfilment inscribed in the myth: *I know* (it's not true that all black guys have big willies), *but* (nevertheless, in my photographs they do).

Within the picture, the binary character of everyday racial discourse is underlined by the jokey irony of the contrast between the black man's exposed private parts and the public display of social respectability signified by the three-piece business suit. The oppositions hidden and exposed, denuded and clothed, play upon the Manichaean dualism of nature and culture, savage and civilized, body and mind, inferior and superior, that informs the logic of dominant racial discourse. In this way, the construction of racial difference in the image suggests that sexuality, and nothing but sexuality, is the essential 'nature' of the black man, because the cheap and tacky quality of the polyester suit confirms his failure to gain access to 'culture'. The camouflage of bourgeois respectability fails to conceal the fact that the black man, as the white man's racial Other, originates, like his dick, from somewhere anterior to civilization.

CONFLICTING READINGS OF MAPPLETHORPE

Notwithstanding the problematic nature of Freud's pathologizing clinical vocabulary, his concept of fetishism can usefully be adapted, via feminist cultural theory, to help conceptualize issues of subjectivity and spectatorship in representations of race and ethnicity. Its account of the splitting of levels of belief may illuminate the prevalence of certain sexual fantasies and their role in the reproduction of racism in contemporary culture. The sexual fetish represents a substitute for something that was never there in the first place: the mother's penis, which the little boy expected to see. Despite conscious acknowledgement of sexual difference, the boy's castration anxiety forces the repression of his initial belief, such that it coexists on an unconscious level and finds manifestation, in adult sexuality, in the form of the erotic fetish.[6] One might say that, despite anatomical evidence, the belief symbolized in the fantasy of the big black willy—that black male sexuality is not only 'different' but somehow 'more'—is one many men and women, black and white, straight or gay, cling on to, because it retains currency and force as an element in the psychic reality of the social fantasies in which our racial and gendered identities have been historically constructed.

Yet because Freud's concept of fetishism is embedded in the patriarchal system of sexual difference that it describes, treating sexual perversion or deviation as a symptom which reveals the unconscious logic of the heterosexual norm, it is less useful as a tool for examining the perverse aestheticism of the modern homoerotic imagination which Mapplethorpe self-consciously employs. Moreover, there are limits to the race and gender analogy drawn from feminist cultural theory in the preceding analysis of visual fetishism: it ignores the obvious homoerotic specificity of the work. As a gay male artist whose sexual identity locates him in a subordinate relation to heterosexual masculinity, Mapplethorpe is hardly representative of the hegemonic model of straight, white, bourgeois male identity traditionally privileged in art history as the centred subject and agent of representation. Above all, as the recent exhibition history of his work attests, far from demonstrating the stability of this supposedly centred white male subject, the vitriol and anxiety expressed in hostile attacks on Mapplethorpe's *oeuvre* (such as those of radical neo-conservative art critic Hilton Kramer) would suggest that there is something profoundly troubling and disturbing about the emotional ambivalence experienced by different audiences through the salient shock effect of Mapplethorpe's work.

In the light of the changed context of reception, the foremost question is how different audiences and readers produce different and conflicting readings of the same cultural text. The variety of conflicting interpretations of the value of Mapplethorpe's work would imply that the text does not bear one, singular and unequivocal meaning, but is open to a number of competing readings. Thus Mapplethorpe's photographic text has become the site for a range of antagonistic interpretations. Once we adopt this view, we need to reconsider the relationship between artist and audience, or author and reader, because although we habitually attempt to resolve the question of the ultimate 'meaning' of a text by appealing to authorial intentions, post-structuralist theory has shown, by way of the 'death of the author' argument, that individual intentions never have the last word in determining the meaning or value of a text. This is because readers themselves play an active role in interpreting a multivalent and open-ended modernist cultural text.

One might say, therefore, that the difficult and troublesome question raised by Mapplethorpe's black male nudes—do they reinforce or undermine racist myths about black sexuality?—is strictly unanswerable, since his aesthetic strategy makes an unequivocal yes/no response impossible. The question is left open by the author and is thus thrown back to the spectator. Our recognition of the unconscious sex-race fantasies which Mapplethorpe's images arouse with such perverse precision does not confirm a stable or centred subject position, but is experienced precisely as an emotional disturbance which troubles the viewer's sense of secure identity.

The recent actual death of the author entails a reconsideration of the issue of authorship and intentionality, and the reciprocal role of the reader, because the articulation of race and homosexuality in Mapplethorpe's art can also be seen as a subversive move that begins to unravel the violent ambiguity at the interface of the social and the emotional. To clarify my suggestion that his black male nudes are open to an alternative evaluation from that of my initial reading, I should come clean with regard to the specific character of my own subject position as a black gay male reader.

My angry emphasis on racial fetishism as a potentially exploitative process of objectification was based on the way in which I felt identified with the black men depicted in the photographs, simply by virtue of sharing the same 'categorical' identity as a black man. As the source of this anger, emotional identification can be best described again in Fanon's words as a feeling that 'I am laid bare. I am overdetermined from without. I am the slave not of the "idea" that others have of me but of my own appearance. I am being dissected under white eyes. I am fixed . . . Look, it's a Negro'.[7] It was my anger at the aestheticizing effect of Mapplethorpe's coolly 'ironic' appropriation of racist stereotypes that informed the description of visual fetishism as a process of reduction, or dehumanization. This argument has many similarities with the early feminist critique of images of women in pornography.[8] But the problem with this view is that it moralizes images in terms of a reductive dichotomy between good and bad, 'positive' and 'negative', and thus fails to recognize the ambivalence of the text. If, on the other hand, we recognize that there is an important difference between saying that an image is racist and saying that it is 'about' racism, then we need a more reflexive approach to the ambiguities set into motion in the destabilizing moment of Mapplethorpe's shock effect.

On this view, the strategic use of visual fetishism is not necessarily a bad thing, as it encourages the viewer to examine his or her own implication in the fantasies which the images arouse. Once I acknowledge my own location in the image reservoir as a gay subject—a desiring subject not only in terms of sharing a desire to look, but in terms of an identical object-choice already there in my own fantasies and wishes—then the articulation of meanings about eroticism, race and homosexuality becomes a lot more complicated. Indeed, I am forced to confront the rather unwelcome fact that as a spectator I actually occupy the very position in the fantasy of mastery previously ascribed to the centred position of the white male subject! In other words, there was another axis of identification—between white gay male author and black gay male reader—that cut across the identification with the black men in the pictures. Could it not be the case that my anger was also mingled with feelings of jealousy, rivalry or envy? If I shared the same desire to look, which would place me in the position of mastery attributed to the author, the anger in the initial critique might also have arisen from a shared, homosexual identification, and thus a rivalry over the same unobtainable object of desire. In so far as the anger and envy were effects of my identification with both object and subject of the look, I would say that my specific identity as a black gay reader placed me in two contradictory positions at one and the same time. I am sure that emotions such as these are at issue in the rivalry of interpretations around Mapplethorpe's most contentious work. Black gay male readers certainly do not have a monopoly on the conflicted and ambivalent structures of feeling they create. My point here is not confessional, but to use my own experience as a source of data about the complex operations of identification and desire that position us in antagonistic and contradictory relations of race, gender and power, which are themselves partly constituted in representations. In revising my views, I have sought to reopen the question of ambivalence, because rather than simply project it on to the author (by asking whether he either perpetuates or challenges racism) one needs to take into account how different readers derive different meanings not only about race, but about sexuality and desire, in Mapplethorpe's work.

THE PERVERSE AESTHETIC

The whole point about the use of textual ambivalence in the modernist tradition is to foreground the uncertainty of any one, singular meaning—which, in the case of Mapplethorpe's double transgressions across race and homosexuality, is a risky business indeed. This is because the open-ended character of the images can provoke a racist reading as much as an anti-racist one, elicit a homophobic reading as much as arouse a homoerotic one. A great deal depends on the reader and the social identity she or he brings to the text. The same statement—the black man is beautiful, say—retains the same denotative meaning, but acquires different connotational values when enunciated by different groups of subjects: the same sentence, uttered by a white man, a black woman, a black man or a white woman, would inevitably take on a qualitatively different 'sound'. Similarly, once we situate the network of relations between author, text and reader, in the contingent, context-bound circumstances in which Mapplethorpe's work currently stands, then we can examine the way in which the open-ended structure of the text gives rise to antagonistic readings that are informed by the social identity of the audience.

Without returning to a naive belief in the author as a godlike figure of authority, it is necessary to argue that it really does matter who is speaking whenever artists, because of their sexual, gender or racial identity, are assigned 'minority' status in the arts and in culture at large. Once we take the biographical dimension of Mapplethorpe's work as a gay artist into account it is possible to reinterpret the black male nudes as the beginning of an inquiry into the archive of 'race' in Western culture and history, which has rendered black men into 'invisible men', in Ralph Ellison's phrase. As Mapplethorpe put it in an interview shortly before his death, 'At some point I started photographing black men. It was an area that hadn't been explored intensively. If you went through the history of nude male photography, there were very few black subjects. I found that I could take pictures of black men that were so subtle, and the form was so photographical.' An awareness of the exclusion of the black subject from one of the most valued canonical genres of Western art—the nude—suggests that it is both possible and necessary to reread Mapplethorpe's work as part of an artistic inquiry into the hegemonic force of a Eurocentric aesthetics which historically rendered invisible not only black people but women, lesbians and gays and others before the radical social transformations of the modern and postmodern period.

By virtue of a perverse aesthetic of promiscuous intertextuality, whereby the overvalued aura of the fine-art nude is contaminated by the filthy and degraded form of the commonplace stereotype, Mapplethorpe transgresses on several fronts to make visible that which is repressed and made invisible in the dominant, and dominating, tradition of the West against the rest. In the contemporary United States, for example, black males constitute one of the 'lowest' social identities in the late-capitalist underclass: disenfranchised, disadvantaged, disempowered. Yet in Mapplethorpe's studio, some of the men who in all probability came from this class are elevated on to the pedestal of the transcendental aesthetic ideal of the male nude in Western culture, which had always excluded the black subject from such aesthetic idealization on account of its otherness. Mapplethorpe's achievement as a postmodern 'society photographer' lies in the way he renders invisible men visible in a cultural system—art photography—that always historically denied or marginalized their existence. One can see in Mapplethorpe's use of homoeroticism a subversive strategy of perversion in which the liberal humanist values inscribed in the idealized fine-art nude are led away from the higher aims of 'civilization' and brought face to face with that part of itself repressed and devalued as 'other' in the form of the banal, commonplace stereotype in everyday culture. What is experienced in the salient shock effect is the disruption of our normative expectations about distinctions that imply a rigid separation between fine art and popular culture, or between art and pornography. Mapplethorpe's transgressive crossing of such boundaries has the effect of calling into question our psychic and social investment in these cultural separations.

CHANGING POLITICAL CLIMATES

If I am now more prepared to offer a defence rather than a critique of Mapplethorpe's representations of race, because of the changed ideological context, it is because the stakes have also changed. I am convinced that it was not the death of the author so much as the cause of his death that was a major factor in the timing of the Helms campaign against the NEA. Almost all the discourse surrounding the furore noted that Mapplethorpe died of AIDS. The new-found legitimacy of political homophobia and the creation of new folk devils through the mismanagement of the AIDS crisis has proved fertile ground for the spread of popular authoritarian tendencies across the left/right spectrum. Yet the Mapplethorpe/NEA crisis in the USA was often perceived, like the Rushdie crisis in Britain, simply in terms of a straightforward opposition between censorship and freedom of artistic expression. This model of a crude binary frontier is unfeasible because what was at stake in the conflicting readings of Mapplethorpe was not a neat dichotomy between bigoted Philistines and enlightened cultured liberals but a new configuration of social actors, some of whom have engaged in unexpected alliances which have transformed the terrain of contestation.

In many ways the right's success in organizing a popular bloc of public opinion on issues like pornography derives from these new alliances. Just like the alliance formed between radical feminist anti-porn activists and the local state legislature in the form of the Dworkin MacKinnon-drafted Minneapolis Ordinance in 1984, or the appropriation of the feminist argument that pornography itself is violence in the official discourse of the Meese Commission in 1986, the Helms campaign has highlighted some significant developments in popular right-wing politics. In his original proposal to regulate public funding of art deemed 'obscene and indecent', Jesse Helms went beyond the traditional remit of moral fundamentalism to add new grounds for legal intervention on the basis of discrimination against minorities. Helms wanted the state to intervene in instances where artistic and cultural materials 'denigrate, debase or revile a person, group or class of citizens on the basis of race, creed, sex, handicap or national origin'. By means of this rhetorical move, he sought to appropriate the language of liberal anti-discrimination legislation to promote a climate of opinion favourable to new forms of coercive intervention. In making such a move, the strategy is not simply to win support from black people and ethnic minorities, nor simply to modernize the traditional 'moral' discourse against obscenity, but to broaden and extend the threshold of illegitimacy to a wider range of cultural texts. As the moral panic unfolds, more and more cultural forms transgress or come up against the symbolic boundary that such prohibitionary legislation seeks to impose. Consider the way in which parental warning labels on rap and rock albums have become commonplace: the Parents' Music Resource Centre that helped to initiate this trend in the 1980s has also inspired prosecutions of rock musicians on the grounds that their cultural texts do not simply 'deprave and corrupt', as it were, but have actually caused violence, in the form of suicides.

Under these conditions—when, despite its initial emancipatory intentions, elements of the radical feminist anti-porn movement of the 1980s have entered into alliance with neo-conservative—it is not inconceivable that a reading of Robert Mapplethorpe's work as racist, however well intended, could serve the ends of the authoritarian trend supported by this new alliance of social actors. The AIDS crisis has also visibly brought to light the way in which homophobia can be used to draw upon conservative forces within minority cultures. In black British communities, the anti-lesbian and gay hostility expressed in the belief that homosexuality is a 'white man's thing', and hence, because of the scapegoating of gay men, that AIDS is a 'white man's disease', has not only helped to cement alliances between black people and the New Right (for example, in the local campaign on 'Positive Images' in Haringey, London, in 1987) but has had tragically self-defeating consequences in the black community itself. Men and women have been dying, but the psychic mechanism of denial and disavowal in such fear of homosexuality has been particularly apparent in many black responses to AIDS.

Yet these contradictory conditions have also shaped the emergence of a new generation of black lesbian and gay cultural activists in Britain and the United States. Their presence is seriously important not only because they contest the repressive precepts of authoritarian politics in both white society and in black communities, but because their creativity points to new ways of making sense of the contemporary situation. Black lesbian and gay artists such as Isaac Julien, Pratibha Parmar, Michelle Parkerson and Marlon Riggs in film and video; or Essex Hemphill, Cheryl Clarke, Barbara Smith and Joseph Beam in writing and critique, or Sunil Gupta, Rotimi Fani-Kayode or Lyle Harris in the medium of photography, have widened and pluralized the political and theoretical debates about eroticism, prohibition, transgression and representation. In films such as Isaac Julien's *Looking for Langston* (1989) some of the difficult and troublesome questions about race and homosexuality that Mapplethorpe raised are taken on in a multifaceted dialogue on the lived experience of black gay desire. In his photographs, Rotimi Fani-Kayode also enters into this dialogue, not through a confrontational strategy but through an invitational mode of address which operates in and against the visual codes and conventions his work shares with Mapplethorpe's. But in this hybrid, Afrocentric, homoerotic image world, significant differences unfold as such artists critically 'signify upon' the textual sources they draw from. In the hands of this new generation of black diaspora intellectuals rethinking sex, such 'signifying' activity simultaneously critiques the exclusions and absences which previously rendered black lesbian and gay identities invisible, and reconstructs new pluralistic forms of collective belonging and imagined community that broaden the public sphere of multicultural society.

Such radical changes in black queer visibility were unthinkable ten or fifteen years ago, and one would hope that their emergence now suggests new possibilities for an alternative set of popular alliances that seek to open up and democratize the politics of desire. In the event that the legislation sought by those opposed to whatever can be called 'pornographic' is ever successful in Britain, it is far more likely that it will first be brought to bear on independent artists such as these rather than on the corporations and businessmen who own the porn industry, edit the tabloids or sell advertising. To propose to outlaw something the definition of which no one seems to agree upon is hardly in the interests of anyone seeking not just the protection of our existing civil rights and liberties (few as they are in Britain) but the necessary changes that would further democratize and deepen new practices of freedom.

Notes

1. Audre Lorde, 'Uses of the Erotic: The Erotic as Power' (1978) and Alice Walker, 'Coming Apart' (1979), both reprinted in Laura Lederer, ed., *Take Back the Night: Women on Pornography* (New York: William Morrow, 1980).
2. Susanne Kappeler, *The Pornography of Representation* (Cambridge: Polity Press, 1986), pp.5–10.

   One important alternative to the race and gender analogy is to open the debate to include racism in both pornography and in the women's movement. This is an important point, raised in the context of a historical overview of the mutual articulation of gender and sexuality in racial oppression, discussed by Tracey Gardner, 'Racism in Pornography and the Women's Movement' (1978), in Lederer, ed., *Take Back the Night.*
3. See Kobena Mercer, 'Imaging the Black Man's Sex', in Patricia Holland, Jo Spence, and Simon Watney, eds, *Photography/Politics: Two* (London: Comedia, 1986) and, for the revision of the initial analysis, 'Skin Head Sex Thing: Racial Difference and the Homoerotic Imaginary', in Bad Object Choices, ed., *How*

Do I Look? Lesbian and Gay Film and Video (Seattle Bay: Press, 1991). Related work on the cultural politics of black masculinity may be found in Isaac Julien and Kobena Mercer, 'Race, Sexual Politics and Black Masculinity: A Dossier', in Rowena Chapman and Jonathan Rutherford, eds, *Male Order: Unwrapping Masculinity* (London: Lawrence & Wishart, 1988).

The black male nude photographs referred to may be found in Robert Mapplethorpe, *Black Males* (Amsterdam: Gallerie Jurka, 1982); *The Black Book* (Munich: Schirme-Mosel, 1986); and Richard Marshall, ed., *Robert Mapplethorpe* (New York: Bullfinch Press, 1990).

4. Homi Bhabha, 'The Other Question: Colonial Discourse and the Stereotype', *Screen* 24:4 (1983), p.18.
5. Frantz Fanon, *Black Skin/White Masks* (London: Pluto Press, 1986 [first published 1952]), p.120.
6. Sigmund Freud, 'Fetishism' (1923), in *The Pelican Freud Library*, vol 7, *On Sexuality* (Harmondsworth: Penguin, 1977).
7. Fanon, *Black Skin/White Masks*, p.82.
8. The humanist critique of objectification is taken up by Essex Hemphill, 'Introduction', in Essex Hemphill, ed., *Brother to Brother: New Writings by Black Gay Men* (Boston: Alyson Press, 1991).

25 Good Girls Look the Other Way

bell hooks

A page in the book *Her Tongue On My Theory* has a single photographic image of a woman's closed painted lips. Next to it the caption raises the question: 'Stripped of history?' Desire has the power to do just that, to make us forget who we are. It both disrupts and deconstructs. It dismembers and disembodies. The power of desire to seduce, to lead us in dangerous directions is explored in Spike Lee's moving film *Girl 6*. Offering audiences intense close-up shots of lips—closed, moving, talking—the passion of this film is there in the mouth, the voice. Contrary to what most viewers imagine before they see *Girl 6* this is not a film that exploits the objectification of women. This is a film that explores the eroticization of stardom, of attention. Is is a long slow narrative about lack, about where the inability to feel pleasure can take one. The film keeps telling us over and over again that there are spaces in our lives, spaces of longing where nothing matters but the quest to fulfill desire. The longing of women and men in this film is not for sexual satisfaction but for undivided, unconditional attention. It is the desire to be seen, to not be erased or rendered invisible that fuels individual longings.

A really sad and tender film, no wonder it is misunderstood, seen by many as a 'bad' movie. It is not as some critics have suggested a failed comedy. While the film has witty, satiric moments that are incredibly funny, it is a serious film. Unlike other Spike Lee films the narrative is not carried along by the persistent humor of vernacular black culture. Race and racism are backdrops, they are not the issues that have center stage. The poetics of unrequited desire is foregrounded in this film. No wonder then that most audiences cannot handle it. And more is the

bell hooks, 'Good Girls Look the Other Way', from *Reel to Real*, bell hooks (Routledge, 1996), 10–19, reprinted by permission of Taylor and Francis/ Routledge Inc.

pity that women, many of them feminist in their thinking, want to dismiss it as just sexism all over again.

Sometimes advertising can kill a movie as much as it can make everyone want to go out and see it. Before anybody sees *Girl 6* the rumor is out that Spike is making a film about phone sex. The previews we see at other movies aim to titillate. Exploiting hidden pornographic longings in the viewer, they imply that the film will be shallow, light, all surface just like your everyday run-of-the-mill heterosexual bad porn. Provocative advertising may lead audiences to the film, but most will not be satisfied with what they see on the screen. Of the nine films that Spike Lee has made this is the most serious, the one that really does not centrally focus on race and racism, the one that uses a lot of technical experimentation in the cinematography.

Before I see *Girl 6* everyone is telling me that this film is 'Spike's answer to the feminists'. As a cultural critic and feminist thinker who began writing on film in response to *She's Gotta Have It*, I wondered what the question was that feminists had asked Spike. In my critical writings on his work I have called for a broader, more complex vision of womanhood in general, and black womanhood in particular, in Lee's work. And of course in the essay 'Whose Pussy Is This' I suggested that it might be great to have a film where when asked that question, an empowered black woman would be seeking her own answer and speaking it with her own sexual voice. In many ways *Girl 6* shows that Spike Lee's artistic vision regarding the representation of female sexuality has expanded. His maturation as a filmmaker is evident, and with it his capacity to represent women characters in more complex ways. This film is not an orgy of pornographic sexism. Audiences voyeuristically enter a world where men 'act out' their patriarchal fantasies, through enlightened commentary by both the phone sex operators and the male characters. The women working in the sex industry whose job it is to respond to those fantasies are never portrayed as victims.

From the get-go, *Girl 6* lets audiences know that women working in this aspect of the sex industry, as in so many other areas, are doing it for the money. And that sometimes it can be pleasurable work like any other job any other worker does for the money, while at other times it is dehumanizing, degrading labor. Headed by a sexy, powerful, full-figured black woman, the team of women Girl 6 joins are depicted as completely detached from their jobs and fairly contemptuous of the men who are seeking phone sex. Everyone is clear that it is boring, tedious work. Mostly, they are doing other things while they talk to the guys on the phone—reading, drawing, eating. Even though undivided attention is what the callers seek, and appear to be getting, the truth is, the operators are only pretending.

The lead character, Girl 6, seeks work in the sex industry only after failing to find gainful employment as an actress. Ironically, it is her refusal to let her naked body be exploited for visual pornographic pleasure that leads her to lose jobs. Blatantly the film reminds audiences that women's bodies are subordinated to patriarchal pleasure in ways that are similar in the movies and on the streets. A critique of sexism in the film industry is made when the movie begins. In a masterfully satiric moment filmmaker-actor Quentin Tarantino plays the role of Q.T., the hottest director in Hollywood. When Girl 6 tries out for a role in his latest film, he humiliates her. He silences her. Basically he tells her to shut up and listen, to be obedient, to do as she is told. When she submits exposing her gorgeous full rounded breasts, shame overwhelms and she leaves. Later her agent admits that he has not informed her that she must audition and possibly work in the nude because he knows she would protest. His deceit and betrayal are part of the seduction. He attacks her principles, pointing out that Sharon Stone has had no such inhibitions. Again and again Girl 6 gets the message that success depends on her willingness to exploit her body, her being. To be a film star she must be willing to go all the way. When she refuses she ends up with no money, no skills, and turns to phone sex.

Girl 6 is utterly seduced by the magic of Hollywood. Her seduction begins in a childhood spent watching television and movies. The filmic heroine whose footsteps she hopes to follow is Dorothy Dandridge, the first black woman ever to be considered for an Academy Award. Dandridge broke down color barriers, and tantalized audiences with her portrayal of a sexually liberated, independent woman in *Carmen Jones*. Dandridge wanted to achieve stardom walking the same path as her white female contemporaries, Grace Kelly, Audrey Hepburn, Judy Garland to name a few. She not only slept with white men, but when a newspaper reported that she had slept with more than a thousand men, she threatened to sue and received a public retraction.

Certain aspects of the film industry, especially the history of black film, are subtly conveyed by the focus on Dorothy Dandridge. And even though Girl 6 overtly deals with the issue of racism, everyone understands that in the world of representations whiteness is the essential ingredient necessary for ultimate fulfillment. This is true of both movie culture and the realm of phone sex. The head of the agency reminds all the women that they must all describe themselves as 'white' unless they are assuming a role in a requested fantasy. Sallie Tisdale's *Talk Dirty to Me* documents the longing for young white, blonde flesh that abounds in the sex industry. The same holds true for Hollywood. At the very same time that critics are unable to see the deeper dimensions of Lee's film, works by white male directors *Casino* and *Leaving Las Vegas* with female leads who are white and blonde working in the sex industry receive critical acclaim. Lee's film subtly critiques the hegemony of white images of glamour even as he explicitly shows the way black women enter a movie industry where their beauty marks them for roles as sexual servants.

Exposing the way in which black female sexuality is imaged in television and movies in all-black productions, Lee reenacts a hilariously funny scene from the sitcom *The Jeffersons* where the daughter is protected from the racy phone calls of a male admirer by her patriarchal dad, who literally shoots the phone. Nuclear-family values intact, the characters dance to celebrate. Yet this image suggests that within the context of conservative black family values sexual repression is the order of the day. This is no more a location where a liberatory black female sexuality can emerge than in the context of whiteness.

The black woman character who is the movie's embodiment of sexual power and agency is the police officer Foxy Brown, whose name, 'Lovely', Girl 6 assumes for her phone callers. Since they are white, she can rely on them to be unfamiliar with this cultural reference. Lee incorporates footage from a black exploitation film featuring Foxy. In the scene we see, Lovely gains power only by destroying black men. She becomes a pseudo male in drag, hence her ability to assert sexual agency. By relying on mass-media images to structure her sense of self and identity, Girl 6 can find no representations of liberatory sexuality. She must be either victim, vamp, or castrator. All of these roles still require that she shape her sexuality in response to the eroticism of the patriarchal phallic imaginary. For that imaginary controls the world of media images—of representations.

Black males, the film suggests, can rely on the realms of sport to constitute a space where they can perform and shape an empowering identity. Jimmy, the friendly neighbor who lives in the same building with Girl 6, collects baseball cards with black players. While he borrows money to survive from Girl 6, he is able to use his childlike fantasies to ensure a future. The imagery that he engages does not require a negation of blackness. Whereas any black actress who wants to make it in Hollywood has to confront a world where glamour, beauty, sensuality and sexuality, desirability are always encoded as white. Therefore the black female who wishes to 'make it' in that cultural sphere must be prepared to disidentify; with her body and be willing to make herself over. As the film progresses we witness the myriad ways Girl 6 makes herself over to become the desired object. Her constant changing of outfits, hairstyles, and so on, reminds viewers that femininity is constructed, not natural. Femininity, like phone sex, was invented to satisfy male fantasy. It is there to affirm the realm of the masculine, of phallic power. The bodies of real women must be sacrificed on the patriarchal altar.

Sexism and racism converge to make this sacrifice all the more tragic and horrific for black women. These factors ensure that Girl 6 and the male friends who are her comrades (her ex-husband, her buddy Jimmy) are likely to be poor. They are psychically damaged. The one black adult male who calls for fun sex is as obsessed with baseball as Jimmy. His clinging to fantasies of phallic stardom contrasts with his flabby body and his lack of a real team. All the major black characters in the film are thwarted in their desire to achieve economic prosperity and stardom. Fantasy is the catalyst for their desire. Even if they cannot make it to the top, they can sustain themselves with fantasies of triumph—of stealing power back from the conquering forces of whiteness (the ex husband bases his identity on Robin Hood). The white woman with whom Girl 6 bonds warns her not to become addicted to fantasy. She does not listen. All her dreams are rooted in fantasy. Addictively attached to the attention she receives from callers, she agrees to meet with Bob, the well-to-do white male businessman who usually talks with her about his mother's impending death. Dressed as though she is starring in a movie, Girl 6 waits for Bob to show up, only he never comes. When a white male walks by not even noticing her, she calls out to him. He does not turn and look her way. Invisible within the realm of whiteness, Girl 6 is powerless to fulfill her fantasies.

Rejection only intensifies the shame that has already been central to the formation of Girl 6's identity. Philosopher Sandra Bartky in her insightful work *Femininity and Domination: Studies in the Phenomenology of Oppression* emphasizes that 'Shame is profoundly disempowering', as 'the need for secrecy and concealment' it creates leads to isolation. Certainly Girl 6 seems unable to share with anyone the extent to which she is trapped by her longings for stardom and her understanding that she cannot really fulfill those longings without destroying parts of herself. Both her shame and her sense of woundedness lead her to identify with the pretty little black girl growing up in Harlem who falls down the broken elevator shaft. Overidentified with the television image of this little girl whose tragedy brings stardom, Girl 6 bandages her head as though she, too, were suffering.

Media images have so much power that they distort reality. They encourage children to seek solace in fantasy. Commenting on her relationship to media images in an interview in *Essence* magazine, Theresa Randle remembers: 'I loved Shirley Temple movies. I used to watch this little girl go in and out of all these different experiences and I hoped to be able to do the same thing.' Throughout the film, Lee suggests that individuals who are psychically wounded are trapped in infantile states. Addiction to fantasies begins in childhood as a way the self is nurtured when there is no real nurturance, when life is without substance or meaning. The mother and aunt of the little girl who is hurt use God as their solace, whereas the wounded 'inner child' relies on fantasy—on dreams of power and glory.

No matter how powerful and materially successful the corporate white men are in *Girl 6*, they are also emotionally wounded, stuck in infantile stages of development. Exploring the origin of male sexual fantasies in *Vogue* magazine, a white male writer comments: 'It seems to me that many men fix on their object of desire at a place that is deep in the recesses of childhood; their libidos are coded at an early age. The childish aspect of lust is for most men the hardest to admit or to come to terms with. It is the childishness that all prostitutes and role players know. For many men the mere fact that something regarded as infantile is a stimulus makes them reluctant to disclose it.' Anonymous phone sex enables these men to speak their desires however strange or perverse. This discharging of the repressed emotion (culminating in jerking off) allows them to reenter the space of real life.

Despite interventions made by the contemporary feminist movement, women are still struggling to find a sexual voice, to find places where our desires and fantasies can be articulated in all their strangeness and perversity. One of the most powerful collections of feminist essays about sexuality, *Pleasure and Danger* edited by Carole Vance, contains work where women talk about the difficulty of naming what we desire sexually. In 'The Forbidden: Eroticism and Taboo' Paula Webster talks about the nature of female fear, the failure to find a sexual voice: 'Like strangers in a strange land, we ask ourselves these poignant questions when we admit our confusions to consciousness. The responsibility of creating a sexual life congruent with our often mute desires seems awesome and very likely impossible . . . Going beyond, the erotic territory that is familiar feels forbidden; we stop even our imaginings when confronted with taboo. Our hearts race, the world seems fragmented and threatening; we say "no" over and over again, convincing ourselves that to act or even to dream of new pleasure would be devastating. We meet the taboo head-on, and we are immobilized.' Girl 6 finds herself voyeuristically drawn to phone sex, getting deeper and deeper into the world of misogynist pornographic male fantasy. Following the lead of the female 'pimp' played by none other than Madonna, she goes where the male imagination takes her. And it is only when the anonymous caller who is into 'snuff' fantasies actually threatens to actualize the fantasy, to really kill her, that she awakens from the seductive trance her erotic voyeurism has lured her into. Patriarchal fantasies require that female desirability be constructed in the space of self-negation, of lack. To be subordinated fully Girl 6 (and all women) must die to her longings and be willing to act as a mirror reflecting male desire. This is what Spike Lee shows us in the film.

When Girl 6 performs her 'sex roles' for her ex-husband only to find that he then expects her to act the role of freak, she steps back into the conservative realm of family values where repression is the sign of respectability. Acting like an outraged virgin, she sees no connection between her performance and his assumption that she will do anything to pleasure him. Despite his addiction to stealing, he is the one person depicted in this film who constantly resists dehumanization in the realm of the sexual. Valuing touch, connection, face to-face encounters, he expresses emotions. He is the real romantic in the film, bringing flowers to Girl 6, giving her the old magazine with Dorothy Dandridge on the cover. In the end he calls her by the name Judy, reminding her of her real identity. Yet even their farewell scene is life imitating the movies. In reality their marriage has failed. In the fantasy they can still be close like newlyweds, dressed in white, they reunite only to part. This is the culture movies create in real life. Jimmy carries the suitcases, looking on, genuinely disappointed that he is losing a friend but pleased that she has awakened from her trance.

Girl 6 has no time for emotional feelings. She is stuck, unable to feel pleasure, swept away by her longings for attention, for stardom. Losing touch with caring black male friends subtextually she symbolically follows the path of Dorothy Dandridge, who late in her career was repulsed by the touch of black men. White men matter more to Girl 6 because they have the power to give her the career she so desires. Once again this signals a symbolic doubling with Dandridge, who was often sexually involved with the white men who helped advance her career. In the last black-and-white 'dream' sequence, Girl 6 is in Hollywood.

This scene dramatizes her desire to inhabit a visual universe where she can be center stage, the glamorous star. The powerful white male who receives her in full diva garb is flanked by servants: Girl 6 is led to the 'cinematic massa' by a fawning black secretary. Enchanted by her presence, he lavishes her with attention. In this fantasy racism does not exist and all is possible. Definitely the perfect actress for the part, Theresa Randle admits in *Interview* magazine that she is totally obsessed with 'old-style movie glamour'. 'I want to be Dorothy Dandridge or Marilyn Monroe walking down a red carpet looking fabulous.' Willingly embracing fantasy, Randle, like her character, finds it easy to look the other way when it comes to the fate of these two stars, whose lives end tragically. They were glamour girls who made it and died young. They were women who wanted sexual agency and never found a way to have it. Even when their dreams of stardom were fulfilled, it was not enough.

In many ways *Girl 6* is a satiric comment on the theme of insatiable female sexual desire that Spike Lee fixated on in *She's Gotta Have It*. Like Nola Darling, Judy claims that she is speaking to clear her name. At this moment she seems to be doubling for Spike Lee, who is also clearing his name with this film, wiping away the charges that he can only create sexist representations of black women. With wry wit, his satiric comment is that he had it wrong in *She's Gotta Have It* by suggesting that sexual desire really mattered to the 'liberated' woman. Now he tells us that what sexy black women (and all women) really want is power and stardom and if they have to, they will prostitute themselves to get it. And of course the white world of cinematic cool (quintessentially embodied in this film by Quentin Tarantino and Madonna) says, What's wrong with a little prostitution between friends? It's all performance.

Like Nola Darling, Girl 6 is conflicted. She wants to go all the way to stardom, but she is not sure she is ready to make the sacrifice especially if in the end she must sacrifice her life. If she does not play the game, if she is not willing to go all the way, she can never be a big success. When Judy resists in Hollywood, refusing to take off her clothes, she leaves with her integrity intact, celebrating by dancing on Dorothy Dandridge's star. In the distance we see that there is no crowd waiting outside to see the movie that is showing. The marquee gives its title—*Girl 6*. Once again Spike Lee signifies on his own work in Hollywood. Up to a point he has played the game and made it, doing more feature films than any other black director to date. Yet he has refused to go all the way. *Girl* 6 is his gesture of resistance. Combining strategies of experimental filmmaking, refusing to give us race as we conventionally see it at the movies, or sex or class, he risks that audiences will be unable to appreciate the significance of this work. He has the power to reclaim the space of artistic integrity. Working against the requirements of Hollywood, Spike Lee offers viewers the most diverse images of black female identity ever to be seen in a Hollywood film in *Girl 6*. Represented as mothers, newscasters, business executives, phone sex operators, black women have center stage in this film.

This does not mean that the story told is not a sad one. When the movie ends Judy's dreams are not fulfilled. They remain fantasy. Girl 6 never finds a sexual voice. We leave her as we find her, swept away by desire. It seems fitting that the sound track to this film would be created by the musical genius of the artist once known as Prince. For he eroticizes the voice in music, making a realm of sexual promise and possibility, of articulated anguish and unfulfilled desire. At times the sound track brings an operatic sensibility to *Girl 6*. Like the world of movies, from Hollywood to bad porn, the tradition of opera has given us a space of performance where women's longings are always betrayed, where negative representations of women abound. At the end of her book *Opera, or the undoing of Women*, Catherine Clement seduces readers with the promise of a world where women can live without betrayal. 'Singing there, scarcely audible, is a voice beyond opera, a voice of the future. A voice from before adulthood: the voice of tenderness and cuddling. The voice of a sweet body, one with no distance, one only a real body can make appear. Sleep will no longer awake to a little girl who is dead. Just as you always stretch your arms when you leave the darkness, these women will always sing.' There is this spirit of hopefulness in Spike Lee's *Girl 6*. It lies not in the narrative but in the representations.

The film acts as a critical intervention, opening up a cinematic space where women can disinvest from and disengage with old representations. Importantly, this exciting critical intervention will be overlooked if we see the film through the eyes of a narrowly formed feminism that clings to what Drucilla Cornell calls in *The Imaginary Domain* 'the configuration of the masculine imagery'. Another way to state this would simply be to say that if audiences are hung up about a black male representing female sexuality, using female nakedness and objectification, then they cannot see the whole picture. Often times when the context of a film is the sex industry, that is all anyone sees. So far reviews of *Girl 6* suggest audiences are unwilling to look past the phallic cultural preoccupation with outlaw sex to see what is really happening in the movie. Surely some of this resistance has to do with the fact that audiences in our culture have yet to learn how to see race and sex while simultaneously looking beyond them. In other words, we still live in a culture where black female bodies are stereotypically 'seen' in a sexual light so that it becomes difficult for audiences of any race to see our image standing for universal themes of identity formation, sexual agency, feminist resistance, unrequited longing, etc.

The cover of *Essence* magazine that highlights the female star of *Girl 6* carries the caption 'Spike Lee Does Phone Sex: Has He Gone Too Far?' This caption misleads. The film takes us into the world of the phone sex industry and beyond it. All the other journeys in the movie seem to be the ones audiences refuse to go on. The temptation to see *Girl 6* as only about the way men sexually exploit female bodies in the sex and movie industries must be resisted if we are to embrace the artistry and vision of this film. Spike Lee gives us new cinematic terrain with this movie, reminding us that resistance is vital if we want to see Hollywood change its ways of doing race, sex, and class. Girl 6 resists. Drucilla Cornell reminds us that women are still struggling to create a space where our sexuality and our sexual voices can speak freely, where female sexual identity and performance can be represented in their diversity and difference. That space has to be imagined and created by both progressive, visionary women and men. Affirming our need to make this cultural journey she writes: 'There is space for the woman with glory in her heart as long as we insist that we are already dwelling in it. We must write that dwelling into being as a place for us to "be" differently, to be beyond accommodation.' This is the cultural space Judy longs for, a world where she will not have to accommodate the desires of others. Spike Lee's *Girl 6* gives us a glimpse of glory. Don't look the other way.

26 The Force of Fantasy

Feminism, Mapplethorpe, and Discursive Excess

Judith Butler

A contemporary feminist interrogation of representation is inevitably caught up in a set of persistently ambivalent ontological claims. Recent feminist criticisms of poststructuralism and poststructuralist feminism take issue with what appears to be a refusal to grant a pre-given, pre-linguistic or self-identical status to the real. The so-called deconstruction of the real, however, is not a simple negation or thorough dismissal of any ontological claim, but constitutes an interrogation of the construction and circulation of what counts as an ontological claim. The critical point is to examine the exclusionary means by which the circumspection of the real has been part of feminist practice prior to there being any question of its status as a poststructuralist intrusion.

One feminist site where this critical problematization of the real has taken place is in theories of fantasy which are either implicitly or explicitly formulated in discussions of representation, feminist fictions, and feminist utopias and dystopias. Fantasy has been crucial to the feminist task of (re)thinking futurity: to that end feminist theory relies on the capacity to postulate through fantasy a future that is not yet (Bartkowski, Haraway). In this formation, fantasy is not equated with what is not real, but rather what is not *yet* real, what is possible or futural, or what belongs to a different version of the real.

In those anti-pornography positions that favor censorship, there is an implicit theory of fantasy that runs counter to the position sketched above. This implicit theory by which I mean this set of untheorized presumptions, relies upon a representational realism that conflates the signified of fantasy with its (impossible) referent and

Judith Butler, from 'The Force of Fantasy: Feminism, Mapplethorpe, and Discursive Excess', edited extract from *A Journal of Feminist Cultural Studies*, 2/2 (1990), 105–25, reprinted by permission of the author.

construes 'depiction' as an injurious act and, in legal terms, a discriminatory action or 'real' effect. This gliding from representation to the ontological claim moves in two directions at once: it establishes the referent first as that which the representation reflects and re-presents and, second, as that which is effectively performed and performatively effected by the representation. This formulation of representation as injurious action operates through an implicit understanding of *fantasy* as that which both produces and is produced by representations and which, then, makes possible and enacts precisely the referent of that representation. According to this implicit theory, the real is positioned both before and after its representation: and representation becomes a moment of the reproduction and consolidation of the real.

This hyperdetermination of the ontological claim in some ways runs precisely counter (although not dialectically opposed) to the poststructuralist effort to problematize the ways in which the ontological claim, whatever the foundational or mimetic place it assumes, is performed as an effect of signifying acts. This kind of problematizing suspension of the ontological has also had its place within feminist critical practice. For part of the task of many feminist critical practices has been to question the line according to which the distinction between the real and unreal is drawn; to ask: what is it that passes as the real, that qualifies the extent or domain of 'reality'? are the parameters of the real acceptable, contestable? in whose name is a given version of the real articulated? is the 'real' a contemporary configuration that precludes any transformation by positing the 'not yet' as the impossible, the unreal, rather than the unrealizable? If what goes under the description of the real is contingent, contrived, and instituted for a set of purposes, then the real is not a ground on which we might easily rely; indeed, it is a postulate that requires a political interrogation.

Whereas anti-pornography feminists presume a mimetic relation between the real, fantasy, and representation that presumes the priority of the real, we can understand the 'real' as a variable construction which is always and only determined in relation to its constitutive outside: fantasy, the unthinkable, the unreal. The positivist version of the real will consign all absence to the unreal, even as it relies on that absence to stabilize its own boundaries. In this sense, the phantasmatic, as precisely such a constitutive exclusion, becomes essential to the construction of the real. If this is so, in what sense, then, can we understand the real as an installation and foreclosure of fantasy, a phantasmatic construction which receives a certain legitimation after which it is called the real and disavowed as the phantasmatic? In what sense is the phantasmatic most successful precisely in that determination in which its own phantasmatic status is eclipsed and renamed as the real? Here the distinction between real and unreal contrives a boundary between the legitimate domain of the phantasmatic and the illegitimate.

When we point to something as real, and in political discourse it is very often imperative to wield the ontological indicator in precisely that way, this is not the end but the beginning of the political problematic: to prove events are real, one must already have a notion of the real within which one operates, a set of exclusionary and constitutive principles which confer on a given indication the force of an ontological designator; and if it is that very notion of the real that one wants, for political reasons, to contest, then the simple act of pointing will not suffice to delimit the principles which constitute the force of the indexical. In fact, the effect of transparency produced by indexical pointing will effectively foreclose the interrogation that is called for. Such a restrictively generated discursive domain provides exclusionary rules which guarantee in advance that that kind of pointing performs or produces the signification 'real' that it appears to find as the simple and exterior referent to which it points. When pointing appears sufficient to designate the real, it is only through implicit recourse to certain entrenched and exclusionary conventions that frame and sanction that version of the real, and the real that is thereby designated would also and at the same time be *restricted* to a pre-given version of itself. To change the real, that is, to change what qualifies as the real, would be to contest the syntax within which pointing occurs and on which it tacitly relies. If the production of the real takes place through a restriction of the phantasmatic—and we shall soon see one political ramification of this thesis—then the phantasmatic emerges necessarily as the variable boundary from which the real is insistently contested. In what follows, I will look at one kind of pointing (Helms's pointing at Mapplethorpe) which functions in both a referential and accusatory sense, that is, which restrains the signified (and the domain of the signifiable) precisely in the moment in which the phantasmatic assumes the status of the real, that is, when the two become compellingly conflated, that the phantasmatic exercises its power most effectively.

Now this might seem like an increasingly philosophic discussion for an essay which on the surface makes some gestures towards thinking about pornography, Mapplethorpe, and fantasy. Although a feminist inquiry—as I will insist—this paper seeks to criticize an alternative feminist theory of fantasy, one that is almost nowhere explicitly theorized, but which is implicit, operative, and politically effective.

In particular, I am concerned then with a theory of fantasy that informs some feminist efforts to read and, on occasion, to call for legal sanctions against pornography. And secondly, I am concerned with a theory of fantasy that appears to inform New Right efforts to prohibit federal funding of artists like Robert Mapplethorpe. The first draft of the bill recently passed by the Congress (HR 2788) which sets restrictions on the kinds of representations fundable by the state virtually cites the MacKinnon/Dworkin bill, known as the Minnesota antipornography bill (Title 7), to make its own case against Mapplethorpe.[1] In a sense, it is this sorry discursive alliance that I seek to understand in exposing what I take to be a common theory of fantasy and the phantasmatic that informs both views. But more broadly, I want to suggest that certain kinds of efforts to restrict practices of representation in the hopes of reigning in the imaginary, controlling the phantasmatic, end up reproducing and proliferating the phantasmatic in inadvertent ways, indeed, in ways that contradict the intended purposes of the restriction itself. The effort to limit representations of homoeroticism within the federally funded art world—an effort to censor the phantasmatic—always and only leads to its production; and the effort to produce and regulate it in politically sanctioned forms ends up effecting certain forms of exclusion that return, like insistent ghosts, to undermine those very efforts.

So what is meant by 'phantasmatic' here? To say that something is phantasmatic is not to say that it is 'unreal' or artificial or dismissable as a consequence. Wielded within political discourse, the real is a syntactically regulated phantasm that has enormous power and efficacy. Fantasy postures *as* the real, it establishes the real through a repeated and persistent posturing, but it also contains the possibility of suspending and interrogating the ontological claim itself, of reviewing its own productions, as it were, and contesting their claim to the real.

According to psychoanalytic theorists Jean Laplanche and J.-B. Pontalis, *fantasy constitutes a dimension of the real*, what they refer to as 'psychic reality'. In a sense, psychic reality is here inclusive of the real, it is the semantic excess, the constant verging on idealization and absolutization that characterizes the referential function and, in particular, the ways in which the phantasmatic assumes the places of the real within an untheorized use of referential language. In Jacqueline Rose's terms, the phantasmatic is also precisely that which haunts and contests the borders which circumscribe the construction of stable identities (90). I propose to revise this theory along Foucaultian lines to question how fantasy informs political discourse in ways that often defeat the very purposes to which political discourse is put. At stake is not the phantasmatic construction of the identity of the pornographer and the identity of the pornographee, but the dissimulation of 'identity' in fantasy (its distribution and concealment), a dissimulation which is I think regularly misunderstood by both the advocates of censorship on the political right and those feminist theorists who, in their critique of pornography, propose to establish a logical or causal continuum among fantasy, representation, and action. Does fantasy compel a phantasmatic identification with aggression or victimization? Does it provide a motivational link between representation and action? If both of these questions are based upon a misconstrual of fantasy, then the arguments in favor of censorship are seriously weakened.

The ordinary language in which the meaning of fantasy is constituted misconstrues the status of fantasy altogether. We say, 'I have a fantasy' or 'this is my fantasy' and what is presupposed is an I, a subject who has a fantasy as a kind of interior and visual projection and possession. 'And in my fantasy,' we say, 'I was sitting in the cafeteria and you came up to me.' Already the 'I' who fantasizes is displaced, for the 'I' occurs at least twice, as the one who 'has' the fantasy, and the 'I' who is *in* the fantasy, indeed, who is in a sense 'had' by that prior I. What is the proper place of the 'I' in its redoubling? It is not enough to say that the 'I' who reports the fantasy, who 'has' it, is somehow 'real' and the 'I' who is 'in' it is phantasmatic, for the reporting 'I' is revealing and constituting its own content in and through the fantasy that is elaborated. The narrator of the fantasy is always already 'in' the fantasy. The 'I' both contributes to and *is* the frame, the complex of perspectives, the temporal and grammatical sequencing, the particular dramatic tempo and conclusion that constitutes the very action of the fantasy. Hence, the 'I' is dissimulated into the entire scene, even as it appears that the 'I' merely watches on as an epistemological observer to the event.

According to Laplanche and Pontalis, fantasy does not entail an identification with a single position within the fantasy; the identification is distributed among the various elements of the scene: the identification is with the 'you' who comes up, the 'me' who is sitting, but further, with the verbs themselves, 'sitting', 'coming up', even variously 'coming' and 'up', even abject as it may seem, the grim landscape of cafeteria life that bespeaks the longing for a sudden and decisive erotic interruption. In any case, or rather in all of these cases, identification is multiple and shifting, and cannot be confined to the 'me' alone. Laplanche and Pontalis write:

> Fantasy is not the object of desire, but its setting. In fantasy the subject does not pursue the object or its sign; one appears oneself caught up in the sequence of images. One forms no representation of the desired object, but is oneself represented as participating in the scene although, in the earliest forms of fantasy, one cannot be assigned any fixed place in it (hence the danger, in treatment [and in politics] of interpretations which claim to do so). As a result, the subject, although always present in the fantasy, may be so in a desubjectivized form, that is to say, in the very syntax of the sequence in question. (Formations 26–27)[2]

There is, then, strictly speaking, no subject who has a fantasy, but only fantasy as the scene of the subject's fragmentation and dissimulation; fantasy enacts a splitting or fragmentation or, perhaps better put a multiplication or proliferation of identifications that puts the very locatability of identity into question. In other words, although we might wish to think, even fantasize, that there is an 'I' who has or cultivates its fantasy with some measure of mastery and possession, that 'I' is always already undone by precisely that which it claims to master.

Within psychoanalytic theory, fantasy is usually understood in terms of wish-fulfillment, where the wish and its fulfillment belong to the closed circuit of a polymorphous auto-eroticism. Hence, sexual fantasies may express a longing for a scene outside the fantasy, but the fantasy always figures that outside within its own terms, that is, as a moment inside the scene, effecting its fulfillment through a staging and distributing of the subject in every possible position. The consequence is that although it may well be some Other that I fantasize about, the fantasizing recasts that Other within the orbit of my scene, for fantasy is self-reflexive in its structure, no matter how much it enacts a longing for that which is outside its reach. And yet, the subject cannot be collapsed into the subject-position of that fantasy; all positions are the subject, even as this subject has proliferated beyond recognition. In a sense, despite its apparent referentiality, fantasy is always and only its own object of desire. And this is not to say that fantasy supplies its own thematic, but that the boundaries of the real against which it is determined are precisely what become problematized in fantasy. Fantasy suspends the ontological claim of that which passes as the real under the usual description.

How does the relationship between fantasy and auto-eroticism suggested by the above account provide insight in to the signifying status of the pornographic text? The psychoanalytic account resonates with an article by Dierdre English in *Mother Jones* from the early 1980s. Contrary to the claim that pornographic representation somehow leads to the action of rape by fueling violent fantasies, her argument was that most men interested in pornography were just benign masturbators for whom the auto-erotic moment was the be all and end all of sex.

Whereas English argued that pornographic fantasy substituted for action and provided for a catharsis in fantasy that made action superfluous, a very different position on fantasy has been operative within the anti-pornography movement and recent New Right calls for censorship. Both of these efforts to restrict or prohibit pornographic fantasy end up inadvertently but inevitably producing and authorizing in their own discursive actions precisely the scenes of sexual violence and aggression that they seek to censor. The effort to enforce a limit on fantasy can only and always fail, in part because limits are, in a sense, what fantasy loves most, what it incessantly thematizes and subordinates to its own aims. They fail because the very rhetoric by which certain erotic acts or relations are prohibited invariably eroticizes that prohibition in the service of a fantasy. These prohibitions of the erotic are always at the same time, and despite themselves, the eroticization of prohibition.

It would be mistaken to understand fantasy as a site of psychic multiplicity subsequently reduced and refused by the onset of a prohibitive law, as if fantasy were unproblematically before the law. Laplanche and Pontalis argue that in the *mise en scène* of desire, prohibition is always present in the very position of desire (*Vocabulaire* 156). This posited simultaneity of prohibition and desire, however, is given a circular temporality in Foucault. For Foucault, prohibition depends upon transgressive fantasies, and reproduces them in order to have an object upon which to act and augment itself. Prohibition appears to *precede* fantasy and to structure it essentially; this is part of what is meant earlier by the claim that fantasy designates the constitutive outside of the real. The moment of exclusion or prohibition produces and sustains the domain of the phantasmatic. The multiple sites through which the subject is dissimulated are produced, then, by the regulatory discourse which would institute the subject as a coherent and singular positionality. The 'syntax' and 'sequencing' that stage the self-dissimulating subject might then be reread as the specific rule-governed discourses of a given regulatory regime. In what follows, I will attempt a Foucaultian rereading of Laplanche and Pontalis in terms of the phantasmatic production that is the Helms amendment.

The recent legislative efforts by Jesse Helms to put a juridical harness on the imaginary by forbidding federal art funds appear in two forms, the original proposal, formulated in July 1989, and the final proposal, claimed as a 'compromise bill' which passed the Senate and became law in late September (Public Law 101-121). Although the bill forbids the National Endowment for the Arts from funding artistic projects that depict 'obscenity', the National Endowment for the Humanities, in the spirit of solidarity, quickly volunteered to adopt the bill as internal policy. In the original formulation of the bill, federal funds were prohibited from being used to 'promote, disseminate [!] or produce obscene *or indecent* materials, including but not limited to depictions of sadomasochism, homoeroticism, the exploitation of children, or individuals engaged in sex acts; *or, material which denigrates the objects or beliefs of the adherents of a particular religion or non-religion*' (italicized portions were subsequently deleted). In the original proposal the following clause also appeared continuous with what I just cited: 'or that denigrates, debases or reviles a person, group or class of citizens on the basis of race, creed, sex, handicap, age or national origin' ('Senate'). This added clause may seem logically and legally discontinuous with the former, for while the last clause appears to protect certain individuals against debasement, the former clause appears to enact the very debasement that the latter disallows. By adding the last clause originally, Helms effectively confounded feminist and conservative discourses, for the latter clause is meant to protect individuals and groups against discrimination. The legal move that would establish as discrimination the depiction or representation of certain groups in subordinate or debased positions finds its precedents in those legislative efforts inspired by some anti-pornography feminists to ban representations of women in sexually debased or subordinated positions. In effect, the feminist legal effort to include 'representations' or 'depictions' as instances and enactments of discrimination has been deployed by Jesse Helms to suggest a legal and discursive alliance with anti-pornography feminists. On the one hand, we can argue that legislative efforts to ban pornography never intended to sanction these other kinds of legal prohibitions, and we can even call for qualifications in those legislative efforts to make sure that representations of 'homoeroticism' and 'individuals engaged in sex acts' escape the censor, although clearly sado-masochists would fare less well—possibly because the action of the prohibitive law resembles or mobilizes that power/dynamic most proximately (interestingly, though, without the qualification of consent insisted upon by libertarian sadomasochists).[3]

I would like to consider this alliance briefly in the context of a shared conception of representation as debasing and discriminatory action. I would suggest that the legal equivalence between representation and action could not be established were it not for an implicit and shared conception of fantasy as the causal link between representation and action, or between a psychic act that remains within the orbit of a visual economy, and an enacted fantasy in which the body literally enters what was previously a purely visualized or fantasized scene. Here the phantasmatic construction of the real is confused with a temporal linkage between fantasy and the real, as if fantasy could suddenly transmute into action, as if the two were separable from the start. I would argue, however, that fantasy constitutes a psychic action, and what is conjured as 'physical action' by the above causal formulation is precisely the condensation and foreclosure of fantasy, not that which follows from it. Accordingly, fantasy furnishes the psychic overdetermination of meaning which is designated by 'the real'. 'Fantasy' and 'the real' are always already linked. If the phantasmatic remains in tension with the 'real' effects it produces—and there is good reason to understand pornography as the erotic exploitation of this tension—then the 'real' remains permanently within quotations i.e. 'action' is suspended or better yet pornographic action is always suspended action.

The anti-pornography effort to impute a causal or temporal relation between the phantasmatic and the real raises a set of problems. If representations of women in subordinate or debased positions—assuming for the moment that some agreement could be achieved on what that is—if such representations *are* discriminatory actions, one way to understand representation is as the incipient moment of an inexorable action, containing within itself a teleological principle whereby the transformation of picture into fantasy is followed by the transformation of fantasy into action. By establishing causal lines among representation, fantasy, and action, one can effectively argue that the representation *is* discriminatory action. Here the view that fantasy motivates action rules out the possibility that fantasy is the very scene which *suspends* action and which, in its suspension, provides for a critical investigation of what it is that constitutes action.

Of course, the other way to argue that representation is discriminatory action is to claim that to see a given representation constitutes an injury, that representations injure, and that viewers are the passive recipients of that visual assault. Here again there is no interpretive leeway between the representation, its meanings, and its effects; they are given together, in one stroke—as it were—as an instantaneous teleology for which there is no alternative. And yet, if this were true, there could be no analysis of pornography. Even from within the epistemological discourse that Dworkin uses, one which links masculinity with agency and aggression, and femininity with passivity and injury, her argument defeats itself: no interpretive possibilities could be opened up by the pornographic text, for no interpretive distance could be taken from its ostensibly injurious effects; and the muted, passive, and injured stance of the woman viewer would effectively preclude a critical analysis of its structure and place within the field of social power.

The shift from an epistemological framework to one which takes the pornographic text as a site of multiple significations allows us to read Dworkin's move differently. The claim that the text permits of a single interpretation is itself a construction of the pornographic text as a site of univocal meaning; if pornography is a textualized fantasy of dissimulated and unstable identifications, then *the claim* that pornography enforces a foreclosure of the text's possible readings is itself the forcible act by which that foreclosure is effected.

The reason why representations do not jump off the page to club us over the head, although sometimes we fantasize precisely that, is that even pornographic representations as textualized fantasy do not supply a single point of identification for their viewers, whether presumed to be stabilized in subject-positions of male or female. Indeed, the postulation of a single indentificatory access to the representation is precisely what stabilizes gender identity; the possibility of a cross-identification spells a kind of gender trouble that the anti-pornography analysis fully suppresses. In point of fact, it may well be more frightening to acknowledge an identification with the one who debases than with the one who is debased or perhaps no longer to have a clear sense of the gender position of either; hence, the insistence that the picture enforces an identification with victimization might be understood not only as a refusal to identify—even in fantasy—with aggression, but, further, as a displacement of that refused aggression onto the picture which then—as a transferential object of sorts—takes on a personified status as an active agent that abuses its passive viewer (or which stands in for the phantasmatic figure of 'patriarchy' itself). Indeed, if pornography is to be understood as fantasy, as anti-pornography activists almost invariably insist, then the effect of pornography is not to force women to identify with a subordinate or debased position, but to provide the opportunity to identify with the entire scene of debasement, agents and recipients alike, when and if those 'positions' are clearly discernable in the actions and landscapes of masturbatory scenes of triumph and humiliation. A feminist critic like Dworkin has shown us the importance of pornographic material in its status as *social text* which facilitates certain kinds of readings of domination. And yet, the pornographic fantasy does not restrict identification to any one position, and Dworkin, in her elaborate textual exegesis, paradoxically shows us how her form of interpretive mastery can be derived from a viewing which, in her own view, is supposed to restrict her to a position of mute and passive injury. The logic of epistemological determinism that stabilizes 'masculine' and 'feminine' within a frame of unilateral oppression is subject to a logical reversal which calls that frame into question: if the pornographic representation is someone else's fantasy, that of 'men'—broadly and ambiguously construed—and if 'the woman viewer' is the injured-object of that fantasy-turned-action, then women are by her definition never agents of pornographic fantasy. The very possibility of identifying in fantasy with a debased position requires an active and persistent foreclosure of other possible identifications. Hence, 'passivity' becomes a privileged mode of identification on which requires the collapse and consolidation of multiple sites of identification into one.

A question to raise here would be, is it even possible to do the kind of reading that Dworkin does, that involves a retelling and repetition of the pornographic scene without making use of precisely the variable identifications that the pornographic fantasy itself occasions? From what source does Dworkin's reading draw its own strength and mastery if not through an identification and redeployment of the very representation of aggression that she abhors? In other words, does the identificatory process that her own reading requires effectively refute the theory of identification that she explicitly holds?

Prohibitions work both to generate and to restrict the thematics of fantasy. In its production, fantasy is as much conditioned as constrained by the prohibitions that appear to arrive only after fantasy has started to play itself out in the field of 'representations'. In this sense, Mapplethorpe's production anticipates the prohibition that will be visited upon it; and that anticipation of disapprobation is in part what generates the representations themselves. If it will become clear that Helms requires Mapplethorpe, it seems only right to admit in advance that Mapplethorpe requires Helms as well. This is not to say that Mapplethorpe knew before he died that Helms would appear with amendment in hand, or that Mapplethorpe should have known better. On the contrary: Helms operates as the *pre*condition of Mapplethorpe's enterprise, and Mapplethorpe attempts to subvert that generative prohibition by, as it were, becoming the exemplary fulfillment of its constitutive sexual wish.

Dworkin's call for sanctions can be read similarly as a *re*emergence of precisely the prohibition which occasioned and produced the pornographic material itself. In this sense, the pornographic text mobilizes and produces both the positionality of victimization and that of the critical agency that attends to that victimization. The text encodes and presupposes precisely the prohibition which will later impose itself as if it were externally related to the text itself.

The ambiguous temporal exchange between fantasy and its prohibition—which comes first?—can be read in those positions, like Dworkin's, which assert at the same time not only that certain fantasies are 'of' force or violence, but are *forcibly imposed* by certain kinds of representations. In this sense, the ostensible content of the representation and its rhetorical force are conflated and exchanged.

Something similar happens I think within the very amendment that Helms formulates. The amendment prohibits three kinds of activities, 'promoting, disseminating, and/or producing obscene or indecent materials', and then goes on to state some of what will be included under that category. Significantly, the language reads, 'including, but not limited to . . .' and then offers its list. 'Including, but not limited to' is a phrase that invites conservative judicial activism and presumes that the kinds of depictions to be deprived of federal funding have the possibility to spread, 'to disseminate . . .' like a disease perhaps, like AIDS, from which Mapplethorpe himself died? The presumption that the obscene and the pornographic have a way of getting out of hand is confirmed repeatedly in this fateful sentence: 'Including, but not limited to depictions of sadomasochism, homoeroticism': here homoeroticism is not distinct from homosexuality, but considered a more inclusive category; indeed, it provides for representations that depict homosexuality both explicitly and implicitly; hence, even the nuance of homosexuality is a site of danger (one might well wonder whether Plato's *Symposium* would receive funding under the guidelines now adopted by the National Endowment for the Arts and the National Endowment for the Humanities). But let us return to the progression of this sentence, for the 'including but not limited to' established a determinate juridical object and an indeterminate one as well, and this rhythm repeats itself throughout the sentence. Sadomasochism is presumed to be clearly and collectively identifiable in its distinction from other sorts of sexual activities but 'homoeroticism' is, I take it, a term that concedes the indeterminate status of this sexuality, for it is not simply the acts that qualify as homosexual under the law, but the ethos, the spreading power of this sexuality, which must also be rooted out.

'The exploitation of children' comes next, at which point I begin to wonder: what reasons are there for grouping these three categories together? Do they lead to each other, as if the breaking of one taboo necessitates a virtual riot of perversion? Or is there, implicit in the sequencing and syntax of this legal text, a figure of the homosexual, apparently male, who practices sadomasochism and preys on young boys, or who practices sadomasochism with young boys, a homosexuality which is perhaps defined as sadomasochism and the exploitation of children? Perhaps this is an effort to define restrictively the sexual exploiter of children *as* the sadomasochistic male homosexual in order, quite conveniently, to locate the source of child sexual abuse outside the home, safeguarding the family as the unregulated sexual property of the father?[4] On one level, the figure of such a homosexual is Mapplethorpe whom the *Washington Post* describes as producing 'photographs, some of which are homo-erotic or sado-masochistic, and some that show children exposing themselves' ('Obscenity'). And yet, the figure of Mapplethorpe is already a stand-in for the figure of the homosexual male, so that the target is a representation of homosexuality which, according to the representational theory Helms presumes, *is* in some sense the homosexual *him*self.

If the legal statute relies on this figure of the male homosexual, then perhaps the legal statute can be understood as its own kind of fantasy. The 'subject' of fantasy, according to Laplanche and Pontalis, is dissimulated in the syntax of the scene. This law contains as the tacit structure of its elliptical syntax a figure of homosexuality whose figurings, whose 'representations' are to be forbidden. In other words, this is a figure who can only be figured by Helms, who belongs to him, as it were, and who will be forbidden to figure anything or anyone in return. Is this a figure that the law contrives in order to prohibit, or perhaps, prohibits in order to produce—time and again—for its own . . . satisfaction? Is this a production of a figure that it itself outlaws from production, a vehement and public way of drawing into public attention the very figure that is supposed to be banned from public attention and public funds? What kind of sadomasochistic performance is this that brings into phantasmatic relief the very object that it seeks to subordinate, revile, debase, and denigrate? Is this not, paradoxically, a public flogging and debasement of the homosexual that is finally necrophilic as well, considering the fact that Mapplethorpe, who is made to stand for homosexuality in general, is but recently dead from AIDS?

In a sense, the Helms amendment in its final form can be read as precisely the kind of pornographic exercise that it seeks to renounce. According to the logic which would identify representations with injurious acts, Helms's amendment ought to be understood as an injury against those whom it demeans through its depiction. According to its own logic, Helms's amendment should then prohibit itself from becoming law. Although a wonderful turn of the screw to contemplate, it is not finally the argumentative tactic that I would promote. The phantasmatic construction of the homosexual in Helms's terms is not unlike the phantasmatic construction of women in pornography, but in each case, the question needs to be asked, at what juncture does that phantasmatic construction call its own ontological claim into question, reveal its own tenuousness, confess its own impossibility? There is no doubt that Helms's fantasy of homosexuality takes place within the scene of child molestation and sadomasochism; let us remember that this is his fantasy, though surely not his alone. Consider that the stability of the homosexual real as a social signification is always negotiated through fantasy; to point at Mapplethorpe's representations as the graphic articulation of homosexuality *soi-même*, is a state-sanctioned pointing (both a referring and a restraining) which effectively produces and stabilizes the homosexual real; in other words, it is a syntactically regulated phantasmatic production which assumes and preempts the claim of the real.

Helms not only extends those legal precedents that categorize homosexuality as obscenity, but, rather, authorizes and orchestrates through those legal statutes a restriction of the very terms by which homosexuality is culturally defined. One interpretation could claim that this tactic is simply an occasion for Helms to assault the gay male artistic community, or gay men generally, as well as the sexual practices phantasmatically imposed upon them. The political response is then to develop a political resistance to this move by simply reversing the argument, claiming that gay men are not as he says, that Mapplethorpe is more significant and more properly artistic. It is not merely that Helms characterizes homosexuality unfairly, but that he constructs homosexuality itself through a set of exclusions that call to be politically interrogated.

One effect of this law, then, is to circumscribe the imaginability of homosexuality; in exchange for the variety of 'representations' produced by Mapplethorpe and 'others like him', there is only one representation that is now sanctioned, the one that is articulately prohibited by Helms's law. Homosexuality becomes thinkable only as the forbidden and sadomasochistic exchange between intergenerational male partners. This prohibition is thus a production, one that takes place through reductive and exclusionary principles that regulate the thinkability or imaginability of homosexuality itself. In a sense, lesbian sexuality is not even thought of as the forbidden, for to be forbidden is still to be produced as a prohibited or censored object; whereas male homosexuality is thought as the forbidden, lesbian sexuality cannot even enter into the parameters of thought itself; lesbianism is here the phantasm of the phantasm. It would be naive, however, to assume that the Helms amendment, though phantasmatically obsessed with men, would not be deployed against depictions of female homoeroticism,[5] and that anyone in academics and in the arts who wishes to study representations of homosexuality or homoeroticism in the history of literature, in history, in popular culture, in sexology, in psychoanalysis, or even in the law, as I am doing now, will likewise now be ruled out of NEA and NEH funding.

By focusing on the homoeroticism of the photographs, the anxiety over interracial homo- and hetero-sexual exchange is contained and permanently deferred. The naked Black men characterized by Mapplethorpe engage a certain racist romanticism of Black men's excessive physicality and sexual readiness, their photographic currency as a sexual sign. Perhaps the most offensive dimension of Mapplethorpe's work, it is never that which is explicitly named as the offense by Helms; the fear of miscegenation operates tacitly here as well, disavowed, contained, and deferred by the stated spectre of 'homoeroticism' or the generalized possibility of 'individuals engaged in sex acts'.

In a paradoxical alliance with Dworkin, I am writing here in opposition to what I take to be violent and violating representations; what Helms performs with the help of MacKinnon/Dworkin is a kind of representational violence. But whereas Dworkin would counter this violent reduction with a call for censorship, that is a restriction which can only displace and reroute the violence it seeks to forestall. If prohibitions invariably *produce and proliferate* the representations that they seek to control, then the political task is to promote a proliferation of representations, sites of discursive production which might then contest the authoritative production produced by the prohibitive law. This kind of preemptive exclusion is enacted in the name of a prohibition that seeks to end the ostensibly injurious power of representation; and yet, this prohibition can work only through producing and proliferating precisely the kind of reductive and phantasmatic representations that it seeks to forestall.

In the *History of Sexuality: Volume I*, Foucault argues for the provisional political efficacy of a 'reverse-discourse' that is inadvertently mobilized by the very regulatory structures that would render that reversal impossible. The example he uses is, not coincidentally, that of 'homosexuality'. The juridical discourse of the medico-legal alliance at the end of the nineteenth century, he argues, seeks to establish homosexuality as a medical category and to institute homosexuality as a kind of identity.[6] Fortuitously, the institution of the category of homosexuality provides a discursive site for the homosexual resistance to its pathologization; hence, homosexuals now have the discursive occasion to resignify and valorize the terms of that identity and to organize against the medico-juridical alliance. Foucault's analysis presupposes that the discursive life of such identity categories always exceeds the purposes to which they are originally put; in this sense, Foucault reappropriates Nietzsche's notion of a 'sign-chain' in which the original purposes to which a discursive sign is devised are reversed and proliferated throughout the history of its usages [hence, also the necessity of a 'genealogy' to trace the meanderings of such terms, rather than a unilinear 'history']. The very uncontrollability of discourse, its penchant for superseding and reversing the purposes for which it is instrumentally deployed, provides for the possibility, if not the necessity, of regulatory regimes producing the very terms by which their purposes are undermined.

Although Foucault points to 'homosexuality' as subject to a 'reverse-discourse', that is, a reappropriation and resignification, it is clear that for 'reversal' to become politically undermining, it must be followed by 'proliferation', where what is proliferated is not the self-identical figure of homosexuality, but, rather, a set of figures which refuse to replicate each other faithfully. In other words, it is not enough to effect a dialectical exchange whereby the group consolidated by the term 'homosexuality', or for that matter, 'feminism', tries to control the meaning of that term; such a tactic could only replace a negatively signified identity term with an equally reductive, but positively signified identity term. In opposition to the prohibition of Mapplethorpe and his figures and to the homophobic figuration of Mapplethorpe, *ACT UP* in San Francisco produced and distributed a wide array of Mapplethorpe photographs as posters which counseled gay men on safe sex practices. The resistance to Helms cannot be the regulatory production of a singular or unified figure of homosexuality, for that figuration can always and only suppress the proliferation of non-self-identical semantic sites of homosexuality that punctuate the contemporary discursive field. Although 'proliferation' is often understood exclusively as the depoliticizing effect of late capitalism, it is also precisely the possibility of deploying politically that domain of discursive excess produced by the identity categories at the center of a reverse-discourse. The singular and authoritative homophobic figuration of homosexuality, which works through the violence of a synthesis (all gay men are 'x') and an erasure of multiple cultural formations of lesbianisms and which defers and contains racist erotic fears, cannot be opposed by remaining within the terms of that binary fight, but by displacing the binary itself through producing again and again precisely the discursive *uncontrollability* of the terms that are suppressed by regulatory violence.

In a sense, I have been arguing some very different points, using fantasy and the phantasmatic as a point of critical departure. The fixed subject-position of 'women' functions within the feminist discourse in favor of censorship as a phantasm that suppresses multiple and open possibilities for identification, a phantasm, in other words, that refuses its own possibilities as fantasy through its self-stabilization as the real. Feminist theory and politics cannot regulate the representation of 'women' without producing that very 'representation': and if that is in some sense a discursive inevitability of representational politics, then the task must be to safeguard the open productivity of those categories, whatever the risk.

As I have tried to argue elsewhere (*Gender*), every description of the 'we' will always do more than describe; it will constitute and construct an imaginary unity and contrived totality, a phantasmatic ideal, which makes the 'representability' of the we into a permanent impossibility. This might be understood linguistically as the inevitable performativity of the representational claim; the categories of identity instate or bring into 'the real' the very phenomenon that they claim to name only after the fact. This is not a simple performative, but one which operates through exclusionary operations that come back to haunt the very claim of representability that it seeks to make.

The Helms amendment reenforces the category of identity as a site of political crisis; who and what wields the power to define the homosexual real? This kind of crisis has been produced as well by the anti-pornography discourse: what is the figure of 'women' to which it objects, and the figure of 'women' in the name of whom the objection is articulated? How does the analysis of pornography delimit in advance the terms of identity to be contested? My recommendation is not to solve this crisis of identity politics, but to proliferate and intensify this crisis. This failure to master the foundational identity categories of feminism or gay politics is a political necessity, a failure to be safeguarded for political reasons.[7] The task is not to resolve or restrain the tension, the crisis, the phantasmatic excess induced by the term, but to affirm identity categories as a site of inevitable rifting, in which the phantasmatic fails to preempt the linguistic prerogative of the real. It is the incommensurability of the phantasmatic and the real that requires at this political juncture to be safeguarded; the task, then, is to make that rift, that insistent rifting, into the persistently ungrounded ground from which feminist discourse emerges.

In other words, it is important to risk losing control of the ways in which the categories of women and homosexuality are represented, even in legal terms, to safeguard the uncontrollability of the signified. In my view, it is in the very proliferation and deregulation of such representations—in the production of a chaotic multiplicity of representations—that the authority and prevalence of the reductive and violent imagery produced by Jesse Helms and other pornographic industries will lose their monopoly on the ontological indicator, the power to define and restrict the terms of political identity.

Notes

I thank Karin Cope, Ruth Leys, and Jeff Nunokawa for helping me to think through this essay.

1. In the original version of the Helms amendment, an anti-discrimination clause was added to an obscenity clause. In a sense, the Helms bill imitates the MacKinnon/Dworkin strategy to restrict or censor pornographical materials through (a) broadening obscenity statutes and (b) establishing pornography as

an instance of discrimination on the basis of sex. In the original version of the Helms amendment, the following clause qualifies the kinds of materials to be excluded from federal funding: 'that denigrates, debases or reviles a person, group, or class of citizens on the basis of race, creed, sex, handicap, age or national origin'. Here Helms clearly appeals to the legal precedent of construing pornography as sex discrimination. In a subsequently deleted section, it appears that he wanted to extend the MacKinnon formulation in such a way that materials offensive to members of certain religions could also be construed as discriminatory actions.

In an amendment to Title 7, Chapter 139 the Minneapolis code of ordinances (#385. 130), discrimination on the basis of sex is said to include 'sexual harassment and pornography': in an included special finding, the amendment reads in part: 'Pornography is a systematic practice of exploitation and subordination based on sex which differentially harms women. This harm includes dehumanization, sexual exploitation, physical injury, intimidation, and inferiority presented as entertainment . . . [it] promote[s] rape, battery and prostitution . . . '; 'pornography' is defined as the 'graphic sexually explicit subordination of women': this phrase will be reworked slightly by the Helms amendment.

Obscenity in the Helms amendment is extended to include depictions of 'Homoeroticism, sadomasochism and child molestation' as well as 'individuals engaged in sex acts': in the Minneapolis code, 'obscene' is given the following legal definition: (i) That the average person, applying contemporary community standards, would find that the work, taken as a whole, appeals to the prurient interest in sex of the average person; (ii) That the work depicts or describes, in a patently offensive manner, sexual conduct specially defined by the clause (b); [clause 'b' includes such acts as sexual intercourse, 'actual or simulated','sadomasochistic abuse', 'masturbation', 'physical contact or simulated physical contact with the clothed or unclothed pubic areas or buttocks of a human male or female . . .']; (iii) That the work, taken as a whole, lacks serious literary, artistic, political or scientific value. The Indianapolis code (#20.120), reads similarly, but under 'b' reads, 'the material depicts or describes patently offensive representations or descriptions of ultimate sex acts, normal or perverted, actual or simulated, or patently offensive representations or descriptions of masturbation, excretory functions, and lewd exhibitions of the genitals.'

The amendment 'a' to the Minneapolis Title 7 declares that pornography is discrimination against women. The Indianapolis ordinance, which was passed in 1984, was found unconstitutional in federal court and rescinded.

2. 'Mais le fantasme n'est pas l'objet du désir, il est scène. Dans le fantasme, en effet, le sujet ne vise pas l'objet désiré ou son signe, le figure lui-même pris dans la séquence d'images. Il ne se représente pas l'objet désiré mais il est représenté participant à la scène, sans que, dans les formes les plus proches du fantasme originaire, une place puisse lui être assignée (d'où le danger, dans la cure, des interprétations qui y prétendent). Conséquences: tout en étant toujours présent dans le fantasme, le sujet peut y'être sous une forme désubjectivée, c'est-à-dire dans la syntaxe même de la séquence en question.' Fantasme 74.
3. Significantly, the determination of obscenity in US law since the advent of obscenity statutes in 1957 has almost always appealed to 'contemporary

community standards', a phrase that is used in the Minneapolis and Indianapolis ordinances and which emerged in the recent controversies over the Mapplethorpe show in Cincinnati courts. The MacKinnon tactic has been, it seems, to extend the obscenity statutes by including pornography as part of sex discrimination. The effect of extending anti-discrimination statutes is not only (a) to diversify the legal tactics through which the putative injuries of pornography can be redressed by establishing sex discrimination as a seperate basis for complaint, but (b) to insure that the anti-pornography statutes are not applied differently against protected groups like homosexuals. Hence, the anti-discrimination clause in the Minneapolis bill states clearly that 'affectional preference' is protected against discrimination, and even goes so far as to protect 'transsexuals' against discrimination via pornography.

The anti-discrimination statute also can be understood to provide a legal safeguard against the invocation of the obscenity statute for discriminatory purposes. Insofar as the obscenity statute seeks recourse to 'community standards' which would almost always (and presently in Cincinnati) culminate in the judgement that any and all representations of homosexuality or homoeroticism are obscene, the extended anti-discrimination clause seeks to protect the rights, which obviously includes free speech, of homosexual minorities and others, even when 'community standards' would find the self-representational 'free speech' of those groups to fall unconditionally under the rubric of obscenity.

In a sense, the recourse to these two different legal bases, obscenity and discrimination, always risks a collision between them. And in the case in which 'community standards' *conflict* with the protection of homosexual free speech, community standards, precisely because the sanction of the community outweighs the constitutional claims of the minorities, will invariably win. Moreover, if depictions are construed as discriminatory and injurious, then the legal precedent has been set (and exploited now by Helms) to claim that any and all depictions of homoeroticism are injurious to those whose moral sensibilities are offended in the process of viewing these depiction. Hence, Helms sought (unsuccessfully) to establish that the depiction of homoeroticism et al. *discriminates* against members of certain unspecified religions. Realizing, it seems, that this very statute might discriminate on the basis of religion, he supplies an absurd supplement that protects the rights of members of non-religions as well.

4. In the Mapplethorpe exhibition, 'The Perfect Moment', which was to show at various art spaces partially financed by the National Endowment for the Arts, and which serves as the basis for the Helms criticism, there are two photographs of children. One 'Honey' (1976) is a picture of a young girl around 5 years old, sitting on a bench with one leg up and one leg crossed in front of her. She is looking somewhat indifferently into the camera; she has no underpants on, and the thin line that marks the closed labia revealed by her sitting position is marked primarily by its unremarkability. An aesthetic formalist and photographic realist, Mapplethorpe's photos work to enforce principles of symmetry and linear order. The vertical line that is the labia is paralleled on either side by the vertical lines of the sides of the bench, by the line between her arm and her dress and, predictably, the side-lines of the canvas itself. The focal point of the photograph is effectively distributed across these lines, and the labia line effectively shields the vagina from view.

The other photograph is of a boy, 7–8 years old, 'Jesse McBride' (1976), which is equally languorous, suggesting as in the above, the final unremarkability (and perhaps innocence) of nudity. As in the above, this photo of Jesse sitting nude on the top of a velvet chair, is an exemplar of the symmetrical distribution of formal elements. His two arms rest comfortably against the velvet chair, his two legs fall against the chair, and his small and decidedly *un*erect penis lounges peacefully against the velvet as well. I would call this composition, 'appendages against velvet'. Both figures look straight into the camera, without shame or sexuality, as if to ask (for us now), 'what is the big deal?' In a sense, the photos engage a pornographic convention only to debunk it; the search for eroticism is rerouted and diffused through the insistence on formal symmetry. In this way the photos of children parallel and extend the photographic technique of Mapplethorpe's still life photos of flowers.

5. Recently it seems that letters emanating from certain Congressional quarters inquiring into the federal funding of lesbian poets and writers have been circulating 'confidentially'. Mab Segrest and others have begun to wage a lesbian-based campaign against Helms.
6. Prior to this move, he argues, there are various homosexual acts and pleasures, but they are not yet taken as symptoms or evidence of a certain typological identity. The forces that would pathologize homosexuality institute that category as an identity, a move which involves the distinction between 'normal' identity *qua* heterosexuality and deviant or deformed identity, now occupied by the (male) homosexual.
7. In other words, I want to resist both the claim that feminism is being 'ruined' by its fragmentations, a position which implicitly or explicitly establishes the dispensability of some crucial constituency, and the claim that fragmentation ought to be overcome through the postulation of a phantasmatically unified ideal.

Works Cited

Bartkowski, Frances. *FeministUtopias.* Lincoln: U of Nebraska P, 1989.

Butler, Judith. *Gender Trouble: Feminism and the Subversion of Identity.* New York: Routledge, 1990.

Dworkin, Andrea. *Pornography: Men Possessing Women.* New York: Seal, 1981.

English, Dierdre. 'The Politics of Porn: Can Feminists Walk the Line?', *Mother Jones* (April 1980): 20–50.

Haraway, Donna. *Primate Visions: Gender, Race, and Nature in the World of Modern Science.* New York: Routledge, 1989.

HR 2788 and HR 4825. Department of Interior and Related Agencies Appropriations bill for FY 1990, 1989.

Indianapolis code of ordinances #20.117–20.150. 1984.

Laplanche, Jean, and J.-B. Pontalis. *Fantasme Originaire.* Paris: Hachette, 1985.

——. *Formations of Fantasy.* Ed. Victor Burgin, James Donald, and Cora Kaplan. London: Methuen, 1986.

——. *Vocabulaire de la psychoanalyse.* Paris: P Universitaires de France, 1967.

'Obscenity Measure Approved', *Washington Post*, 21 Sept. 1989:1.
Public Law 101–121 (103 Stat 701). 1989.
Rose, Jacqueline. *Sexuality in the Field of Vision*. London: Verso 1987.
'Senate Votes to Bar U.S. Support of "Obscene or Indecent" Artwork', *New York Times*, 27 July 1989:1.
Title 7, Ch. 139. Minneapolis code of ordinances #385.130, amendment 'a.' 1987.

'Love Me, Master, Love Me, Son'

A Cultural Other Pornographically Constructed in Time

Rey Chow

THE CULTURAL OTHER: A PORNOGRAPHIC CONSTRUCT IN TIME

In an age in which 'identity' has become a crucial issue in cultural politics, the word we encounter most frequently is 'other'. To think in terms of our 'others' is to think, critically, of differences and boundaries. Often, it is assumed that the differences that define our 'others' imply a subversion, transgression and revolution of the stable boundaries of our existing identities, and thus the return of those boundaries to their constructedness and historicity. And yet, precisely because as a concept the 'other' is no less relative in function than other concepts, it can be the occasion for conservatism as much as it can be the occasion for radical possibilities. This essay is an attempt to demonstrate this ambiguity.

I take as my text a fictional narrative by a male Chinese writer about a lower-class woman: Bai Xianyong's (Pai Hsien-yung) *Yuqing Sao.* As it is almost a commonplace among critics and readers of non-Western culture to select for analysis a lower-class character, let me say at the outset that my interest is not that of idealizing a subaltern figure—an 'other' at multiple levels—as a means of criticizing some 'dominant culture'. Rather, it is to ask what happens when intellectuals such as ourselves—writers, critics, teachers—choose to represent this specific type of 'other' called 'the subaltern'. How do we become fascinated with subaltern figures, and at the same time protect ourselves from

Rey Chow, 'Love Me, Master, Love Me, Son: A Cultural Other Pornographically Constructed in Time', from *Boundaries in China*, ed. John Hay (Reaktion Books, 1994), 243–56, reprinted by permission of the author and the publisher.

them precisely through the means of writing? Central to my concern are two issues: pornography and time.

The representation of subalterns shares a major characteristic with pornographic writing in the sense that it depends on a certain objectification and specularization of the 'other': the depiction of a subaltern, even when it is not replete with violence and aggression, is often replete with details that excite our emotions because of the exoticism of the gender, race and, most importantly, class. I emphasize class because it is, in the most abstract sense, what signifies the difference between 'having' and 'lack', be that difference construed sexually, metaphysically, or, as is most commonly the case, economically. Both 'subaltern' writing and pornographic writing invest their fantasy in breaking the limits of propriety.[1] In each case the specularity/spectacularity of the object is produced not only by the act of representation but also by representation-as-reflection-of-(the object's)-debasement. If the excitement of pornography can be described as something like 'the dirtier, the better', then the excitement of subaltern-representation may be described as something like the more socially deprived, the better'. Both types of excitement depend on the object's lack—that is, her great wantingness (or shall we say wantonness) and thus her invitation to the reader to actively fill that lack. In speaking thus, I am not, of course, against sympathy for the 'lower' classes. My concern is rather with the pornographic use of such classes for forms of intellectual pleasure and closure—conceptual or practical—that actually reproduces rather than challenges existing social injustice.

To see how social injustice is reproduced, another question must be asked: How is the representation of otherness mediated by time, often in ways that escape us? Take the example of East Asian literatures, in which time is frequently a thematic concern. Time is associated with the 'changefulness' that leads to deterioration—a state that is inferior because it lacks the plenitude of that which precedes it. The passage of time thus, it is often said, denotes the fleetingness of human experience, the futility of human endeavours, the transience of beauty, the imminence and certitude of death, and so forth. Bai Xianyong, for instance, describes himself as having been very sensitive to time since he was a young man.[2] This sensitivity depicts time as the supreme aggressor to whom the writer himself becomes subjugated. But unlike the pornographic image of the depicted object, time is invisible; its aggression is always understood only retrospectively, in the marks and traces it has left behind. How then does the belatedly-felt aggressivity of time become an active means of keeping the other in place and thus of intellectual self-defence? What is the structural relation between time and the pornographic?

THE STORY OF *YUQING SAO*

The novella *Yuqing Sao* was first published in 1960 by Bai, who spent his early years in mainland China, Hong Kong and Taiwan. He now resides in the United States and teaches at the University of California, Santa Barbara. It tells the tale of a woman servant, Yuqing Sao, in the early part of the twentieth century in Guilin, a city in southwest China. A widow from a relatively dignified family, Yuqing Sao works at a wealthy household as the nanny to the young boy, Rong Ge, who is the narrator of the story. She is beautiful, clean, gentle and hardworking. She is popular with everyone, especially Rong Ge. She does not seem interested in getting married again. By chance one day, Rong Ge discovers that Yuqing Sao has a younger 'nominal' or adopted brother,[3] Qingsheng, a sickly but refined young man who lives by himself not too far away from the house in which she works. Rong Ge quickly develops a friendship with Qingsheng, taking the latter to restaurants and operas. Only at a later point does Rong Ge discover—uncomprehendingly—that Yuqing Sao and Qingsheng are lovers. The story takes a tragic turn when Yuqing Sao finds out that her lover has fallen for another woman. Trying in vain to keep Qingsheng to herself, she loses all hope in life. She goes to Qingsheng's house one day and stabs him to death. Then she kills herself.

THE DANGEROUS SUPPLEMENT

The fascination with characters from the lower class is a familiar one in modern Chinese literature. One paradigmatic type of narration is that frequently used by Lu Xun (1881–1936), who emphasized the irreparable gap between an intellectual narrator and a lower-class person.[4] The effect of Lu Xun's stories is always that of guilt, which we may describe as an emotion created—in the privileged—by the disparities between privilege and subalternity. In Bai's story, however, the emotional effect created by the object is of a different and arguably more dangerous kind. Whereas the boundary of class—the distinction between high and low—remains clear in Lu Xun, Bai merges the familiar interest (among twentieth-century Chinese writers) in subaltern figures with another interest, the formation of sexual desire *across* class boundaries, by depicting Yuqing Sao as a sexually attractive woman. In doing so, Bai comes much closer than most modern Chinese writers to the paradigmatic amalgamation of sexual excitement and social debasement as described by Peter Stallybrass and Allon White. Stallybrass and White show in their study of European male writers such as Sigmund Freud and Walter Benjamin that 'what is socially excluded or subordinated is symbolically central in the formation of desire'. This kind of desire, aptly summed up in the scenario described by Stallybrass and White as 'the conjunction of the maid kneeling in the dirt and the standing voyeur who looks on with fascination',[5] is usually the desire of the middle-class male for those women who occupy lower-class positions such as maids, nurses, nannies and prostitutes.

In the case of *Yuqing Sao*, the merger of the two types of interest is further complicated by the fact that it is Yuqing Sao, the lower-class woman and the sexual object of the narrative gaze, who is depicted with active sexual desire, while the 'voyeur'—the on-looker from the higher class—is a little boy. As a subaltern, then, Yuqing Sao is a contradiction in terms, a lack and a void (in terms of social power and traditional gender construction) and an excess (in terms of sexual power and individualist agency) at once.

Let us first examine the excess. The excessive reality of love and sex in the modern world always carry with it an emancipatory potential. Someone 'coming out' is someone coming out of the repression of his/her secret but real sexuality; 'revelation' results in a kind of freedom. In *Yuqing Sao*, love and sex represent a form of emancipation as well, since as a widow in feudal China, a woman's active sexuality is supposed to have come to an end: a widow is not supposed to have another man in her life. Yuqing Sao's secret affair is, then, a direct challenge to the Confucian moralistic imprisonment of female sexuality. But this 'emancipation' does not carry with it the meaning of a teleological progress toward happiness and sexual fulfilment; it is the beginning, rather than the end, of her tragedy.

In her love for a younger man, Yuqing Sao's plea is a double one, mediated by two types of social hierarchies, both of which are related to gender. The first of these hierarchies is heterosexual difference, in which male sexuality is dominant; the second is age difference, which in traditional Chinese families means that those who are older are usually dominant, although in the case of an older woman and a younger man—as in this story—that dominance is uncertain. Yuqing Sao wants, in other words, to be loved both as a woman and as an older woman, by someone who is thus simultaneously her master and her son (or younger brother). Her love is as tender and caring as it is overbearing and oppressive. Time and again she begs her lover not to desert her: she will work a few more years, she says, and then they can retire to the countryside together. She would devote her entire life to him as long as he remains unchanged. This love takes the form of holding the loved-one prisoner; she is displeased even by the thought of Qingsheng's leaving the house for a walk by himself.

Yuqing Sao's relationship with Qingsheng is not merely a private subversion of social propriety, but a transgression of it at multiple levels. As a member of the servant class, her 'secret' makes her vulnerable to further degradation. But more important is the way she breaks the rules of kinship. As she and her lover address each other by familial titles (Yu *zhi*, 'older sister Yu' and Qing *di*, 'younger brother Qing'), her love is virtually incestuous. ('Incest' in Chinese—*luanlun* — literally means a 'confusion' of the 'kinship codes' and has nothing to do with biological commingling *per se*.) She is also a nanny, a surrogate mother figure, the popular conception of whom is usually divorced from sex. The many social positions Yuqing Sao occupies—social positions that are demarcated clearly within the kinship system—mean that her transgression is an overdetermined one.

In his criticism of the phonocentrism of Western philosophical thinking, Jacques Derrida has described the activity of writing in terms of what he calls the supplement. As supplement, writing is that which seems to come later than the voice and is thus always attributed an inferior and derivative quality. According to Derrida, the peculiar truth about the supplement is that its secondariness is really a firstness: appearing as a mere addition, the supplement also substitutes, thus fundamentally replacing and reorganizing what came 'before'. It is thus a case in which two apparently incompatible events happen simultaneously. Derrida writes:

> the concept of the supplement... harbors within itself two significations whose cohabitation is as strange as it is necessary. The supplement adds itself, it is a surplus, a plenitude enriching another plenitude, the *fullest measure* of presence. It cumulates and accumulates presence. It is thus that art, *technè*, image, representation, convention, etc., come as supplements to nature and are rich with this entire cumulating function . . .

But the supplement supplements. It adds only to replace. It intervenes or insinuates itself *in-the-place-of*; if it fills, it is as if one fills a void. If it represents and makes an image, it is by the anterior default of a presence . . . the supplement an adjunct, a subaltern instance which *takes-(the)-place* [*tient-lieu*].[6]

The logic of criticism inherent to many contemporary discussions of otherness is the logic of the supplement, which Derrida, interestingly enough, emphasizes as a 'subaltern instance'. By introducing another culture, history, sexuality, class, race, body, etc., what we try to do is to add to but also restructure the boundaries of existing knowledge. In Bai's story we have a depiction of a cultural other, a subaltern figure, in multiple supplementary relations: Yuqing Sao's behaviour is enormously destructive because it throws into open confusion the codes of class, kinship, sexual difference, and age. For instance, Yuqing Sao is not simply a nanny, an older sister, and a member of the lower class; she is a lower-class woman with sexual desire. But her sexual desire is not simply sexual; it is also motherly and sisterly, familial and kin-bound, and containing the affection of the older for the younger.

From the beginning, the narrative describes her in a way that is physically attentive. The little boy likes her immediately on seeing her:

When I came downstairs, the sight of Yuqing Sao standing next to my short aunt took my breath away. How neat and clean, and how pretty a person! She was wearing a moon-white servant's jacket and trousers and a pair of black cloth shoes with laces. Her shiny black hair was tied up loosely in a bun like that of Cantonese women, with a pair of almond-sized white earrings just hanging outside its tips. She had a clean-looking oval face, with eyes clear like water . . .

I could not say why, but I felt I wanted to be close to her the moment I saw her.[7]

By accident one day, Rong Ge catches her in one of her intimate moments with her lover. The image of the quiet pretty Yuqing Sao is now strongly contradicted by a fierce and aggressive picture:

Yuqing Sao looked frightening. Her face was red from being drunk. Her two cheek bones shone so bright that they looked like they would catch fire soon. Her forehead was full of sweat and her hair, soaked through with sweat, stuck to her face. Her eyes were half open and very bright; her mouth was slightly open and she was murmuring something. All of a sudden, she bit into Qingsheng's shoulder as if she had gone mad, gnawing back and forth so much so that her hair was all dancing. Like the claws of an eagle, her hands grabbed Qingsheng's pale back, digging deep into it. After a while, she raised her head and, holding Qingsheng by his hair, pulled him towards her breast with a force

> as strong as if she was trying to mash him into her heart. Qingsheng's two long thin arms kept shaking, much like the trembling small legs of a deeply wounded little rabbit which was paralyzed on the ground, weak and powerless. When Yuqing Sao bit him on his shoulder again, he struggled against her and rolled to the middle of the bed, and started sighing in pain. There was blood at the corner of Yuqing Sao's mouth, and Qingsheng's left shoulder was also bleeding . . .[8]

This violent scene is quickly replaced by one in which, alarmed by the pain she has caused her lover, Yuqing Sao touches him with her usual tenderness.

As a 'part object' of love, Yuqing Sao is thus both the good and the bad object, soliciting from the child the most idealizing and the most fearful emotions at once. But more important, I think, is the pornographic way in which she is described in the act of sexual intimacy. As readers, we share the hole in the paper window with the voyeuristic child. What we see is not simply a picture of a woman having sex but a picture of feminine sexuality-as-insanity-and-animality, even though Bai himself described it afterwards in dignified humanistic terms.[9] In other words, the pornographic view here is 'enticing' not because of the overtness of sex but because sex is represented in an overlapping series of significations and displacements as physical violence, as animal aggressivity, as lower-class and, ultimately, as older female and as servitude.

By drawing attention to this central scene in the story, my point is not exactly that of accusing Bai of dehumanizing Yuqing Sao. (This is a possible reading, but it is not the one I am following.) What I find interesting is that this pornographic scene, like Yuqing Sao herself, occupies a relation to the entire story that we may call, after Derrida, 'supplementary'. It comes second to the good and kind impression we have already formed about her, and its difference from that first impression forces the narrative to take a certain decision. The narrative, as it were, has to make up its mind about how it is going to deal with this 'addition'. The radical logic of the supplement, we remember, is that while it adds, it substitutes. But, as in the case of any boundary, there is nothing intrinsically uncontrollable or unmanipulable about the supplement. If the supplement's radicalism is potentially a source of chaos—a boundary, though seemingly stable, can itself be reconstituted over and over indefinitely—such radicalism also contains the option of conservatism and recontainment: what substitutes anarchically can be treated, retrospectively and deliberately, as *mere* addition, as mere ethnic detail to be bounded and incorporated.

Traditionally, a society has many ways of bounding and neutralizing the significatory force of the dangerous supplement. One effective way is by glorification—by raising the supplement to a different level of signification where it no longer shares the same relation with other members of the same society. For instance, we do this by sanctifying members of the lower classes so that, in a way that is stripped of basic human needs and desires, a lower-class person becomes a kind of sacred figure, raised to a moral level at which we forget precisely her daily cares. Modern Chinese literature is full of examples of this kind of sanctification of the dangerous supplement. Where a lower-class person's conduct may, in fact, threaten to overthrow the moral structure that holds a society together, literature often makes her part of the very support, the very boundary of that structure, by glorifying her. Central to such glorification in the case of lower-class women is a prohibition of their sexuality.[10] We thus have countless women characters who are 'admirable' because they live their lives as self-sacrificing motherly servants with little sexuality and subjectivity.

Yuqing Sao's story, because it transgresses social propriety at several levels at once, does not allow such a glorification/prohibition. As a lower-class woman, she is *also* sexually active. She thus makes it difficult for the usual normalization of the dangerous supplement to take place, but instead, brings the shattering power of that supplementarity—both social and sexual—into full force. She is a woman of the family who invades the stronghold of kinship bonds and emotions from within with the violence of an enemy from without: she is a sister and mother who acts as a woman with her own independent value system. The nature of her love is hopeless; it has no future even though she has invested her entire life (force) in it. She draws her happiness exclusively from this dead-end course of love. It is as if, having rejected the traditional mores of Confucian society, she helps consolidate those mores in a different way by basing her happiness entirely on a heterosexual emotional contract and on the emotional loyalty of her sexual partner. She exchanges her own life for this contract—for the supposed materiality of this contract—only to find that she has been cheated of her payment.

Yuqing Sao's extreme 'violence' and 'aggressivity' are thus the qualities of a woman who, like any despot, seeks to establish her own legitimacy by subjugating others. This, rather than a failed love/failed sexual relationship, rather than the adultery which causes tragedy in more 'proper' settings, is what constitutes the catastrophe of the narrative. The catastrophe is that the familial emotions of kinship representation no longer make sense, not even to Yuqing Sao herself. (Early on in the story, she rejects the chance of a second marriage, which would have repositioned her safely within conventional kinship bonds.) In terms of the 'Law' that is social propriety, Yuqing Sao is not simply opposed to it or resisting it; rather she is substituting her own law for it. Her 'breaking' of the Law is thus as absolute and irrational as the Law itself, and we are left incapable of either reaffirming the Law or (as in many cases of literary representation) affirming (the subversiveness of) the crime.

Bai's conscious frame of representation, however, refuses precisely to grant Yuqing Sao her legitimacy as a new Law and thus, we may say, her full significatory power as the dangerous supplement. Instead, he subordinates Yuqing Sao to a more familial, familiar and *readable* narrative—that of a woman who cannot be sexually aggressive without hurting/killing herself. Thus we have, once again, the conventional ending of a heart-rending female suicide. The act of suicide confirms Yuqing Sao's dependence on her male lover and thus the kinship system—her master—to which her life has in fact posed a fundamental challenge. The narrative decides that as she kills this lover/younger brother/son, she also must kill herself. Only thus can the meaning of her life be 'preserved' by Rong Ge, her other son and her actual master in terms of economic class.

THE INNOCENT CHILD

Bai keeps Yuqing Sao in a reticent position by constructing his narrative in such a way that she is already a memory—a time past. The story is told to us by Rong Ge, her 'master' in terms of class and her 'son'/'younger brother' in terms of gender. Rong Ge is at once the Law that punishes her and a version of the libido to which she submits in her love for a younger man.

In the key scene in which he sees Yuqing Sao in her sexual activity, Rong Ge's 'vision', because it is that of a child, is potentially a kind of indeterminacy. The use of a child is a method with which we can defamiliarize reality—to use the term from the Russian Formalists—for the purpose of shock. And yet, it can also be used for the opposite purpose, as I think is the case with the narration in *Yuqing Sao*. Instead of defamiliarization, the child is used here to make blank (and thus to normalize) a reality that has got out of control, so that the dangers of the other can be safely smoothed away in conventional understanding. Later, at the scene of the murder and suicide, Rong Ge literally 'blanks out', or faints, at the sight of the corpses of the lovers. Subsequently he recovers, grows up and writes the story, and Bai's own description of the novella highlights this 'recovery' and 'growth': 'This story can be classified as "enlightenment fiction". One of its chief themes is the growth of Rong Ge. Therefore the emphasis of the script falls on his psychological transformation on witnessing two major lessons of human life, love and death.'[11]

By distancing us from Yuqing Sao's story through the blanking/transparent frame of a child, Bai leaves many issues unexplored. The more or less innocent young boy intuitively senses the unusual relationship between Yuqing Sao and Qingsheng, but he does not understand it. At this point, it is important for us not to follow the logic of Bai's own description of the story that I quoted above, which, by casting the story in the form of a *Bildungsroman*, would have us conclude that Rong Ge's inability to understand would be overcome subsequently by his maturation. Instead, I want to offer a different kind of reading by highlighting the child as a strategic function of time. The most important feature of the young boy's representational frame is that Yuqing Sao's story is cast in the form of a memory of an *other* time. Why?

The little boy's narrative makes it difficult, if not impossible, for us to say that this is 'male subjectivity' representing female tragedy as spectacle. If it had been, straightforwardly, an adult male narrator, it would be possible perhaps to question the complicity of a male narrator who occupies the same time frame—the same kind of chronological age—as his object. A male narrator of this kind would not be able to claim that he did not understand what was going on. But because the narrative point of view is that of a child, who is, in terms of age, in a different kind of time, we cannot put the burden of responsibility of understanding on him—after all, the child is merely a 'white sheet of paper' recording what he sees, so how can we blame him? What the frame of the child does to the story of the passionate woman is a kind of caption written in the present about the past: 'As seen and remembered by a non-comprehending child.'

Once we stop thinking about the passage of the child to adulthood as a linear progress toward maturity, and instead view the two stages as two different temporal orders, we will see that the child in this story acts as the kind of alibi or turnstile that Roland Barthes describes as the mechanism of ideology in his early work *Mythologies*,[12] the mechanism that works by being precisely what we think it is not. Do we say that Rong Ge understands everything? No, because he is too young (and too much of a 'blank'). But do we say that everything escapes him? No, precisely *also* because he is 'blank' and 'transparent': he sees and records everything. Where the 'content' of Yuqing Sao stands out as a kind of corrupt 'signified', the child's narrative, as signifier, blurs its intricacy and emotional complexity; but where Yuqing Sao's story is subordinated to the more 'innocent' eyes of the child, those eyes have also captured and remembered all the 'pornographic' details vividly.

The questions of the child is thus not a simple one. To what is the child related in order to be the child that he is? To what kind of emotional structure, corresponding to what prospective identification? What 'future' subjectivity lies in wait for the particular childhood as constructed here? To whom is the child a father, and—in what amounts to the same question—who is the father to the child? Most importantly, how is the father–child relationship formed? As Gilles Deleuze and Félix Guattari write in *Anti-Oedipus*:

> . . . social investments are first in relation to the familial investments, which result solely from the application or the reduction (*rabattement*) of the social investments. To say that the father is first in relation to the child really amounts to saying that the investment of desire is in the first instance the investment of a social field into which the father and the child are plunged, simultaneously immersed.[13]

The use of the child suggests a kind of ambivalence of structure as regards the 'female' content of the story. It is as if the author is fascinated enough by Yuqing Sao to want to write her story, and yet wants to defend himself from her destructiveness by pretending he is still a child himself. But what does it mean to represent an other in the past while the self remains a child? It means fixing the other in a specularized time which is dead, while imagining the self as a reversible time-machine that is able to move back and forth between the past and the present as it wishes. This temporal reversibility of the writing/intellectual self thus distinguishes itself from the other, who is cast in what I call a pornographic timelessness.

THE WOMAN THAT IS NOT WOMAN

Bai's treatment of Yuqing Sao is especially thought-provoking if one considers his own background. Bai had a privileged childhood much like Rong Ge's, although his family, which had strong connections with the Guomindang (Chinese Nationalist Party), had to leave China during the 1940s, around the time the Communists took over the mainland. They lived for a period in Hong Kong and then in Taiwan, and Bai eventually studied and settled in the United States. However, if his multiple-outsider identity is anchored fictionally in his characters, it is not much anchored in Yuqing Sao, who is portrayed in an idealized but extreme form, as it is anchored in the relationship between the young child and Qingsheng, Yuqing Sao's lover.

Interestingly, Qingsheng is portrayed in the way that many *heroines* of the traditional Mandarin Duck and Butterfly novels are portrayed: he is orphaned, good-looking, sickly and artistic. In the depiction of this male character, Bai is thus following what has been a strong trend in modern Chinese fiction since the early twentieth century, a trend by which 'woman' occupies a prominent position as the embodiment of social problem, fictional experiment and revolutionary hope. It was through the systemic transformation of women's status at the turn of the twentieth century—through the gradual availability of educational opportunities as well as the burgeoning of mass communications and entertainments in urban areas—that the awareness of the meanings of gender constructions became generally intensified. In this intensification of perceptual processes, the traditional injustices suffered by women became, for the first time, fully articulable as both narrative content *and* method. The appearance and prevalence of 'femininity' in narrative fiction is the mark of a socio-perceptual change, partaken of by both male and female writers alike. To stage women as the objects of narration—as the 'other' that enables the unfolding of narrative time and space—is, by the mid and late twentieth century, a well-used narrative practice.

If both Qingsheng and Yuqing Sao are socially deprived people—we are told that Qingsheng was thrown out of the house by his relatives because of his illness before he was adopted by Yuqing Sao as a nominal brother—Bai seems undecided as to whether to associate the state of deprivation in gender terms with the man or the woman. While by the 'normal' conventions of gender, Yuqing Sao is the deprived woman, in their relationship Qingsheng is completely dependent, feminized and infantilized. The investment of vulnerability and lack in the male rather than female character is perhaps an early sign—early in terms of Bai's writing career—of Bai's effort to come to terms with his own homosexuality,[14] which finds its point of identification with the male lover and male child, both of whom are placed somewhat at the mercy of a powerful female character. Against the background of female power, the intimate brotherly bond between Qingsheng and Rong Ge is important in a way that is easily forgotten. There are episodes in which the male child's fascination with the physical features of his male friend is at least as strong as his fascination with the maternal figure, in a manner that is highly suggestive of homoeroticism.[15] One might say that the dissolution of Qingsheng and Yuqing Sao's relationship (and hence the demise of Yuqing Sao's power) begins when the two males start going out together and the younger boy takes Qingsheng to the opera, where he encounters and falls in love with a young actress.[16]

In his passivity, Qingsheng shares with Rong Ge the same kind of position vis-à-vis Yuqing Sao; that is, he simulates the male *child* whom, in spite of its title, this story is ultimately about. It is as if Bai only wants to 'know' about the difficult sexual relationship between a man and a woman from within the safe boundaries of a child's consciousness; it is as if he is presenting such a relationship in its full complexity and yet declaring that he has nothing to do with it because he does not understand it. The 'it' he does not understand is, precisely, the sexuality of the woman.

Hence we have a divided narrative: on the one hand, a violent sexual story of possessive female love; on the other, a kind of indifference or non-participation in that love even while it is recorded as a story complete with tabooed details. But the 'lack of interest' on the part of the narrative frame is not simply a matter of childlike innocence; it is more, I propose, the lack of interest on the part of someone who belongs to a different sexual economy and who for all his sympathy and affection literally cannot enter Yuqing Sao's world. As in the case of some of his other narratives about women Bai stops short of describing the female character's subjectivity.[17] His female characters thus remain fetishized as external objects—beautiful, fierce, powerful, but strangely unhappy and bound by time. On first meeting Yuqing Sao, Rong Ge thinks:

I really like her outfit, especially her earrings—they were so white that they were glittering, how lovely! But when I looked at her closely, I saw that there were a few wrinkles on her forehead. And when she smiled, there was a fish tail at the corners of her eyes.[18]

Wrinkles and crow's feet: even the child sees that this woman is getting old. (Yuqing Sao is just over 30, but this is old by traditional Chinese standards.) This means that her 'good' life—her youth—is drawing to a close. The weight of time creeping up on her is such that she would not be able to escape. But all of this 'understanding' remains at the level of a careful noting of the woman's visible physical features only. While we know how Rong Ge thinks and feels, we only see Yuqing Sao from the outside.

If the dangerous passion of the woman is a supplement to the dominant law and order in Derrida's sense, then the child's function is to provide an escape route from the anarchic force of the supplement. The child reduces the danger of that supplement to fiction by way of his 'innocence', subtracts the supplement from what it has already substituted, and thereby returns things fantastically to a kind of pre-supplementary reality. The child's narrative undoes things in such a way as to make us feel that time is *reversible*. But precisely because there is no such thing as a child's unmediated narrative, what poses as temporal reversibility must itself be seen as a crafted writing, a conscious means of distraction, and a deliberate way of backing off from the feminine dangers it has introduced. In the language of time, the child's 'innocence' is the nostalgic longing for the infinite futurity that we associate with 'youthfulness'. The real meaning of Bai's self-proclaimed sensitivity to time is thus gerontophobia, the fear of aging that characterizes Western and non-Western literature alike,[19] and that he veils with the fetish of a lower-class woman's sexual life.

Yuqing Sao's plea, which I interpret as 'Love me, master, love me, son', is left in the form of that typical lack/deprivation of femininity which can only be completed by man and the social order he creates. Because that plea can, in terms of that social order, never be fulfilled in the way she desires (to be loved both as mother/sister and as sexual partner, both as insider and outsider), she is reurned to a conventional fate, murder and suicide, as her 'way out'. Throughout the story Yuqing Sao is shown to be someone who knows exactly what she wants and what she is doing. She is put in a kind of time in which her knowledge, will, labour, sexuality and action are 'at one'—time*less*—while the narrator is uncertain, changing and alive.[20] The narrative, constructed in what we might thus call male time, is possible and potent only because it does not understand the woman's point of view, and male time, we might say, is the reward for remaining an uncomprehending child.

Notes

1. '. . . Limits are, in a sense, what fantasy loves most, what it incessantly thematizes and subordinates to its own aims.' Judith Butler, 'The Force of Fantasy: Feminism, Mapplethorpe, and Discursive Excess', *Differences: A Journal of Feminist Cultural Studies*, II/2 (1990), p. 111.
2. Cai Kejian, Interview with Pai Hsien-yung, *Playboy*, Chinese edition, no. 24, July, 1988, p. 39.
3. '*Gan didi*' in Chinese. This title refers to the practice by which persons outside the kinship family are adopted nominally as members of the family.
4. For a discussion of the implications of Lu Xun's narrative method, see Rey Chow, '"It's you, and not me": Domination and "Othering" in Theorizing the "Third World"', in *Coming to Terms: Feminism, Theory, Politics*, ed. Elizabeth Weed (New York, 1989), pp. 152–61.
5. Peter Stallybrass and Allon White, *The Politics and Poetics of Transgression* (Ithaca, 1986) chapter 4, pp. 152, 155.
6. Jacques Derrida, *Of Grammatology*, trans. Gayatri Chakravorty Spivak (Baltimore, 1976), pp. 144—5; emphases in the original.
7. All references to this story are taken from Bai Xianyong, *Yuqing Sao* (Taipei, 1985) and translated from the Chinese by me. This quotation is from p. 111 of the original.
8. Ibid., pp. 143–4.
9. 'Love is sometimes very frightening, especially when it reaches a certain degree. Some people perhaps prefer to describe it mildly, but I feel that when one person falls in love with another, it's really . . . really shaking up heaven and earth! . . . Even the physical love in *Yuqing Sao* is, for me, a manifestation of the explosion of such internal emotions.' Interview in *Playboy*, p. 41
10. I have discussed Xu Dishan's short story 'Big Sister Liu' (*Chuntao*) in this light. See Rey Chow, *Woman and Chinese Modernity: The Politics of Reading between West and East* (Minneapolis, 1991), pp. 145–50.
11. *Yüqing Sao*, p. 5; also quoted on the back cover.
12. Roland Barthes, *Mythologies*, selected and translated from the French by Annette Lavers (London, 1973).
13. Gilles Deleuze and Félix Guattari, *Anti-Oedipus: Capitalism and Schizophrenia*, trans. Robert Hurley et al. (Minneapolis, 1983), pp. 274–5.
14. Unlike most Chinese writers, Bai is open about his sexuality. He describes his homosexuality as *'tiansheng de*—that is, something he was born with. Interview with *Playboy*, p. 43.
15. For instance: 'I was really curious as to why his moustache was so fine and so soft . . .if only I could touch it, it must feel real nice . . .' (*Yuqing Sao*, p. 130). 'I really didn't understand why, but as soon as I saw that soft and smooth moustache I was beside myself with excitement. I couldn't restrain myself from gently touching it. An itchy and numbing feeling made me laugh . . .' (*Yuqing Sao*, p. 131).
16. For an argument of how the constitution of homosocial bonding between

men takes place through women, see Eve Kosofsky Sedgwick, *Between Men: English Literature and Male Homosocial Desire* (New York, 1985). If the bond between males is structured by the object of woman, it is structured also by a lack—the father. This is why, for instance, Bai said that *Niezi* (Hong Kong, 1988), his novel about young male homosexuals in present day Taipei, can be described as 'xun fu ji'—a 'story of looking for the father'. Interview with *Playboy*, p. 42. For an English translation of *Niezi*, see *Crystal Boys*, trans. Howard Goldblatt (San Francisco, 1991).

17. This is a point made by Christopher Lupke in his talk 'Nativism, Modernism and Bai Xianyong's "Wandering in the Garden, Waking from a Dream"', the Association for Asian Studies Annual Convention, New Orleans, April 1991. See, for instance, some of the stories in the collection *Wandering in the Garden, Waking from a Dream: Tales of Taipei Characters*, trans. Pai Hsien-yung and Patia Yasin, edited by George Kao (Bloomington, 1982).
18. *Yuqing Sao*, p. 111.
19. For an argument about the ageist ideology and dominant gerontophobia of twentieth-century Western culture, see Kathleen Woodward, *Aging and Its Discontents: Freud and Other Fictions* (Bloomington and Indianapolis, 1991).
20. Bai is here consciously or unconsciously sharing Freud's biased judgement about femininity. Freud claims that in matters of sexuality women are always *certain* about what they want. While a little boy does not understand the meaning of the female genitals until much later than when he first sees them, a little girl behaves differently: 'She makes her judgement and her decision in a flash. She has seen it and knows that she is without it and wants to have it.' ('Some Psychological Consequences of the Anatomical Distinction between the Sexes', 1925.) This attributed 'certainty' of feminine desire goes hand in hand with the view that women become fixed and rigid—that is, *old*—much earlier than men: 'A man of about thirty strikes us as a youthful, somewhat unformed individual, whom we expect to make powerful use of the possibilities for development opened up to him by analysis. A woman of the same age, however, often frightens us by her psychical rigidity and unchangeability. Her libido has taken up other positions and seems incapable of exchanging them for others. There are no paths open to further development; it is as though the whole process had already taken its course and remains thenceforward insusceptible to influence—as though the difficult developments to femininity had exhausted the possibilities of the person concerned' ('Femininity', 1933.) The two passages are in *The Standard Edition of the Complete Psychological Works of Sigmund Freud*, 24 vols, trans. and ed. James Strachey (London, 1953–74), vol. XIX, p. 252; vol., XXII, pp. 134–5.

Part V. Erotic Hope, Feminine Sexuality, and the Beginnings of Sexual Freedom

28 Polemical Preface

Pornography in the Service of Women

Angela Carter

> Sadism is not a name finally given to a practice as old as Eros; it is a massive cultural fact which appeared precisely at the end of the eighteenth century, and which constitutes one of the greatest conversions of Western imagination: unreason transformed into delirium of the heart, madness of desire, the insane dialogue of love and death in the limitless presumption of appetite.
>
> (*Madness and Civilisation*, Michel Foucault)

> I am not the slave of the Slavery that dehumanised my ancestors.
>
> (*Black Skin White Masks*, Frantz Fanon)

Pornographers are the enemies of women only because our contemporary ideology of pornography does not encompass the possibility of change, as if we were the slaves of history and not its makers, as if sexual relations were not necessarily an expression of social relations, as if sex itself were an external fact, one as immutable as the weather, creating human practice but never a part of it.

Pornography involves an abstraction of human intercourse in which the self is reduced to its formal elements. In its most basic form, these elements are represented by the probe and the fringed hole, the twin signs of male and female in graffiti, the biological symbols scrawled on the subway poster and the urinal wall, the simplest expression of stark and ineradicable sexual differentiation, a universal pictorial language of lust—or, rather, a language we accept as universal because, since it has always been so, we conclude that it must always remain so.

Angela Carter, 'Polemical Preface: Pornography in the Service of Women', edited extract from *The Sadeian Woman and the Ideology of Pornography*, Angela Carter (Pantheon Books, 1979), 3–19, reprinted by permission of the publisher.

In the stylisation of graffiti, the prick is always presented erect, in an alert attitude of enquiry or curiosity or affirmation; it points upwards, it asserts. The hole is open, an inert space, like a mouth waiting to be filled. From this elementary iconography may be derived the whole metaphysic of sexual differences—man aspires; woman has no other function but to exist, waiting. The male is positive, an exclamation mark. Woman is negative. Between her legs lies nothing but zero, the sign for nothing, that only becomes something when the male principle fills it with meaning.

Anatomy is destiny, said Freud, which is true enough as far as it goes, but ambiguous. My anatomy is only part of an infinitely complex organisation, my self. The anatomical reductionalism of graffiti, the *reductio ad absurdum* of the bodily differences between men and women, extracts all the evidence of me from myself and leaves behind only a single aspect of my life as a mammal. It enlarges this aspect, simplifies it and then presents it as the most significant aspect of my entire humanity. This is true of all mythologising of sexuality; but graffiti lets it be *seen* to be true. It is the most explicit version of the idea of different sexual essences of men and women, because it is the crudest. In the face of this symbolism, my pretensions to any kind of social existence go for nothing; graffiti directs me back to my mythic generation as a woman and, as a woman, my symbolic value is primarily that of a myth of patience and receptivity, a dumb mouth from which the teeth have been pulled.

Sometimes, especially under the influence of Jung, a more archaic mouth is allowed to exert an atavistic dominance. Then, if I am lucky enough to be taken with such poetic pseudo-seriousness, my nether mouth may be acknowledged as one capable of speech—were there not, of old, divinatory priestesses, female oracles and so forth? Was there not Cassandra, who always spoke the truth, although admittedly in such a way that nobody ever believed her? And that, in mythic terms, is the hell of it. Since that female, oracular mouth is located so near the beastly backside, my vagina might indeed be patronisingly regarded as a speaking mouth, but never one that issues the voice of reason. In this most insulting mythic redefinition of myself, that of occult priestess, I am indeed allowed to speak but only of things that male society does not take seriously. I can hint at dreams, I can even personify the imagination; but that is only because I am not rational enough to cope with reality.

If women allow themselves to be consoled for their culturally determined lack of access to the modes of intellectual debate by the invocation of hypothetical great goddesses, they are simply flattering themselves into submission (a technique often used on them by men). All the mythic versions of women, from the myth of the redeeming purity of the virgin to that of the healing, reconciling mother, are consolatory nonsenses; and consolatory nonsense seems to me a fair definition of myth, anyway. Mother goddesses are just as silly a notion as father gods. If a revival of the myths of these cults gives women emotional satisfaction, it does so at the price of obscuring the real conditions of life. This is why they were invented in the first place.

Myth deals in false universals, to dull the pain of particular circumstances. In no area is this more true than in that of relations between the sexes. Graffiti, the most public form of sexual iconography, one which requires no training or artistic skill in its execution and yet is always assured of an audience, obtains all its effects from these false universals of myth. Its savage denial of the complexity of human relations is also a consolatory nonsense.

In its schema, as in the mythic schema of all relations between men and women, man proposes and woman is disposed of, just as she is disposed of in a rape, which is a kind of physical graffiti, the most extreme reduction of love, in which all humanity departs from the sexed beings. So that, somewhere in the fear of rape, is a more than merely physical terror of hurt and humiliation—a fear of psychic disintegration, of an essential dismemberment, a fear of a loss or disruption of the self which is not confined to the victim alone. Since all pornography derives directly from myth, it follows that its heroes and heroines, from the most gross to the most sophisticated, are mythic abstractions, heroes and heroines of dimension and capacity. Any glimpse of a real man or a real woman is absent from these representations of the archetypal male and female.

The nature of the individual is not resolved into but is ignored by these archetypes, since the function of the archetype is to diminish the unique 'I' in favour of a collective, sexed being which cannot, by reason of its very nature, exist as such because an archetype is only an image that has got too big for its boots and bears, at best, a fantasy relation to reality.

All archetypes are spurious but some are more spurious than others. There is the unarguable fact of sexual differentiation; but, separate from it and only partially derived from it, are the behavioural modes of masculine and feminine, which are culturally defined variables translated in the language of common usage to the status of universals. And these archetypes serve only to confuse the main issue, that relationships between the sexes are determined by history and by the historical fact of the economic dependence of women upon men. This fact is now very largely a fact of the past and, even in the past, was only true for certain social groups and then only at certain periods. Today, most women work before, during and after marriage. Nevertheless, the economic dependence of women remains a believed fiction and is assumed to imply an emotional dependence that is taken for granted as a condition inherent in the natural order of things and so used to console working women for their low wages. They work; see little profit from it; and therefore conclude they cannot really have been working at all.

This confusion as to the experience of reality—that what I know from my experience is true is, in fact, not so—is most apparent, however, in the fantasy love-play of the archetypes, which generations of artists have contrived to make seem so attractive that, lulled by dreams, many women willingly ignore the palpable evidence of their own responses.

In these beautiful encounters, any man may encounter any woman and their personalities are far less important to their copulation than the mere fact of their genders. At the first touch or sigh he, she, is subsumed immediately into a universal. (She, of course, rarely approaches him; that is not part of the fantasy of fulfillment.) She is most immediately and dramatically a woman when she lies beneath a man, and her submission is the apex of his malehood. To show his humility before his own erection, a man must approach a woman on his knees, just as he approaches god. This is the kind of beautiful thought that has bedevilled the history of sex in Judaeo-Christian culture, causing almost as much confusion as the idea that sex is a sin. Some of the scorn heaped on homosexuals may derive from the fact that they do not customarily adopt the mythically correct, sacerdotal position. The same beautiful thought has elevated a Western European convention to the position of the only sanctified sexual position; it fortifies the missionary position with a bizarre degree of mystification. God is invoked as a kind of sexual referee, to assure us, as modern churchmen like to claim in the teeth of two thousand years of Christian sexual repression, that sex is really sacred.

The missionary position has another great asset, from the mythic point of view; it implies a system of relations between the partners that equates the woman to the passive receptivity of the soil, to the richness and fecundity of the earth. A whole range of images poeticises, kitschifies, departicularises intercourse, such as wind beating down corn, rain driving against bending trees, towers falling, all tributes to the freedom and strength of the roving, fecundating, irresistible male principle and the heavy, downward, equally irresistible gravity of the receptive soil. The soil that is, good heavens, myself. It is a most self-enhancing notion; I have almost seduced myself with it. Any woman may manage, in luxurious self-deceit, to feel herself for a little while one with great, creating nature, fertile, open, pulsing, anonymous and so forth. In doing so, she loses herself completely and loses her partner also.

The moment they succumb to this anonymity, they cease to be themselves, with their separate lives and desires; they cease to be the lovers who have met to assuage desire in a reciprocal pact of tenderness, and they engage at once in a spurious charade of maleness and femaleness.

The anonymity of the lovers, whom the act transforms from me and you into they, precludes the expression of ourselves.

So the act is taken away from us even as we perform it.

We become voyeurs upon our own caresses. The act does not acknowledge the participation of the individual, bringing to it a whole life of which the act is only a part. The man and woman, in their particularity, their being, are absent from these representations of themselves as male and female. These tableaux of falsification remove our sexual life from the world, from tactile experience itself. The lovers are lost to themselves in a privacy that does not transcend but deny reality. So the act can never satisfy them, because it does not affect their lives. It occurs in the mythic dream-time of religious ritual.

But our flesh arrives to us out of history, like everything else does. We may believe we fuck stripped of social artifice; in bed, we even feel we touch the bedrock of human nature itself. But we are deceived. Flesh is not an irreducible human universal. Although the erotic relationship may seem to exist freely, on its own terms, among the distorted social relationships of a bourgeois society, it is, in fact, the most self-conscious of all human relationships, a direct confrontation of two beings whose actions in the bed are wholly determined by their acts when they are out of it. If one sexual partner is economically dependent on the other, then the question of sexual coercion, of contractual obligation, raises its ugly head in the very abode of love and inevitably colours the nature of the sexual expression of affection. The marriage bed is a particularly delusive refuge from the world because all wives of necessity fuck by contract. Prostitutes are at least decently paid on the nail and boast fewer illusions about a hireling status that has no veneer of social acceptability, but their services are suffering a decline in demand now that other women have invaded their territory in their own search for a newly acknowledged sexual pleasure. In this period, promiscuous abandon may seem the only type of free exchange.

But no bed, however unexpected, no matter how apparently gratuitous, is free from the de-universalising facts of real life. We do not go to bed in simple pairs; even if we choose not to refer to them, we still drag there with us the cultural impedimenta of our social class, our parents' lives, our bank balances, our sexual and emotional expectations, our whole biographies—all the bits and pieces of our unique existences. These considerations have limited our choice of partners before we have even got them into the bedroom. It was impossible for the Countess in Beaumarchais' *The Marriage of Figaro* to contemplate sleeping with her husband's valet, even though he was clearly the best man available; considerations of social class censored the possibility of sexual attraction between the Countess and Figaro before it could have begun to exist, and if this convention restricted the Countess's activities, it did not affect those of her husband; he happily plotted to seduce his valet's wife. If middle-class Catherine Earnshaw, in Emily Brontë's *Wuthering Heights*, wants to sleep with Heathcliff, who has the dubious class origins of the foundling, she must not only repress this desire but pay the socially sanctioned price of brain-fever and early death for even contemplating it. Our literature is full, as are our lives, of men and women, but especially women, who deny the reality of sexual attraction and of love because of considerations of class, religion, race and of gender itself.

Class dictates our choice of partners and our choice of positions. When fear, shame and prudery condemn the poor and the ignorant to copulate in the dark, it must be obvious that sexual sophistication is a by-product of education. The primal nakedness of lovers is a phenomenon of the middle-class in cold climates; in northern winters, naked lovers must be able to afford to heat their bedrooms. The taboos regulating the sight of bare flesh are further determined by wider cultural considerations. The Japanese bathed together in the nude for centuries, yet generations of Japanese lovers fucked in kimono, even in the humidity of summer, and did not even remove the combs from their chignons while they did so. And another complication—they did not appreciate the eroticism of the nude; yet they looked at one another's exposed genitalia with a tender readiness that still perturbs the West.

Control of fertility is a by-product of sexual education and of official legislation concerning the availability of cheap or free contraception. Even so, a poor woman may find herself sterilised when all she wanted was an abortion, her fertility taken out of her own control for good by social administrators who have decided that poverty is synonymous with stupidity and a poor woman cannot know her own mind.

The very magical privacy of the bed, the pentacle, may itself only be bought with money, and lack of privacy limits sexual sophistication, which may not be pursued in a room full of children.

Add to these socio-economic considerations the Judaeo-Christian heritage of shame, disgust and morality that stand between the initial urge and the first attainment of this most elementary assertion of the self and it is a wonder anyone in this culture ever learns to fuck at all.

Flesh comes to us out of history; so does the repression and taboo that governs our experience of flesh.

The nature of actual modes of sexual intercourse is determined by historical changes in less intimate human relations, just as the actual nature of men and women is capable of infinite modulations as social structures change. Our knowledge is determined by the social boundaries upon it; for example, Sade, the eighteenth-century lecher, knew that manipulation of the clitoris was the unique key to the female orgasm, but a hundred years later, Sigmund Freud, a Viennese intellectual, did not wish to believe that this grand simplicity was all there was to the business. It was socially permissible for an eighteenth-century aristocrat to sleep with more women than it was for a member of the nineteenth-century bourgeoisie, for one thing, and to retain a genuine curiosity about female sexuality whilst doing so, for another. Yet Freud, the psychoanalyst, can conceive of a far richer notion of human nature as a whole than Sade, the illiberal philosopher, is capable of; the social boundaries of knowledge expand in some areas and contract in others due to historical forces.

Sexuality, in short, is never expressed in a vacuum. Though the archaic sequence of human life—we are born, we fuck, we reproduce, we die – might seem to be universal experience, its universality is not its greatest significance. Since human beings have invented history, we have also invented those aspects of our lives that seem most immutable, or, rather, have invented the circumstances that determine their nature. Birth and death, the only absolute inescapables, are both absolutely determined by the social context in which they occur. There is no longer an inevitable relationship between fucking and reproducing and, indeed, neither fucking nor reproducing have been activities practiced by all men and women at all times, anyway; there has always been the option to abstain, whether it is exercised or not. Women experience sexuality and reproduction quite differently than men do; rich women are more in control of the sequence than poor women and so may actually enjoy fucking and childbirth, when poor women might find them both atrocious simply because they are poor and cannot afford comfort, privacy and paid help.

The notion of a universality of human experience is a confidence trick and the notion of a universality of female experience is a clever confidence trick.

Pornography, like marriage and the fictions of romantic love, assists the process of false universalising. Its excesses belong to that timeless, locationless area outside history, outside geography, where fascist art is born.

Nevertheless, there is no question of an aesthetics of pornography. It can never be art for art's sake. Honourably enough, it is always art with work to do.

Pornographic literature, the specific area of pornography with which we are going to deal, has several functions. On one level, and a level which should not be despised, it might serve as an instruction manual for the inexperienced. But our culture, with its metaphysics of sexuality, relegates the descriptions of the mechanics of sex to crude functionalism; in the sex textbook, intercourse also takes place in a void. So pornography's principal and most humanly significant function is that of arousing sexual excitement. It does this by ignoring the first function; it usually describes the sexual act not in explicit terms—for that might make it seem frightening—but in purely inviting terms.

The function of plot in a pornographic narrative is always the same. It exists purely to provide as many opportunities as possible for the sexual act to take place There is no room here for tension or the unexpected. We know what is going happen; that is why we are reading the book. Characterisation is necessarily limited by the formal necessity for the actors to fuck as frequently and as ingeniously as possible. But they do not do so because they are continually consumed by desire; the free expression of desire is as alien to pornography as it is to marriage. In pornography, both men and women fuck because to fuck is their *raison d'être*. It is their life work.

It follows that prostitutes are favourite heroines of the pornographic writer, though the economic aspects of a prostitute's activity, which is her own main concern in the real world, will be dealt with only lightly.

Her labour is her own private business. Work, in this context, is *really* dirty work; it is unmentionable. Even unspeakable. And we may not talk about it because it reintroduces the question of the world. In this privatised universe pleasure is the only work; work itself is unmentionable. To concentrate on the prostitute's trade *as* trade would introduce too much reality into a scheme that is first and foremost one of libidinous fantasy, and pornographic writers, in general, are not concerned with extending the genre in which they work to include a wider view of the world. This is because pornography is the orphan little sister of the arts; its functionalism renders it suspect, more applied art than fine art, and so its very creators rarely take it seriously.

Fine art, that exists for itself alone, is art in a final state of impotence. If nobody, including the artist, acknowledges art as a means of *knowing* the world then art is relegated to a kind of rumpus room of the mind and the irresponsibility of the artist and the irrelevance of art to actual living becomes part and parcel of the practice of art. Nevertheless, pornographic writing retains this in common with all literature—that it turns the flesh into word. This is the real transformation the text performs upon libidinous fantasy.

The verbal structure is in itself reassuring. We know we are not dealing with real flesh or anything like it, but with a cunningly articulated verbal simulacrum which has the power to arouse, but not, in itself, to assuage desire. At this point, the reader, the consumer, enters the picture; reflecting the social dominance which affords him the opportunity to purchase the flesh of other people as if it were meat, the reader or consumer of pornography is usually a man who subscribes to a particular social fiction of manliness. His belief in this fiction prevents him from realising that, when he picks up a dirty book, he engages in a game with his own desire and with his own solitude, both of which he endlessly titillates but never openly confronts.

Therefore a cerebral insatiability, unacknowledged yet implicit, is a characteristic of pornography, which always throws the reader back on his own resources, since it convinces him of the impotence of his desire that the book cannot in itself assuage, at the same time as he solaces that loneliness through the medium of the fantasy extracted from the fiction.

The one-to-one relation of the reader with the book is never more apparent than in the reading of a pornographic novel, since it is virtually impossible to forget oneself in relation to the text. In pornographic literature, the text has a gap left in it on purpose so that the reader may, in imagination, step inside it. But the activity the text describes, into which the reader enters, is not a whole world into which the reader is absorbed and, as they say, 'taken out of himself'. It is one basic activity extracted from the world in its totality in such a way that the text constantly reminds the reader of his own troubling self, his own reality—and the limitations of that reality since, however much he wants to fuck the willing women or men in his story, he cannot do so but must be content with some form of substitute activity. (The fictional maleness of the pornography consumer encompasses the butch hero of homosexual pornography; it is a *notion* of masculinity unrelated to practice.)

The privacy of the reader is invaded by his own desires, which reach out towards the world beyond the book he is reading. Yet they are short-circuited by the fantastic nature of the gratification promised by the text, which denies to flesh all its intransigence, indeed its sexed quality, since sexuality is a quality made manifest in being, and pornography can only allow its phantoms to exist in the moment of sexual excitation; they cannot engage in the wide range of activity in the real world in which sexual performance is not the supreme business of all people at all times.

Yet the gripping nature of pornography, its directly frontal assault upon the senses of the reader, its straightforward engagement of him at a non-intellectual level, its *sensationalism*, suggest the methodology of propaganda. Indeed, pornography is basically propaganda for fucking, an activity, one would have thought, that did not need much advertising in itself, because most people want to do it as soon as they know how.

The denial of the social fact of sexuality in pornography is made explicit in its audience. Produced in the main by men for an all-male clientele, suggesting certain analogies with a male brothel, access to pornography is usually denied to women at any level, often on the specious grounds that women do not find descriptions of the sexual act erotically stimulating. Yet if pornography is produced by men for a male audience, it is exclusively concerned with relations between the sexes and even the specialised area of homosexual pornography divides its actors into sexual types who might roughly be defined as 'masculine' and 'feminine'. So all pornography suffers the methodological defects of a manual of navigation written by and for land-lubbers.

Many pornographic novels are written in the first person as if by a woman, or use a woman as the focus of the narrative; but this device only reinforces the male orientation of the fiction. John Cleland's *Fanny Hill* and the anonymous *The Story of O*, both classics of the genre, appear in this way to describe a woman's mind through the fiction of her sexuality. This technique ensures that the gap left in the text is of just the right size for the reader to insert his prick into, the exact dimensions, in fact, of Fanny's vagina or of O's anus. Pornography engages the reader in a most intimate fashion before it leaves him to his own resources. This gap in the text may also be just the size of the anus or mouth of a young man, subsuming him, too, to this class that is most present in its absence, the invisible recipients of the pornographic tribute, the mental masturbatory objects.

So pornography reinforces the false universals of sexual archetypes because it denies, or doesn't have time for, or can't find room for, or, because of its underlying ideology, ignores, the social context in which sexual activity takes place, that modifies the very nature of that activity. Therefore pornography must always have the false simplicity of fable; the abstraction of the flesh involves the mystification of the flesh. As it reduces the actors in the sexual drama to instruments of pure function, so the pursuit of pleasure becomes in itself a metaphysical quest. The pornographer, in spite of himself, becomes a metaphysician when he states that the friction of penis in orifice is the supreme matter of the world, for which the world is well lost; as he says so, the world vanishes.

Pornography, like satire, has an inbuilt reactionary mechanism. Its effect depends on the notion that the nature of man is invariable and cannot be modified by changes in his social institutions. The primordial itch in the groin existed before multinational business corporations and the nuclear family and will outlast them just as it illicitly dominates them. The disruptiveness of sexuality, its inability to be contained, the overflowing of the cauldron of id—these are basic invariables of sexuality, opines the pornographer, and in itself pornography is a satire on human pretensions. The judge conceals his erection beneath his robes of office as he passes judgement on the whore. The cabinet minister slips away from his office early to visit the call girl. The public executioner ejaculates as the neck of his victim snaps. And we laugh wryly at the omnipotence of Old Adam, how he will always, somehow or other, get his way, and we do ourselves and Old Adam the grossest injustice when we grant him so much power, when we reduce sexuality to the status of lowest common denominator without asking ourselves what preconceptions make us think it should be so.

Since sexuality is as much a social fact as it is a human one, it will therefore change its nature according to changes in social conditions. If we could restore the context of the world to the embraces of these shadows then, perhaps, we could utilise their activities to obtain a fresh perception of the world and, in some sense, transform it. The sexual act in pornography exists as a metaphor for what people do to one another, often in the cruellest sense; but the present business of the pornographer is to suppress the metaphor as much as he can and leave us with a handful of empty words.

Pornographic pictures, movies and narrative fiction are the pure forms of sexual fiction, of the fiction *of* sex, where this operation of alienation takes place most visibly. But all art which contains elements of eroticism (eroticism, the pornography of the elite) contains the possibility of the same methodology—that is, writing that can 'pull' a reader just as a woman 'pulls' a man or a man 'pulls' a woman.

And all such literature has the potential to force the reader to reassess his relation to his own sexuality, which is to say to his own primary being, through the mediation of the image or the text. This is true for women also, perhaps especially so, as soon as we realise the way pornography reinforces the archetypes of her negativity and that it does so simply because most pornography remains in the service of the status quo. And that is because its elementary metaphysic gets in the way of real life and prevents us seeing real life. If the world has been lost, the world may not be reassessed. Libidinous fantasy in a vacuum is the purest, but most affectless, form of day-dreaming. So pornography in general serves to defuse the explosive potential of all sexuality and that is the main reason why it is made by and addressed to the politically dominant minority in the world, as an instrument of repression, not only of women, but of men too. Pornography keeps sex in its place, that is, under the carpet. That is, outside everyday human intercourse.

The sexuality of the blue movie queen, contained by her social subservience, exhibits no menace. Linda Lovelace does not believe in the Women's Liberation Movement; how could she? Fanny Hill gladly gives up the dominant role of mistress for the subservient role of wife and hands to her Charles all her hard-earned money too, which is an infinitely more far-reaching gesture of submission than that of accepting his sexual mastery and opting for domestic monogamy and motherhood under his exclusive economic sanction. Fanny knows in her heart that her Charles is really her last, most efficient, pimp. O, less complex because her economic means of support are not explored as closely as Cleland explores Fanny's, is more content simply to rejoice in her chains, a model for all women.

It is fair to say that, when pornography serves—as with very rare exceptions it always does—to reinforce the prevailing system of values and ideas in a given society, it is tolerated; and when it does not, it is banned. (This already suggests there are more reasons than those of public decency for the banning of the work of Sade for almost two hundred years; only at the time of the French Revolution and at the present day have his books been available to the general public.) Therefore an increase of pornography on the market, within the purchasing capacity of the common man, and especially the beginning of a type of pornography modelled on that provided for the male consumer but directed at women, does not mean an increase in sexual licence, with the reappraisal of social mores such licence, if it is real, necessitates. It might only indicate a more liberal attitude to masturbation, rather than to fucking, and reinforce a sollipsistic concentration on the relationship with the self, which is a fantasy one at the best of times.

When pornography abandons its quality of existential solitude and moves out of the kitsch area of timeless, placeless fantasy and into the real world, then it loses its function of safety valve. It begins to comment on real relations in the real world. Therefore, the more pornographic writing acquires the techniques of real literature, of real art, the more deeply subversive it is likely to be in that the more likely it is to affect the reader's perceptions of the world. The text that had heretofore opened up creamily to him, in a dream, will gather itself together and harshly expel him into the anguish of actuality.

There is a liberal theory that art disinfects eroticism of its latent subversiveness, and pornography that is also art loses its shock and its magnetism, becomes 'safe'. The truth of this is that once pornography is labelled 'art' or 'literature' it is stamped with the approval of an elitist culture and many ordinary people will avoid it on principle, out of a fear of being bored. But the more the literary arts of plotting and characterisation are used to shape the material of pornography, the more the pornographer himself is faced with the moral contradictions inherent in real sexual encounters. He will find himself in a dilemma; to opt for the world or to opt for the wet dream?

Out of this dilemma, the moral pornographer might be born.

Porn in the USA

The following is taken from interviews with Candida Royalle conducted by Anne McClintock in New York, 1991–1993, and an oral presentation by Royalle at Columbia University.

Candida Royalle

There were three reasons why I started Femme Productions. After a few years of working as an actress in adult films, I began to write for men's magazines and review adult movies. That was when I started looking closely at the films and was horrified to see how sexist they were. So I began to think about making porn movies that were aimed at women, and which couples could share together. I felt that adult entertainment could be very valid and life-enriching, but it wasn't being done with that in mind. Unlike the antiporn movement, I don't think porn causes violence. But the films were very exploitive of women and of sexuality in general. I didn't think that they were offering anything constructive about our sexuality. I also realized that women were beginning to watch porn, and I knew that there was nothing out there for them to watch. So I began Femme with three aims in mind. I wanted to show that it was possible to produce explicit porn that had integrity, I wanted to show that porn could be nonsexist, and I wanted to show that porn could be life-enriching.

I grew up Catholic, fed on the usual menu of guilt and shame. I was a very passionate young woman with urges and feelings that I was not supposed to have. I was almost raped when I was 13 and although I managed to get away, my culture made me feel that I must have been asking for it: I was reaching puberty, I was becoming sexual, I was making men do these things to me. It's a very tough culture for

Candida Royalle, 'Porn in the USA', from *Social Text* (Winter 1993), 23–32, reprinted by permission of the author and the publisher. Every attempt has been made to obtain permission to reproduce this article. Please contact Oxford University Press with queries.

women. So I wanted to make films that made people feel good about their sexuality and about who they are as sexual beings. I wanted to make films that say we all have a right to pleasure, and that women, especially, have a right to our own pleasure.

In the beginning, the men in the business told me that there is no 'couples' market, and that women don't watch porn. 'Honey,' they said, 'you won't make a dollar.' They'd say: 'That's really nice, honey. That's a really nice idea. (She's nuts. She'll be gone in a year.)' But I knew that a new market had opened up that no one was addressing. I knew that, financially, it could be a very good business venture and a way to utilize the name I had created which was following me around now whether I liked it or not. When I started Femme, I was already branded as an evil woman for working in porn, so I felt that I had nothing to lose. I thought I might as well take all my education and training, and use it to my advantage. Now, I think they are really stunned. Now people are saying: 'Well, maybe she's right. Maybe there *is* a "couples" market,' and they've started trying to make movies that are more palatable to women.

I have great respect for the actresses who work in this business. It takes enormous courage to face the condemnation and hypocrisy that will inevitably fall upon women who dare to break with a cultural taboo. People always criticize the actors for lack of talent. But in a culture that condemns you as a no-good whore for acting in a porn film, directors can hardly go to good drama schools to try and recruit talent there. But there are still some very talented erotic performers. It's important to point out that the movies tend to look as bad as they do because it is an industry that is kept in the gutter by the stigma. People who want to be serious producers and directors don't touch the industry because they don't want to ruin their careers.

It is often taken for granted that women get into porn because they are victims or prostitutes or self-destructive. It's very hard for this culture to accept that women could choose to do this as a job, which was certainly the case with me and many other women. So when I interview the talent for my films, I really sit down and talk to them. If women tell me that they want to get into porn, I really put them through the mill. I tell them what it will be like once they have done it, and how people will treat them. You carry it around with you forever. Everyone has skeletons in the closet, but this isn't in the closet, it's right out in public. My skeletons follow me visually wherever I go.

When people say: 'What about the feminists who are against you?' that makes me so angry, because Women Against Pornography does not represent feminist thought. They are a very small minority. To tell us continually that it is unsafe for us to explore our own fantasies is to keep us out of power. We have to take control of our own images and of our own power. But I don't like to present myself as pro-porn/anything goes. Because I've been both in front of and behind the camera, I consider myself balanced about it. My own experience was for the most part okay, and there were some very nice people to work for. The mood on the sets was one of camaraderie. There was a lot of closeness among the talent. Also, I was involved in the late seventies when it was a much smaller, tighter circle. At the same time, there were some real creeps that you could work for. It's like any industry; you really had to use your brains and your wit. But in Hollywood, they make you go on the couch for a hope and a promise. In this industry you know what you are being paid for. I never had to do anything to get a job, because that *was* the job. It was very straightforward: no one was fucking me over.

It's the same today. There are some really decent people to work for. You can make some really good money if you are smart. A beginner might get $250 a day, whereas a top figure might be as high as $2,000 a day, depending on your box office draw and how smart you are at negotiating your salary. There are also some real sleaze-bags who will take advantage of you and who are to be avoided. But when I went for auditions—and they really *were* auditions—they would hand you a checklist, and you would fill out what you would do and what you wouldn't do. I was *never* forced to do anything. Never.

The only time a director wanted me to do something that I didn't want to do, I refused. It wasn't anything injurious to myself. It was just a sex act that I didn't want to be known for doing, involving a scene where the women would urinate on the man who was the villain. I refused, and Annette Haven and I organized all the other actresses and most of us wouldn't do it.

If this were a culture that *genuinely* cared about women, it would create unions for sex workers. It would create places for the women to spread the word: who is good to work for, who isn't; what are your rights; what should you do or not do. Now I own my own company. I produce. I speak internationally. And I have to constantly dodge someone in the business world trying to fuck me over. Especially as a woman in business. It's new terrain. But if this industry is kept underground because of hypocrisy, it makes it much tougher for the people working in it, and creates unique problems. How the experience affects you depends very much on who you are and what you bring to it in the way of mental stability. There *are* some people who come out of porn very damaged. And there are those who are tremendous survivors and end up turning it into a positive thing for ourselves.

There's also an assumption that if you are performing sex for a living, it detracts from your personal and sexual life. When I was in front of the camera I never felt that it interfered with my personal life at all. It was a job, and it was very hard work, and if I could get any pleasure out of it that was all the better. Any work that you can enjoy is much better. But that's what it was: a job. And it's not at all the same as what you experience intimately with someone. My ex-husband was also in the industry. He was a young producer and he really understood that what we did together was different from what I was paid to do on the set. My work and my sexual life really didn't interfere with one another at all. In fact being involved in the field of sexuality has made me much more open, much less judgmental, and very comfortable with sex.

What I did find, though, was that people think that, having been in porn, you have to be a super lover. But that's not true at all. All it teaches you is technique and the mechanics, and I realized that I had to learn all over again what sensuality was about, and I had to get back in touch with my sensual beginnings.

As a director, I find that good erotic performers are people who can lose themselves in the sex while staying in character. No one really thinks about that. After all, it's acting. It's really wonderful when you find a woman who can get off on set, but of course the women are usually faking. The best one was Chelsea Blake, who would be my all-time favorite actress. She was wonderful. She was in her mid-forties when she worked for me. She was in *Urban Heat* and *Christine's Secret*, and if she was faking it even I don't know. In *Urban Heat* she does a torrid scene where she seduced a man in a freight elevator, and the guy was so intimidated by the whole thing that he couldn't get it up. He loved her, but he couldn't get an erection. So I thought, that's not the main thing. We'll just work around it and, boy, she really carried that scene and made it incredibly hot without any really explicit sex happening.

Chelsea left porn only because she got married to a guy who seemed to think he had to do battle with Mary Magdalene to save his own conscience. And he really tortured her. This happens a lot to women in the business. It turns the men on, but then they feel the necessity to turn the woman into a madonna, and they say: 'You can't do this anymore.' Sometimes they never let them forget that they worked in porn. They torture them emotionally.

I don't hire anyone who has a bad attitude. I get guys calling me who say: 'Hey, I got ten inches, and I can get you some new babes.' Believe me, there are women, too, who are very negative about the men they work with. I have had actresses say to me: 'When the cameras are rolling, that's fine. If he touches me otherwise I am going to slap his face.' And will do it. So I try to hire people who are really into each other. I don't even take camera people from the industry, as they are already programmed to shoot things a certain way. The same even applies to female talent, who are used to performing for the male fantasy medium. We are trying to do something different.

There tends to be a lot of camaraderie on set, because you're in such a vulnerable position and so exposed with each other. When I was an actress I felt it was important to make the guy feel that I really wanted him, even if I didn't. The man's got such a tough job. He's got to get it up and he's got to perform. And the men would do the same for me. So, on set you come to expect that consideration. But it can also be a total nightmare if you can't stand each other. I put Jerry Butler with Rhonda Jo Petty, for example, because they were having an affair. Little did I know, by the time they got to the set they were not having an affair anymore and they couldn't stand each other. She had a cold and was sniffling and racing through the scene, and she kept asking him: 'Are you coming, are you coming now?' That doesn't make for a great sex scene

There's always been wonderful energy on the Femme sets. *Three Daughters*, for example, became a very cathartic experience for the actress, Siobhan Hunter. She was one of the Mayflower Madam girls, who had worked as an escort to put herself through medical school. The scene we were shooting was supposed to be a very tender portrayal of her first time and we were shooting in a green room, and the actor had a moustache. All of a sudden, Siobhan started freaking out. She said, 'This is reminding me of my actual first sexual experience. It was a green room, with a man with a moustache, and it was a horrendous experience, and I'm starting to freak.' So I sat her down and I talked to her, and I told her that my first experience was done with someone I loved, but that it was also a dreadful experience. I told her that I use the movies as a form of catharsis—as a way of redoing it, in a way, and making it better. I thought she could try to use this the same way. The man she was working with had so much genuine feeling for her, that is exactly what happened. They did the scene together and at the very end, while the cameras were still rolling, she sat up, they were hugging, and she started crying. If you see the scene, you'll see tears on her face. It was such a release for her.

I have been criticized for not crossing boundaries of class and race, and that is a very difficult issue. People also ask me why I don't do lesbian movies. But since I'm not a lesbian I don't feel I'm the right person to do it. Debi Sundahl and the women at Blush Productions are making fabulous lesbian movies, which is great, as they come from the heart. Whereas I know heterosexuality better. I also think there should be a really strong line of movies that reflect the fantasies and desires of black people. There aren't that many black or Latina/o actors and actresses. This is a very racist culture and a lot of porn that uses black actors and actresses is really racist and very exploitive. I'm told the black community also tends to be more Christian and more conservative about what is sexually proper. So it is very tough for black actresses, who are very condemned by their own community.

Perhaps my biggest complaint about my own movies is that I now like a bit of rawness. I had a relationship after my marriage that really explored power play, and it was the most passionate, powerful, liberating thing I have ever experienced in my life. Since then I've opened up to more of a raw edge within myself. Everyone says: 'Oh, women want sex soft and pretty, like a Harlequin novel.' It's as if women are being protected, and maybe I'm a little guilty of that too. So I really want to bring more of that raw edge into Femme. I think women can handle it. In *Three Daughters*, I have a couple who are engaged to be married and who get into some very light power play. They take turns tying each other's hands to the bed very lightly. He says to her: 'Do you trust me?' She says: 'I trust you.' I mean, it loses all its intensity because it is so safe! But I had to be very careful in the beginning. My message was: what better place to play with your fantasies than with someone you love and trust? When you find a safe environment to play with your fantasies, they can really lose their control over you. It is so hard to keep the sex in a long-term monogamous relationship interesting. Routine is the death of sensuality. Porn can be an enhancement to talking about fantasies, and can offer a safe and erotic way of opening things up.

Some people insist women are masochists by nature. But, ironically, it's usually the man who wants to be submissive. The fantasy of forced sex may be very powerful for women because it relieves us of responsibility and guilt in a culture that tells us we shouldn't have sexual pleasures and lusts. But, of course, these fantasies are nothing like real rape, since women control them for their own pleasure. If it happened in reality it would be so disempowering and terrifying. But if you control the fantasy, you control the power. But the problem, of course, is that if you show women living out a rape fantasy, some men may believe that women really want to be raped. And, unfortunately, we live in a culture where a lot of men think that women who are raped are asking for it. It's a very difficult issue for a filmmaker. If a film shows a woman forced into sex against her will in a genuinely frightening context, and then she's shown to turn around and like it, that is very destructive. Whereas if it is obvious that it is a woman's fantasy and if it's consensual—consensual being the key word here—it's totally different. It's a very delicate balance, though. I've posed this question at sex therapy conferences I've attended. Usually I get answers like: 'Show the couple discussing it.' While this may dilute the fantasy, I've tried that approach in a scene I recently shot and it may work very well.

The primary element in role playing is consent and trust. In S/M, when the submissive says, 'Stop, it's going too far, I'm uncomfortable'—it stops. The irony, then, is that it is the submissive who is in control. It is really the dominant who serves the submissive. Also, the funny thing is, as women get older, they get more comfortable with exploring their fantasies, and I've heard a lot of women my age say: 'Gee, it's really difficult to find a good dominant male.' You can't find them!

Believe me, though, it's one thing to play at being dominant in bed, but if a man starts displaying a macho attitude in real life, he's out the door! No one wants a guy who dominates you all the time. It's just that bed can be the one safe place where you can play out things like power—*play* with power. Traditionally, men are supposed to be in control and be the boss at work. So, typically, in their free time men want to give up control and be submissive to dominant women. But now that women are also entering positions of control and becoming business owners and executives, they, too, feel the need to relinquish control and surrender in a safe consensual setting. Women need to be able to kick off their shoes and let go. But it's actually harder for women to find a good dominant. I hear this from women all the time.

I wish more women were encouraged to make erotic films from a variety of points of view. But as long as porn was strictly male entertainment, it was tolerated. Now that it is being taken into the bedroom, where women—the wives, madonnas, and sisters—can see it, it's very threatening to the Right. That is where I could pose a threat, by making porn more palatable to women.

When I began Femme I was so fed up with seeing the cum shot in every movie—in a context that didn't support women's pleasure—that I decided to have no cum shots in my films. I had always wondered, seeing so many films with cum shots, why men wanted to see other men's penises spurting cum, rather than seeing women's orgasms. The cum shots—the exterior climax shots—are called the money shots in the business because they say if you don't have them, you don't have a movie. Before making our first film, my former partner Lauren Niemi and I went for a consultation with one of the porn filmmakers, and when he heard I wasn't going to use cum shots, he said, 'Oh, my God!' and warned my investors and said, 'She's going to lose all your money.' Years ago, as an actress, I had asked, 'Why are they in there?' They said: 'To prove it's really happening.' I thought, 'If you have to do that to prove this is all really happening, you've lost the game already.' These men are so out of touch with people's sexuality!

Porn is a very narcissistic form of pleasure, where viewers can glorify their own bodily functions by projecting themselves onto the actors. Perhaps the cum shot is also a way of saying to a woman: 'Here, take this.' It's a way of maintaining control. But perhaps there's also something else. I had a lover who had a hard time coming inside. I felt a real desire for him. When he finally did come inside me, it really felt that he was surrendering and losing himself to me. I felt a sense of power. So it would make sense that he might feel he was losing his power. Now, a man who is not afraid of losing himself in a woman's body enjoys that act of surrender. It's only when you fear that you've got something to lose that you can never regain, that it becomes a threat. If men are threatened by their desire for women, the cum shot may be a way of keeping a distance, keeping control. It has to do with men feeling threatened by the power women have over them.

In the beginning, I felt the same about anal sex as I felt about cum shots. Before the eighties, the big thing in porn was women giving men head. Then that became commonplace, so, in the eighties, anal sex took over. My first two movies were distributed by one of the major adult distributors. When I was negotiating with the distributor, the guy says, 'Well, you know, Candida, I got to tell you—I got to tell you that what you need is to put more anal sex in your movies.' More anal sex? I didn't have *any* anal sex. 'I know who watches these films,' he says. 'It's the husbands who buy these movies, to show their wives what they want them to do.' I was horrified. I thought, do you realize who you are talking to? Here I am, a woman wanting to make movies from a woman's point of view, and you're telling me to make something that the husband can bring home and talk their wives into doing. I was really appalled, and after that I started my own distribution.

I would argue that the sense of powerlessness boys feel in infancy, the pain in trying to separate from their mothers, and then the incredible desire they feel for girls in adolescence create a strong need in men to assert their dominance over women. So they develop a real thirst for seeing visual representations of women losing their power to men.

People in the porn business recognize now, though, how large a part of the market women are, and a lot of filmmakers are changing their films to reflect this. Others have decided to stay with the male end of the market. But they also realize how much the business has been hurt by turning out a lot of cheap products. Still, it is hard to spend any real money on porn movies, because everyone else is making and selling them so cheap, just to make a buck. The way most of them function is to make lots of tiny movies and lots of tiny profits, whereas the way we operate is to spend much more time and money on a movie because it is so unique, and have the profits come in indefinitely. There are some exceptions: Andrew Blake, who did *Night Trips*, is really doing some special stuff. But I am really the only one who has any real philosophical or political motive.

I've used safer-sex in all the movies I've done since 1986. I feel it is my responsibility to show people how they can make safer-sex fun and erotic. I also have an age policy: I don't like to use people under the age of 22. I am more strict with women, because the ramifications are so much greater for us. I didn't get into movies until I was 24 or 25 and I feel that before your twenties you haven't done enough thinking and living to fully grasp the consequences of working in this industry. It's not that there is anything inherently wrong with porn work; but we live in a culture that will condemn anyone who chooses this work.

Femme's production costs are higher than most porn movies. We take a lot of care with the quality. But I don't think I pay people any more than any other good production would pay their people. I have a very egalitarian system of paying. Whether you are a big star or a small star, everyone gets paid the same. People love working for me. In some cases, people take less money for working for me. They know that they are working for a woman who has been there, and who has a tremendous sense of compassion and respect for them, who cares about what she's doing. At the most, they'll have one sex scene a day and, with rare exceptions, will not work longer than an eight- to ten-hour day. Other people may demand three sex scenes in a day and keep them there eighteen hours.

The key to my films is sensuality. Every part of our body is an erogenous zone; so I've taken the emphasis off the hard-core. I don't like to focus on the genitals any more than the face or the hands, but I don't want to hide them either. I don't like to use the terms *foreplay* and *afterplay*, because those terms imply that the only real goal of sex is penetration. What does that mean for women's sexuality? There shouldn't even be such terminology as foreplay and afterplay. I wanted to focus on sensuality, tenderness, and mutual respect—a holistic approach, instead of a collection of body parts. And I get a lot of letters of appreciation! The audience for my films is ever-growing. My work has been wonderfully received by the sexology community, which has been very gratifying to me. It's amazing how much mail I get from both men and women, thanking me. I think I have gotten two hate letters in the last eight years.

But there are women who have said my films are too soft. Some women like regular hard porn, and think mine could be harder. On the other hand, there are also a lot of men who don't like hard-core, and feel more comfortable with mine. Porn can cover the whole spectrum. In Europe, porn is very compartmentalized. There's very hard-core pornography, which lately has ventured into the bizarre and unusual, but they also make really beautiful, nonexplicit erotic movies, which is a thriving business we don't have here. We are a very, very puritanical country. In some parts of Europe, they don't know what to do with my movies because my work falls between super hard-core and nonexplicit soft-core. They haven't yet recognized a market for them. Here I recognized and created the market.

But I definitely think you can have explicit adult films that are not sexist and not exploitive of women. It's not showing genitals that is exploitive; it is the philosophy behind it, and the acts and images that philosophy fosters. The Women Against Porn rap assumes that anything that is explicit is automatically exploitive. But then you have to assume that just the act of showing explicit sex is an act of exploitation. Whereas some of the most sexist, exploitive garbage is in our soft R-rated movies. You can get away with just about anything in an R-rated movie. Cut the woman's breasts into little pieces and eat them? It's okay, as long as you don't see any genitals.

At the moment, it is a very bad time for the industry. It has hurt itself financially, and the turn to the Right in this country is very serious. The Right knows it's difficult to get obscenity convictions anymore, so they harass companies and drain their bank accounts with multiple, simultaneous obscenity cases. There was a major sting this year. If things are made tougher for the companies, they'll just end up in the hands of the sleaziest people who are willing to take the chance. The conditions for the performers are going to get worse. The only way to improve adult films and give them more integrity and quality is to encourage more people to go into them and to encourage better production; to encourage young people with fresh new ideas and better consciousness; to encourage people of color to create as well. But who is going to do that now?

30 Pornography's Temptation

Drucilla Cornell

The pornography debate portrays its contestants within sex and gender stereotypes, its contending figures drawn in the broad outlines of a Harlequin romance. Rapacious men with libidos of mythological proportions heartlessly brutalize innocent women as the hopeless victims of their lust, while the anti-pornography feminist poses herself as the sacrificial victim, the barrier to a tide of male sexuality that threatens violence. Bold freedom fighters ride out, drawing their lances against the oppressive feminists, the purported enemy of these brave warriors.

Meanwhile, there thrives an eight to thirteen billion dollar a year industry, churning out hundreds of low-budget videos every month.[1] If pornography was once a powerful political tool, produced in secret places by revolutionary groups, it is now also big business.[2]

How can a feminist approach to pornography that challenges rather than replicates gender stereotypes be developed? How can we both recognize the nitty-gritty reality of the industry and the suffering it can impose upon its workers at the same time that we affirm the need for women to freely explore their own sexuality? The first step in answering these questions is to insist on an important distinction. Feminists need to separate political action from legal action in the sphere of pornography. I advocate an alliance with two forms of representational politics currently being undertaken by women pornographers and porn workers that are challenging the terms of production in the mainstream heterosexual porn industry. Political action, not legal action, should be the main mode of intervention in the *production* of pornography. In accordance with this distinction

Drucilla Cornell, 'Pornography's Temptation', edited extract from *The Imaginary Domain*, Drucilla Cornell (Routledge (NY), 1995), reprinted by permission of the author and Taylor and Francis/Routledge Inc.

between the political and the legal, a second distinction must be made, one which can help us clarify what kind of legal action should be taken—and at what point it should be taken—in the arena of pornography.

We need to separate legal action to be taken in the *production* of pornography from action addressed specifically to the *distribution* of pornography. I insist on these distinctions primarily to serve the feminist purpose of treating women, including porn workers, as selves individuated enough to have undertaken the project of becoming persons. To treat women in the industry as reducible to hapless victims unworthy of solidarity refuses them that basic respect.

The alternative to such solidarity has been an attempt to correct for the abuse in the production of pornography through indirect, primarily legal means that focus on curtailing the distribution of pornography. This approach treats the women in the industry as if they were incapable of asserting their own personhood and, in this way, assumes that others need to act on their behalf. The wealthy woman as moral rescuer has a long history in both the United States and England. The prostitute, in particular, has always been a favourite candidate for rescue. By remaining 'other', the epitome of victimization, she stands in for the degradation of all women. Her life is then reduced to that figuration of her. Now, porn workers have become the ultimate figuration of the victim who needs to be rescued. But this is certainly not how most porn workers see themselves.[3]

Indeed, women in the industry are 'acting up'.[4] Ona Zee, porn star, producer and director, fought in 1990 and 1991 to unionize the mainstream heterosexual pornography industry. Her vigilance led her to be named the 'Norma Rae' of the porn industry and, for some time, she was blackballed for her efforts. Yet, in spite of Ona Zee's difficulties in unionizing the industry, she remains convinced that unionization and self-representation must remain at the heart of the political programme to change working conditions in the production of pornography. Unionization and self-determination both represent and respect the workers' own sense of their worth as persons.

Ona Zee's efforts are also not the only form of political action that has taken place in and around the pornography industry. Two of the women initially involved in the National Organization of Women Against Violence Against Women broke away from that organization over the issue of how to grapple with the reality of the industry and still affirm the exploration of new forms of sexually explicit material.[5]

Those feminists who have primarily directed their work towards experimenting with new expressions of the feminine 'sex' are engaging in a different kind of 'representational politics' than the union efforts of Ona Zee. This is a phrase that accurately describes the effort in these materials to unleash the feminine imaginary into new representational forms that challenge the stereotypes of femininity governing the presentation of the female 'sex' in the mainstream heterosexual porn industry.

The sets used in the production of these explicitly 'femme' videos already incorporate some of the most basic demands of the movement for self-organization. Candida Royalle, for example, insists that condoms be mandatory for all sex acts performed on her sets.[6] Here we have an example of how the formation of two kinds of representational politics has had a major impact on the industry's production of pornography. If academics have difficulty defining pornography, mainstream industry producers have had no such problem. If there is a 'cumshot', then it's pornography.[7] Thus, the simple demand for a condom will be seen as a threat to free expression in the production of pornography.

My affirmation of the representational politics of 'femme' pornographers such as Candida Royalle also expresses the emphasis in my own feminism on unleashing the feminine imaginary, rather than on constraining men.[8] I place myself on the side of those feminists who have stressed the importance of expanding the horizons of feminine sexuality.[9]

The split between feminists who have insisted on sexual exploration and the redefinition of sex itself, and those feminists who have sought to protect women from the imagined brutality of male sexuality, has recurred frequently in Anglo-American history. The social movements to close brothels and shut bars,[10] which stand in sharp contrast to Victoria Woodhull's zealous writings on the transformation of our heterosexual congress on behalf of a feminist revolution for women, exemplify this split.[11] Emma Goldman made it clear that she wanted no part of a revolution which foreclosed the explorations of her sexuality and forbade her 'to dance' differently.[12] Our generation, then, is certainly not unique in this split. Although the previous movements always had at their base some kind of appeal to state and organizational authority, the present situation is unusual in its explicit focus on the role of the law. Perhaps we should not be surprised that this focus occurs within my generation, because it is only within this generation that so many women have entered law schools and have graduated to become lawyers, judges, and law professors.[13] By now it should be clear that I do not believe law is our only mode of intervention into the field of significance laid out by pornography, particularly in the *production of pornography*.

My emphasis on the imaginary domain as crucial to the thriving of feminism demands a different analytical approach, not only to law, but to the problems of sexuality and representation inherent in pornography. The imaginary domain is the moral and psychic space we as sexuate beings need in order to freely play with the sexual persona through which we shape our sexual identity, whether as man or woman, straight, gay, lesbian or transgender. The call for a new feminist approach to pornography, and for an analysis of what law can and cannot achieve in its intervention into the pornographic world is inspired by the recognition of this need. Feminism must struggle to clear the space for, rather than create new barriers to, women's exploration of their sexuality.

I am suspicious of overreliance on law in the regulation of pornography for two specifically feminist reasons. The first is that we must not entrench stereotypes of femininity as the basis of discrimination law. We do not, in other words, want law to endorse the culturally encoded femininity that, in the work of Catharine MacKinnon, reduces woman to the 'fuckee', or the victim and demands her protection as such. Thus, I reject most aspects of MacKinnon and Andrea Dworkin's civil rights ordinance as an appropriate legal means to regulate pornography.[14]

Second, law is, at least in part, a force for accommodation to current social norms, even if it also provides us with a critical edge in its normative concepts such as equality. But feminism expresses an aspiration to struggle beyond accommodation, beyond those symbolic forms that have been deeply inscribed in and by the structures of gender. Feminism, particularly in the complex area of sexuality, demands that we live with the paradox that we are trying to break the bonds of the meanings that have made us who we are as women.

Nevertheless, there should be some legal regulation of pornography. It sentimentalizes pornography to forget that it is anywhere from an eight to thirteen billion dollar industry and that in the mainstream of heterosexual pornography some women are both used and violated for profit on a daily basis. The cynicism of a First Amendment organization sponsored and promoted by the pornography industry is only too evident. In their more honest moments, they readily admit that what is at stake for them in the pornography debate is their profitability and not the value of freedom.[15] Whatever the pornographers' intention, however, the First Amendment and the value of free expression is unavoidably implicated in the debate. The idea of the imaginary domain can help us think more fruitfully about the relationship between freedom of expression, sexual freedom more generally, and equality for women.

We need to recast the debate over whether or not pornography is speech by analysing exactly what the scene is that pornography signifies. Mainstream heterosexual pornography does not communicate an idea as much as it graphically portrays an unconscious scene of rigid gender identities played out in explicit sex acts. But it is not politically or legally desirable to argue that pornography is not speech. We need to explore the temptation of pornography; exactly how and what it communicates. My disagreement with the argument that pornography has direct behavioural implications is inseparable from my overall wariness of too great a reliance on the law to intervene in this field. It also informs my analysis of why pornography is speech. I will argue against Catharine MacKinnon's notion that pornography can simply be reduced to a trigger for sexuality, understood in a mechanistic fashion. MacKinnon's hope that law can and should function as a form of reconditioning and re-education implies a kind of behaviouristic analysis of the structures of desire. If pornography is not removed from the arena of speech altogether, does that mean that it is only representation, only fantasy; that it has no 'real content?' The answer lies in viewing the real content of pornography via its power to lure us into a scene which clearly pervades some of our deepest unconscious fantasies about gender.

For MacKinnon, the reality that sex is performed in pornography leads her to the conclusion that pornography is two-dimensional sex ad therefore more act than speech. It is not a representation of sex in the traditional sense that it is about sex, or that it represents an erotic scene which indicates sex. Due to the fact that sex is not simulated in a pornography scene, MacKinnon concludes that the sex portrayed there should be viewed as sex that has happened as an act on the woman's body and that the portrayal itself is also, in some way, sex itself. The temporal aspect of MacKinnon's ordinance is important for two reasons. First, that MacKinnon is not advocating prior restraint turns on the past happening of the abuse. A woman *was* raped on a porn set and therefore she *has* been harmed and has the right to seek redress for the harm that *has* happened. Second, for MacKinnon the sex itself has happened in real time. It took place on the set and occurs again and again in real time whenever the male viewer sexually responds to it. If there is violence in the sex as presented, the man continues to live out that violence in his sexual response in his own arousal at the violence. The 'past sex' becomes present sex in this specific sense. The past and present become one as the man responds, gets an erection, and then proceeds to masturbate. As MacKinnon writes:

> What is real here is not that the materials are pictures, but that they are part of a sex act. The women are in two dimensions, but the men have sex with them in their own three-dimensional bodies, not in their minds alone. Men come doing this. This, too, is a behavior, not a thought or an argument. It is not ideas they are ejaculating over. Try arguing with an orgasm sometime. You will find you are no match for the sexual access and power the materials provide.[16]

MacKinnon then proceeds to make an argument of 'addiction', premissed on her understanding of the viewing of pornography as two-dimensional sex. The man who has two-dimensional sex will want more. He will want to enact the scene on a real woman. A fantasy object will no longer be enough for him. MacKinnon is arguing here that the presentation of the coercion in pornography and men's response to it has a direct effect on men in terms of their actions; first, as they masturbate and second, as they move to violate actual women.

Before returning to my own psychoanalytic account of why pornography tempts, and what lies at the basis of its power to tempt, consumers into its scene, I want to note here that MacKinnon's view of men and masculine sexuality precisely mirrors the pornographic world which she critiques. Pornography usually involves an abstraction or a reduction of a human being into its elemental body parts. There is no self there, only the body reduced to the genitals in a pictorial language of lust. MacKinnon's argument represents an exact, if gender-inverted, reinscription of Freudian insight that anatomy is destiny.[17] A man becomes his penis. He cannot help it. The penis asserts itself against him. He is reduced to a prick.

In pornography, the prick is always presented as erect, as eternally lustful, as having the positive 'attributes' of the one who at any moment can fuck and come. But this depends on an anatomical reductionism in which a man's sexual difference has had extracted from it all evidence that he is a self, and leaves behind only a single aspect of his life—a being whose sexuality completely takes him over. This fantasy of the dick controlling the man is inseparable from the sexuality of the pornographic world. MacKinnon's own view of masculinity, which enables her to insist that pornography is in no way speech, mirrors the very pornographic world she abhors:

> In the centuries before pornography was made into an 'idea' worthy of First Amendment protection, men amused themselves and excused their sexual practices by observing that the penis is not an organ of thought. Aristotle said, 'it is impossible to think about anything while absorbed in the pleasures of sex.' The Yiddish equivalent translates roughly as 'a stiff prick turns the mind to shit.' The common point is that having sex is antithetical to thinking. It would not have occurred to them that having sex *is* thinking.[18]

I think that men can think and have an erection at the same time. And perhaps more importantly, that they can think themselves out of an erection. This is only the beginning of an analysis of the ways in which the complexity of desire involves the most profound recesses of the mind: unconscious fantasies, semi-conscious constructs, longings and hopes that are inadequately described if they are not rendered as having cognitive competence.

The power of pornography to tempt its consumer is extracted through sexual arousal. In order to give an account of how it tempts the consumer, I will discuss Jacques Lacan's insight that at the very basis of Western culture lies the repressed, abjected figure of the ultimate object of desire, the phallic Mother. We need an analysis of how and why pornography has become so pervasive. MacKinnon's contribution has been to force us to confront the pervasiveness of pornography and the way in which it has become completely enmeshed in our social reality. Some of MacKinnon's critics have implicitly dismissed the extent to which pornography plays a role in our social, cultural, and emotional lives. For example, Ronald Dworkin argues that 'most men find pornography offensive'.[19] In her response to Dworkin, MacKinnon argues that he is denying the extent to which pornography pervades our lives and the extent to which there are harms to women inevitably caused by pornography. An effective answer to MacKinnon must provide us with an account of why pornography is pervasive and how that pervasiveness operates. We need to have an analysis of both of these aspects of pornography if we are to adequately account for an industry in which the market base is continually expanding. Thus, I set forth a psychoanalytic account so that we can adequately come to terms with pornography as a cultural phenomenon. Let me stress again that the analysis that follows is of the portrayal of sex by the mainstream heterosexual pornography industry. It does not address the sexually explicit materials produced by those tangentially related to the industry or outside of it altogether. The psychoanalytic account not only helps us understand the pervasiveness of pornography but serves as the basis for determining the type of display regulation measures we should take; it relies on the work of Jacques Lacan because it is he who provides us with a field of significance for gender and sexuality.

According to Lacan, the genesis of linguistic consciousness, and obviously with it what has come to be called the rational-cognitive aspect of human beings, occurs when the infant is forced to register that the mother is separate from himself.[20] She is not 'just there' as the guarantor of his identity. The registration of the mother's desire beyond the infant's needs is inseparable from the recognition of his separateness from her. And such registration is inevitable because mothers are also women. There can be no desiring mommy in the imaginary infant/mother dyad. Therefore, it is fated to be broken up by the third, the one the mother desires. But does the third necessarily have to be the father? Or, if not the actual father, whatever the father symbolizes? According to Lacan's rendering of the Freudian Oedipal complex, the answer is in the affirmative. But to understand why the third will inevitably be unconsciously identified as the imaginary father, we need to explore the effects of this primary narcissistic wound. It is this wound that can explain the tempting of the consumer/reader into the pornographic scene.

The primordial moment of separation from the mother is literally life threatening because of the absolute dependence of the infant on this Other. The terror of the threat that the mother presents in her separateness initiates a struggle to overcome the dependence and the need the infant has for her. The move from need to demand, to 'give me', is in part the infant's expression of the vulnerability of his need. The resistance is against the mother because it is her desire that is registered as robbing the infant of his security. Of course, this kind of absolute security is a fantasy. The condition of this fantasy is that the mother not 'be sexed'. Thus, the fantasy is inevitably associated with the pre-Oedipal stage, the time before the registration of the full cultural significance of sexual difference, or its imagined graphic simplicity that men have dicks and women have holes.

The fantasy of absolute security rests on the corresponding fantasy that mother is whole in herself, a being unscathed by the rending of desire. This fantasy figure on whom the infant is totally dependent in its need is the Phallic Mother. This fantasy figure is envisioned as 'having it all', thus Lacan names this figure the Phallic Mother; the one with the phallus as well as the one with the female genitalia. Once the fantasized mother/child dyad is shattered, the Phallic Mother remains in the imaginary as all powerful and threatening in her power to both bestow and take away life. One result of the Oedipal phase marked by the infant's awakening to the mother's desire is sheer terror of the fantasized otherness of this imaginary all-powerful mother. The terror of, and yet longing for return to, this figure accounts for the repression of this figure into the unconscious. This terror can also potentially explain the drive to enter into the symbolic realm so as to seek the fulfillment of desire that can no longer be guaranteed by the fantasy of the Phallic Mother who is only 'there for the infant'. Registered as separate from the infant, and therefore as incomplete, the mother as a woman comes to be abjected for her lack, which is inseparable in the unconscious from her failure to be the fantasy figure who can guarantee the fulfillment of the infant's desire.

This primordial moment of separation is not only experienced through sheer terror and fear of loss; it is also the gaining of an identity separate from the mother. The attempt to negotiate the ambivalence of a loss that is also the gaining of identity is demonstrated in the fort-da game of Freud's grandson, Ernst. The game enacts the fantasy that the child is separate, but nonetheless in control of the Mother/Other. But this negotiation, in turn, demands an unconscious identification with the one who is at least imagined as capable of bringing the other back, because he is the site of her desire. The narcissistically wounded infant thus turns toward the imaginary father, because the imaginary father is who mommy desires. But what is it that singles out the imaginary father? What makes him so special? What is it, in other words, that Daddy has that Mommy desires? The simple answer is the penis. For Lacan, however, it is not so simple.

It is the Name of the father and the symbolic register of his potency that is the basis of the identification with him, not the simple fact that he has a penis. The biological penis takes on the significance it does only through its identification with the Big Other that secures identity through the power to control the Mother/Other. But in pornography, it is precisely that biological penis, the simplistic conflation of the penis with the phallus, that is portrayed in the ever-erect prick that mimics 'the great fucker in the sky' who can always take the woman at any moment. The ever-erect prick we see in pornography is the imagined prick of the father who can control the terrifying figure of the Phallic Mother.

It is this fantasy that protects the man from ever having to face the other possibility of unconscious dis-identification between the phallus and the penis. In his anxiety that he too is lack, i.e. that the penis is never the phallus and cannot be because the phallus does not exist except as fantasy, he turns to pornography that portrays and positions him as the one imagined to be the all-powerful Father, the one with the erect prick. It is this prick that keeps him safe from the Phallic Mother. It is this fantasized prick that he uses to dis-identify with her. It is this prick that he uses to ultimately control her, bring her back, and dismember her. That other body is acted out as the phantasmatic Other, the bleeding hole, the lack in having, that lurks in man's consciousness as an unconscious fear of what he truly is.

The beating and stabbings of erotic violence implemented by the prick and its other symbols, as the ultimate weapons against this terrifying Other, protect the man from being overtaken by the unconscious realization that this Other, the bleeding scar left by castration, is a projected image of what he fears he might be. In an ultimate act of dis-identification and abjection, he rips her apart. But precisely because she is a phantasmatic figure, and therefore always there in her absence, she returns to haunt him again. The pornographic scene has to be repeated because the Phallic Mother, pushed under, dismembered ripped apart, will always return on the level of the unconscious. Here we see the connection between the pornographic scene and the abjection of the Phallic Mother, and the unconscious terror that the man himself is the lack-in-having that the woman represents. The pornographic scene is driven by the death drive in the explicit Freudian sense that it is frozen into a repetitive dance of dismemberment that can never achieve its end.[21] And what is that end? That end is to have ascended once and for all into the position of the imaginary father who can absolutely control the Woman/Other. Real women are never successfully reduced in life to objects. A woman can, of course, be killed. But even in her absence, to the degree that she is identified with the Phallic Mother, she will continue to haunt the man.

In *Psycho*, Hitchcock portrayed a serial killer who endlessly had to kill the Phallic Mother. But she forever rises again in the very absence left after each killing. The wake he left behind of mutilated bodies is a terrifying testament to how dangerous and threatening is this unconscious scene.[22] For Lacan, the dismembered pieces of the body of the mother take the form of the 'object a'. We have breast men, leg men. We have women who are only their cunts. In the place of a rich and diversified account of the actual power of women as sexed beings, whose sexuality is defined and lived by them, we have a phantasmatic figure who threatens and lurks and who must be controlled. The excitement and the sexual arousal in pornography is inseparable from the fantasy of transcendence in which one has finally separated himself absolutely from that bodily other upon which one was once utterly dependent. Marquis de Sade understood this when he insisted that killing was the ultimate act of transcendence and control.[23] Ironically, for Sade, all that one did when one 'fucked' was think oneself beyond the body. As one 'fucked', one knew oneself to be the master of the Other. As a believer in the sexual ideology that was part of the rationalist materialism of his day, Sade's ultimate conception of self-knowledge was 'I am, because I fuck and I know that I do it to you.'[24]

But of course Sade's belief that the knowledge given to him was the knowledge that he had mastered the feared Woman is itself a fantasy, one that lies at the very basis of the pornographic scene. Without the fear, I am arguing, there wouldn't be the arousal. Unless one had the fantasy that one has controlled the desired object, and yet also, at least unconsciously, had registered the knowledge that this is impossible, one would not experience the desire for repetition and the desire to return again and again to that woman, bound and chained. The separation of the Phallic Mother from the actual mother explains her profound association with figures of the 'bad girl'. To explain: the Phallic Mother is the ultimate object of desire. She is remembered as a lost paradise. But she is also unconsciously identified as a threatening power, one who can potentially rob the man of his independence. The 'bad girl', the seductress, is the woman who tempts the man to pursue his desire only at risk to himself. The unconscious association of desirability with threatening power is what accounts for desirable women becoming identified as 'bad girls'. These 'bad girls' stand in for the Phallic Mother.

Given the way that race is played out on the level of fantasy, it is not at all surprising to find African-American women figured in pornography as these ultimate 'bad girls', and therefore as ultimately desirable. The raging African-American woman in chains represents exactly that terrifying Other who is controlled, but only barely so. The terror and the fantasy of control come together in the orgasm. Without the terror, without the unconscious fear of the woman fully remembered as herself, without the memory of the actual mother being erased into the unconscious identification with this figure, there would be no explanation of this temptation. Indeed, the whole scene of pornography as forbidden, as an entrance into another 'adult' world, mimics the male child's ascendance into the adult masculine symbolic in which he too becomes a man, proud of his prick, with its power to control women and bring the Other back.

What, then, is the bottom line of my argument? First, pornography tempts because it enacts a powerful fantasy scene. In any sophisticated account of fantasy, we have to note that fantasy never simply consists of the object of desire, but also of the setting in which the subject participates. In fantasy no subject can be assigned a fixed position. The fantasy structure of pornography allows the subject to participate in each one of the established positions. This explains why it is possible for powerful men to fantasize about taking up the position of a dominated Other, and for women to imagine themselves in the position of phallic agency, as the one who 'fucks' back. It explains the possibilities of reversal. But as I have also argued, the dominating pornographic scene is frozen. There are two positions: the prick, the imagined phallus in the position of agency and assertion; and the woman, the controlled dismembered body, reduced to the bleeding hole. The rigidity of the scene and its connection with the death drive explains why the reversal of positions cannot lead to the disruption of the setting itself, or achieve anything like a 'true' heterosexuality in which men and women could meet in a sexual encounter.[25] The result is that male role reversal or cross-identification is not adequate to shift the meaning inherent in the presentation of the scene. For example, the figure of the woman dominatrix as the desired other of phallic agency does not in any way undermine the identification of the phallus as the figuration of sexual agency itself.

Is there a representation of the fantasy of the dominatrix that is more than an unconscious reaffirmation of the identification of the phallus with sexual agency? I believe that it can be found in the explicit presentation of the production of the fantasy of the dominatrix itself. The best example of any such presentation that I have seen is Ona Zee's *Learning the Ropes*,[26] a film which presents us with ritualized sado-masochism. In my analysis, pornographic fantasy has no straightforward connection with what would be presumed to be 'real life', even if the scene cannot be separated from profound unconscious fantasies of how sex and gender are produced. In ritualized sado-masochism, the stylized enactment is part of the performance which remains under the fantasizer's control. In MacKinnon's understanding of pornography, the pervasiveness of sado-masochism goes beyond its ritualized enactment as a specific form of sex. It becomes the truth of heterosexual sex. On the other hand, in this movie the real couple is explicitly separated from the fantasy enactment of one form of sex.

In *Learning the Ropes*, the dominatrix is not presented as 'real'. She is presented as a character who is produced in Ona Zee's performance. Thus, the fantasy of ritualized sado-masochism is separated from the 'real' Ona. In the name of education, Ona and her husband Frank both move into their roles, into sado-masochistic rituals, and out of their roles again. One finds in the film an insistent separation of the pornographic fantasy and the 'real' life of Ona and Frank. The separation of performance and real life is made in the presentation of a 'how to' sado-masochistic performance. It is not simply the reversal of Ona Zee's position of the phallic agency as the dominatrix that makes *Learning the Ropes* subversive of the realism associated with mainstream heterosexual hard-core porn. Rather, it is the presentation of the dominatrix as a performance that undermines the realism of the scene. Thus, the irony in *Learning the Ropes* is that it is in the presentation of a ritualistic sado-masochistic performance that we see what is being produced and the fantasy behind it. Paradoxically, in the presentation of the frozen scene, the scene itself becomes unfrozen as it is presented as ritual. This presentation unfreezes the scene in its encoding as reality.

Let's now turn to another example, a sexually explicit video, but not one produced in the pornography industry, Candida Royalle's *True Stories in the Life of Annie Sprinkle*.[27] In this 'porn film',[28] the Annie Sprinkle character begins to have sex with a man. A mainstream heterosexual porn movie is playing in the background during their sexual encounter. The man becomes increasingly distracted by the image of sexuality playing on the television set. He mimics the sex performed there. The mirroring of sexuality that is often performed outside the setting of pornography as the enactment of the truly masculine persona is mirrored again. Annie, in turn, grows distracted by her lover's distraction. We, the viewers, see a woman watching a man watching a porn movie. We watch as Annie becomes increasingly dissatisfied that her lover is not having sex with 'her', and she eventually opts to throw him out. Annie's ensuing monologue evokes her despair of ever finding a 'true' heterosexual encounter. The monologue is interrupted when her own fantasy object, a genie, appears. The genie is far from the usual porn character. With hair down to his shoulders and the phantasmatic costume of the genie, he mimics a kind of androgynous appearance foreign to the pornographic scene. From there the film proceeds through the imagined lover's continuing and deepening recognition of who Annie Sprinkle is.

Annie and the genie begin to have sex only after a period of dramatic, emphasized eye contact. The genie describes the difference between 'looking' at someone and truly 'seeing' them. For the genie, to truly see into the soul of the Other is the ultimate erotic act. Although the film moves into graphic, explicit sex acts, it does so with a cinematic blurring effect that makes it impossible to tell the difference between oral sex, kissing, and other forms of licking and touching. Finally, there is the ultimate act that purportedly marks the film as pornographic: Annie and the genie have sexual intercourse. The cinematic portrayal of their sexual encounter makes it difficult for the viewer to enter the scene as if he were present as a voyeur. In other words, the cinema appears in its own cinematic role.

Does turning pornography back into a self-conscious presentation of cinematic positioning make the presence of fantasy itself the 'truth' of sex? In this film, it does so on many levels. The first is the so-called challenge that takes place by making the cinematic presence obvious. The second is that the male lover is himself a fantasy object. The third level is the critical distance that the woman maintains from the counter-phantasmatic production of the porn movie her lover is watching. At the conclusion of the sexual act with the genie, and following the lesson of the experience that a 'true' heterosexual encounter is possible, Annie's original lover returns; this time without all the paraphernalia of a so-called hard-core pornography scene. The scene is now set in terms of Annie's fantasy.

Ona Zee and Candida Royalle are, in this way, engaging in 'representational politics'. These politics do not just challenge mainstream pornography as the one possible form of sexually explicit material. They also, as is particularly the case with Candida Royalle, provide representational forms which enrich the imaginary and symbolic resources in which women's sexuality can be expressed. It is a mistake, then, to reject out of hand the argument that 'more speech' is one feminist weapon to take up against the pornography industry. Candida Royalle's films should be understood as a form of feminist practice. Without new images and new words in which to express our sexuality, we will be unable to create a new world for women.

There is yet another reason to affirm the representational politics of women pornographers as a more potent threat to the pornography industry than, for instance, lawsuits. The psychoanalytic account of pornography argues that pornography speaks not to the penis but to the unconscious, and is an expression of the fantasy underpinnings of so-called heterosexuality. Thus, it is not easily reached by the law. Underlying the unconscious structure of pornography is the ultimate forbidden object of desire, the Phallic Mother. The lure of the forbidden object makes the temptation to pornography indissociable from its being a prohibited or shameful activity. The murkiness of the pornographic world is part of its deep attraction. Push it underground and it becomes even more desirable. Thus, the challenge from within by women pornographers may ultimately be more unsettling to the mainstream pornography industry than any outside legal challenge to it: just one more reason why we should focus pornography regulation not on constraining men and their fantasies, but on protecting the breathing space of the feminine imaginary.

Because pornography appeals to powerful unconscious fantasies, it cannot simply be disregarded as speech. If we accepted the behaviorist assumptions that MacKinnon makes about pornography and men's pricks, we not only would be more optimistic than I am about the success of direct legal regulation, we could also accept that pornography was a type of two-dimensional sex. On my analysis, on the other hand, pornography communicates an unconscious fantasy scene. This scene clearly speaks to us. We have to rethink, then, how the analysis of pornography can lead us to justify modes of regulation that give women breathing space and yet, at the same time, accept that it is speech.[29] Without such an analysis, we reinscribe the very kind of mind/body dualism that feminism has critiqued over the years. We need to have a much richer account of the way in which the human mind and body operate together in the complex activity we know as sex. What I have offered is an explanation of why the pornographic fantasy scene has come to be frozen through profoundly and deeply engendered structures.

I recognize the silencing of those of us who have been designated as women as we struggle to find the words to say how we might 'be' differently. But the struggle is possible, the struggle is happening, the struggle has already begun as soon as any woman claims for herself the name 'feminist'. The lack of phenomenality of the female body, profoundly attested to in psychoanalytic literature, leads to the sense that the feminine has been turned over to the gaze of the other. But this is not inevitable, given that the feminine imaginary cannot be foreclosed. When Annie Sprinkle steps out on stage, takes off her blouse, puts her breasts in ink, imprints them, holds them up and says, 'these are not tits, they are other', and then creates an array of names for what that other is, she is critically engaging with the symbolic order's claim to capture her, and the possibility that her breasts are more than just 'tits'. Meaning changes in the flow of words in Annie Sprinkle's monologue, as she holds up the imprint, the seeming object. The distance between the reprint of her breasts, the representation, and correspondingly between the fantasy of them and their reality is brought home to the audience who would otherwise simply see that what is presented are 'tits'.

When Sula, in Toni Morrison's novel of the same name, evokes the time and place when there will be a 'little left for a woman with glory in her heart', she too is evoking the feminine imaginary:

> 'Oh, they'll love me all right. It will take time, but they'll love me.' The sound of her voice was as soft and distant as the look in her eyes. 'After all the old women have lain with the teen-agers; when all the young girls have slept with their old drunken uncles; after all the black men fuck all the white ones; when all the white women kiss all the black ones; when the guards have raped all the jailbirds and after all the whores make love to their grannies; after all the faggots get their mothers' trim; when Lindbergh sleeps with Bessie Smith and Norma Shearer makes it with Stepin Fetchit; after all the dogs have fucked all the cats and every weathervane on every barn flies off the roof to mount the hogs . . . then there'll be a little love left over for me. And I know just what it will feel like.'[30]

There is space for the woman with glory in her heart as long as we insist that we are already dwelling in it. We must write that dwelling into being, as a space for us to 'be' differently, to be beyond accommodation.

Notes

1. See Nick Cohen, 'Reaping Rich Rewards from the Profits of Pornography', *The Independent*, 19 Dec. 1989.
2. One central disagreement that I have with Nadine Strossen is her failure to take into account the fact that there is a pornography industry with documented working conditions. See Nadine Strossen, *Defending Pornography: Free Speech, Sex, and the Fight for Women's Rights* (New York: Scribners, 1995). The vast majority of workers in the mainstream industry are paid off the books, without the secure benefits of contract employment such as health insurance, pensions, etc. Also, most workers in the industry are young and have fairly short careers. Obviously, economic protection of their futures is crucial. There are, of course, other industries in which the working career is relatively short, and, as a result, workers are aware of their need for some sort of economic protection in regard to their futures. Consider, for example, the difference between porn workers and athletes who also rely on physical characteristics associated with youth in their working life. The degree to

which baseball players, for instance, take seriously their need to protect their economic future is evident in the lengthy strike that, as of March 1995, continues.

As a result of Strossen's failure to confront the reality of the industry, she ignores the porn worker's reform struggles for what they are: a challenge to the conditions of their work. She also conflates all pornography with the mainstream heterosexual industry while many pornographers, such as Candida Royalle, work either outside industry norms or peripherally to them. For example, Candida Royalle's insistence on all-condom sets already allies her with the efforts of porn workers aiming to reform working conditions. If we are to take porn workers seriously as workers, then we should also take their reform efforts seriously. There are also problems with Strossen's absolutist interpretation of the First Amendment.

But my primary disagreement with Strossen has to do with her failure to confront the actual working conditions that dominate the mainstream porn industry. As a former union organizer, the title 'Defending Pornography' would be, for me, the equivalent of a demand to defend big business. I do want to stress, however, that Strossen and I share a commitment to a feminist politics that celebrates women's sexuality and demands the protection of sexually explicit materials. Indeed, I would argue that my defence of the imaginary domain is perfectly consistent with the feminist political argument—if not the legal argument—made in Strossen's book.

3. Taped interview with Ona Zee, on file with the author.
4. I borrow this phrase from the name of the gay rights, AIDS awareness group, ACT UP.
5. See Lisa Katzman, 'The Women of Porn: They're not in it for the Moneyshot', *The Village Voice*, 24 Aug. 1993, 31 and Gary Indiana, 'A Day in the Life of Hollywood's Sex Factory', *The Village Voice*, 24 Aug. 1993, 27–37.
6. Ibid.
7. Ibid.
8. Please see Drucilla Cornell, 'Feminine Writing, Metaphor and Myth', in *Beyond Accommodation* (New York: Routledge, 1991).
9. See, for instance, Judith Butler, *Bodies That Matter: On the Discursive Limits of 'Sex'* (New York: Routledge, 1993) and Wendy Brown, *States of Injury: Essays on Power and Freedom in Late Modernity* (Princeton: Princeton University Press, 1995).
10. See Bonnie Bullogh, *Women and Prostitution: A Social History* (Buffalo, NY: Prometheus Books, 1987) and Jack Blocker, Jr, *Retreat from Reform: The Prohibition Movement in the United States, 1890–1913* (Westport, Conn.: Greenwood Press, 1976).
11. See Marion Meade, *The Life and Times of Victoria Woodhull* (New York: Knopf, 1976).
12. See Emma Goldman, *Anarchism & Other Essays*, intro. by Richard Drinnon (New York: Dover Publications, 1969).
13. See Dorothy and Carl Schneider, *U.S. Women in the Workplace* (Santa Barbara, Calif.: Clio Companion Series, 1993).
14. See Andrea Dworkin and Catharine MacKinnon, *Pornography and Civil Rights: A New Day for Women's Equality* (Minneapolis: Organizing Against Pornography, 1988).

15. Katzman, 'The Women of Porn'.
16. MacKinnon, *Only Words* (Cambridge Mass.: Harvard University Press, 1993), 17.
17. See the lecture on 'Femininity' in Sigmund Freud, *New Introductory Lectures on Psychoanalysis* (Norton: New York, 1965).
18. MacKinnon, *Only Words*, 17. I reject this kind of dichotomization between thought and sexuality as reinstating a divide between mind and body that I believe has been profoundly undermined in the last 50 if not 100, years of philosophical discourse. See, generally, Drucilla Cornell, *Beyond Accommodation.*
19. See Ronald Dworkin's response to MacKinnon's reply to his review of *Only Words* in *The New York Review of Books*, 3 Mar. 1994, vol. 151, no. 5.
20. My use of the male pronoun here is true to Lacan's (and Freud's) narrative which is of an explicitly masculine subject.
21. See Sigmund Freud, *Beyond the Pleasure Principle* (Norton: New York, 1975).
22. See Slavoj Žižek, *The Sublime Object of Ideology* (London: Verso, 1989).
23. For an excellent portrayal of the graphic representation of the heterosexual relationship inevitably failing, see Marquis de Sade, *Juliette* (New York: Grove Press, 1968).
24. For a discussion of the relationship between 18th-century materialism and pornography, see Margaret C. Jacob, 'The Materialist World of Pornography', in *The Invention of Pornography*, ed. Lynn Hunt (New York: Zone Books, 1993), 157–202.
25. Catharine MacKinnon, *Feminism Unmodified: Discourses on Life and Law* (Cambridge, Mass.: Harvard University Press, 1987), 149.
26. See *Learning the Ropes* (Ona Zee Productions, 1993).
27. See Candida Royalle's *True Stories in the Life of Annie Sprinkle* (Femme Productions, 1992).
28. I place 'porn' in quotation marks precisely because Candida Royalle's films would not be pornographic under the definition I have offered.
29. See Stanley Fish, *There is no such Thing as Free Speech and it's a Good Thing Too* (New York: Oxford University Press, 1993). Ultimately I agree with Fish that First Amendment analysis does not proceed wisely by trying to establish a continuum of what forms of expression are to count as speech.
30. Toni Morrison, *Sula* (New York: Knopf, 1973), 145–6.

31 Uses of the Erotic

The Erotic as Power

Audre Lorde

There are many kinds of power, used and unused, acknowledged or otherwise. The erotic is a resource within each of us that lies in a deeply female and spiritual plane, firmly rooted in the power of our unexpressed or unrecognized feeling. In order to perpetuate itself, every oppression must corrupt or distort those various sources of power within the culture of the oppressed that can provide energy for change. For women, this has meant a suppression of the erotic as a considered source of power and information within our lives.

We have been taught to suspect this resource, vilified, abused, and devalued within western society. On the one hand, the superficially erotic has been encouraged as a sign of female inferiority; on the other hand, women have been made to suffer and to feel both contemptible and suspect by virtue of its existence.

It is a short step from there to the false belief that only by the suppression of the erotic within our lives and consciousness can women be truly strong. But that strength is illusory, for it is fashioned within the context of male models of power.

As women, we have come to distrust that power which rises from our deepest and nonrational knowledge. We have been warned against it all our lives by the male world, which values this depth of feeling enough to keep women around in order to exercise it in the service of men, but which fears this same depth too much to examine the possibilities of it within themselves. So women are maintained at a distant/inferior position to be psychically milked, much the same way ants

Audre Lorde, 'Uses of the Erotic: The Erotic as Power', from *Sister Outsider: Essays and Speeches* (Crossing Press, 1984), 53–9, reprinted by permission of the publisher. Paper delivered at the Fourth Berkshire Conference on the History of Women, Mount Holyoke College, August 24, 1978. Published as a pamphlet by Out & Out Books.

maintain colonies of aphids to provide a life-giving substance for their masters.

But the erotic offers a well of replenishing and provocative force to the woman who does not fear its revelation, nor succumb to the belief that sensation is enough.

The erotic has often been misnamed by men and used against women. It has been made into the confused, the trivial, the psychotic, the plasticized sensation. For this reason, we have often turned away from the exploration and consideration of the erotic as a source of power and information, confusing it with its opposite, the pornographic. But pornography is a direct denial of the power of the erotic, for it represents the suppression of true feeling. Pornography emphasizes sensation without feeling.

The erotic is a measure between the beginnings of our sense of self and the chaos of our strongest feelings. It is an internal sense of satisfaction to which, once we have experienced it, we know we can aspire. For having experienced the fullness of this depth of feeling and recognizing its power, in honor and self-respect we can require no less of ourselves.

It is never easy to demand the most from ourselves, from our lives, from our work. To encourage excellence is to go beyond the encouraged mediocrity of our society is to encourage excellence. But giving in to the fear of feeling and working to capacity is a luxury only the unintentional can afford, and the unintentional are those who do not wish to guide their own destinies.

This internal requirement toward excellence which we learn from the erotic must not be misconstrued as demanding the impossible from ourselves nor from others. Such a demand incapacitates everyone in the process. For the erotic is not a question only of what we do; it is a question of how acutely and fully we can feel in the doing. Once we know the extent to which we are capable of feeling that sense of satisfaction and completion, we can then observe which of our various life endeavors bring us closest to that fullness.

The aim of each thing which we do is to make our lives and the lives of our children richer and more possible. Within the celebration of the erotic in all our endeavors, my work becomes a conscious decision—a longed-for bed which I enter gratefully and from which I rise up empowered.

Of course, women so empowered are dangerous. So we are taught to separate the erotic demand from most vital areas of our lives other than sex. And the lack of concern for the erotic root and satisfactions of our work is felt in our disaffection from so much of what we do. For instance, how often do we truly love our work even at its most difficult?

The principal horror of any system which defines the good in terms of profit rather than in terms of human need, or which defines human need to the exclusion of the psychic and emotional components of that need—the principal horror of such a system is that it robs our work of its erotic value, its erotic power and life appeal and fulfillment. Such a system reduces work to a travesty of necessities, a duty by which we earn bread or oblivion for ourselves and those we love. But this is tantamount to blinding a painter and then telling her to improve her work, and to enjoy the act of painting. It is not only next to impossible, it is also profoundly cruel.

As women, we need to examine the ways in which our world can be truly different. I am speaking here of the necessity for reassessing the quality of all the aspects of our lives and of our work, and of how we move toward and through them.

The very word *erotic* comes from the Greek word *eros*, the personifi cation of love in all its aspects—born of Chaos, and personifying creative power and harmony. When I speak of the erotic, then, I speak of it as an assertion of the lifeforce of women; of that creative energy empowered, the knowledge and use of which we are now reclaiming in our language, our history, our dancing, our loving, our work, our lives.

There are frequent attempts to equate pornography and eroticism, two diametrically opposed uses of the sexual. Because of these attempts, it has become fashionable to separate the spiritual (psychic and emotional) from the political, to see them as contradictory or antithetical. 'What do you mean, a poetic revolutionary, a meditating gunrunner?' In the same way, we have attempted to separate the spiritual and the erotic, thereby reducing the spiritual to a world of flattened affect, a world of the ascetic who aspires to feel nothing. But nothing is farther from the truth. For the ascetic position is one of the highest fear, the gravest immobility. The severe abstinence of the ascetic becomes the ruling obsession. And it is one not of self-discipline but of self-abnegation.

The dichotomy between the spiritual and the political is also false, resulting from an incomplete attention to our erotic knowledge. For the bridge which connects them is formed by the erotic—the sensual—those physical, emotional, and psychic expressions of what is deepest and strongest and richest within each of us, being shared: the passions of love, in its deepest meanings.

Beyond the superficial, the considered phrase, 'It feels right to me,' acknowledges the strength of the erotic into a true knowledge, for what that means is the first and most powerful guiding light toward any understanding. And understanding is a handmaiden which can only wait upon, or clarify, that knowledge, deeply born. The erotic is the nurturer or nursemaid of all our deepest knowledge.

The erotic functions for me in several ways, and the first is in providing the power which comes from sharing deeply any pursuit with another person. The sharing of joy, whether physical, emotional, psychic, or intellectual, forms a bridge between the sharers which can be the basis for understanding much of what is not shared between them, and lessens the threat of their difference.

Another important way in which the erotic connection functions is the open and fearless underlining of my capacity for joy. In the way my body stretches to music and opens into response, hearkening to its deepest rhythms, so every level upon which I sense also opens to the erotically satisfying experience, whether it is dancing, building a bookcase, writing a poem, examining an idea.

That self-connection shared is a measure of the joy which I know myself to be capable of feeling, a reminder of my capacity for feeling. And that deep and irreplaceable knowledge of my capacity for joy comes to demand from all of my life that it be lived within the knowledge that such satisfaction is possible, and does not have to be called *marriage*, nor *god*, nor *an afterlife*.

This is one reason why the erotic is so feared, and so often relegated to the bedroom alone, when it is recognized at all. For once we begin to feel deeply all the aspects of our lives, we begin to demand from ourselves and from our life-pursuits that they feel in accordance with that joy which we know ourselves to be capable of. Our erotic knowledge empowers us, becomes a lens through which we scrutinize all aspects of our existence, forcing us to evaluate those aspects honestly in terms of their relative meaning within our lives. And this is a grave responsibility, projected from within each of us, not to settle for the convenient, the shoddy, the conventionally expected, nor the merely safe.

During World War II, we bought sealed plastic packets of white, uncolored margarine, with a tiny, intense pellet of yellow coloring perched like a topaz just inside the clear skin of the bag. We would leave the margarine out for a while to soften, and then we would pinch the little pellet to break it inside the bag, releasing the rich yellowness into the soft pale mass of margarine. Then taking it carefully between our fingers, we would knead it gently back and forth, over and over, until the color had spread throughout the whole pound bag of margarine, thoroughly coloring it.

I find the erotic such a kernel within myself. When released from its intense and constrained pellet, it flows through and colors my life with a kind of energy that heightens and sensitizes and strengthens all my experience.

We have been raised to fear the *yes* within ourselves, our deepest cravings. But, once recognized, those which do not enhance our future lose their power and can be altered. The fear of our desires keeps them suspect and indiscriminately powerful, for to suppress any truth is to give it strength beyond endurance. The fear that we cannot grow beyond whatever distortions we may find within ourselves keeps us docile and loyal and obedient, externally defined, and leads us to accept many facets of our oppression as women.

When we live outside ourselves, and by that I mean on external directives only rather than from our internal knowledge and needs, when we live away from those erotic guides from within ourselves, then our lives are limited by external and alien forms, and we conform to the needs of a structure that is not based on human need, let alone an individual's. But when we begin to live from within outward, in touch with the power of the erotic within ourselves, and allowing that power to inform and illuminate our actions upon the world around us, then we begin to be responsible to ourselves in the deepest sense. For as we begin to recognize our deepest feelings, we begin to give up, of necessity, being satisfied with suffering and self-negation, and with the numbness which so often seems like their only alternative in our society. Our acts against oppression become integral with self, motivated and empowered from within.

In touch with the erotic, I become less willing to accept powerlessness, or those other supplied states of being which are not native to me, such as resignation, despair, self-effacement, depression, self-denial.

And yes, there is a hierarchy. There is a difference between painting a back fence and writing a poem, but only one of quantity. And there is, for me, no difference between writing a good poem and moving into sunlight against the body of a woman I love.

This brings me to the last consideration of the erotic. To share the power of each other's feelings is different from using another's feelings as we would use a kleenex. When we look the other way from our experience, erotic or otherwise, we use rather than share the feelings of those others who participate in the experience with us. And use without consent of the used is abuse.

In order to be utilized, our erotic feelings must be recognized. The need for sharing deep feeling is a human need. But within the european-american tradition, this need is satisfied by certain proscribed erotic comings-together. These occasions are almost always characterized by a simultaneous looking away, a pretense of calling them something else, whether a religion, a fit, mob violence, or even playing doctor. And this misnaming of the need and the deed give rise to that distortion which results in pornography and obscenity—the abuse of feeling.

When we look away from the importance of the erotic in the development and sustenance of our power, or when we look away from ourselves as we satisfy our erotic needs in concert with others, we use each other as objects of satisfaction rather than share our joy in the satisfying, rather than make connection with our similarities and our differences. To refuse to be conscious of what we are feeling at any time, however comfortable that might seem, is to deny a large part of the experience, and to allow ourselves to be reduced to the pornographic, the abused, and the absurd.

The erotic cannot be felt secondhand. As a Black lesbian feminist, I have a particular feeling, knowledge, and understanding for those sisters with whom I have danced hard, played, or even fought. This deep participation has often been the forerunner for joint concerted actions not possible before.

But this erotic charge is not easily shared by women who continue to operate under an exclusively european-american male tradition. I know it was not available to me when I was trying to adapt my consciousness to this mode of living and sensation.

Only now, I find more and more women-identified women brave enough to risk sharing the erotic's electrical charge without having to look away, and without distorting the enormously powerful and creative nature of that exchange. Recognizing the power of the erotic within our lives can give us the energy to pursue genuine change within our world, rather than merely settling for a shift of characters in the same weary drama.

For not only do we touch our most profoundly creative source, but we do that which is female and self-affirming in the face of a racist, patriarchal, and anti-erotic society.

32 Lovers and Workers

Screening the Body in Post-Communist Hungarian Cinema

Catherine Portuges

Eastern Europe's emergence from its Stalinist past is dramatically inscribed in the politics of its recent cinema. Relegated to a secondary status in favor of more pressing economic priorities, filmmakers accustomed to the security of a state-supported industry now find themselves competing for scarce resources in the midst of accusations of complicity with and defenses of opposition to former regimes. In Hungary as elsewhere, cinema continues nonetheless to play a vital role as public forum for the ongoing reassessment of the nation's political past.[1] Yet despite—or perhaps on account of—the transformations that have overtaken East-Central Europe, there persists in Hungarian cinema a lingering double vision, a depressive symptom of the profound alienation that is a legacy of the post-totalitarian psyche.[2]

In the vanguard of the 'other Europe's' increasingly oppositional stance throughout the 1980s, Hungarian filmmakers boldly represented contested political terrain, especially the central event of Hungary's postwar history: the uprising of 1956. The status, nomenclature and ultimate reclaiming of that event by the opposition movement became a cornerstone of Hungary's 'quiet revolution' of 1989, finding its way into nearly every film produced that year. The urgency displayed by artists and intellectuals to examine, with obsessional repetition, that period of their country's history with its stories of deceit and accommodation, collaboration and resistance, seems in fact to have displaced other, more contemporary projects that had been on the agenda, creating a transitional space between collective

Catherine Portuges, 'Lovers and Workers: Screening the Body in Post-Communist Hungarian Cinema', edited extract from *Nationalities and Sexualities*, ed. Andrew Parker, Mary Russo, Doris Somer, and Patricia Yaeger (Routledge (NY), 1992), 285–99, reprinted by permission of the author and Taylor and Francis/Routledge Inc.

discourse and individual subjectivity, between official narrative and private memory.[3]

Suppressed under the aegis of Stalinist internationalism, culturally-specific questions of gender, sexuality and politics invite today renewed articulation, cloaked though these questions may be in the mantle of a Western 'look' that bears little resemblance to the Stalinist aesthetic of previous decades.[4] Although economic constraints are likely to foreclose temporarily the exploration of these issues, whether in the cinema or in other cultural media, an enduring (albeit seldom examined) dialectic of sexuality and nationalism may well become the site of future representational enactments. Joining the ever-increasing list of joint capitalist ventures and 'limited corporations' that characterize Hungary's post-communist transitional moment, the culture of cinema has been forced to reinvent itself if indeed it is to survive under a new order. To that end, such 1989–90 films as *The Dokumentator*, *Sexploitation* and *Fast and Loose* suggest that some Hungarian film-makers have responded to the demands of liberalization by embracing the more commercially viable trajectory of the eroticized spectacle.[5]

Long banned by the Communist Party as a symptom of the more decadent aspects of Western capitalism, pornography now can be found at local kiosks graphically displayed on the covers of such publications as *Sexexpress*, *Apollo*, and *Lesbi Girls*. X-rated videos constitute a new growth industry, as suggested in *The Dokumentator* in which a successful video-store owner, having profited by trafficking in black-market trade, spends his time suturing video footage of international catastrophes before turning the camcorder on his own suicidal impulses. A pornography kingpin celebrates this tendency, hoping customers will 'spend their sorrow' and thereby enrich his successful enterprise consisting of sex magazines, massage parlors, and sexual tourism. A female teacher, aware that the repressive sexuality of Stalinism is in part accountable for the escalation of such images, nevertheless voices a concern, familiar to Western feminists but far less so in Eastern Europe, for the exploitation of women: 'But what is missing from the debate is the articulation of the view that this is offensive to women. People are mixing liberty with bad taste.'[6]

One of the most popular of the newly 'liberated' films, Gyorgy Szomjas's *Fast and Loose* (*Konnyu Ver*) features the adventures of two platinum-blonde 'models' in search of foreign clients with hard currency. Compensating in audience appeal for its good-natured lack of high production values, the film is an index of current spectatorial cravings for uninhibited exploration of heterosexual titillation in the wake of puritanical censorship. For representation of the body is inseparable from political discourse, implicated as it is in the circulation of desire between production and spectatorship.[7]

In these and other works in which youthful bodies are exhibitionistically fetishized, the ardently sought free-market economy is both symptom and cause, and the Western observer accustomed to the more subdued look of films of the 1970s and early 1980s is understandably confused by this appearance of eroticized excess. Among the few filmmakers who have consistently addressed the intersections of state ideology, sexuality, and everyday life—rural and urban, work place and domestic—Márta Mészáros has courageously and consistently explored the highly charged intersections of gender and nationality. After a distinguished career as a documentary filmmaker trained in Moscow at the Institute of Cinematographic Art, she made her first feature films in the late 1960s and early 1970s. These works, which catapulted her to a degree of international celebrity hitherto unequalled by any other East European woman director, established the concerns for which she is now recognized: the representation of the struggle of working women and men attempting to create a new society against the background of modern political and socioeconomic life in postwar Hungary.[8]

In contrast to most of her male colleagues, Mészáros's films raise issues of class relations and gender, love and sexuality, deception and honesty in an unsentimental and at times even ruthless fashion. They have been particularly troubling for Hungarian audiences and critics discomfited by her uncompromising meditations on the double imperatives of national identity and gender inscription in post-Stalinist and post-communist Eastern Europe. One of over a dozen features released between 1968 and 1988, her 1980 film *The Heiresses*, with Isabelle Huppert as the leading actress, received favorable notices in France for its audacious treatment of such subversive issues as infertility, class difference, and the solidarity of female friendship. Unable to produce an heir, a wealthy Jewish couple contracts a young working-class woman to act as surrogate mother while fascism overtakes the country. It is worth noting that this highly controversial topic emerged in Hungarian cinema more than half a decade before the 'Baby M.' case, anticipating contemporary debates on surrogacy and maternity within the politically and historically charged atmosphere of wartime Nazism and the historical specificity of East European anti-semitism. Cinematic references to this topic are rare in Hungary, and Mészáros did not endear herself to critics of the time by focusing on highly controversial—and officially denied—problems of class, religion, ethnicity, and gender. The unorthodox arrangement backfires in the film, transgressing its purported object—the perpetuation of the married couple's upper-class family—as the husband and his wife's friend fall in love.

The film's reception was far from welcoming; critics and audiences in Hungary were resistant, if not outraged. Communist Party leaders displeased by its portrayal of a 'decadent' bourgeois relationship and its exploitation of a working-class woman saw in it a distinction officially discouraged and, for that matter, denied by the socialist state. Critics and spectators alike read the film as a confirmation of their deepest fears of the consequences of the weakening of family bonds and the amorality of contemporary Hungarian domestic life.[9]

At once encoding and disclosing a critical stance with regard to the interpenetration of sexuality and the state, Mészáros's films may be seen as consistent with other East European cinematic discourses previously compelled to perform their textual operations through nuance, subversion, and covert systems of reference. But her cinema diverges inescapably from those representations, I think, by virtue of the specificity of its inscription of masculinity and femininity compared, for example, to the work of an Agnieska Holland in Poland or of Vera Chytilova in Czechoslovakia.[10] For Mészáros's texts embody an unrelenting conflict and persistent sense of unease between men and women, be they factory workers (as in *The Girl*, 1968, and *Nine Months*, 1976), communist party officials (as in *Diary for My Children*, 1983), or bourgeois intellectuals (as in *Mother and Daughter*, 1981, and *The Heiresses*, 1980). Intimacy and sensuality, Mészáros seems to suggest, are possible primarily between female coworkers or in solitary moments of respite from the unceasing turmoil of the rigors of contemporary socialist life:

> I am an East European director, and my whole life, unfortunately, has been filled with politics. It is a tradition that, good or bad, you must deal with politics, especially for my generation educated under Stalinism. . . . An independent woman—one who finds herself in a situation where she must make a decision on her own—is the central character in each of the pictures I have made so far.[11]

In *Adoption* (1975), two women are framed together, at first contentedly drinking and smoking in a bar, later harassed by the mocking laughter and gestures of male patrons. The men appear envious of the women's obvious pleasure in their own conversation and are discomfited by the obvious display of intimacy between them. Visually and semiotically, these sequences foreground the women's friendship while acknowledging their vulnerability in a society whose socialist party rhetoric of sexual equality is often dramatically at odds with traditional cultural practice.[12]

Like *The Heiresses*, *Adoption* trangresses codes of national and sexual chauvinism, opening with a long sequence that portrays a woman in her forties named Kata awakening alone, preparing breakfast, showering and leaving for work in the practiced gestures of solitary habit. Later she is examined by a male physician: we suspect from her rather haggard appearance that she might be suffering from tuberculosis; yet as the doctor pronounces her fit, it becomes clear that she wishes to conceive a child, a fact she subsequently announces to her married lover when they arrange to meet in a cafe. The scene is played without pathos or self-pity, and Mészáros's characteristic restraint evinces not blame but painfully realistic acceptance of the lover's limitations, unwilling (and, we are meant to understand, unable) as he is to commit himself fully to his mistress. Encouraged later by her friendship with a young woman from a nearby orphanage, Kata finds herself able to adopt a baby on her own. The camera tracks back in the final sequence of *Adoption* as Kata boards a bus with her newly acquired infant; they appear all the more vulnerable in an urban landscape indifferent to the middle-aged woman's subjective drama.

But there is in Mészáros's cinematic construction an affecting visual ambiguity, for, however great the cost, Kata has triumphed over entrenched priorities of nation and gender to achieve the 'object of her desire'—the opportunity to raise a child as a single, older woman, without the family or male companion normally considered as prerequisites for adoption by the values of the socialist state of the time. Seen today in a Western context, this gesture of defiance should be inserted within its proper historical frame in a national agenda that, while encouraging natalism and gender equality under socialism, was only beginning to emerge from a legacy of communism that privileged collectivity above individual psychology and hence offered little opportunity for emotional support for such social experiments. The woman's body becomes, for Mészáros, a sign of opposition to prevailing post-Stalinist gender policies in which sexual difference was to be elided in favor of the project of building 'socialist man' and 'socialist woman'. Mészáros's treatment of gender thus contrasts markedly with the work of Miklós Jancsó, Mészáros's husband at the time and an internationally renowned film director, celebrated for historical dramas portraying Hungary's nineteenth-century revolutionary period in films such as *Red Psalm* (1971), in which long-haired young peasant women are made to undress before the gaze of uniformed soldiers who then encircle and run toward them across the vast *puszta*. Jancsó's camera appropriates the female body both as provocation and erotic object, and never grants it the measure of authorial subjectivity which it is accorded in Mészáros's diegetic universe.[13]

Like many Hungarian films of the past twenty years produced in the wake of a socialist-realist aesthetics, Mészáros's works bear the traces of an implicit critique of the problematics of desire, of male domination and female suffering. Almost seductively engaged with the political issues of their time, these films also strike many Western audiences as inordinately depressing, hopeless, or resigned. Erotic encounters are often represented as pleasurable only when illicit—whether because of class differences or oedipal triangulation, as in *The Heiresses* (1980)—or as mythical, idealized by the temporal distance of childhood memory, such as in her later *Diary* trilogy. Mészáros's lovers are often young workers seeking relief from foreclosed possibilities in the early period of Stalinism, as in *Riddance* (1973); middle-aged couples growing apart under the weight of unrealized hopes, as in *The Two of Them* (1977), and older people attempting to reconcile harsh objective conditions with thwarted individual desires, as in the *Diary* films.

Mészáros's first feature film, *The Girl* (1968), initiates the interrogation of parentage and family history that has persisted throughout the director's work to date. Symbolically, parentage converges with the Stalinist state in the 1950s when Matyas Rákosi, the country's leader from 1948–56, followed Stalin's example by proclaiming himself the metaphorical progenitor of all Hungarian children.[14] A number of her feature films employ the narrative strategy of a child or young girl who accuses her parents—and, through them, the state—of lying about the past, and, in so doing, insists on discovering the truth at great personal cost. In sexual, familial, and political matters, then, the evasions and half-truths typical of Stalinist culture are investigated with unflinching vision, whether they concern the trauma of a little girl witnessing her father's degrading alcoholic cure in a detoxification clinic (as in *The Two of Them*), or the more abstract ideological consequences of repression (as in the *Diary* trilogy). Such relentless probing testifies eloquently to the prescience of Mészáros's agenda; further, it demonstrates the leading role of filmmakers in opening the discursive boundaries that gave voice to that which had so long been silenced far in advance of the transformations in East-Central Europe and the Soviet Union.

The Two of Them (1977), Mészáros's seventh feature, shifts its focus to concentrate on a friendship between two women, and is, according to the director, the first of her narrative films to have a 'sympathetic male character—albeit an alcoholic . . . a sensitive person who sees life in its complexity and profundity'.[15] As the self-possessed director of a working women's hostel, Marina Vlady as Mari maintains her composed serenity in principled stands against the hostel administration's inhumane regulations on behalf of a troubled younger woman still deeply attracted to her alcoholic husband. But it is Juli's daughter Zuzsi whose point of view indicts the adult world of deception and compromise, and the child actress who plays her, Zsuzsa Czinkoczy, in fact becomes the central protagonist in Mészáros's subsequent films, an alter ego for the director's fascination with the experience of a child abandoned by her parents.[16] Despite Mari's efforts to shelter and assist her friend, Juli finds it difficult to resist her irresponsible, childlike husband. In a darkly lit yet revealing sequence, they make love on a kitchen chair, two bodies hopelessly lost, acting out a primally brutal physical attraction. In contrast, Mari's own deteriorating middle-class marriage has become psychologically abusive through her husband's absences and is devoid of the erotic passion that controls Juli and her husband. This difference is demonstrated in a sequence of visually shocking sexual humiliations when Mari is left lying on the floor, legs spread, by her usually passive husband after a brief and, we are meant to suspect, typical moment of intercourse. Afterward, we see Mari, water streaming from her blonde hair, enjoying herself in a steamy shower, joined by her fully-clothed friend Juli, as the two women embrace and share a moment of sensuous release through the complicit laughter that momentarily transcends even the barriers of class and gender.

Such sensual moments portraying a woman nude in the shower recur frequently in Mészáros's work, often counterbalancing anguished episodes of distress resulting from the material as well as the sexual conditions of existence. The female body is imaged—but not, I think, fetishized—through the purificatory ritual of bathing, either alone or in the company of other women. While the unclothed female figure was hardly unknown in post-Stalinist East European cinema, other Hungarian renderings, among which the most celebrated are those of Miklós Jancsó, are clearly presented primarily for the visual, erotic pleasure of the male spectator. A telling sequence of shots from *Riddance* (1973) dramatically integrates issues of class, domestic abuse, and gender within a state-socialist context. A young factory worker ashamed of her working class origins pretends to be a university student in order to please a young man she meets at a dance and to rid herself of her working-class boyfriend. When she confronts the latter by admitting she does not love him, he slaps her face several times in the presence of patrons at an outdoor cafe. Only after repeated blows does a nearby waitress come to her aid, while onlookers (both male and female) appear either to ignore or to take pleasure in her humiliation. Mészáros cuts again to a shower sequence where the young woman is framed in close-up, the camera panning unhurriedly down small, graceful breasts toward her trim belly as the water's spray mingles with her tears. It is obviously a pleasurable moment for the protagonist, and we share her complicated yet enjoyable sense of catharsis and renewal. Such unflinching cinematic representation of domestic violence mirrored social conditions perhaps rather too accurately, and as a result was met with particularly hostile reception in the popular and critical press. That the director was a woman willing to express such truths in uncompromising visual terms may have left audiences with a sense of unbearable exposure.

The critical realism of Márta Mészáros's method works to situate her bourgeois women and factory workers in the homes, offices, and factories in which they spend much of their time; we learn in deliberate, documented detail about the machines they operate, the domestic tasks they accomplish, the financial, political, and sexual anxieties that preoccupy them. We are allowed, for instance, to see women of all ages and physical types showering together in the factory washroom at the end of a shift, arguing heatedly about working conditions and teasing each other about their love lives.

Even the rural and urban antagonisms characteristic of Hungarian society are examined with cinematographic rigor and the impeccable editing attributable in part to Mészáros's documentary training. When a young urban woman worker returns to her village to seek her father in *Binding Sentiments* (1969), Mészáros gives the story a twist that highlights urban–rural tensions with regard to gender: a peasant mother, now remarried, denies her own daughter, now a city dweller, thereby illustrating as well the deeper suspicion with which each group has traditionally regarded the other in Hungarian society. The young woman is subjected first to the unwelcome advances of her mother's husband and then to those of her half-brother at a village dance, suggesting the family's acceptance of this form of incestuous behavior and its rejection of her as both class traitor and now unattainably sophisticated, desired object. Mészáros thus combines several layers of social critique by foregrounding the alienation between mother and daughter as inescapably embedded within the complexities of class tension, national antagonisms between city and countryside, and the gender politics that encompass both.

Within those contexts, disparities and affinities between generations emerge as young village women come to live and work with older women in workers' hostels in Budapest, a common theme of Mészáros's early features. At first glance, these women appear to gain autonomy because of their excursion into the labor force. But at a deeper level, Mészáros's treatment is grounded in the reality of the sexual antagonism of Hungarian working class relations: these women are depicted as increasingly alienated from familial ties because of their displacement into urban workers' hostels, thereby making them more vulnerable to the advances of similarly solitary males.[17]

Subverting the official party program of an East European state claiming to have created a homogeneous society in which gender as well as class contradictions have been eliminated, Márta Mészáros places the cinematic apparatus in the service of a deconstruction of that ideology. In so doing, she reveals how deeply embedded within the culture such contradictions remain, how resistant to transformation by purely external dictates. But her most searching critique thus far emanates from the two completed segments of her *Diary* trilogy, the director's autobiographical *magnum opus.*

Having been denied permission for fifteen years to embark upon that project, Mészáros was able to complete the first installment in 1984. *Diary for My Children*, its 1986 sequel *Diary for My Loves*, and the last of the trilogy *Diary for My Father and Mother* (1990) represent the director's return to Hungary following several years of international coproductions. As such, they exemplify the conflict facing many East European artists—and, for that matter, any exiled artist—trapped between the desire to return to the site of national origin or leave it behind, perhaps forever. Confronting her own past by returning to Budapest, she once more chronicles through these films the tumultuous period of Hungarian and East European history between 1949 and 1989. More important still, they narrate the director's own life story from the perspective of her adolescent alter ego, Juli, using what was a highly innovative and, since, much-imitated combination of semi-fictionalized and documentary material.

By validating the importance of reconciliation with what had been repressed or denied—be it family, political affiliation, or inequalities inadmissible under Stalinism and in its aftermath, these films affirm the right and responsibility of both individual and nation to claim their experience, no matter how fraught with guilt, betrayal, or fear. And as in her first feature, Mészáros again focuses upon the protagonist's quest for her lost father, according him a more overtly political role. For this time, not only the small Hungarian but also the mighty Soviet state is interrogated and indicted: Juli's father disappears in the Stalinist purges, as did Mészáros's own father, the sculptor László Mészáros, who vanished in 1938. Juli subsequently returns to Hungary as an orphan, unwilling to accept the powerful influence, potential support, and concomitant control of Magda, a devoted communist party cadre in search of a surrogate daughter. In the final instalment of the *Diary* trilogy, Mészáros restages the destruction of a monumental statue of Stalin as her heroine completes the odyssey of reassessment begun a decade earlier in *Diary for My Children*. The completion of the *Trilogy* corresponds with the end of an era of Hungarian filmmaking, opening new directions for filmmakers and spectators at the site of the border crossings between sexuality and nationality.

Notes

1. For an overview of the effects of *glasnost* on film culture in the USSR, East Germany, Hungary, Poland, Czechoslovakia, Yugoslavia and Rumania, see Daniel J. Goulding (ed.), *Post New Wave Cinema in the Soviet Union and Eastern Europe* (Bloomington: Indiana University Press, 1989). My comments on current developments in Hungarian film are based in part on screenings of 43 feature and documentary films produced in 1989 and presented 2–8 February 1990 in Budapest at the 22nd Hungarian National Film Festival, at which I was an invited observer.
2. See Timothy Garton Ash, *The Uses of Adversity: Essays on the Fate of Central Europe* (New York: Random House, 1989); also Milan Kundera, 'The Tragedy of Central Europe', *New York Review of Books*, 26 April 1984, for further elaboration of this syndrome.
3. This spatial metaphor originates with the British psychoanalyst and pediatrician D. W. Winnicott in *Playing and Reality* (London: Routledge & Kegan Paul, 1986) and refers to his theory of the psychological distance between mother and infant presumably indispensable to the development of the child's sense of creativity and cultural experience.

4. According to *Variety* (23 May 1990), Universal Pictures plans to schedule release of some 200 American films on Hungarian screens in 1990 alone, more than eight times the total number of films produced in an average year by Hungarian studios.
5. Screened at the 22nd Hungarian National Film Festival in Budapest, 2–8 February 1990.
6. Quoted in the *New York Times*, 12 May 1990, p. 6.
7. Szomjas' *Fast and Loose* was Hungary's only feature entry in the 27th International Film Festival at Karlovy Vary, Czechoslovakia, in July 1990, a decision suggestive of how the country wishes to see itself represented in the international market.
8. Best known among Mészáros's films of this period are *Riddance* (1973), *Adoption* (1975), and *The Two of Them* (1977). See my *Screen Memories: The Hungarian Films of Mártá Mészáros* (Bloomington: Indiana University Press, 1991).
9. French critical reception was considerably more positive (the film was a Franco-Hungarian coproduction), and Mészáros's reputation continued to rise in that country as elsewhere in Western Europe, in contrast to the negative view a number of her Hungarian colleagues evinced in response to her work. This may have been due in part to the dissolution of her marriage to Miklós Jancsó, the best-known Hungarian filmmaker of that period, whose avant-garde works such as *The Red and the White* (1967) and *Red Psalm* (1971) were highly esteemed by such influential journals as *Cahiers du Cinéma.*
10. See Peter Hames, *The Czechoslovak New Wave* (Berkeley: University of California Press, 1985); and Boleslaw Michalek and Frank Turaj, *The Modern Cinema of Poland* (Bloomington: Indiana University Press, 1988), for discussions of these and other Polish and Czechoslovak filmmakers.
11. From a series of interviews conducted by the author in Budapest between 1986 and 1990.
12. I am grateful to Prof. F. T. Zsuppan of St Andrews University, Scotland, for his illuminating presentation on the seeming anachronism of the history of feminist activism in Hungary (cf. 'Rozsika Schwimmer and Hungarian Feminism, 1904–1918,' Conference of the American Association for the Advancement of Slavic Studies, October, 1990, Washington, DC).
13. It should be noted that Jancsó's experimental avant-garde work was nevertheless an instrumental intervention in the rupture of contemporary Hungarian cinema from the stronghold of post-Stalinist puritanism.
14. A fascinating example of this tendency may be found in *Somewhere in Europe*, the classic Hungarian film by Radvanyi in which homeless children—mostly boys—are cared for by the state, a powerful reference to the ideology of the then-new socialist state's function *in loco parentis.*
15. See Barbara Koenig Quart, *Women Directors: The Emergence of a New Cinema* (New York: Praeger, 1988), pp. 191–208.
16. Like François Truffaut's use of the 12-year-old Jean-Pierre Léaud in *The 400 Blows*—the actor who became the primary figure of the director's autobiographical Antoine Doinel cycle of films—Mészáros has sustained with Czinkoczy (at first a nonprofessional actress and a village girl) an evolving on-screen relationship of extraordinary depth and delicacy.

17. See for example Miklós Haraszti, *A Worker in a Worker's State* (New York: Universe Books, 1978), for an insightful overview of the 1960s in Hungary; and László Kürti, 'Hierarchy and Workers' Power in a Csepel Factory', *Journal of Communist Studies*, 6: 2, special issue on Market Economy and Civil Society in Hungary, ed. C. M. Hann (London: Frank Cass, June 1990), pp. 61–84, for an excellent analysis of working-class youth in a socialist firm during this period.

What We're Rollin Around in Bed With
Sexual Silences in Feminism

Amber Hollibaugh and Cherríe Moraga

Is lesbianism by definition an advanced form of feminism? Some lesbian activists have assumed that women only choose heterosexuality under some kind of coercion from men. In this piece Hollibaugh and Moraga challenge the view that lesbianism is necessarily a privileged, an ideal sexuality. Rather, they argue, feminism has jumped too quickly to its judgments of what is or is not 'politically correct'. Instead, they suggest, feminists need to return to the techniques of the early women's liberation movement, to the discursive description of individual experiences called consciousness raising, if we are to find out more about sexuality and particularly sexual differences. Hollibaugh and Moraga discuss variables of temperament and ethnic background that elude generalization, bringing us up against the complex reality of differing sexual styles and tastes; they surmise that sexual boundaries may well begin at our own skins. Every sexual relation involves a crossing of borders.

Feminists have often seen an improved sexual technique and a more assertive sexuality as the essential ingredients in women's fulfillment. This is the line of thinking that, at its baldest, underlay the mechanistic injunctions of The Hite Report, *which posited masturbation as the most efficient and possibly most pleasurable mode of female satisfaction, In contrast, Hollibaugh and Moraga suggest that arousal depends not so much on technique as on emotional dynamics: one can deeply excite a lover, Hollibaugh notes, without 'doing' anything. In 'openly' acknowledging the psychological play that can touch upon the 'hurt places' in all of us, this colloquial conversation underscores in its*

Amber Hollibaugh and Cherríe Moraga, 'What We're Rollin Around in Bed With: Sexual Silences in Feminism', from *Powers of Desire* (Monthly Review Press, 1983), 395–405, reprinted by permission of the publisher.

own way Jessica Benjamin's highly theoretical analysis of similar themes.

This article was derived from a series of conversations we entertained for many months. Through it, we wish to illuminate both our common and different relationship to a feminist movement to which we are both committed.

THE CRITIQUE

Ironically, the whole notion of 'the personal is political', which surfaced in the early part of the women's liberation movement (and which many of us have used to an extreme), is suddenly dismissed when we begin to discuss sexuality. We have become a relatively sophisticated movement, so many women think they now have to have the theory before they expose the experience. It seems we simply did not take our feminism to heart enough. This most privatized aspect of ourselves, our sex lives, has dead-ended into silence within the feminist movement.

For a brief moment in its early stages, the feminist movement did address women's sexual pleasure, but this discussion was quickly swamped by recognition of how much pain women had suffered around sex in relation to men (e.g., marriage, the nuclear family, wife-battering, rape, etc.). In these early discussions, lesbianism was ignored and heterosexuality was not understood as both an actual sexual interaction *and* a system. No matter how we play ourselves out sexually, we are all affected by the system inasmuch as our sexual values are filtered through a society where heterosexuality is considered the norm. It is difficult to believe that there is anyone in the world who hasn't spent some time in great pain over the choices and limitations that characterize the system.

By analyzing the institution of heterosexuality, feminists learned what's oppressive about it and why people cooperate with it or don't but we didn't learn what is *sexual*. We don't really know, for instance, why men and women are still attracted to each other, even through all that oppression. There is something genuine that happens between heterosexuals, but gets perverted in a thousand different ways. There *is* heterosexuality outside of heterosexism.

What grew out of this kind of 'nonsexual' theory was a 'transcendent' definition of sexuality where lesbianism (since it exists outside the institution of heterosexuality) came to be seen as the practice of feminism. It set up a 'perfect' vision of egalitarian sexuality, where we could magically leap over our heterosexist conditioning into mutually orgasmic, struggle-free, trouble-free sex. We feel this vision has become both misleading and damaging to many feminists, and in particular to lesbians. Who created this sexual model as a goal in the first place? Who can really live up to such an ideal? There is little language, little literature that reflects the actual sexual struggles of most lesbians, feminist or not.

The failure of feminism to answer all the questions about women, in particular about women's sexuality, is the same failure the homosexual movement suffers from around gender. It's a confusing of those two things—that some of us are both female and homosexual—that may be the source of some of the tension between the two movements and of the inadequacies of each. When we walk down the street, we are both female and lesbian. We are working-class white and working-class Chicana. We are all these things rolled into one and there is no way to eliminate even one aspect of ourselves.

THE CONVERSATION

CM: *In trying to develop sexual theory, I think we should start by talking about what we're rollin around in bed with. We both agree that the way feminism has dealt with sexuality has been entirely inadequate.*

AH: Right. Sexual theory has traditionally been used to say *people have been forced to be this thing; people could be that thing.* And you're left standing in the middle going, 'Well, I am here; and I don't know how to get there.' It hasn't been able to talk realistically about what people *are* sexually.

I think by focusing on roles in lesbian relationships, we can begin to unravel who we really are in bed. Hiding how profoundly roles shape your sexuality can be seen as an example of how other things about sex get hidden. There's a lot of different things that shape the way that people respond—some not so easy to see, some more forbidden, as I perceive sadomasochism to be. Like with sadomasochism—when I think of it I'm frightened. Why? Is it because I might be sexually fascinated with it and I don't know how to accept that? Who am I there? The point is that when you deny that roles, sadomasochism, fantasy, or any sexual differences exist in the first place, you can only come up with neutered sexuality, where everybody's got to be basically the same because anything different puts the element of power and deviation in there and threatens the whole picture.

CM: *Exactly. Remember how I told you that when growing up what turned me on sexually, at a very early age, had to do with the fantasy of capture, taking a woman, and my identification was with the man, taking? Well, something like that would be so frightening to bring up in a feminist context—fearing people would put it in some sicko sexual box. And yet, the truth is, I do have some real gut-level misgivings about my sexual connection with capture. It might feel very sexy to imagine 'taking' a woman, but it has sometimes occurred at the expense of my feeling, sexually, like I can surrender myself to a woman; that is, always needing to be the one in control, calling the shots. It's a very butch trip and I feel like this can keep me private and protected and can prevent me from fully being able to express myself.*

AH: But it's not wrong, in and of itself, to have a capture fantasy. The real question is: Does it *actually* limit you? For instance, does it allow you to eroticize someone else, but never see yourself as erotic? Does it keep you always in control? Does the fantasy force you into a dimension of sexuality that feels very narrow to you? If it causes you to look at your lover in only one light, then you may want to check it out But if you can't even dream about wanting a woman in this way in the first place, then you can't figure out what is narrow and heterosexist in it and what's just play. After all, it's only *one* fantasy.

CM: *Well, what I think is very dangerous about keeping down such fantasies is that they are forced to stay unconscious. Then, next thing you know, in the actual sexual relationship, you become the capturer, that is, you try to have power over your lover, psychologically or whatever. If the desire for power is so hidden and unacknowledged it* will *inevitably surface through manipulation or what-have-you. If you couldn't* play *capturer, you'd be it.*

AH: Part of the problem in talking about sexuality is *it's so enormous* in our culture that people don't have any genuine sense of dimension. So that when you say 'capture', every fantasy you've ever heard of from Robin Hood to colonialism comes racing into your mind and all you really maybe wanted to do was have your girlfriend lay you down.

But in feminism, we can't even explore these questions because what they say is, in gender, there is a masculine oppressor and a female oppressee. So whether you might fantasize yourself in a role a man might perform or a woman in reaction to a man, this makes you sick, fucked-up, and you had better go and change it.

If you don't speak of fantasies, they become a kind of amorphous thing that envelops you and hangs over your relationship and you get terrified of the silence. If you have no way to describe what your desire is and what your fear is, you have no way to negotiate with your lover. And I guarantee you, six months or six years later, the relationship has paid. Things that are kept private and hidden become painful and deformed.

When you say that part of your sexuality has been hooked up with capture, I want to say that absolutely there's a heterosexist part of that, but what part of that is just plain dealing with power, sexually? I don't want to live outside of power in my sexuality, but I don't want to be trapped into a heterosexist concept of power either. But what I feel feminism asks of me is to throw the baby out with the bathwater.

For example, *I think the reason butch/femme stuff got hidden within lesbian feminism is because people are profoundly afraid of questions of power in bed.* And though everybody doesn't play out power the way I do, the question of power affects who and how you eroticize your sexual need. And it is absolutely at the bottom of all sexual inquiry. Given the present state of the movement, it's impossible to say I'm a femme and I like it—no apologies—without facing the probability of a heavy fight.

CM: *But what is femme to you? I told you once that what I thought of as femme was passive, unassertive, and so forth, and you didn't fit that image. And you said to me, 'Well, change your definition of femme.'*

AH: My fantasy life is deeply involved in a butch/femme exchange. I never come together with a woman, sexually, outside of those roles. It's saying to my partner, 'Love me enough to let me go where I need to go and take me there. Don't make me think it through. Give me a way to be so in my body that I don't have to think; that you can fantasize for the both of us. You map it out. You are in control.'

It's hard to talk about things like giving up power without it sounding passive. I am willing to give myself over to a woman equal to her amount of wanting. I expose myself for her to see what's possible for her to love in me that's female. I want her to respond to it. I may not be doing something active with my body, but more eroticizing her need that I feel in her hands as she touches me.

In the same way, as a butch, you want and conceive of a woman in a certain way. You dress a certain way to attract her and you put your sexual need within these certain boundaries to communicate that desire. . . . And yet, there's a part of me that feels maybe all this is not even a question of roles. Maybe it's much richer territory than that.

CM: *Yes, I feel the way I want a woman can be a very profound experience. Remember I told you how when I looked up at my lover's face when I was making love to her (I was actually just kissing her breast at the moment), but when I looked up at her face, I could feel and see how deeply every part of her was present? That every pore in her body was entrusting me to handle her, to take care of her sexual desire. This look on her face is like nothing else. It fills me up. She entrusts me to determine where she'll go sexually. And I honestly feel a power inside me strong enough to heal the deepest wound.*

AH: Well, I can't actually see what I look like, but I can feel it in my lover's hands when I look the way you described. When I open myself up more and more to her sensation of wanting a woman, when I eroticize that in her, I feel a kind of ache in my body, but it's not an ache to *do* something. I can feel a hurt spot and a need and it's there and it's just the tip of it, the tip of that desire and that is what first gets played with, made erotic. It's light and playful. It doesn't commit you to exposing a deeper part of yourself sexually. Then I begin to pick up passion. And the passion isn't butch or femme. It's just passion.

But from this place, if it's working, I begin to imagine myself being the *woman that a woman always wanted.* That's what I begin to eroticize. That's what I begin to feel from my lover's hands. I begin to fantasize myself becoming more and more female in order to comprehend and meet what I feel happening in her body. I don't want her not to be female to me. Her need is female, but it's butch because I am asking her to expose her desire through the movement of her hands on my body and I'll respond. I want to give up power in response to her need. This can feel profoundly powerful and very unpassive.

A lot of times how I feel it in my body is I feel like I have this fantasy of pulling a woman's hips into my cunt. I can feel the need painfully in another woman's body. I can feel the impact and I begin to play and respond to that hunger and desire. And I begin to eroticize the fantasy that *she can't get enuf of me.* It makes me want to enflame my body. What it feels like is that I'm in my own veins and I'm sending heat up into my thighs. It's very hot.

CM: *Oh honey, she feels the heat*, too.

AH: Yes, and I am making every part of my body accessible to that woman. I completely trust her. There's no place she cannot touch me. My body is literally open to any way she interprets her sexual need. My power is that I know how to read her inside of her own passion. I can hear her. It's like a sexual language; it's a rhythmic language that she uses her hands for. My body is completely in sync with a lover, but I'm not deciding where she's gonna touch me.

CM: *But don't you ever fantasize yourself being on the opposite end of that experience?*

AH: Well, not exactly in the same way, because with butches you can't insist on them giving up their sexual identity. You have to go through that identity to that other place. But you don't have to throw out the role to explore the sexuality. There are femme ways to orchestrate sexuality. I'm not asking a woman not to be a butch. I am asking her to let me express the other part of my own character, where I am actively orchestrating what's happening. I never give up my right to say that I can insist on what happens sexually. . . . quite often what will happen is I'll simply seduce her. Now, that's very active. The seduction can be very profound, but it's a seduction as a femme.

CM: *What comes to my mind is something as simple as you comin over and sittin on her lap. Where a butch, well, she might just go for your throat if she wants you.*

AH: Oh yes, different areas for different roles! What's essential is that your attitude doesn't threaten the other person's sexual identity, but plays with it. That's what good seduction is all about. I play a lot in that. It's not that I have to have spike heels on in order to fantasize who I am. Now that's just a lot of classist shit, conceiving of a femme in such a narrow way.

CM: *Well, I would venture to say that some of these dynamics that you're describing happen between most lesbians, only they may both be in the same drag of flannel shirts and jeans. My feeling, however, is—and this is very hard for me—what I described earlier about seeing my lover's face entrusting me like she did, well,* I want her to take me to that place, too.

AH: Yes, but you don't want to have to deny your butchness to get there. Right?

CM: *Well, that's what's hard. To be butch, to me, is not to be a woman. The classic extreme-butch stereotype is the woman who sexually refuses another woman to touch her. It goes something like this: She doesn't want to feel her femaleness because she thinks of you as the 'real' woman and if she makes love to you, she doesn't have to feel her own body as the object of desire. She can be a kind of 'bodiless lover'. So when you turn over and want to make love to her and make her feel physically like a woman, then what she is up against is QUEER. You are a woman making love to her. She feels queerer than anything in that. Get it?*

AH: Got it. Whew!

CM: *I believe that probably from a very early age the way you conceived of yourself as female has been very different from me. We both have pain, but I think that there is a particular pain attached you identified yourself as a butch queer from an early age as I did. I didn't really think of myself as female, or male. I thought of myself as this hybrid or somethin. I just kinda thought of myself as this free agent until I got tits. Then I thought, oh oh, some problem has occurred here. . . . For me, the way you conceive of yourself as a woman and the way I am attracted to women sexually reflect that butch/femme exchange—where a woman believes herself so woman that it really makes me want her.*

But for me, I feel a lot of pain around the fact that it has been difficult for me to conceive of myself as thoroughly female in that sexual way. So retaining my 'butchness' is not exactly my desired goal. Now that, in itself is probably all heterosexist bullshit—about what a woman is supposed to be in the first place—but we are talkin about the differences between the way you and I conceive of ourselves as sexual beings.

AH: I think it does make a difference. I would argue that a good femme does not play to the part of you that hates yourself for feelin like a man, but to the part of you that knows you're a woman. Because it's absolutely critical to understand that femmes are women to women and dykes to men in the straight world. *You and I are talkin girl to girl.* We're not talkin what I was in straight life.

I was ruthless with men, sexually, around what I felt. *It was only with women I couldn't avoid opening up my need to have something more than an orgasm.* With a woman, I can't refuse to know that the possibility is just there that she'll reach me some place very deeply each time we make love. That's part of my fear of being a lesbian. I can't refuse that possibility with a woman.

You see, I want you as a woman, not as a man; but, I want you in the way *you* need to be, which may not be traditionally female, but which is the area that you express as *butch.* Here is where in the other world you have suffered the most damage. Part of the reason I love to be with butches is because I feel I repair that damage. I make it right to want me that hard. Butches have not been allowed to feel their own desire because that part of butch can be perceived by the straight world as male. I feel that as a femme I get back my femaleness and give a different definition of femaleness to a butch. That's what I mean about one of those unexplored territories that goes beyond roles but goes through roles to get there.

CM: *How I fantasize sex roles has been really different for me with different women. I do usually enter into an erotic encounter with a woman from the kind of butch place you described, but I have also felt very ripped off there, finding myself taking all the sexual responsibility. I am seriously attracted to butches sometimes. It's a different dynamic, where the sexuality may not seem as fluid or comprehensible, but I know there's a huge part of me that wants to be handled in the way I described I can handle another woman. I am very compelled toward that 'lover' posture. I have never totally reckoned with being the 'beloved' and, frankly, I don't know if it takes a butch or a femme or what to get me there. I know that it's a struggle within me and it scares the shit out of me to look at it so directly. I've done this kind of searching emotionally, but to combine sex with it seems like very dangerous stuff.*

AH: Well, I think everybody has aspects of roles in their relationships, but I feel pretty out there on the extreme end. . . . I think what feminism did, in its fear of heterosexual control of fantasy, was to say that there was almost no fantasy safe to have, where you weren't going to have to give up power or take it. There's no sexual fantasy I can think of that doesn't include some aspect of that. But I feel like I have been forced to give up some of my richest potential sexually in the way feminism has defined what is, and what's not, 'politically correct' in the sexual sphere.

CM: *Oh, of course when most feminists talk about sexuality, including lesbianism, they're not talkin about Desire, It is significant to me that I came out only when I met a good feminist, although I knew I was queer since eight or nine. That's only when I'd risk it because I wouldn't have to say it's because I want her. I didn't have to say that when she travels by me, my whole body starts throbbing.*

AH: Yes, it's just *correct*.

CM: *It was okay to be with her because we all knew men were really fuckers and there were a lot of 'okay' women acknowledging that. Read: white and educated. . . . But that's not why I 'came out'. How could I say that I wanted women so bad I was gonna die if I didn't get me one, soon! You know, I just felt the pull in the hips, right?*

AH: Yes, really— . . . well, the first discussion I ever heard of lesbianism among feminists was: 'We've been sex objects to men and where did it get us? And here when we're just learning how to be friends with other women, you got to go and sexualize it.' That's what they said! 'Fuck you. Now I have to worry about you looking down my blouse.' That's exactly what they meant. It horrified me. 'No no no,' I wanted to say, 'that's not me. I promise I'll only look at the sky. *Please* let me come to a meeting. I'm really okay. I just go to the bars and fuck like a rabbit with women who want me. You know?'

Now from the onset, how come feminism was so invested in that? They would not examine sexual need with each other except as oppressor/oppressee. Whatever your experience was you were always the victim. So how do dykes fit into that? Dykes who wanted tits, you know?

Now a lot of women have been sexually terrorized and this makes sense, their needing not to have to deal with explicit sexuality, but they made men out of every sexual dyke. 'Oh my god, *she* wants me, too!'

So it became this really repressive movement, where you didn't talk dirty and you didn't want dirty. It really became a bore. So after meetings, we *ran* to the bars. You couldn't talk about wanting a woman, except very loftily. You couldn't say it hurt at night wanting a woman to touch you. . . . I remember at one meeting breaking down after everybody was talking about being a lesbian very delicately. I began crying. I remember saying, 'I can't help it. I just . . . want her. I want to feel her.' And everybody forgiving me. It was this atmosphere of me exorcising this *crude* sexual need for women.

CM: *Shit, Amber . . . I remember being fourteen years old and there was this girl, a few years older than me, who I had this crush on. And on the last day of school, I knew I wasn't going to see her for months! We had hugged good-bye and I went straight home. Going into my bedroom, I got into my unmade bed and I remember getting the sheets, winding them into a kind of rope, and pulling them up between my legs and just holding them there under my chin. I just sobbed and sobbed because I knew I couldn't have her, maybe never have a woman to touch. It's just pure need and it's whole. It's like using sexuality to describe how deeply you need/want intimacy, passion, love.*

Most women are not immune from experiencing pain in relation to their sexuality, but certainly lesbians experience a particular pain and oppression. Let us not forget, although feminism would sometimes like us to, that lesbians are oppressed in this world. Possibly, there are some of us who came out through the movement who feel immune to 'queer attack' but not the majority of us (no matter when we came out), particularly if you have no economic buffer in this society. If you have enough money and privilege, you can separate yourself from heterosexist oppression. You can be sapphic *or somethin, but you don't have to be queer.*

The point I am trying to make is that I believe most of us harbor plenty of demons and old hurts inside ourselves around sexuality. I know, for me, that each time I choose to touch another woman, to make love with her, I feel I risk opening up that secret, harbored, vulnerable place . . . I think why feminism has been particularly attractive to many 'queer' lesbians is that it kept us in a place where we wouldn't have to look at our pain around sexuality anymore. Our sisters would just sweep us up into a movement. . . .

AH: Yes, it's not just because of feminism we were silent. Our own participation in that silence has stemmed from our absolute terror of facing that profound sexual need. Period.

There is no doubt in my mind that the feminist movement has radically changed, in an important way, everybody's concept of lesbianism, straight or gay. There's not a dyke in the world today (in or out of the bars) who can have the same conversation that she could have had ten years ago. It seeps through the water system or something, you know? Still, while lesbianism is certainly accepted in feminism, it's more as a political or intellectual concept. It seems feminism is the last rock of conservatism. It will not be sexualized. It's *prudish* in that way. . . .

Well, I won't give my sexuality up and I won't *not* be a feminist. So I'll build a different movement, but I won't live without either one.

Sometimes, I don't know how to handle how angry I feel about feminism. We may disagree on this. We have been treated in some similar ways, but our relationship to feminism has been different. Mine is a lot longer. I really have taken a lot more shit than you have, specifically around being femme. I have a personal fury. The more I got in touch with how I felt about women, what made me desire and desirable, the more I felt outside the feminist community and that was just terrifying because, on the one hand, it had given me so much. I loved it. And then, I couldn't be who I was. I felt that about class, too. I could describe my feelings about being a woman, but if I described it from my own class, using that language, my experience wasn't valid. I don't know what to do with my anger, particularly around sexuality.

CM: *Well, you've gotta be angry. . . . I mean what you were gonna do is turn off the tape, so we'd have no record of your being mad. What comes out of anger . . . if you, one woman, can say* I have been a sister all these years and you have not helped me . . . *that speaks more to the failure of all that theory and rhetoric than more theory and rhetoric.*

AH: Yeah. . . . Remember that night you and me and M. was at the bar and we were talkin about roles? She told you later that the reason she had checked out of the conversation was because she knew how much it was hurting me to talk about it. You know, I can't tell you what it meant to me for her to know that. The desperation we all felt at that table talking about sexuality was so great, wanting people to understand why we are the way we are.

CM: *I know. . . . I remember how at that forum on sadomasochism that happened last spring, how that Samois* [a lesbian-feminist S/M group in the San Francisco Bay Area] *woman came to the front of the room and spoke very plainly and clearly about feeling that through sadomasochism she was really coping with power struggles in a tangible way with her lover. That this time, for once, she wasn't leaving the relationship. I can't write her off. I believed her. I believed she was a woman in struggle. And as feminists, Amber, you and I are interested in struggle.*

THE CHALLENGE

We would like to suggest that, for dealing with sexual issues both personally and politically, women go back to consciousness-raising (CR) groups. We believe that women must create sexual theory in the same way we created feminist theory. We simply need to get together in places where people agree to suspend their sexual values, so that all of us can feel free to say what we do sexually or want to do or have done to us. We do have fear of using feelings as theory. We do not mean to imply that feelings are everything. But they are the place to start if we want to build a broad-based, cross-cultural movement that recognizes the political implications of sexual differences.

We believe our racial and class backgrounds have a huge effect in determining how we perceive ourselves sexually. Since we are not a movement that is working-class-dominated or a movement that is Third World, we both hold serious reservations as to how this new CR will be conceived. In our involvement in a movement largely controlled by white middle-class women, we feel that the values of their cultures (which may be more closely tied to an American-assimilated puritanism) have been pushed down our throats. The questions arise then: *Whose* feelings and *whose* values will be considered normative in these CR groups? If there is no room for criticism in sexual discussion around race and class issues, we foresee ourselves being gut-checked from the beginning.

We also believe our class and racial backgrounds have a huge effect in determining how we involve ourselves politically. For instance why is it that it is largely white middle-class women who form the visible leadership in the anti-porn movement? This is particularly true in the Bay Area, where the focus is less on actual violence against women and more on sexist ideology and imagery in the media. Why are women of color not particularly visible in this sex-related single-issue movement? It's certainly not because we are not victims of pornography.

More working-class and Third World women can be seen actively engaged in sex-related issues that *directly* affect the life-and-death concerns of women (abortion, sterilization abuse, health care, welfare, etc.). It's not like we choose this kind of activism because it's an 'ideologically correct' position, but because we are the ones pregnant at 16 (straight *and* lesbian), whose daughters get pregnant at 16, who get left by men without childcare, who are self-supporting lesbian mothers with no childcare, and who sign forms to have our tubes tied because we can't read English. But these kinds of distinctions between classes and colors of women are seldom absorbed by the feminist movement as it stands to date.

Essentially, we are challenging other women and ourselves to look where we haven't, to arrive at a synthesis of sexual thought that originates and develops from our varied cultural backgrounds and experiences. We refuse to be debilitated one more time around sexuality race, or class.

34 Porn

Alice Walker

Like many thoughtful women of the seventies, she had decided women were far more interesting than men. But, again like most thoughtful women, she rarely admitted this aloud. Besides, again like her contemporaries, she maintained a close connection with a man.

It was a sexual connection.

They had met in Tanzania when it was still Tanganyika; she was with an international group of students interested in health care in socialist African countries; he with an American group intent upon building schools. They met. Liked each other. Wrote five or six letters over the next seven years. Married other people. Had children. Lived in different cities. Divorced. Met again to discover they now shared a city and lived barely three miles apart.

A strong bond between them was that they respected their former spouses and supported their children. They had each arranged a joint custody settlement and many of their favorite outings were amid a clash of children. Still, her primary interest in him was sexual. It was not that she did not respect his mind; she did. It was a fine mind. More scientific than hers, more given to abstractions. But also a mind curious about nature and the hidden workings of things (it was probably this, she thought, that made him such a good lover) and she enjoyed following his thoughts about the distances of stars and whole galaxies from the earth, the difference between low clouds and high fog, and the complex survival mechanisms of the snail.

But sex together was incredibly good: like conversation with her women friends, who were never abstract, rarely distant enough from nature to be critical in their appraisal of it, and whose own mechan-

Alice Walker, 'Porn', from *You Can't Keep a Good Woman Down*, Alice Walker (Harcourt Brace & Co., 1981), 77–84,

isms for survival were hauled out in discussion for all to see. The touch of his fingers—sensitive, wise, exploring the furthest reaches of sensation—were like the tongues of women, talking, questing, searching for the *true* place, the place which, when touched, has no choice but to respond.

She was aflame with desire for him.

On those evenings when all the children were with their other parents, he would arrive at the apartment at seven. They would walk hand in hand to a Chinese restaurant a mile away. They would laugh and drink and eat and touch hands and knees over and under the table. They would come home. Smoke a joint. He would put music on. She would run water in the tub with lots of bubbles. In the bath they would lick and suck each other, in blissful delight. They would admire the rich candle glow on their wet, delectably earth-toned skins. Sniff the incense—the odor of sandal and redwood. He would carry her in to bed.

Music. Emotion. Sensation. Presence.
Satisfaction like rivers
flowing and silver.

On the basis of their sexual passion they built the friendship that sustained them through the outings with their collective children, through his loss of a job (temporarily), through her writer's block (she worked as a free-lance journalist), through her bouts of frustration and boredom when she perceived that, in conversation, he could only *be* scientific, only *be* abstract, and she was, because of her intrepid, garrulous women friends—whom she continued frequently, and often in desperation, to see—used to so much more.

In short, they had devised an almost perfect arrangement.

One morning at six o'clock they were making 'morning love'. 'Morning love' was relaxed, clearheaded. Fresh. No music but the birds and cars starting. No dope.

They came within seconds of each other.

This inspired him. He thought they could come together.

She was sated, indifferent, didn't wish to think about the strain.

But then he said: 'Did I ever show you [he knew he hadn't] my porn collection?'

'What could it be?' she inevitably wondered. Hooked.

His hands are cupping her ass. His fingers like warm grass or warm and supple vines. One thumb—she fancies she feels the whorled print—makes a circle in the wetness of her anus. She shivers. His tongue gently laps her vulva as it enters her, his top lip caressing the clitoris. For five minutes she is moving along as usual. Blissed *out*, she thinks to herself. Then she stops.

'What have you got?' she has asked him.

'This,' he replied. 'And this.'

. . .

A gorgeous black woman who looks like her friend Fannie has a good friend (white boy from her hometown down South) who is basically gay. Though—. 'Fannie' and let us call him 'Fred' pick up a hick tourist in a bar. They both dig him, the caption says. He is not gorgeous. He is short, pasty, dirty blond. Slightly cross-eyed. In fact, looks retarded. Fred looks very much the same. 'Fannie' invites them to her place where without holding hands or eating or bathing or putting on music, they strip and begin to fondle each other. 'Fannie' looks amused as they take turns licking and sucking her. She smiles benignly as they do the same things to each other. . . .

'And this.'

A young blonde girl from Minnesota [probably kidnapped, she thinks, reading] *is far from home in New York, lonely and very horny. She is befriended by two of the blackest men on the East Coast. (They had been fighting outside a bar and she had stopped them by flinging her naive white self into the fray.) In their gratitude for her peacemaking they take her to their place and do everything they can think of to her. She grinning liberally the whole time. Finally they make a sandwich of her: one filling the anus and the other the vagina, so that all that is visible of her body between them is a sliver of white thighs.* [And we see that these two pugilists have finally come together on something.]

She is sitting with her back against the headboard of the bed so that her breasts hang down. This increases sensation in her already very aroused nipples. He crawls up to her on all fours like a gentle but ravenous bear and begins to nuzzle her. He nuzzles and nuzzles until her nipples virtually aim themselves at him. He takes one into his mouth. She begins to flow.

But the flow stops

Once he said to her: 'I could be turned on by bondage' No, he said 'by a "little light bondage"'. She had told him of a fantasy in which she lay helpless, bound, waiting for the pleasure worse than death.

There is no plot this time. No story of an improbable friendship down South, no goldilocks from the Midwestern plains. Just page after page of women: yellow, red, white, brown, black [she had let him tie her up very loosely once; it was not like her fantasy at all. She had wanted to hold him, caress him, snuggle and cuddle] *bound, often gagged. Their legs open. Forced to their knees.*

He is massaging the back of her neck, her shoulders. Her buttocks. The backs of her thighs. She has bent over a hot typewriter all day and is tired. She sinks into the feeling of being desired and pampered. Valued. Loved. Soon she is completely restored. Alert. She decides to make love to him. She turns over. She cradles his head in her arms. Kisses his forehead. His eyes. Massages his scalp with her fingers. Buries her nose in his neck. Kisses his neck. Caresses his chest. Flicks his nipples, back and forth, with her tongue. Slowly she moves down his body. His penis (which he thinks should not be called 'penis'—'a white boy's word'; he prefers 'cock') is standing. She takes it—she is on her knees—into her mouth.

She gags.

The long-term accommodation that protects marriage and other such relationships is, she knows, forgetfulness. She will forget what turns him on.

'No, no,' he says, very sorry he has shown her his collection; in fact, vowing passionately to throw it away. 'The point is for *you* to be turned on by it *too!*'

. . .

She thinks of the lovely black girl—whom she actually thinks of as her friend Fannie—and is horrified. What is Fannie doing in such company? she wonders. She panics as he is entering her. Wait! she says, and races to the phone.

The phone rings and rings.

Her friend Fannie is an out of-work saleswoman. She is also a lesbian. She proceeds to write in her head a real story about Fannie based on what she knows. Her lover at work on her body the whole time.

Fannie and Laura share a tiny loft apartment. They almost never make love. Not because they are not loving—they do a lot of caressing and soothing—but they are so guilty about what they feel that sexuality has more or less dried up. [She feels her own juices drying up at this thought.]

They have both been out of work for a long time. Laura's mother is sick. Fannie's young brother has entered Howard University. There is only Fannie to send him money for books, clothes and entertainment. Fannie is very pretty but basically unskilled in anything but selling, and salespersons by the thousands have been laid off in the recession. Unemployment is not enough.

But Fannie is really very beautiful. Men stop her on the street all the time to tell her so. It is the way they chose to tell her so, when she was barely pubescent, that makes her return curses for 'compliments' even today.

But these men would still stop her on the street, offer her money 'for a few hours' work.'. . .

By now she has faked all kinds of things, and exhausted her lover. He is sound asleep. She races to Fannie and Laura's apartment. Sits waiting for them on the stoop. Finally they come home from seeing a Woody Allen movie. They are in high spirits, and besides, because she shares part of her life with a man, care much less for her than she does for them. They yawn loudly, kiss her matronizingly on both cheeks, and send her home again.

Now, when he makes love to her, she tries to fit herself into the white-woman, two-black-men story. But who will she be? The men look like her brothers, Bobo and Charlie. She is disgusted, and worse, bored, by Bobo and Charlie. The white woman is like the young girl who, according to the *Times, was* seduced off a farm in Minnesota by a black pimp and turned out on 42nd Street. She cannot stop herself from thinking: *Poor: Ignorant: Sleazy: Depressing.* This does not excite or stimulate.

He watches her face as he makes expert love to her. He knows his technique is virtually flawless, but he thinks perhaps it can be improved. Is she moving less rhythmically under him? Does she seem distracted? There seems to be a separate activity in her body, to which she is attentive, and which is not connected to the current he is sending through his fingertips. He notices the fluttering at the corners of her eyelids. Her eyes could fly open at any moment, he thinks, and look objectively at him. He shudders. Holds her tight.

He thinks frantically of what she might be thinking of him. Realizes he is moving in her *desperately*, as if he is climbing the walls of a closed building. As if she reads his mind, she moans encouragingly. But it is a distracted moan—that offends him.

He bites the pillow over her head: Where is she? he thinks. Is she into fantasy or not?

He must be.

He slips her into the role of 'Fannie' with some hope. But nothing develops. As 'Fannie' she refuses even to leave her Southern town. Won't speak to, much less go down on, either of the two gays.

He races back and forth between an image of her bound and on her knees, to two black men and a white woman becoming acquainted outside a bar.

This does not help.

Besides, she is involved in the activity inside herself and holding him—nostalgically.

He feels himself sliding down the wall that is her body, and expelled from inside her.

A Little Hungarian Pornography

Péter Esterházy

PREFACE

Life in a dictatorship is not the same as life in a democracy. You live in a different way. And you write in a different way, too. You also read in a different way. And though literary considerations everywhere are equally 'lasting as steel', literature is nevertheless affected by the just-mentioned difference. Some books are irrevocably the prisoners of the time in which they were written. The author hopes (not that he's got a choice) that his book is perhaps an exception, that time has not done too much damage. Of course, all sorts of shackles and loose bindings flapping this way and that are in evidence throughout its pages, which, to say the least, have their own special logic.

This is the author's most East-European book, and his most helpless, too. It was written in 1982–3, in the overripe period of the Kádár era, under small, Hungarian, pornographic circumstances where pornography should be understood as meaning lies, the lies of the body, the lies of the soul, our lies. Let us imagine, if we can, a country where everything is a lie, where the lack of democracy is called socialist democracy, economic chaos socialist economy, revolution anti-revolution, and so on.

The dictatorship of the time was a real dictatorship, though it was neither bloody nor crude. For all practical purposes, it meant the potential threat of dictatorship, a ubiquitous and unavoidable threat that tainted every moment of our lives. *If*, you thought to yourself, *if it should happen*. And you felt helpless. But usually there was no *if*. *It* did not happen.

Péter Esterházy, 'A Little Hungarian Pornography', from *A Little Hungarian Pornography*, Péter Esterházy (Quartet Books/Northwestern University Press, 1997), 106–16 and Preface, reprinted by permission of the author and the publisher.

Such a total, all-encompassing lie, when from history through green-pea soup, when from our father's eyebrows and our lover's lap everything is a lie, not to mention this theoretical yet very tangible presence of threat, all this makes for a highly poetic situation. The language of the real dictatorship of the fifties was silence, keeping mum. That of the seventies and the eighties was the avoidance of speech, not talking about *it*. The time was not yet ripe to speak out 'properly'. But you could at least *hint* that you could not speak out properly. Under the circumstances, the literature of the period automatically took advantage of the aesthetic possibility suggested by a constant cramp in one's stomach. It took advantage of the elemental terror that certain words hold (Stalin, Rákosi, ÁVÓ). It used terror as an aesthetic creative force.

This book was written during a so-called time of transition (though who has ever heard of a time that was not transitional?) when Hungarian literature (or part of it at least) was fed up to here with this encoded, oblique, reading-between-the-lines type of writing and collusion, and rejected the help coming from the cramp in the stomach, all the while taking advantage of it, inadvertently of course.

Putting an end to this bad situation should have been the business of the readers and not the writers. It should have been something for society to attend to. But at the time, the readers (for reasons of their own) did not yet want to chase the Russians out of Hungary.

Whether in the end it was the Hungarians who chased the Russians out or not is debatable. But leave they did. And with that, some of the political edge of the book, if ever there was any, was blunted. The author nevertheless relies on the circumstance that all countries everywhere will surely have small Hungarian-type pornographic stories of their own.

Péter Esterházy

III
('?')

> Of course there are then no questions left, and this itself is the answer.
>
> (Wittgenstein)

What are we saying?

Take off your glasses? Come clean, sir? We know everything anyhow? Don't shit in your pants, Kossuth?[1]. Look, little schmuck, we know the sun is shining and we know it is raining? Come, come? Why this show of obstinacy?

The speaker uses the interrogative sentence to express his thirst for knowledge and to call upon his listener to quench said thirst? As a rule, the speaker's point of view is dubious in one respect only? Generally, this is a lie? When we feel the necessity of looking for a loophole in this manner, shouldn't we feel honour bound to admit: we've got nothing left in stock? Which is expressed by the most emphatic word in the interrogative sentence?

All that beating about the bush, where did it get us?[2] Where is Pálfi by now and what is he about? You crave rotten meat? With loving care for gravy? How is your worship's disposition for barren maidens tonight? Is the wolfman's power limited to a specific terrain, or is it universal?[3] How did distance beckon to Puss 'n Boots and take him away from us?

The riddle does not exist? If a question can be framed at all, it is also *possible* to answer it? For doubt can exist only where a question exists, a question only where an answer exists, and an answer only where something *can be said*?

I am in the *proper* place? I am here? I'm okay, I go for myself in a really big way? Are you open-hearted? A gentleman? Bellicose, proud, fearless and above-board? Brash, defiant, pleasure-seeking, apprehensive? Baleful? Obstinate, silent, withdrawn, a bit facetious, even? Is that why you lack trust? Are independence and autonomy your greatest treasures? Are you a freedom-loving Kurucz?

At the foot of the tall, luxuriant pines the bit of quivering snow appears ludicrous, the faded forest litter jotting through, while on the branches of the scant thicket the flakes of snow tremble like a fancy net that's seen better days? In the gardens the tenacious bindweed creeps up the birch trunks while haphazard spaces open up to make room for the piercing rays of the sun among the boughs?

The backs of our scawny hags are steaming?

But if one or another of our capricious clouds-in-the-sky so enjoins, a dull drabness descends swiftly on the land, greyness coming upon greyness; only very high up in the firmament does a hint of colour appear, a blemished shade of red, giving the land an even more sordid aspect?

Tortured, tormented, like a weeping eye? The traditional Magyar costumes, see them dangle from the branches of the big, leafy trees, an elaborately trimmed cloak, a short *mente* lined with fox fur, a kerchief wrought with spun gold, a wide pleated skirt and a cherry-coloured hussar's pelisse, of velvet? The grey slush settles on the soft leather boots? *Do you approve of this*? Conversely, do you disapprove? You couldn't care less? Not a fig? Or you know not what to think? You have never experienced great difficulties, you have never been made to run the gauntlet? Well? The memory of a childhood humiliation, at least?

A helpless *shifting in place*? A creaking parquet floor? Mayonnaise potatoes slithering around your plate? Have you been made to eat humble pie? How many? Or have they broken off your horns? Been cut down to size? Life's thrown you *a bad curve*? In grammar school? In high school?

Once, for instance, you had to bring the skeleton of a frog to biology class, *quasi* as your reward? A mistake, having joined that stupid study circle? You should've had more pluck? No use crying over spilled milk? Wandering aimlessly by the Danube between the Árpád Bridge, named after the first Magyar chieftain, and that other, christened after Liberty, the one outcome of which was that you became the *terror of the fishermen*, which ain't nothin'? In the end it hit you and you drove out to City Park lake? Cussing your pretty biology teacher in no uncertain terms, you strolled along the stone footbridge while in the distance two girls giggled in a boat? One of them was Drahosch?

Leaning over the side, you rubbed your groin against the balustrade hard as you could and for as long as you could? Working in minuscule, invisible circles, you clenched your teeth while your poor little heart went pit-a-pat? Frightened like a doe, you glanced around but could see nothing suspicious? *A stone groin?* Well worth it, shame notwithstanding? *As a general rule do you suppress or sublimate*? Work *through* it? Work it *in*? Artistic form? Or ethical bedrock? Are you plotting, scheming, conspiring, double-dealing *amiably*? Setting traps in the old manner? Stab in the back, abort and torpedo? Are you some sort of vermin? A rat? Or the transition that eases remembering?

What did you do the first time it hit you? You were 19 and you were sitting for all you were worth on the school john and when you got home you tried not to look anyone in the eye?

Are you passionate?

Kurucz and passion, Kurucz and manly verve are as inseparable as the Bobsy twins? Are you in favour of manly verve *without democracy*? Have you ever had a real democratic experience to begin with? Do you think it is important that you should?

Do you have (have had, could have) such an experience under the following conditions: self-delusion—bloody battles—nationalistic sentiments (a little manual democracy)—grammar?

What are the symptoms? What position are your legs in?

Does it give you a thrill? Have you, jocularly speaking, laid an egg and liked it? You wouldn't give it up for a bushel of gold? You're as pleased with it as a fool is with his own shadow or a blind man with a wooden penny? Or is it six in the morning and half a dozen at night? Perish the thought?

Even the scum are delighted?

Never say die? Or is that going too far? How far? Everything leading to the dictatorship of the proletariat is heavenly, divine? Of course, the end does not justify the means? (Who knows why, but some go in for full openness and abandon, while others opt for constraint, dogmatism, it being their hobby-horse? Still others fall to their knees and raise their voices in supplication while, conversely, certain people, their feet beating about in the air, wheeze with every breath as if they were playfully practising standing on their heads?)

First impressions can be decisive? The times? '49, '67, '19, '45, '56, '68? Do you play the lottery, madame? There is always a number, *rational, positive*, even *whole*, which is surrounded by either silence or fanfare whereas it should be reflection, deliberation and ethics? And the like?
To be a democrat means first and foremost not to be afraid?
Let us speak for once the way the Lord would have us?
The time is not ripe, friends?

Who're you calling friend, friend? Oh, don't, sweetie pie, you mustn't? As we straddle the borderline of our knowledge and opportunities, mum's the word? Let us predicate the way we are used to? I'm okay, you're okay, he goes for himself in a really big way? We should make bold? Clear out of the way, lose our edge, lose interest, denounce, take to wing, wander about aimlessly, die of mortal fear? Settle for the common denominator? Impose burdens, fume with rage, shy away, dance the shilly-shally, hold out to the last breath, be wary and circumspect? Or *guardedly* credulous?

Let's synchronise our intentions?

Nurse a yellow streak, go for it, worm our way, side-stepping, flake off; get the hell out? Slavering and drivelling at the mouth? Full peace-environment, peace supplies? You betcha? We should stammer and stutter, act deplorably, colour our efforts individually, be *demi-mondain*, go for the fun? Oh, ye crowds of rags and patches, frail, sinful and beggarly, what about it? I hate you, my homeland, may a fly walk across your open eyes?

What's going on here?

Where here? Let us make a fuss, be base, not worth our weight in salt? You are content? Oh, young sir, how refined, the way your cute little heart doth pound pound pound? Or will this a discreet shading yet receive? The Kurucz craves understanding? There's such a whole lot we could give one another?

In short, we're easy as pie? A song stands ready to burst trippingly from the tongue? THE WATCHWORD: INGRATIATE? Democracy is rebirth, the awakening of life, springtime, pleasure, radiant, exciting, exquisite, outta sight? The ideal way to relax after a hard day's day? Who're you kidding?

In your joy you wag your own tail? Wiggle your ass? Or eager and explosive, generally grab yourself a woman on the run? What do you think: does the dictatorship of the proletariat *happen* to you, so to speak, or, conversely, are you making *it* happen? The woman does not speak, nor does she move, she merely grabs the corner of the hearth, lowering her eyes like one who does not mind what is going on behind her in the night? She imagines what she hankers for? An old hag enters to put more wood on the fire? When she sees the two of you, her face breaks into a devilish grimace, but you don't mind her presence in the least, and grinning she cackles, *ride her, your excellency, ride my good, kind mistress*? The woman straightens up and, sighing, fatigued, shaking at the knees, her innards battered, a moist, wet smile playing on her lips, she lowers her big round eyes and stumbles out?

The second shall be Clara of the eloquent behind, grab her boobs, see if she minds? Her beaver scrapes the Kurucz's belly?

I prefer to be wearing tight blue jeans, sometimes I apply baby oil to my tits and belly, and I don't mind telling you what it feels like when I unscrew the head of the shower hose—a rose is a rose is a rose—a gallant Kurucz am I? (*Wow!!! what a question, even with my panties on . . .*) Timid and anxiety-ridden, easygoing and blindly trusting, morose and spiteful, my intellect subdivided, working in large units, even-keeled, simple, compact? I can heave a donkey off the ground by the tail? I can take care of myself, I keep in tune with my self and my body, I am *here*, I'm okay, I go for myself in a really big way? We declare war on lies, hypocrisy, dullness and cowardice? We are shooting at random, not so much at given targets, but rather to impress the populace we've jolted out of its slumber? To disturb the peace?

It is time somebody tied a knot on this endless string of thread? Sons-of-bitches-of-the-soul?

Embedded in cultural history, the balls nailed down?

Trust to time to find a way? From the walls of the former besieged castles (*ex:* Brasov), unflagging and obstinate, the rain continues to wash away the traces, the centuries dull the high brilliance of the towers, the firmament like a piece of pergamon crowded with writing a long, long time ago, at the bottom the seal crumbling like the disc of the sun going down in a storm before anyone could have supposed that at dawn the fog would lift from the funereal plains, the flax open its blue flowers, and the dew wash clean the berries glistening from their poisonous deadly nightshade? It is cold, says Miska Halassi, then turns away from the window? The wind creeps through the thick walls?

My lips chapped, I stand in front of the large oval tray, of silver, hung on the wall in place of a mirror? It hardly distorts at all, my face dignified and pale, *beaten silver*, as night descends? Outside the black trees disappear, the hard-packed snow gleams icy-white, the loathsome Labancz lurk on the edge of the woods, sweet German lords adorned with ribands, raven-black grenadiers, cavaliers, lean-flanked dogs, hairy-legged canines with rib of woven twigs, the moonlight gleaming on their eye-teeth, the melancholy woven of this light, the wild pack of moon-coloured dogs? I smooth my hand over the indelible grooves on my forehead, an uncertain fire crackling in the hearth, what ignominious, abject poverty!—am I hoping to sail away on a sea of bliss?

Will you kindly provide a couple of *sketches* of situations in which you saw a chance, however slight, for the dictatorship of the proletariat? In these uncertain times you can see by anybody, and try, too, what's in people's hearts, who you should bend a knee to, or bow your head?

Are they teasing your sense of justice? How? Hypothetically speaking, for the sake of argument? Does this particular form of manly verve mean a lot to you? How much of a lot? They're teasing your linguistic sense too? D'ya dig it daddy-o like, so much fiddle-faddle, or enraged and terrified, your life's blood is drained from you?

How do you achieve the delicate balance of your sense of justice? Lengthy shilly-shallying, indirect teasing? Is an alert conscience of the essence, or just a matter of custom? What's yours like? Groggy? It even snores? And now a word or two about lullabies? Well? The projection of colourful wish-fulfilment images on the water-stained wall of the imagination? Or in the wake of a substantial surprise attack from the flanks, holding the poor somnolent city to ransom, do you prefer to reduce its stone walls to rubble and carry off the city elders?

If in the midst of a bloody battle a democratic experience should happen to advance on the scene, what do you prefer, the politics of the hard fist—the soft—the fast—the slow? Complete or partial penetration into problems, penetration, then holding still? Do you give primacy to a thought's greatness and shape? Which in your opinion is *most fortunate:* the long and traditional, the short and traditional, the thin but resourceful, and so on?

Or lying low and holding your breath? Waiting breathlessly for that breathless moment? At which juncture you unwittingly play with the bonds of social responsibility? I should have it so good? Do you like to do it from the back? Are you often asked to? In what manner? Who asks you? Does the little devil with the horns and hoofs appear from the murky corners of nondescript bus stations? Or do you happen to be sitting with your beautiful sweetheart at a table spread with a yellow cloth, a candle burning with a sputter because the wick is long, an accordion player seated nearby and a single man on the drums, as in the manner of two old maids you discuss the weather, the soccer scores and the difficulty of making ends meet—when one of the waiters describes a big circle with a hazel switch? Whereupon the food turns saltless in the blinking of an eye, the women can't conceive even amidst pain, all becoming fertile, all of them, and the candles stink? But it mustn't phaze you, the two of you should just look on? The waiters wink encouragingly, the accordion player, jocularly speaking, takes over, circling dreamily among the tables, sprinkling white powder from his filthy pocket, in all probability salt? To quiet her we grasp our beautiful sweetheart's trembling alabaster hands? The vodka glasses depleted, the marrow desiccated in the bone, vermin in the potato croquettes, the griddle cakes crumbling, pink worms in the meat, the liver dumplings dry as stone?

The accordion player throws outdated slang around, real cool, the single drummer is real cool, an awkward virtuoso, while at our table the waiter bows confidently and begs your pardon for the slight *malheur*? The accordion player breaks into the national anthem for all he's worth, with possibly even a false note slipping in now and then, and with an obsequious smile the waiter asks whether your sweetheart mightn't be *needing* something *more*, whereupon you spring to your feet and with conviction though awkwardly slap the waiter's face? Then they beat the shit out of you?

Are other forms of manly verve and passion (social work, tree planting, aiding the underprivileged, the peace movement, retirement, etc.) important to you? Or would you rather, *sans gene*, be a party to a bit of irredentist nationalism? Onward to the breach, dear friends?

Are you a regular? Since when? Those droll years again, in ascending order? Does this affect your passions in any way? Have you any experience being *irregular*? Have you dipped the cold steel in anyone's bosom yet? What was it like? Did it affect your relationship, and if so, in what manner? How 'bout the trade union? Are you a materialist, or do you prefer to turn in supplication to the god of the Magyars while you brazenly blaspheme against the Virgin Mary herself? Conversely, would you rather keep all eventualities in mind? If you are a lone wolf, to what extent does this depend on choice? Have you any idea who is whose wolf? Who is whose what?[4]

Are you in favour of internecine war? Hungarian scratching out the eye of Hungarian? Of course, who *is* Hungarian? All enemies—yours—are *ab ovo* homeless villains? Are you of Hungarian mother born? Did you suck milk that was *likewise*? You, if they ask you nice, will give the shirt off your back (by the way, are you familiar with Hungarian sayings?), but not your wild oats? You're of two minds? Is the second of any use? Any use at all? You cry, laughing into your beer? A stranger to fear and trembling? With no need of a pardon? How about an interpreter? You carry your heart on the tip of your tongue? It is easy to seat you on a high horse but hard to get you off? Might you be wearing blinders?

If for some reason and regardless of the price (!?) you are opposed to slaughter because a severed arm, even if bourgeois, makes you retch and the sight of a man's guts hanging out of his belly neither fills you with joy, nor can you see any benefit in it—in short, if you are a squeamish humanitarian—what do you think of this state of suspended animation? Would you recommend it to others? What are your plans? How much longer?

The defiant troops come sweeping down the gulf, the stirrups working overtime, the hoofs thundering, the gentle valley reigning over the peaks; a bullet whizzes past with noble death for its passenger—but you just stand around, feeling desperate at best? You think we should crack down on this sort of national passion? When? In early childhood? Grammar school? High school? Or if not, why? It already is?

Notes

1. Lajos Kossuth: leader of the 1848–49 Hungarian freedom fights against the House of Habsburg which, although they produced some impressive partial results, ended, as always, etc., etc., etc.
2. Oh, all that indolent beating about the bush, it got us nowhere.
3. A difficult question to answer (given the present state of things).
4. If the text is from the thirties of the 20th century, then this is an oblique thrust at Admiral Horthy (who headed the country's semi-bourgeois, semi-democratic government), but in a way so that his fascistoid prime minister Gömbös should also get the message. If not, not.

Newsletter

Sexual Workers from AMSS Introduce a Demand Platform

Association of Women 'Flowers of Stone' for the Dignity of Sexual Workers

The Demand platform is composed from now on of reflected and organized processes generated by sexual workers in their fight to be recognized as full fledged citizens.

The former municipal governments directed repressive and discriminatory actions towards sexual workers, who are blamed for the existence of prostitution. With these actions, activists, who by means of direct or indirect challenge to the constant violations to women's human rights, have been immobilized.

With this current municipal gesture, objective conditions have been created for the participation of citizens. From this point on, sexual workers, after achieving their autonomy as such, have begun a process of reflection — an action that would allow them to further the elaboration of important proposals concerning prostitution.

We are aware that the institution known as prostitution comes from and is developed by the patriarchal system, and that it pre-dates from ancient times. It's an institution that exploits women, and thus why we are engaged in the search for better alternatives based on the following criteria:

(a) preventative actions directed to children and to the young in the most vulnerable sectors so that they can live and develop in conditions that were lacked by many of the current sexual workers;

Association of Women 'Flowers of Stone', 'Newsletter: Sexual Workers from AMSS Introduce a Demand Platform', reprinted with their permission.

(b) close attention to current sexual workers so that their human rights can be respected;
(c) special attention to women who wish to enter voluntarily into another way of life.

We believe firmly that the consolidation of democracy in the city of San Salvador as well as on the national level won't be possible without everyone's participation in every social sector and especially without the participation of those who have been historically discriminated against and marginalized.

Prostitution in Latin America and in the Caribbean

Economist Zoraida Ramirez Rodriguez for the Coalition Against the Trafficking of Women

Zoraida Ramirez Rodriguez

(For the campaign against Sexual Exploitation in Venezuela, 2/8/98)

Speaking about prostitution's causes in an isolated manner, avoiding the origin and the effects of sexual exploitation of women wouldn't produce an ideal instrument for this important event, therefore that is the reason why I will try to consider these aspects throughout the conference.

ORIGIN, CAUSES, AND EFFECTS

It's necessary to define the Patriarchal System and Ideology as the origin of prostitution in the world. By dedicating ourselves to the works of investigation and action inside prostitution, we will achieve easily the short, medium, and long-term objectives, if we begin with patriarchy's identification with the area that insists in perpetuating the slavery of women.

The causes that we may find might be structural, based upon patriarchy and conjectures founded on some observed characteristics in some cross-sections of the population: the level of education, the breakdown of the family, the deterioration and/or inversion of moral values, destitution, hunger, the many levels of poverty, and ignorance about Human Rights. In a brief historical analysis about prostitution and the women therein we saw that a high number were illiterate. This

Zoraida Ramirez Rodriguez, 'Prostitution in Latin America and the Caribbean', previously unpublished, reprinted by permission of the author.

relationship was always present among women; the lesser a woman's level of education, the greater her poverty, her destitution, the corrosion of her moral values, and the greater the likelihood that she came from a broken home. The actual statistics of prostitution show women of different social rankings, and far from being illiterate, sometimes they are students in universities, colleges, and high school. We also find that the concept of poverty varies based on the region in which it's studied and the culture in which it takes place. Finally, we can't forget that during the last few decades, well-developed countries have imposed a model of development upon Third World countries, which in a single blow smashed the essence of human beings and opened a passageway between those who live in the Northern Hemisphere and those of us who are located in the Southern Hemisphere. It is thus the subjugation imposed by the International Monetary Fund and the World Bank, in order to perpetuate poverty, a concept that becomes more feminized in all of our nations.

And since there are no effects without causes, due to that ignorance about Human Rights which we should impugn, we will find each time more women that are being exploited through prostitution that are organizing in order to demand 'better contractuals' and thus continue to be exploited. Among the other results are the many variations of prostitution that don't escape from other regions in the world, including among them a presence within certain technological advances, and among others countless abhorrent practices with human beings.

We can also include as an effect traumatized sexuality, expressed in different ways, beginning with the low self-esteem that occurs after being made into a sexual object, up to the chains that we have been conditioned to accept succinctly by means of, among others, consumerism.

CONSUMERISM, CONSUMPTION AND THE ECONOMIC PROCESS

Women become the society's object of consumption by means of consumerism, and are then exploited sexually, among other ways, by the patriarchy. Consumerism can be defined solely as excessive consumption that doesn't have as a means the satisfaction of the consumer's basic needs. Consumerism has several causes, among them stand out: the buying of goods and services in order to attain status, competition among peers, trying to be fashionable, the conditioning effects of publicity, or as a substitution for human feelings such as love or affection.

There is, however, a difference between that which we have just seen as consumerism and that which we will designate as consumption. The latter refers to the final act of the economic process and consists in the personal and direct use of goods and services produced to satisfy basic human necessities. For economy, needs are a 'lack of something'. For Francisco Zamora, 'need is fundamentally a sense of lacking, of a lack of means, the psychological reaction that provokes in the subject a rupture in the balance between the internal forces of their organism and those of the cosmic medium which surrounds them'.[1] In other words, needs can be defined as certain cravings experienced by human beings which cause a lack of balance which must be re-established as soon as the agent of satisfaction is administered.

Many specialists of the economy producer of consumers (a term which we could use to identify the 'excessive' consumer, or those who are trapped by consumerism), propose that the use of the term 'consumerism' is only to criticize the free production market, that those who are anti-consumerists are moralists and invoke morality to create a controversy out of this productive process, only to question the capacity of acquisition by those who demand consumer goods.

The Economic Process generates by means of publicity a mutual influence that operates in every society, and that is transmitted from person to person creating a similar response. Then begins the conditioning designed for the consumption of goods of certain brands, colours, models, and the prices never go in favour of the society in question, but rather in favour of those who are the owners of the means of production. This process doesn't consider the consumer's standard of living, and therefore their economic capacity to satisfy their vital needs, and thus by the traps of exploitation, the growing lines of consumerism are allowed.

PROSTITUTION, POVERTY, CONSUMERISM

In all of those populations in the diverse regions of Latin America, and others in the Third World, we witness an alarming increase in prostitution, poverty, and consumerism. The economic and political inequalities have become more intensified. Women are discriminated against more frequently, and their true participation in the process of development becomes more limited, but opening a 'puerta franca' to prostitution. The social means of communication and publicity situate them solely as and for sexual objects. The woman's body becomes a piece of merchandise that can be bought and sold by means of prostitution inside any system of production wherever a patriarchy may be present.

Concurrently, in Latin America and in the Caribbean the lack of opportunities and options for women so that they can live at least in minimally satisfactory conditions has increased. The economic marginality in which many families live becomes greater each time, due to the unequal distribution of the national income, holding of land (the same for both the rural and urban sectors), racism, and economical politics imposed by the different governments, in order to pay the exorbitant External Debt. The Economic Plans imposed by the state, after watching their social results become poorer, women in prostitution, young girls and boys on the streets, etc., let us define economic planning as a simple technique, that limits our active and conscious participation to achieve the well-being of all of the members of society. Our realities in Latin America and in the Caribbean come expressed with macroeconomic indicators that hide the truth. The supposed allocations for education, health care, culture, housing, and scientific investigations are reduced annually. The job market becomes more closed to women, especially when there is a preference for women who are between 18 and 35 years of age, that may be single and of a 'pleasant appearance'. Our children and young people are in every region 70 per cent of the total population, and lack the appropriate funding for a good education and a system of health care. We women are already 51 per cent of the global populace.

But women, young women, and girls, without opportunities of employment and study, have to assert their income in order to survive through prostitution and all of the variants therein: sexual tourism, the prostitution of children, militarized prostitution, informal prostitution, the traffic of women and girls on a local and international level, print pornography, as well as in videos, cassettes, the Internet, etc.

Sexual exploitation has become an industry in a society of consumption, the demand and supply being met through transnational enterprises and their affiliates. The female population is 'trained' so as to indulge in a cult of beauty for their bodies, and the subterfuge of which the feminine sexuality is at man's disposal. In order to consume their goods and immediate necessities, such as food, housing, and clothing, women and girls that don't have a source of employment, make prostitution their way of life. In the cases pertaining to high society, they use their income to satisfy their comfort, situations that have been generated by consumerism and that easily can be seen in every population that has prostitution and whose mark is felt on the higher classes. Both real and created needs use prostitution to maintain unbreakable chains of 'reproducing the creation of value for the country', and thus the patriarchy recurs to the systems of production to maintain women's condition. Other institutions allow the patriarchy to manifest itself as well: churches, governments, corporations, monarchies, etc.

Both women and girls are the first victims claimed by sexual exploitation due to the fragility they embody before it. Sex has become a consumer good that produces women and girls within a 'sexual industry generated source of *employment* in the process of crisis'. This creates within the subject of exploitation (women and girls) an income akin to a salary, perhaps the reason for its existence. Many of the organized women in our region which are exploited through prostitution call themselves 'sexual workers', without thinking of the consequences, that by so doing they perpetuate their own exploitation.

From the Coalition Against the Trafficking of Women, we are developing campaigns to inform the female populace about their Human Rights, the trap of consumerism, the myths of prostitution and of masculine and feminine sexuality, since these are the fundamental bases for the eradication of all manners in which sex becomes merchandise. This in unison, of course, to the public demand before their governing agents to create political structures by which the conditions of poverty can be improved, and through which the satisfaction of the basic human needs: nourishment, health care, housing, education, clothing, shoes, minimum communication can be attained, as well as the security to have access to the basic satisfying agents: affection, participation, creation, identity, and liberty.

Note

1. Economic Theory Treaty, Francisco Zamora, Administration of Economic Culture, (Mexico, 1977).

From Research to Action

Foundation for Women in Thailand

The second phase of the Research and Action project on Traffic in Women (RATW), from November 1993 to October 1994, focused on working co-operatively with women in their communities to address the issue of trafficking. The primary objective was to identify appropriate strategies, both at the village level and nationally, to combat the traffic in women. The approach was to be participatory, that is, led by the people most directly affected by trafficking. The role of the research team was to assist with devising and developing such strategies. This was to include spreading information, raising awareness, and organising groups to decide on and to implement the strategies. This chapter details the results of this phase of the project.

Three villages were selected; the choice was based on the extent of trafficking and on the degree of interest shown by village women. Project activities were also pursued in the urban centres of Bangkok and Pattaya. In the north, the project team worked in Rim Mon village, which had a long history of migration for prostitution and a large number of returned sex workers. In the north-east, Ton Yang village was included, but Khon Na was replaced by a neighbouring village, 'Na Thong'. Na Thong was the home of 15 young women trafficked to Japan between 1989 and 1991, and the mothers of these women had contacted the research team for assistance in bringing them home. This seemed a good starting point from which to develop strategies for resistance to trafficking. In Pattaya, the researchers worked with local sex workers; in Bangkok, mostly with agency personnel.

Foundation for Women in Thailand, 'From Research to Action', from *The Traffic in Women: Human Realities of the International Sex Trade*, by Siriporn Skrobanek, Nattaya Boonpakdi, and Chutima Janthakeero, (Zed Books, 1997), 89–97, reprinted by permission of the publisher.

MOTHERS IN NA THONG VILLAGE

When the research team first visited Na Thong, ten mothers there had lost contact with daughters who had gone to Japan. They wanted help in bringing their daughters home. They had borrowed money, sold cattle or mortgaged land to pay the broker's fee of 25,000 baht (US$l,042). The broker, who lived locally and was a relative of one mother, had told them that their daughters would be working in a restaurant for 20,000 baht a month. The women now believed that they were working as prostitutes. The promised remittances had failed to arrive, and the debts incurred at home were still unpaid. The mothers did not dare ask for assistance from government officers, because they had been warned against sending their daughters away.

A public tribunal on traffic in women, organised by the Asian Women's Human Rights Council, was held in Tokyo in March 1994, and this provided an opportunity for the group to talk openly about their experiences. The research team had suggested that they send a representative to Tokyo, and Nee was elected as spokesperson.

Before she went, Nee met all the mothers to discuss their experiences. Some had already changed their minds about wanting their daughters to return, either because they had heard from them in the meantime or because they had received money from Japan. One daughter had written to her mother, warning her to trust nobody. This frightened others, who decided to leave things alone. During her visit to Japan, Nee met migrant workers, visited agencies which help migrants, and visited Thai women imprisoned for killing their moneylender. She came to understand more about the difficulties faced by illegal migrant workers, and about Thai women coerced into working as prostitutes in bars and clubs.

With assistance from a local agency, Mizura, and the Japanese police, Nee found her daughter. She had just finished paying off her debt and had become a sex worker in a restaurant. The local media covered the work of the tribunal and Nee's search for her daughter. When Nee returned with her daughter to Na Thong, she told others about the working conditions and the contracts which bound the workers. A public discussion was held in Na Thong, led by Nee, and attended by people from neighbouring villages. She inspired others to write to their daughters, asking for the truth about their work in Japan. Some were shocked to learn that their daughters were employed as sex workers, but others were more pragmatic about the need to earn fast money

The 300 people who attended the first meeting saw a video and slides dealing with the circumstances in which migrant Thai women live in Japan. For a majority, this was the first they had heard or seen of the reality. Similar meetings were held in the district and provincial centres, where Nee was joined by a number of returned women migrants, who spoke of their experiences in Singapore and Japan. These meetings were well attended, and there were requests for Nee to visit other districts where the emigration rate was high. A returned migrant from Rim Mon in the north came to one meeting, and went back to her village to organise a women's group there.

COMMUNITY REACTION

Reactions to the meetings and the disclosure of the conditions in which women were living were not all positive or compassionate. One woman complained:

> Nee said too much. She should not say that our daughters are prostitutes and suffer misfortune. Some believe their daughters are doing the right thing. Nee talked too much because she wanted others to believe her. Staying a few days there, how could she know the country thoroughly?

Others, who had received money from their daughters, were angry because they now knew how it had been earned. One suggested Nee should go and work in Japan herself. This anger reflected the strength of the social and moral divisions between 'good girls' and 'bad girls'. The same attitude compels returned women to remain silent about their experiences. Many returnees do not stay in their home villages, but prefer to go and live elsewhere in Thailand.

Communities do not necessarily support those who have been forced into prostitution. Following Nee's personal disclosure about her daughter's experience, some villagers blamed the daughter. The researchers also became targets for anger. One government officer accused the research team of humiliating the young women for their own ends. The village head, who was related to Nee, told her to desist because it brought disgrace on the family, and hence upon him also. These reactions made the research team more cautious about using local women to recall their experiences in public. The presentation of such stories clearly runs the risk of exposing them to possible further abuse.

It is clear that much of the traffic in women remains in shadow, and that a collusive unknowing sometimes unites families with agents, traffickers and exploiters. While the whole nexus remains hidden, face may be saved; but the young women must suffer in secrecy and silence.

THE MIGRANT WOMEN'S NETWORK

Following the provincial meeting in Nong Khai, three women who had been abused by traffickers and employers worked with the research team to record their personal histories. All these women, Mali, Chantra and Duangta, also organised groups in their home villages to spread awareness of migration and trafficking. The telling of their stories gave them real comfort, because, in doing so, they came to perceive that what had happened to them was only part of wider social and economic processes, and was not a consequence of personal error or fault. They were able to understand the relationship between individual experience and the unbalanced social and economic conditions of men and women, rich and poor, both nationally and internationally.

Ton Yang village information centre

Experience gained from activities in Na Thong village clarified the need to make known what life is really like for migrant women. Mali, who had worked in Singapore, started a group with the purpose of educating the people of Ton Yang, and a neighbouring village, 'Kham Wan'. This group was supported by the research project, especially with books and videos about migration, prostitution and the kind of life women can expect when they work in foreign countries. Members of the group started discussions after women had given testimony about their own experiences, the sufferings and sorrows they had endured.

The reaction from young people taking part was very powerful. Many said they would never go overseas in search of work now that they had some idea of what to expect. The women themselves, when they came to reflect on these sessions, struck up a strong rapport with their audiences.

The way Thai prostitutes in Japan are treated is depressing. People are not aware it is like this. You feel sad for the parents whose daughters have gone away to work. It would be all right if they knew the sacrifices their daughters are making, if they knew the real cost of the money they earn. It is very sad for the parents who do not know.

The ones who went abroad came back and built a big house; they have more money to spend. Some people still want to follow them. Migration brings problems to the community

The women and young people in Ton Yang agreed to set up an information centre. To begin with, this was done in Mali's living room but later, they extended her house to provide a space for reading matter and information relating to migration. Government officers have also contributed documentary material. Among visitors to the centre have been people from Na Thong, who are keen for something similar in their village.

More and more women and men approached Mali, seeking advice on migration or information about what they could do when employment contracts were not fulfilled. Mr Kham and his friend sought her help following their deportation from New Zealand, when they had paid large fees to brokers on the promise of agricultural jobs. Mali suggested they sue the broker's company. In spite of this experience, they were still anxious to migrate far for work, because, they said, the wages in neighbouring countries were too low. Brokers are quick to promote new destinations with promises of even greater potential earnings.

The existence of the centre and the work of the group have made Mrs Tan, who is the mother of Paeng and Peaun, unhappy. It has interfered with her work of recruitment for her daughters in Japan. Her youngest daughter has even joined the group.

Returned migrants group in Rim Mon

While Ton Yang and Na Thong saw women leave for what turned out to be sex work abroad, the people of Rim Mon observed foreigners coming to their village for sex. Women with experience of sex work overseas were coming back to Rim Mon having amassed considerable wealth. Some were being supported by foreign men. It was assumed that those who had not yet returned had been less successful.

The researchers worked with some of these women in Rim Mon, particularly with those who had experienced discrimination when they came home, or who were still suffering from the trauma of working abroad.

Kham Por had been forced into prostitution by the Yakuza in

Japan. She had tried to escape, but only when a Japanese customer paid her debt was she allowed to leave. She lived as the second wife of this man, but when her baby died, she came home. Her husband still visits her and gives financial support. Kham Por suffers from nightmares that the Yakuza are still after her. She has been in hospital several times. The villagers think she is neurotic. After revisiting Kham Por in 1996, the Foundation for Women learned that she had been forced to disown her baby, and to pass it over to the Japanese wife, so that the child should not end up as illegitimate under Japanese law.

Kham Por sought out the researchers, because she was sorely in need of friends. Later, she was elected president of the returned women's group. The village head could see the potential power of the group, if only because they were better off than most, but he would not offer his support. He was cynical about migrant women workers.

> If they need money, they just go south, or send their daughters. It's more comfortable than bag-weaving until their backs ache.

Kham Por started to teach other returned women, and was involved in planning vocational training for young women villagers. This had to stop when she went back into hospital.

Kham Por had introduced the researchers to other returned women, who provided valuable information which would either validate or deny the evidence collected in the first phase of the project. Most of these women had been outside the mainstream of village life. In spite of the obvious benefit the village had received from remittances, the women who had been the instruments of making this money were sometimes rejected. They were asked to help out at Songkran (the traditional Thai new year festival), because they could afford the elaborate Thai costumes required for the ceremony. In talking with the researchers, these women were able to speak of their dissatisfactions with their life as returnees, and to identify a possible new role for themselves.

> We should work with the housewives' group, because there are no other appropriate groups or programmes for women in the village.

> I would like it if there were other work for the people in our community.

> I wish that women in the community could cook properly so that we could welcome visitors, and not feel inferior. And it's a pity they don't know better manners when it comes to eating.

The researcher contacted government agencies to arrange for instruction in cookery. Field visits to other women's groups were organised. In the event, the members of the group decided that the high cost of investment in food production and the limited market were against them. They moved on to look at other ideas.

Women need to learn and understand other people's skills and tricks of the trade, because women have to work also.

If women are not developed, how can the country be developed?

We are the women of a new age, we can do what we want by ourselves. We don't have to wait for men. We can do it, but we have never been given the opportunity,

They learned that working together is effective, and earns respect. Even the village head changed his mind and lent his support to the group.

When we worked together and showed how useful we are to the village, people appreciated us more. Women came to understand that responsibility has to be shared. Although each one had to help herself, she also needed to contribute to the wider group. In the meetings, everyone had the right to express her opinion. There was no need to whisper behind our hands.

Visits to other women's groups encouraged and strengthened their resolve. They named themselves the Women's Development Group, Rim Mon village. Following Duangta's visit to the north-east, they organised a seminar on migration and prostitution in co-operation with the local sub-district committee and the Community Development Division of the Ministry of the Interior. The seminar was titled 'Unemployment after the farming season'. Those who took part agreed that the main reason for migration was poverty, and lack of knowledge on how to make and market other produce. The success of the meeting led them on to other activities, and women from neighbouring villages began to talk about the way the traffic in women affected their own communities.

BENEFITS OF PARTICIPATION

The idea behind participatory research, and especially feminist research, is that through collective working, women will be able to articulate problems and work together on solutions. It was most clearly successful in Rim Mon, partly because the women there had not previously formed themselves into a collective entity. In Ton Yang and Na Thong, vocational groups had been established earlier. In Rim Mon, the practice of pooling and sharing ideas was new for some women. Most had had direct experience of prostitution, and this gave life and authenticity to the discussions. The researchers did not have to provide information on trafficking, as was the case with some other groups; and this left the women free to focus more on the process of working together in groups.

The group in Ton Yang consisted mainly of women who were anxious about the issue in relation to the fate of their children. The history of sex work migration in Ton Yang can be traced back to a single individual—a woman called Pang—returning from Japan, who set about recruiting others. The story runs that she brought home a million baht; and this is said to have convinced parents that big money was there for the making in Japan. More recently, two other women came back, also with considerable wealth. The members of the group felt that they had to make sure that people in the village received a more balanced picture than this rosy view of easy money. They arranged video and slide presentations on trafficking and migration, and these were followed by discussions.

> These children face many difficulties, they have to endure a great deal. The girls had to put up with whatever they found there but the parents at home thought they were having a good time. They believed what their children wrote and told them.

Stories from real life inspired those taking part to devise concrete solutions that could actually be put into practice in the village. In Na Thong, there had been many women's development activities, but none which concentrated on finding solutions through collective effort. The group started soon after the meetings which Nee had organised. One of the more popular seminars was about the law and legal procedures in foreign countries, and the kinds of help which migrant workers can draw on. This was also the first time that men had taken part in large numbers.

Spreading information

The second phase of the research confirmed that many villages lacked accurate information on migration—how it came about, what would happen to those who left, the pitfalls as well as the advantages. This was, therefore, a major focus of the women's energies. Activities included:

- core group members who had been directly caught up in trafficking, and who spoke about their personal experiences;
- researchers and others who could give out accurate information on legal issues—labour regulations, immigration laws, marriage to foreigners and the support available to children;
- documentary videos on child labour; prostitution, migration and trafficking;
- printed material— books, posters, picture books;
- presentation of the real life stories of trafficked women.

Other events included debates between children on the issues, and role-play on the stories in the books. Everything was designed to promote two-way communication, and to build understanding of all the implications of migrant sex work.

Changes in attitude and behaviour

The overwhelming impression people have of work in Japan is that it pays well. Women were sending home enough money to buy land and to renovate houses. Parents were unaware of the dangerous and damaging circumstances in which their daughters were working.

I never thought it was cruel. I only knew that she sent a lot of money home. (Ton Yang)

Seeing the video gave her sleepless nights. She was unhappy to see Thai girls being hit and even killed. She was afraid she would see her own daughter on the video. (Na Thong)

The reality of the conditions of work was shrouded in silence. Even returnees rarely spoke of their experiences, preferring to collude with the illusion that everything was fine. Families continued to borrow money and to mortgage their land to pay agents' fees. As they came to learn more about the life of migrant women workers, and the routine sexual exploitation they suffered, the enthusiasm of people became tempered; they showed more compassion.

I feel sorry for those who went away to work, and who risked their lives, lost their virginity for money. If only I had known this before, I would not have let them go. (Na Thong)

During the courses of the research, people came to talk about doing things differently. Young people said they would be more cautious in seeking work outside the village. Wealthier families spoke of furthering their children's education before they would permit them to look for work. In Na Thong, the youth leader reported that all the students who finished their six years of compulsory education that year went on to secondary school. The circumstances that led young people to want to leave still existed, but it was hoped that the new awareness that had come might make them more alert and think twice before leaving home. By the time the project was concluded in Na Thong, women were still leaving for work abroad, but it was found that they were now applying to travel legally, through the Department of Labour. The destination now was more likely to be Taiwan than Japan. The women most immediately involved with the project gained confidence from working with others, and were more ready to contact agencies for assistance. They became more hopeful that they would be instrumental in effecting change.

Vocational activities

Apart from alerting people to the reality of migration for sex work, the women's groups saw the urgent need for wider local work opportunities for women and girls. In Na Thong, they gave this priority over everything else, and focused on the weaving group. In Ton Yang and Rim Mon, they combined vocational skills and the spread of information. They did not expect vocational projects to lead to a wider range of new work possibilities.

Weaving group in Na Thong: Early in the Na Thong discussions, one woman community leader mentioned the availability of interest-free loans for income-generating projects from the Community Development Department of the Interior Ministry. The women thought that reviving traditional weaving skills, using the local designs of their area, might be a possible means of creating extra income. The researchers helped with the application for the loan, and arranged visits to existing weaving groups. When no response came from the Community Development Department, the researcher suggested taking a low-interest loan from elsewhere. But the group, fearful of further debt, became discouraged. They decided to disband the weaving group, at least until the harvest was over.

Sewing group in Ton Rang: The women's group was attracted by sewing, and contacted the Non-Formal Education Department for training. They could use equipment they already owned, but needed a wider market for selling the garments. They pursued this for a time, but when demand dropped away, the sewing project was abandoned.

The experience of these two groups demonstrates the obstacles to local employment-creation, including delays in obtaining loans, the lack of outlets for products, and the absence of organising skills for co-operative enterprises.

Bag-making in Rim Mon: Vocational training in Rim Mon served as a means of bringing women together to talk about migration. Income-generating work was used to get the group to work in harmony, although the income was not the main purpose of the group. The women worked well together; and there was talk of extending the idea to other groups within the village. The alternative emphasis in this group, whereby the dynamics of the group took precedence over income-generation, is, in part, the key to its success. The Rim Mon women were, in general, better off than the other groups, so they could afford to adopt a more relaxed attitude towards additional earnings. For the others, improvement in finances was a major consideration, and the obstacles to this led to frustration and conflict.

Casework assistance

Help and counselling with individual problems was part of the overall purpose of the project. The benefits extend beyond the particular family: the example helps to win credibility and support from other people in the village and community leaders.

Assistance with documents: The difficulties over arranging documents for migrants were similar in all villages. These included government officers who demanded unofficial additional payments for preparing documents. People were often confused about which documents were required, and in what language they should be drawn up. The researchers were able to help with translations, and they accompanied villagers on their visits to government offices. The presence of researchers inhibited the officials from demanding extra fees. The confusion over official documents and correct government procedures leads to a situation which traffickers can easily exploit.

Locating women abroad: The researchers, in collaboration with staff from the Foundation for Women, helped parents trace daughters who had disappeared overseas. Some searches were happily concluded, others ended with the sad news that the women had died. There were many cases where parents had lost contact with their daughters.

Applications for scholarships: One means of combating the traffic in women is by prolonging the education of girls. The advantages are twofold: they are kept busy with study, and at the same time they are enhancing their skills for when they enter the labour market. For poor families, keeping children at school beyond the compulsory limit is too costly. In the second phase of the research, 12 scholarships were provided from project funds, and these were offered to young girls thought to be vulnerable to recruiters.

Tuition: The researchers helped young women with literacy. They also ran typing classes in Na Thong, particularly Thai/English typing skills. The equipment for this was provided by the Foundation for Women. The enthusiasm for acquiring new skills and becoming literate, especially among young women, gives some indication of the reservoir of unmet need for further education and the desire to work outside traditional agricultural labour. Some women returning from abroad hesitated before joining classes run by the Non-Formal Education Division.

I want to study, but I don't want to be in a large class. I am shy. If the government officer is the teacher; I won't study. (Rim Mon)

The officers were impatient with this.

We don't understand why they are shy. They've worked in Bangkok and other places. They shouldn't be shy.

The researchers tried an approach that would put them at ease. Their teaching was based upon an exchange of ideas and feelings. Many young women acknowledged this.

At first I was shy, but now if there is anything to learn, I will do it. Reading develops our minds.

OBSTACLES ENCOUNTERED

The project encountered some hostility, particularly from those families receiving money from daughters overseas.

Why are you concerned with other people's business? If they want to go, what does it matter? It's better to go and earn money to spend than to stay home and starve. (Ton Yang)

The promotion of understanding had to be structured in such a way that it did not offend families whose daughters were abroad, and so that it did not add to the discrimination against returned sex workers.

One unanticipated outcome of the project was that recruitment agents and brokers were praised and congratulated by families who felt their daughters had been successful. This was the opposite of the response of those women whose stories featured in the videos and books. In Rim Mon in particular; from where there is a well-beaten path to overseas prostitution, there were many wealthy returned women. Their very presence was an eloquent denial of the message which the project was seeking to convey.

> This job is not a mistake. Right now, money can save our lives, never mind our honour. Disparaging prostitution only makes villagers dissatisfied, especially the parents of the women in prostitution.

The researchers had to make clear the difference between trafficking and prostitution. Traffic, it was explained, was about coercing women into prostitution, or into any other work, denying them adequate wages and dignified working conditions.

PARTICIPATION OF EXTERNAL AGENCIES

Local government personnel

Officials co-operated with and, in some cases, took part in the activities surrounding the project. Local community development officers assisted by advertising the seminars. Senior officers chaired some meetings. They were clearly familiar with the problems of migration and trafficking, but, so far, no official programmes have been set up to deal with the issue. The work of the women's groups gave them a chance to become involved without waiting for official permission.

In Rim Mon, the local teachers had already been working against trafficking and child prostitution. They had set up a counselling project specifically for girls at risk, and had arranged exhibitions illustrating the dangers of child prostitution. They had also gone with students to Bangkok for college entrance exams, and helped with applications for scholarships designed to prevent poorer children from dropping out of school. They were supported in this by the District Education Office. They reported that a higher proportion of girls are now completing their six years of compulsory education and going on to further study.

The Community Development Department has also given practical help by offering interest-free loans for income-generating schemes. This worked well in Rim Mon, as reported above, but delays in approval in Udon Thani province prevented any benefit being derived from it in Na Thong. The need for loans in Rim Mon confirms the observation that remittances from women's work in urban centres or overseas were being used mainly for capital expenditure—repairing houses or buying white goods—and little of the money was saved. A few women had started a convenience store with their earnings, but, overall, the money was deployed on conspicuous consumption and the flaunting of wealth.

Central government activity

The beginning of the FFW project coincided in 1992 with a government crackdown on child prostitution. The Chuan Leekpai Government gave the primary responsibility for the fight against child prostitution to the Department of Public Welfare. The Department set up a committee to oversee the achievement of this objective. This committee distributed a manual to the agencies involved, with an outline of their campaign and ideas for co-operative efforts. The National Commission on Women's Affairs, part of the Office of the Prime Minister; also formed a committee to inquire into the sex entertainment business.

Social programmes: The Government established social programmes to focus on women who have worked in the sex industry. These include the 'welfare home' of the Department of Public Welfare, for women released into their custody following conviction on criminal charges related to prostitution. Other aspects of the programme include vocational training, both for convicted women and for young people considered to be at risk.

Educational programmes: The Education Department provided opportunities for further education for young people, through scholarship programmes and 'welfare schools' for girls at risk. The scholarships were established in the northern provinces, from where many girls migrate for sex work, and where there are limited places in secondary schools.

Media projects: The Department of Public Welfare published information for families on child prostitution and trafficking. The Ministry of Foreign Affairs also ran a media campaign on illegal migration to Japan, intended to inform and deter potential migrants.

Legal programmes: The national strategy in terms of the law was to foster greater co-operation and co-ordination between government departments in implementing existing laws. These departments included Public Welfare, Provincial Administration, Foreign Affairs and the Police.

Perhaps more significant was the drafting of a bill to reform the 1960 Abatement of Prostitution Act. Non-governmental organisations lobbied vigorously in favour of the decriminalisation of prostitution, and harsher penalties against traffickers and the clients of child prostitutes. The bill did include more rigorous punishment for procurers and for the clients of under-age prostitutes, and a reduction in penalties for adult prostitutes. This bill was enacted in December 1996, and is now in force.

A second bill currently before Parliament seeks to replace the 1928 Anti-Trafficking Act, which would extend protection to boys, and provide for assistance rather than punishment for victims of trafficking. Penalties for trafficking would also be increased. This bill still awaits the final reading and approval by Parliament (January 1997).

Health programmes: The Ministry of Public Health screens prostitutes for sexually transmitted diseases, including HIV. There have been difficulties in offering this service to immigrant sex workers, mainly because of the lack of translation and interpretation facilities. The Ministry has also surveyed the sex industry, with a view to targeting its programmes more effectively.

Following an evaluation of these projects, a number of limitations were identified. Vocational and educational support programmes have been set up only in the northern provinces. This takes no account of the existence of child prostitution and trafficking in other regions, notably in the north-east. The vocational programme of the Public Welfare Department provided skills-training to 2,000 young women a year. The average income generated by this amounted to between 60 and 150 baht per day (US$2.50–6.25), which was considered too low to sustain a commitment by the young women to the work. Participants complained that the skills they acquired were limited and not adapted to their needs. Many were not convinced that prostitution was a bad choice of occupation. The Department of Industry also ran a skills-training programme in an effort to resist child prostitution. It set up projects in 72 villages, but only 1,363 individuals completed the programme, and, of these, only 262 were girls between the ages of 13 and 18.

Non-governmental activity

There were not many non-governmental organisations (NGOs) working directly on trafficking. However, the research team was able to collaborate with four organisations for the purpose of collecting data and in the analysis of service-delivery to trafficked persons. The operations of NGOs can be divided into four main areas of work designed to resist trafficking and child prostitution.

Social programmes: These include making available emergency shelter for victims of trafficking, counselling, health care education and some vocational training. Each NGO has a particular target group and a specific way of working: the Centre for the Protection of Children's Rights, for example, provides assistance, shelter and rehabilitation to abused children under 18. The religious-based groups focus on services to women who have been arrested or trafficked, but are rarely in a position to do much about the underlying factors which contribute towards trafficking.

Legal programmes: Some agencies provided legal advice and assistance during court hearings and proceedings. The overall level of expertise was not high, and there was not a great deal of interest in using the law to combat trafficking or to seek compensation for its victims. The difficulties in this respect were exacerbated by the indifference of law enforcers, and inadequate protection of the privacy of witnesses and victims.

Disseminating information: Part of each NGO's purpose was to bring home to the public the scale and extent of trafficking and prostitution. The most effective work through the media was accomplished in co-operative ventures between governmental and non-governmental agencies. Great care had to be taken to ensure that the women involved were not placed in further jeopardy by publicising their real-life stories.

NGOs and the international dimension: To dismantle international trafficking networks, co-operation between NGOs across national boundaries is required. Campaigns to change government policies and to provide effective help for trafficked persons must be co-ordinated by popular movements and NGOs in both sending and receiving countries. Such collaboration has worked well in tracing missing persons, in the joint provision of social and legal assistance in both the country of residence and the country of origin, and in media campaigns to inform the public. One good example of this has been the co-operation between NGOs in Japan and in Thailand to plead for leniency in the Shimodate case. The obstacles to such international efforts include language difficulties and cultural differences in ways of looking at and dealing with the issue. Some organisations underestimate the capacity of the women themselves to act on their own behalf.

Co-operation to combat trafficking

Powerful national and international strategies are needed to combat international trafficking. At present the level of co-operation between agencies within countries and between countries is inadequate.

Between government departments: The researchers found evidence of duplication between departments in their efforts to counter child prostitution. Co-operation between representatives of different departments was more effective in implementing the law which deals with the detention and 'rehabilitation' of sex workers. This has little impact on the sex industry itself. When it came to the Department of Public Welfare and the Ministry of Foreign Affairs working together to check applications for passports, this proved to be an unsuccessful tactic to discover whether trafficking was involved. The Public Welfare Department had instructions to check the background of young Thai women who applied for passports, to ensure that traffickers were not involved. The Foreign Affairs Ministry, however, refused to pass on information about applicants, on the grounds that it might be accused of unnecessary interference and discrimination.

The best examples of co-operation between governments are to be found in the detention and repatriation of illegal immigrants. The police officer interviewed in Malaysia by the project researcher stressed the co-operation with the Thai branch of Interpol in providing interpreters for cases against migrant sex workers. The Thai government, however, exhibited little interest in the plight of Thai women forced into prostitution overseas. During one case in Germany, in which defendants were prosecuted for forced prostitution, requests to the Thai police for witnesses were refused (Rayanakorn 1995).

Between government and NGOs: The response to the issue and to the women themselves is a source of conflict between government and non-governmental agencies. During the second phase of the research, the team was supporting a witness for a prosecution in Germany. They sought the compliance of the Thai police department. The police later released the information, including the identity of the victim, to the local press. They continued to defend their action, even though this threatens further collaboration between them and the Foundation for Women.

There were, however, examples of effective co-operation. The Thai Embassy in Tokyo is responsive to Japanese NGOs in bringing assistance to Thai women in distress. The Thai Ministry of Labour and Social Welfare and the Ministry of Foreign Affairs have provided some financial support to these Japanese NGOs.

Between NGOs: Transnational co-operation between NGOs in providing material help to individual women is well established. This is impaired to some degree by agencies supplying inadequate background information to cases that they refer and failing to follow them up. Co-operation within the country is also limited. Where it occurs, it is mostly on the basis of individual cases, rather than in a concerted effort to lobby government on the particular legislative measures required to address the problems.

International organisations: In October 1994, the Foundation for Women, together with the VENA Centre of the University of Leiden, and the Women's Studies Centre of Chiang Mai University, organised an international workshop on migration and trafficking of women. Some 70 people from 22 countries took part. The event concluded with an action plan for international co-operation, and recommendations were drawn up for national and international policies.

The Global Alliance Against Traffic in Women (GAATW) was formed. Its function is to co-ordinate efforts across national boundaries to promote international law reform and the adoption and enforcement of laws to combat trafficking. Part of its mandate is also to spread information and to promote research. It has set up working groups in a number of countries, including a group for research and co-ordination at the Foundation for Women in Bangkok.

CONCLUSION

Evidence emerged from the second phase of the project of the ability of migrant women themselves, their families and communities, to take on the issue of trafficking. Governmental and non-governmental agencies can provide support and information to active groups rooted in village and community. Outside agencies can contribute by linking women's groups across the country, and by arranging fact-finding trips. The participation of women in discussions and decisions about trafficking and migration is vital at all levels, for it is their livelihood, their lives, and their freedoms that are at stake.

The research also identified gaps in co-operation between agencies, many of which derive from conflicting views on prostitution and women migrants. Efforts to eradicate trafficking can be made more difficult by negative attitudes towards sex workers. This not only leads to gratuitous humiliation of the women, but also undermines co-operation on the prosecution of traffickers.

At present, prostitution represents the most hopeful option for some women. This, in turn, raises other vital questions. Is it more useful to apply the law to improve their working conditions, or to seek to eliminate the whole industry? The distinction must be maintained between issues of trafficking and of prostitution. Where prostitution is forced by coercion or violence, the law must be deployed against recruiters, brokers, agents and employers, and all those who collude with this damaging and degrading trade.

39 Editing Pornography

Isabelle V. Barker

Is pornography relevant to Western feminism in the late 1990s? Or did the 'sex wars' of the 1980s deal sufficiently with the challenges posed by pornography? These apparently pivotal feminist debates set forth a clear set of terms for dealing with pornography—as a feminist, one would need to choose sides, one was either for pornography or against it.[1] Fought largely as a legal matter, the debate took on a contentious, legalistic tone of 'either/or'. At base, the 'for pornography' argument relies on upholding First Amendment rights of free speech. This approach has been charged with defending First Amendment freedoms at the expense of women, as it seems to overlook the real violence that women around the world continue to endure. The anti-pornography argument considered all pornography as doing violence to women and fought hard to make pornography illegal. This view has been countered on many levels, but generally is considered too narrow of an approach with results too costly. For example, in the USA, anti-pornography feminists have found themselves in strange alliance with moral conservatives, partnering to eradicate all representations of sexuality deemed obscene.

This collection brings together essays from a wide tradition of feminist thought to develop more complicated means of thinking about and engaging with pornography. The polarized nature of the debate continues to shape conversations about pornography. For example, when I told someone that I was writing an essay about pornography, she asked me 'are you for pornography or against it?' Simply responding 'yes, I'm for it' or 'no, I abhor all things pornographic' seems impossible without a string of qualifiers attached. In the face of the complicated nature of pornography can any of us really answer this seemingly simple question?

We continue to be limited to thinking of pornography as an either/or issue. This is in part the legacy of feminist efforts to make pornography illegal. This approach requires that we come up with a definition of what pornography is. Following this, we must then funnel every instance of pornography into this narrow definition and simply look away when confronted with exceptions, or examples which cannot be contained by our now limited conception of pornography. It has become clear that the question, 'are you for or against pornography?' cannot provide us with the tools necessary to confront pornography. The complicated forms that pornography assumes makes the question insufficient; being limited to choosing sides in this way keeps us from effectively confronting pornography in all of its complexities.

If we pause to consider the history of pornography, we begin to see why simply being for or against pornography would limit the radical potential of feminist interventions. History shows us how pornography has been deployed to measure morality: an incident or an image labelled 'pornographic' has been generally considered immoral. Pornography has come to be defined as interchangeable with all that is considered immoral. At the same time, pornography's history reminds us that pornography has often functioned as a site for transgression. To enter into the realm of the pornographic is to call into question all that a society deems 'moral'. The history of morality in the context of the Western world is one that has hinged on hierarchical explications of a split between good and evil and mind and body. As historians have shown us, these dichotomous modes of thought have in turn hinged on stratifications of difference defined according to sexuality, race, class, and nation. Ethical feminist theories and practices will take into account how, at various moments, pornography has been deployed to reinforce these hierarchical orderings. At other times pornographic representations have been instances of the undoing of these very stratifications.

At the level of representation, violent and offensive images fuel the notion that we are expendable. Pornography provides a medium by which to represent this violence along the lines of sexuality. In some pornography, social hierarchies are folded into one another, and are objectified, represented, and fetishized. And certainly, there is much phallocentric pornography that lends to the idea that the female characters exist only as objects of male pleasure and male violence. It is fair to say, however, and has been said again and again, that not all pornography represents these violent orderings. So, an effective feminist intervention into pornography will include means of discerning how pornography can at times represent violence, while at other times, it merely functions to ethically represent the complexities of human sexuality.

If we consider how pornography exists currently in the world, 'choosing sides' becomes irrelevant. Choosing sides lends itself to a politics of resentment and frustration, and leads to stagnant political practice. In the face of contemporary forms of pornography this polarized debate as a basis for theoretical and political practice is ineffective. As we work to carve our selves out in a world replete with sexual imagery, we are confronted with the violent and the sublime on a daily basis; we contend with images that give pleasure, as well as with images that offend. In this era of hyper-technological, global capitalist consumerism, these well marketed images of sexuality come at us from all directions. If we are to function in—much less have a critical engagement with—this world, we will need to develop mechanisms to respond to these complicated and ever-present images. We will need to sift and cull representations of sexuality—in other words we need to come up with ways to edit pornography.

What is the goal of feminist intervention in pornography? While there is great disagreement about how to get there, the goal of an ethical feminist struggle is to work to create a world that, ultimately, is safe for all, and that gives us each the space to work out our sense of who we are and who we would like to be. If this is the ideal, how are we to contend with today's reality? Obviously, each individual will answer this question in ways that make sense to them—there is no one answer to this question. But on the level of feminist theory and feminist policy, we must challenge the violence that women continue to face on a daily basis while continuing to also insist on freedom and justice. So, in the context of the United States, we must refuse the path of censorship, while developing ethical interventions to counter violence against women as instanced in some pornography.

In the face of pornography in its current forms, we have to resist temptations to simplify and instead hold onto the complexities of our realities. With these complexities, we can develop dynamic feminist theories and practice to counter the challenges presented by pornography. We must hone our editing skills, developing our own individual rapid responses to the sex industry. I am not suggesting that we throw in the towel and accept the violent and the offensive. Quite the opposite. I am suggesting that feminists continue to edge towards what Wendy Brown terms the 'risky experiments with resignification and emancipation'.[2] Within the framework of Western liberalism, these 'risky experiments' will require a theoretical and political definition of feminist subjectivity.[3]

In order to edit pornography we have to develop theoretical and political conceptions of the feminist editor, the individual who is capable of making determinations for herself as to how pornography will figure in her life. Moreover, in order to recognize the feminist editor, we have to understand her as a subject. By imagining the feminist subject, we can position ourselves as editors, and by editing, we resignify the world around us. The feminist subject, at least in the context of contemporary Western subjectivity, will likely define herself with respect to representations of sexuality. The feminist subject I imagine is capable of thinking of herself as a whole sexual being in the face of a world that attempts to sell pleasure at the expense of women at every turn. We live in a violent world and must contend with violence on a daily basis. In Western modernity, this violence is trafficked along the lines of categories of sexual, racial, ethnic, national, and class difference. We develop our subjectivity in the face of the misogyny, racism, and xenophobia that structures the modern Western world. How we choose to integrate these current realities into our lives is personal, but we have to be accountable for the choices that we make. Otherwise we edge into an apolitical and unethical way of being which helps sustain a world that thrives on violent orderings.

In order to develop an ideal of a feminist subject, we must first consider how we represent our own sexuality. If we truly desire a just society, we are ethically called upon to do more than simply act as free sexual agents. We cannot counter the violence of the social hierarchies that order our world by simply and brazenly asserting our sexuality, although, in recent years, this very approach has been seductively proposed as an alternative to the supposedly dated arguments of feminism. Packaged as 'post-feminism' by the mass media, this trend has gathered strength, at least in the media, and seemingly represents a common sentiment on the part of young women.

The 'post-feminist' label seems to refer to primarily young white women who are readily writing off the 'old feminist order'[4] as morally conservative and politically and socially archaic. Charging that feminists have developed a politics of 'women as victims', young women are running the other way, unabashedly reclaiming their sexuality—proudly and loudly. Camille Paglia's legacy can be found in the very publishable work of Katie Roiphe and, most recently, Elizabeth Wurtzel, a young 'post-feminist' who recently put out a book titled *Bitch: In Praise of Difficult Women.*[5] Most striking (and most worrisome) is the irony that these young women are appropriating feminist language of agency and self-determinism to in fact prop up phallocentric logic of gender hierarchy. It remains unclear, however, if there exist multitudes of women who self-identify as post-feminist, or if this is in fact a media creation. Perhaps this is simply a clumsy application of the ubiquitous and trendy prefix 'post'. It is important to note, however, that the term, and the views it seems to represent, have taken hold in the Anglo-American cultural landscape. While post-feminism may or may not reflect a widespread sentiment on the part of young women, its rally has captured media attention. Young women are voicing that they are over 'prudish' feminism and—apparently—the media believes it can sell this shelving of out-of-date feminism. Out with the old and in with the new.

The post-feminist challenge is not tremendously substantive; perhaps this is why it functions extraordinarily well in contemporary consumer culture. The apparent popularity of post-feminism should give feminists pause particularly because the post-feminist strain veils deep-seated conservatism. It is no surprise that arguments deemed 'post-feminist' emerged from women of my generation, the generation that came of age in the Reagan years—an era that led citizens of the United States to believe that we could own it all. For example, the 1980s witnessed the making of Madonna, who possessed unprecedented notoriety for a female pop star, and who capitalized on the idea that feminism could be sexy. Her persona heralded the power of the purse, and seemed to promise young (implicitly white) women that we too could be sexy material girls—we could have it all, sex and nice clothes. Post-feminism picks up where Madonna left off (she is now embracing the more subdued arts of Zen meditation and motherhood). Post-feminist rhetoric seems obsessed with sex as commodity. bell hooks has aptly pinpointed the 'hedonistic consumerism' of what is deemed the 'new' feminism. She writes that she 'repudiate(s) the notion of a "new feminism" and (sees) it being created in the mass media mainly as a marketing ploy to advance the opportunistic concerns of individual women while simultaneously acting as an agent of antifeminist backlash by undermining feminism's radical/revolutionary gains'.[6]

In its myopic and redundant insistence that women need to simply assert their sexuality and stop being victims, post-feminism callously ignores how sexualized violence has historically been deployed to reinforce social hierarchies. The logic of post-feminism is one of simple inversion: 'we are not the victims that feminists say we are', goes the message. Post-feminism tells women to stop their whining, suggesting that incidents of gendered violence are figments of feminist imagination. This logic of inversion blatantly ignores the historical and identifiable fact of sexualized violence. Moreover, it ignores that sexualized violence in the USA has functioned as a means of maintaining racial and sexed divides. The history of slavery in this country is steeped in incidents of racialized sexual violence, and this past haunts us in ways that cut across intersectional axes of difference. Kimberlé Crenshaw, who has written much on 'intersectionality', writes of the effects of racialized sexuality: 'while the fallen-woman imagery that white feminists identify does represent much of black women's experience of gender domination, given their race, black women have in a sense always been within the fallen-women category.'[7] The charge that the 'fallen women' image is a figment of feminist imagination necessarily dismisses the fact that, throughout modern history in the USA, this image has been enacted on multiple levels to enact both misogyny and racism. In so easily dismissing violence against women, post-feminism ignores that this violence is shaped via complicated histories of race and ethnicity.

The post-feminist line of argument would seem to say that politics has no place in the bedroom. Post-feminism cannot and will not recognize that sociohistorical contexts shape our sexualities. It is perhaps no coincidence that the movie *Boogie Nights* was so popular in the 1990s. The movie depicts the pornography industry in its supposed heyday, reaping the benefits of the sexual revolution of the 1970s. There is no threat of AIDS looming, nor does there appear to be any threat of men being charged with rape. Everyone seems to be having the ultimate experience of sex with no consequences. This melancholic nostalgia for a sexual era seemingly void of any political ramifications is reminiscent of post-feminism's desire for a sexual world void of any political and ethical accountability. A just world will require that we take into account—and be accountable for—sociohistorical circumstances as they intersect with our sexualities. The post-feminist line of argument which has attracted so much media attention is simply inadequate as a political and theoretical response to the challenges posed by contemporary pornography.

An ethical intervention into pornography will confront the sociohistorical forces that shape contemporary pornography. For example, in order to have an effect, contemporary feminist interventions in pornography must take into consideration global culture and global economies. More and more, borders between nations are fading, particularly with regard to the sex industry. After all, the sex industry thrives in the free market, therefore, magazines, videos, and prostitutes are well travelled commodities in the international free market. The free market has so thoroughly dehumanized and commodified prostitutes, that women working in the sex trade come to be seen as interchangeable with magazines and videos. In the face of this global society, Western feminists will need to be extraordinarily cautious of mimicking imperialist impulses by simply imposing our theories and practices around the world. For example, Eastern European feminists have been critical of Catharine MacKinnon's fact-finding mission regarding the role of pornography in the Serbo-Croatian war. Following her visit, MacKinnon concluded that gender hierarchy, reinforced by pornography, was the root cause of the sexualized violence that took place during the war. Eastern European feminists charged that by simply transplanting her equation of 'pornography equals rape', MacKinnon dangerously overlooks the specificities of the region and of the war.[8] This story should give us pause. Clearly, we in the West need to develop theoretical and political means of comprehending how pornography functions differently throughout the world. This will require that we develop global conversations among feminists; these conversations will be most fruitful when those who are not used to listening actually assume the role of listeners.

In the context of Anglo-American culture, effective intervention requires that we consider pornography on two levels—on the level of production and on the level of consumption. A complex ideal of feminist subjectivity can assist on both levels. By demanding safe and fair labour practices in the production of pornography, on the one hand, and, on the other hand, by demanding that pleasure be represented in ways that do not prescribe the erasure of the feminine, we will more effectively counter violence against women. When we conceive of women as three-dimensional subjects, we challenge the masculinist instance as elaborated in pornography; feminist subjects are not static characters in a well-worn sexual fantasy—we lift off of the page or the screen. We have complicated lives that are not contained in the fantasy world imagined by phallocentric pornography. Quite simply, we need to pay the rent, we need health insurance, we experience successes and failures, pleasure and violence. Pornography is not in the business of selling reality, of course, but its employees and its customers have complicated real lives.

On the level of the production of pornography, one feminist intervention into the sex industry includes improving the working conditions by demanding fair wages, safe working environments, and good benefits. Because of the current shifts and perhaps unpredictable forces in today's labour market, these demands may seem unrealistic. Yet, we must continue to work to make these standards real and to redefine the sex industry so that these standards apply. The level of consumption requires an ethical intervention that will shape how we can conceive of a feminist sexual future.[9] Again, I turn to the notion of a feminist subjectivity as a way of thinking about how we, as individuals, can edit pornography. To consider women as *ethical* agents of our own sexuality is, in and of itself, a way of 'jamming the machinery' of phallocentric pornography.

Most pornography fashions fantasy through the rigidity of scripted performance. In pornographic films there literally exists a script with characters, sets, plots, etc. The script of phallocentric pornography rehearses the same story again and again—and it is a story that is steeped in hierarchies. It is a story that turns around and around masculine sexual pleasure. Actresses serve merely as the conduits by which male pleasure is achieved. The pre-eminence of male pleasure at the expense of the feminine dominates the film and reinstates the hierarchy of gender difference. The Achilles' heal of masculinist pornography lies in this redundancy—in the remarkable (often times laughable) predictability of its story. Luce Irigaray points us towards laughter as an emancipatory practice: 'Isn't laughter the first form of liberation from a secular form of power? *Isn't the phallic tantamount to the seriousness of meaning*? Perhaps woman, and the sexual relation, transcend [phallogocentrism] "first" in laughter?'[10] How many times and in how many ways can the same story be told?

In 'Fighting Bodies, Fighting Words: A Theory and Politics for Rape Prevention', Sharon Marcus applied poststrucuralist theories of narrative to identify and undo the tropes of heterosexual gender hierarchy that are enacted in incidents of rape. The script of phallocentric pornography, like the script of rape, is not infallible. Marcus shows how we can unwrite the script of violence against women:

> by defining rape as a scripted performance, we enable a gap between script and actress which can allow us to rewrite the script, perhaps refusing to take it seriously and treating it as a farce, perhaps by resisting the physical passivity which it directs us to adopt. Ultimately we must eradicate this social script. In

the meantime, we can locally interfere with it by realizing that men elaborate masculine power in relation to imagined feminine powerlessness; since we are solicited to help create this power, we can act to destroy it.[11]

Ironically, phallocentric pornographic representation gives us an example of misogyny writ large. If we dare to look, the glaring weaknesses of phallocentric story shine through the hyperbole that is pornographic representation. Then, we can more easily identify how an ethical feminist intervention can unravel the story. I am not denying the horrific violence and degradation that are often depicted and even enacted in phallocentric pornography. However, if we consider phallocentric pornography as performance of a story that can be interrupted, we begin to shake the foundations of this violence and degradation. It is only through undoing the foundations of a profoundly unjust social world that we can begin to imagine a different world—one that could be home to dynamic and fully embodied feminist subjects.

Notes

1. I refer here only to the debates that gained national attention. While there existed a range of other feminist voices that did not engage in this polarized debate, these were given little attention either by the mainstream media or by feminists engaged in the 'central' debate.
2. Wendy Brown, 'The Mirror of Pornography', in *States of Injury* (Princeton: Princeton University Press, 1995), 94.
3. I am aware that by calling for a feminist conception of subjectivity, I limit this discussion within a Western context. Moreover, for the purposes of this paper, I turn to the concept of the feminist subject purely as a political strategy that is relevant within liberal political thought.
4. Rene Denfeld, *The New Victorians: A Young Woman's Challenge to the Old Feminist Order* (New York: Warner Books, 1996).
5. Katie Roiphe's most defining publication as of yet is *The Morning After: Sex, Fear, and Feminism on Campus* (Boston: Little, Brown and Co., 1993). Elizabeth Wurtzel, *Bitch: In Praise of Difficult Women* (New York: Anchor Books, 1998).
6. bell hooks, *Outlaw Culture* (New York: Routledge, 1994), 74.
7. Kimberle Crenshaw, 'Whose Story is it Anyway?: Feminist and Antiracist Appropriations of Anita Hill', in Toni Morrison (ed.) *Race-ing Justice En-gendering Power: Essays on Anita Hill, Clarence Thomas, and the Construction of Social Reality* (New York: Pantheon Books, 1992), 414.
8. Maja Korać, 'Representation of Mass Rape in Ethnic Conflicts in What Was Yugoslavia', in *Sociologija*, 36 (4), Oct.–Dec. 1994. and Catharine MacKinnon, 'Turning Rape into Pornography: Postmodern Genocide', in *Ms.*, 4 (1), July 1993.
9. Brown, 'The Mirror of Pornography', 89.

10. Luce Irigaray, *This Sex Which is Not One*, trans. Catherine Porter (Ithaca, NY: Cornell University Press, 1985), 163.
11. Sharon Marcus, 'Fighting Bodies, Fighting Words: A Theory and Politics of Rape Prevention', in Judith Butler and Joan Wallace Scott (eds.), *Feminists Theorize the Political* (New York: Routledge, 1992), 392.

Further Reading (1988–1998)

Compiled by Christa Kelleher and Katrin Kriz

Arcand, Bernard. 1993. *The Jaguar and the Anteater: Pornography and the Modern World.* Toronto: McClelland and Stewart.

Asian Women's Rights Council. 1990. *Crimes Against Gender: Rape and Pornography.* Quezon City, Philippines: AWHRC.

Assiter, Alison. 1989. *Pornography, Feminism and the Individual.* London: Pluto Press.

Bell, Shannon. 1995. 'Pictures Don't Lie: Pictures Tell It All.' *Journal of the History of Sexuality* 6: 284–321.

Bensinger, Terralee. 1992. 'Lesbian Pornography: The Re/Making of (a) Community.' *Discourse* 15: 69–93.

Berger, Ronald J. 1991. *Feminism and Pornography.* New York: Praeger.

Bracher, Mark. 1991. 'Writing and Imaging the Body in Pornography: The Desire of the Other and Its Implications for Feminism.' *American Journal of Semiotics* 8: 105–130.

Brod, Harry. 1988. 'Pornography and the Alienation of Male Sexuality.' *Social Theory and Practice* 14. 265–284.

Brottman, Mikita. 1997. 'Blue Prints and Bodies: Paradigms of Desire in Pornography.' *Critical Studies* 8: 203–216.

Butler, Judith. 1994. 'Against Proper Objects [Queer and Feminist Theory].' *Differences* 6: 1–26.

Carse, Alisa L. 1995. 'Pornography: An Uncivil Liberty?' *Hypatia* 10: 155–182.

Chancer, Lynn S. 1998. *Reconcilable Differences: Confronting Beauty, Pornography, and the Future of Feminism.* Berkeley: University of California Press.

Gibson, Pamela Church, and Roma Gibson (Eds.). 1993. *Dirty Looks: Women, Pornography, Power.* London: British Film Institute.

Cole, Susan, 1992. *Pornography and the Sex Crisis.* Toronto: Second Story.

——1995. *Power Surge: Sex, Violence and Pornography.* Toronto: Second Story.

Collins, Patricia Hill, 1995. 'Pornography and Black Women's Bodies.' Pp. 279–286 in *Gender; Race, and Class in Media: A Text Reader*, edited by Gail Dines and Jean M. Humez. Thousand Oaks, California.: Sage.

COWAN, GLORIA. 1992. 'Feminist Attitudes Toward Pornography Control.' *Psychology of Women Quarterly* 16: 165–177.

——and ROBIN R. CAMPBELL. 1994. 'Racism and Sexism in Interracial Pornography: A Content Analysis.' *Psychology of Women Quarterly* 18: 323–338.

CREITH, ELAINE. 1996. *Undressing Lesbian Sex: Popular Images, Private Acts and Public Consequences.* New York: Cassell.

DAILEADER, CELIA. 1997. 'The Uses of Ambivalence: Pornography and Female Heterosexual Identity.' *Women's Studies* 26: 73–88.

DALECKI, MICHAEL, and JAMMIE PRICE. 1994. 'Dimensions of Pornography.' *Sociological Spectrum* 14: 205–219.

DINES, GAIL. 1997. *Pornography: The Consumption of Inequality.* New York: Routledge.

DOLBY, LAURA M. 1995. 'Pornography in Hungary: Ambiguity of the Female Image in a Time of Change.' *Journal of Popular Culture* 29: 119–27.

DUGGAN, LISA, and NAN D. HUNTER. 1995. *Sex Wars: Sexual Dissent and Political Culture.* New York: Routledge.

DUNCKER, PATRICIA. 1995. '"Bonnie Excitation, Orgasme Assuré." The Representation of Lesbianism in Contemporary French Pornography.' *Journal of Gender Studies 4: 5–15.*

EASTON, SUSAN M. 1994. *The Problem of Pornography: Regulation and the Right to Free Speech.* London: Routledge.

ELLIS, KATE. 1990. 'I'm Black and Blue from the Rolling Stones and I'm Not Sure How I Feel about It: Pornography and the Feminist Imagination.' Pp. 431–450 in *Women, Class, and the Feminist Imagination: A Socialist-Feminist Reader*, edited by Karen V. Hansen and Ilene J. Philipson. Philadelphia: Temple University Press.

ELMAN, AMY R. 1997. 'Disability Pornography: The Fetishization of Women's Vulnerabilities.' *Violence Against Women* 3: 257–270.

FALK, PASI. 1993. 'The Representation of Presence: Outlining the Anti-Aesthetics of Pornography.' *Theory, Culture & Society* 10: 1–42.

GOLDSCHMIDT, PAUL W. 1995. 'Legislation on Pornography in Russia.' *Europe Asia Studies* 47: 909–922.

GUBAR, SUSAN, and JOAN HOFF-WILSON (Eds.). 1989. *For Adult Users Only: The Dilemma of Violent Pornography.* Bloomington: Indiana University.

HARDY, SIMON. 1998. *The Reader, the Author; his Woman and her Lover: Soft-core Pornography and Heterosexual Men.* London: Cassell.

HENDERSON, LISA. 1991. 'Lesbian Pornography: Cultural Transgression and Sexual Demystification.' *Women and Language* 14: 3–12.

HERMAN, DIDI. 1995. 'Law and Morality Re-Visited: The Politics of Regulating Sado-Masochistic Porn/Practice.' *Studies in Law, Politics, and Society* 15: 147–166.

HODGSON, DOUGLAS. 1995. 'Combating the Organized Sexual Exploitation of Asian Children: Recent Developments and Prospects.' *International Journal of Law and the Family* 9: 23–53.

Howell, Colleen 1994. 'Violence Against Women: The Pornography Debate in South Africa.' *Women's Global Network for Reproductive Rights* 16: 19–20.

Jackson, Emily. 1995. 'The Problem with Pornography: A Critical Survey of the Current Debate.' *Feminist Legal Studies* 3: 49–70.

Jensen, Robert. 1996. 'Knowing Pornography.' *Violence Against Women* 2: 82–102.

Kaite, Berkeley. 1995. *Pornography and Difference.* Indianapolis: Indiana University Press,

Kelly, Peggy. 1991. 'Pornography: A Feminist Existentialist Analysis.' *Atlantis* 17: 129–136.

Kimmel, Michael. 1990. *Men Confront Pornography.* New York: Crown.

Lacombe, Dany. 1994. *Blue Politics: Pornography and the Law in the Age of Feminism.* Toronto: University of Toronto Press.

Lederer, Laura J., and Richard Delgado (Eds.). 1995. *The Price We Pay: The Case Against Racist Speech, Hate Propaganda, and Pornography.* New York: Hill and Wang.

McCormack, Thelma. 1993. 'If Pornography Is the Theory, Is Inequality the Practice?' *Philosophy of the Social Sciences* 23: 298–326.

McElroy, Wendy. 1995. *XXX: A Woman's Right to Pornography.* New York: St. Martin's Press.

Maschke, Karen J. (Ed.). 1997. *Pornography, Sex Work and Hate Speech.* New York: Garland.

Mayall, Alice, and Diana Russell. 1993. 'Racism in Pornography.' *Feminism and Psychology* 3: 275–281.

Morgan, David. 1997. 'Sexual Politics and the European Union: The New Feminist Challenge. *Gender; Work, and Organization 4: 134–135.*

Morgan, Thais. 1989. 'A Whip of One's Own: Dominatrix Pornography and the Construction of a Post-Modern (Female) Subjectivity.' *American Journal of Semiotics* 6: 109–136.

Patterson, Katherine J. 1994. 'Pornography Law as Censorship: Linguistic Control as (Hetero)sexist Harness.' *Feminist Issues* 14: 91–115.

Randall, Richard. 1989. *Freedom and Taboo: Pornography and the Politics of a Self Divided.* Berkeley: University of California Press.

Rayanakorn, K. 1993. *Study of the Law Relating to Prostitution and Traffic in Women.* Bangkok: Foundation for Women.

Russell, Diana. 1998. *Dangerous Relationships: Pornography, Misogyny, and Rape.* Thousand Oaks, California.: Sage.

Schuijer, Jan, and Benjamin Rossen. 1992. 'The Trade in Child Pornography.' *Issues in Child Abuse Accusations* 4: 55–107.

Segal, Lynne, and Mary McIntosh (Eds.). 1993. *Sex Exposed: Sexuality and the Pornography Debate.* New Brunswick, NJ: Rutgers University Press.

Smyth, Cherry. 1990. 'The Pleasure Threshold: Looking at Lesbian Pornography on Film.' *Feminist Review* 34 : 152–160.

Stark, Cynthia A. 1997. 'Is Pornography an Action? The Causal vs. the Conceptual View of Pornography's Harm.' *Social Theory and Practice* 23: 277–306.

Stoller, Robert J. 1991. *Porn: Myths for the Twentieth Century.* New Haven: Yale University Press.

Strossen, Nadine. 1996. *Defending Pornography: Free Speech, Sex, and the Fight for Women's Rights.* New York: Anchor Books.

Swedberg, Deborah. 1989. 'What Do We See When We See Woman/ Woman Sex in Pornographic Movies?' *NWSA Journal* 1: 602–616.

COYOTE Bibliography and Sex Worker Resource Listing

Sex Work: Developing Countries

Africa

HALL, LAUREL MEREDITH. 1989. '"Night Life" in Kenya'. In Gail Pheterson (ed.), *A Vindication of the Rights of Whores.* Seattle: Seal Press.

MOODIE, T. DUNBAR (with VIVIENNE NDATSHE and BRITISH SIBUYI). 1989. 'Migrancy and Male Sexuality on the South African Gold Mines'. In Martin Bauml Duberman, Martha Vicinius, and George Chauncey, Jr. (eds.), *Hidden from History: Reclaiming the gay and lesbian past.* New York: New American Library.

NEEQUAYE, ALFRED. 'Prostitution in Accra'. In Martin Plant (ed.), *AIDS, Drugs, and Prostitution.* London: Tavistock Publications.

NELSON, NICI. 1987 '"Selling her Kiosk": Kikuyu Notions of Sexuality and Sex for Sale in Mathare Valley, Kenya'. In Pat Caplan (ed.), *The Cultural Construction of Sexuality.* London: Tavistock Publications.

OOSTENK, ANNEMIEK. 1989. 'A Visit to Burkina Faso'. In Gail Pheterson (ed.), *A Vindication of Rights of Whores.* Seattle: Seal Press.'

PICKERING, HELEN *et al.*, 1992. 'Prostitutes and their Clients: A Gambian Survey'. *Soc. Sci. Med.* 34 (1): 75–88.

TABET, PAOLA. 1989. 'I'm the Meat, I'm the Knife: Sexual Service, Migration, and Repression in Some African Societies'. In Gail Pheterson (ed.), *A Vindication of the Rights of Whores.* Seattle: Seal Press.

WHITE, LUISE. 1990. *The Comforts of Home: Prostitution in Colonial Nairobi.* Chicago: University of Chicago Press.

—— 1986. 'Prostitution, Identity, and Class Consciousness during World War II'. *Signs: Journal of Women in Culture and Society* 11 (2): 255–73.

WILSON, DAVID *et al.*. 1990. 'A Pilot Study for an HIV Prevention Programme among Commercial Sex Workers in Bulawayo, Zimbabwe'. *Soc. Sci. Med.* 31 (5): 609–18.

Asia

Asia Watch and the Women's Rights Project. 1993. *A Modern Form of Slavery: Trafficking of Burmese Women and Girls into Brothels in Thailand.* New York: Human Rights Watch.

DESQUITADO, MARVIC R. 1992. *Behind the Shadows: Towards a Better*

Understanding of Prostituted Women. Davao City: Talikala, Inc. Published by a community organizing project in Davao City, the Phillipines. The project was formed by a group that included social workers and prostitutes.

ENLOE, CYNTHIA. 1989. *Bananas, Beaches & Bases: Making Feminist Sense of International Politics.* London: Pandora Press. See the chapters, 'On the Beach: Sexism and Tourism' and 'Base Women'.

—— 1983. *Does Khaki Become You? The Militarisation of Women's Lives.* Boston: South End Press. See the chapters, 'The Military Needs Camp Followers' and 'The Militarisation of Prostitution'.

GRONEWOLD, SUE. 1985. *Beautiful Merchandise: Prostitution in China 1860–1936.* New York: Harrington Park Press.

HAERI, SHAHLA. 1989. *Law of Desire: Temporary Marriage in Shi'i Iran.* Syracuse: Syracuse University Press.

KAPUR, PROMILLA. 1979. *The Indian Call Girls.* New Delhi; Orient Paperbacks. This book comes with an insert that says, 'This book has now been exonerated from obscenity charge by Delhi High Court'.

NANDA, SERENA. 1990. *Neither Man Nor Woman: The Hijras of India.* Belmont, California.: Wadsworth Publishing Company.

ODZER, CLEO. 1994. PATPONG SISTERS: AN AMERICAN WOMAN'S VIEW OF THE BANGKOK SEX WORLD. New York: Blue Moon Books/Arcade Publishing.

PHONGPAICHIT, PASUK. 1982. *From Peasant Girls to Bangkok Masseuses.* Geneva: International Labour Office.

RAGHURAMAIAH, K. LAKSHMI. 1991. *Night Birds: Indian Prostitutes from Devadasis to Call Girls.* Delhi: Chankya Publications.

STURDEVANT, SAUNDRA POLLACK, and STOLTZFUS, BRENDA. 1992. *Let the Good Times Roll: Prostitution and the U.S. Military in Asia.* New York: The New Press.

THORBEK, SUZANNE. 1987. *Voices from the City: Women of Bangkok.* London: Zed Books.

TRUONG, THANH-DAM. 1990. *Sex, Money and Morality: Prostitution and Tourism in South-East Asia.* London: Zed Books.

——1986. *Virtue, Order, Health and Money: Towards a Comprehensive Perspective on Female Prostitution in Asia.* Bangkok: United Nations, Economic and Social Commission for Asia and the Pacific.

Sex Work: Sexually Transmitted Diseases (HIV) and Working Conditions

ALEXANDER, PRISCILLA. In press. *Making Sex Work Safer: A Guide to HIV/AIDS Prevention Interventions.* Geneva: World Health Organization, Global Programme on AIDS.

—— 1987. 'Prostitutes are being Scapegoated for Aids'. In Delacoste, Frederique and Priscilla Alexander (eds.), *Sex Work: Writings by Women in the Sex Industry*. San Fransisco: Cleis Press. London: Virago Press, 1988. Translations: German: Sex Arbeit. Heyne Verlag, 1989.

—— 1994. 'Sex Workers Fight Against AIDS: An International Perspective'. In Beth E. Schneider and Nancy Stoller (eds.), *Women Resisiting AIDS: Strategies of Empowerment*. Philadelphia: Temple University Press.

Brandt, Allan M. 1985. *No Magic Bullet: A Social History of Venereal Disease in the United States since 1880*. New York: Oxford University Press (Paperback, 1987).

——1987. 'A Historical Perspective'. In Harlon L. Dalton and Scott Burris (eds.), *AIDS and the Law: A Guide for the Public*. New Haven: Yale University press.

——1988. 'AIDS: From Social History to Social Policy'. In Elizabeth Fee and Daniel M. Fox (eds.), *AIDS: The Burdens of History*. Berkeley: University of California Press.

Cohen, Judith B., Alexander, Priscilla, and Wofsy, Constance. 1988. 'Prostitutes and AIDS: Public Policy Issues'. *AIDS & Public Policy Journal* 3 (2): 16–22.

Cohen, Judith B., and Alexander, Priscilla. In press. 'Female Prostitutes: Scapegoats in the AIDS Epidemic'. In Ann O'Leary and Loretta Sweet Jemmott (eds.), *Women and Aids: Primary Prevention* New York: Plenum Press.

Davenport-Hines, Richard. 1990. *Sex, Death and Punishment: Attitudes to Sex and Sexuality in Britain since the Renaissance*. London: Fontana Press/ Harper Collins.

Gibson Mary. 1986. *Prostitution and the State in Italy, 1860–1915*. New Brunswick, NJ: Rutgers University Press.

Harsin, Jill. 1985. *Policing Prostitution in Nineteenth Century Paris*. Princeton, NJ: Princeton University Press.

Hyam, Ronald. *Empire and Sexuality: The British Experience*. Manchester: Manchester University Press.

Mahood, Linda. 1990. *The Magdelenes: Prostitution in the Nineteenth Century*. London: Routledge.

Mort, Frank. 1987. *Dangerous Sexualities: Medico-Moral Politics in England since 1830*. London: Routledge & Kegan Paul.

Plant, Martin (ed.). 1990. *AIDS, Drugs, and Prostitution*. London: Tavistock/Routledge. A series of papers on the epidemiology of HIV infection among prostitutes and the impact of AIDS prevention and community organizing interventions in Europe, the United States, Australia, and Africa.

Quetel, Claude. 1990. *History of Syphilis*. Baltimore: The Johns Hopkins University Press. Translated by Judith Braddock and Brian Pike, originally *Le Mal de Naples: Histoire de la syphilis*, Paris: Editions Seghers, 1986.

Rosenberg, Michael J. 1988. 'Prostitutes and AIDS: A Health Department Priority?'. *American Journal of Public Health*. 78 (4): 418–423.

Walkowitz, Judith R. 1980. *Prostitution and Victorian Society: Women, Class, and the State*. Cambridge: Cambridge University Press.

Sex Worker Organizations

United States

North American Task Force on Prostitution (NTFP)
2785 Broadway 4L
New York, NY 10025–2834 USA

COYOTE/San Francisco
2269 Chestnut Street #452
San Francisco, CA 94123

COYOTE/Los Angeles
1626 N Wilcox Avenue #580
Hollywood, CA 90028

COYOTE/Seattle
16625 Redmond Way Box M237
Redmond, Washington 98052 USA

Hooking is Real Employment (HIRE)
847 Monroe Drive
Atlanta, GA 30308

Sex Workers Action Coalition (SWAC)
PO Box 210256
San Francsico, CA 94121

P.O.N.Y. (Prostitutes of New York)
271 Madison Avenue #908
New York, New York 10016

International Affiliates

Europe

Network of Sexwork Projects
54 Bryantwood Road
London N77BE UK

De Rode Draad (The Red Thread)
Kloveniersburgwal, 47
Amsterdam, Nederlands

PAYOKE
Zirksttraat 27 2000
Antwerpen, Belgium

HWG
Karlsruher Str. 5
60329 Frankfurt Germany

HYDRA
Rigaer Strasse 3
10247 Berlin
Germany

Kassandra
Kopernikusplatz 12
90459 Nurnberg
Germany

Straps & Grips
c/o Aids Hilfe
Herwarthstr. 2
48143 Munster
Germany

Cinderella
Postfach 10 18 14
40009 Dusseldorf
Germany

Phoenix e. V
Postfach 47 62
Bergmannstr. 3
30159 Hannover
Germany

Nitribitt
Stader Str 1
28205 Bremen
Germany

Hurenselbst–hilfe Saabrucken
Forsterstr. 39
66125 Saabrucken
Germany

Hurizonte e. V
Archiv und
Dokumentationszentrum fur
Prostitution
Postfach 30 35 53
10727 Berlin
Germany

Madonna
Gusstahlstr. 34
44793 Bochum
Germany

Nutten & Nuttchen
Fredericiastr. 14
14059 Berlin Germany

Café Sperre
Schillerstr. 69
34117 Kassel Germany

Bathseba
Steinwegpassage 42 A
38100 Braunschweig
Germany

Callboy's Organizations (Germany)
Querstrich Auguststr. 84
10117 Berlin
Germany

Strichweise Heiter
c/o Basisprojekt
Hamburg St. Georg–Kirchhof 26
2009 Hamburg
Germany

Comitato per i Diritti Civili delle
Prostitute
Casella Postal 67
33170 Pordenone
Italy

Scot–PEP
21A Torphican Street
Edinburgh EH3 8HX
Scotland

Aspasie
10 r. Charles Cusin
Geneva
Switzerland

Centre de Documentation
International sur la Prostitution
24, rue Neuchatel
1201 Geneva
Switzerland

Xenia
Mauerain 1
3012 Bern
Switzerland

Americas

Maggie's
Sex Workers Alliance of Toronto
(SWAT)
P.O Box 1143, Station F
Toronto, ON M4Y 2T8

Sex Workers' Alliance of Vancouver
Post Office Box 3075
Vancouver, British Columbia
V6B 3X6
Canada

MUSA A.C.
Col. Alamos C.P. Mexico,
DF 03400, Mexico

Prostitution & Civil Rights
ISER Ladenn da Gloria
98 Rio de Janeiro, RJ 22211
Brazil

Programma Pegacao
NOSS Rua Visconde de Piraja
127/201
Ipanema Rio de Janeiro/ RJ
CEP 22410–001
Brazil

Associacao de Prostitutas do Estato
de Rio de Janeiro
R Miguel de Frias 718, Estacao
Rio de Janeiro, RJ
Brazil

Australasia

SWEETLY
c/o Art Scape Yoshida – Honmachi –4
Sakyo-ku Kyoto
606 Japan

EMPOWER
National Office
57/60 Tivanont Road
Nonthburi 11000
Thailand

Scarlet Alliance
P.O. Box 811
Fyshwick 2609 ACT
Australia

ACT (WISE)
Workers in Sex Employment
P.O. Box 811
Fyshwick 2609 ACT
Australia

S.W.O.P.
Sex Workers Outreach Project
P.O. Box 1453 Darlinghurst
N.S.W. 2010
Australia

SQWISI
Self Help for Queensland Workers in the Sex Industry
P.O. Box 689
West End Q4101
Queensland
Australia

New Zealand Prostitutes Collective
P.O. Box 11–412
Manners Street
Wellington
New Zealand

New Zealand Prostitutes Collective
P.O. Box 13–561
Christchurch
New Zealand

New Zealand Prostitutes Collective
P.O. Box 6407
Dunedin
New Zealand

Allied Organizations

United States

Waikiki Health Center
277 Ohua Ave.
Honolulu, Hawaii 96815–3695

Europe

Mr A. de Graaf Stichting
Instituut voor Prostitutie
Vraagstukken

Outsiders (for disabled people)
P.O. Box 4ZB
London, England W1A 4ZB

4, Westermarkt
1016 DK Amsterdam Netherlands

Australasia

Action for REACH OUT
P.O. Box 98108
T.S.T.Post Office
Tsim Sha Tsui, Kowloon, Hong Kong

Index